THE BARBOUR COLLECTION OF CONNECTICUT TOWN VITAL RECORDS

THE BARBOUR COLLECTION OF CONNECTICUT TOWN VITAL RECORDS

PORTLAND 1841–1850

PROSPECT 1827–1853

REDDING 1767–1852

RIDGEFIELD 1709–1850

Compiled by
Wilma J. Standifer Moore

General Editor
Lorraine Cook White

Copyright © 2000
Genealogical Publishing Co., Inc.
Baltimore, Maryland
All Rights Reserved
Library of Congress Catalogue Card Number 94-76197
International Standard Book Number 0-8063-1651-9
Made in the United States of America

INTRODUCTION

As early as 1640 the Connecticut Court of Election ordered all magistrates to keep a record of the marriages they performed. In 1644 the registration of births and marriages became the official responsibility of town clerks and registrars, with deaths added to their duties in 1650. From 1660 until the close of the Revolutionary War these vital records of birth, marriage, and death were generally well kept, but then for a period of about two generations until the mid-nineteenth century, the faithful recording of vital records declined in some towns.

General Lucius Barnes Barbour was the Connecticut Examiner of Public Records from 1911 to 1934 and in that capacity directed a project in which the vital records kept by the towns up to about 1850 were copied and abstracted. Barbour previously had directed the publication of the Bolton and Vernon vital records for the Connecticut Historical Society. For this new project he hired several individuals who were experienced in copying old records and familiar with the old script.

Barbour presented the completed transcriptions of town vital records to the Connecticut State Library where the information was typed onto printed forms. The form sheets were then cut, producing twelve small slips from each sheet. The slips for most towns were then alphabetized and the information was then typed a second time on large sheets of rag paper, which were subsequently bound into separate volumes for each town. The slips for all towns were then interfiled, forming a statewide alphabetized slip index for most surviving town vital records.

The dates of coverage vary from town to town, and of course the records of some towns are more complete than others. There are many cases in which an entry may appear two or three times, apparently because that entry was entered by one or more persons. Altogether the entire Barbour Collection--one of the great genealogical manuscript collections and one of the last to be published--covers 137 towns and comprises 14,333 typed pages.

TABLE OF CONTENTS

PORTLAND 1

PROSPECT 41

REDDING 57

RIDGEFIELD 137

ABBREVIATIONS

ae.-------------age
b. -------------born, both
bd.------------buried
B. G.----------Burying Ground
d. ------------died, day, or daughter
decd.---------deceased
f. --------------father
h. -------------hour
J. P. -----------Justice of Peace
m. -------------married or month
res. -----------resident
s. --------------son
st. -------------stillborn
w. -------------wife
wid. -----------widow
wk. ------------week
y. --------------year

THE BARBOUR COLLECTION OF CONNECTICUT TOWN VITAL RECORDS

PORTLAND VITAL RECORDS
1841 - 1850

	Page
ABBEY, ABBY, Harriet A., m. Edwin **BELL**, Sept. 13, 1852, by Rev. H. Talcott	29
Lucy Elizabeth, m. James Dwight **JOHNSON**, b. of Portland, Jan. 20, 1846, at Edwin Bell's house, by Rev. Sam[ue]l M. Emery	14
ACKERT, ACKERD, Maria, m. John **PENFIELD**, b. of Portland, Jan. 5, 1848, at Peter Ackert's house, by Rev. Sam[ue]l M. Emery	18
Maria, ae 18, b. in Glastonbury, res. Portland, m. John **PENFIELD**, joiner, ae 23, of Portland, Jan. 5, 1848, by Rev. S. M. Emery	261
AHERN, Hannah, ae 24, b. in Ireland, res. Portland, m. Thomas **BURKE**, quarryman, b. in Ireland, res. Portland, Dec. 6, 1847, by Rev. John Brady	261
ALEXANDER, Frances J., d. Moses F., farmer, ae 33, & Lucy, ae 30, b. Apr. 27, 1850	272
Mary Jane, d. Moses F., farmer, ae 29, & Lucy, ae 29, b. Aug. 12, 1847	259
ALLEN, Alfred Hurlburt, m. Jerusha Ufford **CHURCHILL**, b. of Portland, [ ], 1846, at Henry Churchill's house, by Rev. Sam[ue]l M. Emery	15
David Churchill, s. Alfred H., carpenter, ae 29, & Jerusha U., ae 29, b. Nov. 8, 1847	256
ALVORD, Abigail, b. in R. I., res. Portland, d. Nov. 18, 1847, ae 64	263
AMES, Jane A., of Portland, m. William T. **TIBBALS**, of Middle Haddam, Oct. 6, 1852, by Rev. H. Talcott	29
Margaret A., m. Francis **HALE**, May 2, 1852, by Rev. H. Talcott	27
ANDERSON, Ellen, m. James **TAYLOR**, Apr. 14, 1850, by Rev. Hervey Talcott	22
Ellen, b. in Scotland, m. James **TAYLOR**, laborer, b. in Scotland, res. Portland, Apr. 14, 1850, by Rev. H. Talcott	273
ANDREWS, John Jones, s. Gideon S., coaster, ae 30, & Mary Ann, ae 29, b. Oct. 11, 1847	256
ARNOLD, John, pauper, b. in Haddam, res. Portland, d. Dec. 11, 1849, ae 68	274
ARTHUR, Alexander, stone cutter, b. in Scotland, res. Portland, d. Sept. 15, 1848	271
Maria A., m. Selden S. **COOK**, Apr. 4, 1852, by Rev. Hervey Talcott	27
AXTELL, Frances Harley, of Amhurst, Mass., m. Mary Emeline **ROSBROOK**, of Northampton, Mass., Apr. 6, 1849, at Charles A. Rosbrook's house, by Rev. Samuel M. Emery	20
AYRES, Daniel, Jr., of Brooklyn, N. Y., m. Charlotte Augusta **RUSSELL**, of Portland, Oct. 6, 1848, at Daniel Russell's house, by Rev. Samuel M. Emery	19
Daniel, Jr., physician, ae 26, b. in N. Y. City, res. Portland, m.	

1

	Page
AYRES, (cont.)	
Charlotte Augusta **RUSSELL**, ae 20, of Portland, Oct. 6, 1848, by Rev. S. M. Emery	269
BACON, Lyman M., of Hartford, m. Louisa M. **ROWLEY**, of Portland, Dec. 19, 1849, by Rev. Hervey Talcott	21
BAILEY, Mary Ann, of Portland, m. Samuel C. **SPAULDING**, of Middletown, Sept. 26, 1841, by Rev. Samuel M. Emery	1
Mary Lucinda, of Portland, m. George Henry **WILLIAMS**, of Middletown, Mar. 21, 1847, by Rev. Samuel M. Emery	16
BAKER, John, laborer, b. in Ireland, res. Portland, m. Mary **TRACY**, b. in Ireland, res. Portland, July 13, 1851, by Rev. John Brady	279
Thomas, of Middletown, m. Vienna **HALE**, of Portland, Aug. 23, 1846, by Rev. H. Talcott	14
Thomas, m. Lucy E. **HALE**, Nov. 25, 1852, by S. G. W. J. Rankin	29
BANK, William D., of Portland, m. Hannah Laura **HERCKNET**, of Middletown, Feb. 2, 1853, by Rev. Sam[ue]l M. Emery	30
BARRIGAN, Jeremiah, s. Patrick, quarryman, ae 30, & Marcelia, ae 22, b. Nov. 7, 1847	256
BARRY, Catharine, ae 20, b. in Ireland, res. Portland, m. Patrick **MOORE**, quarryman, ae 23, b. in Ireland, res. Portland, Jan. 28, 1849, by Rev. John Brady	269
Ellen, d. Michael, quarryman, & Ellen, ae 35, b. Aug. 8, 1848	258
Ellen, d. James, quarryman, ae 30, & Margaret, ae 29, b. Oct. 20, 1848	265
Esther, ae 21, b. in Ireland, res. Portland, m. Edward **LYNCH**, quarryman, ae 26, b. in Ireland, res. Portland, Nov. 12, 1848, by Rev. John Brady	269
Helen, d. Patrick, quarryman, ae 28, & Margaret, ae 25, b. June 3, 1849	265
Honora, d. James, 2d, laborer, b. Aug. 6, 1850	275
Johanna, d. Patrick, laborer, b. Apr. [ ], 1851	276
John B., of Haddam, m. Maria **NORCOTT**, of Portland, May 5, 1847, by Rev. Hervey Talcott	17
Mary Ann, d. Patrick, quarryman, ae 29, & Margaret, ae 24, b. Apr. 1, 1848	258
Patrick, laborer, b. in Ireland, res. Portland, d. May 23, 1851, ae 28	281
BARTLETT, Abel, laborer, b. in Chatham, res. Portland, d. Dec. 9, 1849, ae 69	274
Anne Louisa, [d. William H. & Mary C.], b. Sept. 11, 1870	251
Charles Fisk, s. [Joel & Betsey], b. Mar. 10, 1811; d. [ ], 1849	250
Eunice C., [w. of William H.], d. Aug. 24, 1867	251
Jane, of Portland, m. Billings **NEFF**, of Chaplin, Sept. 5, 1841, by Rev. Samuel M. Emery	1
Joel, m. Betsey **WILCOX**, Jan. 18, 1809	250
Mary, [d. Joel & Betsey], b. May 27, 1817	250
Mary Elizabeth, [d. William H. & Mary C.], b. June 9, 1869	251
Mary Elizabeth, [d. William H. & Mary C.], d. Apr. 28, 1880	251
Mary W., d. of Joel, decd., of Portland, m. William T. **WILLIAMS**, Oct. 24, 1852, by Mark Tucker	29
Moses Wilcox, s. [Joel & Betsey], b. Apr. [ ], 1813	250

	Page
BARTLETT, (cont.)	
Moses Wilcox, s. [Joel & Betsey], b. [ ]; d. [ ]	250
W[illia]m H., m. Eunice C. **WILLCOX**, Oct. 20, 1840	251
W[illia]m H., m. Mary C. **COOMES**, May 6, 1868	251
W[illia]m Hall, [s. Joel & Betsey], b. Feb. 25, 1815	250
BECKWITH, Roxana, of Hartford, m. Joseph **ROWLEY**, of Portland, Dec. 30, 1849, by Sylvester Stocking, J. P.	21
BEEBE, William Henry, m. Sarah **SMITH**, b. of Portland, Dec. 24, 1845, by Rev. Sam[ue]l M. Emery	13
BEERS, Amelia D., m. William B. **DINGWELL**, Nov. 5, 1851, by Sylvester Stocking, J. P.	26
Eunice, m. Joseph **YOUNG**, July 13, 1851, by Sylvester Stocking, J. P.	26
Eunice, b. in Chatham, m. Joseph **YOUNG**, quarryman, of Portland, July 13, 1851, by S. Stocking (Her 2d marriage)	280
BELL, Edwin, m. Harriet A. **ABBY**, Sept. 13, 1852, by Rev. H. Talcott	29
Edwin P., s. Edwin, blacksmith, ae 37, & Prudence, ae 38, b. Sept. 17, 1848	265
George W., m. Helen M. **HOPKINS**, Dec. 23, 1845, by Rev. H. Talcott	13
Helen G., d. George W., blacksmith, ae 29, & Helen M., ae 25, b. Sept. 3, 1850	275
Joseph, laborer, b. in England, res. Portland, d. July 13, 1851, ae 27	281
Mary Ann, of Portland, m. Horace F. **HICKOK**, of Chickopee Falls, Nov. 4, 1849, by Rev. Hervey Talcott	21
Mary Ann, ae 24, b. in Portland, res. Springfield, m. Horace F. **HICKOK**, merchant, ae 27, b. in Rocky Hill, res. Springfield, Nov. 4, 1849, by Rev. H. Talcott	273
Prudence, b. in Chatham, res. Portland, d. Feb. 19, 1851, ae 39	280
Susan, d. Enos, carpenter, ae 45, & Sarah, b. Mar. 9, 1851	275
BENNETT, Anna, d. Jan. 25, 1848, ae 55	263
BIDWELL, Alice, of Glastenbury, m. David **HILLS**, July 31, 1842, by Rev. H. Talcott	5
Martha G., m. Jabez E. **JONES**, Dec. 20, 1841, by Rev. H. Talcott	2
BILLINGS, Elizabeth, of Portland, m. Lorenzo **WHEELER**, of Columbia, Dec. 1, 1841, by Rev. Samuel M. Emery	2
BINGHAM, William, joiner, ae 21, b. in E. Haddam, res. Portland, m. Elizabeth **TAYLOR**, ae 18, of Portland, June 26, 1850, by Rev. H. Talcott	273
William W., of E. Haddam, m. Elizabeth **TAYLOR**, June 26, 1850, by Rev. Hervey Talcott	23
BISHOP, Jame[s] White, s. Hiram, cooper, ae 41, & Maria, ae 39, b. Jan. 15, 1850	272
BLACK, Harriet A., b. in Glastonbury, res. N. Y. City, d. Dec. 6, 1850, ae 36	280
BLOODGOOD, Isaac, of New York City, m. Jane Maria **CARY**, of Portland, Nov. 18, 1851, by Rev. Sam[ue]l M. Emery	26
BRADY, Sarah, m. Robert **STREETHERS**, June 27, 1842, by Rev. S. Nash, of Middle Haddam	5
BRAINARD, BRAINERD, Benj[amin] P., overseer in Quarry, ae 29, b. in	

4 BARBOUR COLLECTION

Page

BRAINARD, BRAINERD, (cont.)
Chatham, res. Portland, m. Amelia A. **DAVIS**, ae 28, b. in
Chatham, res. Portland, Mar. 26, 1851, by Rev. Townsend 279
Elizabeth, of Portland, m. Benjamin B. **WILLCOX**, of Saybrook, May
29, 1842, by Rev. H. Talcott 4
Erastus, Jr., m. Emily Hall **CHURCHILL**, b. of Portland, Oct. 10, 1843,
by Rev. Sam[ue]l M. Emery 7
Jane Maria, of Portland, m. Rev. Giles Henry **DESHON**, of Mereden,
May 25, 1853, by Rev. Sam[ue]l M. Emery 30
Jerusha D., ae 17, b. in Portland, res. Boston, m. W[illia]m P.
TEWKSBURY, book-merchant, ae 30, of Boston, Apr. 12, 1848,
by Rev. S. M. Emery 261
Jerusha Dickinson, of Portland, m. William Plumer **TEWKSBURY**, of
Boston, Mass., Apr. 12, 1848, at Erastus Brainerd's house, by Rev.
Sam[ue]l M. Emery 18
Maria, m. Sherman **COWLES**, of Kensington, Sept. 20, 1846, by Rev.
Hervey Talcott 15
Norman Leslie, of N. Y., m. Leara **CAMPBELL**, of Portland, May 18,
1847, by Rev. Sam[ue]l M. Emery, at William Campbell's house 17
Sarah D., of Portland, m. Edward J. **LANGDON**, of Berlin, Nov. 26,
1846, by Rev. Hervey Talcott 15
Sarah Jane, m. Jeremiah H. **TAYLOR**, b. of Portland, Nov. 25, 1847,
by Rev. F. B. Woodward, of Chatham 20
-----, s. W[illia]m H., painter, ae 43, & Emily, ae 39, b. Jan. 20, 1848 259
BRANSFIELD, BRONSFIELD, Catharine, d. James, quarryman, ae 26, &
Catharine, ae 34, b. Mar. 25, 1849 268
James, quarryman, b. in Ireland, res. Portland, d. Mar. 10, 1849, ae 23 271
Jeremiah, s. Maurice, quarryman, ae 30, & Abby, ae 27, b. Nov. 20,
1848 266
Johanna, d. Maurice, quarryman, & Abby, ae 27, b. Oct. 14, 1847 256
Margaret, b. in Ireland, res. Portland, d. Feb. [ ], 1849, ae 14 271
Mary, d. W[illia]m, quarryman, ae 29, & Margaret, ae 22, b. Oct. 7,
1848 268
Mary, ae 19, b. in Ireland, res. Portland, m. Cornelius **LENNIHAN**,
ferryman, ae 26, b. in Ireland, res. Portland, Jan. 28, 1849, by Rev.
John Brady 269
Mary, ae 22, b. in Ireland, res. Portland, m. Cornelius **LENNAHAN**,
quarryman, ae 25, b. in Ireland, res. Portland, July 20, 1849, by
Rev. John Brady 270
William, laborer, b. in Ireland, res. Portland, d. July 15, 1851, ae 28 281
BRONSON, Henry, of Bristol, Ct., m. Penelope Elizabeth **SHEPARD**, of
Portland, Jan. 3, 1847, at Edward Shepard's house, by Rev.
Sam[ue]l M. Emery 16
BROOKS, Roswell, m. Julia Ann **BUCK**, b. of Portland, June 8, 1845, at
Frederick Miller's house, by Sylvester Stocking, J. P. 11
Roswell Bidwell, s. Roswell, farmer, ae 64, & Julia, ae 37, b. Jan. 26,
1848 256
BROWN, Alvin F., s. Sam[ue]l, Jr., laborer, ae 28, & Mary A., ae 22,

	Page
BROWN, (cont.)	
b. Nov. 20, 1850	275
Charles H., s. George M., farmer, ae 37, & Harriet M., ae 36, b. June 1, 1849	267
Chester G., d. Apr. 19, 1848, ae 15 m.	263
Cecero, m. Mary Ann **STRICKLAND**, Feb. 6, 1851, by Rev. S. G. W. J. Rankin	25
Cicero, mariner, ae 24, b. in Chatham, res. Portland, m. Mary Ann **STRICKLAND**, ae 25, b. in Chatham, res. Portland, Feb. 6, 1851, by Rev. S. G. W. J. Rankin	280
Frances E., d. Apr. 19, 1848, ae 5	263
Frederic W., farmer, b. in Chatham, res. Portland, d. Nov. 10, 1848, ae 18	271
Geo[rge] M., farmer, b. in Chatham, res. Portland, d. Sept. 23, 1850, ae 38	281
John Russell, m. Sarah Ann **STEVENSON**, b. of Portland, Dec. 7, 1845, by Rev. Sam[ue]l M. Emery	12
Mary, of Portland, m. Henry Edward **SIMPSON**, of Ellington, Dec. 20, 1841, by Rev. Sam[ue]l M. Emery	3
Mary Emma, d. John R., laborer, ae 25, & Sarah, ae 25, b. May 13, 1851	275
Morris, miner, ae 23, b. in Philadelphia, res. Portland, m. Grace **CHILD**, ae 25, b. in Chatham, June 1, 1851, by Joseph Law	280
Reuben, s. John R., quarryman, ae 23, & Sarah A., ae 23, b. Oct. 11, 1848	265
Samuel F., s. Samuel, Jr., quarryman, ae 26, & Mary, ae 20, b. Dec. 8, 1848	265
Sam[ue]l F., d. Jan. 9, 1849, ae 4 w.	271
Sarah, m. Joel **STRICKLAND**, Jr., Nov. 29, 1843, by Rev. H. Talcott	8
W[illia]m A., d. Mar. 31, 1848, ae 9	263
BUCK, Harvey T., s. James F., farmer, ae 33, & Adaline, ae 32, b. Aug. 12, 1847	260
Horace B., m. Eliza A. **HALL**, b. of Portland, Mar. 2, 1845, by Edmund A. Standish	10
Julia Ann, m. Roswell **BROOKS**, b. of Portland, June 8, 1845, at Frederick Miller's House, by Sylvester Stocking, J. P.	11
Martha E., d. Sept. 1, 1848, ae 2 1/2	271
Mary Jane, m. Luther **SAVAGE**, Nov. 17, 1850, by Rev. H. Talcott	23
Mary Joy, ae 24, b. in Chatham, res. Portland, m. Luther **SAVAGE**, carpenter, ae 23, b. in Chatham, res. Portland, Nov. 17, 1850, by Rev. H. Talcott	280
BUCKINGHAM, Herman, s. Sam[ue]l S., merchant, ae 41, & Julia R., ae 36, b. Sept. 10, 1849	272
Jonah Clark, of Barnwell, S. C., m. Esther Rebecca **GILDERSLEEVE**, of Portland, Sept. 8, 1846, at Sylvester Gildersleeve's house, by Rev. Sam[ue]l M. Emery	14
Laura, m. Abel **STRICKLAND**, Nov. 27, 1851, by S. G. W. J. Rankin	26
BUGGY, Alicia, d. Thomas, truckman, ae 29, & Julia, ae 26,	

6 BARBOUR COLLECTION

	Page
BUGGY, (cont.)	
b. Apr. 11, 1848	258
Bridget, d. Martin, quarryman, ae 27, & Mary, ae 33, b. June 4, 1848	258
Michael, d. Aug. 25, 1850, ae 1 1/2	280
BULKLEY, Margaret, d. Maurice, laborer, b. Sept. 18, 1850	276
Walter, of Glastonbury, m. Electa **HUNT**, of Portland, May 9, 1852, by Rev. H. Talcott	27
William Riley, of Rocky Hill, m. Emma **FREEMAN**, of Glastonbury, Jan. 6, 1850, by Rev. Sam[ue]l M. Emery	21
BURKE, BURK, Ellen Maria, d. James F., farmer, ae 35, & Adaline, ae 34, b. Nov. 26, 1850	278
John, s. Thomas, laborer, b. Nov. 25, 1850	276
Michael, s. Thomas, quarryman, ae 30, & Johanna, ae 25, b. Sept. 15, 1848	265
Thomas, quarryman, b. in Ireland, res. Portland, m. Hannah **AHERN**, ae 24, b. in Ireland, res. Portland, Dec. 6, 1847, by Rev. John Brady	261
BURNS, Charles, s. William, quarryman, ae 30, & Mary Ann, ae 25, b. Nov. 16, 1848	265
James, s. Michael, quarryman, ae 39, & Elizabeth, ae 27, b. Jan. 21, 1848	257
Michael, d. Nov. 25, 1847, ae 13 m.	263
William, s. William, laborer, b. Oct. 13, 1850	276
BURTON, Edmund, laborer, b. in England, res. Portland, d. July 13, 1851, ae 23	281
BUTTON, Daniel, m. Emily S. **SANDERSON**, Dec. 24, 1846, by Rev. H. Talcott	16
Egbert Oswald, m. Mary **SHEPARD**, b. of Portland, Feb. 16, 1845, at Jonathan Shepard's house, by Rev. Sam[ue]l M. Emery	10
Fanny, m. Frederick **TRYON**, Dec. 30, 1846, by Rev. H. Talcott	16
Franklin S., s. Daniel, laborer, ae 25, & Emily, ae 17, b. Feb. 3, 1848	259
Harriet, m. Jeremiah **GOFF**, b. of Portland, Jan. 8, 1846, by Rev. Sam[ue]l Emery	13
Jeremiah P., shoemaker, b. in Chatham, res. Portland, m. Eliza **SAGE**, b. in Chatham, res. Portland, Dec. 2, 1850, by Rev. S. M. Emery	279
Jeremiah Pelton, m. Eliza **SAGE**, b. of Portland, Dec. 2, 1850, at Charles L. Sage's house, by Rev. Sam[ue]l M. Emery	24
CADWELL, Angeline Elizabeth, of Portland, m. Hillard **CLEVELAND**, of Munson, Mass., May 9, 1842, by Rev. Sam[ue]l M. Emery	4
CAMP, Alfred Erastus, of Mereden, m. Adaline **JOHNSON**, of Portland, Aug. 15, 1854, by Rev. Sam[ue]l M. Emery	31
CAMPBELL, Leara, of Portland, m. Norman Leslie **BRAINERD**, of N. Y., May 18, 1847, by Rev. Sam[ue]l M. Emery, at William W. Campbell's house	17
CANTWELL, Peter, s. John, quarryman, ae 33, & Mary, ae 26, b. Apr. 13, 1848	258
CAREY, CARY, James, s. Maurice, quarryman, ae 31, & Catharine, ae 30, b. July 27, 1849	267
Jane Maria, of Portland, m. Isaac **BLOODGOOD**, of New York City,	

	Page
CAREY, CARY, (cont.)	
Nov. 18, 1851, by Rev. Sam[ue]l M. Emery	26
Rosa Ann, d. Maurice, quarryman, & Catharine, b. Aug. 10, 1847	256
CARRIER, Mary, d. Philip, laborer, b. Jan. 23, 1851	277
CARROLL, CARROL, Eliza, d. Michael, quarryman, & Johanna, ae 22, b. Jan. 1, 1848	257
Michael, s. Michael, laborer, b. July 10, 1851	277
CARTHY, [see also **McCARTHY**], Daniel, s. John, quarryman, ae 30, & Mary, ae 26, b. Dec. 15, 1847	260
CARTY, [see also **CRARTY** and **McCARTHY**], James, d. Oct. 14, 1847, ae 3 y.	264
John, d. Oct. 15, 1847, ae 5	264
CASE, John, quarryman, b. in Ireland, res. Portland, m. Frances **WELCH**, ae 24, b. in Ireland, Aug. 1, 1848, by Rev. John Brady	261
CASEY, Betsey, b. in Ireland, res. Portland, d. May 8, 1848, ae 26	264
Mary, ae 19, b. in Ireland, m. Michael **CRATY**, quarryman, ae 28, b. in Ireland, res. Portland, Aug. 6, 1848, by Rev. John Brady	261
CASHMAN, Patrick, laborer, b. in Ireland, res. Portland, d. Feb. [ ], 1851, ae 21	280
Thomas, s. Thomas, laborer, b. Dec. 12, 1850	276
CASWELL, Dwight K., d. Apr. 16, 1850, ae 2 m.	274
Dwight William, s. Harlow H., joiner, ae 30, & Jane G., ae 27, b. Feb. 16, 1850	272
Harlow, of Glastonbury, m. Jane G. **PENFIELD**, May 23, 1844, by Rev. Warren G. Jones, of Glastonbury	8
Harlow H., s. Harlow H., joiner, & Jane, b. Oct. 1, 1848	265
Harlow H., d. Oct. 11, 1848, ae 10 d.	271
CHAPMAN, Adalaide, d. Martin, laborer, ae 46, & Clarissa, ae 43, b. Dec. 13, 1848	269
Alonzo, b. in Glastonbury, res. Portland, d. Oct. 17, 1848, ae 5	271
Arthur D., s. Martin, farmer, ae 44, & Clarissa, ae 42, b. Jan. 2, 1848	260
Arthur D., d. Jan. 30, 1848, ae 28 d.	264
Emily E., d. Rufus, laborer, ae 33, & Thankful, ae 27, b. Apr. 5, 1848	259
Harriet E., d. Mar. 8, 1848, ae 1	264
Lavinia, m. Edward **PEASE**, Mar. 3, 1850, by Rev. Hervey Talcott	22
Lovina, ae 18, b. in Glastonbury, res. Portland, m. Edward **PEASE**, carpenter, ae 23, of Portland, Mar. 3, 1850, by Rev. H. Talcott	273
Washington, m. Eliza **ROBINSON**, July 3, 1845, by Rev. Hervey Tallcott	11
William E., of Westchester, Conn., m. Rosannah M. **VALENTINE**, of Portland, Conn., July 3, [1851], by Rev. F. W. Bill	26
CHENEY, Daniel, farmer, d. Apr. 18, 1850, ae 48	274
CHILD, Grace, ae 25, b. in Chatham, m. Morris **BROWN**, miner, ae 23, b. in Philadelphia, res. Portland, June 1, 1851, by Joseph Law	280
CHURCHILL, David, mariner, b. in Portland, res. Staten Island, d. Dec. [ ], 1847, ae 21	263
Emily Hall, m. Erastus **BRAINERD**, Jr., b. of Portland, Oct. 10, 1843, by Rev. Sam[ue]l M. Emery	7

BARBOUR COLLECTION

	Page
CHURCHILL, (cont.)	
Jerusha Ufford, m. Alfred Hurlburt **ALLEN**, b. of Portland, [ ], 1846, at Henry Churchill's house, by Rev. Sam[ue]l M. Emery	15
Mary Brown, of Portland, m. Nathan Denison **MORGAN**, of Brooklyn, N. Y., Feb. 14, 1842, by Rev. Sam[ue]l M. Emery	3
Ruth, b. in Chatham, res. Portland, d. Jan. 1, 1849, ae 86	271
CLARK, Clara Emily, d. Edward, mariner, ae 27, & Emily H., ae 23, b. Mar. 13, 1851	275
John Harris, m. Sarah Jane **PENFIELD**, b. of Portland, Dec. 24, 1853, by Rev. Sam[ue]l M. Emery	30
Martha B., m. Sylvester **STOCKING**, Feb. 23, 1811	251
Samuel F., of Middletown, m. Mary W. **PENFIELD**, of Portland, Nov. 3, 1844, by Rev. Samuel M. Emery	9
CLEVELAND, Hillard, of Munson, Mass., m. Angeline Elizabeth **CADWELL**, of Portland, May 9, 1842, by Rev. Sam[ue]l M. Emery	4
CLINCH, Margaret, d. James, quarryman, ae 30, & Bridget, ae 30, b. Nov. 26, 1847	257
CODEY, -----, d. John, laborer, b. Dec. 9, 1850	276
COE, Julia Williams, d. Wellington S., coaster, ae 31, & Elizabeth, ae 30, b. Sept. 19, 1847	256
COLBERT, John, s. Joseph, quarryman, ae 30, & Margaret, ae 28, b. July 26, 1849	267
-----, d. Joseph, quarryman, & Margaret, b. July 11, 1848	258
COLEMAN, Daniel, laborer, b. in Ireland, res. Portland, m. Ellen [ ], b. in Ireland, res. Portland, Dec. [ ], 1850, by Rev. John Brady	279
Mary, d. Dan[ie]l, laborer, & Ellen, b. July 27, 1851	277
Timothy, d. Mar. 20, 1848, ae 2 1/2	263
Timothy, d. Apr. 12, 1848, ae 2	264
CONCKLING, Augusta, d. Richard B., carpenter, ae 37, & Elizabeth, ae 30, b. Dec. 25, 1849	272
Malvina, ae 20, b. in Chatham, res. Portland, m. Timothy R. **PARKER**, shoemaker, ae 24, b. in Chatham, res. Portland, Nov. 18, 1850, by Rev. S. M. Emery	279
Sarah Malvina, m. Timothy Russell **PARKER**, b. of Portland, Nov. 18, 1850, at Henry Conckling's house, by Rev. Sam[ue]l M. Emery	24
CONDON, David, d. Mar. [ ], 1849, ae 15 d.	271
Maurice, s. Michael, quarryman, ae 40, & Mary, ae 39, b. Nov. 27, 1848	266
Michael, d. July 17, 1851, ae 2 y.	281
CONE, Silas, of Granby, m. Caroline M. **NORCOTT**, of Portland, Sept. 30, 1849, by Rev. Hervey Talcott	20
Silas, manufacturer, ae 55, res. W. Granby, m. 2d w. Caroline M. **NORCOTT**, ae 37, b. in Portland, res. W. Granby, Sept. 30, 1849, by Rev. H. Talcott	273
CONKLIN, [see under **CONCKLING**]	
CONLEY, Patrick, quarryman, ae 24, b. in Ireland, res. Portland, m. Jane **KELLY**, ae 19, b. in Ireland, res. Portland, Nov. 23, 1848,	

PORTLAND VITAL RECORDS 9

	Page
CONLEY, (cont.)	
by Rev. John Brady	269
CONNELL, Abby, d. Thomas, laborer, b. Sept. [ ], 1850	276
Johanna, d. Matthew, quarryman, ae 37, & Enerah, ae 30, b. May 17, 1849	268
CONNERS, Bridget, d. Jeremiah, quarryman, ae 24, & Ann, ae 22, b. Nov. 20, 1847	257
Bridget, d. Oct. [ ], 1848, ae 10 m.	271
Bridget, d. Jeremiah, quarryman, ae 26, & Ann, ae 24, b. Jan. 18, 1849	266
Katharine, d. John, quarryman, ae 40, & Hannah, age 30, b. Mar. 17, 1848	260
Katharine, d. Apr. 3, 1848, ae 2	264
William, s. W[illia]m, laborer, & Margaret, b. May 15, 1851	276
CONNERY, Esther, d. Thomas, laborer, b. Mar. 8, 1851	276
CONROY, Ann, d. Joseph, quarryman, ae 40, & Elizabeth, ae 38, b. May 8, 1849	266
COOK, Antoinette, d. John J., farmer, ae 29, & Antoinette, ae 19, b. Jan. 20, 1848	259
Sally, b. in Chatham, res. Portland, d. Dec. 22, 1849, ae 59	274
Selden S., m. Maria A. **ARTHUR**, Apr. 4, 1852, by Rev. Hervey Talcott	27
COOMES, Mary C., m. W[illia]m H. **BARTLETT**, May 6, 1868	251
COOPER, Henry S., spectacle-case maker, ae 20, m. Julia Ann **KELSEY**, ae 15, b. of Portland, May 24, 1848, by Rev. S. M. Emery	261
Henry Salisbury, m. Julia Ann **KELSEY**, b. of Portland, May 24, 1848, at Edwin Kelsey's house by Rev. Sam[ue]l M. Emery	19
Lydia Maria, b. in St. Lawrence Co., N. Y., res. Portland, d. Sept. 19, 1849, ae 5 y.	274
Mortimer, b. in Little Falls, N. Y., res. Portland, d. Oct. 3, 1849, ae 10	274
Sally G., Mrs., d. Oct. 29, 1849, ae 45	274
Sarah S., of Portland, m. George W. **LINSLEY**, of Fair Haven, Apr. 13, 1851, by Rev. Sam[ue]l M. Emery	25
Sarah S., b. in Chatham, res. Portland, m. Geo[rge] W. **LINSLEY**, Apr. 13, 1851, by Rev. S. M. Emery	279
CORBIT, Hannah N., d. July 23, 1851, ae 22 m.	282
CORNWALL, Andrew, m. Elizabeth **WHITMORE**, Jan. 30, 1843, by Rev. Hervey Talcott	6
Anna, b. in Newington, res. Portland, d. Sept. 29, 1848, ae 90	271
Carrie Augusta, d. W[illia]m E., merchant, ae 27, & Carrie A. N., ae 27, b. Nov. 12, 1850	277
Emily Ann, of Portland, m. John Gaylord **WELLS**, of Hartford, Sept. 13, 1847, by Rev. Sam[ue]l M. Emery, at Sylvester Gildersle[e]ve's	17
Emily Ann, ae 25, b. in Portland, res. Hartford, m. John G. **WELLES**, printer, ae 25, b. in Newington, res. Hartford, Sept. 13, 1847, by Rev. S. M. Emery	261
Jemima, b. in Chatham, res. Portland, d. Apr. 3, 1850, ae 69	274
Julia Ann, of Portland, m. David Sage **STOCKING**, of Charleston,	

CORNWALL, (cont.)
S. C., Oct. 30, 1845, at David Cornwall's house, by Rev. Sam[ue]l
M. Emery   12
Julia Ann, m. David Sage **STOCKING**, Oct. 30, 1845   251
Sophia, of Portland, m. Solomon **PHELPS**, of Windsor, May 27, 1850,
at David Cornwall's house, by Rev. Sam[ue]l M. Emery   23
Sophia, ae 50, b. in Portland, res. Windsor, m. Solomon **PHELPS**,
farmer, ae 57, of Windsor, May 27, 1850, by Rev. S. M. Emery   273
-----, s. Harvey B., housejoiner, ae 27, & Janette L., ae 21, b. Mar. 2,
1851   277
-----, s. Andrew, farmer, ae 29, & Elizabeth, ae 30, b. July 14, 1851   277
COTTER, Edward, quarryman, b. in Ireland, res. Portland, d. Aug. 19, 1850,
ae 40   282
Hannah, d. Patrick, quarryman, ae 35, & Hannah, ae 25, b. Mar. 8,
1848   260
Hannah, d. Mar. 9, 1848, ae 1 d.   264
Hannah, d. Mar. 16, 1848, ae 25, b. in Ireland   264
John, s. Edmond, quarryman, ae 30, & Johanna, ae 30, b. July 20, 1849   268
Mary, d. Timothy, laborer, b. Sept. 15, 1850   276
Mary, d. James, quarryman, ae 35, & Fanny, ae 30, b. July 2, 1851   278
William, quarryman, ae 27, b. in Ireland, res. Portland, m. Julia
FITZGERALD, ae 19, b. in Ireland, res. Portland, June 28, 1849,
by Rev. John Brady   269
William, quarryman, ae 24, b. in Ireland, res. Portland, m. July
FITZGERALD, ae 22, b. in Ireland, res. Portland, July 15, 1849,
by Rev. John Brady   270
COTTRELL, Catharine, d. John, quarryman, ae 22, & Eliza, ae 20, b. July
14, 1849   267
COUGHLIN, John, quarryman, ae 25, b. in Ireland, res. Portland, m. Eliza
DAILEY, ae 20, b. in Ireland, res. Portland, Jan. 6, 1848, by Rev.
John Brady   261
William, s. John, laborer, b. Aug. 17, 1850   275
COURTNEY, Catherine, d. Oct. 17, 1847, ae 21 m.   263
Dan, d. Oct. [ ], 1848, ae 9 m.   271
Daniel, s. Daniel, quarryman, ae 30, & Catharine, ae 31, b. Dec. 11,
1847   257
Frances, b. in Ireland, res. Portland, d. June [ ], 1849, ae 5   271
Johanna, b. in Ireland, res. Portland, d. Oct. 3, 1847, ae 5   263
COVELL, Charlotte N., ae 28, b. in Glastonbury, res. E. Windsor, m. Henry
SMITH, farmer, ae 24, b. in Ellington, res. E. Windsor, Mar. 17,
1850, by Rev. S. M. Emery   273
Charlotte Newell, of Portland, m. Henry **SMITH**, of Ellington, Mar. 17,
1850, at Elisha Covell's house, by Rev. Sam[ue]l M. Emery   22
COWLES, Sherman, of Kensington, m. Maria **BRAINERD**, Sept. 20, 1846,
by Rev. Hervey Talcott   15
CRARTY, [see also **CARTY**], Eliza, d. Michael, quarryman, ae 28, & Mary,
ae 21, b. June 27, 1849   267
CRATY*, Michael, quarryman, ae 28, b. in Ireland, res. Portland, m. Mary

PORTLAND VITAL RECORDS 11

CRATY*, (cont.)
    CASEY, ae 19, b. in Ireland, Aug. 6, 1848, by Rev. John Brady
    (*Perhaps "**CRARTY**"?)   261
CRAW, Chester Gilbert, s. Ebenezer, farmer, ae 25, & Cornelia, ae 22, b.
    May 6, 1851   275
-----, s. Ebenezer, farmer, ae 22, & Cornelia, ae 20, b. July 14, 1849   265
CURTIN, CURTEN, Edmund, s. Thomas, quarryman, ae 25, & Margaret,
    ae 29, b. Jan. 6, 1849   266
    Ellen, d. Thomas, laborer, b. June 30, 1851   277
    Michael, d. Nov. 8, 1847, ae 14 m.   263
DAGLE, Sam[ue]l J., d. Apr. 19, 1851, ae 6 m.   281
DAILEY, Bridget, d. Mar. 5, 1848, ae 4   264
    Catharine, d. John, quarryman, ae 25, & Ann, ae 24, b. Feb. 20, 1851   278
    Eliza, ae 20, b. in Ireland, res. Portland, m. John **COUGHLIN,**
    quarryman, ae 25, b. in Ireland, res. Portland, Jan. 6, 1848, by
    Rev. John Brady   261
D'ANGELIST, Ann Amelia, m. David M. **STAPLIN,** Sept. 5, 1852, by
    S. G. W. J. Rankin   29
    Charles S., of Chester, m. Ann **HOLMES,** of Chatham, Jan. 18, 1846,
    by Huntington Selden, J. P.   13
DANIELS, Edgar A., s. Hiram A., blacksmith, ae 29, & Hannah E., ae 30,
    b. May 17, 1851   278
DARLING, Samuel, m. Paulina **HOPKINS,** Feb. 6, 1852, by S. G. W. J.
    Rankin   27
DAVIS, Amelia, m. William Sage **STRICKLAND,** b. of Portland, June 1,
    1854, by Rev. Sam[ue]l M. Emery   31
    Amelia A., ae 28, b. in Chatham, res. Portland, m. Benj[amin] F.
    BRAINERD, overseer in quarry, ae 29, b. in Chatham, res.
    Portland, Mar. 26, 1851, by Rev. Townsend   279
    Mary, b. in Chatham, res. Portland, d. Sept. 12, 1850, ae 35   281
    Mary E., d. Samuel, brass founder, ae 33, & Mary, ae 34, b. June 12,
    1850   272
DAY, Guy B., m. Mary Ann **LEWIS,** Sept. 30, 1849, by Rev. Hervey Talcott   20
    Guy B., Rev. teacher, ae 28, b. in Colchester, res. Apalacicola(?),
    Florida, m. Mary Ann **LEWIS,** ae 26, b. in Portland, res.
    Apalacicola, Florida, Sept. 30, 1849, by Rev. H. Talcott   273
DEAN, Lucy, m. Thomas S. **DEAN,** Oct. 31, 1847, by Rev. Hervey Talcott   17
    Lucy, ae 25, of Portland, m. Tho[ma]s S. **DEAN,** quarryman, ae 24, b.
    in E. Haddam, res. Portland, Oct. 31, 1847, by Rev. H. Talcott
    (Her 2d marriage)   262
    Pulaski M., child of Thomas S., quarryman, ae 24, & Lucy, ae 25,
    b. Nov. 16, 1847   259
    Theodore, of E. Haddam, m. Lucy **DICKERSON,** of Portland, Dec. 3,
    1844, at Zaccheus Waldo's house, by Rev. Sam[ue]l M. Emery   9
    Thomas S., m. Lucy **DEAN,** Oct. 31, 1847, by Rev. Hervey Talcott   17
    Tho[ma]s S., quarryman, ae 24, b. in E. Haddam, res. Portland, m. Lucy
    DEAN, ae 25, of Portland, Oct. 31, 1847, by Rev. H. Talcott   262
    -----, d. Thomas S., quarryman, ae 24, & Lucy, ae 25, b. Aug. 5, 1848   268

	Page
DEARNE, Daniel, d. July 16, 1851, ae 14 m.	281
DELAY, Margaret, d. John, quarryman, ae 36, & Hannah, ae 38, b. May 20, 1851	278
DESHON, Giles Henry, Rev., of Mereden, m. Jane Maria **BRAINERD**, of Portland, May 25, 1853, by Rev. Sam[ue]l M. Emery	30
DESMOND, Margaret, d. William, quarryman, ae 32, & Ellen, ae 28, b. May 20, 1849	268
Michael, s. Dennis, laborer, b. July 14, 1851	277
Peter, s. Daniel, quarryman, ae 24, & Catherine, ae 22, b. Apr. 3, 1848	258
DICKERSON, Lucy, of Portland, m. Theodore **DEAN**, of E. Haddam, Dec. 3, 1844, at Zaccheus Waldo's house, by Rev. Sam[ue]l M. Emery	9
DICKINSON, Ellen, d. Elijah, Jr., quarryman, ae 30, & Vienna, ae 26, b. Nov. 30, 1847	260
Ellen, d. Dec. 10, 1847, ae 2 w.	264
Elijah, of Glastonbury, m. Vienna D. **HALL**, of Portland, Feb. 24, 1845, at Hiram Penfield's house, by Rev. Sam[ue]l Emery	10
DINGWELL, Wiliam B., m. Amelia D. **BEERS**, Nov. 5, 1851, by Sylvester Stocking, J. P.	26
DINNEEN, Catharine, d. Lawrence, quarryman, ae 30, & Margaret, ae 30, b. Oct. 8, 1848	265
DONOVAN, John, s. Thomas, quarryman, ae 25, & Mary, ae 23, b. Oct. 7, 1847	256
William, quarryman, ae 25, b. in Ireland, res. Portland, m. Johanna **HORNETT**, ae 19, b. in Ireland, res. Portland, Feb. 18, 1849, by Rev. John Brady	269
-----, s. Edmond, laborer, b. June 25, 1851	277
DOOLING, Henry, laborer, b. in Ireland, res. Portland, d. Apr. 10, 1848, ae 26	263
DOWING, Richard, s. Patrick, laborer, b. Aug. 20, 1850	276
DRERY, [see under **DURY**]	
DUMAY, DAMAY, George C., m. Melissa B. **SCOVILLE**, July 16, 1848, by Rev. H. Talcott	19
George C., blacksmith, ae 24, b. in Salem, res. Portland, m. Melissa **SCOVILL**, ae 24, b. in Chatham, res. Portland, July 16, 1848, by Rev. H. Talcott	262
-----, s. George C., blacksmith, ae 26, & Melissa, ae 27, b. May 30, 1851	275
DUNHAM, Arvilla, of Portland,m. John A. **ILSLEY**, of Thetford, Vt., Dec. 4, 1842, by Rev. Hervey Talcott	6
Daniel, m. Mary **SMITH**, Sept. 28, 1845, by Rev. H. Talcott	12
Edwin G., m. Julia A. **STRICKLAND**, b.of Portland, Dec. 3, 1848, by Rev. Sam[ue]l M. Emery	19
Edwin G., quarryman, ae 25, m. Julia A. **STRICKLAND**, ae 23, b. of Portland, Dec. 3, 1848, by Rev. S. M. Emery	269
Edwin G., m. Jane **STRICKLAND**, Dec. 21, 1851, by S. G. W. J. Rankin	26
Ermina L., of Portland, m. William **ILSLEY**, of Thetford, Vt., June 12, 1842, by Rev. Rob[er]t Southgate	5

	Page
DUNHAM, (cont.)	
Julia, of Portland, m. Albert **GARDNER**, of Vernon, July 24, 1842, by Rev. Aaron Snow, of Eastbury	5
Orvilla, of Portland, m. Roswell **WALBRIDGE**, of Sharon, Vt., May 9, 1843, by Rev. Hervey Talcott	7
-----, d. Edwin G., laborer, b. Aug. 11, 1850	275
DUNN, Ellen, d. William, quarryman, ae 30, & Johanna, ae 27, b. Dec. 11, 1847	257
Ellen, d. James, laborer, b. May 1, 1851	276
Mary, d. July [ ], 1851, ae 1	281
DURY*, Joseph, m. Mary J. **WILLIAMS**, Nov. 16, 1851, by S. G. W. J. Rankin (*Perhaps "**DRERY**"?)	26
EDDY, Cordelia, b. in Chatham, res. Portland, d. July 24, 1851, ae 62	281
Hannah Gaines, m. Frederick Augustus **PARKER**, b. of Portland, Apr. 18, 1852, by Rev. Sam[ue]l M. Emery	27
ELY, Ann, d. May 27, 1849, ae 75	271
Nancy, of Portland, m. Daniel G. **WARNER**, of Hartford, Jan. 26, 1842, at Rufus Sears' house, by Rev. Sam[ue]l M. Emery	3
EMERY, Louisa Jane, d. Sam[ue]l M., clergyman, ae 43, & Mary, ae 31, b. July 29, 1849	267
ERVIN, William, s. William, laborer, b. June 21, 1851	277
EVANS, Isaac, m. Maria **GROVER**, of Portland, June 27, 1852, by Rev. F. B. Woodward	28
Zachary T., d. Jan. 16, 1848, ae 1 1/2	264
FISH, Henry F., m. Lucy C. **WILLCOX**, Jan. 21, 1850, by Rev. Hervey Talcott	21
Henry F., chemist, ae 35, of Waterbury, m. Lucy C. **WILLCOX**, ae 25, b. in Portland, res. Waterbury, Jan. 21, 1850, by Rev. H. Talcott	273
Lucy, d. Henry F., druggist, ae 36, of Waterbury, & Lucy C., b. Jan. 12, 1851	277
FITZGERALD, John, quarryman, ae 23, b. in Ireland, res. Portland, m. Margaret **SHERIDAN**, ae 20, b. in Ireland, res. Portland, Oct 17, 1848, by Rev. John Brady	270
John, s. John, quarryman, ae 23, & Margaret, ae 20, b. July 26, 1849	268
Julia, ae 19, b. in Ireland, res. Portland, m. William **COTTER**, quarryman, ae 27, b. in Ireland, res. Portland, June 28, 1849, by Rev. John Brady	269
July, ae 22, b. in Ireland, res. Portland, m. William **COTTER**, quarryman, ae 24, b. in Ireland, res. Portland, July 15, 1849, by Rev. John Brady	270
W]illia]m, quarryman, b. in Ireland, res. Portland, m. Elizabeth **O'NEIL**, ae 25, b. in Ireland, July 4, 1848, by Rev. John Brady	261
FLETCHER, Lawrence, m. Margaret **GRAY**, b. of Portland, Sept. 9, 1850, by Rev. Sam[ue]l M. Emery	23
Lawrence, laborer, b. in England, res. Portland, m. Margaret **GRAY**, b. in England, res. Portland, Sept. 9, 1850, by Rev. S. M. Emery	279
FLINT, Oliver Newell, s. James J., quarryman, ae 41, & Mary W., ae 37, b. June 18, 1851	277

	Page
FLOOD, Andrew, b. in Chatham, res. Portland, d. Jan. 16, 1850, ae 40	274
FLOWERS, George, m. Catharine **RAGIN**, b. of Portland, May 18, 1851, by Rev. Sam[ue]l M. Emery	25
George, laborer, b. in England, res. Portland, m. Catharine **ROGERS**, b. in Ireland, res. Portland, May 18, 1851, by Rev. S. M. Emery	279
FORREST, Richard, s. Thomas, quarryman, ae 28, & Katharine, ae 24, b. June 25, 1848	260
FORRESTEL, Ellen, d. John, Quarryman, ae 29, & Ellen, ae 27, b. Mar. 15, 1848	257
FREEMAN, Emma, of Glastonbury, m. William Riley **BULKLEY**, of Rocky Hill, Jan. 6, 1850, by Rev. Sam[ue]l M. Emery	21
Mary Ann, of So. Glastonbury, m. Henry Huntington **WELLS**, of Portland, Aug. 25, 1845, by Rev. Sam[ue]l M. Emery	11
FULLER, David T., of Deleware, Ohio, m. Harriet M. **SPARKS**, of Portland, Oct. 8, 1849, by Rev. Sam[ue]l M. Emery	20
Joseph A., of Middletown, m. Betsey E. **SMITH**, of Portland, Feb. 20, 1845, at the house of the late Capt. Daniel Smith, by Rev. Sam[ue]l M. Emery	10
GAMMONS, [see also **GANNON**], Christopher, d. Jan. 12, 1851, ae 16 m.	282
GANNON, GANNAN, [see also **GAMMONS**], Esther, d. John, laborer, b. Sept. 11, 1850	276
Hugh, s. Dennis, quarryman, ae 34, & Margaret, ae 28, b. July 22, 1848	258
Jesse, s. John, laborer, b. Sept. 11, 1850	276
John, s. Peter, quarryman, ae 25, & Mary, ae 22, b. Apr. 7, 1848	258
Julia, d. Christopher, quarryman, ae 29, & Bridget, ae 26, b. Apr. 11, 1848	258
Sarah, d. Peter, quarryman, ae 27, & Mary, ae 24, b. Oct. 1, 1850	278
GARDNER, Albert, of Vernon, m. Julia **DUNHAM**, of Portland, July 24, 1842, by Rev. Aaron Snow, of Eastbury	5
GIDDINGS, Martha, b. in Middletown, res. Portland, d. Oct. 24, 1850, ae 58	280
GILBERT, G. C. H., m. Harriette **TALCOTT**, May 6, 1845, by Rev. H. Talcott	11
GILDERSLEEVE, GILDERSLEVE, Annah, d. Henry, shipbuilder, ae 33, & Emily, ae 30, b. Feb. 28, 1850	272
Esther Rebecca, of Portland, m. Jonah Clark **BUCKINGHAM**, of Barnwell, S. C., Sept. 8, 1846, at Sylvester Gildersleeve's house, by Rev. Sam[ue]l M. Emery	14
Isabella, m. Henry Hobart **GILLAM**, b. of Portland, Aug. 19, 1854, by Rev. Sam[ue]l M. Emery	31
Mary Bartlett, d. Henry, ship builder, ae 31, & Emily F., ae 27, b. Mar. 9, 1848	256
Statira, m. Charles Alpheas **JARVIS**, b. of Portland, Jan. 17, 1854, at Sylvester Gildersleve's house, by Rev. Sam[ue]l M. Emery	31
GILLAM, GILLIAM, GILLUM, GILHAM, George, Jr., m. Charlotte Maria **JARVIS**, b. of Portland, Oct. 8, 1850, by Rev. Sam[ue]l M. Emery	23
Geo[rge], Jr., overseer in quarry, b. in Chatham, res. Portland, m. Charlotte M. **JARVIS**, b. in Chatham, res. Portland, Oct. 8, 1850, by Rev. S. M. Emery	279

	Page
GILLAM, GILLIAM, GILLUM, GILHAM, (cont.)	
Henry Hobart, m. Isabella **GILDERSLE[E]VE**, b. of Portland, Aug. 19, 1854, by Rev. Sam[ue]l M. Emery	31
Pamelia, d. May 5, 1848, ae 49	263
Sophia, d. Apr. 4, 1849, ae 43	271
GLADWIN, Leara, m. Theodore F. **LEWIS**, May 23, 1852, by Rev. H. Talcott	28
GLEASON, William, rr. agent, ae 33, of Bethel, Vt., m. 2d w. Abby G. **WILCOX**, ae 29, b. in Portland, res. Bethel, Vt., Mar. 18, 1850, by Rev. S. M. Emery	273
William Trowbridge, of Bethel, Vt., m. Abigail Gleason **WILLCOX**, of Portland, Mar. 18, 1850, at the house of Mrs. Eliza Willcox, by Rev. Sam[ue]l M. Emery	22
-----, d. W[illia]m, quarryman, & Abby, b. June 16, 1851	276
GOFF, Catharine, d. Jesse, quarryman, ae 48, & Mary, ae 40, b. Jan. 29, 1851	278
Isabella, d. Jesse, quarryman, ae 46, & Mary, ae 38, b. Feb. 7, 1849	268
Jeremiah, m. Harriet **BUTTON**, b. of Portland, Jan. 8, 1846, by Rev. Sam[ue]l M. Emery	13
Sarah, d. Jeremiah, quarryman, ae 27, & Hannah, ae 22, b. Mar. 20, 1848	260
Sarah E., d. Jesse, quarryman, ae 46, & Mary, ae 37, b. Sept. 27, 1847	259
GOODRICH, Ann Augusta, d. Stephen, ship carpenter, ae 37, & Esther, ae 34, b. Nov. 3, 1849	273
Archibald, s. Elizur, Jr., shoemaker, ae 25, & Caroline, ae 23, b. June 8, 1848	258
Cora Maria, d. Aug. 30, 1847, ae 17 m.	263
Dolly, of Portland, m. Samuel G. W. J. **RANKIN**, of Ripley, Ohio, Aug. 27, 1845, by Rev. Hervey Talcott	11
Elizabeth C., of Portland, m. Oliver S. **MEECH**, of E. Haddam, May 19, 1850, by Rev. Hervey Talcott	23
Elizabeth C., ae 18, b. in Glastonbury, res. E. Haddam, m. Oliver **MEACH**, joiner, ae 23, of E. Haddam, May 19, 1850, by Rev. H. Talcott	273
Elizur, m. Caroline **SHEPARD**, b. of Portland, Sept. 7, 1844, by William Case	9
Flora A., d. Charles A., farmer, ae 26, & Nancy J., ae 20, b. Feb. 9, 1851	277
George W., of Glastonbury, m. Lucy **HURLBURT**, of Portland, Nov. 21, 1841, by Rev. H. Talcott	2
Jane, of Portland, m. William L. **ROGERS**, of East Hartford, Nov. 28, 1850, by Rev. Sam[ue]l M. Emery	24
Jane, b. in Chatham, res. Portland, m. William L. **ROGERS**, school-teacher, of Portland, Nov. 28, 1850, by Rev. S. M. Emery	279
John, s. Stephen, ship carpenter, ae 35, & Esther, ae 30, b. Nov. 7, 1847	259
Laurette, of Portland, m. Samuel **WARRINER**, of New Britain, Feb. 23, 1851, by Rev. Hervey Talcott	25

	Page
GOODRICH, (cont.)	
Laurette, ae 41, m. Samuel **WARRINER**, book-keeper, ae 56, b. in Springfield, Mass., res. New Britain, Feb. 23, 1851, by Rev. H. Talcott	280
Maria M., d. [1849], ae 2	274
Nancy Maria, d. Joseph E., farmer, ae 42, & Nancy W., ae 39, b. Apr. 16, 1850	273
Phebe, b. in Chatham, res. Portland, d. Dec. 11, 1850, ae 76	281
Rebecca, ae 25, b. in Chatham, m. William **LOWRY**, joiner, ae 35, b. in Tenn., res. Ripley, Ohio, Apr. 6, 1851, by Rev. Rankin	280
Rebeckah, m. William R. **LAWREY**, Apr. 7, 1851, by S. G. W. J. Rankin	26
Sarah, of Glastonbury, d. Jan. 23, 1849, ae 84	271
Sarah W., d. J. Edwards, farmer, ae 40, & Nancy, ae 37, b. June 13, 1848	259
GORMAN, John, laborer, b. in Ireland, res. Portland, m. Honora **MURPHY**, b. in Ireland, res. Portland, Oct. 23, 1850, by Rev. John Brady	279
John, s. John, laborer, b. June 11, 1851	276
John, d. July 15, 1851, ae 10 d.	281
GOSMAN, John, m. Ruth **READ**, Apr. 29, 1852, by Rev. Hervey Talcott (Perhaps "**GORMAN**)	27
GRAHAM, Edmund L., s. Edmund, quarryman, b. Aug. 2, 1850	275
Edmund L., d. Sept. 22, 1850, ae 7 w.	280
Joseph, laborer, b. in Chatham, res. Portland, d. Mar. 24, 1849, ae 70	271
GRAVES, William Barnabus, of Hebron, m. Catharine Maria **OVERTON**, of Portland, Sept. 10, 1843, by Rev. Sam[ue]l M. Emery	7
GRAY, Margaret, m. Lawrence **FLETCHER**, b. of Portland, Sept. 9, 1850, by Rev. Sam[ue]l M. Emery	23
Margaret, b. in England, res. Portland, m. Lawrence **FLETCHER**, laborer, b. in England, res. Portland, Sept. 9, 1850, by Rev. S. M. Emery	279
GREEN, Martin, s. Martin, laborer, b. Aug. 1, 1851	275
GRISWOLD, Harris, of Wethersfield, m. Ellen M. **SHEPARD**, of Portland, Sept. 23, 1852, by Rev. H. Talcott	29
Nathan Sparks, s. Charles, silversmith, b. Dec. 12, 1850	276
Sarah Jane, d. Nov. 29, 1847, ae 3 1/2 y.	263
Theodore, m. Sarah Augusta **HALL**, b. of Portland, Mar. 28, 1842, at Chester Pelton's house, by Rev. Sam[ue]l M. Emery	4
-----, s. Theodore, joiner, ae 31, & Sarah Augusta, ae 27, b. Feb. 29, 1848	257
GROVER, Maria, of Portland, m. Isaac **EVANS**, June 27, 1852, by Rev. F. B. Woodward	28
HADDEN, Hannah, d. William, quarryman, ae 24, & Margaret, ae 23, b. May 18, 1849	266
HALE, Alexander, farmer, b. in Chatham, res. Portland, d. Oct. 2, 1849, ae 57	274
Daniel, m. Sophronia M. **HALL**, b. of Portland, Oct. 24, 1841, by Rev. H. Talcott	1

HALE, (cont.)

Eliza A., of Portland, m. John H. **THOMAS**, of Orange, Ct., Nov. 24, 1844, by Rev. Hervey Tallcott	9
Eliza Ann, Mrs., d. Mar. 10, 1849, ae 38	271
Francis, m. Margaret A. **AMES**, May 2, 1852, by Rev. H. Talcott	27
Gardner, s. Titus, quarryman, ae 24, & Mary, ae 24, b. Dec. 28, 1847	256
Lucy E., m. Thomas **BAKER**, Nov. 25, 1852, by S. G. W. J. Rankin	29
Sarah A., of Portland, m. Daniel **SLOPER**, of Southington, [Mar.] 9, [1851], by Frederick W. Chapman,of Glastonbury	25
Sarah A., ae 22, b. in Chatham, res. New Britain, m. Daniel **SLOPER**, joiner, ae 25, b. in Southington, res. New Britain, Mar. 10, 1851, by Rev. F. W. Chapman	280
Susan F., d. William, farmer, ae 43, & Laura, ae 40, b. Nov. 9, 1848	268
Titus, of Glastonbury, m. Mary K. **STRONG**, of Portland, Dec. 22, 1846, at Kellogg Strongs house, by Rev. Samuel M. Emery	15
Vienna, of Portland, m.Thomas **BAKER**, of Middletown, Aug. 23, 1846, by Rev. H. Talcott (See also Vienna **HALL**)	14
William Hudson, s. Henry, quarryman, ae 28, & Clarissa, ae 32, b. June 11, 1849	266
-----, child of Daniel, farmer, ae 31, & Sophronia, ae 29, b. May 24, 1846	260
-----, d. Elisha, farmer, ae 32, & Ruth, ae 29, b. Feb. 10, 1849	268
-----, d. Titus, farmer, ae 27, & Mary K., ae 27, b. Mar. 19, 1851	275
HALEY, John, s. Dennis, quarryman, ae 35, & Mary, ae 26, b. July 26, 1851	278
HALING, Emily, m. David **ROBINSON**, b. of Portland, Jan. 12, 1853, at Jeremiah Haling's house, by Rev. Sam[ue]l M. Emery	30
Rebecca, b. in Glastonbury, res. Portland, d. July 28, 1849, ae 50	271
HALL, Abner, Jr., m. Mary A. **TAYLOR**, Mar. 7, 1847, by Rev. Hervey Talcott	16
Charles, m. Abby J. **WELLS**, Sept. 21, 1851, by S. G. W. J. Rankin	26
Eliza, m. Charles Henry **SAGE**, b. of Portland, Dec. 10, 1845, by Rev. W[illia]m Bliss Ashley, of Derby	13
Elisa A., m. Horace B. **BUCK**, b. of Portland, Mar. 2, 1845, by Edmund A. Standish	10
Eliza Stocking, d. Joel, farmer, ae 35, & Eliza Ann, ae 38, b. Feb. 11, 1849	266
Elizabeth, of Portland, m. David Sumner **NORTON**, of Hebron, Apr. 15, 1846, by Rev. Sam[ue]l M. Emery	14
Frederic Nelson, s. Sam[ue]l Nelson, quarryman, ae 28, & Olive S., ae 32, b. Dec. 4, 1847	257
Frederic S., d. Oct. 24, 1847, ae 15 m.	263
Harriet, of Portland, m. Luther H. **PERKINS**, of Hartford, [Nov.] 10, [1841], at Henry Hall's house, by Rev. W[illia]m Bliss Ashley, of Glastonbury	2
James Phillip, s. Alfred & Maria L., b. May 18, 1844. Recorded Feb. 15, 1912	254
John Henry, s. Alfred, merchant, ae 39, & Maria L, ae 35, b. Mar. 24, 1849	266

HALL, (cont.)

	Page
Lucy Brown, d. Edward, quarryman, ae 46, & Charity Brown, ae 33, b. Sept. 30, 1847	256
Maria E., d. Mar. 24, 1851, ae 9 m.	280
Mary Ann, d. Mar. 8, 1851, ae 2	281
Mary Ann, d. Abner, Jr., laborer, ae 24, & Mary Ann, ae 23, b. Jan. 24, 1849	269
Mary F., d. June 3, 1849, ae 2	271
Nathaniel Brown, m. Cynthia **SOUTHMAYED**, b. of Portland, Oct. 12, 1841, by Rev. Samuel M. Emery	1
Sarah Augusta, m.Theodore **GRISWOLD**, b. of Portland, Mar. 28, 1842, at Chester Pelton's house, by Rev. Sam[ue]l M. Emery	4
Sophronia m., m. Daniel **HALE**, b. of Portland, Oct. 24, 1841, by Rev. H. Talcott	1
Vienna D., of Portland, m. Elijah **DICKINSON**, of Glastonbury, Feb. 24, 1845, at Hiram Penfield's house, by Rev. Sam[ue]l M. Emery (see also Vienna **HALE**)	10
HARNEY, Hannah, d. Michael, quarryman, ae 35, & Catharine, ae 30, b. Dec. 14, 1847	257
HARRIS, George Washington, of Middletown, m. Amelia **JOHNSON**, of Portland, Feb. 10, 1842, by Rev. Sam[ue]l M. Emery	3
HARVEY, Wheelock Nye, of N. Y. City, m. Margaret B. **LEWIS**. of Portland, Aug. 26, 1852, by Rev. Sam[ue]l H. Elliott, of Westville	29
HAWKES, John, of St. Johns, New Brunswick, m. Sarah Smith **TRYON**, of Portland, Nov. 8, 1846, at the house of H. E. Simpson, by Rev. Samuel M. Emery	15
HAYES, Robert, s. Stephen, quarryman, ae 32, & Hannah, ae 29, b. July 8, 1848	258
HENNISON, Thomas, s. Patrick, quarryman, ae 29, & Mary, ae 26, b. Oct. 9, 1848	265
HERCKNET, Hannah Laura, of Middletown, m. William D. **BANK**, of Portland, Feb. 2, 1853, by Rev. Sam[ue]l M. Emery	30
HEWITT, Richard, quarryman, ae 25, b. in Ireland, res. Portland, m. Mary **JOYCE**, ae 21, b. in Ireland, res. Portland, Oct. 25, 1848, by Rev. John Brady	269
HICKOK, Horace F., of Chickopee Falls, m. Mary Ann **BELL**, of Portland, Nov. 4, 1849, by Rev. Hervey Talcott	21
Horace F., merchant, ae 27, b. in Rocky Hill, res. Springfield, m. Mary Ann **BELL**, ae 24, b. in Portland, res. Springfield, Nov. 4, 1849, by Rev. H. Talcott	273
Mary Frances, d. Horace F., merchant, ae 27, of Northampton, & Mary Ann, ae 25, b. Nov. 3, 1850	275
HIGGINS, Bartholomew, s. Williams, laborer, b. June [ ], 1851	276
Bartholo[mew], d. July 16, 1851	281
Elizabeth, d. William, quarryman, ae 23, & Joanna, ae 30, b. July 4, 1848	260
Margaret, d. William, quarryman, ae 32, & Hannah, ae 30, b. May 10, 1851	278

	Page
HILLS, David, m. Alice **BIDWELL**, of Glastenbury, July 31, 1842, by H. Talcott, Minister	5
Martha, of Portland, m. Edwin **STEVENS**, of Hartford, Oct. 16, 1842, by Rev. William Jarvis	6
HODGE, Caroline H., m. Harvey Young **PHILLIPS**, b. of Leicester, N. Y., Oct. 28, 1847, at Sherman Kelsey's house, by Rev. Sam[ue]l M. Emery	18
Caroline Hale, m. Harvey Young **PHILLIPS**, b. of Leicester, N. Y., Oct. 28, 1847, by Rev. S. M. Emery	261
Charles Williams, m. T[h]eresa Mason **KELSEY**, b. of Portland, Oct. 18, 1846, at Sherman Kelsey's house, by Rev. Sam[ue]l M. Emery	15
Lucy P., m. Leonard E. **POST**, Aug. 3, 1851, by J. L. Dudley	26
Sarah, of Glastonbury, m. Charles Alonzo **ROSBROOK**, of Portland, Nov. 21, 1847, at Edward Hall's house, by Rev. Sam[ue]l M. Emery	18
Sarah, ae 20, of Glastonbury, m. Charles M. **ROSBROOK**, quarryman, ae 28, of Glastonbury, Nov. 21, 1847, by Rev. S. M. Emery	261
HOLLISTER, Mary Jane, d. Ashbel, quarryman, ae 46, & Emily, ae 40, b. July 23, 1848	259
HOLMES, Ann, of Chatham, m. Charles S. **D'ANGELIST**, of Chester, Jan. 18, 1846, by Huntington Selden, J. P.	13
HOPKINS, Ebenezer M., of Portland, m. Laura U. **RICH**, of Chatham, Jan. 5, 1851, by Sylvester Stocking, J. P.	24
Ebenezer W., carpenter, b. in Chatham, res. Portland, m. Laura U. **RICH**, b. in Chatham, res. Portland, Jan. 5, 1851, by S. Stocking	279
Helen M., m. George W. **BELL**, Dec. 23, 1845, by Rev. H. Talcott	13
Jemima, b. in Chatham, res. Portland, d. May 31, 1850, ae 44	274
Paulina, m. Samuel **DARLING**, Feb. 6, 1852, by S. G. W. J. Rankin	27
Russell, m. Fanny **SHEPARD**, Dec. 20, 1846, by Rev. Hervey Talcott	16
Russell Daniel, s. Russell, wicker worker, ae 53, & Fanny, ae 31, b. Mar. 30, 1850	272
Ruth, d. Russell, wicker worker, ae 52, & Fanny, ae 30, b. Mar. 6, 1849	267
-----, s. Eber M., carpenter, ae 36, & Jemima B., ae 43, b. Apr. 25, 1849	267
HORNETT, Johanna, ae 19, b. in Ireland, res. Portland, m. William **DONOVAN**, quarryman, ae 25, b. in Ireland, res. Portland, Feb. 18, 1849, by Rev. John Brady	269
HOUSTON, Alexander, of Hartford, m. Emily Elizabeth **PELTON**, of Portland, [Aug. 21, 1842], by Rev. Sam[ue]l M. Emery	5
HUBBARD, Clarissa W., ae 21, of Portland, m. Edwin Dean **KELSEY**, quarryman, ae 30, of Portland, Jan. 16, 1848, by Rev. S. M. Emery	261
Joanna, d. Thomas J., shoemaker, ae 44, & Catharine, ae 36, b. Feb. 7, 1848	256
Ruth, b. in Chatham, res. Portland, d. Apr. 25, 1849, ae 78	271
-----, d. Tho[ma]s J., shoemaker, ae 46, & Katharine, ae 35, b. June 13, 1850	272
HUNT, Electa, of Portland, m. Walter **BULKLEY**, of Glastonbury, May 9,	

	Page
HUNT, (cont.)	
1852, by Rev. H. Talcott	27
HURLBURT, Catherine, m. George **STOCKING**, Apr. 26, 1843, by Rev. H. Talcott	7
Clarissa W., m. Edwin Deane **KELSEY**, b. of Portland, Jan. 16, 1848, at Job Hurlburt's house, by Rev. Sam[ue]l M. Emery	18
Emma Jewett, d. Chester, farmer, ae 41, & Eliza, ae 38, b. Nov. 2, 1849	272
Eugenia, d. Halsey & Malantha, b. Dec. 13, 1834, in Chatham	250
James M., farmer, ae 33, b. in Chatham, res. Portland, m. Mary Jane **JOHNSON**, ae 28, b. in Hebron, res. Portland, May 12, 1851, by Rev. S. M. Emery	279
Jesse, of Portland, m. Elizabeth **WELCH**, of Chatham, Dec. 10, 1843, by Selden Cook, J. P.	8
Joseph Gurney, s. Alonzo, farmer, ae 49, & Charlotte, ae 35, b. May 6, 1849	267
Leonora, d. Halsey & Malantha, b. Mar. 26, 1839, in Chatham	250
Lucy, of Portland, m. George W. **GOODRICH**, of Glastonbury, Nov. 21, 1841, by Rev. H. Tallcott	2
W[illia]m Welch, s. Alanson, farmer, ae 51, & Charlotte, ae 32, b. June 6, 1851	277
ILSLEY, John A., of Thetford, Vt., m. Arvilla **DUNHAM**, of Portland, Dec. 4, 1842, by Rev. Hervey Talcott	6
William, of Thetford, Vt., m. Ermina L. **DUNHAM**, of Portland, Ct., June 12, 1842, by Rev. Rob[er]t Southgate	5
INGRAHAM, Jane, b. in Colchester, res. Portland, d. June 27, 1850, ae 18	274
John, miller, b. in Chatham, res. Portland, d. Jan. 25, 1848, ae 54	263
JAMES, Elizabeth C., m. William H. **SPENCER**, July 11, 1852, by Rev. H. Talcott	28
JARVIS, Charles Alpheas, m. Statira **GILDERSLEVE**, b. of Portland, Jan. 17, 1854, at Sylvester Gildersleeve's house, by Rev. Sam[ue]l M. Emery	31
Charlotte M., b. in Chatham, res. Portland, m. Geo[rge] **GILLUM**, Jr., overseer in quarry, b. in Chatham, res. Portland, Oct. 8, 1850, by Rev. S. M. Emery	279
Charlotte Maria, m. George **GILHAM**, Jr., b. of Portland, Oct. 8, 1850, by Rev. Sam[ue]l M. Emery	23
JOHNSON, Adaline, of Portland, m. Alfred Erastus **CAMP**, of Mereden, Aug. 15, 1854, by Rev. Sam[ue]l M. Emery	31
Amelia, of Portland, m. George Washington **HARRIS**, of Middletown, Feb. 10, 1842, by Rev. Sam[ue]l M. Emery	3
James Dwight, m. Lucy Elizabeth **ABBEY**, b. of Portland, Jan. 20, 1846, at Edwin Bell's house, by Rev. Sam[ue]l M. Emery	14
Mary Jane, ae 28, b. in Hebron, res. Portland, m. James M. **HURLBURT**, farmer, ae 33, b. in Chatham, res. Portland, May 12, 1851, by Rev. S. M. Emery	279
Seth Terry, s. James Dwight, coaster, ae 25, & Lucy Elizabeth, ae 22, b. Mar. 20, 1848	257

	Page
JONES, Harriet Augusta, d. Jabez E., quarryman, ae 28, & Martha, ae 27, b. Sept. 22, 1847	256
Henry Warren, of E. Haddam, m. Julia Ann **KELSEY**, of Portland, Sept. 20, 1848, at Erastus Kelsey's house, by Rev. Samuel M. Emery	19
Jabez E., m. Martha G. **BIDWELL**, Dec. 20, 1841, by Rev. H. Talcott	2
JOYCE, Mary, ae 21, b. in Ireland, res. Portland, m. Richard **HEWITT**, quarryman, ae 25, b. in Ireland, res. Portland, Oct. 25, 1848, by Rev. John Brady	269
Michael, s. Edmund, quarryman, ae 35, & Margaret, ae 30, b. Sept. 17, 1848	265
KEEFE, John, s. John, laborer, b. Feb. 6, 1851	276
Mary Ann, ae 26, b. in Ireland, res. Portland, m. Bartholomew **POMFRET**, quarryman, ae 24, b. in Ireland, res. Portland, Feb. 10, 1849, by Rev. John Brady	269
KELLY, Jane, ae 19, b. in Ireland, res. Portland, m. Patrick **CONLEY**, quarryman, ae 24, b. in Ireland, res. Portland, Nov. 23, 1848, by Rev. John Brady	269
Julia, d. John, laborer, ae 24, & Mary, ae 22, b. Mar. 17, 1849	266
KELSEY, Edwin Deane, m. Clarissa W. **HURLBURT**, b. of Portland, Jan. 16, 1848, at Job Hurlburt's house, by Rev. Sam[ue]l M. Emery	18
Edwin Dean, quarryman, ae 30, of Portland, m. Clarissa W. **HUBBARD**, ae 21, of Portland, Jan. 16, 1848, by Rev. S. M. Emery	261
Julia Ann, m. Henry Salisbury **COOPER**, b. of Portland, May 24, 1848, at Edwin Kelsey's house, by Rev. Sam[ue]l M. Emery	19
Julia Ann, ae 15, m. Henry S. **COOPER**, spectacle-case maker, ae 20, b. of Portland, May 24, 1848, by Rev. S. M. Emery	261
Julia Ann, of Portland, m. Henry Warren **JONES**, of E. Haddam, Sept. 20, 1848, at Erastus Kelsey's house by Rev. Samuel M. Emery	19
Lydia S., m. Sherman **KELSEY**, Sept. 29, 1844, by Rev. Hervey Talcott	9
Sherman, m. Lydia S. **KELSEY**, Sept. 29, 1844, by Rev. Hervey Talcott	9
T[h]eresa Mason, m. Charles Williams **HODGE**, b. of Portland, Oct. 18, 1846, at Sherman Kelsey's house, by Rev. Sam[ue]l M. Emery	15
KENNEDY, -----, d. Daniel, quarryman, ae 22, & Catharine, ae 18, b. Nov. 19, 1848	265
KENT, David, s. John, laborer, b. Jan. 10, 1851	276
KILEY, KYLEE, Francis, s. John, shoemaker, b. June 1, 1851	276
Thomas, s. Michael, shoemaker, ae 38, & Ellen, ae 38, b. Mar. 17, 1849	266
KIMBALL, John, blacksmith, ae 25, b. in Middletown, res. Middletown, m. Rebecca **RICHMOND**, ae 19, b. in Chatham, res. Portland, Nov. 21, 1847, by T. P. Abell	261
KING, Margaret, d. Nov. 10, 1850, ae 17 m.	282
Mary Ann, d. Nov. 28, 1848, ae 9 m.	271
Walter, laborer, b. in England, res. Portland, d. Nov. 28, 1850, ae 28	280

KYLEE, [see under **KILEY**]
LANGDON, Edward J., of Berlin, m. Sarah D. **BRAINERD**, of Portland, Nov. 26, 1846, by Rev. Hervey Talcott — 15
LAVERTY, Mary, m. Alexander **McHAFFEY**, b. of Portland, Jan. 1, 1854, by Rev. Sam[ue]l M. Emery — 30
LAWTON, James, s. John, quarryman, ae 30, & Johanna, ae 28, b. May 28, 1849 — 266
    John, d. Jan. 9, 1848, ae 2 1/2 — 263
    John, s. John, laborer, b. May 10, 1851 — 276
    William, s. Patrick, quarryman, ae 37, & Margaret, ae 32, b. Dec. 11, 1847 — 257
LENNIHAN, LENNAHAN, LINAHEE, Cornelius, ferryman, ae 26, b. in Ireland, res. Portland, m. Mary **BRANSFIELD**, ae 19, b. in Ireland, res. Portland, Jan. 28, 1849, by Rev. John Brady — 269
    Cornelius, quarryman, ae 25, b. in Ireland, res. Portland, m. Mary **BRANSFIELD**, ae 22, b. in Ireland, res. Portland, July 20, 1849, by Rev. John Brady — 270
    Mary, d. Cornelius, quarryman, ae 35, & Margaret, ae 32, b. Dec. 15, 1850 — 278
LEWELLYN, Thomas, m. Grace **OULD**, of Portland, Apr. 15, 1854, by Rev. F. B. Woodward, of Middle Haddam — 31
LEWIS, Margaret B., of Portland, m. Wheelock Nye **HARVEY**, of N. Y. City, Aug. 26, 1852, by Rev. Sam[ue]l H. Elliott, of Westville — 29
    Mary Ann, m. Guy B. **DAY**, Sept. 30, 1849, by Rev. Hervey Talcott — 20
    Mary Ann, ae 26, b. in Portland, res. Apalacicola(?), Florida, m. Rev. Guy B. **DAY**, teacher, ae 28, b. in Colchester, res. Apalacicola, Florida, Sept. 30, 1849, by Rev. H. Talcott — 273
    Theodore F., m. Leara **GLADWIN**, May 23, 1852, by Rev. H. Talcott — 28
    William, m. Mary **STEWART**, Mar. 17, 1844, by Rev. Harvey Talcott — 8
LINAHEE, [see under **LENNIHAN**]
LINSLEY, George W., of Fair Haven, m. Sarah S. **COOPER**, of Portland, Apr. 13, 1851, by Rev. Sam[ue]l M. Emery — 25
    Geo[rge] W., m. Sarah S. **COOPER**, b. in Chatham, res. Portland, Apr. 13, 1851, by Rev. S. M. Emery — 279
LOVELAND, Eliza Ann, d. of Glastonbury, d. June 21, 1851, ae 16 — 280
LOWRY, LAWREY, William, joiner, ae 35, b. in Tenn., res. Ripley, Ohio, m. 2d w. Rebecca **GOODRICH**, ae 25, b. in Chatham, Apr. 6, 1851, by Rev. Rankin — 280
    William R., m. Rebeckah **GOODRICH**, Apr. 7, 1851, by S. G. W. J. Rankin — 26
LYNCH, Edward, quarryman, ae 26, b. in Ireland, res. Portland, m. Esther **BARRY**, ae 21, b. in Ireland, res. Portland, Nov. 12, 1848, by Rev. John Brady — 269
    Jeremiah, s. Michael, laborer, b. Apr. 27, 1851 — 276
    Michael, laborer, b. in Ireland, res. Portland, m. Bridget [   ], b. in Ireland, res. Portland, Apr. [   ], 1851, by Rev. John Brady — 279
MACK, -----, d. Oliver W., quarryman, b. Jan. 10, 1851 — 276
MAHER, Michael, d. May 26, 1851, ae 1 — 281

	Page
MAHER, (cont.)	
Michael, s. Patrick, laborer, b. June 16, 1851	276
William, s. Patrick, quarryman, ae 40, & Margaret, ae 27, b. Dec. 12, 1848	266
MARKHAM, Sarah L., d. Horace C., farmer, ae 28, & Elizabeth, ae 27, b. Nov. 3, 1850	278
MATSON, Mary A., ae 32, b. in Glastonbury, res. Portland, m. Pierpoint S. **PORTER**, blacksmith, ae 30, b. in Glastonbury, res. Portland, Sept. 22, 1848, by Rev. Lemuel	270
Melissa Josephine, d. Almond, factory spinner, ae 27, & Asenath, ae 26, b. Apr. 6, 1849	268
McCARTY, [see also **CARTHY** and **CARTY**], Daniel, s. John, quarryman, ae 26, & Mary, ae 25, b. Dec. 21, 1847	257
Honora, d. Charles, laborer, b. Mar. 15, 1851	276
Richard, s. John, quarryman, ae 30, & Mary, ae 30, b. Dec. 20, 1848	266
McCLEVE, Emma J., d. John, coaster, ae 30, & Martha, ae 26, b. Feb. 25, 1848	260
James, farmer, ae 29, of Portland, m. Maria **WARD**, ae 27, b. in Middletown, res. Portland, Oct. 28, 1848, by Rev. Phelps	270
Jane, ae 24, b. in Catham, res. New Haven, m. William **WARD**, tinner, ae 24, b. in Middletown, res. New Haven, Feb. 3, 1851, by Rev. S. M. Emery	280
Jane, of Portland, m. William Henry **WARD**, of New Haven, Feb. 4, 1851, at Mrs. Ruth McCleve's house, by Rev. Sam[ue]l M. Emery	24
McFARLAND, -----, d. David, laborer, b. Sept. 10, 1850	276
McHAFFEY, Alexander, m. Mary **LAVERTY**, b. of Portland, Jan. 1, 1854, by Rev. Sam[ue]l M. Emery	30
McNAMARA, John, s. Sheda, quarryman, ae 41, & Johan[n]a, ae 33, b. Feb. 21, 1848	257
MEECH, MEACH, Oliver, joiner, ae 23, of E. Haddam, m. Elizabeth C. **GOODRICH**, ae 18, b. in Glastonbury, res. E. Haddam, May 19, 1850, by Rev. H. Talcott	273
Oliver S., of E. Haddam, m. Elizabeth C. **GOODRICH**, of Portland, May 19, 1850, by Rev. Hervey Talcott	23
MENEY, Margaret, d. Andrew, quarryman, ae 21, & Mary, ae 19, b. July 20, 1849	267
MILLER, Frederika, d. Frederic, farmer, ae 41, & Juliett, ae 32, b. Aug. 2, 1850	277
MINAHAN, Mary, ae 20, b. in Ireland, res. Portland, m. Thomas **PUNCH**, quarryman, ae 31, b. in Ireland, res. Portland, Sept. 15, 1847, by Rev. John Brady	261
MITCHELL, Robert S., s. Robert A., butcher, ae 29, & Susan, ae 29, b. Nov. 21, 1848	265
MOLLAND, Lydia F., of Nantucket, m. Samuel **POTTER**, of Liverpool, Eng., July 11, 1852, by Rev. H. Talcott	28
MOORE, Patrick, quarryman, ae 23, b. in Ireland, res. Portland, m. Catharine **BARRY**, ae 20, b. in Ireland, res. Portland, Jan. 28, 1849, by Rev. John Brady	269

	Page
MORGAN, Mary J., d. July 26, 1851, ae 8 m.	281
Nathan Denison, of Brooklyn, N. Y., m. Mary Brown **CHURCHILL**, of Portland, Feb. 14, 1842, by Rev. Sam[ue]l M. Emery	3
-----, d. Nathan D., laborer, & Mary, b. Nov. 17, 1850	276
MOULTON, -----, st. b. d. Turner, farmer, ae 24, & Samantha, ae 19, b. June 28, 1849	265
MULKEY, Ellen, d. Timothy, quarryman, ae 35, & Mary, ae 25, b. May 16, 1849	266
Margaret, d. Timothy, quarryman, ae 35, & Mary, ae 25, b. Jan. 21, 1848	257
Timothy, s. Timothy, laborer, b. May 15, 1851	276
MURPHY, Honora, b. in Ireland, res. Portland, m. John **GORMAN**, laborer, b. in Ireland, res. Portland, Oct. 23, 1850, by Rev. John Brady	279
John, s. Daniel, quarryman, & Ellen, ae 24, b. Apr. 10, 1848	258
John, s. John, laborer, b. June 29, 1851	277
Michael, laborer, b. in Ireland, res. Portland, m. Bridget **TRACY**, b. in Ireland, res. Portland, Aug. 20, 1850, by Rev. John Brady	279
MYERS, John, laborer, b. in Ireland, res. Portland, d. Mar. 24, 1851	280
MYRICK, Esther, m. George J. **WHITE**, Oct. 15, 1845, by Rev. H. Talcott	12
NEFF, Billings, of Chaplin, m. Jane **BARTLETT**, of Portland, Sept. 5, 1841, by Rev. Samuel M. Emery	1
-----, st. b. d. Billings, quarryman, & Jane, b. Feb. [ ], 1851	275
NOLAN, John, s. John, laborer, b. Oct. 18, 1850	276
NOLAND, Margaret, d. Daniel, quarryman, ae 34, & Mary, ae 27, b. Jan. 21, 1849	266
NORCOTT, Caroline M., of Portland, m. Silas **CONE**, of Granby, Sept. 30, 1849, by Rev. Hervey Talcott	20
Caroline M., ae 37, b. in Portland, res. W. Granby, m. Silas **CONE**, manufacturer, ae 55, res. W. Granby, Sept. 30, 1849, by Rev. H. Talcott	273
Charles Albert, s. William, ship carpenter, ae 45, & Mary, ae 35, b. Feb. 3, 1848	256
Harriet M., m. Asaph **STRONG**, Mar. 7, 1852, by S. G. W. J. Rankin	27
Henry R., s. Richard P., ship carpenter, ae 33, & Mary, ae 23, b. Aug. 20, 1847	259
Maria, of Portland, m. John B. **BARRY**, of Haddam, May 5, 1847, by Rev. Hervey Talcott	17
Reuben Henry, s. Richard P., carpenter, ae 37, & Mary N., ae 26, b. Oct. 12, 1850	277
NORTH, William E., of Middletown, m. Ellen S. **TRYON**, of Portland, June 18, 1846, by Rev. H. Talcott	14
NORTON, Belinda Smith, m. Edward Augustus **PENFIELD**, Mar. 22, 1835	249
Charles Williams, s. Parker Pelton, mariner, ae 37, & Julia, ae 26, b. June 8, 1848	258
David Sumner, of Hebron, m. Elizabeth **HALL**, of Portland, Apr. 15, 1846, by Rev. Sam[ue]l M. Emery	14
Parker Pelton, of N. Y., m. Betsey **WILLIAMS**, of Portland, Apr. 9, 1844, at Charles Williams' house, by Rev. Sam[ue]l M. Emery	8

	Page
NORTON, (cont.)	
Parker Pelton, m. Julia **WILLIAMS**, b. of Portland, Aug. 18, 1847, by Rev. Samuel M. Emery	18
Parker Pelton, mariner, ae 37, b. in Chatham, res. Portland, m. 3d w. Julia **WILLIAMS**, ae 25, of Portland, Aug. 18, 1847, by Rev. S. M. Emery	261
-----, s. Parker P., shipmaster, b. Sept.16,1850	276
O'BRIEN, Catharine, d. John, laborer, b. Mar. 16, 1851	276
Harriet, d. John, 2d, quarryman, ae 34, & Margaret, ae 25, b. Mar. 17, 1848	257
James, quarryman, b. in Ireland, res. Portland, m. Catherine **POWER**, ae 29, b. in Ireland, res. Portland, Oct. 14, 1847, by Rev. John Brady	261
James, s. James, laborer, b. Aug. 6, 1850	275
John, d. July 14, 1849, ae 14 m.	271
Mary, d. Sept. 23, 1847, ae 9 m.	263
Michael, s. John, laborer, ae 25, & Mary, ae 23, b. Feb. 3, 1849	266
O'NEIL, Elizabeth, ae 25, b. in Ireland, m. W[illia]m **FITZGERALD**, quarryman, b. in Ireland, res. Portland, July 4, 1848, by Rev. John Brady	261
OULD, Grace, of Portland, m. Thomas **LEWELLYN**, Apr. 15, 1854, by Rev. F. B. Woodward, of Middle Haddam	31
OVERTON, Catharine Maria, of Portland, m. William Barnabus **GRAVES**, of Hebron, Sept. 10, 1843, by Rev. Sam[ue]l M. Emery	7
PARKER, Ellen Elizabeth, d. Timo[thy] R., shoemaker, & Sarah M., b. Mar. [ ], 1851	276
Frederick Augustus, m. Hannah Gaines **EDDY**, b. of Portland, Apr. 18, 1852, by Rev. Sam[ue]l M. Emery	27
Timothy R., shoemaker, ae 24, b. in Chatham, res. Portland, m. Malvina **CONCKLING**, ae 20, b. in Chatham, res. Portland, Nov. 18, 1850, by Rev. S. M. Emery	279
Timothy Russell, m. Sarah Malvina **CONCKLING**, b. of Portland, Nov. 18, 1850, at Henry Conckling's house, by Rev. Sam[ue]l M. Emery	24
PATTEN, Esther, b. in Eastbury, res. Portland, d. Nov. 5, 1850, ae 66	280
Joel, of Glastonbury, m. Sarah M. **REEVES**, of Portland, Dec. 25, 1849, by Rev. H. Talcott	21
John S., s. Joel, joiner, ae 27, & Sarah, ae 28, b. Sept. 20, 1850	278
PAYNE, Alfred A., m. Laura Ann **STRONG**, b. of Portland, [Nov.?] 2, 1845, at Kellogg Strong's house, by Rev. Sam[ue]l M. Emery	12
Daniel, of Windsor, Ct., m. Grace E. **STEWART**, of Portland, Nov. 22, 1855, by Rev. F. B. Woodward, of Middle Haddam	32
Eliza, m. Harvey **WILLIAMS**, June 24, 1850, by Rev. Hervey Talcott	23
Eliza, ae 23, b. in Portland, res. Hartford, m. Harvey **WILLIAMS**, clerk, ae 28, b. in Canaan, res. Hartford, June 24, 1850, by Rev. H. Talcott	273
Franklin, s. Franklin, farmer, ae 32, & Almira, ae 30, b. Sept. 28, 1847	259
Franklyn, d. Sept. 28, 1847, ae 1 d.	263
PEACE, [see also **PEASE**], Elizabeth, d. July 24, 1851, ae 3 m.	280

PEASE, [see also PEACE], Edward, m. Lavinia CHAPMAN, Mar. 3, 1850,
    by Rev. Hervey Talcott — 22
    Edward, carpenter, ae 23, of Portland, m. Lovina CHAPMAN, ae 18, b.
        in Glastonbury, res. Portland, Mar. 3, 1850, by Rev. H. Talcott — 273
PELTON, Elizabeth, d. Hezekiah G., farmer, ae 43, & Elizabeth, ae 41, b.
        June 23, 1849 — 268
    Emily Elizabeth, of Portland, m. Alexander HOUSTON, of Hartford,
        [Aug. 21, 1842], by Rev. Sam[ue]l M. Emery — 5
    Emma Augusta, d. Geo[rge] E., silversmith, ae 38, & Caroline, ae 37,
        b. Apr. 2, 1849 — 268
    Fanny, b. in Chatham, res. Portland, d. Feb. 8, 1851, ae 60 — 281
    Maria, m. Haynes Porter RANSOM, b. of Portland, Jan. 18, 1854, by
        Rev. Sam[ue]l M. Emery — 31
    Sarah, d. Lewis, wagonmaker, ae 39, of California, & Sarah, ae 33, b.
        Nov. 15, 1849 — 272
    -----, d. William, pewterer, ae 32, & Eliz[   ], ae 28, b. July 15, 1849 — 267
PENFIELD, Edward Augustus, m. Belinda Smith NORTON, Mar. 22, 1835 — 249
    Edward Parker, s. Edward Augustus & Belinda Smith, b. July 21, 1836 — 249
    Emma A., d. Julia, ae 22, b. Nov. 23, 1847 — 260
    Jane G., m. Harlow CASWELL, of Glastonbury, May 23, 1844, by
        Rev. Warren G. Jones, of Glastonbury — 8
    John, m. Maria ACKERT, b. of Portland, Jan. 5, 1848, at Peter Ackert's
        house, by Rev. Sam[ue] M. Emery — 18
    John, joiner, ae 23, of Portland, m. Maria ACKERD, ae 18, b. in
        Glastonbury, res. Portland, Jan. 5, 1848, by Rev. S. M. Emery — 261
    Lucy, b. in Chatham, res. Portland, d. Feb. 28, 1849, ae 103 — 271
    Marionette U., m. Demas S. WHITMORE, June 25, 1848, by Rev.
        Hervey Talcott — 19
    Marinette U., ae 28, of Portland, m. Demas S. WHITMAN, mariner, ae
        32, b. in Chatham, res. Portland, June 25, 1848, by Rev. H. Talcott — 262
    Mary W., of Portland, m. Samuel F. CLARK, of Middletown, Nov. 3,
        1844, by Rev. Samuel M. Emery — 9
    Oliver S., s. John, joiner, ae 27, & Maria, ae 22, b. Oct. 8, 1850 — 278
    Sarah Jane, m. John Harris CLARK, b. of Portland, Dec. 24, 1853, by
        Rev. Sam[ue]l M. Emery — 30
    Vienna, m. Philip SAGE, June 26, 1813 — 249
    William Dixon, s. Edward Augustus & Belinda Smith, b. Nov. 7, 1837 — 249
    W[illia]m Sylvester, s. George, laborer, ae 27, & Polly, ae 25, b. July
        18, 1849 — 267
PERKINS, Luther H., of Hartford, m. Harriet HALL, of Portland, [Nov.] 10,
    [1841], at Henry Hall's house, by Rev. W[illia]m Bliss Ashley, of
    Glastonbury — 2
PETTIS, George, d. Sept. 29, 1849, ae 14 m. — 274
    George, s. George W., shoemaker, & Cordelia, ae 29, b. Nov. 7, 1849 — 272
PHELPS, Solomon, of Windsor, m. Sophia CORNWALL, of Portland, May
    27, 1850, at David Cornwall's house, by Rev. Sam[ue]l M. Emery — 23
    Solomon, farmer, ae 57, of Windsor, m. 2d w. Sophia CORNWALL,
        b. in Portland, res. Windsor, May 27, 1850, by Rev. S. M. Emery — 273

	Page
PHILLIPS, Harvey Young, m. Caroline H. HODGE, b. of Leicester, N. Y., Oct. 28, 1847, at Sherman Kelsey's house, by Rev. Sam[ue]l M. Emery	18
Harvey Young, m. Caroline Hale HODGE, b. of Leicester, N. Y., Oct. 28, 1847, by Rev. S. M. Emery	261
POLLEY, Albertina, of Portland, m. Walcott WATSON, of E. Haddam, Sept. 7, 1845, by Rev. H. Tallcott	11
POMFRET, Bartholomew, quarryman, ae 24, b. in Ireland, res. Portland, m. Mary Ann KEEFE, ae 26, b. in Ireland, res. Portland, Feb. 10, 1849, by Rev. John Brady	269
PORTER, Lydia, d. P. Sabin, blacksmith, ae 33, & Mary Ann, ae 32, b. Oct. 17, 1850	278
Maria, b. in Entbury(?), res. Portland, d. Apr. 18, 1848, ae 28	264
Pierpoint S., blacksmith, ae 30, b. in Glastonbury, res. Portland, m. 2d w. Mary A. MATSON, ae 32, b. in Glastonbury, res. Portland, Sept. 22, 1848, by Rev. Lemuel	270
Sarah, d. Pierpoint S., blacksmith, ae 30, & Maria, ae 28, b. Apr. 10, 1848	260
POST, Jedediah G., of Gilead, Ct., m. Henrietta S. WELCH, of Portland, Oct. 24, 1847, by Rev. Henry Torbush	17
Jedediah G., minister, ae 36, b. in Hebron, res. Portland, m. 2d w. Henrietta S. WELCH, school teacher, ae 28, b. in Chatham, res. Portland, Oct. 24, 1847, by Henry Torbush	261
Leonard E., m. Lucy P. HODGE, Aug. 3, 1851, by J. L. Dudley	26
POTTER, Jemima Chapman, m. Rufus SEARS, b. of Portland, Apr. 29, 1850, by Rev. Sam[ue]l M. Emery	22
Joel H., joiner, ae 28, b. in Glastonbury, res. Portland, m. Sarah M. REEVES, ae 29, of Portland, Dec. 25, 1849, by Rev. H. Talcott	273
Samuel, of Liverpool, Eng., m. Lydia F. MOLLAND, of Nantucket, July 11, 1852, by Rev. H. Talcott	28
POWER, Catherine, ae 29, b. in Ireland, res. Portland, m. James O'BRIEN, quarryman, b. in Ireland, res. Portland, Oct. 14, 1847, by Rev. John Brady	261
PRENDERGAST, Auster, d. John, mason, & Auster, b. Aug. 15, 1850	278
Auster, d. Aug. 25, 1850, ae 10 d.	282
PUNCH, Ellen, d. Thomas, quarryman, ae 32, & Mary, ae 20, b. Sept. 24, 1848	265
Mary, d. Thomas, laborer, b. Sept. 8, 1850	276
Thomas, quarryman, ae 31, b. in Ireland, res. Portland, m. Mary MINAHAN, ae 20, b. in Ireland, res. Portland, Sept. 15, 1847, by Rev. John Brady	261
RAGIN, [see also ROGERS], Catharine, m. George FLOWERS, b. of Portland, May 18, 1851, by Rev. Sam[ue]l M. Emery	25
RANKIN, Samuel G. W. J., of Ripley, Ohio, m. Dolly GOODRICH, of Portland, Aug. 27, 1845, by Rev. Hervey Talcott	11
RANNEY, Lucy Ann, m. Daniel STRONG, b. of Portland, Feb. 12, 1843, by Rev. Sam[ue]l M. Emery	7
RANSOM, Haynes Porter, m. Maria PELTON, b. of Portland, Jan. 18,	

28 BARBOUR COLLECTION

Page

RANSOM, (cont.)
    1854, by Rev. Sam[ue]l M. Emery   31
RARIDEN, Mary, b. in Ireland, res. Portland, d. Nov. 28, 1850, ae 26   282
RATHBONE, Charles, C., m. Angeline **WELLS**, Feb. 29, 1852, by
    S. G. W. J. Rankin   27
READ, REED, John, s. John, laborer, b. Nov. 30, 1850   276
    Ruth, m. John **GOSMAN**, Apr. 29, 1852, by Rev. Hervey Talcott   27
REEVES, Emily, d. Sam[ue]l B., quarryman, ae 44, & Lucy Ann, ae 33, b.
    Feb. 17, 1851   275
    Julia, b. in Chatham, res. Portland, d. Dec. 21, 1850, ae 37   282
    Sarah M., of Portland, m. Joel **PATTEN**, of Glastonbury, Dec. 25,
    1849, by Rev. H. Talcott   21
    Sarah M., ae 29, of Portland, m. Joel H. **POTTER**, joiner, ae 28, b. in
    Glastonbury, res. Portland, Dec. 25, 1849, by Rev. H. Talcott   273
RICH, Laura U., of Chatham, m. Ebenezer M. **HOPKINS**, of Portland, Jan.
    5, 1851, by Sylvester Stocking, J. P.   24
    Laura U., b. in Chatham, res. Portland, m. Ebenezer W. **HOPKINS**,
    carpenter, b. in Chatham, res. Portland, Jan. 5, 1851, by
    S. Stocking   279
    Melissa, m. Samuel **ROWLEY**, Feb. 22, 1852, by Sylvester
    Stocking, J. P.   27
RICHARDSON, Artemus, blacksmith, ae 23, b. in Mass., res. Portland, m.
    Charlotte **STRONG**, ae 18, of Portland, Feb. 24, 1850, by Rev. H.
    Talcott   273
    Artemas P., m. Charlotte A. **STRONG**, Feb. 24, 1850, by Rev. Hervey
    Talcott   22
RICHMOND, Mary M., m. Harvey B. **SIMPSON**, Feb. 9, 1851, by Rev.
    Hervey Talcott   25
    Mary M., ae 18, b. in Chatham, res. Portland, m. Harvey B. **SIMPSON**,
    quarryman, ae 25, b. in Springfield, Mass., res. Portland, Feb. 9,
    1851, by Rev. H. Talcott   280
    Rebecca, ae 19, b. in Chatham, res. Portland, m. John **KIMBALL**,
    blacksmith, ae 25, b. in Middletown, res. Middletown, Nov. 21,
    1847, by T. P. Abell   261
ROBBINS, James, laborer, b. in Ireland, res. Portland, d. June 20, 1848   263
ROBINSON, David, m. Emily **HALING**, b. of Portland, Jan. 12, 1853, at
    Jeremiah Haling's house, by Rev. Sam[ue]l M. Emery   30
    Eliza, m. Washington **CHAPMAN**, July 3, 1845, by Rev. Hervey
    Tallcott   11
    Henry, m. Maria **ROBINSON**, b. of Portland, Dec. 26, 1853, at Mrs.
    Maria Robinson's house, by Rev. Sam[ue]l M. Emery   30
    Maria, m. Henry **ROBINSON**, b. of Portland, Dec. 26, 1853, at Mrs.
    Maria Robinson's house, by Rev. Sam[ue]l M. Emery   30
    -----, d. Burrage, blacksmith, ae 34, & Maria, ae 34, b. Mar. 29, 1849   266
ROGERS, [see also **RAGIN**], Catharine, b. in Ireland, res. Portland, m.
    George **FLOWERS**, laborer, b. in England, res. Portland, May 18,
    1851, by Rev. S. M. Emery   279
    Jane, teacher, b. in Chatham, res. Bristol Ct., d. May 6, 1851, ae 18   281

PORTLAND VITAL RECORDS

ROGERS, (cont.)

William L., of East Hartford, m. Jane **GOODRICH**, of Portland, Nov. 18, 1850, by Rev. Sam[ue]l M. Emery — 24

William L., school-teacher, of Portland, m. Jane **GOODRICH**, b. in Chatham, res. Portland, Nov. 28, 1850, by Rev. S. M. Emery — 279

ROSBROOK, Charles Alonzo, of Portland, m. Sarah **HODGE**, of Glastonbury, Nov. 21, 1847, at Edward Hall's house, by Rev. Sam[ue]l M. Emery — 18

Charles M., quarryman, ae 28, of Glastonbury, m. Sarah **HODGE**, ae 20, of Glastonbury, Nov. 21, 1847, by Rev. S. M. Emery — 261

Mary Emeline, of Northampton, Mass., m. Frances Harley **AXTELL**, of Amhurst, Mass., Apr. 6, 1849, at Charles A. Rosbrook's house, by Rev. Samuel M. Emery — 20

ROWLEY, Caroline Amelia, d. George W., laborer, ae 37, & Lydia L., ae 31, b. June 8, 1851 — 275

Charles S., s. Jesse, laborer, ae 29, & Prudence U., ae 23, b. Feb. 18, 1849 — 268

Elizabeth, d. John, carpenter, ae 31, & Lucy, ae 29, b. Sept. 7, 1849 — 272

Emma Louisa, d. Joseph, laborer, ae 27, & Roxana J., ae 20, b. Nov. 26, 1850 — 275

James Henry, s. George W[illia]m, quarryman, ae 34, & Lydia, ae 28, b. Mar. 24, 1848 — 257

Jesse, s. Jesse, laborer, ae 31, & Prudence U., ae 23, b. Feb. 14, 1851 — 275

Joseph, of Portland, m. Roxana **BECKWITH**, of Hartford, Dec. 30, 1849, by Sylvester Stocking, J. P. — 21

Louisa M., of Portland, m. Lyman M. **BACON**, of Hartford, Dec. 19, 1849, by Rev. Hervey Talcott — 21

Samuel, m. Melissa **RICH**, Feb. 22, 1852, by Sylvester Stocking, J. P. — 27

-----, child of George W., quarryman, & Lydia, b. Mar. 24, 1848 — 256

-----, s. Jesse, laborer, ae 29, & Prudence, ae 22, b. Feb. 18, 1849 — 267

-----, d. George W., laborer, ae 36, & Lydia L., ae 30, b. May 10, 1850 — 272

RUSSELL, Charlotte Augusta, of Portland, m. Daniel **AYRES**, Jr., of Brooklyn, N. Y., Oct. 6, 1848, at Daniel Russell's house, by Rev. Samuel M. Emery — 19

Charlotte Augusta, ae 20, of Portland, m. Daniel **AYRES**, Jr., physician, ae 26, b. in N. Y. City, res. Portland, Oct. 6, 1848, by Rev. S. M. Emery — 269

John C., mariner, b. in Haddam, res. Portland, d. July 5, 1849, ae 42 — 271

John Chatfield, s. John C., mariner, ae 42, & Abigail, ae 33, b. Oct. 16, 1848 — 267

RYAN, Michael, quarryman, ae 25, b. in Ireland, res. Portland, m. Bridget **WELCH**, ae 21, b. in Ireland, res. Portland, Aug. 1, 1849, by Rev. John Brady — 269

SAGE, Charles Henry, s. Philip & Vienna, b. May 5, 1816 — 249

Charles Henry, m. Eliza **HALL**, b. of Portland, Dec. 10, 1845, by Rev. W[illia]m Bliss Ashley, of Derby — 13

Charles L., farmer, ae 55, of Portland, m. 3d w. Harriet **WILCOX**, ae 46, Mar. 17, 1850, by Rev. S. M. Emery — 273

	Page
SAGE, (cont.)	
Charles L., m. Harriet **WILLCOX**, b. of Portland, May 6, 1850, at the house of Miss Harriet Willcox, by Rev. Sam[ue]l M. Emery	22
Eliza, m. Jeremiah Pelton **BUTTON**, b. of Portland, Dec. 2, 1850, at Charles L. Sage's house, by Rev. Sam[ue]l M. Emery	24
Eliza, b. in Chatham, res. Portland, m. Jeremiah P. **BUTTON**, shoemaker, b. in Chatham, res. Portland, Dec. 2, 1850, by Rev. S. M. Emery	279
Enoch, s. Philip & Vienna, b. Mar. 26, 1814	249
Enoch, m. Sarah **WILLCOX**, Feb. 23, 1836	250
Frances Lawton, child of Philip & Vienna, b. May 28, 1820; d. Nov. 13, 1820	249
Frances Lawton, child of Philip & Vienna, b. Apr. 12, 1825; d. Aug. 25, 1837	249
John Hall, s. Charles Henry, ae 31, & Eliza Hall, ae 23, b. Apr. 20, 1847. Recorded Feb. 15, 1901	254
Lavinia Elizabeth, d. Philip & Vienna, b. July 6, 1829	249
Mary Ann, m. Edward Collins **WHITMORE**, b. of Portland, May 20, 1852, at Mrs. Hannah Hale's house, by Rev. Sam[ue]l M. Emery	28
Mary Frances, d. Enoch & Sarah, b. Dec. 30, 1836	250
Oliver P., book-keeper, b. in Chatham, res. Portland, d. Aug. 13, 1849, ae 27	274
Oliver Penfield, s. Philip & Vienna, b. May 21, 1822	249
Philip, m. Vienna **PENFIELD**, June 26, 1813	249
Philip, s. Enoch, farmer, ae 37, & Mary, ae 34, b. Nov. 4, 1850	277
Sarah E., of Portland, m. Henry L. **STEWART**, of Chatham, Nov. 9, 1843, by Rev. H. Talcott	8
-----, d. Edward, farmer, ae 33, & Abigail, ae 32, b. Mar. 11, 1849	267
SANDERSON, Emily S., m. Daniel **BUTTON**, Dec. 24, 1846, by Rev. H. Talcott	16
Franklin, b. in Middletown, res. Portland, d. Oct. 13, 1847, ae 5	263
SAVAGE, Luther, m. Mary Jane **BUCK**, Nov. 17, 1850, by Rev. H. Talcott	23
Luther, carpenter, ae 23, b. in Chatham, res. Portland, m. Mary Joy **BUCK**, ae 24, b. in Chatham, res. Portland, Nov. 17, 1850, by Rev. H. Talcott	280
SCOVILL, SCOVILLE, David S., d. July 24, 1851, ae 4	281
Melissa, ae 24, b. in Chatham, res. Portland, m. George C. **DUMAY**, blacksmith, ae 24, b. in Salem, res. Portland, July 16, 1848, by Rev. H. Talcott	262
Melissa B., m. George C. **DUMAY**, July 16, 1848, by Rev. H. Talcott	19
William, d. July 6, 1851, ae 3	281
W[illia]m Henry, s. Isaac, Jr., quarryman, ae 21, & Susan, ae 29, b. July 16, 1848	258
SEARS, Betsey, b. in Chatham, res. Portland, d. Feb. 22, 1849, ae 45	271
Charles Abbott, s. Rufus, quarryman, ae 45, & Betsey, ae 45, b. Feb. 21, 1849	268
Jane, d. Mar. 30, 1849, ae 14	271
Rufus, m. Jemima Chapman **POTTER**, b. of Portland, Apr. 29, 1850,	

PORTLAND VITAL RECORDS 31

Page

SEARS, (cont.)
by Rev. Sam[ue]l M. Emery 22
SELLECK, Gershom, of N. Y., m. Hannah Maria **TAYLOR**, of Portland, Apr. 2, 1849, by Rev. F. B. Woodward 28
SHEPARD, Amy B., of Portland, m. Homer **SKINNER**, of Marlborough, June 17, 1846, by Rev. H. Talcott 14
Caroline, of Portland, m. Frederick **WILLCOX**, of Middletown, Oct. 25, 1842, by Rev. G. Washington Nichols, of So. Glastonbury 6
Caroline, m. Elizur **GOODRICH**, b. of Portland, Sept. 7, 1844, by William Case 9
David, farmer, b. in Chatham, res. Portland, d. Oct. 24, 1850, ae 98 281
Edward, farmer, d. Jan. 16, 1848, ae 31 263
Elizabeth, d. Nelson, farmer, ae 27, & Elizabeth, ae 26, b. May 29, 1848 259
Elizabeth, b. in Chatham, res. Portland, d. June 22, 1849, ae 87 271
Ellen M., of Portland, m. Harris **GRISWOLD**, of Wethersfield, Sept. 23, 1852, by Rev. H. Talcott 29
Fanny, m. Russell **HOPKINS**, Dec. 20, 1846, by Rev. Hervey Talcott 16
Isabella L., d. Nelson, farmer, ae 30, & Elizabeth T., ae 28, b. Nov. 11, 1850 277
Mary, m. Egbert Oswald **BUTTON**, b. of Portland, Feb. 16, 1845, at Jonathan Shepard's house, by Rev. Sam[ue]l M. Emery 10
Noah, m. Eliza E. **SPENCER**, b. of Portland, Nov. 23, 1842, at Mrs. Abner Pelton's house, by Rev. Sam[ue]l M. Emery 6
Noah, m. Harriet E. **SPENCER**, b. of Portland, Jan. 1, 1845, at David William's house, by Rev. Sam[ue]l M. Emery 10
Penelope Elizabeth, of Portland, m. Henry **BRONSON**, of Bristol, Ct., Jan. 3, 1847, at Edward Shepard's house by Rev. Sam[ue]l M. Emery 16
-----, d. Noah, farmer, ae 24, & Harriet E., ae 22, b. May 6, 1848 259
SHERIDAN, Margaret, ae 20, b. in Ireland, res. Portland, m. John **FITZGERALD**, quarryman, ae 23, b. in Ireland, res. Portland, Oct. 17, 1848, by Rev. John Brady 270
SHINCK, Catharine, ae 19, b. in Ireland, res. Portland, m. Peter **WOOD**, quarryman, ae 20, b. in Ireland, res. Portland, Jan. 2, 1849, by Rev. John Brady 269
SIMPSON, Chales W., s. W[illia]m N., farmer, ae 26, & Lucy T., ae 33, b. Oct. 9, 1850 277
Harvey B., m. Mary M. **RICHMOND**, Feb. 9, 1851, by Rev. Hervey Talcott 25
Harvey B., quarryman, ae 25, b. in Springfield, Mass., res. Portland, m. Mary M. **RICHMOND**, ae 18, b. in Chatham, res. Portland, Feb. 9, 1851, by Rev. H. Talcott 280
Henry Edward, of Ellington, m. Mary **BROWN**, of Portland, Dec. 20, 1841, by Rev. Sam[ue]l M. Emery 3
Nelson, m. Lucy M. **TAYLOR**, Apr. 8, 1849, by Rev. H. Talcott 20
William N., farmer, ae 24, m. Lucy M. **TAYLOR**, ae 21, b. of Portland, Apr. 8, 1849, by Rev. H. Talcott 269

	Page
SKINNER, Homer, of Marlborough, m. Amy B. **SHEPARD**, of Portland, June 17, 1846, by Rev. H. Talcott	14
SLOPER, Daniel, of Southington, m. Sarah A. **HALE**, of Portland, [Mar.] 9, [1851], by Frederick W. Chapman, of Glastonbury	25
Daniel, joiner, ae 25, b. in Southington, res. New Britain, m. Sarah A. **HALE**, ae 22, b. in Chatham, res. New Britain, Mar. 10, 1851,by Rev. F. W. Chapman	280
SMITH, Betsey E., of Portland, m. Joseph A. **FULLER**, of Middletown, Feb. 20, 1845, at the house of the late Capt. Daniel Smith, by Sam[ue]l M. Emery	10
George, laborer, b. in England, res. Portland, d. May 27, 1851, ae 23	281
Henry, of Ellington, m. Charlotte Newell **COVELL**, of Portland, Mar. 17, 1850, at Elisha Covell's house, by Rev. Sam[ue]l M. Emery	22
Henry, farmer, ae 24, b. in Ellington, res. E. Windsor, m. 2d w. Charlotte N. **COVELL**, ae 28, b. in Glastonbury, res. E. Windsor, Mar. 17, 1850, by Rev. S. M. Emery	273
Margaret; d. Mar. 16, 1848, ae 65	263
Mary, m. Daniel **DUNHAM**, Sept. 28, 1845, by Rev. H. Talcott	12
Sarah, m. William Henry **BEEBE**, b. of Portland, Dec. 24, 1845, by Rev. Sam[ue]l M. Emery	13
SOUTHMAYD, SOUTHMAYED, Cynthia, m. Nathaniel Brown **HALL**, b. of Portland, Oct. 12, 1841, by Rev. Samuel M. Emery	1
Elizabeth Perkins, m. Gilbert **STONCLIFF**, Dec. 24, 1845, by Rev. Sam[ue]l M. Emery	13
-----, d. Clark G., quarryman, b. Dec. 1, 1850	276
SPARKS, Harriet M., of Portland, m. David T. **FULLER**, of Deleware, Ohio, Oct. 8, 1849, by Rev. Sam[ue]l M. Emery	20
SPAULDING, Samuel C., of Middletown, m. Mary Ann **BAILEY**, of Portland, Sept. 26, 1841, by Rev. Samuel M. Emery	1
Samuel Curtis, s. Sam[ue]l C., joiner, ae 26, & Mary Ann, ae 26, b. Mar. 10, 1848	256
-----, d. Sam[ue]l c., joiner, ae 29, & Mary Ann, ae 29, b. Mar. 15, 1850	272
SPENCER, Eliza E., m. Noah **SHEPARD**, b. of Portland, Nov. 23, 1842, at Mrs. Abner Pelton's house, by Rev. Sam[ue]l M. Emery	6
Harriet E., m. Noah **SHEPARD**, b. of Portland, Jan. 1, 1845, at David Williams' house, by Rev. Sam[ue]l M. Emery	10
William H. m. Elizabeth C. **JAMES**, July 11, 1852, by Rev. H. Talcott	28
SPLAN, James, s. James, laborer, ae 39, & Catherine, ae 36, b. July 1, 1851	277
Mary, d. John, quarryman, ae 35, & Margaret, ae 35, b. Mar. 25, 1849	266
STANCLIFF, STANDCLIFF, STONCLIFF, [see also **STANDFIFT**], Charlotte Jarvis, d. Gilbert, blacksmith, ae 25, & Elizabeth P., ae 21, b. Oct. 3, 1847	256
George declared intention of so signing his name instead of George **STANDFIFT** as he formerly did	253
Gilbert, m. Elizabeth Perkins **SOUTHMAYD**, Dec. 24, 1845, by Rev. Sam[ue]l M. Emery	13
STANDFIFT, [see also **STANCLIFF**], George declared his intention	

PORTLAND VITAL RECORDS

	Page
STANDFIFT, (cont.) of signing his name George **STANDCLIFF**, instead of **STANDFIFT**	253
STAPLIN, David M., m. Ann Amelia D. **ANGELIST**, Sept. 5, 1852, by S. G. W. J. Rankin	29
STEVENS, Edwin, of Hartford, m. Martha **HILLS**, of Portland, Oct. 16, 1842, by Rev. William Jarvis	6
Isaac, farmer, b. in Glastonbury, res. Portland, d. Feb. 24, 1848, ae 58	263
STEVENSON, Sarah Ann, m. John Russell **BROWN**, b. of Portland, Dec. 7, 1845, by Rev. Sam[ue]l M. Emery	12
STEWART, Grace E., of Portland, m. Daniel **PAYNE**, of Windsor, Ct., Nov. 22, 1855, by Rev. F. B. Woodward, of Middle Haddam	32
Henry L., of Chatham, m. Sarah E. **SAGE**, of Portland, Nov. 9, 1843, by Rev. H. Talcott	8
Mary, m. William **LEWIS**, Mar. 17, 1844, by Rev. Harvey Talcott	8
STOCKING, David Sage, [s. Sylvester & Martha B.], b. Jan. 16, 1812	251
David Sage, of Charleston, S. C., m. Julia Ann **CORNWALL**, of Portland, Oct. 30, 1845, at David Cornwall's house, by Rev. Sam[ue]l M. Emery	12
David Sage, m. Julia Ann **CORNWALL**, Oct. 30, 1845	251
George, m. Catherine **HURLBURT**, Apr. 26, 1843, by Rev. H. Talcott	7
Julia, [d. David Sage & Julia Ann], b. Sept. 13, 1846	251
Mary Ann, [d. Sylvester & Martha B.], b. Aug. 10, 1813	251
Mary Ann, m. Brackett M. **WEST**, Oct. 26, 1834	251
Sarah Maria, [d. Sylvester & Martha B.], b. Jan. 11, 1818	251
Sylvester, m. Martha B. **CLARK**, Feb. 23, 1811	251
STODDARD, -----, Mrs., d. Feb. 11, 1851, ae 90	281
STONE, Edward, b. in England, res. Portland, d. June 30, 1851, ae 4	281
Thomas, b. in England, res. Portland, d. May 27, 1851, ae 31	281
STOTT, Elasa, laborer, b. in Ireland, res. Portland, d. Apr. 29, 1851, ae 19 y.	281
STOUGHTON, Amelia, d. Feb. 9, 1851, ae 60	281
STRACHER, George, d. Feb. 24, 1848, ae 25	263
STREETHERS, Robert, m. Sarah **BRADY**, June 27, 1842, by Rev. S. Nash, of Middle Haddam	5
STRICKLAND, Abel, m. Laura **BUCKINGHAM**, Nov. 27, 1851, by S. G. W. J. Rankin	26
Ammuel, tanner, d. Aug. 3, 1848, ae 55	263
Charles, shoemaker, b. in Chatham, res. Portland, d. Nov. 14, 1850, ae 34	281
Emily, m. William Starr **WHITE**, b. of Portland, June 2, 1847, at Mr. Strickland's house, by Rev. Sam[ue]l M. Emery	17
Jane, m. Edwin G. **DUNHAM**, Dec. 21, 1851, by S. G. W. J. Rankin	26
Joel, Jr., m. Sarah **BROWN**, Nov. 29, 1843, by Rev. H. Talcott	8
Julia A., m. Edwin G. **DUNHAM**, b. of Portland, Dec. 3, 1848, by Rev. Sam[ue]l M. Emery	19
Julia A., ae 23, m. Edwin G. **DUNHAM**, quarryman, ae 25, b. of Portland, Dec. 3, 1848, by Rev. S. M. Emery	269
Mary Ann, m. Cecero **BROWN**, Feb. 6, 1851, by Rev.	

BARBOUR COLLECTION

	Page
STRICKLAND, (cont.)	
S. G. W. J. Rankin	25
Mary Ann, ae 25, b. in Chatham, res. Portland, m. Cicero **BROWN**, mariner, ae 24, b. in Chatham, res. Portland, Feb. 6, 1851, by Rev. S. G. W. J. Rankin	280
Phebe Ann, d. Dan[ie]l B., farmer, ae 33, & Harriet, ae 31, b. June 16, 1847	259
William Sage, m. Amelia **DAVIS**, b. of Portland, June 1, 1854, by Rev. Sam[ue]l M. Emery	31
-----, d. Joel, Jr., laborer, ae 27, & Sarah, ae 23, b. Aug. 5, 1848	259
STRONG, Asaph, m. Harriet M. **NORCOTT**, Mar. 7, 1852, by S. G. W. J. Rankin	27
Augusta S., d. Oct. 6, 1848, ae 2	271
Betsey L., of Portland, m. Elery B. **TAYLOR**, of So. Glastonbury, Feb. 2, 1851, by Rev. H. Talcott	24
Betsey L., ae 22, b. in Chatham, res. Portland, m. Elery B. **TAYLOR**, joiner, ae 22, b. in Glastonbury, res. Portland, Feb. 2, 1851, by Rev. H. Talcott	279
Charlotte, ae 18, of Portland, m. Artemus **RICHARDSON**, blacksmith, ae 23, b. in Mass., res. Portland, Feb. 24, 1850, by Rev. H. Talcott	273
Charlotte A., m. Artemas P. **RICHARDSON**, Feb. 24, 1850, by Rev. Hervey Talcott	22
Daniel, m. Lucy Ann **RANNEY**, b. of Portland, Feb. 12, 1843, by Rev. Sam[ue]l M. Emery	7
Laura Ann, m. Alfred A. **PAYNE**, b. of Portland, [Nov. ?] 2, 1845, at Kellogg Strong's house, by Rev. Sam[ue]l M. Emery	13
Mary K., of Portland, m. Titus **HALE**, of Glastonbury, Dec. 22, 1846, at Kellogg Strong's house, by Rev. Samuel M. Emery	15
-----, s. Adonijah, quarryman, ae 33, & Julia, ae 34, b. Nov. 18, 1848	265
-----. s. Adonijah, quarryman, ae 34, & Julia, ae 36, b. July 22, 1851	275
SULLIVAN, Sarah, d. John & Sarah, laborer, b. Mar. 18, 1851	276
SUMMERS, Dudley, laborer, d. June 20, 1851, ae 82	281
Sally, d. Feb. 11, 1851, ae 70	281
TALCOTT, Harriette, m. G. C. H. **GILBERT**, May 6, 1845, by Rev. H. Tallcott	11
Maria, d. June 27, 1848, ae 17	263
TAYLOR, Cha[rle]s P., d. Dec. 30, 1850, ae 4 1/2	280
Elery B., of So. Glastonbury, m. Betsey L. **STRONG**, of Portland, Feb. 2, 1851, by Rev. H. Talcott	24
Elery B., joiner, ae 22, b. in Glastonbury, res. Portland, m. Betsey L. **STRONG**, ae 22, b. in Chatham, res. Portland, Feb. 2, 1851, by Rev. H. Talcott	279
Elizabeth, m. William W. **BINGHAM**, of E. Haddam, June 26, 1850, by Rev. Hervey Talcott	23
Elizabeth, ae 18, of Portland, m. William **BINGHAM**, joiner, ae 21, b. in E. Haddam, res. Portland, June 26, 1850, by Rev. H. Talcott	273
Ellen, d. Gurdon, quarryman, ae 51, & Ruth M., ae 42, b. Apr. 25, 1849	268

PORTLAND VITAL RECORDS 35

	Page
TAYLOR, (cont.)	
Ellen, b. in Chatham, res. Portland, d. May 4, 1849, ae 9 d.	271
Frances E., d. Geo[rge] W., quarryman, ae 32, & Mary, ae 37, b. Nov. 27, 1848	268
George Washington, m. Mary Rogers **WOLCOTT**, b. of Portland, May 15, 1842, by Rev. Sam[ue]l M. Emery	4
Gilbert Russell, s. Harvey T., merchant, ae 28, & Nancy, ae 30, b. Dec. 31, 1849	272
Hancy M., d. Harvey T., clerk, ae 26, & Nancy, ae 28, b. Dec. 28, 1847	256
Hannah Maria, of Portland, m. Gershom **SELLECK**, of N. Y., Apr. 2, 1849, by Rev. F. B. Woodward	28
James, m. Ellen **ANDERSON**, Apr. 14, 1850, by Rev. Hervey Talcott	22
James, laborer, b. in Scotland, res. Portland, m. Ellen **ANDERSON**, b. in Scotland, Apr. 14, 1850, by Rev. H. Talcott	273
Jason Almond, s. David, quarryman, ae 36, & Jane, ae 28, b. May 1, 1849	268
Jeremiah H., m. Sarah Jane **BRAINERD**, b. of Portland, Nov. 25, 1847, by Rev. F. B. Woodward, of Chatham	20
Knowles H., m. Frances Emma **WHITE**, May 18, 1851, by Rev. H. Talcott	25
Knowles H., harnessmaker, ae 22, b. in Brooklyn, N. Y., res. Portland, m. Frances Emma **WHITE**, ae 19, May 18, 1851, by Rev. H. Talcott	279
Lucy M., m. Nelson **SIMPSON**, Apr. 8, 1849, by Rev. H. Talcott	20
Lucy M., ae 21, m. William N. **SIMPSON**, farmer, ae 24, b. of Portland, Apr. 8, 1849, by Rev. H. Talcott	269
Mary A., m. Abner **HALL**, Jr., Mar. 7, 1847, by Rev. Hervey Talcott	16
TEWKSBURY, W[illia]m P., book-merchant, ae 30, of Boston, m. Jerusha D. **BRAINERD**, ae 17, b. in Portland, res. Boston, Apr. 12, 1848, by Rev. S. M. Emery	261
William Plumer, of Boston, Mass., m. Jerusha Dickinson **BRAINERD**, of Portland, Apr. 12, 1848, at Erastus Brainerd's house, by Rev. Sam[ue]l M. Emery	18
THOMAS, John H., of Orange, Ct., m. Eliza A. **HALE**, of Portland, Nov. 24, 1844, by Rev. Hervey Tallcott	9
THOMPSON, -----, child of John L., farmer, ae 38, & Marietta, ae 31, b. July 3, 1848	260
TIBBALS, Rufus D., of Chatham, m. Harriet M. **TREAT**, of Northampton, Ohio, Aug. 24, 1852, by Rev. H. Talcott	28
William T., of Middle Haddam, m. Jane A. **AMES**, of Portland, Oct. 6, 1852, by Rev. H. Talcott	29
TRACY, Bridget, b. in Ireland, res. Portland, m. Michael **MURPHY**, laborer, b. in Ireland, res. Portland, Aug. 20, 1850, by Rev. John Brady	279
Mary, b. in Ireland, res. Portland, m. John **BAKER**, laborer, b.in Ireland, res. Portland, July 13, 1851, by Rev. John Brady	279
TREAT, Harriet M., of Northampton, Ohio, m. Rufus D. **TIBBALS**, of Chatham, Aug. 24, 1852, by Rev. H. Talcott	28
TRYON, Abigail, b. in Chatham, res. Portland, d. June 28, 1848, ae 69	264

36 BARBOUR COLLECTION

Page

TRYON, (cont.)
Daniel, d. Mar. 5, 1848, ae 6 — 264
Edward, quarryman, d. Nov. 13, 1848, ae 21 — 271
Elizabeth A., d. Mar. 30, 1848, ae 2 — 264
Ellen S., of Portland, m. William E. **NORTH**, of Middletown, June 18, 1846, by Rev. H. Talcott — 14
Eunice, b. in Glastonbury, res. Portland, d. Mar. 28, 1849, ae 85 — 271
Frederic, m. Fanny **BUTTON**, Dec. 30, 1846, by H. Talcott — 16
Sarah Smith, of Portland, m. John **HAWKES**, of St. Johns, New Brunswick, Nov. 8, 1846, at the house of H. E. Simpson, by Rev. Samuel M. Emery — 15
Thomas, carpenter, b. in Glastonbury, res. Portland, d. Mar. 25, 1849, ae 86 — 271
UFFORD, Sarah, b. in Chatham, res. Portland, d. Feb. 10, 1851, ae 92 — 281
VALENTINE, Rosannah M., of Portland, Conn., m. William E. **CHAPMAN**, of Westchester, Conn., July 3, [1851], by Rev. F. W. Bill — 26
WALBRIDGE, Roswell, of Sharon, Vt., m. Orvilla **DUNHAM**, of Portland, May 9, 1843, by Rev. Hervey Talcott — 7
WALDO, Leroy, s. Zacheas, quarryman, ae 32, & Sarah, ae 31, b. Apr. 1, 1851 — 278
Wesley, s. Zecheas, quarryman, ae 31, & Sarah C., ae 30, b. Nov 2, 1847 — 259
WARD, Maria, ae 27, b. in Middletown, res. Portand, m. James **McCLEVE**, farmer, ae 29, of Portland, Oct. 28, 1848, by Rev. Phelps — 270
William, shoemaker, d. Mar. 3, 1848, ae 38 — 263
William, tinner, ae 24, b. in Middletown, res. New Haven, m. Jane **McCLEVE**, ae 24, b. in Chatham, res. New Haven, Feb. 3, 1851, by Rev. S. M. Emery — 280
William Henry, of New Haven, m. Jane **McCLEVE**, of Portand, Feb. 4, 1851, at Mrs. Ruth McCleve's house, by Rev. Sam[ue]l M. Emery — 24
WARNER, Daniel G., of Hartford, m. Nancy **ELY**, of Portland, Jan. 26, 1842, at Rufus Sears' house, by Rev. Sam[ue]l M. Emery — 3
WARRINER, Samuel, of New Britain, m. Laurette **GOODRICH**, of Portland, Feb. 23, 1851, by Rev. Hervey Talcott — 25
Samuel, book-keeper, ae 56, b. in Sringfield, Mass., res. New Britain, m. 2d w. Laurette **GOODRICH**, ae 41, Feb. 23, 1851, by Rev. H. Talcott — 280
WATSON, Walcott, of E. Haddam, m. Albertina **POLLEY**, of Portland, Sept. 7, 1845, by Rev. H. Tallcott — 11
WEIR, -----, s. Alanson, quarryman, ae 48, & Emma, ae 42, b. Jan. 17, 1848 — 257
WELCH, Ann, d. July 16, 1851, ae 24 — 281
Bridget, ae 21, b. in Ireland, res. Portland, m. Michael **RYAN**, quarryman, ae 25, b. in Ireland, res. Portland, Aug. 1, 1849, by Rev. John Brady — 269
Elizabeth, of Chatham, m. Jesse **HURLBURT**, of Portland, Dec. 10, 1843, by Selden Cook, J. P. — 8
Frances, ae 24, b. in Ireland, m. John **CASE**, quarryman, b. in Ireland, res. Portland, Aug. 1, 1848, by Rev. John Brady — 261

WELCH, (cont.)
    Henrietta S., of Portland, m. Jedediah G. **POST**, of Gilead, Ct., Oct. 24,
        1847, by Rev. Henry Torbush   17
    Henrietta S., school-teacher, ae 28, b. in Chatham, res. Portland, m.
        Jedediah G. **POST**, minister, ae 36, b. in Hebron, res. Portland,
        Oct. 24, 1847, by Henry Torbush   261
    Martin, s. Martin, laborer, b. Aug. 3, 1850   275
    Richard, s. Martin, quarryman, ae 30, & Wingfred, ae 26, b. May 1,
        1848   258
WELLS, WELLES, Abby J., m. Charles **HALL**, Sept. 21, 1851, by
        S. G. W. J. Rankin   26
    Allen, s. Henry H., farmer, ae 27, & Mary, ae 26, b. Feb. 5, 1848   259
    Angeline, m. Charles C. **RATHBONE**, Feb. 29, 1852, by S. G. W. J.
        Rankin   27
    Henry Huntington, of Portland, m. Mary Ann **FREEMAN**, of So.
        Glastonbury, Aug. 25, 1845, by Rev. Sam[ue]l M. Emery   11
    John G., printer, ae 25, b. in Newington, res. Hartford, m. Emily Ann
        CORNWALL, ae 25, b. in Portland, res. Hartford, Sept. 13, 1847,
        by Rev. S. M. Emery   261
    John Gaylord, of Hartford, m. Emily Ann **CORNWALL**, of Portland,
        Sept. 13, 1847, at Sylvester Gildersle[e]ve's house, by Rev.
        Sam[ue]l M. Emery   17
WEST, Brackett M., m. Mary Ann **STOCKING**, Oct. 26, 1834   251
    Emma Isabella, d. Brackett M., joiner, ae 40, & Mary Ann, ae 36, b.
        Apr. 28, 1849   267
    Mary Ann Gates, [d. Brackett M. & Mary Ann], b. July 2, 1839   251
    William Wilfred, [s. Brackett M. & Mary Ann], b. Aug. 7, 1835   251
WETHERELL, Hancy Elora, d. Jonathan, quarryman, ae 32, & Mary Ann, ae
    36, b. May 26, 1849   269
    Henry M., d. [1849]   274
    Ruhaman, b. in Glastonbury, res. Portland, d. Jan. 11, 1849, ae 66   272
WHEELER, Elizabeth, d. Sept. 2, 1850, ae 71   281
    Lorenzo, of Columbia, m. Elizabeth **BILLINGS**, of Portland, Dec. 1,
        1841, by Rev. Samuel M. Emery   2
WHITE, Charlotte Ann, ae 29, b. in Portland, res. Bolton, m. Edward
        WHITE, farmer, ae 29, b. in Bolton, res. Bolton, June 19, 1849, by
        Rev. W. G. Jones   270
    Edward, farmer, ae 29, b. in Bolton, res. Bolton, m. Charlotte Ann
        WHITE, ae 29, b. in Portland, res. Bolton, June 19, 1849, by Rev.
        W. G. Jones   270
    Elizabeth, d. William S., farmer, ae 24, & Emily, ae 23, b. Apr. 14,
        1848   256
    Frances Emma, m. Knowles H. **TAYLOR**, May 18, 1851, by Rev. H.
        Talcott   25
    Frances Emma, ae 19, m. Knowles H. **TAYLOR**, harnessmaker, ae 22,
        b. in Brooklyn, N. Y., res. Portland, May 18, 1851, by Rev. H.
        Talcott   279
    Frederick H., s. George J., farmer, ae 30, & Esther, ae 23, b.

BARBOUR COLLECTION

	Page
WHITE, (cont.)	
Aug. 12, 1848	265
George, farmer, d. June 1, 1848, ae 85	263
George J., m. Esther **MYRICK**, Oct. 15, 1845, by Rev. H. Talcott	12
Ward, d. Sept. 15, 1847, ae 15	263
William Starr, m. Emily **STRICKLAND**, b. of Portland, June 2, 1847, at Mr. Strickland's house, by Rev. Sam[ue]l M. Emery	17
WHITMAN, Demas S., mariner, ae 32, b. in Chatham, res. Portland, m. Marinette U. **PENFIELD**, ae 28, of Portland, June 25, 1848, by Rev. H. Talcott	262
WHITMORE, Demas S. m. Marionette U. **PENFIELD**, June 25, 1848, by Rev. Hervey Talcott	19
Edward Collins, m. Mary Ann **SAGE**, b. of Portland, May 20, 1852, at Mrs. Hannah Hale's house, by Rev. Sam[ue]l M. Emery	28
Elizabeth, m. Andrew **CORNWALL**, Jan. 30, 1843, by Rev. Hervey Talcott	6
WILCOX, WILLCOX, Abby G., ae 29, b. in Portland, res. Bethel, Vt., m. William **GLEASON**, rr. agent, ae 33, of Bethel, Vt., Mar. 18, 1850, by Rev. S. M. Emery	273
Abigail Gleason, of Portland, m. William Trowbridge **GLEASON**, of Bethel, Vt., Mar. 18, 1850, at the house of Mrs. Eliza Wilcox, by Rev. Sam[ue]l M. Emery	22
Benjamin B., of Saybrook, m. Elizabeth **BRAINARD**, of Portland, May 29, 1842, by Rev. H. Talcott	4
Betsey, m. Joel **BARTLETT**, Jan. 18, 1809	250
Eunice C., m. W[illia]m H. **BARTLETT**, Oct. 20, 1840	251
Frederick, of Middletown, m. Caroline **SHEPARD**, of Portland, Oct. 25, 1842, by Rev. G. Washington Nichols, of So. Glastonbury	6
Harriet, ae 46, m. Charles L. **SAGE**, farmer, ae 55, of Portland, Mar. 17, 1850, by Rev. S. M. Emery	273
Harriet, m. Charles L. **SAGE**, b. of Portland, May 6, 1850, at the house of Miss Harriet Willcox, by Rev. Sam[ue]l M. Emery	22
Lucy C., m. Henry F. **FISH**, Jan. 21, 1850, by Rev. Hervey Talcott	21
Lucy C., ae 25, b. in Portland, res. Waterbury, m. Henry F. **FISH**, chemist, ae 35, of Waterbury, Jan. 21, 1850, by Rev. H. Talcott	273
Sarah, m. Enoch **SAGE**, Feb. 23, 1836	250
W[illia]m Bartlett, s. Horace B., farmer, ae 28, & Flavia, ae 26, b. July 23, 1849	267
WILLIAMS, Abigail, b. in Chatham, res. Portland, d. June 20, 1851, ae 60	281
Betsey, of Portland, m. Parker Pelton **NORTON**, of N. Y., Apr. 9, 1844, at Charles Williams' house, by Rev. Sam[ue]l M. Emery	8
Charles, quarryman, d. Mar. 30, 1848, ae 54	263
George Henry, of Middletown, m. Mary Lucinda **BAILEY**, of Portland, Mar. 21, 1847, by Rev. Samuel M. Emery	16
Harvey, m. Eliza **PAYNE**, June 24, 1850, by Rev. Hervey Talcott	23
Harvey, clerk, ae 28, b. in Canaan, res. Hartford, m. Eliza **PAYNE**, ae 23, b. in Portland, res. Hartford, June 24, 1850, by Rev. H. Talcott	273
Julia, m. Parker Pelton **NORTON**, b. of Portland, Aug. 18, 1847,	

	Page
WILLIAMS, (cont.)	
by Rev. Samuel M. Emery	18
Julia, ae 25, of Portland, m. Parker Pelton **NORTON**, mariner, ae 37, b. in Chatham, res. Portland, Aug. 18, 1847, by Rev. S. M. Emery	261
Mary J., m. Joseph **DURY***, Nov. 16, 1851, by S. G. W. J. Rankin (* Pershaps "**DRERY**")	26
William, laborer, black, b. in Enfield, res. Portland, d. Nov. 4, 1847, ae 100	263
William T., m. Mary W. **BARTLETT**, d. of Joel, decd., of Portland, Oct. 24, 1852, by Mark Tucker	29
-----, d. Joseph, hotel-keeper, & Laura, b. Mar. 18, 1851	276
WOLCOTT, Mary Rogers, m. George Washington **TAYLOR**, b. of Portland, May 15, 1842, by Rev. Sam[ue]l M. Emery	4
WOOD, Peter, quarryman, ae 20, b. in Ireland, res. Portland, m. Catharine **SHINCK**, ae 19, b. in Ireland, res. Portland, Jan. 2, 1849, by Rev. John Brady	269
YOUNG, Joseph, m. Eunice **BEERS**, July 13, 1851, by Sylvester Stcoking, J. P.	26
Joseph, quarryman, of Portland, m. Eunice **BEERS**, b. in Chatham, July 13, 1851, by S. Stocking	280
NO SURNAME	
Bridget, b. in Ireland, res. Portland, m. Michael **LYNCH**, laborer, b. in Ireland, res. Portland, Apr [ ], 1851, by Rev. John Brady	279
Ellen, b. in Ireland, res. Portland, m. Daniel **COLEMAN**, laborer, b. in Ireland, res. Portland, Dec. [ ], 1850, by Rev. John Brady	279

PROSPECT VITAL RECORDS
1827 - 1853

	Page
ADAMS, Laura Preston, [ ]	96
ANDREWS, Angeline, m. Tiba **ANDREWS**, Feb. 17, 1828, by Rev. John E. Brag	1
Cornelia, m. Lauren P. **BLAKESLEE**, May 13, 1843, by Thomas Wilmot, J. P.	20
Fanny, d. Dec. 23, 1838; ae 49 y. Samuel Williams, Jr., Adm.	98
Harriet, of Prospect, m. Hanford **ISBELL**, of Salem, Oct. 28, 1838, by W. W. Brewer	15
Miles R., m. Cornelia **MIX**, b. of Prospect, Apr. 2, 1837, by Thomas Wilmot	13
Tiba, m. Angeline **ANDREWS**, Feb. 17, 1828, by Rev. John E. Brag	1
ANTHONY, Eliza, of Mereden, m. Russell **BEACH**, of Bethaney, Dec. 5, 1853, by Asa H. Train	31
Lafayette, of Middlefield, m. Julia **JOHNSON**, of Harwinton, [Aug.] 26, [1849], by John L. Ambler	26
ATKINS, Julia, of Prospect, m. Garry **SPERRY**, of Waterbury, June 19, 1842, by Horace Porter, J. P.	18
AUSTIN, Aaron A., m. Betsey C. **GUN**, Jan. 16, 1834, by Lemuel Preston, J. P.	10
Abigail, d. Jan. 22, 1836	97
Amos, of Prospect, m. Hannah Louisa **GAYLORD**, of Hamden, Dec. 6, 1845, by Rev. Samuel W. Smith, Int. Pub.	23
Esther Jane, d. Aaron & Betsey C., b. Oct. 17, 1834	89
BALDWIN, Luther, of Harwinton, m. Nancy S. **TALMAGE**, of Prospect, Dec. 16, [1849], by John L. Ambler	27
Miles, m. Abigail **PAYNE**, July 29, 1834, by Samuel Peck, J. P.	10
BARBER, Phebe C., of Wolcottville, m. Spencer C. **THOMAS**, of Prospect, [ ] 27, [1847(?)], by Rev. Reuben Torrey	24
BARNES, BARNS, Elizabeth, of Prospect, m. John **WARNER**, of Derby, July 27, 1828, by Rev. John E. Brag	3
Emeline, of Northampton, Mass., m. Reuben M. **HITCHCOCK**, of Cheshire, [May] 5, 1849], by John L. Ambler	26
Jeremiah R., of New Haven, m. Catharine M. **PLATT**, of Prospect, Aug. 7, 1836, by Rev. Zephaniah Swift	13
BEACH, Mary, m. Major **HOTCHKISS**, Sept. 14, 1845, by Thomas Wilmot, J. P.	23
Russell, of Bethaney, m. Eliza **ANTHONY**, of Mereden, Dec. 5, 1853, by Asa H. Train	31
BEECHER, Anna, m. Sam[ue]l **DOOLITTLE**, b. of Prospect, Aug. 18, 1850, by Thomas Wilmot, J. P.	28
Chloe, m. Henry Peck **PLATT**, b. of Prospect, Oct. 16, 1836, by Rev. Zephaniah Swift	13

BEECHER, (cont.)
Elizabeth, of Prospect, m. Benjamin **BROCKET**, of Waterbury, May 29, 1831, by Rev. John E. Brag 7
Harriet, of Prospect, m. Jonathan **BRISTOL**, of Wallingford, Aug. 19, 1844, by Rev. Reuben Torrey 21
Hezekiah, d. Apr. 22, 1833 96
Stephen, m. Mary **TYLER**, Apr. 1, 1852, by Thomas Wilmot, J. P. 29
Temerence, m. Eben C. **TUTTLE**, b. of Prospect, Apr. 27, 1829, by Rev. John E. Brag 3
BENHAM, Almeda, m. Joseph **HULL**, Dec. 22, 1850, by Thomas Willmot, J. P. 28
Bennet, of Prospect, m. Harriet **JOHNSON**, of Woodbury, July 5, 1852, by J. Killburn 30
Edward Franklin Spencer, s. Franklin D. & Charlotte P., b. Sept. 14, 1832 91
Franklin D., m. Charlotte **PLATT**, b. of Prospect, Apr. 6, 1828, by Rev. John E. Brag 2
Lewis, m. Jennett A. **MATTHEWS**, Jan. 3, 1847, by Thomas Wilmot, J. P. 24
Miles, m. Elizabeth **PRESTON**, b. of Prospect, Jan. 11, 1829, by Rev. Hershal Sandford 3
Welcome E., of Cheshire, m. Martha **STREET**, Feb. 8, 1854, by Asa H. Train 31
[BIRMINGHAM], BURMINGHAM, Daniel S., m. Mary Ann **KNOWLTON**, of Waterbury, Apr. 18, 1837, by Thomas Wilmot, J. P. 13
BLAKESLEE, BLACKESLEY, BLAKESLEY, BLAKELEY, BLAKSLEY,
Hannah, of Prospect, m. Stephen **MERRIMAN**, of Southington, Nov. 30, 1843, by Rev. Reuben Torrey 21
Lauren P., m. Cornelia **ANDREWS**, May 13, 1843, by Thomas Wilmot, J. P. 20
Lydia Ann, of Prospect, m. John **STANLEY**, of Waterbury, Nov. 15, 1835, by Aaron Austin, J. P. 12
Maria, of Prospect, m W. M. **SPERRY**, of Cheshire, Sept. 7, 1843, by Rev. Reuben Torrey 20
Mary, of Prospect, m. Elizur **YALE**, of Mereden, Oct. 3, 1848, by Rev. Ira H. Smith 25
Sarah, m. Isaac **BRADLEY**, Oct. 13, 1839, by Ammi Linsley, V. D. M. 16
Sarah, m. Sheldon **HOTCHKISS**, b. of Prospect, Dec. 14, 1839, by Samuel Williams, Jr., J. P. 16
Sherman, m. Nancy Maria **MIX**, b. of Prospect, Oct. 28, 1838, by Samuel Williams, Jr., J. P. 15
William, of Prospect, m. Sarah **PARKER**, of Wallingford, Nov. 8, 1846, by Isaac Bradley, J. P. 24
Willitt R., of Bristol, m. Mary Ann **RICHARD**, of Waterbury, Nov. 27, 1834, by Rev. Sylvester Selden 11
BOTSFORD, William, of Mereden, m. Azubah **BRONSON**, of Prospect, Mar. 4, 1832, by Rev. John E. Brag 8
BRADLEY, Charlotte B., of Bethany, m. William E. **KIMBALL**, of

	Page
BRADLEY, (cont.)	
Prospect, Nov. 18, [1849], by John L. Ambler	27
Isaac, m. Sarah **BLAKESLEY**, of Prospect, Oct. 13, 1839, by Ammi Linsley, V. D. M.	16
Isaac, m. Sally **SPENCER**, b. of Prospect, June 6, 1852, by J. Killburn	29
BRAG, Edward Parmelee, s. John E. & Esther, b. Oct. 17, 1829	91
BRISTOL, Charles B., of Cheshire, m. Nancy **NETTLETON**, of Prospect, Oct. 6, 1850, by John L. Ambler	28
Hannah, m. David M. **HOTCHKISS**, b. of Prospect, May 1, [1850], by John L. Ambler	27
Henry, of Cheshire, m. Hannah **DOOLITTLE**, of Prospect, Mar. 15, 1830, by Rev. John E. Brag	6
John, of Oxford, m. Hannah **HITCHCOCK**, of Prospect, Mar. 15, 1838, by Samuel Williams, Jr., J. P.	14
Jonathan, of Wallingford, m. Harriet **BEECHER**, of Prospect, Aug. 19, 1844, by Rev. Reuben Torrey	21
BROCKET, Benjamin, of Waterbury, m. Elizabeth **BEECHER**, of Prospect, May 29, 1831, by Rev. John E. Brag	7
George, of Hamden, m. Abigail **SANDFORD**, of Prospect, Apr. 22, 1830, by Rev. Hershal Sandford	4
BRONSON, Abigail A., m. Levi **DAVIS**, Jan. 16, 1834, by Lauren Preston, J. P.	10
Azubah, of Prospect, m. William **BOTSFORD**, of Mereden, Mar. 4, 1832, by Rev. John E. Brag	8
Benjamin B., of New York State, m. Emily B. **HOTCHKISS**, of Prospect, July 9, 1843, by Aaron C. Beach	20
Eliza, 2nd w. [Samuel C.], b. June 4, 1804	102
Eliza, m. Samuel C. **BRONSON**, Nov. 20, 1831, by Rev. John E. Brag	7
Hannah, of Prospect, m. Sheldon **JUDD**, of Watertown, June 25, 1830, by Samuel Peck, J. P.	5
Jerusha, m. Hobart C. **PORTER**, b. of Prospect, Apr. 6, 1842, by Rev. Edw[ard] Bull	18
John, of Waterbury, m. Polly **HITCHCOCK**, of Prospect, Dec. 24, 1829, by Rev. John E. Brag	4
Lydia, w. Sam[ue]l C., d. Feb. 12, 1830	102
Lydia An[n], [d. Samuel C.], b. Apr. 22, 1833	102
Norsha, m. William **PLATT**, b. of Prospect, [Apr.] 30, [1845], by Rev. Reuben Torrey	22
Permella, w. Benjamin, d. July 14, 1848, ae 65 y.	102
Sally, of Prospect, m. Daniel **HAMISTON**, of Wallingford, Nov. 29, 1829, by Rev. John E. Brag	4
Sally, d. Cornelus, d. July 10, 1833	96
Sam[ue]l C., b. Aug. 5, 1801	102
Samuel C., m. Eliza **BRONSON**, Nov. 20, 1831, by Rev. John E. Brag	7
Spencer, s. Samuel C., b. Nov. 23, 1826	102
Susan, of Prospect, m. Archibald E. **RICE**, of Woodbridge, May 16, 1832, by Rev. John E. Brag	9
BROOKS, Joel, of Wolcott, m. Laura Ann **HOTCHKISS**, Nov. 15, 1846,	

44 BARBOUR COLLECTION

Page

BROOKS, (cont.)
    by Rev. Reuben Torrey 24
    Laura, of Bethany, m. Silas **WILMOT**, Jr., of Wallingford, May 4,
        1851, by Rev. Henry Gill 28
BROWN, Isaac, d. Sept. 6, 1833 96
BURMINGHAM, [see under **BIRMINGHAM**]
CARRINGTON, Augusta, m. John R. **PLATT**, b. of Prospect, June 5, 1850,
    by John L. Ambler 28
CARTER, Phebe, m. Lauren **CURTISS**, b. of Goshen, Apr. 10, 1845, by
    Rev. Reuben Torrey 22
CASTLE, Emeline, m. Edward **CHITTENDEN**, b. of Prospect, Apr. 6, 1828,
    by Rev. John E. Bray 2
CHANDLER, Almon E., m. Julia A. **MATTHEWS**, b. of Prospect, May 26,
    1850, by [ ] 27
    Betsey A., m. Franklin J. **MATTHEWS**, Sept. 17, 1853, by Asa H.
    Train 30
    Marcus D., m. Julia A. C. **GRISWOLD**, Jan. 15, 1854, by Asa H. Train 31
CHITTENDEN, Edward, m. Emeline **CASTLE**, b. of Prospect, Apr. 6, 1828,
    by Rev. John E. Bray 2
    Emelin[e], d. Edward & Emeline, b. May 23, 1829 91
CLARK, CLARKE, Emily, of Prospect, m. Henry B. **SKELTON**, of
    Watertown, Nov. 19, 1838, by Ammi Linsley, V. D. M. 15
    Harriet, m. Lucius **RUSSELL**, b. of Prospect, [June] 6, [1845], by Rev.
    Reuben Torrey 23
    Smith S., m. Margaret A. **WILLIAMS**, b. of Prospect, [May] 8, 1849,
    by John L. Ambler 26
COOK, Thelbert, of Cheshire, m. Philenda **SANFORD**, of Prospect, Mar. 2,
    1828, by Rev. Henshal Sandford 1
CURTISS, Lauren, m. Phebe **CARTER**, b. of Goshen, Apr. 10, 1845, by
    Rev. Reuben Torrey 22
DAILEY, Henry P., m. Esther **MATTHEWS**, b. of Prospect, Mar. 24, 1850,
    by Rev. John L. Ambler 27
DAVIS, Levi, m. Abigail A. **BRONSON**, Jan. 16, 1834, by Lauren
    Preston, J. P. 10
DEMING, Johnson J., of Hamden, m. Abbey **DOOLITTLE**, of Prospect,
    Nov. 23, 1831, by A. A. Perkins, J. P. 7
DOOLITTLE, Abbey, of Prospect, m. Johnson J. **DEMING**, of Hamden,
    Nov. 23, 1831, by A. A. Perkins, J. P. 7
    Benjamin, m. Nancy **HOTCHKISS**, b. of Prospect, May 2, 1838, by
    Samuel Williams, Jr., J. P. 14
    Hannah, of Prospect, m. Henry **BRISTOL**, of Cheshire, Mar. 15, 1830,
    by Rev. John E. Brag 6
    Harriet D., of Prospect, m. John W. **SULLIVAN**, of New Milford, Sept.
    12, 1847, by Rev. Reuben Torrey 25
    Sam[ue]l, m. Anna **BEECHER**, b. of Prospect, Aug. 18, 1850, by
    Thomas Wilmot, J. P. 28
DUDLEY, Whiting B., m. Rosannar **HOTCHKISS**, Mar. 24, 1844, by Rev.
    Reuben Torrey 21

	Page
DURAND, Return, m. Nancy J. **HOTCHKISS**, Feb. 22, 1825, by Thomas Willmot	11
[**FERREL**], Asa, [s. Benjamin & Patience], b. June 9, 1809, in Waterbury	98
Clarrisa, [d. Benjamin & Patience], b. May 9, 1805, in Waterbury; d. Sept. 22, 1805	98
Garry, [s. Benjamin & Patience], b. Jan. 24, 1812, in Waterbury	98
Rhoda, [d. Benjamin & Patience], b. Jan. 10, 1806, in Waterbury	98
FORD, George, [s. Jared B.], b. June 1, 1827	99
Georg[e] M., of Prospect, m. Sarah L. **PAINTER**, of Plymouth, [May] 13, [1849], by John L. Ambler	26
Jared B., [s. Jared B.], b. Mar. 29, 1829	99
Jared B., m. Harriet **RUSSELL**, b. of Prospect, June 3, 1841, by Lauren Preston, J. P.	17
Lucy A., [d. Jared B.], b. Feb. 2, 1831	99
-----, w. Jared P., d. Apr. 22, 1833	96
GAYLORD, Hannah Louisa, of Hamden, m. Amos **AUSTIN**, of Prospect, Dec. 6, 1845, by Rev. Samuel W. Smith, Int. Pub.	23
GIBBARD, Israel T., of Naugatuck, m. Esther E. **HOTCHKISS**, of Prospect, [Jan.] 18, [1846], by Rev. Reuben Torrey	23
GILLET, Abigail, of Prospect, m. Lucius **TALMAGE**, of Oxford, May 12, 1830, by Rev. John E. Bray	5
Garret, see Damaris **TUTTLE**	97
John, m. Elizabeth R. **PAYNE**, June 8, 1842, by Rev. Edw[ard] Bull	18
GOODRICH, William H., of Cheshire, m. Harriet **PRESTON**, of Prospect, Sept. 13, 1829, by Rev. John E. Brag	4
GRILLEY, Davis, m. Jane C. **SCOVILL**, b. of Waterbury, Apr. 28, 1832, by Rev. John E. Brag	8
GRISWOLD, Julia A. C., m. Marcus D. **CHANDLER**, Jan. 15, 1854, by Asa H. Train	31
Marintha, of Litchfield, m. Edward S. **JEURLDS**, of Wallingford, [Nov.] 4, [1849]	27
GUN, Betsey C., m. Aaron A. **AUSTIN**, Jan. 16, 1834, by Lamuel Preston, J. P.	10
HALL, Fanny, of Wallingford, m. Franklin **WALLACE**, of Prospect, [Jan.] 12, [1845], by Rev. Reuben Torrey	22
W[illia]m, m. Maria O. **HOTCHKISS**, Mar. 16, 1845, by L. C. Collins	22
HAMICK, Striphon, of Southington, m. Lucy **PORTER**, of Prospect, June 10, 1839, by W. W. Brewer	16
HAMISTON, Daniel, of Wallingford, m. Sally **BRONSON**, of Prospect, Nov. 29, 1829, by Rev. John E. Brag	4
HANCKLEY, George, m. Julia **SHERMAN**, Aug. 17, 1842, by Thomas Wilmot, J. P.	18
HANDY, Loly, of Hamden, m. Eli **SANFORD**, of Prospect, Nov. 20, 1842, by Lauren Preston, J. P.	19
HEADLEY, Minerva, of Waterbury, m. Stephen **WILLIAMS**, of Prospect, Mar. 28, 1832, by Rev. John E. Brag	8
HINE, Ann A., of Cheshire, m. Nelson **HOTCHKISS**, of Prospect, July 4, 1847, by Thomas Wilmot, J. P.	25

46   BARBOUR COLLECTION

                                                                         Page
HITCHCOCK, Carver, of Windsor, N. Y., m. Sally SCOTT, of Prospect,
    Oct. 11, 1830, by Rev. John E. Brag   6
Hannah, of Prospect, m. John BRISTOL, of Oxford, Mar. 15, 1838, by
    Samuel Williams, Jr., J. P.   14
Ichabod, m. Lucy E. HITCHKISS, b. of Prospect, Aug. 30, 1835, by
    Aaron Austin, J. P.   12
Mary W., of Prospect, m. Henry S. WILMOT, of Cheshire, Sept. 20,
    1847, by Rev. Reuben Torrey   25
Polly, of Prospect, m. John BRONSON, of Waterbury, Dec. 24, 1829,
    by Rev. John E. Brag   4
Reuben M., of Cheshire, m. Emeline BARNES, of Northampton, Mass.,
    [May] 5, [1849], by John L. Ambler   26
Susan A., of Prospect, m. Horace P. WELTON, of Waterbury, Nov. 13,
    1831, by A. A. Perkins, J. P.   7
Sylyleel, of Prospect, m. Titus PECK, of Bethaney, June 13, 1852, by
    Thomas Wilmot, J. P.   29
Titus, m. Hannah SANDFORD, b. of Prospect, Oct. 10, 1830, by Rev.
    Hershal Sandford   5
HOADLEY, Charles, of Cheshire, m. Lucinda WOODIN, of Cheshire, Dec.
    12, 1853, by Asa H. Train   31
HOPPIN, Andrew H., s. Allen & Charlotte, b. Oct. 26, 1811   94
Andrew H., s. Allen & Charlotte, b. Jan. 8, 1813, in Waterbury   92
Benjamin, [s. Allen & Charlotte], d. Mar. 9, 1828   95
Esther, [d. Allen & Charlotte], b. Jan. [1813 or 1814], in Waterbury   92
Esther, [d. Allen & Charlotte], b. Jan. 3, 1813   94
Esther, [d. Allen & Charlotte], d. Jan. 31, 1828   95
Flora, [d. Allen & Charlotte], b. Feb. 24, 1824   94
Flora, of Prospect, m. Lucellus H. JOHNSON, of Leyden, N. Y.,
    [   ] 18, 1848, by Rev. Ira H. Smith   25
Nancy, [d. Allen & Charlotte], b. Feb. 14, 1829   94
Reuben, s. [Allen & Charlotte], b. July 18, 1814, in Waterbury   92
Reuben, [s. Allen & Charlotte], b. July 18, 1814   94
Sally, d. [Allen & Charlotte], b. Nov. 24, 1814, in Waterbury   92
Sally, [d. Allen & Charlotte], b. Nov. 24, 1819   94
Sally, m. Harry HOTCHKISS, b. of Prospect, Feb. 24, 1839, by Ammi
    Linsley   15
HOTCHKISS, HITCHKISS, Abigail, m. Charles STODDARD, Jan. 16,
    1849, by Thomas Wilmot, J. P.   19
Alma, m. Jared PRITCHARD, June 24, 1832, by Rev. John E. Brag   9
Bele E., m. Nancy S. PLATT, b. of Prospect, [June] 11, 1843, by Rev.
    Reuben Torrey   20
Betsey E., m. Charles R. HOTCHKISS, b. of Prospect, Oct. 18, 1843,
    by Rev. Reuben Torrey   20
Charles R., m. Betsey E. HOTCHKISS, b. of Prospect, Oct. 18, 1843,
    by Rev. Reuben Torrey   20
David M., m. Hannah BRISTOL, b. of Prospect, May 1, [1850], by
    John L. Ambler   27
Ebin, m. Ruth MARTIN, b. of Prospect, May 4, 1835, by

	Page
HOTCHKISS, HITCHKISS, (cont.)	
Sylvester Selden	11
Emily B., of Prospect, m. Benjamin B. **BRONSON**, of New York State, July 9, 1843, by Aaron C. Beach	20
Ervin B., m. Nancy J. **WALLACE**, Sept. 17, 1853, by Asa H. Train	30
Esther E., of Prospect, m. Israel T. **GIBBARD**, of Naugatuck, [Jan.] 18, [1846], by Rev. Reuben Torrey	23
Harriet, of Prospect, m. Julius **WAY**, of Mereden, Oct. 28, 1838, by David M. Hotchkiss, J. P.	15
Harry, m. Sally **HOPPIN**, b. of Prospect, Feb. 24, 1839, by Ammi Linsley	15
Harvey, m. Eliza **SMITH**, May 25, 1845, b. of Prospect, by Rev. R. Torrey	23
Isaac, of Prospect, m. Mrs. Ann **ROBERTS**, of Barkhamsted, June 1, 1851, by Rev. William H. Whitmore	29
Laura Ann, m. Joel **BROOKS**, of Wolcott, Nov. 15, 1846, by Rev. Reuben Torrey	24
Lauren, of Prospect, m. Algenon S. **PLUMB**, of Wolcott, June 12, 1854, by Rev. Asa H. Train	31
Lucy E., m. Ichabod **HITCHCOCK**, b. of Prospect, Aug. 30, 1835, by Aaron Austin, J. P.	12
Major, m. Mary **BEACH**, Sept. 14, 1845, by Thomas Wilmot, J. P.	23
Maria O., m. W[illia]m **HALL**, Mar. 16, 1845, by L. C. Collins	22
Mary N., of Prospect, m. George S. **SLOPER**, of Bethany, Feb. 17, 1839, by Ammi Linsley	15
Nancy, m. Benjamin **DOOLITTLE**, b. of Prospect, May 2, 1838, by Samuel Williams, Jr., J. P.	14
Nancy J., m. Return **DURAND**, Feb. 22, 1835, by Thomas Willmot	11
Nelson, of Prospect, m. Ann A. **HINE**, of Cheshire, July 4, 1847, by Thomas Wilmot, J. P.	25
Polly, m. Harvey **NORTON**, b. of Prospect, Apr. 13, 1828, by Rev. Lucius Baldwin	2
Rosannar, m. Whiting B. **DUDLEY**, Mar. 24, 1844, by Rev. Reuben Torrey	21
Sarah C., d. Nov. 16, 1848, ae 30 y. 2 m. 8 d.	102
Sheldon, m. Sarah **BLAKESLEY**, b. of Prospect, Dec. 14, 1839, by Samuel Williams, Jr., J. P.	16
HUGHES, William W., of New Haven, m. Martha A. **NETTLETON**, Feb. 28, [1847], by Rev. Reuben Torrey	24
HULL, Joseph, m. Almeda **BENHAM**, Dec. 22, 1850, by Thomas Willmot, J. P.	28
ISBELL, Hanford, of Salem, m. Harriet **ANDREWS**, of Prospect, Oct. 28, 1838, by W. W. Brewer	15
JACKSON, Emulus B., of Waterbury, m. Julia J. **SCOTT**, of Prospect, Mar. 13, 1830, by Rev. John E. Brag	6
JEURLDS(?), Edward S., of Wallingford, m. Marintha **GRISWOLD**, of Litchfield, [Nov.] 4, [1849], by Rev. John L. Ambler	27
JOHNSON, Harriet, of Woodbury, m. Bennet **BENHAM**, of Prospect,	

	Page
JOHNSON, (cont.)	
July 5, 1852, by J. Killburn	30
Julia, of Harwinton, m. Lafayette **ANTHONY**, of Middlefield, [Aug.] 26, [1849], by John L. Ambler	26
Lucellus H., of Leyden, N. Y., m. Flora **HOPPIN**, of Prospect, [ ] 18, 1848, by Rev. Ira H. Smith	25
JUDD, Eliza, d. Sheldon & Hannah, b. Jan. 30, 1831	91
Sheldon, of Watertown, m. Hannah **BRONSON**, of Prospect, June 25, 1830, by Samuel Peck, J. P.	5
William, of Naugatuck, m. Esther R. **WILMOTT**, of Prospect, [Aug.] 5, [1849], by John L. Ambler	26
KIMBALL, Ele[a]zer, m. Fan[n]y E. **ROWE**, b. of Prospect, June 29, 1828, by Rev. Hershal Sandford	2
William E., of Prospect, m. Charlotte B. **BRADLEY**, of Bethany, Nov. 18, [1849], by John L. Ambler	27
KNOWLTON, Mary Ann, of Waterbury, m. Daniel S. **BURMINGHAM**, Apr. 18, 1837, by Thomas Wilmot, J. P.	13
KYES, Hiram H., of New Hartford, m. Harriet E. **SCOTT**, of Prospect, Sept. 2, 1832, by Rev. John E. Brag	10
LORD, Julia, of Prospect, m. Joel **MATTHEWS**, of Southington, July 4, 1830, by Rev. John E. Brag	5
LOUNSBURY, Allen, [s. Allen & Maria], b. Sept. 6, 1824	100
Cook, [ch. of Allen & Maria], b. Apr. 20, 1828	100
Lelitia, [ch. of Allen & Maria], b. Dec. 13, 1831	100
Mariah, [d. Allen & Maria], b. Oct. 8, 1826	100
Mariah, [d. Allen & Maria], d. Oct. 23, 1836	100
Sarah, [d. Allen & Maria], b. Nov. 21, 1822	100
MANHUGH, [see under **MARRIHUGH**]	
MARRIHUGH, MERRYHUGH, MANHUGH, Gideon S., of Canton, N. Y., m. Damares L. **TUTTLE**, of Prospect, June 3, 1830, by Rev. John E. Brag	5
William T., s. Gideon S. & Damaris, b. Jan. 28, 1836	99
-----, ch. of Gideon, d. July 7, 1833	96
MARTIN, Ruth, m. Ebin **HOTCHKISS**, b. of Prospect, May 4, 1835, by Sylvester Selden	11
MATTHEWS, Anna, m. Elijah J. **WILLIAMS**, Apr. 7, 1834, by W[illia]m Mix, J. P.	10
Esther, m. Henry P. **DAILEY**, b. of Prospect, Mar. 24, 1850, by Rev. John L. Ambler	27
Franklin J., m. Betsey A. **CHANDLER**, Sept. 17, 1853, by Asa H. Train	30
Jennett A., m. Lewis **BENHAM**, Jan. 3, 1847, by Thomas Wilmot, J. P.	24
Joel, of Southington, m. Julia **LORD**, of Prospect, July 4, 1830, by Rev. John E. Brag	5
Julia A., m. Almon E. **CHANDLER**, b. of Prospect, May 26, 1850, by [ ]	27
Mary Ann, m. Ira G. **TERREL**, July 20, 1840, by David M. Hotchkiss, J. P.	16

	Page
MERRIMAN, Stephen, of Southington, m. Hannah **BLAKESLEY**, of Prospect, Nov. 30, 1843, by Rev. Reuben Torrey	21
MIX, Cornelia, m. Miles R. **ANDREWS**, b. of Prospect, Apr. 2, 1837, by Thomas Wilmot	13
Emily A., m. George F. **TYLER**, b. of Prospect, July 4, 1853, by Rev. Asa M. Train	30
Henry H., m. Charlotte **TYLER**, b. of Prospect, Apr. 7, 1852, by James Killburn	29
Mary E., of Prospect, m. Silas **PERKINS**, of Bethaney, Apr. 13, 1849, by John L. Ambler	26
Nancy Maria, m. Sherman **BLAKSLEY**, b. of Prospect, Oct. 28, 1838, by Samuel Williams, Jr., J. P.	15
Orvil, of Wallingford, m. Elizabeth **WILMOT**, of Prospect, Nov. 19, 1837, by Sylvester Smith	14
MORGAN, Laura, m. Olcott H. **PAYNE**, Jan. 16, 1838, by Samuel Williams, Jr., J. P.	14
MORSE, [see also **MOSS** & **MOSES**], Lent, m. Clara **TUTTLE**, b. of Prospect, Sept. 24, 1827, by Rev. John E. Brag	1
MOSS, [see also **MORSE** & **MOSES**], Albert, m. Loly **THOMAS**, Oct. 4, 1840, by A. A. Perkins, J. P. (Perhaps **MOSS**?)	17
Ashrah, m. George **PAYNE**, b. of Prospect, Dec. 2, 1837, by Ammi Linsley, V. D. M.	14
Loyd, of Cheshire, m. Marthy **PLATT**, of Prospect, June 19, 1828, by Rev. John E. Brag	3
Luther, m. Adelia **PRATT**, b. of Prospect, Feb. 5, 1835, by Sylvester Selden	11
NETTLETON, Martha A., m. William W. **HUGHES**, of New Haven, Feb. 28, [1847], by Rev. Reuben Torrey	24
Nancy, of Prospect, m. Charles B. **BRISTOL**, of Cheshire, Oct. 6, 1850, by John L. Ambler	28
-----, ch. of Ephraim, d. July 4, 1833	96
NORTON, Friend C., m. Mrs. Betsey **TUTTLE**, b. of Waterbury, Sept. 23, 1827, by Rev. John E. Brag	1
Harvey, m. Polly **HOTCHKISS**, b. of Prospect, Apr. 13, 1828, by Rev. Lucius Baldwin	2
PAINTER, Sarah L., of Plymouth, m. Georg[e] M. **FORD**, of Prospect, [May] 13, [1849], by John L. Ambler	26
PARKER, Sarah, of Wallingford, m. William **BLAKESLEE**, of Prospect, Nov. 8, 1846, by Isaac Bradley, J. P.	24
PAYNE, Abigail, m. Miles **BALDWIN**, July 29, 1834, by Samuel Peck, J. P.	10
Edward, of Prospect, m. Hannah **SPERRY**, of Westville, Dec. 25, 1844, by Rev. R. Torrey	21
Elizabeth R., m. John **GILLET**, June 8, 1842, by Rev. Edw[ard] Bull	18
George, m. Ashrah **MOSS**, b. of Prospect, Dec. 2, 1837, by Ammi Linsley, V. D. M.	14
Olcott H., m. Laura **MORGAN**, Jan. 16, 1838, by Samuel Williams, Jr., J. P.	14
PECK, Elizabeth A., m. David **RICHARDSON**, b. of Prospect, Oct. 7, 1850,	

PECK, (cont.)
by John L. Ambler 28
Titus, of Bethaney, m. Sylyleel **HITCHCOCK**, of Prospect, June 13,
1852, by Thomas Wilmot, J. P. 29
PERKINS, Charlotte, of Prospect, m. Sheldon **WOODING**, of Pittsfield,
N. Y., Oct. 4, 1835, by Thomas Willmot 12
Edward, of Waterbury, m. Delight **SMITH**, of Prospect, May 11, 1828,
by Rev. Hershall Sandford 2
Silas, of Bethaney, m. Mary E. **MIX**, of Prospect, Apr. 13, 1849, by
John L. Ambler 26
PLATT, Catharine M., of Prospect, m. Jeremiah R. **BARNES**, of New
Haven, Aug. 7, 1836, by Rev. Zephaniah Swift 13
Charlotte, m. Franklin D. **BENHAM**, b. of Prospect, Apr. 6, 1828, by
Rev. John E. Brag 2
Harris, m. Lucinda **TYLER**, June 27, 1841, by Rev. Edw[ard] Bull 17
Henry Peck, m. Chloe **BEECHER**, b. of Prospect, Oct. 16, 1836, by
Rev. Zephaniah Swift 13
John R., m. Augusta **CARRINGTON**, b. of Prospect, June 5, 1850, by
John L. Ambler 28
Marthy, of Prospect, m. Loyd **MOSS**, of Cheshire, June 19, 1828, by
Rev. John E. Brag 3
Nancy S., m. Bele E. **HOTCHKISS**, b. of Prospect, [June] 11, 1843, by
Rev. Reuben Torrey 20
William, m. Norsha **BRONSON**, b. of Prospect, [Apr.] 30, [1845], by
Rev. Reuben Torrey 22
PLUMB, Algenon S., of Wolcott, m. Lauren **HOTCHKISS**, of Prospect, June
12, 1854, by Rev. Asa H. Train 31
PORTER, Hobart C., m. Jerusha **BRONSON**, b. of Prospect, Apr. 6, 1842,
by Rev. Edw[ard] Bull 18
Lucy, of Prospect, m. Striphon **HAMICK**, of Southington, June 10,
1839, by W. W. Brewer 16
Melecent A., of Prospect, m. Simeon **WHITE**, of Colebrook, Mar. 30,
1828, by Rev. John E. Brag 1
William S., of Waterbury, m. Catharine M. **SCOTT**, of Prospect, Sept.
2, 1832, by Rev. John E. Brag 10
PRATT, Adelia, m. Luther **MOSS**, b. of Prospect, Feb. 5, 1835, by Sylvester
Selden 11
PRESTON, Elizabeth, m. Miles **BENHAM**, b. of Prospect, Jan. 11, 1829, by
Rev. Hersal Sandford 3
Harriet, of Prospect, m. William H. **GOODRICH**, of Cheshire, Sept. 13,
1829, by Rev. John E. Brag 4
PRITCHARD, Jared, m. Alma **HOTCHKISS**, June 24, 1832, by Rev. John E.
Brag 9
RICE, Archibald, E., of Woodbridge, m. Susan **BRONSON**, of Prospect,
May 16, 1832, by Rev. John E. Brag 9
RICHARD, Mary Ann, of Waterbury, m. Willitt R. **BLACKESLEY**, of
Bristol, Nov. 27, 1834, by Rev. Sylvester Selden 11
RICHARDSON, David, m. Elizabeth A. **PECK**, b. of Prospect, Oct. 7, 1850,

PROSPECT VITAL RECORDS 51

	Page
RICHARDSON, (cont.)	
by John L. Ambler	28
RIGGS, Charles Samuel, s. William B. & Eliza, b. July 13, 1832	91
ROBERTS, Ann, Mrs., of Barkhamsted, m. Isaac **HOTCHKISS**, of Prospect, June 1, 1851, by Rev. William H. Whitmore	29
ROWE, Fan[n]y E., m. Ele[a]zer **KIMBALL**, b. of Prospect, June 29, 1828, by Rev. Hershal Sandford	2
RUSSELL, Harriet, m. Jared B. **FORD**, b. of Prospect, June 3, 1841, by Lauren Preston, J. P.	17
Henry E., m. Sarrah **TYLER**, Sept. 9, 1855, by Rev. Edw[ard] Bull, at Cheshire	31
Henry E., m. Sarah **TYLER**, Sept. 9, 1855, by Rev. Edward Bull, at Cheshire	32
Lucius, m. Harriet **CLARK**, b. of Prospect, [June] 6, [1845], by Rev. Reuben Torrey	23
Malinda, m. Alonzo **WORSTER**, b. of Waterbury, Oct. 12, 1828, by Rev. Samuel Potter, of Woodbridge & Salem	2
SANFORD, SANDFORD, Abigail, of Prospect, m. George **BROCKET**, of Hamden, Apr. 22, 1830, by Rev. Hershal Sandford	4
Eli, of Prospect, m. Loly **HANDY**, of Hamden, Nov. 20, 1842, by Lauren Preston, J. P.	19
Hannah, m. Titus **HITCHCOCK**, b. of Prospect, Oct. 10, 1830, by Rev. Hershal Sandford	5
Mary, of Bethany, m. Elizur **YOUNGS**, of Prospect, May 27, 1852, by J. Killburn	29
Philenda, of Prospect, m. Thelbert **COOK**, of Cheshire, Mar. 2, 1828, by Rev. Henshal Sandford	1
Rhoda, m. Leonard **TUTTLE**, June 7, 1832, by Rev. John E. Brag	9
SCOTT, Catharine M., of Prospect, m. William S. **PORTER**, of Waterbury, Sept. 2, 1832, by Rev. John E. Brag	10
David, m. Elizabeth **TERREL**, b. of Prospect, May 15, 1832, by Rev. John E. Brag	9
Harriet E., of Prospect, m. Hiram H. **KYES**, of New Hartford, Sept. 2, 1832, by Rev. John E. Brag	10
Julia J., of Prospect, m. Emulus B. **JACKSON**, of Waterbury, Mar. 13, 1830, by Rev. John E. Brag	6
Matilda, m. Lauren **TUTTLE**, b. of Prospect, Mar. 26, 1829, by Rev. John E. Brag	3
Sally, of Prospect, m. Carver **HITCHCOCK**, of Windsor, N. Y., Oct. 11, 1830, by Rev. John E. Brag	6
SCOVILL, Jane C., m. Davis **GRILLEY**, b. of Waterbury, Apr. 28, 1832, by Rev. John E. Brag	8
SHERMAN, Albert, [s. James J. & Julia], b. Nov. 23, 1722* *(Probably 1832)	98
James J., of Oxford, m. Julia **TUTTLE**, of Prospect, July 2, 1830, by Samuel Peck, J. P.	6
Julia, m. George **HANCKLEY**, Aug. 17, 1842, by Thomas Wilmot	18
SKELTON, Henry B., of Watertown, m. Emily **CLARKE**, of Prospect,	

	Page
SKELTON, (cont.)	
Nov. 19, 1838, by Ammi Linsley, V. D. M.	15
SLOPER, George S., of Bethany, m. Mary N. HOTCHKISS, of Prospect,	
Feb. 17, 1839, by Ammi Linsley	15
SMITH, Adeline Mary, d. [Leverit & Betsey], b. Mar. 9, 1814, in Waterbury	90
Delight, of Prospect, m. Edward PERKINS, of Waterbury, May 11,	
1828, by Rev. Hershall Sandford	2
Ebenezer Elmer, s. [Leverit & Betsey], b. May 23, 1816, in Waterbury	90
Eliza, m. Harvey HOTCHKISS, b. of Prospect, May 25, 1845, by Rev.	
R. Torrey	23
Emily A., m. Wales L. WEADON, b. of Prospect, Feb. 25, 1849, by	
Rev. John L. Ambler	26
Fidelia, d. [Leverit & Betsey], b. Apr. 9, 1807, in Wallingford	90
George Evelin, s. Leverit & Betsey, b. Mar. 28, 1805, in Wallingford	90
Laura, m. Sherman SMITH, b. of Milford, Jan. 29, 1832, by Rev. John	
E. Brag	8
Leverett Mansfield, s. [Leverit & Betsey], b. Aug. 26, 1808, in	
Wallingford	90
Nancy Elizabeth, d. [Leverit & Betsey], b. Nov. 4, 1821, in Waterbury	90
Sherman, m. Laura SMITH, b. of Milford, Jan. 29, 1832, by Rev. John	
E. Brag	8
Simeon Pardee, s. [Leverit & Betsey], b. Mar. 10, 1810, in Wallingford	90
Thankful Brocket, d. [Leverit & Betsey], b. Aug. 17, 1818, in	
Waterbury	90
William Beverly Barnerd Hartley, s. [Leverit & Betsey], b. Oct. 25,	
1825, in Waterbury	90
SPENCER, Sally, m. Isaac BRADLEY, b. of Prospect, June 6, 1852,	
by J. Killburn	29
Samuel, m. Harriet WALLACE, b. of Prospect, Aug. 1, 1852,	
by J. Killburn	30
SPERRY, Garry, of Waterbury, m. Julia ATKINS, of Prospect, June 19,	
1842, by Horace Porter, J. P.	18
Hannah, of Westville, m. Edward PAYNE, of Prospect, Dec. 25, 1844,	
by Rev. R. Torrey	21
W. M., of Cheshire, m. Maria BLAKESLEE, of Prospect, Sept. 7, 1843,	
by Rev. Reuben Torrey	20
STANLEY, John, of Waterbury, m. Lydia Ann BLAKELEY, of Prospect,	
Nov. 15, 1835, by Aaron Austin, J. P.	12
STODDARD, Charles, m. Abigail HOTCHKISS, Jan. 16, 1849, by Thomas	
Wilmot, J. P.	19
STREET, Martha, d. James & Betsey, b. June 14, 1829	91
Martha, m. Welcome E. BENHAM, of Cheshire, Feb. 8, 1854, by	
Asa H. Train	31
SULLIVAN, John W., of New Milford, m. Harriet D. DOOLITTLE, of	
Prospect, Sept. 12, 1847, by Rev. Reuben Torrey	25
SYKES, Francis A., m. Sarah TALMAGE, Nov. 14, 1842, by Thomas	
Wilmot, J. P.	19
TALMAGE, Lucius, of Oxford, m. Abigail GILLET, of Prospect, May 12,	

PROSPECT VITAL RECORDS 53

Page

TALMAGE, (cont.)
1830, by Rev. John E. Bray 5
Nancy S., of Prospect, m. Luther **BALDWIN**, of Harwinton, Dec. 16,
   [1849], by John L. Ambler 27
Sarah, m. Francis A. **SYKES**, Nov. 14, 1842, by Thomas Wilmot, J. P. 19
TERREL, Elizabeth, m. David **SCOTT**, b. of Prospect, May 15, 1832, by
   Rev. John E. Brag 9
Elizabeth, m. Alonzo **THOMPSON**, Oct. 23, 1842, by Thomas
   Wilmot, J. P. 19
Ira G., m. Mary Ann **MATTHEWS**, of Prospect, July 20, 1840, by
   David M. Hotchkiss, J. P. 16
THOMAS, Loly, m. Albert **MOSES**, Oct. 4, 1840, by A. A. Perkins, J. P. 17
Lyman, m. Eliza Ann **WILMOT**, b. of Prospect, Mar. 27, 1840, by
   Samuel Williams, Jr., J. P. 16
Sarah A., of Prospect, m. William **THRALL**, of Branford, [Feb.] 11,
   [1849], by John L. Ambler 25
Spencer C., of Prospect, m. Phebe C. **BARBER**, of Wolcottville, [ ]
   27, [1847(?)], by Rev. Reuben Torrey 24
THOMPSON, Alonzo, m. Elizabeth **TERREL**, Oct. 23, 1842, by Thomas
   Wilmot, J. P. 19
THRALL, William, of Branford, m. Sarah A. **THOMAS**, of Prospect, [Feb.]
   11, [1849], by John L. Ambler 25
TUTTLE, Betsey, Mrs., m. Friend C. **NORTON**, b. of Waterbury, Sept. 23,
   1827, by Rev. John E. Brag 1
Charles Sherman, [s. Zopher & Nancy], b. Nov. 20, 1829 91
Clara, m. Lent **MORSE**, b. of Prospect, Sept. 24, 1827, by Rev.
   John E. Brag 1
Damaris, d. July 28, 1835. Garret Gillet, Executor 97
Damares L., of Prospect, m. Gideon S. **MANGHUGH**, of Canton,
   N. Y., June 3, 1830, by Rev. John E. Brag 5
Eben C., m. Temerence **BEECHER**, b. of Prospect, Apr. 27, 1829, by
   Rev. John E. Brag 3
Eliza Jane, [d. Zopher & Nancy], b. Nov. 5, 1830 91
Emily Augusta, [d. Zopher & Nancy], b. Feb. 3, 1831 91
George, [s. Zopher & Nancy], b. Apr. 9, 1833, in Oxford 91
Julia, of Prospect, m. James J. **SHERMAN**, of Oxford, July 2, 1830, by
   Samuel Peck, J. P. 6
Julius Riley, [s. Vincent & Mary], b. Jan. 27, 1830 91
Lauren, m. Matilda **SCOTT**, b. of Prospect, Mar. 26, 1829, by Rev.
   John E. Brag 3
Leonard, m. Rhoda **SANDFORD**, June 7, 1832, by Rev. John E. Brag 9
Louisa Amelia, [d. Vincent & Mary], b. Mar. 9, 1827, in Waterbury 91
Mary Jane, d. Vincent & Mary, b. Jan. 17, 1836 91
Moses, d. Jan. 18, 1835 97
Philo Burr, [s. Vincent & Mary], b. Apr. 5, 1833 91
TYLER, Charlotte, m. Henry H. **MIX**, b. of Prospect, Apr. 7, 1852, by James
   Killburn 29
George F., m. Emily A. **MIX**, b. of Prospect, July 4, 1853, by Rev.

	Page
TYLER, (cont.)	
Asa M. Train	30
Lucinda, m. Harris **PLATT**, June 27, 1841, by Rev. Edw[ard] Bull	17
Mary, m. Stephen **BEECHER**, Apr. 1, 1852, by Thomas Wilmot, J. P.	29
Sarrah, m. Henry E. **RUSSELL**, Sept. 9, 1855, by Rev. Edw[ard] Bull, at Cheshire	31
Sarah, m. Henry E. **RUSSELL**, Sept. 9, 1855, by Rev. Edward Bull, at Cheshire	32
WALLACE, Franklin, of Prospect, m. Fanny **HALL**, of Wallingford, [Jan.] 12, [1845], by Rev. Reuben Torrey	22
Harriet, m. Samuel **SPENCER**, b. of Prospect, Aug. 1, 1852, by J. Killburn	30
James, Jr., m. Sarah **WILMOT**, Nov. 11, 1842, by Thomas Wilmot, J. P.	19
	30
Nancy J., m. Ervin B. **HOTCHKISS**, Sept. 17, 1853, by Asa H. Train	
WARNER, Amanda, of Waterbury, m. Albert **WILLIAMS**, of Prospect, July 4, 1841, by Rev. Edw[ard] Bull	17
John, of Derby, m. Elizabeth **BARNS**, of Prospect, July 27, 1828, by Rev. John E. Brag	3
WAY, Julius, of Mereden, m. Harriet **HOTCHKISS**, of Prospect, Oct. 28, 1838, by David M. Hotchkiss, J. P.	15
WEADON, Wales L., m. Emily A. **SMITH**, b. of Prospect, Feb. 25, 1849, by Rev. John L. Ambler	26
WELTON, Horace P., of Waterbury, m. Susan A. **HITCHCOCK**, of Prospect, Nov. 13, 1831, by A. A. Perkins, J. P.	7
WHITE, Simeon, of Colebrook, m. Melecent A. **PORTER**, of Prospect, Mar. 30, 1828, by Rev. John E. Brag	1
WILLIAMS, Albert, of Prospect, m. Amanda **WARNER**, of Waterbury, July 4, 1841, by Rev. Edw[ard] Bull	17
	10
Elijah J., m. Anna **MATTHEWS**, Apr. 7, 1834, by W[illia]m Mix, J. P.	
Margaret A., m. Smith S. **CLARK**, b. of Prospect, [May] 8, 1849, by John L. Ambler	26
Richard, m. Martha Maria **WILMOT**, May 5, 1836, by Samuel Williams, Jr., J. P.	12
	98
Samuel, Jr., see Fanny Andrews	
Stephen, of Prospect, m. Minerva **HEADLEY**, of Waterbury, Mar. 28, 1832, by Rev. John E. Brag	8
WILMOT, WILMOTT, Asa, 2nd, of Burton, O., m. Sylvia **WILMOT**, of Prospect, Mar. 28, 1841, by Laurens Preston, J. P.	17
Eliza Ann, m. Lyman **THOMAS**, b. of Prospect, Mar. 27, 1840, by Samuel Williams, Jr., J. P.	16
Elizabeth, of Prospect, m. Orvil **MIX**, of Wallingford, Nov. 19, 1837, by Sylvester Smith	14
Esther R., of Prospect, m. William **JUDD**, of Naugatuck, [Aug.] 5, [1849], by John L. Ambler	26
Henry S., of Cheshire, m. Mary W. **HITCHCOCK**, of Prospect, Sept. 20, 1847, by Rev. Reuben Torrey	25
Martha Maria, m. Richard **WILLIAMS**, May 5, 1836, by Samuel	

	Page
WILMOT, WILMOTT, (cont.)	
Williams, Jr., J. P.	12
Sarah, m. James **WALLACE**, Jr., Nov. 11, 1842, by Thomas Wilmot, J. P.	19
Silas, Jr., of Wallingford, m. Laura **BROOKS**, of Bethany, May 4, 1851, by Rev. Henry Gill	28
Sylvia, of Prospect, m. Asa **WILMOT**, 2nd, of Burton, O., Mar. 28, 1841, by Laurens Preston, J. P.	17
WOODING, WOODIN, Lucinda, of Cheshire, m. Charles **HOADLEY**, of Cheshire, Dec. 12, 1853, by Asa H. Train	31
Sheldon, of Pittsfield, N. Y., m. Charlotte **PERKINS**, of Prospect, Oct. 4, 1835, by Thomas Willmot	12
WORSTER, Alonzo, m. Malinda **RUSSELL**, b. of Waterbury, Oct. 12, 1828, by Rev. Samuel Potter, of Woodbridge & Salem	2
YALE, Elizur, of Mereden, m. Mary **BLAKESLEY**, of Prospect, Oct. 3, 1848, by Rev. Ira H. Smith	25
YOUNGS, Elizur, of Prospect, m. Mary **SANFORD**, of Bethany, May 27, 1852, by J. Killburn	[29]

REDDING VITAL RECORDS
1767 - 1852

	Page
ABBOT, ABBOTT, Betsey, [d. Thaddeus & Rebeckah], b. Apr. 1, 1794	56
Philo W., m. Elosia **BEERS**, b. of Redding, Jan. 6, 1839, by Rev. Charles J. Todd	144
Polly, [d. Thaddeus & Rebeckah], b. Nov. 8, 1788	56
Sarah, [d. Thaddeus & Rebeckah], b. Jan. 15, 1792	56
Thaddeus, m. Rebecah **MARWIN**, May 24, 1788, by Barnabus Marwin, certified	56
ADAMS, Aaron, [s. Joseph & Joanna], b. Feb. 22, 1775	88
Aaron, s. [Hezekiah & Bettey], b. July 21, 1795 [?]	89
Abigail, [d. Joseph & Joanna], b. Oct. 1, 1767	88
Abigail, d. Oct. 27, 1824, ae 48 y. 6 m. 16 d. Entry from Daniel Stowe's Bible	77
Bettey, [d. Hezekiah & Bettey], b. July 6, 1789	89
Elen, [d. Joseph & Joanna], b. Aug. 30, 1765	88
Ellen, d. Hezekiah & Betty, b. Apr. 10, 1799	102
Harriet, m. Burr **EDMONDS**, b. of Redding, Dec. 24, 1840, by Rev. P. R. Brown	149
Hezekiah, [s. Joseph & Joanna], b. Aug. 14, 1764	88
Hezekiah, m. Bettey **PARSONS**, Sept. 11, 1788, by Rev. Nathaniel Bartlett. Witness Joseph Adams	89
Israel, [s. Joseph & Joanna], b. Sept. 5, 1772	88
Israel, m. Abigail **STOW**, Mar. 28, 1796. Witness Anna Barnum	52
Jedediah, s. Hezekiah & Betty, b. Oct. 26, 1805	103
Jedediah, m. Amelia **MOREHOUSE**, b. of Redding, this day [May 12, 1824], by Rev. Lemuel B. Hull	118
Joseph, m. Joanna **DISBROW**, Sept. 9, 1761	88
Joseph, [s. Joseph & Joanna], b. Aug. 27, 1770	88
Julia A., m. Joseph E. **CLARK**, Oct. 2, 1848, by Daniel D. Frost, M. G.	162
Lemuel, s. [Hezekiah & Bettey], b. Dec. 18, 1792	89
Lucinda, of Redding, m. David O. **GRAY**, of Weston, Sept. 12, [1824], at the house of Israel Adams, by John Reynolds, Elder	119
Lynda, [d. Israel & Abigail], b. Nov. 18, 1798	52
Mary, m. Daniel **MALLERY**, Jr., Jan. 15, 1792	66
Nathan, [s. Joseph & Joanna], b. Jan. 27, 1778	88
Philo, s. [Israel & Abigail], b. May 12, 1797	52
Stephen, [s. Joseph & Joanna], b. July 15, 1762	88
Stephen, [s. Hezekiah & Bettey], b. Jan. 22, 1791	89
Stephen, d. Mar. 8, 1890	89
ALVORD, Mary, of Greenfield, m. Jonathan **KNAP[P]**, of Redding, Sept. 7, 1772. Witnesses John Alvord, Abigail Alvord	30
AMBLER, Diodate, of Danbury, m. Polly **GOODSELL**, of Redding, Sept. 14, 1805	102

58   BARBOUR COLLECTION

	Page
AMES, Anna Maria, of Craigvill, N. Y., m. Daniel SANFORD, of Redding, Apr. 10, 1845, by Morris Hill	157
ANDREWS, Daniel, of Redding, m. Catharine DOWNS, of Weston, Jan. 17, 1830, by Rev. Hawley Sanford	129
Ebenezer, m. Hannah WHEELER, June [ ], 1781, by Rev. Nath[anie]ll Bartlett	1
Ebenezer, s. [Seth & Rachel], b. Feb. 17, 1783	52
Eleanor, d. [Seth & Rachel], b. Oct. 17, 1789	52
Elias, m. Ruth MOREHOUSE, b. of Redding, June 3, 1837, by James A. Batterson, Dea.	141
Eliza, m. Dan[ie]l CHAPMAN, Jr., b. of Redding, this day, [Feb. 24, 1824], by Jonathan Bartlett, M. G.	118
Ethiel, of Danbury, m. Chary CHAPMAN, of Redding, this day [May 28, 1826], by Jonathan Bartlett, M. G.	122
Eunice, m. Ezekiel FAIRCHILD, b. of Redding, Jan. 8, 1767, by Rev. Nath[anie]l Bartlet	6
Francis, m. Sabra PARSONS, Mar. 5, 1778, by Nath[anie]ll Bartlet	1
Maria, of Redding, m. Burr WOOD, of Weston, this day [ ], by Jonathan Bartlett, M. G. Recorded Mar. 28, 1827	124
Mary, m. John HULL, b. of Redding, Feb. 3, 1763, by Rev. Nathaniel Bartlet	29
Molle, m. John HULL, Feb. 3, 1763, by Nathaniel Bartlett	48
Pamelia, m. Harvy ROWEL, Jan. 30, 1839, by Rev. John Crawford	144
Priscilla, of Redding, m. Silliman GODFREY, of Wilton, June 22, 1842, by Rev. Daniel Smith	152
Rachel, [w. Seth], b. Feb. 2, 1761	52
Seth, b. May 16, 1763; m. Rachel [ ], May 1, 1782	52
Seth, m. Mabel O. BANKS, Oct. 23, 1828, by Rev. Henry Stead	128
William E., of Danbury, m. Priscilla BANKS, of Weston, Oct. 17, [1832], by Abram Stow, J. P.	134
ASHTON, James Henry, m. Polly COUCH, June 29, 1825, by Rev. Aaron Hunt	121
BALDWIN, Hiram I., m. Sarah B. GOULD, of Redding, Mar. 8, 1841, by Rev. P. R. Brown	149
Wakeman, of Weston, m. Emily GRAHAM, of Greenfield, Dec. 8, 1841, by David S. Duncomb, J. P.	150
BANKS, Aaron, m. Mary Ann COLEY, b. of Redding, Mar. 4, 1835, by Rev. W[illia]m L. Strong	137
Adaline L., m. Alanson LYON, b. of Redding, June 5, 1848, by Rev. J. D. Marshall	161
Amanda M., of Redding, m. Nathan CORNWALL, of Danbury, Nov. 29, 1848, by Rev. Jacob Shaw	163
Anna, [d. Jesse, Jr. & Martha], b. Nov. 8, 1798	4
Betsey, m. Bradley HILL, b. of Redding, Nov. 5, 1822, by Rev. Daniel Crocker	115
David, [s. Jesse, Jr. & Martha], b. May 1, 1792	4
Ebenezer, s. [Hyatt & Sarah], b. Apr. 15, 1790	5
Eben[eze]r, s. [Hyatt & Sarah], d. Mar. 29, 1794	5

	Page
BANKS, (cont.)	
Eli, [s. Jesse, Jr. & Martha], b. June 22, 1794	4
Esther, [d. Seth & Sarah], b. July 3, 1785	23
Gershom, s. [Hyatt & Sarah], b. Apr. 7, 1792	5
Gershom, s. [Hyatt & Sarah], d. Feb.* 15, 1795 *(First written "March")	5
Gershom W., m. Emma **EDMONDS**, of Redding, July 9, 1848, by Rev. Tho[ma]s K. Witsil	162
Hannah, m. Isaac W. **HOYT**, Oct. 8, 1796, certified by Jemimah Biggsby	65
Hannah W., m. Nathan E. **WILCOX**, Sept. 17, 1837, by John Crawford	142
Harriet, of Redding, m. George **SILLICK**, of Norwalk, Nov. 28, 1825, by Marvin Richardson	121
Henry S., m. Harriet **PARSONS**, b. of Redding, July 9, 1844, by Rev. W[illia]m F. Collins	154
Hyatt,* [s. Jesse & Mehetable], b. Dec. 9, 1764 *(First written "Jesse")	23
Hyatt, m. Sarah **SUMMERS**, Dec. 1, 1785	5
Jeremiah, s. [Hyatt & Sarah], b. Mar. 18, 1794	5
Jesse, m. Mehetabel **WHEELER**, b. of Redding, June 11, 1764, by Rev. Nathaniel Bartlet	23
Jesse, Jr., [s. Jesse & Mehetable], b. Oct. 29, 1766	23
Jesse, Jr., m. Martha **SUMMERS**, Dec. 14, 1787, by Hyatt Banks	4
Jesse, s. Hyatt & Sarah, b. Mar. 15, 1800	102
Jesse, 3rd, m. Sally **STOWE**, Jan. 3, 1822, by Rev. Laban Clark	112
Joanna, d. [Jesse & Mehetable], b. July 27, 1768	23
Joseph, m. wid. Ann **MOREHOUSE**, b. of Redding, Nov. 29, 1767	23
Joseph, s. [Hyatt & Sarah], b. May 3, 1788	5
Joseph, Dea., d. July 8, 1802	1
Josiah P., [s. Seth & Sarah], b. July 5, 1774	23
Josiah P. [s. Seth & Sarah], d. Sept. 19, 1775	23
Laura, d. [Hyatt & Sarah], b. July 21, 1796	5
Laurey, [s. Thomas & Sarah], b. Apr. 6, 1794	83
Lydia, see Lucy **HOYT**	76
Mable, [d. Jesse & Mehetable], b. Oct. 2, 1772; d. Nov. [ ]	23
Mabel, d. [Jesse & Mehetable], b.Nov. 17, 1778	23
Mabel, m. Ebenezer **FOOT**, Aug. 29, 1797, by Jonathan Bartlett	5
Mabel, d. Hyatt & Sarah, b. May 3, 1802	102
Mabel, m. Gould Dimond **CROFUT**, Jan. 10, 1822, by Rev. Laban Clark	112
Mabel O., m. Seth **ANDREWS**, Oct. 23, 1828, by Rev. Henry Stead	128
Mary, d. [Jesse & Mehetable], b. June 23, 1774	23
Mary Ann, of Redding, m. Charles H. **HAY**, of Newton, Aug. 11, 1822, by Hawley Sanford, Elder	114
Mehetabel, [d. Seth & Sarah], b. Jan. 15, 1768	23
Mehitable, of Redding, m. Thomas **HOYT**, of Danbury, Sept. 1, 1822, by Rev. Samuel Cochran	114
Morgan, [s. Thomas & Sarah], b. May 31, 1797	83

BARBOUR COLLECTION

BANKS, (cont.)

	Page
Nathan S., s. [Hyatt & Sarah], d. Feb. 18, 1795	5
Nathan Summers, s. [Hyatt & Sarah], b.May 21, 1786	5
Platt, [s. Thomas & Sarah], b. Feb. 24, 1796; d. May 27, 1796	83
Priscilla, of Weston, m. William E. **ANDREWS**, of Danbury, Oct. 17, [1832], by Abram Stow, J. P.	134
Rachel, of Weston, m. Isaac **FAIRCHILD**, of Redding, Apr. 8, 1802	100
Rufus B., of Fairfield, m. Mary B. **BARTRAM**, of Redding, July 24, 1850, by Rev. J. L. Gilder	165
Sally, [d. Seth & Sarah], b. Feb. 25, 1782	23
Sally, d. [Hyatt & Sarah], b. Apr. 15, 1798	5
Sally, d. June 21, 1845, ae 40 y.	77
Sally Maria, of Walton, m. Henry D. **KEELER**, of Wilton, this day, [Oct. 9, 1836], by Jonathan Bartlett, M. G.	140
Sarah, [d. Jesse, Jr. & Martha], b. June 22, 1788	4
Sarah, [d. Jesse, Jr. & Martha], d. Apr. 29, 1791	4
Sarah, m. Noah M. **LEE**, b. of Redding, Jan. 28, 1835, by Rev. W[illia]m L. Strong	137
Seth, m. Sarah **PICKET**, b. of Redding, Nov. 20, 1766, by Rev. Nathaniel Bartlet	23
Summers, m. Electa **STURGES**, b. of Redding, Oct. 10, 1825, by Rev. H. Humphreys	121
Susan Caroline, m. George A. **SANFORD**, b. of Redding, Mar. 15, 1846, by Morris Hill	158
Thomas, [s. Seth & Sarah], b. May 17, 1770	23
Thomas, m. Sarah **WOOD**, Jan. 21, 1792, by Elias Lee. Witnesses Sarah Banks & Hannah Banks	83
BARBER, Henry, of Danbury, m. Achsa **STONE**, of Redding, Nov. 3, 1844, by Morris Hill	155
BARLOW, Aaron, m. Rebeckah **SANFORD**, Dec. 27, 1772, by Nathaniel Bartlet	22
Anson, m. Rebeckah **SANFORD**, b. of Redding, Dec. 17, 1772, by Rev. Nathaniel Bartlet [This entry crossed out]	25
Betsey, [d. Jane], b. Aug. 2, 1778	35
Eliza Ann, m. Enoch Augustus **SANFORD**, b. of Redding, Oct. 10, 1821, by Rev. Daniel Crocker	110
Elnathan, s. Aaron & Rebeckah, b. Oct. 14, 1773	22
Elnathan, s. [Aaron & Rebeckah], d. Aug. 31, 1774	22
Huldah, m. Alfred **GREGORY**, b. of Redding, this day [May 13, 1830], by Rev. Lemuel B. Hull	130
Jane, had daughters Sarah, b. Jan. 16, 1770 & Betsey, b. Aug. 2, 1778	35
Joel, m. Deborah **SANFORD**, b. of Redding, Oct. 9, 1821, by Rev. Daniel Crocker	110
Ruama, m. John **GRAY**, b. of Redding, Aug. 7, 1759, by Rev. Nath[anie]l Bartlet	7
Sally, m. Miles **STRATTON**, b. of Redding, Jan. 28, 1849, by Daniel D. Frost	163
Sarah, [d. Jane], b. Jan. 16, 1770	35

	Page
BARLOW, (cont.)	
Sarah Ann, of Sharon, m. Lewis B. **SHEPARD**, of Danbury, May 4, 1835, by Jared Olmstead, J. P.	138
BARNUM, Anna, wid., d. Aug. 28, 1822. Entry from Daniel Stowe's Bible	77
Rachel, of Redding, m. W[illia]m **TAYLOR**, of Ridgefield, Oct. 29, 1826, by W[illia]m C. Kniffin, M. G.	123
Zar B., of Bethel, m. Amanda **BENEDICT**, of Redding, Feb. 4, 1852, by Rev. J. L. Gilder	167
BARTLETT, BARTLET, Abigail, d. Dan[ie]l C. & Esther, b. June 26, 1778	47
Abigail, d. Dan[ie]l C. & Est[h]er, b. June 26, 1778	50
Anna, had d. Sally, b. Feb. 18, 1784	54
Betsey, w. Rev. Jonathan, d. Mar. 12, 1811	54
Clarre, d. Russel & Rachel, b. Feb. 7, 1777	47
Daniel Collins, m. Esther **READ**, Jan. 7, 1778, by Nathaniel Bartlet	47
Eunice, m. Ezekiel **JACKSON**, b. of Redding, Dec. 24, 1806	103
Eunice, wid., d. Aug. 12, 1810	2
Jonathan, m. Rhoda **SANFORD**, Aug. 16, 1795	54
Jonathan, m. Betsey **MARWIN**, Sept. 10, 1798, by Nathaniel Bartlett	54
Jonathan, m. Abigail **SANFORD**, Apr. 6, 1812	54
Lucretia, b. Jan. 4, 1768	2
Nathaniel, Rev., d. Jan. 11, 1810	2
Rhoda, w. Rev. Jonathan, d. Dec. 23, 1796	54
Russel, m. Rachel **TAYLOR**, Feb. 28, 1776, by Rev. Ebenezer Baldwin, of Danbury. Witnesses Nathaniel Bartlet, Daniel C. Bartlet	47
Sally, d. Anna, b. Feb. 18, 1784	54
BARTRAM, BATRAM, Aaron R., m. Harriet **BATES**, of Redding, Jan. 15, 1827, by W[illia]m C. Kniffin, M. G.	124
Aaron Read, s. [Gurdon & Lorrain], b. Nov. 15, 1804	102
Adaline, of Redding, m. Asa P. **CLAPP**, of Sharon, Oct. 9, 1850, by Rev. J. L. Gilder	165
Anna, [d. Daniel], b. Jan. 21, 1773; d. Sept. 27, 1777	78
Anna, [d. Daniel], b. Aug. 18, 1778	78
Barna, s. Gurdon & Laurain, b. Sept. 20, 1808	105
Belinda, [d. Eli & Dolle], b. Nov. 24, 1798	31
Belinda, of Redding, m. Samuel **CAMP**, of Old Milford, Aug. 26, 1832, by James Coleman	134
Betsey, d. Gurdon & Laurain, b. May 23, 1813	105
Betsey, of Redding, m. Ebenezer **WILSON**, of Weston, Apr. 16, 1835, by Rev. Josiah Bowen	138
Betsey M., of Redding, m. Charles B. **RICH**, of Batavia, Genesee Co., N. Y., Oct. 29, 1833, by Rev. Hawley Sanford	136
Coley, s. Gurdon & Laurain, b. Nov. 1, 1810	105
Dan[ie]ll, m. Ann **MERCHANT**, b. of Redding, Oct. 10, 1769, by [ ]	2
Daniel Sanford, s. Gurdon & Lorrain, b. Jan. 14, 1818	107
David, m. Phebe **MOREHOUSE**, b. of Redding, Apr. 30, 1762, by Rev. Nath[anie]l Bartlet	2

BARTRAM, BATRAM, (cont.)

	Page
David, [s. Daniel], b. June 5, 1795	78
Eleanor, [d. Daniel], b. Nov. 1, 1774; d. Sept. 21, 1777	78
Eleanor, [d. Daniel], b. Feb. 4, 1780; d. May 24, 1781	78
Eleanor, [d. Daniel], b. Oct. 28, 1783	78
Eli, [s. Paul & Mary], b. Mar. 30, 1767	22
Eli, m. Dolle **LYON**, Sept. 9, 1794, by Nathaniel Bartlett	31
Esther, [d. Daniel], b. Apr. 16, 1770	78
Eunice, [d. Paul & Mary], b. Jan. 3, 1765	22
Eunice, m. Daniel **PARSONS**, Mar. 15, 1783, by Nathaniel Bartlett	68
Ezekiel, [s. Paul & Mary], b. July 9, 1770	22
Ezekiel, m. Esther **PARSONS**, on or about Jan. 26, 1793, by Nathaniel Bartlett	31
Gurdon, [s. Daniel], b. Dec. 25, 1771; d. Mar. 20, 1772	78
Gurdon, [s. Daniel], b. Sept. 21, 1776	78
Gurdon, m. Lorrain **SANFORD**, b. of Redding, Jan. 1, 1804	102
Hugh S., of Danbury, m. Alma **PICKETT**, of Redding, Mar. 24, 1839, by Aaron Sanford, Jr., J. P.	145
Jared, s. [Ezekiel & Esther], b. Dec. 25, 1794	31
Joseph, [s. Paul & Mary], b. Jan. 28, 1758; d. Feb. 2, 1758	22
Laura, m. Sanford **PLATT**, Dec. 7, 1826, by William Sanford	123
Levi, [s. Daniel], b. Nov. 26, 1787	78
Lucy, of Redding, m. Cha[rle]s W. **LOCKWOOD**, of Monroe, Apr. 23, 1850, by Rev. Jacob Shaw	165
Lucey Ann, d. Gurdon & Lorrain, b. Aug. 27, 1806	103
Lucy Ann, of Redding, m. Milo **LEE**, of Milford, N. Y., Apr. 8, 1830, by Rev. E. Washburn	130
Lydia, of Redding, m. Levi **DREW**, of Bethel, Oct. 13, 1847, by Rev. J. D. Marshall	159-60
Mary, [d. Paul & Mary], b. May 12, 1760	22
Mary, d. [Ezekiel & Esther], b. Aug. 18, 1792	31
Mary Ann, of Redding, m. Levi **GODFREY**, of Ridgefield, May 21, 1843, by David C. Comstock	152
Mary B., of Redding, m. Rufus B. **BANKS**, of Fairfield, July 24, 1850, by Rev. J. L. Gilder	165
Milo, s. [Ezekiel & Esther], b. Sept. 8, 1797	31
Oliver, s. Gurdon & Lorrain, b. July 11, 1815	107
Oliver, s. Gurdon & Lorrain, d. July 23, 1816	106
Paul, m. Mary **HAWLEY**, b. of Redding, Nov. 9, 1756, by Rev. Nathaniel Bartlet	22
Paul & w. Mary, had twins, b. Jan. 12, 1757; d. same day	22
Phebe, [d. Daniel], b. Sept. 19, 1790	78
Ruth, [d. Paul & Mary], b. June 17, 1769; d. same day	22
Sally H., m. Aaron **SQUIRE**, b. of Redding, Apr. 14, 1835, by Rev. Hawley Sanford	138
Sarah, [d. Paul & Mary], b. Aug. 6, 1762	22
Sarah, m. Milo **PALMER**, Sept. 26, 1790	83
Sarah, m. Jonathan **MIDDLEBROOKS**, b. of Redding, Oct. 21,	

	Page
BARTRAM, BATRAM, (cont.)	
1826, by W[illia]m C. Kniffin, M. G.	123
Ulily, [child of Daniel], b. Nov. 12, 1785	78
Uriah, [s. Daniel], b. Jan. 9, 1782	78
William, [s. Eli & Dolle], b.May 3, 1795	31
BASSETT, George, of Redding, m. Nancy **JENKINS**, of Danbury, Mar. 17, 1851, by Rev. Daniel D. Frost	166
Lucy A., m. Edwin L. **CANFIELD**, June 30, 1847, by Rev. Jos. P. Taylor	159
BATES, Armaziah, m. David **SANFORD**, b. of Redding, Nov. 30, 1820, by Rev. Daniel Crocker	109
Charles H., [s. George & Polly], b. Aug. 26, 1833	125
Elias, s. Justus [& Hannah], b. Aug. 29, 1772; m. [ ], Nov. 9, 1793	20
George, m. Polly **SHERWOOD**, [18]	125
Harriet, m. Aaron R. **BARTRAM**, b. of Redding, Jan. 15, 1827, by W[illia]m C. Kniffin, M. G.	124
Harry B., m. Frances J. **GRAY**, b. of Redding, Jan. 4, 1846, by Jonathan Bartlett, M. G.	157
Henry W., [s. George & Polly], b. July 28, 1828	125
Huldah, m. Samuel S. **LOCKWOOD**, b. of Redding, Mar. 20, 1831, by Rev. Oliver E. Amerman	132
Justus, m. Hannah **COLEY**, b. of Redding, May 23, 1771, by Rev. Nath[anie]l Bartlet	20
Justus, Jr., s. Justus, b. Aug. 19, 1771; d. Aug. 20, 1771	20
Lucy A., [d. George & Polly], b. Oct. 25, 1835	125
Roena, of Redding, m. Daniel B. **WOOD**, of Danbury, Mar. 7, 1833, by James A. Batterson, Dea.	135
Ruth, m. Enos **LEE**, Apr. 22,* 1778, by Nathaniel Bartlett *(23?)	11
Samuel, of Fairfield, m. Elizabeth **BURGESS**, of Wilton, Nov. 10, 1850, by James A. Batterson, Dea.	165
Walker, s. Elias, b. June 4, 1796	20
BATTERE, William, of Redding Ridge, m. Dorathy **BOTHWELL**, of Wilton, Mar. 24, 1851, by D. D. Frost, M. G.	166
BATTERSON, Wilkey W., of Wilton, m. Eunice **SHERWOOD**, of Redding, July 10, 1831, by James A. Batterson, Dea.	132
BEACH, Abigail, [d. Lazarus & Lydia], b. Sept. 13, 1778	79
Betsey, d. [Isaac & Hannah], b. Nov. 12, 1798	79
Charles, s. Isaac, b. Nov. 27, 1801	103
Elisabeth, [w. Isaac], d. Feb. 14, 1796	79
Eunice, [d. Lazarus & Lydia], b. Nov. 23, 1769	79
Hannah, [d. Lazarus & Lydia], b. Apr. 14, 1767	79
Isaac, [s. Lazarus & Lydia], b. May 19, 1773	79
Isaac, m. Elisabeth **SILLIMAN**, Dec. 7, 1794, by Rev. Stephen W. Stebbins, of Stratford	79
Isaac, m. Hannah **HILL**, Sept. 26, 1797, by Nathaniel Bartlet	79
Isaac, m. Mary Rebecca **WINTON**, b. of Redding, Nov. 1, 1840, by Rev. Charles J. Todd	148

64 BARBOUR COLLECTION

Page

BEACH, (cont.)
Joseph, of Sullivan, N. Y., m. Charlotte **TYRREL**, of Weston, Jan. 24,
 [1827], by John M. Heron, J. P. Int. Pub. 124
Lazarus, Jr., [s. Lazarus & Lydia], b. Dec. 1, 1760 79
Lazarus, m. Betsey **FOSTER**, b. of Redding, this day [May 14, 1829],
 by Jonathan Bartlett, M. G. 128
Lemuel, [s. Lazarus & Lydia], b. Mar. 31, 1763 79
Lydia, w. Lazarus, d. Nov. 28, 1797 79
Lydia, d. Isaac, b. Feb. 27, 1800 103
Lydia, m. James R. **HAWLEY**, Mar. 28, 1822, by Rev. Ambrose S.
 Todd 113
Sarah, [d. Lazarus & Lydia], b. Sept. 27, 1758; d. Nov. 21, 1759 79
Sarah, [d. Lazarus & Lydia], b. Nov. 19, 1764 79
Wyllys, s. Isaac, b. Aug. 20, 1803 103
BEARD, Abigail, w. Dr. William, d. Oct. 7, 1802 101
William, Dr., m. Hannah **FARMAN**, Nov. 6, 1803 100
BEARDSLEY, Aaron T., [s. William], b. Aug. 8, 1809 46
Jesse, [s. William], b. July 9, 1802 46
Lois, [d. William], b. Apr. 4, 1799 46
Lydia, [d. William], b. Nov. 21, 1800 46
Polly Ann, [d. William], b. May 19, 1804 46
Ruth, [d. William], b. Feb. 16, 1806 46
W[illia]m, of Redding, m. Molly **SANFORD**, of Newton, July 28,
 1798, by [   ]. Witnesses Jesse Beardsley, Jr., &
 Aaron Beardsley 31
W[illia]m, Jr., [s. William], b. Feb. 12, 1808 46
BEATTYS, Daniel S., of Danbury, m. Caroline **HUBBEL**, of Redding,
 Mar. 19, 1826, by W[illia]m C. Kniffin, M. G. 122
BEECHER, BEACHER, Hannah, Mrs. of Redding, m. Lyman **BENNETT**, of
 Easton, June 8, 1845, by John Edwards, J. P. 159
Samuel, of Cheshire, m. Hannah **WHEELER**, of Redding, Aug. 22,
 1830, by Aaron Sanford, Jr., J. P. 130
BEERS, BEARS, Abigail, m Levi **FANTON**, Feb. 26, 1797, by Jonathan
 Bartlett 61
Almira, m. David **KEELER**, b. of Redding, this day [Feb. 3, 1828], by
 Rev. Lemuel B. Hull 127
Angeline, m. George R. **PECK**, b. of Redding, Dec. 3, 1848, by Rev.
 Joseph P. Taylor 163
Aseneth, d. [Gershom & Mary], b. Mar. 3, 1798 56
Cyrus, s. [Gershom & Mary], b. June 13, 1784 56
Eli, s. [Gershom & Mary], b. Apr. 12, 1789 56
Elosia, m. Philo W. **ABBOTT**, b. of Redding, Jan. 6, 1839, by Rev.
 Charles J. Todd 144
Ephraim I., m. Sarah A. **PLOWS**, b. of Redding, Mar. 12, 1837, by
 Rev. H. Humphreys 141
Eunice, d. [Gershom & Mary], b. Feb. 15, 1796 56
Gershom, m. Mary **PARSONS**, Nov. 13, 1783. Certified by Betty Mead 56
Hannah, m. Jabez **GORHAM**, May 22, 1797, by Nathaniel Bartlett 92

REDDING VITAL RECORDS 65

Page

BEERS, BEARS, (cont.)
Henry, m. Mary Esther **WHITLOCK**, b. of Norwalk, Aug. 4, 1852, by
  Cortis Merchant, J. P. 168
Hezekiah, of Weston, m. Betsey **SQUIRE**, of Weston, Jan. 3, 1841, by
  Rev. Charles J. Todd 149
Jeremiah, m. Flora **SHERWOOD**, Dec. 12, 1821, by Rev. Laban Clark 111
Lyman, of Aurelius, Cayuga Co., N. Y., m. Eliza **GORHAM**, of
  Redding, May 5, 1839, by Rev. Hawley Sanford 145
Mary, m. Benjamin **BIGELOW**, b. of Redding, Nov. 2, 1845, by
  Edward Starr, J. P. 157
Philo, m. Mary **GOULD**, Feb. 22, 1838, by John Crawford 143
Polly, m. Hezekiah **GRAY**, Sept. 24, 1826, by Marvin Richardson 123
Simeon, [s. Gershom & Mary], b. July 1, 1792 56
BELDEN, Eunice, m. Zalmon **HULL**, Mar. 4, 1784, by Rev. Isaac Lewis.
  Witnesses Polly Smith & S. Sam[ue]l Smith 63
Harriet, of New York City, m. Charles **HILL**, of Redding, Oct. 21,
  1845, by Rev. W[illia]m F. Collins 157
BENEDICT, Amanda, of Redding, m. Zar B. **BARNUM**, of Bethel, Feb. 4,
  1852, by Rev. J. L. Gilder 167
Betsey, [d. Daniel & Rebeckah], b. Mar. 6, 1791 46
Charles, s. Thadeus [& Deborah], b. Aug. 22, 1783 40
Daniel, m. Rebeckah **MEEKER**, Mar. 16, 1786, by Nathaniel Bartlett 46
Daniel, of Vermont, m. Sally Ann **LEE**, of Redding, June 6, 1828, by
  W[illia]m C. Kniffin, M. G. 127
Ebenezer, of Danbury, m. Charry **COUCH**, of Redding, [Jan.] 6,
  [1823], by Rev. Daniel Crocker 116
Ebenezer, m. Julia **BURR**, b. of Redding, Sept. 29, 1827, by W[illia]m
  C. Kniffin, M. G. 126
Eunice, of Redding, m. Lewis **SHERWOOD**, of Weston, Apr. 2, 1834,
  by Rev. W[illia]m L. Strong 137
Henry, s. Thaddeus [& Deborah], b. July 18, 1785 40
Hiram, s. Thaddeus [& Deborah], b. Nov. 21, 1779 40
Jared Meeker, [s. Daniel & Rebeckah], b. Mar. 22, 1795 46
Mabel, [d. Daniel & Rebeckah], b. Nov. 13, 1798 46
Mabel, of Redding, m. Samuel **STEVENS**, of Darien, [Dec.] 11, [1831],
  by Jonathan Bartlett, M. G. 133
Maria, Mrs., of Wilton, m. Isaac **OSBORN**, of Redding, Oct. 29, 1843,
  by James A. Batterson, Dea. 153
Michael, [s. Dan[ie]l & Rebeckah], b. Feb. 14, 1787 46
Sarah, d. Thaddeus [& Deborah], b. Mar. 3, 1776 40
Sarah, [d. Daniel & Rebeckah], b. Mar. 20, 1789; d. Mar. 27, 1794 46
Thaddeus, m. Deborah **READ**, b. of Redding, July 12, 1775, by
  Nathaniel Bartlet 40
Thaddeus, s. Thaddeus [& Deborah], b. July 29, 1791 40
W[illia]m, s. Thaddeus [& Deborah], b. Feb. 14, 1778 40
BENNETT, BENNET, Aaron, of Redding, m. Polly **HULL**, of Weston, Dec.
  24, 1833, by Rev. W[illia]m L. Strong 137
Burr, m. Sally Ann **LEE**, b. of Redding, [May] 1, [1838], by Rev.

BENNETT, BENNET, (cont.)

	Page
Jeremiah Miller	143
Elousia,* 1st d. [Platt & Martha], b. Dec. 16, 1792 *(First written "Eleanor")	41
Fanny, 3rd d. [Platt & Martha], b. Nov. 20, 1798	41
Lucinda, 2nd d. [Platt & Martha], b. Feb. 20, 1795	41
Lyman, of Easton, m. Mrs. Hannah **BEECHER**, of Redding, June 8, 1845, by John Edwards, J. P.	159
Mary, m. Augustus **LYON**, Mar. 20, 1788	13
Phebe, m. John **WANZER**, b. of Weston, this day [Sept. 10, 1839], by Rev. W[illia]m Denison	147
Platt, m. Martha **WHEELER**, July 29, 1792	41
Polly Ann, m Stephen **FAIRCHILD**, b. of Redding, Sept. 1, 1833, by Rev. Jesse Hunt	136
Sherman, m. Angenett **SHERWOOD**, b. of Redding, Jan. 28, 1837, by James A. Batterson, Dea.	141
Shubel, m. Rebeckah **PICKIT**, b. of Redding, Feb. 17, 1767, by Rev. Nath[anie]ll Bartlet	2

BERT, Sarah Ann, of Ridgefield, m. Leander **HODGE**, of Redding, Jan. 3, 1839, by W[illia]m Bowen — 144

BETTS, Dan[ie]l, [s. Stephen, Jr. & Sarah], b. Feb. 19, 1776 — 44

Daniel, m. Abigail **ROGERS**, Nov. 25, 1798. Certified by James Rogers	57
Daniel, m. Abigail **ROGERS**, Nov. 25, 1798	100
Eliza, [d. Daniel & Abigail], b. Apr. 26, 1802	100
Hannah, [d. Stephen, Jr. & Sarah], b. Dec. 19, 1773; d. Apr. 13, 1777	44
Julia, d. [Daniel & Abigail], b. Sept. 19, 1799	100
Julia, d. Dan[ie]l & Abigail, d. Dec. 27, 1804	101
Julia, d. Daniel & Abigail, b. Oct. 27, 1805	102
Martha, wid., m. Theophilus **HULL**, b. of Redding, Jan. 25, 1759, by Rev. Nath[anie]ll Bartlet	8
Polly, [d. Stephen, Jr. & Sarah], b. Apr. 19, 1786; d. Feb. 29, 1788	44
Polly, d. [Stephen, Jr. & Sarah], b. May 29, 1789	44
Sarah, m. Ephraim **DeFOREST**, b. of Norwalk, Oct. 25, 1764, by Rev. Nath[anie]ll Bartlet	4
Sarah, [d. Stephen, Jr. & Sarah], b. Nov. 23, 1779	44
Stephen, Jr., of Redding, m. Sarah **CLARK**, of Danbury, Apr. 30, 1776, by Rev. Ebenezer Baldwin, of Danbury	44

BIGELOW, Benjamin, m. Mary **BEERS**, b. of Redding, Nov. 2, 1845, by Edward Starr, J. P. — 157

BIGGS, Jonas, of Weston, m. Laura Juliaette **SHERMAN**, of Redding, Jan. 27, 1851, by Aaron Sanford, J. P. — 166

BIRCHUM, Sam[ue]l, m. Almyra **GREEN**, b. of Redding, Oct. 8, 1843, by David C. Comstock — 153

BISHOP, Seth L., of Woodbury, m. Harriet **CROFUT**, of New Town, Feb. 2, 1829, by Rev. Henry Stead — 128

BIXBY, Eleanor, m. Seth **MEEKER**, Mar. 14, 1770; d. Aug. 6, 1774 — 33

Elinor, m. Seth **MEEKER**, b. of Redding, Mar. 27, 1770, by Rev. Nathaniel Bartlet — 12

	Page
BIXBY, (cont.)	
Mehetabel, m. Nathan **COLEY**, b. of Redding, Nov. 15, 1770, by Rev. Nath[anie]ll Bartlett	3
BOOTH, Betsey Ann, Mrs., of Redding, m. Benedict **HAYES**, of California, Apr. 17, 1851, by Rev. J. L. Gilder	167
Maria H., m. Walter **SANFORD**, Dec. 6, 1821, by Rev. Laban Clark	111
BOSWORTH, Mary, of New Milford, m. Elijah **COUCH**, of Redding, Nov. 5, 1772. Witnesses Daniel Couch, Sarah Couch	24
BOTHWELL, Dorathy, of Wilton, m. William **BATTERE**, of Redding Ridge, Mar. 24, 1851, by D. D. Frost, M. G.	166
BOTSFORD, Abiel K., of Huntington, m. Eliza **HAWLEY**, of Redding, June 22, 1820, by Rev. Daniel Crocker	108
BOUGHTON, Annis, m. Stephen **GRAY**, Nov. 1, 1792, by Timothy Langdon. Witness Samuel Hull	62
Benjamin S., m. Sarah Maria **SANFORD**, b. of Redding, Jan. 19, 1850, by D. D. Frost, M. G.	164
Fanny, d. Orrin & Sally, b. Mar. 7, 1810	59
Mary, m. John H. **LEE**, b. of Redding, [Dec.] 27, [1837], by Rev. Jeremiah Miller	142
Orrin, m. Sally **GRAY**, Jan. 9, 1809. Witness Charles Smith	59
Richard S., of Danbury, m. Betsey **BURR**, of Redding, this day [Sept. 14, 1825], by Rev. Lemuel B. Hull	121
BRADLEY, Elizabeth, m. Daniel **PLATT**, Sept. 21, 1808	105
Hannah, m. Enos **WHEELER**, May 15, 1760. Witness Martha Wheeler	74
Harriet, of Weston, m. Theodore **FREEMAN**, of Redding, Nov. 10, 1826, by W[illia]m C. Kniffin, M. G.	123
Lucinda, m. Joseph **BURR**, Jr., Apr. 8, 1795, by Rev. James Johnson. Witnesses Ebenezer Merritt & Tamesin Burr	98
Molly B., m. Ephraim **SANFORD**, Dec. 22, 1795, by Rev. James Johnson. Witness Gershom Bradley	77
Nancy, m. Ishmael **COLEY** (colored), Feb. 8, last [1821], by Rev. Daniel Crocker	109
Phyllis, of Weston, m. Harry **WAKEMAN**, of Redding (colored), Oct. 6, 1839, by Rev. Hawley Sanford	146
Prisscilla, m. Daniel **CHAPMAN**, Nov. 3, 1795, by Rev. Nath[anie]ll Bartlett	3
Robert, m. Jane **PIKE**, May 4, 1852, by Orasmus H. Smith	168
Sarah, m. Jesse **SHERWOOD**, Sept. 20, 1795. Witnesses Joseph Banks & w. Sarah Banks	72
Tamesin, m. Aaron **BURR**, Apr. 7, 1799, by Rev. James Johnson. Witnesses Joseph Burr, Jr., Lucinda Burr	98
BRISCO, Samuel, of Brooklyn, N. Y., m. Huldah **HILL**, of Redding, (colored), Oct. 23, 1828, by Rev. Hawley Sanford	128
BRISTOL, Jerusha, m. John R. **WHEELER**, June 27, 1793. Witness Florilla Crofut	75
BROOKS, Charles, of Danbury, m. Lucy **MIDDLEBROOK**, of Redding, Dec. 18, 1831, by Rev. W[illia]m L. Strong	133
Thomas E., of Clinton, N. Y., m. Julia **GRAY**, of Redding, Aug. 31,	

BROOKS, (cont.)
1825, by W[illia]m C. Kniffin 121
BROWN, Betsey, of Brookfield, m. Harry **COUCH,** of Redding, Jan. 10,
1850, by D. D. Frost, M. G. 164
BUCSH, Rosanna, of Newton, m. Tunis **GREEN,** of Redding, Nov. 28, 1822,
by Hawley Sanford, Elder 114
BULKLEY, BULKLY, Andrew, [s. Peter], b. Oct. 14, 1785 95
Daniel Starling, [s. Peter], b. Dec. 27, 1790 95
Eben[eze]r Green, [s. Peter], b. Dec. 30, 1787 95
Elisabeth, [d. Peter], b. Sept. 8, 1781 95
Gershom, [s. Peter], b. July 30, 1779 95
Hannah, m. Benjamin **HAMBLETON,** b. of Redding, Apr. 5, 1754, by
Rev. Nath[anie]l Bartlet 8
Josiah, of Stratford, m. Eunice **MONROE,** of Weston, July 6, 1833, by
Rev. James A. Batterson 136
Lucy, [d. Peter], b. Nov. 14, 1783 95
Marcy, [d. Peter], b. June 6, 1772 95
Mary, m. Joseph **JOICE,** Feb. 16, 1794, by Rev. Timothy Langdon.
Witnesses Phebe Bulkley & Sarah Bulkley 96
Peter, m. [   ], Oct. 2, 1768 95
Peter, [s. Peter], b. July 7, 1769 95
Phebe, [d. Peter], b. Feb. 9, 1776 95
Sarah, [d. Peter], b. May 7, 1774 95
BURGESS, Elizabeth, of Wilton, m. Samuel **BATES,** of Fairfield, Nov. 10,
1850, by James A. Batterson, Dea. 165
BURLOCK, Elisabeth, m. Sam[ue]l **GUYER,** Mar. 24, 1782 7
BURR, BURS, Aaron, [s. Joseph & Grace], b. Sept. 1, 1777 2
Aaron, m. Tamesin **BRADLEY,** Apr. 7, 1799, by Rev. James Johnson.
Witnesses Joseph Burr, Jr. & Lucinda Burr 98
Abel, m. Sarah **WOOD,** Dec. 20, 1775, by Rev. Mr. Baldwin. Witness
Anne Salmon 22
Abel, [s. Jacob C. & Eunice], b. Aug. 27, 1787 57
Ann, d. [Jacob C. & Eunice], b. Feb. 19, 1793 57
Betsey, of Redding, m. Richard S. **BOUTON,** of Danbury, this day,
[Sept. 14, 1825], by Rev. Lemuel B. Hull 121
Clarissa, m. Moses **DIMON,** b. of Redding, Feb. 22, 1830, by Jared
Olmstead, J. P. 129
Clarry, [d. Stephen & Molly], b. June 8, 1788 90
David, [s. Jacob C. & Eunice], b. Jan. 25, 1791 57
Deborah, m. Seth **TODD,** b. of Redding, Oct. 1, 1845, by Rev.
W[illia]m F. Collins 156
Eli, [s. Seth & Elisabeth], b. July 16, 1797 57
Elijah, m. Rodah **SANFORD,** b. of Redding, Apr. 2, 1767, by Rev.
Nathaniel Bartlet 46
Eliza Ann, m. Marvin C. **SANFORD,** b. of Redding, Nov. 3, 1841, by
Rev. Warner Hoyt, of Ridgefield 153
Elisabeth, m. Jonathan **MIDDLEBROOK,** Jan. 6, 1793, by Nath[anie]l
Bartlett 3

	Page
BURR, BURS, (cont.)	
Euncie, m. Onesemous **COLEY**, on or about Dec. 22, 1762, by Nathaniel Bartlett	34
Fanny E., of Redding, m. Samuel B. **STURGES**, of Westport, Oct. 15, 1845, by Rev. W[illia]m F. Collins	157
Grace, m. Joseph **BURR**, May 28, 1758	2
Hannah, m. Henry **HOPKINS**, stranger, July 26, 1769	29
Harvey, s. [Jacob C. & Eunice], b. Feb. 13, 1795	57
Huldah, m. Abijah **FAIRCHILD**, b. of Redding, Nov. 5, 1767, by Rev. Nath[anie]ll Bartlet	6
Huldah, m. Daniel **MALLERY**, Jr., Oct. 12, 1806	105
Jacob C., m. Eunice **WOOD**, Feb. [ ], 1787, by Rev. Mr. Goodrich. Witness Abel Burr	57
James L., m. Clarissa **HULL**, Oct. 18, 1837, by John Crawford	143
Jesse, [s. Seth & Elisabeth], b. Aug. 5, 1791; d. Feb. 9, 1793	57
John, s. [Jacob C. & Eunice], b. Sept. 15, 1798	57
John, m. Sally Keeler **TAYLOR**, Feb. 4, 1824, by Nathan Burton	119
Joseph, m. Grace **BURR**, May 28, 1758	2
Joseph, [s. Joseph & Grace], b. July 26, 1772	2
Joseph, Jr., m. Lucinda **BRADLEY**, Apr. 8, 1795, by Rev. James Johnson. Witnesses Ebenezer Merrit & Tamesin Burr	98
Joseph, s. [Lemuel & Anna], b. Sept. 7, 1796	52
Julia, m. Ebenezer **BENEDICT**, b. of Redding, Sept. 29, 1827, by W[illia]m C. Kniffin, M. G.	126
Lemuel, m. Anna **HULL**, on or about Dec. 7, 1793, by Nathaniel Bartlett	52
Lucey, b. Dec. 3, 1780	103
Lucy, m. Jonathan **KNAPP**, b. of Redding, Apr. 10, 1800	103
Molly, [d. Stephen & Molly], b. July 10, 1793; d. July 15, 1793	90
Moses, m. Delia **KEELER**, Nov. 22, 1832, by Levi Brunson	134
Rachel, of Redding, m. Robert **TOWN**, of Weston, Mar. 3, 1839, by Aaron Sanford, Jr., J. P.	145
Rebe[c]kah, m. Seth **SANFORD**, b. of Redding, Apr. 25, 1759, by Rev. Nathaniel Bartlet	18
Sarah, [d. Jacob C. & Eunice], b. Feb. 4, 1789	57
Sarah, d. [Lemuel & Anna], b. Jan. 15, 1794	52
Seth, m. Elisabeth **LOBDEL**, Jan. 23, 1788, by John Benedict. Witness Abel Burr	57
Stephen, Dea. of Redding, m. Abigail **HALL**, of New Jersey, Apr. 12, 1761, by Rev. Nath[anie]ll Bartlet	2
Stephen, m. Molly **GRIFFIN**, Feb. 19, 1787. Witnesses Isaac Coley & Sarah Coley	90
Stephen, [s. Stephen & Molly], b. Dec. 28, 1795	90
Sturges, [s. Seth & Elisabeth], b. Apr. 22, 1788	57
Walter, m. Julia Ann **NORTHROP**, b. of Redding, Feb. 1, 1846, by Rev. Hawley Sanford	158
BURRET, Philip, m. Rachel **READ**, Mar. 1, 1774, by Nathaniel Bartlet	16
[BUSH], [see under **BUCSH**]	

	Page
BUTLER, William R., of Wilton, m. Abby J. **HENDRICK**, of Bridgeport, Jan. 5, 1845, by James A. Batterson, Dea.	154
BYUNGTON, BYINTON, Aaron, [s. John & Sarah], b. Sept. 14, 1775	23
Aaron, m. Mary **DARLING**, Jan. 2, 1797, by Nathaniel Bartlett	86
Alonzo, m. Betsey **COMSTOCK**, b. of Redding, this day [Aug. 20, 1835], by Jonathan Bartlett, M. G.	139
Belinda, d. Joel & Deborah, b. Aug. 16, 1798	102
George, s. Joel & Deborah, b. Mar. 1, 1802	102
Joel, [s. John & Sarah], b. Mar. 1, 1771	23
Joel, of Redding, m. Deborah **ROCKWELL**, of Ridgefield, Oct. 1, 1795	102
John, m. Sarah **GRAY**, b. of Redding, Nov. 16, 1763, by Rev. Nathaniel Bartlet	23
John, [s. John & Sarah], b. Sept. 17, 1764	23
Lucina, [d. John & Sarah], b. July 4, 1766	23
Lucy, [d. John & Sarah], b. May 19, 1780	23
Mary, d. Joel & Deborah, b. Apr. 28, 1807	104
Rachel, [d. John & Sarah], b. Sept. 4, 1785; d. Jan. 26, 1788	23
Reuben, [s. John & Sarah], b. May 2, 1769	23
St. John, of New Canaan, m. Delia **COLE**, of Redding, Feb. 21, 1830, by Rev. E. Washburn	130
Sarah, [d. John & Sarah], b. Apr. 22, 1778	23
CABLE, Sarah, m. Abraham **TAYLOR**, Dec. 1, 1784, by Jno Benedict. Witnesses Preserved Taylor & Justus Whitlock	85
CAMP, Samuel, of Old Milford, m. Belinda **BATRAM**, of Redding, Aug. 26, 1832, by James Coleman	134
CANFIELD, Betsey Ann, m. Asahel S. **DUNCOMB**, b. of Redding, [Dec.] 25, [1837], by Rev. Jeremiah Miller	142
Edwin L., m. Lucy A. **BASSETT**, June 30, 1847, by Rev. Jos. P. Taylor	159
Eliza, of Redding, m. Charles **OSBORN**, of Monroe, this day [Nov. 25, 1835], by Jonathan Bartlett, M. G.	140
Josiah, m. Abigail **SANFORD**, of Redding, Oct. 27, 1799, by Rev. Nathaniel Bartlett	99
Mary, d. Josiah & Abigail, b. May* 9, 1801 *(First written "Oct.")	99
Rachel, m. Oliver **TURKINGTON**, Sr., b. of Redding, Oct. 22, 1849, by Rev. Jacob Shaw	164
CARL, CARLE, Martha, Mrs., m. Joel **GRAY**, b. of Redding, Nov. [ ], 1850, by Rev. Daniel D. Frost	166
Zechariah, m. Martha **MEEKER**, of Redding, June 4, 1826, by Rev. W[illia]m Andrews	122
CARTER, Ezra, of Stockridge, Mass., m. Harriet **COLE**, of Redding, [July] 16, [1837], by Rev. Jeremiah Miller	141
CHAMBERS, Ruth, of Ridgefield, m. Daniel **SHERWOOD**, of Redding, Aug. 30, 1795	103
CHAPMAN, Chary, of Redding, m. Ethiel **ANDREWS**, of Danbury, this day, [May 28, 1826], by Jonathan Bartlett, M. G.	122
Daniel, b. Nov. 28, 1774	86

CHAPMAN, (cont.)
Daniel, m. Prisscilla **BRADLEY**, Nov. 3, 1795, by Rev. Nath[anie]ll
  Bartlett — 3
Dan[ie]l, Jr., m. Eliza **ANDREWS**, b. of Redding, this day [Feb. 24,
  1824], by Jonathan Bartlett, M. G. — 118
Electa M., of Redding, m. Daniel B. **SHERWOOD**, of Weston, Nov.
  27, 1827, by W[illia]m C. Kniffin — 126
Eliza, m. Abraham **HULL**, Nov. 24, 1838, by Rev. John Crawford — 144
Eliza Ann, m. Henry B. **FANTON**, Sept. 26, 1843, by P. L. Hoyt — 153
Harriot, d. Dan[ie]l & Priscilla, b. Sept. 29, 1796 — 3
Lucy, m. Daniel **FOSTER**, b. of Redding, Dec. 13, 1831, by Rev.
  W[illia]m L. Strong — 133
Mary, m. Benj[ami]n **DARLING**, Nov. 6, 1777, by Nathaniel Bartlet — 48
Mary, m. Benj[ami]n **DARLING**, Nov. 6, 1777, by Nathaniel Bartlett — 86
Permelia, m. Orson **MARCHANT**, b. of Redding, [Mar.] 23, [1823], by
  Rev. Daniel Crocker — 116
Sarah, of Redding, m. Daniel B. **ROCKWELL**, of Ridgebury, Dec. 12,
  1848, by Daniel D. Frost — 163
CLAPP, Asa P., of Sharon, m. Adaline **BATRAM**, of Redding, Oct. 9, 1850,
  by Rev. J. L. Gilder — 165
CLARK, Joseph E. Dr., m. Julia A. **ADAMS**, Oct. 2, 1848, by Daniel D.
  Frost, M. G. — 162
Sarah, of Danbury, m. Stephen **BETTS**, Jr., of Redding, Apr. 30, 1776,
  by Rev. Ebenezer Baldwin, of Danbury — 44
CLARKSON, Daniel, m. Charlotte **NASH**, July 22, 1821, by Dea. Hawley
  Sanford — 110
CLUCKSTON, CLUGSTONE, John, m. Eunice **MALLERY**, b. of Redding,
  July 7, 1760, by Rev. Nath[anie]ll Bartlett — 3
John, of Redding, m. Charity **GENNINGS**, of Fairfield, Nov. 20, 1764,
  by Rev. Nath[anie]ll Bartlett — 3
Sarah, m. Barnabard **KEEKER**,* on or about Jan. 1, 1793, by Nathaniel
  Bartlett   *(**KEELER?**) — 19
COLE, Delia, of Redding, m. St. John **BYINGTON**, of New Canaan, Feb.
  21, 1830, by Rev. E. Washburn — 130
Eli, of Wilton, m. Emily A. **MORGAN**, of Redding, July 16, 1848, by
  James A. Batterson, Dea. — 162
Harriet, of Redding, m. Ezra **CARTER**, of Stockbridge, Mass., [July]
  16, [1837], by Rev. Jeremiah Miller — 141
Mehetabel, m. Jared **MEEKER**, May 3, 1770, by Isaac Lewis — 33
COLEY, Abigail, of Redding, m. Zachariah **STEVENS**, Oct. 22, 1794,
  certified by Nathaniel Bartlett — 77
Azariah, [s. Onesemous & Eunice], b. Mar. 6, 1776 — 34
Betsey, d. [Isaac & Sarah], b. June 6, 1791 — 90
Betsey, m. Edward **MARCHANT**, b. of Redding, [Apr.] 4, [1839], by
  Rev. Jeremiah Miller — 145
Betsey Ann, d. Eben[eze]r B. & Amelia], b. May 30, 1815 — 107
David, m. Tama **SQUIRE**, Dec. 21, 1788 — 1
David, m. 2nd w. Parthenia **MEAD**, of Wilton, Dec. 5, 1802 — 1

COLEY, (cont.)

	Page
Dorcas, [d. Onesemous & Eunice], b. June 25, 1769; d. Nov. 6, 1774	34
Eben[eze]r, of Redding, m. Rachel **STURGES**, of Greensfarms, Nov. 12, 1771, by [　　　　]	24
Ebenezer Bradley, s. [Isaac & Sarah], b. May 17, 1786	90
Eben[ezer]r Bradley, m. Amelia **SANFORD**, Oct. 16, 1810, [by] Daniel Crocker	99
Ebenezer Bradley, d. Apr. 5, 1816	106
Elisabeth, [d. Onesemous & Eunice], b. May 5, 1763	34
Elisabeth, m. Ezra **HULL**, on or about Dec. 23, 1784, by Nathaniel Bartlett	63
Elisabeth, [d. David & Tama], b. June 4, 1791	1
Elisabeth, [d. David & Tama], d. Aug. 22, 1794	1
Eunice, m. Isaac **MEEKER**, b. of Redding, May 29, [　　], by Rev. Nathaniel Bartlet	12
Gershom, d. Dec. 16, 1798. Admr. Isaac Coley	90
Hannah, m. Justus **BATES**, b. of Redding, May 23, 1771, by Rev. Nath[anie]l Bartlet	20
Harry, s. [Isaac & Sarah], b. July 26, 1795	90
Henry, [s. David & Tama], b. June 16, 1793	1
Henry, [s. David & Tama], d. Aug. 13, 1794	1
Isaac, m. Sarah **GRIFFIN**, Sept. 8, 1785, certified by Stephen Burr & Molley Burr	90
Ishmael, m. Nancy **BRADLEY**, (colored), Feb. 8, last [1821], by Rev. Daniel Crocker	109
Lonson, of Westport, m. Emily **SANFORD**, of Redding, Aug. 30, 1848, by David C. Comstock	162
Lucretia, d. Amos & Phyllis (colored), b. Feb. 10, 1828	125
Lucretia, m. George **PETERSON**, b. of Redding (colored), Dec. 13, 1846, by Rev. Hawley Sanford	158
Mabel, m. Abijah **PERSONS**, Aug. [　　], 1782	75
Mary Ann, m. Aaron **BANKS**, b. of Redding, Mar. 4, 1835, by Rev. W[illia]m L. Strong	137
Myra, m. Henry **GLOVER**, Oct. 10, 1843, by Jared Olmstead, J. P.	153
Nathan, m. Mehetabel **BIXBY**, b. of Redding, Nov. 15, 1770, by Rev. Nath[anie]ll Bartlet	3
Nathan, of Redding, m. wid. Eleanor **CRAFT**, of Westport, this day, [Aug. 24, 1845], by Rev. W[illia]m Denison of Easton	156
Onesemous, m. Eunice **BURR**, on or about Dec. 22, 1762, by Nathaniel Bartlett	34
Onisimus, d. May 5, 1806	101
Peter, s. Amos & Phyllis, b. Dec. 5, 1819 (colored)	125
Peter Sanford, s. Eben[eze]r B. & Amelia, b. Oct. 21, 1812	107
Rachel, of Northfield, m. Oliver **SANFORD**, of Redding, Apr. 9, 1767, by Rev. Samuel Sherwood. Witness David Lyon	49
Rachael, m. Dan[ie]ll **MALLERY**, Jr., Oct. 13, 1778, by Rev. Mr. Bartlett. Witnesses Isaac Coley & John Davis	66
Rebeckah, [d. David & Tama], b. Apr. 16, 1789	1

REDDING VITAL RECORDS 73

Page

COLEY, (cont.)
Samuel, [s. David & Tama], b. Sept. 18, 1795   1
Samuel W., m. Ann Augusta **SANFORD**, Oct. 18, 1848, by Daniel D.
   Frost, M. G.   162
Tama, w. David, d. May 17, 1802   1
Zalmon, [s. David & Tama], b. May 1, 1799   1
COLLINS, Samuel J., m. Mary **SANFORD**, b. of Redding, Oct. 22, 1827, by
   W[illia]m C. Kniffin, M. G.   126
COMSTOCK, Andrew, [s. Billy & Rebecca], b. Jan. 23, 1803   59
Betsey, m. Alonzo **BYINGTON**, b. of Redding, this day {Aug. 20,
   1835], by Jonathan Bartlett, M. G.   139
Billy, m. Rebecca **STARR**, b. of Danbury, Mar. 26, 1797, by Rev.
   John Ely   59
Cornelia, [d. Billy & Rebecca], b. Feb. 16, 1800   59
Sally Maria, [d. Billy & Rebecca], b. Apr. 25, 1806   59
W[illia]m Starr, [s. Billy & Rebecca], b. Dec. 12, 1810   59
COPLY, Calvin, [s. Daniel & Theody], b. Jan. 20, 1791   28
Daniel, m. Theody **COUCH**, Apr. 3, 1777. Certified by Elijah Couch   28
Eunice, of Woodbury, m. Elijah **COUCH**, of Redding, July 20, 1777,
   by Jeremiah Day. Witnesses Daniel Couch & Lucy Couch   49
Lucy, [d. Daniel & Theody], b. Feb. 14, 1798   28
Theody Ann, [d. Daniel & Theody], b. July 24, 1794   28
CORNWALL, Nathan, of Danbury, m. Amanda M. **BANKS**, of Redding,
   Nov. 29, 1848, by Rev. Jacob Shaw   163
COUCH, Aaron, s. Eben[eze]r, Jr., b. June 17, 1772   24
Abigail, m. Edward **STARR**, b. of Redding, Dec. 9, 1824, by Rev.
   Lemuel B. Hull   119
Adria, m. Stephen **CROOFOT**, b. of Redding, Aug. 27, 1761, by Rev.
   Nathaniel Bartlet   30
Betty, m. John **SANFORD**, b. of Redding, Mar. 19, 1822, by Dea.
   Hawley Sanford   113
Calvin, [s. Elijah & Mary], b. Aug. 14, 1788   24
Charry, of Redding, m. Ebenezer **BENEDICT**, of Danbury, [Jan.] 6,
   [1823], by Rev. Daniel Crocker   116
Dan[ie]l, b. July 30, 1739; m. Sarah **HOWS**, Jan. 23, 17[ ]   50
Daniel, of Redding, m. Sarah **HOWES**, of Stanford, Jan. 23, 1763.
   Witnesses Ebenezer Couch & Preserved Taylor   24
Dan[ie]l, Jr., s. [Daniel & Sarah], b. Apr. 2, 1764   50
Daniel, s. Daniel & Sarah, b. Apr. 22, 1764   24
Dan[ie]l, [s. Elijah & Mary], b. Dec. 15, 1790   24
Ebenezer, [s. Elijah & Mary], b. Mar. 23, 1793   24
Ebenezer, d. Mar. 23, 1797, in the 88th y. of his age   24
Edward, [s. Simon, Jr. & Eleanor], b. July 14, 1792   58
Edward, m. Betsey **MARCHANT**, b. of Redding, Jan. 1, 1822, by Rev.
   Daniel Crocker   112
Eleanor, [d. Simon, Jr. & Eleanor], b. Aug. 26, 1782   58
Elijah, of Redding, m. Mary **BOSWORTH**, of New Milford, Nov. 5,
   1772. Witnesses Daniel Couch & Sarah Couch   24

COUCH, (cont.)

	Page
Elijah, of Redding, m. Euncie **COPLY**, of Woodbury, July 20, 1777, by Jeremiah Day. Witnesses Daniel Couch & Lucy Couch	49
Elijah, [s. Elijah & Mary], b. Mar. 14, 1782	24
Elisabeth Nash, [d. Simon, Jr. & Eleanor], b. Oct. 9, 1776	58
Esther, d. [Thomas, Jr. & Mary], b. Jan. 29, 1799	79
Esther, m. Stephen S. **MEAD**, Nov. 25, 1821, by Rev. Laban Clark	111
Harriet, m. James B. **CROFUT**, b. of Redding, Oct. 6, 1828, by W[illia]m C. Kniffin, M. G.	127
Harry, of Redding, m. Betsey **BROWN**, of Brookfield, Jan. 10, 1850, by D. D. Frost, M. G.	164
Hiram, [s. Thomas N. & Abigail], b. July 27, 1791	58
Horace H., of Danbury, m. Lucy **STOW**, of Redding, Feb. 2, 1831, by Rev. E. Washburn	132
Ira, s. [Daniel & Sarah], b. Sept. 29, 1766	50
Ira Howes, s. [Daniel & Sarah], b. Sept. 29, 1766	24
Jane Ann, of Redding, m. Aaron **SHERWOOD**, of Manlius, N. Y., Feb. 29, 1848, by Rev. J. D. Marshall	160-1
John, m. Maria **SANFORD**, b. of Redding, May 19, 1822, by Rev. Daniel Crocker	114
Jonathan, m. Eunice **GRIFFIN**, b. of Redding, Aug. 15, 1759, by Rev. Nath[anie]l Bartlet	3
Jonathan, m. Mehetabel **MEEKER**, Sept. 23, 1777, by N. Bartlet. Witnesses Ebenezer Couch & Elijah Couch	48
Jonathan, [s. Elijah & Mary], b. Jan. 15, 1780	24
Joseph, [s. Simon, Jr. & Eleanor], b. Aug. 3, 1778	58
Lydia, [d. Thomas N. & Abigail], b. [ ]	58
Lydia, m. Andrew **FAIRCHILD**, Jr., Feb. 16, 1792. Witnesses Simon Couch & Tho[ma]s N. Couch	61
Mary, [d. Elijah & Mary], b. July 20, 1784	24
Nash, [s. Simon, Jr. & Eleanor], b. Apr. 23, 1787	58
Nash, [s. Thomas N. & Abigail], b. Oct. 17, 1794	58
Polly, m. James Henry **ASHTON**, June 29, 1825, by Rev. Aaron Hunt	121
Priscilla, [d. Simon, Jr. & Eleanor], b. June 27, 1790	58
Rebeckah, [d. Thomas N. & Abigail], b. June 19, 1788	58
Sally, d. [Daniel & Sarah], b. Feb. 4, 1770	50
Sam[ue]l, s. Elijah & Eunice, b. Jan. 29, 1778	49
Sarah, of Redding, m. Ephraim **ROBBINS**, formerly of Killingley, June 20, 1769, by Rev. Nathaniel Bartlet	38
Sarah, d. [Daniel & Sarah], b. Feb. 4, 1770	24
Sarah, 2nd, m. Seth **SANFORD**, Jr., b. of Redding, Oct. 8, 1803	100
Sarah, m. Ebenezer B. **SANFORD**, b. of Redding, [Nov.] 25, [1838], by Rev. Jeremiah Miller	144
Seth, [s. Simon, Jr. & Eleanor], b. Aug. 31, 1780	58
Silas Crane, [s. Elijah & Mary], b. June 8, 1786	24
Simon, Jr., m. Eleanor **NASH**, Jan. 7, 1776, by Hezekiah Ripley, V. D. M.	58
Simon, 3rd, [s. Simon, Jr. & Eleanor], b. Dec. 2, 1784; d. Feb. 14, 1794	58

REDDING VITAL RECORDS 75

	Page
COUCH, (cont.)	
Simon, 3rd, [s. Simon, Jr. & Eleanor], b. Dec. 6, 1794	58
Stephen, [s. Elijah & Mary], b. Oct. 28, 1797	24
Theody, m. Daniel **COPLY**, Apr. 3, 1777. Certified by Elijah Couch	28
Tho[ma]s, Jr., m. Mary **SANFORD**, Sept. 25, 1797, by Jonathan Bartlett	79
Thomas, s. Timothy & Polly (colored), b. Mar. 3, 1818	117
Thomas N., m. Abigail **STEBBENS**, Dec. 13, 1787. Witnesses Simon Couch & Anna Couch	58
Timothy Sanford, s. [Thomas, Jr. & Mary], b. Feb. 12, 1797	79
William, [s. Elijah & Mary], b. Feb. 18, 1774	24
W[illia]m T., m. Eunice H. **LOCKWOOD**, Apr. 29, 1840, by David C. Comstock	148
CRAFT, Eleanor, wid. of Westport, m. Nathan **COLY**, of Redding, this day, [Aug. 24, 1845], by Rev. W[illia]m Denison	156
CRAWFORD, Charlotte, m. Ezra **SANFORD**, Sept. 20, 1795, by Nathaniel Bartlett	53
James Lewis, b. July 20, 1769	3
CROCKER, John A., m. Sally **HULL**, Apr. 8, 1810. Witness Anna Crocker	99
CROFUT, CROFOOT, CROOFOT, CROWFUT, Abel, of Danbury, m. Sophia **SMITH**, of Redding, Sept. 23, 1827, by Henry Stead	126
Ambros C., [s. Zalmon], b. Feb. 25, 1792	25
Anner Maria, [d. Zalmon], b. Nov. 25, 1798	25
Annis, d. Oct. 28, 1802	101
Benedict, m. Harriet **HULL**, b. of Redding, Mar. 30, 1831, by Rev. W[illia]m L. Strong	132
Betsey Ann, [d. Israel & Annis], b. Jan. 20, 1793	34
David, of Redding, m. Elisabeth [ ], Nov. 15, 1775, by Rev. [ ] Lewis, of Norwalk. Witness Thankful Whitlock	15
Gould Dimond, m. Mabel **BANKS**, Jan. 10, 1822, by Rev. Laban Clark	112
Harriet, of New Town, m. Seth L. **BISHOP**, of Woodbury, Feb. 2, 1829, by Rev. Henry Stead	128
Israel, m. Annis **SANFORD**, Sept. 19, 1784, certified by Elijah Couch	34
Israel, m. Elizabeth **STUART** (2nd w.), June 9, 1803	100
James B., m. Harriet **COUCH**, b. of Redding, Oct. 6, 1828, by W[illia]m C. Kniffin, M. G.	127
Joel Dunning, [s. Israel & Annis], d.* Feb. 15, 1798 *(First written "born")	34
Jonathan, s. Nathan & Phebe, b. Aug. 22, 1796	103
Jonathan, [s. Nathan & Phebe], b. Aug. 22, 1797	47
Josiah **SANFORD**, [s. Israel & Annis], b. Dec. 30, 1786	34
Lucy Ann, of Redding, m. Grandison **GLOVER**, of Newton, Mar. 31, 1831, by Rev. Lemuel B. Hull	133
Mabel, of Danbury, m. Monson **KEELER**, of Redding, this day [Mar. 20, 1825], by Rev. Lemuel B. Hull	120
Maraney, [d. Zalmon], b. Apr. 28, 1794	25
Mary, d. [Zalmon], b. Sept. 20, 1809	25

76   BARBOUR COLLECTION

                                                                    Page
CROFUT, CROFOOT, CROOFOT, CROWFUT, (cont.)
  Mary, m. Hiram **POLLY**, Jan. 27, 1831, by Rev. Lemuel B. Hull   133
  Nathan, m. Phebe **HENDRIX**, Aug. 2, 1796, by Enos Wheeler   47
  Peter, s. Nathan & Phebe, b. May 16, 1802   103
  Ruth, m. Ephraim **WHITLOCK**, June 15, 1786, certified by
    Israel Crofut   74
  Ruth, d. Zalmon, b. Mar. 11, 1801   25
  Solomon C., [s. Zal[mo]n], b. May 7, 1779   25
  Stephen, s. John, b. Mar. 27, 1757   26
  Stephen, m. Adria **COUCH**, b. of Redding, Aug. 27, 1761, by Rev.
    Nathaniel Bartlet   30
  Susan, of Redding, m. Edwin **PIERCE**, of New Fairfield, Jan. 12, 1845,
    by Rev. W. F. Collins   155
  Silve, [d. Nathan & Phebe], b. Feb. 26, 1799   47
  Sylvia, d. Nathan & Phebe, b. Feb. 26, 1799   103
  Sylvia, of Redding, m. Jeremiah **HUBBEL**, of Weston, Dec. 29, 1826,
    by John M. Heron, J. P. Int. Pub.   124
  Zalmon, s. John, b. May 16, 1759; d. Dec. following   26
  Zalmon, had s. b. Jan. 13, 1803; d. Jan. 18, 1803   25
CROSSMAN, Polly Ann, of Redding, m. James N. **DAVIS**, of South East,
    N. Y., Nov. 22, 1846, by Rev. J. D. Marshall   160
CURTIS, CURTICE, David, m. Charry **MONROE**, Nov. 27, 1838, by Rev.
    John Crawford   144
  Stiles, m. Amelia **MONROE**, Mar. 10, 1839, by Rev. John Crawford 145
  William B., m. Louisa **MOREHOUSE**, Nov. 26, 1837, by John
    Crawford   143
DARLING, Anna Maria, of Easton, m. Aaron B. **HULL**, of Redding, June
    23, 1850, by James A. Batterson, Dea.   167
  Benj[ami]n, m. Mary **CHAPMAN**, Nov. 6, 1777, by Nathaniel Bartlet 48
  Benj[ami]n, m. Mary **CHAPMAN**, Nov. 6, 1777, by Nathaniel Bartlett 86
  Benj[ami]n A., [s. Benjamin & Mary], b. Apr. 2, 1786   86
  Benjamin A., of Redding, m. Sally B. **ODELL**, of Norwalk,
    Nov. 2, 1808   25
  Eli, m. Eliza **GRAY**, b. of Redding this day [Apr. 18, 1830], by
    Jonathan Bartlett, M. G.   130
  Eli Andrus, s. Benj[ami]n A. & Sally B., b. Oct. 12, 1809   25
  Elizabeth, [d. Benjamin & Mary], b. Feb. 24, 1784   86
  Harry Ferris, s. Joseph & Betsey, b. Aug. 16, 1809; d. Oct. 13, 1811 59
  Harry Ferris, s. [Joseph & Betsey], b. June 13, 1812   59
  Joseph, [s. Benjamin & Mary], b. July 27, 1780   86
  Joseph, of Redding, m. Betsey **FERRIS**, of Salem, Jan. 1, 1807   59
  Love, [d. Benjamin & Mary], b. Apr. 8, 1788   86
  Mary, m. Joseph **MEEKER**, b. of Redding, Mar. 12, 1767   12
  Mary, [d. Benjamin & Mary], b. Oct. 25, 1778   86
  Mary, m. Aaron **BYINGTON**, Jan. 2, 1797, by Nathaniel Bartlett   86
  Minot Odell, s. Benj[amin] A. & Sally B., b. Apr. 22, 1811   25
  Paulina, of Redding, m. Samuel **DINTON**, of Middletown, N. Y.,
    Dec. 2, 1823, by Sylvanus Haight   117

REDDING VITAL RECORDS 77

	Page
DARLING, (cont.)	
Sally, d. Joseph & Betsey, b. June 1, 1807; d. May 8, 1810	59
Sarah, [d. Benjamin & Mary], b. Oct 11, 1791	86
Selina, [d. Benjamin & Mary], b. Dec. 27, 1794	86
Selina, m. Timothy **PARSONS**, b. of Redding, Sept. 29, 1839, by Rev. P. R. Brown	146
Urania, m. Eliphalet **TAYLOR**, Mar. 15, 1826, by M. Richardson	122
DARROW, Anna, m. Robert **STOW**, Jan. 26, 1774, certified by Samuel Gold	82
Anne, m. Robert **STOW**, b. of Redding, Jan. 26, 1775, by Nathaniel Bartlet	40
DAUCHY, Mary, m. Ebenezer **SANFORD**, Feb. 24, 1787	39
DAVIES, [see under **DAVIS**]	
DAVIS, DAVIES, Aaron, [s. John], b. Nov. 2, 1787	85
Daniel, [s. John], b. Dec. 8, 1783; d. Mar. 13, 1784	85
Esther, m. John **GRAY**, Oct. 17, 1790. Witnesses Joel Gray & Stephen Gray	62
Eunice, m. Azariah **MEEKER**, May 19, 1789, by Nathaniel Bartlet	76
Hezekiah, [s. John], b. Feb. 19, 1797	85
James N., of South East, N. Y., m. Polly Ann **CROSSMAN**, of Redding, Nov. 22, 1846, by Rev. J. D. Marshall	160
John, m. Eunice **GRAY**, Oct. 21, 1779, by Rev. Nathaniel Bartlett. Witnesses Joel Gray & Ruhamah Gray	85
Maria, m. Jonathan R. **SANFORD**, Oct. 17, 1808	104
Moses, [s. John], b. July 16, 1792	85
Nancy, d. [Dr. Thomas], d. Mar. 6, 1795	80
Roxy, [d. John], b. Apr. 24, 1786	85
Thomas F., s. Dr. Tho[ma]s, b. Aug. 22, 1793	80
Thomas Frederic, s. Dr. Thomas & Hannah, b. Aug. 22, 1793	104
DAVISON, Melleson, m. Seth **MEEKER**, Mar. 14, 1775	33
DeFOREST, Ephraim, m. Sarah **BETTS**, b. of Norwalk, Oct. 25, 1764, by Rev. Nath[anie]ll Bartlet	4
Mary, d. May 7, 1810	101
DENISON, Abigail Jane, m. Joseph **JENNINGS**, Nov. 26, 1851, by Orsamus H. Smith	167
Clarissa D., of Redding, m. William C. **MOREHOUSE**, of Amenia, N. Y., June 11, 1848, by Rev. Joseph P. Taylor	162
DIBBLE, Elizabeth T., m. Moses **SHERWOOD**, b. of Redding, Nov. 7, 1850, by Rev. J. L. Gilder	166
Eveline F., of Bethel, m. Hiram **LOCKWOOD**, of Norwalk, Apr. 6, 1851, by Rev. J. L. Gilder	167
Sarah, of Ridgefield, m. Nehemiah **SEELEY**, Jr., of Redding, Sept. 26, 1769, by Rev. Nath[anie]l Bartlet	38
DICKENS, Alonzo, m. Caroline **MIDDLEBROOK**, b. of Redding, Nov. 23, 1848, by Rev. Jacob Shaw	163
DIKEMAN, DEKEMAN, Levi, s. Frederick & Ann, b. Apr. 13, 1750	25
Levi, m. Rebeckah **LYNES**, Feb. 9, 1774, by Rev. Nathaniel Bartlet. Witnesses John Couch & Sarah Couch	25
Mary Ann, m. Thomas **WOOD**, Mar. 10, 1852, by Rev. C. Bartlett	168

	Page
DIKEMAN, DEKEMAN, (cont.)	
Samuel, s. Levi & Rebeckah, b. Nov. 2, 1774	25
DIMON, Harriet, m. Harry **HULL**, b. of Redding, Dec. 31, 1829, by Rev. E. Washburn	129
Laura, of Redding, m. Zalmon **EDWARDS**, of New Fairfield, Feb. 2, 1831, by Rev. W[illia]m L. Strong	132
Mary E., of Redding, m. Samuel B. **MEAD**, of Bethel, May 20, 1850, by Daniel D. Frost, M. G.	165
Moses, m. Clarissa **BURR**, b. of Redding, Feb. 22, 1830, by Jared Olmstead, J. P.	129
DINTON, Samuel, of Middletown, N. Y., m. Paulina **DARLING**, of Redding, Dec. 2, 1823, by Sylvanus Haight	117
DISBROW, Joanna, m. Joseph **ADAMS**, Sept. 9, 1761	88
DOWNS, Anna, m. George **STARR**, b. of Redding, June 8, 1822, by Hawley Sanford, Elder	114
Catharine, of Weston, m. Daniel **ANDREWS**, of Redding, Jan. 17, 1830, by Rev. Hawley Sanford	129
Hannah, m. Daniel **MOREHOUSE**, May [ ], 1785, by Nathaniel Bartlett	96
Peter, of Weston, m. Sally **LYON**, of Redding, this day [Sept. 23, 1827], by Rev. Lemuel B. Hull	127
DREW, Amelia, m. Hiram **KNAPP**, b. of Redding, Sept. 23, 1827, by John M. Heron, J. P., Int. Pub.	126
Anna, [d. John & Joanna], b. Oct. 30, 17[ ]* *(Crossed out)	4
Anna, [d. John & Joanna], b.Oct. 30, 1765	4
Asabel, m. Grissel **WHEELER**, Nov. 25, 1795. Witnesses Enos Wheeler & Peter Wheeler	59
Daniel, [s. John & Joanna], b. Apr. 24, 1764	4
Hannah, [d. John & Mary], b. Feb. 9, 1760	4
Isaac, [s. John & Mary], b. June 17, 1752	4
John, m. Mary **NORTHROP**, Jan. 16, 1746	4
John, Jr., [s. John & Mary], b. Dec. 16, 1749	4
John, m. Joanna **THORP**, June 24, 1760	4
Levi, of Bethel, m. Lydia **BARTRAM**, of Redding, Oct. 13, 1847, by Rev. J. D. Marshall	159-60
Mary, [d. John & Mary], b. Mar. 29, 1758	4
Mary, w. John, d. Mar. 5, 1760	4
Noah, [s. John & Joanna], b. Aug. 8, 1768	4
Peter, [s. John & Mary], b. Apr. 22, 1754	4
Rebecca W., m. Orin W. **THORP**, b. of Redding, Apr. 3, 1842, by David C. Comstock	151
Samuel, [s. John & Joanna], b. Mar. 21, 1770	4
Sarah, [d. John & Joanna], b. May 12, 1762	4
William, [s. John & Mary], b. July 28, 1746	4
DUNCOMB, Aaron H., m. Mary G. **EDMUNDS**, b. of Redding, Oct. 9, 1849, by Rev. Jacob Shaw	164
Asahel S., m. Betsey Ann **CANFIELD**, b. of Redding, [Dec.] 25, [1837], by Rev. Jeremiah Miller	142

REDDING VITAL RECORDS 79

DUNCOMB, (cont.) Page
   Charles, m. Eliza **FANTON**, b.of Redding, Sept. 29, 1839, by
     Rev. P. R. Brown 146
   Harriet, m. John L. **HILL**, b. of Redding, May 4, 1840, by Rev.
     P. R. Brown 148
   Henry, m. Anna **HULL**, [   ], by Rev. Jesse Hunt 135
   Lydia Ann, m. John **OSBORN**, b. of Redding, Apr. 18, 1842, by
     Rev. Daniel Smith 151
DUTTON, Thomas, of Guilford, m. Sarah Maria **WHITING**, of Redding,
   Nov. 17, 1840, by Rev. D. C. Comstock 149
EDMONDS, EDMOND, EDMUNDS, Betsey, of Ridgefield, m. Rodney
   PENNOYER, of Redding, Mar. 26, 1843, by James A.
   Batterson, Dea. 151
   Burr, m. Harriet **ADAMS**, b. of Redding, Dec. 24, 1840, by Rev.
     P. R. Brown 149
   Daniel, of Ridgefield, m. Caroline **SANFORD**, of Redding, Nov. 28,
     1827, by W[illia]m C. Kniffin, M. G. 127
   Emma, m. Gershom W. **BANKS**, b. of Redding, July 9, 1848, by Rev.
     Tho[ma]s K. Witsil 162
   Mary G., m. Aaron H. **DUNCOMB**, b. of Redding, Oct. 9, 1849, by
     Rev. Jacob Shaw 164
EDWARDS, Anne, [d. Isaac & Hannah], b. Oct. 10, 1795 60
   Benj[ami]n, [s. Isaac & Hannah], b. Sept. 1, 1793 60
   Isaac, b. Apr. 7, 1762; m. Hannah **HALL**, Dec. 22, 1786 60
   Lanson, [s. Isaac & Hannah], b. Feb. 1, 1799 60
   Polly, [d. Isaac & Hannah], b. Jan. 1, 1791 60
   Zalmon, [s. Isaac & Hannah], b. Dec. 26, 1787 60
   Zalmon, of New Fairfield, m. Laura **DIMON**, of Redding, Feb. 2, 1831,
     by Rev. W[illia]m L. Strong 132
EVERTS, George, of New Haven, m. Ann Eliza **SILLECK**, of Redding,
   Sept. 26, 1847, by Rev. J. D. Marshall 160
FAIRCHILD, Aaron, [s. Samuel & Abigail], b. Oct. 9, 1786; d.
   May 31, 1787 80
   Aaron, [s. Samuel & Abigail], b. Jan. 9, 1792 80
   Abigail, m. Lymon **THORP**, Nov. [   ], 1790, by Justus Hull.
     Witnesses Stephen Gray & Samuel Hull 12
   Abigail, of Redding, m. William **LEE**, of Ridgefield, May 2, 1822, by
     Rev. Ambrose S. Todd 115
   Abijah, m. Huldah **BURR**, b. of Redding, Nov. 5, 1767, by Rev.
     Nath[anie]ll Bartlet 6
   Abraham, [s. Abram], d. July 9, 1764 84
   Andrew, Jr., m. Lydia **COUCH**, Feb. 16, 1792. Witnesses Simon Couch
     & Tho[ma]s N. Couch 61
   Betsey, [d. Samuel & Abigail], b. Jan. 20, 1789 80
   Dan, m. Sarah **LANE**, b. of Redding, Dec. 25, 1770, by Rev.
     Nath[anie]l Bartlet 7
   Daniel, [s. Abram], d. May 20, 1760 84
   Daniel, s. [Stephen & Elisabeth], b. Oct. 20, 1780 64

	Page
FAIRCHILD, (cont.)	
Daniel, m. Betsey **MEAD**, b. of Redding, Jan. 15, 1801	100
David, [s. Abram], d. May 16, 1777	84
David, [s. John & Abigail], b. Mar. 9, 1797	72
David, m. Charlotte **GUYRE**, Sept. 6, 1820, by Rev. Daniel Crocker	108
Elen, [d. Abram], b. Oct. 16, 1767	84
Elen, [d. Abram], d. Sept. 25, 1794	84
Elen, d. [Stephen & Elisabeth], b. Aug. 24, 1796	64
Eli, [s. John & Abigail], b. Nov. 15, 1794	72
Ezekiel, m. Eunice **ANDREWS**, b. of Redding, Jan. 8, 1767, by Rev. Nath[anie]l Bartlet	6
Hezekiah, [s. Stephen & Elisabeth], b. Apr. 19, 1785	64
Isaac, [s. Abram], d. Oct. 25, 1776	84
Isaac, [s. Stephen & Elisabeth], b. Jan. 27, 1783	64
Isaac, of Redding, m. Rachel **BANKS**, of Weston, Apr. 8, 1802	100
John, [s. Abram], b. Mar. 13, 1764	84
John, m. Abigail **WAKEMAN**, Jan. 6, 1792. Witnesses Stephen Fairchild & Samuel Fairchild	72
John, m. Elizabeth **MEEKER**, June 17, 1821, by Rev. Ambrose S. Todd	110
Lydia, d. Andrew, Jr. [& Lydia], b. Mar. 3, 1799	61
Peter, of Redding, m. Mary **LOCKWOOD**, of Fairfield(?), Mar. 27, 1768, by Rev. Nath[anie]l Bartlet	6
Peter, s. [Andrew, Jr. & Lydia], b. Aug. 2, 1794	61
Polly, m. Nathan E. **WILCOX**, Dec. 12, 1841, by Rev. Eli Barnett	150
Rachel, [d. Abram], b. Feb. 2, 1761	84
Rachel, w. Abram, d. July 23, 1801	101
Rachel, of Redding, m. Frederick **STEVENS**, of Danbury, Mar. 9, 1829, by Rev. Henry Stead	128
Rebeckah, d. [Andrew, Jr. & Lydia], b. Aug. 13, 1796	61
Samuel, m. Abigail **PLATT**, Mar. 31, 1785, by Nathaniel Bartlett	80
Sarah, m. John **HULL**, Jr., Feb. 22, 1782, by Nathaniel Bartlett	16
Simon, s. [Andrew, Jr. & Lydia], b. Sept. 29, 1792	61
Stephen, m. Elisabeth **FITCH**, Dec. 30, 1779. Witnesses Sam[ue]l Fairchild & Isaac Gorham	64
Stephen, m. Polly Ann **BENNETT**, b. of Redding, Sept. 1, 1833, by Rev. Jesse Hunt	136
Uriah, [s. Samuel & Abigail], b. May 20, 1794; d. Aug. 9, 1795	80
FANTON, Altha, m. John Wheeler **SANFORD**, Mar. 5, 1822, by Rev. Laban Clark	113
Caroline S., of Redding, m. John M. **REID** (Rev.), of Jamaica, L. I., May 3, 1848, by Rev. J. D. Marshall	161
Eliza, m. Charles **DUNCOMB**, b. of Redding, Sept. 29, 1839, by Rev. P. R. Brown	146
Henry B., m. Eliza Ann **CHAPMAN**, Sept. 26, 1843, by P. L. Hoyt	153
Julia, m. Moses **HILL**, Mar. 28, 1826, by M. Richardson	122
Levi, m. Abigail **BEERS**, Feb. 26, 1797, by Jonathan Bartlett	61
Prussia, m. Robert **PLATT**, Nov. 31, 1796. Witness Hezekiah Platt, Jr.	68
FARMAN, Hannah, m. Dr. William **BEARD**, Nov. 6, 1803	100

REDDING VITAL RECORDS 81

Page

FENNY, [see under **FERRY** & **PHINNEY**]
FERRIS, Betsey, of Salem, m. Joseph **DARLING**, of Redding, Jan. 1, 1807   59
FERRY, Anna, of Danbury, m. Jeremiah **STURGES**, of Redding, Oct. 3,
    1837, by Rev. Hawley Sanford   142
FINCH, Dimon, of Norwalk, m. Lucinda **HULL**, of Redding, Oct. 24, 1830,
    by W[illia]m L. Strong   131
FITCH, Abigail A., m. Levi **SANFORD**, Sept. 13, 1801, by Rev. Jonathan
    Bartlett. Witnesses Oliver Sanford, & Rachel Sanford   98
Abigail A., m. Levi **SANFORD**, Sept. 13, 1801, certified by David
    Sanford   99
Elisabeth, m. Stephen **FAIRCHILD**, Dec. 30, 1779. Witnesses Sam[ue]l
    Fairchild & Isaac Gorham   64
James Gale, s. Asahel, b. Aug. 31, 1773   27
FLEMIN, Benjamin, of Danbury, m. Mary Ann **MALLORY**, of Redding,
    Oct. 25, 1820, by Rev. Daniel Crocker   108
FOOT, Ebenezer, m. Mabel **BANKS**, Aug. 29, 1797, by Jonathan Bartlett   5
Frederick, [s. Reuben], b. June 8, 1811   61
Lucretia, [d. Reuben], b. Aug. 31, 1802   61
Peter, [s. Reuben], b.May 4, 1795   61
Phebe, [d. Reuben], b. July 15, 1806   61
Sally, m. Lewis **LOBDELL**, Apr. 4, 1827, by M. Richardson   124
FOSTER, Angeline, of Redding, m. Hezekiah D. **TAYLOR**, of Ridgefield,
    Nov. 23, 1846, by Morris Hill   158
Betsey, d. Joel & Esther, b. Jan. 6, 1811   117
Betsey, m. Lazarus **BEACH**, b. of Redding, this day [May 14, 1829],
    by Jonathan Bartlett, M. G.   128
Charles Thatcher, s. Joel & Esther, b. Mar. 2, 1818   117
Daniel, s. Joel & Esther, b. Apr. 23, 1804   117
Daniel, m. Lucy **CHAPMAN**, b. of Redding, Dec. 13, 1831, by Rev.
    W[illia]m L. Strong   133
E. Francis, of Ridgefield, m. Harriet **PLATT**, of Redding, Dec. 3, 1851,
    by Rev. Shaler J. Hillyer   167
Eliza, d. Joel & Esther, b. Apr. 2, 1816   117
Eliza, of Redding, m. Warren W. **SELLECK**, of Bridgeport, this day,
    [Apr. 22, 1839], by Jonathan Bartlett, M. G.   145
FREEMAN, Anne, [d. John & Elizabeth], b. Feb. 21, 1785   94
Charles, [s. John & Elizabeth], b. Dec. 15, 1790   94
Ebenezer, [s. John & Elizabeth], b. Sept. 15, 1786   94
Mary, of New Milford, m. Henry **HILL**, of Redding (colored), Oct. 3,
    1846, by Rev. Hawley Sanford   158
Nancy, [d. John & Elizabeth], b. Nov. 5, 1797   94
Thaddeus, [s. John & Elizabeth], b. Feb. 15, 1793   94
Theodore, of Redding, m. Harriet **BRADLEY**, of Weston, Nov. 10,
    1826, by W[illia]m C. Kniffin, M. G.   123
FRENCH, Eliza, of Weston, m. James **SANFORD**, Jr., of Redding, Jan. 27,
    1822, by Rev. Ambrose S. Todd   113
Mary Ann, m. Henry **MILLER**, b. of Redding, Jan. 17, 1833, by Rev.
    W[illia]m L. Strong   135

	Page
FRISBY, Jane, m. Davis **TAYLOR**, Dec. 9, 1824, by Nathan Burton	119
FROST, Adria, [child of Jabez & Deborah], b. Jan. 21, 1748	27
Betse, [d. Jabez & Deborah], b. May 16, 1764	27
Dan[ie]l, [s. Jabez & Deborah], b. Sept. 21, 1771	27
Deborah, [d. Jabez & Deborah], b. Nov. 5, 1753	27
Ezra, [s. Jabez & Deborah], b. Aug. 21, 1766	27
Griszel, [d. Jabez & Deborah], b. Oct. 10, 1751	27
Hannah, [d. Jabez & Deborah], b. Apr. 24, 1761	27
Jabez, m. Deborah **KING**, Dec. 3, 1746	27
Mary, [d. Jabez & Deborah], b. Feb. 23, 1756	27
Stephen, [s. Jabez & Deborah], b. Aug. 7, 1768	27
William, [s. Jabez & Deborah], b. Dec. 20, 1749	27
FOX, Charles, of Weston, m. Alma G. **GORHAM**, of Redding, [Oct.] 10, [1837], by Rev. Jeremiah Miller	142
GAUL, Aaron, of Danbury, m. Nancy **SANFORD**, of Redding (colored), Jan. 1, 1822, by Dea. Hawley Sanford	112
GILBERT, Eunice, of Redding, m. Zalmon **WHITLOCK**, of Danbury, Oct. 17, 1839, by Rev. Charles J. Todd	146
Seth, of Newton, m. Nancy **SANFORD**, of Redding, this day [Mar. 20, 1825], by Rev. Lemuel B. Hull	120
GILES, Joseph, of Redding, m. Ann **OLMSTEAD**, of Wilton, Feb. 14, 1835, by Rev. Josiah Bowen	138
GLOVER, Augustus, m. Eliza **PLUMB**, b. of Monroe, Jan. 13, 1850, by D. D. Frost, M. G.	164
Elias, m. Emeline **STOWE**, Nov. 12, 1837, by John Crawford	143
Elsa, m. Francis **PRICE**, b. of Redding (colored), Mar. 30, 1846, by Jonathan Bartlett, M. G.	158
Grandison, of Newtown, m. Lucy Ann **CROFUT**, of Redding, Mar. 31, 1831, by Rev. Lemuel B. Hull	133
Henry, m. Laura **SHERWOOD**, b. of Redding, Dec. 26, 1841, by Rev. Daniel Smith	151
Henry, m. Myra **COLEY**, of Redding, Oct. 10, 1843, by Jared Olmstead, J. P.	153
Lem[ue]l, m. Sarah **MEEKER**, June 29, 1786, by Rev. Nathaniel Bartlett. Certified by Jonathan Meeker, Jr., John Meeker & Stephen Betts	7
Lemuel, s. [Lemuel & Sarah], b. Apr. 26, 1791	7
GODFREY, GODFRY, Edmund, m. Ann Maria **SANFORD**, Oct. 16, 1848, by Daniel D. Frost, M. G.	162
Jeremy, of Weston, m. Hannah **PATCHEN**, of Redding, this day [Dec. 15, 1824], by Rev. Lemuel B. Hull	120
Levi, of Ridgefield, m. Mary Ann **BARTRAM**, of Redding, May 21, 1843, by David C. Comstock	152
Sarah, d. Selivent, b. Sept. 17, 1771; m. Burton **OSBURN**, Nov. 14, 1792, by Rev. Mr. Noyes. Witnesses Hezekiah Osborn & David Osborn	93
Silliman, of Wilton, m. Priscilla **ANDREWS**, of Redding, June 22, 1842, by Rev. Daniel Smith	152

Page

GODFREY, GODFRY, (cont.)
Wakeman, of Weston, m. Nancey **PERRY**, of Redding, Dec. 31, 1829,
   by Rev. E. Washburn   129
GOLD, [see also **GOULD**], Aaron, [s. Samuel & Sarah], b. Aug. 19, 1798   88
Burr, [s. Samuel & Sarah], b. Sept. 2, 1793   88
Dan[ie]l, [s. Samuel & Sarah], b.Feb. 20, 1791   88
Grace, [d. Samuel & Sarah], b. Apr. 29, 1779   88
Grace, [d. Samuel & Sarah], d. Jan. 8, 1794   88
Hezekiah, [s. Samuel & Sarah], b. May 30, 1785   88
Samuel, m. Sarah **PLATT**, Apr. 9, 1778   88
Sarah, of Redding, m. David **TURNEY**, of Fairfield, Nov. 4, 1766, by
   Rev. Nath[anie]l Bartlet   19
Sarah, [d. Samuel & Sarah], b. July 29, 1782   88
GOODSELL, Eunice, of Redding, m. Nathan **WELLS**, of Easton, Sept. 19,
   1847, by Rev. J. D. Marshall   161
Lewis, of Weston, m. Edna **LACEY**, of Redding, Feb. 19, 1840, by
   Rev. Charles T. Prentice   147
Polly, of Redding, m. Diodate **AMBLER**, of Danbury, Sept. 14, 1805   102
Sarah, m. Geo[rge] **OSBORN**, b. of Redding, Dec. 12, 1832, by Rev.
   W[illia]m L. Strong   134
GOODYEAR, Eleanor, m. Harry **MEEKER**, b. of Redding, this day [Nov.
   24, 1824], by Jonathan Bartlett, M. G.   119
Theophilus M., m. Louisa Jane **LOCKWOOD**, b. of Redding, Nov. 23,
   1836, by Rev. E. Cole   140
GORHAM, GOREHAM, Alma G., of Redding, m. Charles **FOX**, of Weston,
   [Oct.] 10, [1837], by Rev. Jeremiah Miller   142
Anna, m. Hezekiah **READ**, May 14, 1775, by Nathaniel Bartlett   55
Anna, [d. Isaac, Jr. & Sarah], b. Sept. 1, 1782   60
Anna, wid., d. June 11, 1807, ae 79   101
David, m. Fanny B. **JENNINGS**, Jan. 29, 1823, by Samuel Cochran   116
Eliza, of Redding, m. Lyman **BEERS**, of Aurelius Cayuga Co., N. Y.,
   May 5, 1839, by Rev. Hawley Sanford   145
Hannah, m. Lazarus **WHEELER**, b. of Redding, Jan. 24, 1773, by Rev.
   Nathaniel Bartlet   21
Hannah, [d. Isaac, Jr. & Sarah], b. Aug. 17, 1790   60
Isaac, Jr., m. Sarah **MORGAN**, Mar. 4, 1780, by Rev. Mr. Lewis.
   Witness Joseph Morgan   60
Isaac, d. July 4, 1798   60
Jabez, m. Sarah **MORGAN**, Aug. 5, 1784, by Nathaniel Bartlett   92
Jabez, [s. Jabez & Sarah], b. Dec. 24, 1793   92
Jabez, m. Hannah **BEERS**, May 22, 1797, by Nathaniel Bartlett   92
Joseph Wakeman, [s. Isaac, Jr. & Sarah], b. Mar. 17, 1788   60
Lydia, [d. Jabez & Sarah], b. Nov. 26, 1785   92
Maretta, d. [Jabez & Hannah], b. Jan. 1, 1800   92
Patty, [d. Jabez & Sarah], b. Feb. 14, 1790   92
Polly, [d. Jabez & Sarah], b. Jan. 28, 1787   92
Polly, [d. Isaac, Jr. & Sarah], b. June 4, 1796   60
Sally, [d. Isaac, Jr. & Sarah], b. Sept. 20, 1784   60

84   BARBOUR COLLECTION

                                                                    Page
GORHAM, GOREHAM, (cont.)
Sally, [d. Jabez & Hannah], b. Jan. 15, 1798   92
Sarah, [w. Jabez], d. Mar. 9, 1797   92
Tamar, (colored), d. Sept. 15, 1807, ae 59   101
GOULD, [see also **GOLD**], Aaron, m. Fanny **SHERWOOD**, July 7, 1820, by
  Rev. Laban Clark, Int. Pub.   108
Mary, m. Philo **BEERS**, Feb. 22, 1838, by John Crawford   143
Polley, [d. Samuel & Sarah], b. Jan. 12, 1787   88
Sarah B., m. Hiram I. **BALDWIN**, Mar. 8, 1841, by Rev. P. R. Brown 149
GRAHAM, Emily, of Greenfield, m. Wakeman **BALDWIN**, of Weston, Dec.
  8, 1841, by David S. Duncomb, J. P.   150
GRAY, Alford, [s. Justus & Rachel], b. Sept. 15, 1793   91
Ann, m. Eli **MALLERY**, b. of Redding, Sept. 27, 1820, by Rev. Daniel
  Crocker   108
Anne, b. Aug. 2, 1732; m. Timothy **HULL**, Dec. 14, 1749   34
Anne, [d. Stephen & Annis], b. Mar. 4, 1797   62
Annis, of Redding m. Reuben **ROCKWELL**, of Southeast, N. Y., Nov.
  19, 1839, by Jonathan Bartlett, M. G.   147
Barzilla, of Weston, m. Milla **KEELER**, of Redding, Mar. 8, 1840, by
  Rev. Hawley Sanford   147
Betsy, d. [James, Jr. & Mabel], b. Oct. 9, 1773   42
Betsey, [d. Justus & Rachel], b. Oct. 25, 1795   91
Charles, s. Buel, b. Mar. 5, 1796   44
David O., of Weston, m. Lucinda **ADAMS**, of Redding, Sept. 12,
  [1824], at the house of Israel Adams, by John Reynolds, Elder   119
Edward, [s. Justus & Rachel], b. July 25, 1791   91
Eleanor, m. Frederick **READ**, b. of Redding, this day [Nov. 20, 1839],
  by Jonathan Bartlett, M. G.   147
Eli, [s. Justus & Rachel], b. June 28, 1787   91
Eliza, d. Stephen & Annis, b. Jan. 20, 1809   104
Eliza, m. Eli **DARLING**, b. of Redding, this day [Apr. 18, 1830], by
  Jonathan Bartlett, M. G.   130
Eunice, m. John **DAVIS**, Oct. 21, 1779, by Rev. Nathaniel Bartlett.
  Witnesses Joel Gray & Ruhamah Gray   85
Eunice, [d. Joel & Phebe], b. Feb. 24, 1785   20
Frances J., m. Harry B. **BATES**, b. of Redding, Jan. 4, 1846, by
  Jonathan Bartlett, M. G.   157
Hannah, [d. Justus & Rachel], b. Aug. 23, 1782   91
Hannah, m. Ezekiel **JACKSON**, Apr. 30, 1786, by Rev. Nathaniel
  Bartlet   9
Hezekiah, m. Polly **BEERS**, Sept. 24, 1826, by Marvin Richardson   123
Huldah, m. Zalmon **READ**, Jr., Nov. [   ], 1780   38
James, Jr., m. Assena **TAYLOR**, b. of Redding, Mar. 27, 1760, by Rev.
  Nath[anie]l Bartlet*   *(Crossed out)   7
James, Jr., m. Assena **TAYLOR**, b. of Redding, Mar. 27, 1760, by Rev.
  Nathaniel Bartlet   28
James, Jr., m. wid. Mehetabel **FENNY**, b. of Redding, Feb. 9, 1764,
  by [   ]   28

GRAY, (cont.)
James, Jr., m. Mabel **PHINNY**, Feb. 9, 1764, by Nathaniel Bartlet	42
Jerry, s. [James, Jr. & Mabel], b. Jan. 11, 1766	42
Joel, m. Phebe **SMITH**, Mar. 18, 1784, by Nathaniel Bartlett	20
Joel, [s. John & Esther], b. Feb. 3, 1796	62
Joel, m. Mrs. Martha **CARL**, b. of Redding, Nov. [ ], 1850, by Rev. Daniel D. Frost	166
John, m. Ruama **BARLOW**, b. of Redding, Aug. 7, 1759, by Rev. Nath[anie]l Bartlet	7
John, m. Esther **DAVIS**, Oct. 17, 1790. Witnesses Joel Gray & Stephen Gray	62
John, f. of Joel, d. Oct. 25, 1793	1
Julia, of Redding, m. Thomas E. **BROOKS**, of Clinton, N. Y., Aug. 31, 1825, by W[illia]m C. Kniffin	121
Justus, m. Rachel **WEED**, Jan. 10, 1780	91
Laura, [d. John & Esther], b. Apr. 24, 1794	62
Mabel, [d. James, Jr. & Mabel], b. Nov. 29, 1766	42
Mary Levine, [d. Justus & Rachel], b. Jan. 29, 1781	91
Rachel, [d. Justus & Rachel], b. Apr. 13, 1784	91
Rachel, Jr., [d. Justus & Rachel], d. Apr. 13, 1784	91
Rachel, [d. Justus & Rachel], b. July 18, 1789	91
Rachel, w. [Justus], d. Dec. 4, 1795	91
Sally, [d. Justus & Rachel], b. June 12, 1785	91
Sally, d. [John & Esther], b. Sept. 3, 1791	62
Sally, m. Orrin **BOUGHTON**, Jan. 9, 1809. Witness Charles Smith	59
Sally Ann, m. James **POYLLON**, b. of Redding, Aug. 26, 1823, by Hawley Sanford, Elder	116
Samuel Smith, [s. Joel & Phebe], b. Aug. 1, 1797	20
Sarah, m. John **BYINGTON**, b. of Redding, Nov. 16, 1763, by Rev. Nathaniel Bartlet	23
Stephen, m. Sarah **TERRY**, b. of Redding, Sept. 3, 1758, by Rev. Nath[anie]ll Bartlet	7
Stephen, m. Annis **BOUGHTON**, Nov. 1, 1792, by Timothy Langdon. Witness Samuel Hull	62
Stephen, f. of Stephen, d. Feb. 26, 1796	7
Uriah, [s. Stephen & Annis], b. June 8, 1793	62

GREEN, Almyra, m. Sam[ue]l **BIRCHUM**, b. of Redding, Oct. 8, 1843, by David C. Comstock — 153
Caroline, d. Tunis & Maria (colored), b. Aug. 11, 1819 — 110
George Henry, s. Tunis & Maria (colored), b. May 28, 1817 — 110
Tunis, of Redding, m. Rosanna **BUCSH**, of Newtown, Nov. 28, 1822, by Hawley Sanford, Elder — 114

GREGORY, Alfred, m. Huldah **BARLOW**, b. of Redding, this day [May 13, 1830], by Rev. Lemuel B. Hull — 130
Benjamin, m. Abigail **SANFORD**, Nov. 14, 1797, by Nathaniel Bartlett — 71
Mary C., of Redding, m. Aaron **OSBORN**, of Weston, July 29, 1841, by James A. Batterson, Dea. — 149
Matthew, s. [Matthew], b. Apr. 10, 1791 — 62

86   BARBOUR COLLECTION

                                                                        Page
GREGORY, (cont.)
 Rebeckah, [d. Matthew], b. May 11, 1789   62
 Seymour, formerly of New Milford, m. Lydia **WILSON**, of Ridgefield
  (colored), Mar. 31, 1833, by Rev. Hawley Sanford   135
 Walter, s. [Benjamin & Abigail], b. Feb. 14, 1798   71
GRIFFIN, Ebenezer, s. {Joseph & Esther], b. Aug. 21, 1768; d. [   ] 92
 Ebenezer, 2nd, [s. Joseph & Esther], b. Aug. 24, 1781   92
 Esther, d. [Joseph & Esther], b. Apr. 16, 1767   92
 Esther, d. Joseph, m. John **WYNKOOP**, b. of Redding, Mar. 18, 1790,
  by Nathaniel Bartlett   43
 Eunice, m. Jonathan **COUCH**, b. of Redding, Aug. 15, 1759, by Rev.
  Nath[anie]l Bartlet   3
 Eunice, d. [Joseph & Esther], b. Mar. 25, 1777   92
 Eunice, d. [Joseph & Esther], b. Sept. 4, 1784   92
 Hannah, d. [Joseph & Esther], b. Aug. 4, 1770; d. [   ]   92
 Hannah, [d. Joseph & Esther], b. Apr. 29, 1778   92
 Hepsabeth, m. Joseph **SANFORD**, b. of Redding, Nov. 2, 1762, by
  Rev. Nathaniel Bartlet   39
 Huldah, m. Joel **SANFORD**, May 1, 1788   89
 John, m. wid. Catharine **JOHNSON**, b. of Redding, Dec. 23, 1761, by
  Rev. Nathaniel Bartlet   28
 Joseph, m. Esther **HALL**, [   ], 1766   92
 Joseph, s. [Joseph & Esther], b. Nov. 9, 1774   92
 Joseph, Jr., m. Eunice **HAMILTON**, Jan. 25, 1798   92
 Joseph, m. Esther **HALL**, b. of Redding, Sept. 18, [   ]   28
 Molly, m. Stephen **BURR**, Feb. 19, 1787. Witnesses Isaac Coley &
  Sarah Coley   90
 Sarah, m. Isaac **COLEY**, Sept. 8, 1785. Witnesses Stephen Burr &
  Molley Burr   90
 Sebey, s. [Joseph, Jr. & Eunice], b. Mar. 17, 1799   92
GRUMMON, Elijah, m. Cornelia **HOLMES**, b. of Redding, Mar. 1, 1835, by
 Rev. W[illia]m L. Strong   137
GUYER, GUYRE, GUIER, Charrity, [d. Sam[ue]l & Elisabeth], b.
 Mar. 2, 1787   7
 Charlotte, m. David **FAIRCHILD**, Sept. 6, 1820, by Rev. Daniel
  Crocker   108
 Deborah, of Redding, m. Seymour **TAYLOR**, of Fairfield, Nov. 21,
  1820, by Rev. Daniel Crocker   109
 Esther, [d. Sam[ue]l & Elisabeth], b. Jan. 2, 1784   7
 John, [s. Sam[ue]l & Elisabeth], b. Sept. 7, 1782   7
 John Darling, m. Rebeckah **HILL**, b. of Redding, Nov. 29, 1768, by
  Rev. N. Bartlet   7
 Joseph Benjamin, [s. Samuel & Elisabeth], b. Nov. 7, 1791   7
 Ruth, m. Billey **MOREHOUSE**, Mar. 11, 1778, by Nathaniel Bartlett 66
 Sam[ue]l, m. Elisabeth **BURLOCK**, Mar. 24, 1782   7
 Samuel, hus. of Elisabeth, d. Apr. 24, 1793, in the 33rd y. of his age 7
 Sarah, w. John, d. June 16, 1795   28
HALL, Abigail, of New Jersey, m. Stephen **BURR**, Dea., of Redding, Apr.

	Page
HALL, (cont.)	
12, 1761, by Rev. Nath[anie]ll Bartlet	2
Abigail, m. Samuel **PLATT**, Oct. 17, 1773, by Nathaniel Bartlet	15
Esther, m. Joseph **GRIFFIN**, b. of Redding, Sept. 18, [ ]	28
Esther, m. Joseph **GRIFFIN**, [ ], 1766	92
Hannah, m. Isaac **EDWARDS**, Dec. 22, 1786	60
HAMILTON, HAMBLETON, Benjamin, m. Hannah **BULKLY**, b. of Redding, Apr. 5, 1754, by Rev. Nath[anie]l Bartlet	8
Eunice, m. Joseph **GRIFFIN**, Jr., Jan. 25, 1798	92
Hannah, m. Chauncy **MARCHANT**, May 19, 1773, by Nathaniel Bartlet	13
Hannah, m. Chauncy **MARCHANT**, Nov. 28, 1773	45
HANFORD, Elizabeth, of Darien, m. Daniel S. **SANFORD**, of Redding, this day [Nov. 17, 1822], by Jonathan Bartlett, M. G.	115
[HARRINGTON], [see under **HERRINGTON**]	
HAWLEY, HAWLY, Aaron, [s. Joseph & Chloe], b. Nov. 1, 1794	63
Bille, [s. William & Lydia], b. Feb. 9, 1767	29
Eliza, of Redding, m. Abiel K. **BOTSFORD**, of Huntington, June 22, 1820, by Rev. Daniel Crocker	108
Harriet, m. Leman **PHILLIPS**, Jan. 1, 1838, by John Crawford	143
Hezekiah, [s. William & Lydia], b. Mar. 10, 1772	29
Hezekiah, m. Rebeckah **SANFORD**, Apr. 4, 1796, by Jonathan Bartlett	8
Hezekiah, [twin with Rebecca], s. Hezekiah & Rebecca, b. Aug. 10, 1801	8
James R., m. Lydia **BEACH**, Mar. 28, 1822, by Rev. Ambrose S. Todd	113
James Rogers, [s. Joseph & Chloe], b. Sept. 18, 1797	63
Joel, m. Sarah **HAWLY**, Jan. 13, 1850, by D. D. Frost, M. G.	164
Joseph, [s. William & Lydia], b. June 3, 1762	29
Joseph, m. Chloe **ROGERS**, Aug. 3, 1785	63
Joseph, [s. Joseph & Chloe], b. July 23, 1792	63
Lemuel, [s. Joseph & Chloe], b. Dec. 8, 1785	63
Lydia, [d. William & Lydia], b. Sept. 6, 1759; d. Dec. 5, 1761	29
Lydia, 2nd, [d. William & Lydia], b. Dec. 13, 1760	29
Lydia, m. Aaron **SANFORD**, Nov. 2, 1780, by Nathaniel Bartlett	37
Mariah, [d. Joseph & Chloe], b. Mar. 16, 1788	63
Maria, m. Aaron **READ**, b. of Redding, Oct. 2, 1806	103
Mary, m. Paul **BARTRAM**, b. of Redding, Nov. 9, 1756, by Rev. Nathaniel Bartlett	22
Rebecca, [twin with Hezekiah], d. Hezekiah & Rebecca, b. Aug. 10, 1801	8
Sarah, m. William **READ**, b. of Redding, Dec. 11, 1753, by Rev. Nathaniel Bartlet	17
Sarah, m. Joel **HAWLY**, Jan. 13, 1850, by D. D. Frost, M. G.	164
Sarah Sanford, [d. Hezekiah & Rebeckah], b. Jan. 31, 1797	8
Uriah Rogers, [s. Joseph & Chloe], b. June 14, 1790	63
William, s. Joseph, of Redding, m. Lydia **NASH**, d. Thom[a]s, of Greensfarms, July 12, 1758. Witnesses Joseph Hawley & Thomas Nash	29

HAWLEY, HAWLY, (cont.)
William, [s. William & Lydia], b. [   ] 1, [   ]; d. [   ],
   3, 1766 — 29
William, d. Feb. 16, 1797, in the 59th y. of his age. Hezekiah Hawlet,
   Admr. — 29
William, [s. Hezekiah & Rebeckah], b. Jan. 9, 1799 — 8
HAY, [see under **HAYES**]
HAYES, HAY, Benedict, of California, m. Mrs. Betsey Ann **BOOTH,** of
   Redding, Apr. 17, 1851, by Rev. J. L. Gilder — 167
Charles H., of Newtown, m. Mary Ann **BANKS,** of Redding, Aug. 11,
   1822, by Hawley Sanford, Elder — 114
HENDRICK, HENDRIX, Abby J., of Bridgeport, m. William R. **BUTLER,**
   of Wilton, Jan. 5, 1845, by James A. Batterson, Dea. — 154
Mary, m. John **LINES,** Mar. 17, 1779, by Nathaniel Bartlett — 32
Phebe, m. Nathan **CROFOOT,** Aug. 2, 1796, by Enos Wheeler — 47
HERON, Sally, m. Lemuel **SANFORD,** Jr., b. of Redding, Jan. 1, 1795, by
   Nathaniel Bartlett — 53
HERRINGTON, Jerusha, m. Zalmon **MAIN,** Sept. 13, 1837, by John
   Crawford — 142
HICKERSON, Ellen J., m. Nathan B. **KEELER,** b. of Redding, Apr. 6, 1850,
   by Rev. Jacob Shaw — 165
HILL, Aaron S., m. Phebe **HUNT,** b. of Redding, Oct. 9, 1822, by Rev.
   Sam[ue]l Cochran — 114
Aaron Sanford, s. Jno R. & Betsey, b. Mar. 23, 1800 — 107
Abby Jane, m. Aaron **MALLET,** Oct. 4, 1837, by John Crawford — 143
Abby M., m. Lemuel **SANFORD,** b. of Redding, Jan. 13, 1847, by
   Daniel D. Frost, M. G. — 159
Abel, m. Anna **LYON,** May 11, 1773. Witnesses James Jonson &
   Abel Adams — 95
Amos, of Redding, m. Eleanor **JACKLIN,** of Greenfield, (colored), Oct.
   6, 1839, by Rev. Hawley Sanford — 146
Andrew L., m. Hannah **LYON,** Apr. 23, 1775, by Rev. John Beach.
   Witnesses Sim[o]n Munger & Lois Munger — 55
Andrew Lane, s. [Capt. Dan[ie]l], b. Dec. 14, 1755 — 35
Anne, m. Daniel **REED,** Dec. 7, 1773, by Nathaniel Bartlet — 41
Barlow, s. [Ebenezer], b. [   ], 23, 1793 — 10
Beach, [s. Abel & Anna], b. Apr. 2, 1777 — 95
Betsey, d. Jno R. & Betsey, b. Mar. 6, 1806 — 107
Betsey, w. John R., d. July 29, 1818 — 106
Betty, m. Eli **LYON,** Apr. 26, 1795. Witness Abel Hill — 13
Bradley, m. Betsey **BANKS,** b. of Redding, Nov. 5, 1822, by Rev.
   Daniel Crocker — 115
Charles, of Redding, m. Harriet **BELDEN,** of New York City, Oct. 21,
   1845, by Rev. W[illia]m F. Collins — 157
Clarry, d. [Andrew L. & Hannah], b. Aug. 24, 1788 — 55
Daniel, s. [Capt. Dan[ie]l], b. Apr. 12, 1761 — 35
Daniel, s. [Andrew L. & Hannah], b. Sept. 1, 1793 — 55
Ebenezer, s. [Ebenezer], b. Oct. 11, 1797 — 10

	Page
HILL, (cont.)	
Eliza, of Redding, m. Samuel **JACKSON**, of Weston, Nov. 23, 1828, by Rev. Lemuel B. Hull	128
Elisabeth, m. Thomas **STARR**, Dec. 15, 1789, by Rev Mr. Hull. Witnesses Ezekiel Hill & Rebekah Guyer	93
Fanny, d. [Andrew L. & Hannah], b. Sept. 18, 1795	55
Gershom, s. [Ebenezer], b. Mar. 10, 1796	10
Hannah, d. [Capt. Dan[ie]l], b. Feb. 27, 1753; d. Sept. 27, 1755	35
Hannah, 2nd, [d. Capt. Dan[ie]l], b. Sept. 25, 1758	35
Hannah, m. Asahel **LYON**, 6th mo. 2nd da., 1775. Witness Daniel Hill	65
Hannah, d. [Andrew L. & Hannah], b. Jan. 7, 1776	55
Hannah, m. Isaac **BEACH**, Sept. 26, 1797, by Nathaniel Bartlet	79
Henry, of Redding, m. Mary **FREEMAN**, of New Milford (colored), Oct. 3, 1846, by Rev. Hawley Sanford	158
Huldah, of Redding, m. Samuel **BRISCO**, of Brooklyn, N. Y., (colored), Oct. 23, 1828, by Rev. Hawley Sanford	128
John L., m. Hester **SANFORD**, May 26, 1837, by Rev. Edward J. Darken	141
John L., m. Harriet **DUNCOMB**, b. of Redding, May 4, 1840, by Rev. P. R. Brown	148
John Lee, s. Jno R. & Betsey, b. June 15, 1810	107
John R., b. Apr. 26, 1775; m. Betsey [ ], Mar. 23, 1799	107
John R. m. Deborah **READ**, Sept. 1, 1819	109
Joseph, s. John R. & Betsey, b. Aug. 21, 1817	109
Lucy, [d. Abel & Anna], b. Mar. 4, 1783; d. Mar. 9, 1794	95
Lydia, d. John R. & Betsey, b. Mar. 26, 1815	109
Mabel, [d. Ebenezer], b. Dec. 17, 1791	10
Mabel, m. Daniel **MALLETT**, b. of Redding, Nov. 8, 1829, by Rev. Ebenezer Washburn	129
Mary, of Redding, m. Zalmon **LYON**, of Weston, Feb. 4, 1835, by Rev. Nathan Wildman	137
Morris, s. Jno R. & Betsey, b. Oct. 6, 1812	107
Moses, s. John R. & Betsey, b. Feb. 5, 1802	107
Moses, m. Julia **FANTON**, Mar. 28, 1826, by M. Richardson	122
Polly, of Redding, m. Aaron **SEARS**, of Monroe, Mar. 16, 1831, by Rev. Lemuel B. Hull	133
Rebeckah, m. John Darling **GUYER**, b. of Redding, Nov. 29, 1768, by Rev. N. Bartlet	7
Sarah, d. [Capt. Dan[ie]l], b. Mar. 24, 1764; d. June 19, 1764	35
Sarah, m. Timothy **PLATT**, Feb. 8, 1793. Witness Joannah Adams	61
William Hawley, s. Jno R. & Betsey, b. Mar. 29, 1804	107
HILLARD, Anna, [d. Thurston & Eunice], b. July 31, 1793	97
Betsey, d. Isaac & Sarah, b. Sept. 11, 1780	4
Charles, [s. Thurston & Eunice], b. July 24, 1791	97
Henry, [s. Thurston & Eunice], b. Sept. 28, 1795	97
Thurston, m. Eunice **JACKSON**, June 1, 1790. Witness Ephraim Jackson	97
Zoa, m. John **READ**, Jr., June 15, 1783, certified by Daniel C. Bartlett	71

90   BARBOUR COLLECTION

	Page
HINES, Frances F., m. Alfred **LOUDEN**, Nov. 5, 1829, by G. Pierce, Elder	129
HODGES, HODGE, Leander, of Redding, m. Sarah Ann **BERT**, of Ridgefield, Jan. 3, 1839, by W[illia]m Bowen	144
Mary A., m. Bela St. **JOHN**, b. of Redding, Dec. 29, 1850, by James A. Batterson, Dea.	165
Minerva, of Redding, m. Roswell **TAYLOR**, of Wilton, Aug. 16, [1835], by James A. Batterson	138
Sarah Ann, of Redding, m. Amos S. **SCHOONMAKER**, of Danbury, Aug. 3, 1845, by James A. Batterson, Dea.	156
HOLLY, Closson, of Danbury, m. Sarah **JUDD**, of Redding, this day [Jan. 1, 1824], by Nathan Seelye, J. P.	118
HOLMES, Cornelia, m. Elijah **GRUMMON**, b. of Redding, Mar. 1, 1835, by Rev. W[illia]m L. Strong	137
HOPKINS, Henry, stranger, m. Hannah **BURR**, July 26, 1769	29
HOWES, HOWS, Sarah, b. July 19, 1744; m. Dan[ie]l **COUCH**, Jan. 23, 17[ ]	50
Sarah, of Stanford, m. Daniel **COUCH**, of Redding, Jan. 23, 1763. Witnesses Ebenezer Couch & Preserved Taylor	24
HOYT, Amos, of Danbury, m. Ann **TURKINGTON**, of Redding, Apr. 10, [1833], by Rev. Jesse Hunt	136
Charles, [s. Isaac W. & Hannah], b. Oct. 2, 1797	65
Isaac W., m. Hannah **BANKS**, Oct. 8, 1796, certified by Jerimah Biggsby	65
Lucy, * b. Mar. 23, 1781; m. Daniel **STOWE**, [ ] *(First written "Lucy Banks" and erased)	76
Molley, m. William **MEAD**, Nov. 17, 1788	67
Ruth, m. John **SANFORD**, Dec. 30, 1797, by Nath[anie]l Bartlett	27
Thomas, of Danbury, m. Mehitable **BANKS**, of Redding, Sept. 1, 1822, by Rev. Samuel Cochran	114
HUBBELL, HUBBEL, Abraham, of Redding, m. Hannah **LINDLEY**, of Danbury, Oct. 11, 1835, by Rev. H. Humphreys	139
Caroline, of Redding, m. Daniel S. **BEATTYS**, of Danbury, Mar. 19, 1826, by W[illia]m C. Kniffin, M. G.	122
Jeremiah, of Weston, m. Sylvia **CROWFUT**, of Redding, Dec. 29, 1826, by John M. Heron, J. P., Int. Pub.	124
Moses, Jr., m. Betsey **PERRY**, b. of Redding, Jan. 13, 1828, by Henry Stead	127
Sarah, m. Cyrus **SANFORD**, of Redding, Oct. 7, 1826, by W[illia]m C. Kniffin, M. G.	123
HULL, Aaron, [s. John, Jr. & Sarah], b. Oct. 19, 1782	16
Aaron B., of Redding, m. Anna Maria **DARLING**, of Easton, June 23, 1850, by James A. Batterson, Dea.	167
Abigail, [d. Seth & Elisabeth], b. Jan. 28, 1762	46
Abigail, m. Hezekiah **READ**, Feb. 22, 1789, by Nathaniel Bartlett	55
Abigail, m. Timothy **PERRY**, Apr. 26, 1796, by Nathaniel Bartlett	87
Abraham, s. [Timothy & Anne], b. Mar. 30, 1761	34
Abraham, m. Eliza **CHAPMAN**, Nov. 24, 1838, by Rev. John Crawford	144
Amelia,* d. Lazarus & Anna, b. Jan. 10, 1797 *(The words	

HULL, (cont.)

	Page
"daughter to Lazarus" erased)	42
Anna, m. Henry **DUNCOMB**, [ ], by Rev. Jesse Hunt	135
Anna, m. Lemuel **BURR**, on or about Dec. 7, 1793, by Nathaniel Bartlett	52
Anne, d. [Timothy & Anne], b. Dec. 7, 1771	34
Betsey S., [twin with Sally B.], b. Dec. 12, 1792. [Probably children of Sally **HULL** who married Eli **SHERWOOD**, in 1796]	87
Clarissa, m. James L. **BURR**, Oct. 18, 1837, by John Crawford	143
Daniel, s. [David & Chloe], b. Apr. 19, 1795	26
David, s. [Timothy & Anne], b. Mar. 22, 1763	34
David, m. Chloe **LEE**, on or about Sept. [ ], 1788, by Nathaniell Bartlett	26
Denney, m. Mary **PLATT**, Apr. 2, 1786, by Rev. Mr. James Johnson. Witness Eunice Brush	81
Denney, [s. Denney & Mary], b. May 15, 1789	81
Eleanor, d. [John & Molle], b. Dec. 3, 1763	48
Eliphelet, [s. Seth & Elisabeth], b. Dec. 18, 1765	46
Eliza, d. Samuel & Anna, b. Mar. 3, 1804	102
Elizabeth, of Fairfield, m. Stephen **JACKSON**, of Redding, May 17, 1775, by Andrew Eliot, V. D. M.	86
Elisabeth, d. Feb. 22, 1795; Execur. Lazarus Hull	42
Esther, m. Daniel **SANFORD**, b. of Redding, Apr. 18, 1758, by Rev. Nathaniel Bartlet	18
Esther, of Redding, m. Gould **NICHOLS**, of Weston, Sept. 8, 1827, by Levi Brunson	126
Eunice, d. [Timothy & Anne], b. Aug. 26, 1757	34
Eunice, [d. Ezra & Elisabeth], b. July 6, 1785	63
Ezekiel, [s. John, Jr. & Sarah], b. Apr. 4, 1787	16
Ezra, [s. Timothy & Anne], b. Apr. 5, 1756	34
Ezra, m. Elisabeth **COLEY**, on or about Dec. 23, 1784, by Nathaniel Bartlett	63
Hanford, of Newtown, m. Lois **ROWLAND**, of Redding, Nov. 24, 1831, by Rev. Lemuel B. Hull	134
Hannah, [d. Timothy & Anne], b. July 27, 1751	34
Harriet, m. Benedict **CROFUT**, b. of Redding, Mar. 30, 1831, by Rev. W[illia]m L. Strong	132
Harry, m. Harriet **DIMON**, b. of Redding, Dec. 31, 1829, by Rev. E. Washburn	129
Henry, [s. Zalmon & Eunice], b. Dec. 25, 1794	63
Hezekiah, s. [Timothy & Anne], b. Oct. 22, 1769	34
Hezekiah, [s. Seth & Elisabeth], b. Mar. 24, 1772	46
Hezekiah, [s. Zalmon & Eunice], b. Nov. 20, 1788	63
Hezekiah, [s. John, Jr. & Sarah], b. July 6, 1796	16
Isaac Platt, [s. Denney & Mary], b. Oct. 5, 1797	81
James, d. Feb. 20, 1805	101
John, s. [Timothy & Anne], b. June 26, 1759	34
John, m. Mary **ANDREWS**, b. of Redding, Feb. 3, 1763,	

92   BARBOUR COLLECTION

Page
HULL, (cont.)
by Rev. Nathaniel Bartlet 29
John, m. Molle **ANDREWS**, Feb. 3, 1763, by Nathaniel Bartlett 48
John, Jr., m. Sarah **FAIRCHILD**, Feb. 22, 1782, by Nathaniel Bartlett 16
Jonathan, [s. Seth & Elisabeth], b. Oct. 25, 1763 46
Laure, [d. Ezra & Elisabeth], b. Aug. 4, 1788 63
Lazaurs, [s. Seth & Elisabeth], b. Jan. 16, 1770 46
Lazarus, m. Anna **READ**, Nov. 2, 1794. Witnesses Sturges Sanford &
  Sarah Sanford 42
Lucinda, of Redding, m. Dimon **FINCH**, of Norwalk, Oct. 24, 1830, by
  W[illia]m L. Strong 131
Lydia, [d. Zalmon & Eunice], b. Dec. 28, 1790 63
Lydia, m. William **SANFORD**, Jan. 8, 1792, by Nathaniel Bartlett 80
Martha, m. Ephraim **JACKSON**, Jr., b. of Redding, June 26, 1766, by
  Rev. Nathaniel Bartlet 9
Martha, [d. Seth & Elisabeth], b. Apr. 28, 1774 46
Mary Chapman, [d. Denney & Mary], b. Dec. 9, 1786 81
Molle, [d. John & Molle], b. Feb. 3, 1765 48
Nehemiah, m. Grezel **PERRY**, b. of Redding, Feb. 5, 1767, by Rev.
  Nath[anie]l Bartlet 8
Polly, [d. John, Jr. & Sarah], b. Apr. 2, 1785 16
Polly, of Weston, m. Aaron **BENNETT**, of Redding, Dec. 24, 1833, by
  Rev. W[illia]m L. Strong 137
Sally, m. John A. **CROCKER**, Apr. 8, 1810. Witness Anna Crocker 99
Sally B., [twin with Betsey S.], b. Dec. 12, 1792. [Probably children of
  Sarah **HULL**, who married Eli **SHERWOOD** in 1796] 87
Samuel, s. [Timothy & Anne], b. June 22, 1766 34
Samuel, m. Anna **WAKEMAN**, Jan. 22, 1797, by Nath[anie]l Bartlett 26
Sarah, [d. Timothy & Anne], b. Feb. 5, 1754 34
Sarah, [d. Zalmon & Eunice], b. June 20, 1784 63
Sarah, m. Eli **SHERWOOD**, Oct. 25, 1796, by Jonathan Bartlett 87
Seth, d. Apr. 5, 1795. Execur. Lazarus Hull 42
Theophilus, m. wid. Martha **BETTS**, b. of Redding, Jan. 25, 1759, by
  Rev. Nath[anie]l Bartlet 8
Theophilus, [s. Zalmon & Eunice], b. Nov. 5, 1785 63
Timothy, b. Sept. 4, 1726; m. Anne **GRAY**, Dec. 14, 1749 34
Walter, [s. Seth & Elisabeth], b. Nov. 21, 1767 46
Zalmon, m. Eunice **BELDEN**, Mar. 4, 1784, by Rev. Isaac Lewis.
  Witnesses Polly Smith & S. Sam[uel] Smith 63
HUNT, Phebe, m. Aaron S. **HILL**, b. of Redding, Oct. 9, 1822, by Rev.
  Sam[ue]l Cochran 114
HURD, Roswell W., of Newtown, m. Rebecca J. **TURNEY**, of Redding, this
  day [Jan. 24, 1836], by Rev. J. Lyman Clark 164
William Curtis, m. Mary Ann **TURNEY**, May 25, 1837, by Rev.
  Edward J. Darken 141
HUTCHINSON, Catharine A., m. Levi **PATCHEN**, b. of Redding, Aug. 31,
  1845, by Rev. Hawley Sanford 156
HYATT, Aaron Sanford, of Ridgefield, m. Lydia **SANFORD**, of Redding,

REDDING VITAL RECORDS 93

	Page
HYATT, (cont.)	
Apr. 20, 1831, by Rev. E. Washburn	132
ICLLIFF,* Sherman, of Ridgefield, m. Sally M. **SHERWOOD**, of Redding, Jan. 30, 1842, by James A. Batterson, Dea. *(Probably "**JELLEFF**")	150
JACKLIN, Eleanor, of Greenfield, m. Amos **HILL**, of Redding, (colored), Oct. 6, 1839, by Rev. Hawley Sanford	146
JACKSON, Abigail, [d. David & Esther], b. June 22, 1780	91
Aaron, [s. David & Esther], b. Mar.* 31, 1783 *(First written "August")	91
Anna, [d. David & Hannah], b. Aug. 28, 1770; d. May 29, 1771	9
Anna, [d. David & Hannah], b. May 6, 1772	9
Anna, d. [Ezekiel & Hannah], b. Dec. 21, 1786	9
Anna, d. Ezekiel, d. Apr. 21, 1802	101
Clarissa, [d. Ezekiel & Hannah], b. Dec. 25, 1792	9
David, m. Hannah **SANFORD**, b. of Redding, Nov. 18, 1762, by Rev. Nathaniel Bartlet	9
David, [s. David & Hannah], b. Dec. 29, 1765	9
David, m. Esther **WARD**, Jan. 23, 1774, by Nathaniel Bartlett	91
Edward, m. Lydia Ann **SANFORD**, Aug. 14, 1826, by Marvin Richardson	122
Ephraim, Jr., m. Martha **HULL**, b. of Redding, June 26, 1766, by Rev. Nathaniel Bartlet	9
Ephraim, [s. David & Esther], b. Jan. 12, 1781	91
Esther, [d. Stephen & Elizabeth], b. Apr. 1, 1776	86
Esther, [d. David & Esther], b. Jan. 20, 1777	91
Eunice, [d. David & Hannah], b. Jan. 26, 1768	9
Eunice, m. Thurston **HILLARD**, June 1, 1790. Witness Ephraim Jackson	97
Ezekiel, s. [David & Hannah], b. Sept. 20, 1763	9
Ezekiel, m. Hannah **GRAY**, Apr. 30, 1786, by Rev. Nathaniel Bartlet	9
Ezekiel, m. Eunice **BARTLETT**, b. of Redding, Dec. 24, 1806	103
Hannah, w. Ezekiel, d. June 8, 1805	101
Hariot, d. [Ezekiel & Hannah], b. Dec. 18, 1795	9
Henry, [s. David & Esther], b. Aug. 12, 1785; d. Mar. 13, 1786	91
Henry, [s. David & Esther], b. Oct. 8, 1797	91
Hiram, s. [Ezekiel & Hannah], b. Apr. 22, 1788	9
Laura, d. [Ezekiel & Hannah], b. Feb. 28, 1794	9
Laura, m. Samuel **READ**, b. of Redding, Nov. 25, 1821, by Rev. Daniel Crocker	111
Martha, [d. Stephen & Elizabeth], b. Oct. 29, 1778	86
Moses, [s. David & Esther], b. Oct. 16, 1774; d. Oct. 28, 1775	91
Moses, 2nd, [d. David & Esther], b. Jan. 15, 1779	91
Sam[ue]l, s. [Ezekiel & Hannah], b. Dec. 29, 1789	9
Samuel, of Weston, m. Eliza **HILL**, of Redding, Nov. 23, 1828, by Rev. Lemuel B. Hull	128
Sarah, [d. David & Esther], b. Apr. 20, 1788	91
Stephen, of Redding, m. Elizabeth **HULL**, of Fairfield, May 17, 1775,	

94 BARBOUR COLLECTION

	Page
JACKSON, (cont.)	
by Andrew Eliot, V. D. M.	86
Stephen, [s. David & Esther], b. Jan. 30, 1793	91
JARVIS, Abigail, [twin with Samuel, d. Samuel], b. July 28, 1782	64
Amelia, [d. Samuel], b. Mar. 2, 1796	64
Benj[ami]n Sturges, [s. Samuel], b. Apr. 18, 1784	64
Eli Starr, [s. Samuel], b. Jan. 23, 1786	64
Henry, [s. Samuel], b. Nov. 26, 1788	64
Nathan, Jr., of Norwalk, m. Betsey SANFORD, of Redding, Nov. 16, 1802, by Rev. Jonathan Bartlett, certified by David Sanford	99
Sam[ue]l, m. [ ], Dec. 7, 1780	64
Samuel, [twin with Abigail, s. Samuel], b. July 28, 1782	64
Sarah, [d. Samuel], b. Aug. 24, 1791	64
Will[ia]m Augustus, [s. Samuel], b. Dec. 19, 1793	64
JELLEFF, Hiram, of Redding, m. Fanny MEEKER, of Redding, July 20, 1845, by Rev. W. F. Collins	156
Sherman,* of Ridgefield, m. Sally M. SHERWOOD, of Redding, Jan. 30, 1842, by James A. Batterson, Dea. *(Written "Sherman ICLLIFF")	150
JENKINS, Nancy, of Danbury, m.George BASSETT, of Redding, Mar. 17, 1851, by Rev. Daniel D. Frost	166
Sarah Ann, of Redding, m. Charles WILSON, of Ridgefield, Dec. 26, 1826, by W[illia]m C. Kniffin, M. G.	124
JENNINGS, GENNINGS, Angeline, m. George SHUTE, b. of Redding, Sept. 5, 1830, by Rev. Oliver E. Amermon	131
Charity, of Fairfield, m. John CLUCKSTON, of Redding, Nov. 20, 1764, by Rev. Nath[anie]ll Bartlet	3
Fanny B., m. David GORHAM, Jan. 29, 1823, by Samuel Cochran	116
Joseph, m. Abigail Jane DENISON, Nov. 26, 1851, by Orsamus H. Smith	167
Morris, of Ridgefield, m. Angeline S. WHITEHEAD, of Redding, Apr. 9, 1845, by D. C. Comstock	155
Sally, of Wilton, m. Beach WHITEHEAD, of Redding, May 31, [1824], by Rev. Daniel Crocker	118
JOHNSON, Catharine, wid., m. John GRIFFIN, b. of Redding, Dec. 23, 1761, by Rev. Nathaniel Bartlet	28
Eliza Ann, m. Seth SQUIRES, Sept. 9, 1839, by Rev. P. R. Brown	146
JONES, Abigail, m. W[illia]m NICHOLS, b. of Redding, Sept. 26, 1830, by W[illia]m L. Strong	131
Mary Ann, m. Charles ROCKWELL, Nov. 9, 1842, by David C. Comstock	152
JOYCE, JOICE, Hannah B., [d. Joseph & Mary], b. Apr. 27, 1796	96
Joseph, m. Mary BULKLEY, Feb. 16, 1794, by Rev. Timothy Langdon. Witnesses Phebe Bulkley & Sarah Bulkley	96
Joseph A., [s. Joseph & Mary], b. Apr. 18, 1798	96
Polly G., [d. Joseph & Mary], b. Oct. 6, 1794	96
JUDD, Ebenezer Silliman, of Danbury, m. Harriet STOW, of Redding, Jan. 3, 1826, by Marvin Richardson	122

	Page
JUDD, (cont.)	
Hannah, d. [Elijah], b. Jan. 15, 1785	64
Rebeckah, [twin with Sarah, d. Elijah], b. Nov. 29, 1788	64
Samuel, [s. Elijah], b. Sept. 21, 1783	64
Sarah, [twin with Rebeckah, d. Elijah], b. Nov. 29, 1788	64
Sarah, of Redding, m. Closson **HOLLY**, of Danbury, this day, [Jan. 1, 1824], by Nathan Seelye, J. P.	118
KAY, Daniel, of New Haven, m. Paulina **MONROE**, [Dec.] 25, [1831], by Abram Stow, J. P., Int. Pub.	133
KEEKER, [see also **KEELER**], Barnabard*, m. Sarah **CLUGSTONE**, on or about Jan. 1, 1793, by Nathaniel Bartlett *(Written "Barnabard **KEEKER**")	19
Barnabard*, m. Esther **SHERWOOD**, Apr. [ ], 1797, by Nathaniel Bartlet *(Written "Barnabard **KEEKER**")	19
KEELER, Abigail, m. Peter **SANFORD**, Jan. 1, [1786*], by Rev. Mr. Camp. Witnesses Timothy Keeler, Jr. & Esther Keeler (*correction (1786) handwritten in space with "6" underlined)	37
Barnabard, see Barnabard **KEEKER**	19
Catherine, of Redding, m. Rufus S. **PICKET**, of Ridgefield, Oct. 16, 1849, by D. D. Frost, M. G.	164
David, m. Almira **BEERS**, b. of Redding, this day [Feb. 3, 1828], by Rev. Lemuel B. Hull	127
Delia, m. Moses **BURR**, Nov. 22, 1832, by Levi Brunson	134
Henry D., of Wilton, m. Sally Maria **BANKS**, of Walton, this day, [Oct. 9, 1836], by Jonathan Bartlett, M. G.	140
Milla, of Redding, m. Barzilla **GRAY**, of Weston, Mar. 8, 1840, by Rev. Hawley Sanford	147
Monson, of Redding, m. Mabel **CROFUT**, of Danbury, this day, [Mar. 20, 1825], by Rev. Lemuel B. Hull	120
Nathan B., m. Ellen J. **HICKERSON**, b. of Redding, Apr. 6, 1850, by Rev. Jacob Shaw	165
Sarah, of Redding, m. James **WORDEN**, of New York, June 18, 1837, by Rev. Hawley Sanford	141
William K., of Ridgefield, m. Esther **MEAD**, of Redding, Oct. 25, 1835, by Rev. H. Humphreys	139
KETCHUM, Sally, m. Hawley **SANFORD**, Nov. 20, 1823, by Rev. Aaron Hunt	117
KING, Deborah, m. Jabez **FROST**, Dec. 3, 1746	27
KNAPP, KNAP, Andrew, m. Rebeckah **MANROW**, b. of Redding, Apr. 7, 1769, by Rev. Nathaniel Bartlet	31
Anna, [d. Jonathan & Mary], b. Apr. 22, 1798	30
Aquila, [s. Jonathan & Mary], b. Dec. 5, 1785	30
David, [s. David, Jr.], b. Nov. 3, 1796	19
David, d. Oct. 18, 1797. Eben[eze]r Mallery Admr.	19
Hiram, m. Amelia **DREW**, b. of Redding, Sept. 23, 1827, by John M. Heron, J. P., Int. Pub.	126
Jonathan, of Redding, m. Mary **ALVORD**, of Greenfield, Sept. 7, 1772. Witnesses John Alvord & Abigail Alvord	30

	Page
KNAPP, KNAP, (cont.)	
Jonathan, b. Dec. 29, 1777	103
Jonathan, m. Lucy **BURR**, b. of Redding, Apr. 10, 1800	103
Lucy H., m. Francis A. **SANFORD**, b. of Redding, Sept. 16, 1845, by Rev. W. F. Collins	156
Lydia Ann, [d. David, Jr.], b. Oct. 5, 1793	19
Mary, [d. Jonathan & Mary], b. Apr. 15, 1774	30
Mauris, [s. David, Jr.], b. July 2, 1791	19
Moses, [s. Jonathan & Mary], b. Jan. 8, 1790	30
Moses Hawley, s. Jonathan & Lucey, b. Apr. 2, 1801	103
Polly, [d. David], b. Feb. 11, 1789	19
Priscilla, [d. Jonathan & Mary], b. Apr. 25, 1788	30
Rachel, [d. Jonathan & Mary], b. Sept. 6, 1792	30
LACEY, Edna, of Redding, m. Lewis **GOODSELL**, of Weston, Feb. 19, 1840, by Rev. Charles T. Prentice	147
LANE, Sarah, m. Dan **FAIRCHILD**, b. of Redding, Dec. 25, 1770, by Rev. Nath[anie]l Bartlet	7
LEACH, Daniel, of Fishkill, N. Y., m. Esther **WHEELER**, of Redding, Apr. 20, 1830, by Aaron Sanford, Jr., J. P.	130
Hannah, m. Peter **WHEELER**, Nov. 25, 1796, certified by Ebenezer Crofut	74
LEE, Abig[ai]l, d. [John], b. Sept. 26, 1783	10
Ann, m. Stephen **MEEKER**, b. of Redding, Mar. 25, 1768, by Rev. Nathaniel Bartlet	39
Chloe, [d. Silas & Whitley], b. Aug. 26, 1770	32
Chloe, m. David **HULL**, on or about Sept. [ ], 1788, by Nathaniel Bartlett	26
Dan[ie]l, [s. John], b. Jan. 23, 1775	10
Edmund B., m. Electa M. **SHERWOOD**, b. of Redding, Apr. 11, 1848, by Rev. J. D. Marshall	161
Eleanor, m. Samuel S. **OSBORN**, b. of Redding, this day [Nov. 18, 1835], by Jonathan Bartlett, M. G.	139
Eli, [s. Enos & Ruth], b. May 28, 1779	11
Enos, m. Ruth **BATES**, Apr. 22 or 23, 1778, by Nathaniel Bartlett	11
Enos, f. of Jno., d. Apr. 25, 1796	10
Eunice, [d. Silas & Whitley], b. Dec. 13, 1778; d. Nov. 16, 1780	32
Eunice, [d. Silas & Whitley], b. Feb. 24, 1781	32
Eunice, m. David **STARR**, 3rd, b. of Redding, Nov. 24, 1802	100
Hiram, [s. Enos & Ruth], b. Apr. 9, 1789	11
John, [s. Daniel], b. Jan. 19, 1799	70
John H., m. Mary **BOUGHTON**, b. of Redding, [Dec.] 27, [1837], by Rev. Jeremiah Miller	142
Mariah, [d. Enos & Ruth], b. July 24, 1798	11
Mary B., of Ridgefield, m. Eli **STARR**, of Redding, Mar. 8, 1800	100
Milo, of Milford, N. Y., m. Lucy Ann **BARTRAM**, of Redding, Apr. 8, 1830, by Rev. E. Washburn	130
Nathan, [s. Enos & Ruth], b. May 17, 1781	11
Noah, [s. Silas & Whitley], b. Dec. 25, 1775	32

REDDING VITAL RECORDS

LEE, (cont.)
Noah, m. Eleanor **OSBURN**, May 3, 1798, by Rev. Mr. Noyes.
  Witnesses John Byington & Asahel Salmon — 16
Noah M., m. Sarah **BANKS**, b. of Redding, Jan. 28, 1835, by Rev.
  W[illia]m L. Strong — 137
Salina, [d. Enos & Ruth], b. Nov. 17, 1791 — 11
Saloma, [d. John], b. Dec. 25, 1777 — 10
Sally, [d. Daniel], b. Mar. 20, 1797 — 70
Sally Ann, of Redding, m. Daniel **BENEDICT**, of Vermont, June 6,
  1828, by W[illia]m C. Kniffin, M. G. — 127
Sally Ann, m. Burr **BENNETT**, b. of Redding, [May] 1, [1838], by
  Rev. Jeremiah Miller — 143
Silas, m. Whitley **MEEKER**, b. of Redding, Aug. 23, 1769, by Rev.
  Nath[anie]l Bartlet — 32
Thurston, [s. Silas & Whitley], b. May 30, 1788 — 32
William, of Ridgefield, m. Abigail **FAIRCHILD**, of Redding, May 2,
  1822, by Rev. Ambrose S. Todd — 115
LEWIS, Charles, of Redding, m. Nancy **REED**, of Wilton, Mar. 28, [1833],
  by James A. Batterson — 135
LINDLEY, Hannah, of Danbury, m. Abraham **HUBBELL**, of Redding, Oct.
  11, 1835, by Rev. H. Humphreys — 139
Noah H., m. Laura **WINTON**, b. of Redding, Nov. 14, 1830, by
  W[illia]m L. Strong — 131
LINES, LYNES, John, m. Mary **HENDRICK**, Mar. 17, 1779, by Nathaniel
  Bartlett — 32
Rebeckah, d. Sam[ue]l & Mary], b. Apr. 11, 1750 — 25
Rebeckah, m. Levi **DEKEMAN**, Feb. 9, 1774, by Rev.Nathaniel Bartlet.
  Witnesses John Couch & Sarah Couch — 25
LOBDELL, LOBDEL, Elisabeth, m. Seth **BURR**, Jan. 23, 1788, by John
  Benedict. Witness Abel Burr — 57
Lewis, m. Sally **FOOT**, Apr. 4, 1827, by M. Richardson — 124
LOCKWOOD, Angeline, m. David **SHERWOOD**, b. of Redding, Dec. 2,
  1850, by Rev. J. L. Gilder — 166
Cha[rle]s W., of Monroe, m. Lucy **BARTRAM**, of Redding, Apr. 23,
  1850, by Rev. Jacob Shaw — 165
Eunice H., m. W[illia]m T. **COUCH**, Apr. 29, 1840, by David C.
  Comstock — 148
Hiram, of Norwalk, m. Eveline F. **DIBBLE**, of Bethel, Apr. 6, 1851, by
  Rev. J. L. Gilder — 167
Louisa Jane, m. Theophilus M. **GOODYEAR**, b. of Redding, Nov. 23,
  1836, by Rev. E. Cole — 140
Mary, of Fairfield(?), m. Peter **FAIRCHILD**, of Redding, Mar. 27,
  1768, by Rev. Nath[anie]l Bartlet — 6
Munson, m. Frances Mary **PLATT**, b. of Redding, Jan. 25, 1846, by
  Rev. W[illia]m F. Collins — 157
Samuel S., m. Huldah **BATES**, b. of Redding, Mar. 20, 1831, by Rev.
  Oliver E. Amerman — 132
Sarah, of Redding, m. Israel H. **WILSON**, of Bethel, Oct. 16, 1836, by

98 BARBOUR COLLECTION

	Page
LOCKWOOD, (cont.)	
Rev. E. Cole	140
LORD, James, of Monroe, m. Emeline **WILSON**, of Redding, this day [Oct. 4, 1846], by Jonathan Bartlett, M. G.	158
Sarah, m. Hezekiah **PLATT**, Apr. [ ], 1756	68
LOUDEN, Alfred, m. Frances F. **HINES**, Nov. 5, 1829, by G. Pierce, Elder	129
LYNES, [see under **LINES**]	
LYON, Aaron, s. [Daniel, Jr. & Any], b. Nov. 12, 1789	65
Alanson, m. Adaline L. **BANKS**, b. of Redding, June 5, 1848, by Rev. J. D. Marshall	161
Anna, m. Abel **HILL**, May 11, 1773. Witnesses James Jonson & Abel Adams	95
Asahel, m. Hannah **HILL**, 6th mo. 2nd da., 1775. Witness Daniel Hill	65
Augustus, b. Apr. 4, 1765; m. Mary **BENNET**, Mar. 20, 1788	13
Camilla, m. Samuel Bradley **READ**, b. of Redding, Mar. 6, 1825, by Rev. Lemuel B. Hull	120
Cyrus, s. [David & Hannah], b. June 10, 1777	11
Daniel, Jr., m. Any **SUMMERS**, Mar. 26, 1789, certified by Daniel Lyon	65
Daniel H., of Washington, N. Y., m. Hannah **LYON**, of Redding June 2, 1839, by Rev. Charles J. Todd	145
David, m. Hannah **SANFORD**, b. of Redding, Sept. 19, 1756, by Rev. Nathaniel Bartlet	11
Dolly, [d. Jabez & Grace], b. June 6, 1774	83
Dolle, m. Eli **BARTRAM**, Sept. 9, 1794, by Nathaniel Bartlett	31
Eleanor, m. Thaddeus B. **READ**, this day [Jan. 1, 1824], by Lemuel B. Hull	117
Eli, [s. Lemuel & Huldah], b. Jan. 19, 1790	96
Eli, m. Betty **HILL**, Apr. 26, 1795. Witness Abel Hill	13
Eli, of Redding, m. Esther Ann **NORTHROP**, of Newtown, Dec. 25, 1820, by Rev. Daniel Crocker	109
Eli, m. Louisa A. **WINTON**, b. of Redding, Nov. 17, 1839, by Rev. Charles J. Todd	147
Eliza Maria, [d. Augustus & Mary], b. Feb. 3, 1798	13
Eunice, [d. Jabez & Grace], b. Dec. 3, 1773	83
Grace, wid., m. Jabez **LYON**, Aug. 18, 1768	83
Grace, [d. Jabez & Grace], b. Mar. 4, 1776	83
Hannah, m. Andrew L. **HILL**, Apr. 23, 1775, by Rev. John Beach. Witnesses Sim[o]n Munger & Lois Munger	55
Hannah, w. [David], d. May 8, 1779	11
Hannah, of Redding, m. Daniel H. **LYON**, of Washington, N. Y., June 2, 1839, by Rev. Charles J. Todd	145
Jabez, m. Wid. Grace **LYON**, Aug. 18, 1768	83
Jabez, [s. Jabez & Grace], b. Jan. 7, 1777	83
Jabez, hus. of Grace, d. Oct. 20, 1777	83
Lemuel, m. Huldah **SANFORD**, Oct. 25, 1787, by James Jonson, of Weston. Witnesses James Sanford & Elisabeth Morgain	96
Lois, m. Sim[o]n **MUNGER**, Nov. 5, 1775, by Rev. Jno Beach	12

	Page
LYON, (cont.)	
Lois, [d. Augustus & Mary], b. Oct. 13, 1788	13
Mabel, m. Ele **READ**, May 20, 1783. Witnesses Zalmon Read & Huldah Read	17
Maria, m. Aaron **OAKLEY**, b. of Redding, Apr. 20, 1840, by Aaron Sanford, Jr., J. P.	148
Mary, [d. Jabez & Grace], b. Feb. 4, 1771	83
Mary, m. Nathan **WHITLOCK**, Mar. 3, 1793. Witnesses Jesse Beardsley & Daniel Beardsley	75
Peter, s. [Asahel & Hannah], b. 3rd mo. 29th da., 1784	65
Rebeckah Ann, [d. Lemuel & Huldah], b. Jan. 11, 1799	96
Sally, of Redding, m. Peter **DOWNS**, of Weston, this day [Sept. 23, 1827], by Rev. Lemuel B. Hull	127
Sarah, d. [Asahel & Hannah], b. 1st mo. 10th da., 1776	65
Sarah, [d. Daniel, Jr. & Any], b. Mar. 26, 1791	65
Sarah, m. Eli **SANFORD**, Apr. 22, 1792, by Nathaniel Bartlett	73
Simeon, [s. Lemuel & Huldah], b. June 13, 1792; d. Mar. 15, 1795	96
Stephen, [s. Jabez & Grace], b. May 9, 1769	83
Suse, [d. Lemuel & Huldah], b. Jan. 10, 1795	96
Zalmon, of Weston, m. Mary **HILL**, of Redding, Feb. 4, 1835, by Rev. Nathan Wildman	137
MAIN, MAINE, W[illia]m P., of Wilton, m. Eliza **MIDDLEBROOKS**, of Redding, Sept. 16, 1827, by W[illia]m C. Kniffin, M. G.	126
Zalmon, m. Jerusha **HERRINGTON**, Sept. 13, 1837, by John Crawford	142
MALLERY, Aaron, of Warren, m. Elizabeth **SKILLENGER**, of Redding, Feb. 14, 1827, by W[illia]m C. Kniffin, M. G.	124
Aaron Burr, s. Daniel, Jr. & Huldah, b. Aug. 17, 1809	105
Charles, [twin with Samuel], b. Apr. 6, 1780	98
Dan[ie]l, Jr., m. Rachael **COLEY**, Oct. 13, 1778, by Rev. Mr. Bartlett. Witnesses Isaac Coley & John Davis	66
Daniel, s. [Daniel, Jr. & Rachel], b. Nov. 26, 1783	66
Daniel, Jr., m. Mary **ADAMS**, Jan. 15, 1792	66
Daniel, Jr., m. Huldah **BURR**, Oct. 12, 1806	105
David, [s. Joseph], b. July 29, 1798	33
Eli, s. [Daniel, Jr. & Mary], b. Mar. 13, 1797	66
Eli, m. Ann **GRAY**, b. of Redding, Sept. 27, 1820, by Rev. Daniel Crocker	108
Eli, m. Delia **SHERWOOD**, b. of Redding, this day [Apr. 20, 1825], by Jonathan Bartlett, M. G.	120
Esther, [d. Samuel & Hannah], b. Oct. 22, 1781	17
Eunice, m. John **CLUCKSTON**, b. of Redding, July 7, 1760, by Rev. Nath[anie]ll Bartlet	3
Eunice, d. [Daniel, Jr. & Rachael], b. July 30, 1779	66
Ezra, s. [Samuel & Hannah], b. Feb. 20, 1785	17
Hannah, [d. Samuel & Hannah], b. Dec. 16, 1788	17
James, b. July 28, 1773	98
Joseph, s. Dan[ie]l, b. Sept. 2, 1766	33
Lucy, [twin with Lydia], b. Apr. 23, 1786	98

MALLERY, (cont.)
	Page
Lydia, [twin with Lucy], b. Apr. 23, 1786	98
Mary Ann, [d. Joseph], b. Aug. 7, 1796	33
Mary Ann, of Redding, m. Benjamin **FLEMIN**, of Danbury, Oct. 25, 1820, by Rev. Daniel Crocker	108
Rachel, 1st w. [Daniel, Jr.], d. June 16, 1791	66
Rena, d. Daniel & Huldah, b. Nov. 16, 1807; d. Mar. 2, 1808	105
Sam[ue]l, m. Hannah **NICHOLS**, Oct. 16, 1777. Witness Dan[ie]l Mallery, Jr.	17
Sam[ue]l, [twin with Charles], b. Apr. 6, 1780	98
Samuel, [s. Joseph], b. Sept. 10, 1794	33
Sarah, m. Billey **MOREHOUSE**, Sept. 23, 1797, by Nathaniel Bartlett	66
William, b. May 2, 1778	98
William, s. [Samuel & Hannah], b. Sept. 16, 1778	17

MALLETT, MALLET, Aaron, m. Abby Jane **HILL**, Oct. 4, 1837, by John Crawford — 143
Daniel, m. Mabel **HILL**, b. of Redding, Nov. 8, 1829, by Rev. Ebenezer Washburn — 129

MANCE, Joseph, of Newtown, m. Sarah **SQUIRES**, of Newtown, July 19, 1835, by Rev. H. Humphreys — 138

MARCHANT, MERCHANT, Aaron Meeker, [s. Enoch & Molly], b. Oct. 14, 1791 — 11
Abel, s. [Chauncy & Hannah], b. Feb. 8, 1789	45
Ahaz, [child of Silas & Huldah], b. Mar. 16, 1794	70
Ann, m. Dan[ie]ll **BARTRAM**, b. of Redding, Oct. 10, 1769, by [ ]	2
Asher, s. Joel & Molly, b. May 18, 1810	104
Benjamin, [s. Chauncy & Hannah], b. Nov. 28, 1774	45
Betsy, [d. Joel], b. Jan. 29, 1795	76
Betsey, m. Edward **COUCH**, b. of Redding, Jan. 1, 1822, by Rev. Daniel Crocker	112
Charles, [s. Silas & Huldah], b. Jan. 5, 1799	70
Chauncy, m. Hannah **HAMBLETON**, May 19, 1773, by Nathaniel Bartlet	13
Chauncy, m. Hannah **HAMILTON**, Nov. 28, 1773	45
Chauncey, d. Aug. 25, 1804; "suicide"	101
Clary, [d. Joel], b. Dec. 17, 1791	76
Cortes, [s. Joel], b. June 9, 1797	76
Edward, s. Joel & Molly, b. July 29, 1806	104
Edward, m. Betsey **COLEY**, b. of Redding, [Apr.] 4, [1839], by Rev. Jeremiah Miller	145
Eleanor, d. [Chauncy & Hannah], b. May 13, 1781	45
Eliza Ann, d. Joel & Molly, b. Nov. 15, 1808	104
Eliza Ann, of Redding, m. Alva **SHERWOOD**, of Fairfield, this day, [Oct. 23, 1835], by Jonathan Bartlett, M. G.	139
Enoch, m. Molly **MEEKER**, May 16, 1790, by Azariah Meeker	11
Eunice, m. John **MARCHANT**, Aug. 20, 1797	94
George, s. Joel & Molley, b. Feb. 13, 1814	33

	Page
MARCHANT, MERCHANT, (cont.)	
George, b. Feb. 13, 1814	168
George, b. Feb. 15, 1814	51
Hannah, d. [Chauncy & Hannah], b. Feb. 28, 1779	45
Hannah, w. Chauncey, d. Aug. 25, 1804; "murdered by her husband"	101
Huldah, [d. Silas & Huldah], b. July 15, 1790	70
Joel, s. [Chauncy & Hannah], b. Sept. 28, 1786	45
John, [s. Chauncy & Hannah], b. Mar. 15, 1777	45
John, m. Eunice **MARCHANT**, Aug. 20, 1797	94
Lusinda, [d. John & Eunice], b. Sept. 21, 1798	94
Lucy, d. [Chauncy & Hannah], b. Nov. 29, 1783	45
Lydia, [d. Enoch & Molly], b. Mar. 3, 1795	11
Orson, m. Permelia **CHAPMAN**, b. of Redding, [Mar.] 23, [1823], by Rev. Daniel Crocker	116
Rebecca, [d. Silas & Huldah], b. May 9, 1796	70
Salina, d. [Enoch & Molly], b. Mar. 6, 1798	11
Sally, d. [Chauncy & Hannah], b. Apr. 25, 1793	45
Silas, m. Huldah **PLATT**, June 1, 1788, [by] Thaddeus Abbott	70
MARVIN, [see also **MARWIN**], Charles, [twin with George], s. Curtis B. & Huldah, b. Oct. 18, 1814	107
Curtis B., of New York, m. Huldah **READ**, of Redding, May 27, 1805	103
Frederick Bartlett, s. Curtis B. & Huldah, b. July 8, 1811	105
George, [twin with Charles], s. Curtis B. & Huldah, b. Oct. 18, 1814	107
Sally Read, d. Curtis B. & Huldah, b. June 7, 1807	104
Sarah, of Redding, m. Charles D. **SMITH**, of Manlius, N. Y., this day, [Sept. 19, 1831], by Jonathan Bartlett, M. G.	132
MARWIN, [see also **MARVIN**], Betsey, m. Jonathan **BARTLETT**, Sept. 10, 1798, by Nathaniel Bartlett	54
Rebecah, m. Thaddeus **ABBOT**, May 24, 1788, certified by Barnabus Marwin	56
MEAD, Barnard Keeler, s. [William & Molley], b. Nov. 20, 1790	67
Betsey, m. Daniel **FAIRCHILD**, b. of Redding, Jan. 15, 1801	100
David Hoyt, s. [William & Molley], b. July 20, 1796	67
Esther, of Redding, m. William K. **KEELER**, of Ridgefield, Oct. 25, 1835, by Rev. H. Humphreys	139
Gershom, [s. Uriah], b. Mar. 8, 1791	67
Hannah, [d. Uriah], b. Sept. 25, 1795	67
Henry B., Rev. of West Point, N. Y., m. Lydia **SANFORD**, of Redding, June 3, 1852, by Rev. J. L. Gilder	168
Lewis, of New Haven, m. Zilpha **NICHOLS**, of Redding, May 31, 1807	104
Parthenia, of Wilton, m. David **COLEY**, Dec. 5, 1802	1
Rebeckah, [twin with Samuel, d. Uriah], b. June 4, 1787	67
Samuel, [twin with Rebeckah], s. [Uriah], b. June 4, 1787	67
Samuel B., of Bethel, m. Mary E. **DIMON**, of Redding, May 20, 1850, by Daniel D. Frost, M. G.	165
Stephen S., m. Esther **COUCH**, Nov. 25, 1821, by Rev. Laban Clark	111
Step[he]n St. John, s. [William & Molley], b. June 21, 1798	67
Uriah, [s. Uriah], b. Jan. 6, 1793	67

MEAD, (cont.)

	Page
[Uriah], his 1st w. [ ], d. Sept. 25, 1795	67
Uriah, m. 2nd w. [ ], May 1, 1796	67
Ursuly, s. [William & Molley], b. Oct. 12, 1793	67
William, m. Molley **HOYT**, Nov. 17, 1788	67
Will[ia]m, s. [William & Molley], b. Mar. 15, 1789	67
Zalmon, [s. Uriah & 2nd w. [ ], b. Apr. 15, 1797	67

MEEKER, MEAKER, Aaron, [s. Seth & Melleson], b. June 12, 1784; d. Nov. 5, 1784 — 33
Abigail, 3rd child [Jonathan & Elisabeth], b. Feb. 1, 1766 — 21
Abigail, of Redding, m. Justus **WHITLOCK**, formerly of Greenfield, July 19, 1781, by Hezekiah Ripley, V. D. M. — 13
Abigail, m. Jacob **PATCHEN**, Feb. 26, 1787, by Rev. Nath[anie]l Bartlett — 6
Alfred, [s. Azariah & Eunice], b. Mar. 30, 1790 — 76
Andrew, m. Lydia Ann **SANFORD**, b. of Redding, June 16, 1845, by Rev. W. F. Collins — 155
Arza, s. [Jonathan, Jr. & Esther], b. Mar. 8, 1799 — 21
Azariah, m. Eunice **DAVIS**, May 19, 1789, by Nathaniel Bartlet — 76
Azariah Edgar, s. Dan[ie]l & Eunice, b. Jan. 14, 1838 — 125
Benjamin, s. [Seth & Eleanor], b. Feb. 1, 1771 — 33
Benjamin, f. of Azariah, d. Aug. 13, 1787 — 12
Benjamin, m. Sarah **MEEKER**, Oct. 14, 1792, by Nathaniel Bartlet — 10
Benjamin, Jr., m. Mary J. **SHERWOOD**, July 25, 1852, by Rev. D. D. Frost — 168
Betsey, d. [Seth & Melleson], b. Mar. 19, 1793 — 33
Bodema, d. [Seth & Melleson], b. Apr. 23, 1782 — 33
Burr, [s. Azariah & Eunice], b. Nov. 25, 1791 — 76
Catharine, d. [Seth & Melleson], b. Oct. 22, 1790 — 33
Catharine, of Redding, m. Sam[ue]l S. **SHERWOOD**, of New York, Apr. 26, 1828, by W[illia]m C. Kniffin, M. G. — 127
Charlotte, d. [Seth & Melleson], b. Dec. 10, 1785 — 33
Daniel, [s. Jared & Mehetabel], b Mar. 5, 1772 — 33
Daniel, 7th child [Jonathan & Elisabeth], b. May 15, 1774; d. Mar. 20, 1778 — 21
Daniel, [s. Azariah & Eunice], b. May 23, 1796 — 76
David, [s. Jared & Mehetabel], b. Jan. 5, 1774 — 33
David, 8th child [Jonathan & Elizabeth], b. July 5, 1776; d. Mar. 9, 1788 — 21
Dile, [d. Benjamin & Sarah], b. Oct. 24, 1798 — 10
Eleanor, w. Seth, d. Aug. 6, 1774 — 33
Eleanor, [d. Seth & Melleson], b. Mar. 21, 1780 — 33
Eleanor, [d. Benjamin & Sarah], b. Sept. 5, 1796 — 10
Elisabeth, 4th child [Jonathan & Elisabeth], b. June 20, 1768 — 21
Elisabeth, w. [Jonathan], d. Apr. 5, 1783 — 21
Elizabeth, m. John **FAIRCHILD**, June 17, 1821, by Rev. Ambrose S. Todd — 110
Elizabeth, d. Daniel & Eunice, b. May 23, 1827 — 125

	Page
MEEKER, MEAKER, (cont.)	
Esther, d. [Seth & Melleson], b. Feb. 26, 1778	33
Eunice, wid. of Redding, m. Ebenezer **STURGES**, of Stamford, July 31, 1803	100
Fanny, d. [Jonathan, Jr. & Esther], b. Dec. 20, 1796; d. Sept. 18, 1798	21
Fanna, [d. Azariah & Eunice], b. Sept. 8, 1798	76
Fanny, m. Bradley **TREADWELL**, b. of Redding, Oct. 14, 1844, by Rev. W. F. Collins	154
Fanny, m. Hiram **JELLEFF**, b. of Redding, July 20, 1845, by Rev. W. F. Collins	156
Hannah, [5th child Jonathan & Elisabeth], b. Apr. 24, 1770	21
Harry, m. Eleanor **GOODYEAR**, b. of Redding, this day [Nov. 24, 1824], by Jonathan Bartlett, M. G.	119
Isaac, m. Eunice **COLEY**, b. of Redding, May 29, [ ], by Rev. Nathaniel Bartlet	12
Jared, m. Mehetabel **COLE**, May 3, 1770, by Isaac Lewis	33
John, 6th child [Jonathan & Elisabeth], b. May 15, 1772	21
John, s. [Seth & Melleson], b. Mar. 30, 1776	33
John, m. Sarah **MUNGER**, b. of Redding, Oct. 18, 1800	100
Jonathan, 2nd child [Jonathan & Elisabeth], b. Oct. 23, 1763	21
Jonathan, Jr., m. Esther [ ], Jan. 8, 1792, by Rev. Philo Perry. Witnesses Richard Hawley & Richard Hawley, Jr.	21
Joseph, m. Mary **DARLING**, b. of Redding, Mar. 12, 1767, by [ ]	12
Joseph, of Redding, m. Hannah **STREET**, of Ridgbury, May 4, 1774, in Ridgfield, by Samuel Camp, V. D. M.	33
Lois, 9th child [Jonathan & Elisabeth], b. Oct. 5, 1778	21
Maria, m. Edmond **OLMSTEAD**, Nov. 24, 1847, by D. D. Frost, M. G.	159
Martha, m. Zechariah **CARLE**, June 4, 1826, by Rev. W[illia]m Andrews	122
Martha A., of Redding, m. W[illia]m B. **SELLICK**, of Ridgefield, Jan. 17, 1843, by Rev. Daniel Smith	152
Mary S., m. Stephen R. **RIDER**, b. of Redding, Jan. 16, 1849, by Daniel D. Frost	163
Mehetabel, m. Jonathan **COUCH**, Sept. 23, 1777, by N. Bartlet. Witnesses Ebenezer Couch & Elijah Couch	48
Molly, d. [Seth & Eleanor], b. Nov. 19, 1773	33
Molly, m. Enoch **MARCHANT**, May 16, 1790, by Azariah Meeker	11
Molly, d. [Benjamin & Sarah], b. Apr. 6, 1794	10
Moses, s. [Seth & Melleson], b. Mar. 13, 1796	33
Pamela, d. [Seth & Melleson], b. June 18, 1788	33
Rebeckah, [d. Jared & Mehetabel], b. Dec. 21, 1770	33
Rebeckah, m. Daniel **BENEDICT**, Mar. 16, 1786, by Nathaniel Bartlett	46
Sarah, 1st child [Jonathan & Elisabeth], b. Feb. 17, 1762	21
Sarah, m. Lem[ue]l **GLOVER**, June 29, 1786, by Rev. Nathaniel Bartlett. Certified by Jonathan Meeker, Jr., John Meeker & Stephen Betts	7
Sarah, m. Benjamin **MEEKER**, Oct. 14, 1792, by Nathaniel Bartlet	10

MEEKER, MEAKER, (cont.)

	Page
Sarah, w. Isaac, d. Oct. 20, 1805	101
Seth, m. Elinor **BIXBY**, b. of Redding, Mar. 27, 1770, by Rev. Nathaniel Bartlet	12
Seth, m. Eleanor **BIXBY**, Mar. 14, 1770	33
Seth, m. 2nd w. Melleson **DAVISON**, Mar. 14, 1775	33
Stephen, m. Ann **LEE**, b. of Redding, Mar. 25, 1768, by Rev. Nathaniel Bartlet	39
Susan, m. John B. **MERRITT**, b. of Redding, this day [May 15, 1825], by Rev. Lemuel B. Hull	120
Susannah, d. John & Sarah, b. Aug. 12, 1801	100
Whitley, m. Silas **LEE**, b. of Redding, Aug. 23, 1769, by Rev. Nath[anie]l Bartlet	32

MERCHANT, [see under **MARCHANT**]

MERRITT, MERRIT, Anna, d. [Eben[eze]r & Hannah], b. Feb. 25, 1783 — 97

Eben[eze]r, m. Hannah **WHEELER**, Nov. 10, 1782, by Rev. James Johnson. Witnesses Calvin Wheeler & Calvin Wheeler, Jr.	97
Eben[eze]r, s. [Ebenezer & Hannah], b. Jan. 13, 1795	97
John B., m. Susan **MEEKER**, b. of Redding, this day [May 15, 1825], by Rev. Lemuel B. Hull	120
John Burr, s. [Ebenezer & Hannah], b. Feb. 11, 1789	97

MIDDLEBROOK, MIDDLEBROOKS, Betsey, [d. Jonathan & Elisabeth], b. Oct. 4, 1793 — 3

Betsey, of Redding, m. Seth **OBEDIENT**, of Weston, Apr. 7, 1842, by Rev. Daniel Smith	151
Caroline, m. Alonzo **DICKENS**, b. of Redding, Nov. 23, 1848, by Rev. Jacob Shaw	163
Eliza, of Redding, m. W[illia]m P. **MAINE**, of Wilton, Sept. 16, 1827, by W[illia]m C. Kniffin, M. G.	126
Hubbell, m. Julia **PLATT**, b. of Redding, Oct. 5, 1835, by Rev. Hawley Sanford	139
Jonathan, m. Elisabeth **BURR**, Jan. 6, 1793, by Nath[anie]ll Bartlett	3
Jonathan, m. Sarah **BARTRAM**, b. of Redding, Oct. 21, 1826, by W[illia]m C. Kniffin, M. G.	123
Lorry, [s. Jonathan & Elisabeth], b. Mar. 3, 1798	3
Lucy, of Redding, m. Charles **BROOKS**, of Danbury, Dec. 18, 1831, by Rev. W[illia]m L. Strong	133
Norman T., of Weston, m. Felida **SANFORD**, of Redding, Dec. 15, 1822, by Rev. Ambrose S. Todd	115

MILLER, Charlotte, m. Joseph S. **OLMSTEAD**, b. of Redding, Mar. 25, 1832, by Rev. W[illia]m L. Strong — 134

Henry, m. Mary Ann **FRENCH**, b. of Redding, Jan. 17, 1833, by Rev. W[illia]m L. Strong	135
Oliver, of Pound Ridge, N. Y., m. Myra **STOWE**, of Redding, Dec. 3, 1845, by Morris Hill	157

MONROE, MANROW, MUNROE, MUNROW, Amelia, m. Stiles **CURTIS**, Mar. 10, 1839, by Rev. John Crawford — 145

Amos, m. Lucy **STILSON**, of Newtown, June 25, 1795. Witnesses

	Page
MONROE, MANROW, MUNROE, MUNROW, (cont.)	
Elijah Judd & Benj[ami]n Judd	84
Betsey A., of Redding, m. Warren G. **WOODROUGH**, of New Milford, Mar. 1, 1843, by Rev. Daniel Smith	152
Charry, m. David **CURTICE**, Nov. 27, 1838, by Rev. John Crawford	144
David, [s. David], b. Apr. 7, 1777	84
Elisabeth, [d. David], b. May 31, 1780	84
Eunice, of Weston, m. Josiah **BUCKLEY**, of Stratford, July 6, 1833, by Rev. James A. Batterson	136
Julay, d. [Amos & Lucy], b. Feb. 11, 1799	84
Liman, [s. David], b. Aug. 26, 1774	84
Mary A., of Redding, m. Henry B. **OSBORN**, of New Milford*, Oct. 21, 1847, by Rev. J. D. Marshall *(First written "Redding")	160
Paulina, m. Daniel **KAY**, of New Haven, [Dec.] 25, [1831], by Abram Stow, J. P., Int. Pub.	133
Rebeckah, m. Andrew **KNAP[P]**, b. of Redding, Apr. 7, 1769, by Rev. Nathaniel Bartlet	31
MOREHOUSE, [Aaron], m. Rune **STARR**, Aug. 19, 1787	25
Aaron, [s. Billey & Ruth], b. Sept. 14, 1795	66
Almira, of Redding, m. Nelson **SHERMAN**, of Trumbull, this day [Nov. 15, 1826], by Rev. Lemuel B. Hull	123
Amelia, m. Jedediah **ADAMS**, b. of Redding, this day [May 12, 1824], by Rev. Lemuel B. Hull	118
Ann, wid., m. Joseph **BANKS**, b. of Redding, Nov. 29, 1767	23
Anna, [d. Aaron & Rune], b. May 13, 1795	25
Bettsey, [d. Aaron & Rune], b. Jan. 11, 1793	25
Billey, m. Ruth **GUIER**, Mar. 11, 1778, by Nathaniel Bartlett	66
Billey, m. Sarah **MALLERY**, Sept. 23, 1797, by Nathaniel Bartlett	66
Charles, [s. Billey & Ruth], b. Nov. 30, 1785	66
Charles, m. Fidelia **STARR**, b. of Redding, Mar. 21, 1824, by Rev. Lemuel B. Hull	118
Clary, [d. John & Grace], b. Mar. 10, 1791	45
Daniel, m. Hannah **DOWNS**, May [ ], 1785, by Nathaniel Bartlett	96
Daniel, d. Aug. 9, 1798. Exec. Hannah Morehouse	96
Floria, [d. Aaron & Rune], b. Nov. 19, 1789	25
Jane, m. Daniel **OSBURN**, Jan. 28, 1778, by Nathaniel Bartlet	14
John, m. Grace **WHEELER**, Nov. 4, 1784. Certified by Nathaniel Bartlett	45
Louisa, m. William B. **CURTIS**, Nov. 26, 1837, by John Crawford	143
Olive, [d. Billey & Ruth], b. July 4, 1779	66
Olive, m. Daniel **SANFORD**, Dec. 14, 1799, by Nathaiel Bartlett	77
Peter, [s. Billey & Ruth], b. July 22, 1781	66
Phebe, m. David **BARTRAM**, b. of Redding, Apr. 30, 1762, by Rev. Nath[anie]l Bartlet	2
Ruth, 1st w. Billey, d. Oct. 23, 1796	66
Ruth, m. Elias **ANDREWS**, b. of Redding, June 3, 1837, by James A. Batterson, Dea.	141
Sally, d. John & Grace, b. Oct. 6, 1799	100

MOREHOUSE, (cont.)

	Page
Starr Hill, [s. Aaron & Rune], b. Jan. 29, 1788	25
Tabitha, [d. Billey & Ruth], b. Apr. 26, 1788	66
William, [s. Aaron & Rune], b. Apr. 25, 1797	25
William C., of Amenia, N. Y., m. Clarissa D. **DENISON**, of Redding, June 11, 1848, by Rev. Joseph P. Taylor	162
Zacheus, [s. John & Grace], b. Feb. 17, 1787	45
MORGAN, Aaron, s. Mary, b. Aug. 18, 1793	78
Aaron, [s. Joseph & Mabel], b. Dec. 3, 1797	89
Abijah, m. [ ], July 7, 1767	78
Abijah, had d. [ ], b. Sept. 12, 1784	78
[Abijah], his d. [ ], d. Sept. 22, 1784	78
Anna, [d. Joseph & Mabel], b. Sept. 20, 1786; d. Feb. 12, 1794	89
Anne, d. [Abijah], b. Oct. 30, 1768	78
Anne, had d. Polly, b. Feb. 24, 1796	78
Charles, m. Mary **ODELL**, b. of Weston, May 7, 1843, by Rev. Daniel Smith	152
Emily A., of Redding, m. Eli **COLE**, of Wilton, July 16, 1848, by James A. Batterson, Dea.	162
Ezra, s. Hezekiah & Elisabeth, b. Feb. 22, 1801	102
Hannah, [d. Joseph & Mabel], b. Nov. 18, 1790	89
Harriet, Mrs., of Redding, m. Jasper **OLMSTEAD**, of Wilton, Dec. 20, 1840, by Rev. Elizur W. Griswold	149
Henry, [s. Joseph & Mabel], b. Apr. 15, 1795	89
Hezekiah, m. [ ], Dec. 27, 1796	66
Joseph, m. Mabel **OSBURN**, Nov. 24, 1785, certified by Nathaniel Bartlett	89
Mabel, [d. Joseph & Mabel], b. Jan. 12, 1793	89
Mary, [d. Abijah], had son Aaron **MORGAN**, b. Aug. 18, 1793. She d. Jan. 23, 1794	78
Minerva, d. Phebe, b. Nov. 24, 1801	102
Molly, [d. Joseph & Mabel], b. Sept. 12, 1788	89
Phebe, had d. Minerva, b. Nov. 24, 1801	102
Polly, d. Anne, b. Feb. 24, 1796	78
Russell, s. Caleb, b. Feb. 10, 1797	67
Sally, d. [Abijah], b. Oct. 7, 1787	78
Sally, d. [Abijah], d. Jan. 25, 1794	78
Sarah, m. Isaac **GORHAM**, Jr., Mar. 4, 1780, by Rev. Mr. Lewis. Witness Joseph Morgan	60
Sarah, m. Jabez **GORHAM**, Aug. 5, 1784, by Nathaniel Bartlett	92
William, s. [Abijah], b. Nov. 26, 1782	78
William, of New York City, m. Abby **THORP**, of Redding, Sept. 6, 1841, by Rev. John Crawford	150
Zira, s. [Hezekiah], b. July 2, 1797	66
MOSIER, David, of Trumbull, m. Eunice **PLATT**, of Redding, Apr. 23, 1833, by Rev. Hawley Sanford	135
MUNGER, Sarah, [d. Sim[o]n & Lois], b. Aug. 4, 1776	12
Sarah, m. John **MEEKER**, b. of Redding, Oct. 18, 1800	100

	Page
MUNGER, (cont.)	
Sim[o]n, m. Lois **LYON**, Nov. 5, 1775, by Rev. Jno Beach	12
Susanna, [d. Sim[o]n & Lois], b. Oct. 6, 1779	12
NASH, Charlotte, m. Daniel **CLARKSON**, July 22, 1821, by Dea. Hawley Sanford	110
Eleanor, m. Simon **COUCH**, Jr., Jan. 7, 1776, by Hezekiah Ripley, V. D. M.	58
Lydia, d. Thom[a]s, of Greensfarms, m. William **HAWLEY**, s. Joseph, of Redding, July 12, 1758. Witnesses Joseph Hawley & Thomas Nash	29
NEPTUNE, Elisha, d. July 23, 1795	41
NICHOLS, David Coley, b. Sept. 9, 1787	29
Gould, of Weston, m. Esther **HULL**, of Redding, Sept. 8, 1827, by Levi Brunson	126
Hannah, m. Sam[ue]l **MALLERY**, Oct. 16, 1777. Certified by Dan[ie]l Mallery, Jr.	17
Polly, d. Jeremiah & Polly, b. Sept. 19, 1803	100
W[illia]m, m. Abigail **JONES**, b. of Redding, Sept. 26, 1830, by W[illia]m L. Strong	131
Zilpha, of Redding, m. Lewis **MEAD**, of New Haven, May 31, 1807	104
NORTHROP, NORTHRUP, Esther Ann, of Newtown, m. Eli **LYON**, of Redding, Dec. 25, 1820, by Rev. Daniel Crocker	109
Julia Ann, m. Walter **BURS**, b. of Redding, Feb. 1, 1846, by Rev. Hawley Sanford	158
Mary, m. John **DREW**, Jan. 16, 1746	4
Smith, of Newtown, m. wid. Eunice **THORP**, of Redding, this day [Apr. 5, 1821], by Calvin Wheeler, Jr., J. P.	113
Zilpha, of Redding, m. Zira **WEED**, of Danbury, [Sept.] 24, [1823], by Rev. Daniel Crocker	116
OAKLEY, Aaron, m. Maria **LYON**, b. of Redding, Apr. 20, 1840, by Aaron Sanford, Jr., J. P.	148
William, s. Beers, d. Apr. 10, 1814	106
OBEDIENT, Seth, of Weston, m. Betsey **MIDDLEBROOKS**, of Redding, Apr. 7, 1842, by Rev. Daniel Smith	151
ODELL, Mary, m. Charles **MORGAN**, b. of Weston, May 7, 1843, by Rev. Daniel Smith	152
Sally B., of Norwalk, m. Benjamin A. **DARLING**, of Redding, Nov. 2, 1808	25
OLMSTED, OLMSTEAD, Ann, of Wilton, m. Joseph **GILES**, of Redding, Feb. 14, 1835, by Rev. Josiah Bowen	138
Edmond, m. Maria **MEEKER**, Nov. 24, 1847, by D. D. Frost, M. G.	159
Eleazer, m. Grace **PICKET**, b. of Redding, Jan. 17, 1765, by Rev. Nathaniel Bartlet	14
Eleazer, [s. Elias & Elisabeth], b. Apr. 13, 1796	81
Elias, m. Elisabeth **WHITLOCK**, Jan. 5, 1794, by Rev. Samuel Goodrich. Witness Polle Olmsted	81
Elias, [s. Elias & Elisabeth], b. Dec. 26, 1794	81
Frederick, s. Jared & Polly, b. Aug. 7, 1820	68

OLMSTED, OLMSTEAD, (cont.)

	Page
Hiram, s. Jared & Polly, b. Apr. 15, 1823	68
Jasper, of Wilton, m. Mrs. Harriet **MORGAN**, of Redding, Dec. 20, 1840, by Rev. Elizur W. Griswold	149
Joseph S., m. Charlotte **MILLER**, b. of Redding, Mar. 25, 1832, by Rev. W[illia]m L. Strong	134
Samuel, m. Zeruah Ann **WILDMAN**, b. of Redding, Sept. 1, 1841, by Rev. Daniel Smith	150

OSBORN, OSBURN, ORSBURN, Aaron, of Weston m. Mary C. **GREGORY**, of Redding, July 29, 1841, by James A. Batterson, Dea. 149

Burton, b. Sept. 28, 1765; m. Sarah **GODFRY**, d. Selivent, Nov. 14, 1792, by Rev. Mr. Noyes. Witnesses Hezekiah Osborn & David Osborn 93

Charles, of Monroe, m. Eliza **CANFIELD**, of Redding, this day [Nov. 25, 1835], by Jonathan Bartlett, M. G. 140

Daniel, m. Jane **MOREHOUSE**, Jan. 28, 1778, by Nathaniel Bartlet 14

Eleanor, m. Noah **LEE**, May 3, 1798, by Rev. Mr. Noyes. Witnesses John Byington & Asahel Salmon 16

Geo[rge], m. Sarah **GOODSELL**, b. of Redding, Dec. 12, 1832, by Rev. W[illia]m L. Strong 134

Hannah, of Fairfield, m. Asahel **PATCHIN**, of Redding, May 10, 1762, by Rev. Nathaniel Bartlet 15

Henry B., of New Milford*, m. Mary A. **MUNROE**, of Redding, Oct. 21, 1847, by Rev. J. D. Marshall   *(First written "Redding") 160

Hezekiah Read, [s. Burton & Sarah], b. Aug. 5, 1793 93

Isaac, of Redding, m. Mrs. Maria **BENEDICT**, of Wilton, Oct. 29, 1843, by James A. Batterson, Dea. 153

John, m. Lydia Ann **DUNCOMB**, b. of Redding, Apr. 18, 1842, by Rev. Daniel Smith 151

Mabel, m. Joseph **MORGAN**, Nov. 24, 1785, certified by Nathaniel Bartlett 89

Mary, [d. Burton & Sarah], b. Apr. 21, 1796 93

Ruth, m. Orace* **SMITH**, [Apr.] 27, [1825], by Rev. Aaron Hunt *(Brace?, Horace?) 120

Samuel S., m. Eleanor **LEE**, b. of Redding, this day [Nov. 18, 1835], by Jonathan Bartlett, M. G. 139

PALMER, Ezra Bartram, [s. Milo & Sarah], b. Oct. 27,* 1799   *(First written "26") 83

Fanny, [d. Milo & Sarah], b. Mar. 3, 1795 83

Homer, [s Milo & Sarah], b. Mar. 4, 1797 83

Milo, m. Sarah **BARTRAM**, Sept. 26, 1790 83

Polly, [d. Milo & Sarah], b. May 9, 1791 83

Zalmon C., [s. Milo & Sarah], b. Nov. 11, 1792 83

PARSONS, PERSONS, PAIRSONS, Abijah, m. Mabel **COLEY**, Aug. [ ], 1782 75

Betsey, of Redding, m. Rufus H. **PICKET**, of Ridgefield, Oct. 9, 1825, by W[illia]m C. Kniffin 121

PARSONS, PERSONS, PAIRSONS, (cont.)

	Page
Bettey, m. Hezekiah **ADAMS**, Sept. 11, 1788, by Rev. Nathaniel Bartlett. Witness Joseph Adams	89
Betty, [d. Daniel], b. July 26, 1790	68
Clarissy, [d. Daniel], b. Aug. 18, 1792	68
Daniel, m. Eunice **BARTRAM**, Mar. 15, 1783, by Nathaniel Bartlett	68
Elias, s. [Jonathan & Elisabeth], b. Feb. 24, 1781	30
Esther, d. [Jonathan & Elisabeth], b. Feb. 21, 1775	30
Esther, m. Ezekiel **BARTRAM**, on or about Jan. 26, 1793, by Nathaniel Bartlett	31
Eunice, [d. Daniel], b. Mar. 5, 1797	68
Hannah, [d. Daniel], b. Nov. 20, 1794	68
Harriet, d. Timothy & Margarett, b. Dec. 12, 1819	69
Harriet, m. Henry S. **BANKS**, b. of Redding, July 9, 1844, by Rev. W[illia]m F. Collins	154
Jonathan, m. Elisabeth **THOMAS**, Aug. 22, 1774, by Nathaniel Bartlett	30
Mary, m. Gershom **BEARS**, Nov. 13, 1783. Certified by Betty Mead	56
Mary Ann, d. Timothy & Margarett, b. Aug. 27, 1817	69
Noah, s. [Jonathan & Elisabeth], b. Jan. 30, 1795	30
Noah, m. Harriet **SANFORD**, b. of Redding, Jan. 27, 1822, by Rev. Daniel Crocker	112
Phebe, d. [Jonathan & Elisabeth], b. Mar. 25, 1797	30
Phebe, m. Alfred **ROCKWELL**, b. of Redding, this day [Nov. 23, 1823], by Jonathan Bartlett, M. G.	117
Polly, [d. Abijah & Mabel], b. Oct. 9, 1783	75
Sabra, m. Francis **ANDREWS**, Mar. 5, 1778, by Nath[anie]l Bartlet	1
Samuel, [s. Dan[ie]l], b. July 30, 1786	68
Sam[ue]l Gregory, [s. Jonathan & Elisabeth], b. July 2, 1786	30
Sarah, d. [Jonathan & Elisabeth], b. Aug. 29, 1783	30
Timothy, d. Nov. 30, 1810, ae 78	101
Timothy, m. Selina **DARLING**, b. of Redding, Sept. 29, 1839, by Rev. P. R. Brown	146
Uriah, [s. Daniel], b. July 12, 1788	68
PARTRICK, John, of Wilton, m. Eleanor C. **WHITEHEAD**, of Redding, July 3, 1843, by James A. Batterson, Dea.	153
PATCHEN, PATCHIN, Abigail, d. [Andrew], b. Oct. 24, 1762	36
Andrew, had s. [ ], b. Aug. 15, 1758	36
Asahel, of Redding m. Hannah **ORSBURN**, of Fairfield, May 10, 1762, by Rev. Nathaniel Bartlet	15
Betsey, d. [Jacob & Abigail], b. Mar. 15, 1787	6
David, s. [Jacob & Abigail], b. Apr. 22, 1789	6
Esther, [d. Andrew], b. May 5, 1764	36
Hannah, [d. Jacob & Abigail], b. Jan. 24, 1797	6
Hannah, of Redding, m. Jeremy **GODFREY**, of Weston, this day, [Dec. 15, 1824], by Rev. Lemuel B. Hull	120
Jacob, s. [Andrew], b. Nov. 11, 1759	36
Jacob, m. Abigail **MEAKER**, Feb. 26, 1787, by Rev. Nath[anie]l Bartlett	6

110   BARBOUR COLLECTION

Page

PATCHEN, PATCHIN, (cont.)
John, s. [Andrew], b. May 13, 1761   36
Levi, m. Catharine A. **HUTCHINSON**, b. of Redding, Aug. 31, 1845,
    by Rev. Hawley Sanford   156
Molly, m. Elijah **PEARSONS**, May 29, 1790   69
Mott(?), s. [Andrew], b. Apr. 6, 1772   36
Polly, d. [Jacob & Abigail], b. Sept. 3, 1794   6
Ralph, s. [Andrew], b. Jan. 6, 1768   36
Sally, d. [Jacob & Abigail], b. July 7, 1791   6
Sarah, [d. Andrew], b. Mar. 13, 1766   36
Zebpha, d. [Andrew], b. June 21,1770   36
PEARCE, [see under **PIERCE**]
PEARSON, PEARSONS, PIERSONS, Abraham, m. [   ],
    Mar. 25,1792   69
Betey, [d. Abraham], b. Apr. 20,1794   69
Elijah, m. Molly **PATCHEN**, May 29, 1790   69
Jared, s. [Elijah & Molly], b. July 5, 1796   69
Lorra, [d. Abraham], b. Feb. 18, 1798   69
Starr, [s. Abraham], b. Feb. 15, 1793   69
Timothy, s. [Elijah & Molly], b. Mar. 18, 1791   69
PECK, Caroline, m. Zalmon **SANFORD**, b. of Redding, Oct. 1, 1822, by
    Rev. Ambrose S. Todd   115
George R., m. Angeline **BEERS**, b. of Redding, Dec. 3, 1848, by Rev.
    Joseph P. Taylor   163
Mary, w. Dr. Tho[ma]s, d. May 29, 1798   54
Mary, d. Nath[anie]l, b. June 23, 1798   36
Sophia, d. Thomas & Mary, b. Apr. 26, 1797   54
Thomas, m. Mary **SANFORD**, Mar. 27, 1796, by Rev. Jonathan Bartlett   54
PENNOYER, Rodney, of Redding, m. Betsey **EDMOND**, of Ridgefield, Mar.
    26, 1843, by James A. Batterson, Dea.   151
PERRY, Aaron, [s. John], b. Sept. 4, 1782   14
Betsey, m. Moses **HUBBELL,** Jr., b. of Redding, Jan. 13, 1828, by
    Henry Stead   127
Dan[ie]l, Jr., [s. Daniel & Elisabeth], b. May 2, 1782   48
Deborah, [d. John], b. Mar. 21, 1786; d. June 24, 1802   14
Eli, [s. Daniel & Elizabeth], b. Feb. 6, 1776; d. June 12, 1784   48
Eli, [s. Timothy & Abigail], b. Oct. 14, 1796   87
Elisabeth, [d. Daniel & Elisabeth], b. Dec. 11, 1783   48
Elisabeth, w. [Daniel], d. Aug. 3, 1794   48
Ellen, [d. John], b. Apr. 18, 1784   14
Esther, m. Sam[ue]l **SMITH**, Aug. 16, 1799. Witness Hezekiah Ogden   95
George, s. [Timothy & Abigail], b. Mar. 14, 1799   87
Grezel, m. Nehemiah **HULL,** b. of Redding, Feb. 5, 1767, by Rev.
    Nath[anie]l Bartlet   8
Isaac, [s. Daniel & Elisabeth], b. Apr. 28, 1778; d. Apr. 11, 1791   48
Nancey, of Redding, m. Wakeman **GODFREY,** of Weston, Dec. 31,
    1829, by Rev. E. Washburn   129
Nehemiah, Dr., of Ridgefield, m. Mary **SANFORD**, of Redding, Oct.

REDDING VITAL RECORDS

	Page
PERRY, (cont.)	
10, 1821, by Rev. Daniel Crocker	111
Tim[oth]y, [s. Dan[ie]l & Elisabeth], b. Nov. 10, 1772	48
Timothy, m. Abigail **HULL**, Apr. 26, 1796, by Nathaniel Bartlett	87
PETERSON, George, m. Lucretia **COLEY**, b. of Redding (colored), Dec. 13, 1846, by Rev. Hawley Sanford	158
PHILLIPS, Leman, m. Harriet **HAWLEY**, Jan. 1, 1838, by John Crawford	143
PHINNY, FENNY, Mabel, m. James **GRAY**, Jr., Feb. 9, 1764, by Nathaniel Bartlet	42
Mehetabel,* wid., m. James **GRAY**, Jr., b. of Redding, Feb. 9, 1764 *(Written Mehetabel **FENNY**")	28
PICKETT, PICKET, PICKIT, Alma, of Redding, m. Hugh S. **BARTRAM**, of Danbury, Mar. 24, 1839, by Aaron Sanford, Jr., J. P.	145
Clarissa, m. Platt **WOOD**, Mar. 7, 1822, by Levi Brunson	113
Grace, m. Eleazer **OLMSTED**, b. of Redding, Jan. 17, 1765, by Rev. Nathaiel Bartlet	14
John, of Redding, m. Mercy **ROWLEY**, Jan. [ ], 1732	14
Mary, m. Isaac **PLATT**, b. of Redding, Oct. 3, 1765, by Rev. Nathaniel Bartlet	15
Rebeckah, m. Shubel **BENNET**, b. of Redding, Feb. 17, 1767, by Rev. Nath[anie]ll Bartlet	2
Rufus H., of Ridgefield, m. Betsey **PARSONS**, of Redding, Oct. 9, 1825, by W[illia]m C. Kniffin	121
Rufus S., of Ridgefield, m. Catherine **KEELER**, of Redding, Oct. 16, 1849, by D. D. Frost, M. G.	164
Sarah, m. Seth **BANKS**, b. of Redding, Nov. 20, 1766, by Rev. Nathaniel Bartlet	23
PIERCE, PEARCE, Edwin, of New Fairfield, m. Susan **CROFUT**, of Redding, Jan. 12, 1845, by Rev. W. F. Collins	155
Hosea O., of Danbury, m. Nancy **STONE**, of Redding, Nov. 20, 1842, by Morris Hill	151
PIERSONS, [see under **PEARSON**]	
PIKE, Jane, m. Robert **BRADLEY**, May 4, 1852, by Orasmus H. Smith	168
PLATT, Aaron, [s. Hezekiah & Sarah], b. Oct. [ ], 1758	68
Abigail, [d. Hezekiah & Sarah], b. May 9, 1760	68
Abigail, m. Samuel **FAIRCHILD**, Mar. 31, 1785, by Nathaniel Bartlett	80
Betsey, [d. Hezekiah & Sarah], b. Dec. [ ] 1771	68
Daniel, m. Elizabeth **BRADLEY**, Sept. 21, 1808	105
David, [s. Isaac & Mary], b. Apr. 3, 1784; d. Nov. 27, 1784	15
David, s. [Philip P. & Elisabeth], b. Jan. 28, 1792	69
Eben[eze]r, s. [Hezekiah & Sarah], b. Nov. 27, 1756	68
Elizabeth, of Redding, m. Eli **THORP**, of Weston, Feb. 16, 1845, by Rev. W. F. Collins	155
Eunice, of Redding, m. David **MOSIER**, of Trumbull, Apr. 23, 1833, by Rev. Hawley Sanford	135
Frances Mary, m. Munson **LOCKWOOD**, b. of Redding, Jan. 25, 1846, by Rev. W[illia]m F. Collins	157
Grissel, [s. Hezekiah & Sarah], b. Oct. 16, 1768	68

PLATT, (cont.)

	Page
Harriot, d. [Philip P. & Elisabeth], b. Mar. 31, 1798	69
Harriet, of Redding, m. E. Francis **FOSTER**, of Ridgefield, Dec. 3, 1851, by Rev. Shaler J. Hillyer	167
Hezekiah, m. Sarah **LORD**, Apr. [ ], 1756	68
Hezekiah, [s. Hezekiah & Sarah], b. Oct. 28, 1764	68
Huldah, [d. Isaac & Mary], b. Nov. 12, 1769	15
Huldah, m. Silas **MARCHANT**, June 1, 1788, [by] Thaddeus Abbott	70
Isaac, m. Mary **PICKIT**, b. of Redding, Oct. 3, 1765, by Rev. Nathaniel Bartlet	15
Julia, m. Hubbell **MIDDLEBROOKS**, b. of Redding, Oct. 5, 1835, by Rev. Hawley Sanford	139
Justus, [s. Hezekiah & Sarah], b. Feb. 11, 1762	68
Laura, m. William **SHERWOOD**, b. of Redding, this day [Jan. 1, 1837], by Jonathan Bartlett, M. G.	140
Lucey, m. David **SANFORD**, b. of Redding, Sept. 28, 1803	100
Marcy, [d. Isaac & Mary], b. June 5, 1775	15
Mary, m. Denney **HULL**, Apr. 2, 1786, by Rev. James Johnson. Witness Eunice Brush	81
Moses Hill, [s. Timothy & Sarah], b. Jan. 13, 1801	61
Moses Munson, [s. Timothy & Sarah], b. Sept. 3, 1797; d. Feb. 11, 180[ ]	61
Philip P., [s. Isaac & Mary], b. Feb. 13, 1766	15
Philip P., m. Elisabeth **RUSCO**, Feb. 28, 1788	69
Polly, [d. Hezekiah & Sarah], b. Oct. 24, 1760	68
Polly, [d. Philip P. & Elisabeth], b. Apr. 15, 1790	69
Polly, d. Dan[ie]l & Elizabeth, b. June 2, 1809	105
Rhoda, [d. Isaac & Mary], b. June 8, 1772	15
Robert, [s. Hezekiah & Sarah], b. July [ ], 1773	68
Robert, m. Prussia **FANTON**, Nov. 31, 1796. Witness Hezekiah Platt, Jr.	68
Sally, [d. Isaac & Mary], b. May 19, 1767	15
Samuel, m. Abigail **HALL**, Oct. 17, 1773, by Nathaniel Bartlet	15
Sanford, m. Laura **BARTRAM**, Dec. 7, 1826, by William Sanford, J. P.	123
Sarah, [d. Hezekiah & Sarah], b. May 26, 1758	68
Sarah, m. Samuel **GOLD**, Apr. 9, 1778	88
Sarah, [d. Timothy & Sarah], b. Nov.* 27, 1793 *(First written "Feb")	61
Timothy, [s. Hezekiah & Sarah], b. Oct. [ ], 1766	68
Timothy, m. Sarah **HILL**, Feb. 8, 1793. Witness Joannah Adams	61
Timothy, Jr., s. Timothy & Sarah, b. Dec. 28, 1805	103
William, [s. Hezekiah & Sarah], b. Mar. [ ], 1767; d. Sept. 29, 1797	68
W[illia]m, [s. Robert & Prussia], b. Nov. 11, 1797	68

PLOWS, Sarah A., m. Ephraim I. **BEERS**, b. of Redding, Mar. 12, 1837, by Rev. H. Humphreys — 141

PLUMB, Eliza, m. Augustus **GLOVER**, b. of Monroe, Jan. 13, 1850, by D. D. Frost, M. G. — 164

POLLY, George, of Danbury, m. Harriet Almira **WHITE**, of Redding,

REDDING VITAL RECORDS 113

	Page
POLLY, (cont.)	
Dec. 23, 1830, by Rev. Hawley Sanford	131
Hiram, m. Mary **CROFUT**, Jan. 27, 1831, by Rev. Lemuel B. Hull	133
POYLLON, James, m. Sally Ann **GRAY**, b. of Redding, Aug. 26, 1823, by Hawley Sanford, Elder	116
PRICE, Francis, m. Elsa **GLOVER**, b. of Redding (colored), Mar. 30, 1846, by Jonathan Bartlett, M. G.	158
RAMSEY, Abigail, of Redding, m. Nath[anie]l **TURREL**, of the Jerseys, Jan. 23, 1770, by Rev. Nathaniel Bartlet	19
RAYMOND, John, of Redding, m. Abigail **SHERWOOD**, Apr. 6, 1766	17
Justus, [s. John & Abigail], b. Mar. 8, 1770	17
Molley, d. [John & Abigail], b. June 20, 1768	17
READ, REED, REID, Aaron, [s. Zalmon & Huldah], b. Apr. 23, 1781	38
Aaron, m. Maria **HAWLEY**, b. of Redding, Oct. 2, 1806	103
Abigail, d. [John, Jr. & Zoa], b. July 22, 1795	71
Anna, [d. Hezekiah & Anna], b. Dec. 1, 1775	55
Anna, w. Hezekiah, d. Feb. 3, 1785	55
Anna, d. [William, Jr.], b. Apr. 22, 1787	43
Anna, d. W[illia]m, Jr. & Esther, b. Apr. 22, 1787	102
Anna, m. Lazarus **HULL**, Nov. 2, 1794. Witnesses Sturges Sanford & Sarah Sanford	42
Betsey, d. [John, Jr. & Zoa], b. Apr. 15, 1790	71
Betsey, of Redding, m. Geo[rge] H. **WINTON**, of Weston, Feb. 19, 1845, by D. C. Comstock	155
Betey, [d. Zalmon & Huldah], b. Feb. 24, 1792	38
Charles, s. [John, Jr. & Zoa], b. Apr. 8, 1784	71
Charles, Jr., [s. Will[ia]m, Jr.], b. Nov. 16, 1785	43
Charles Henry, s. Aaron & Maria, b. Nov. 12, 1811	105
Clarissa, [d. Zalmon & Huldah], b. Apr. 8, 1795	38
Clarissa, m. Jonathan R. **SANFORD**, May 16, 1847, at the Cong. Church, by Rev. Daniel D. Frost	159
Collins, s. [John, Jr. & Zoa], b. Jan. 7, 1799	71
Daniel, m. Anne **HILL**, Dec. 7, 1773, by Nathaniel Bartlet	41
Deborah, m. Thaddeus **BENEDICT**, b. of Redding, July 12, 1775, by Nathaniel Bartlet	40
Deborah, [d. Hezekiah & Abigail], b. May 23, 1790	55
Deborah, m. John R. **HILL**, Sept. 1, 1819	109
Ele, m. Mabel **LYON**, May 20, 1783. Witnesses Zalmon Read & Huldah Read	17
Elisabeth, [d. Hezekiah & Abigail], b. June 6, 1795	55
Esther, m. Daniel Collins **BARTLET**, Jan. 7, 1778, by Nathaniel Bartlet	47
Frederick, m. Eleanor **GRAY**, b. of Redding, this day [Nov. 20, 1839], by Jonathan Bartlett, M. G.	147
Harriot, d. Aaron & Maria, b. July 10, 1807	104
Henry, [s. Zalmon & Huldah], b. Nov. 11, 1787	38
Hezekiah, m. Anna **GORHAM**, May 14, 1775, by Nathaniel Bartlett	55
Hezekiah, [s. Hezekiah & Anna], b. Mar. 23, 1783	55
Hezekiah, m. Abigail **HULL**, Feb. 22, 1789, by Nataniel Bartlett	55

READ, REED, REID, (cont.)

	Page
Huldah, [d. Ele & Mabel], b. Aug. 16, 1784	17
Huldah, of Redding, m. Curtis B. **MARVIN**, of New York, May 27, 1805	103
John, Jr., m. Zoa **HILLARD**, June 15, 1783, certified by Daniel C. Bartlett	71
John, s. [John, Jr. & Zoa], b. Feb. 8, 1786	71
John M., Rev. of Jamaica, L. I., m. Caroline S. **FANTON**, of Redding, May 3, 1848, by Rev. J. D. Marshall	161
Mabel, d. [John, Jr. & Zoa], b. Mar. 6, 1797	71
Mary, m. William **SLOAN**, b. of Redding, Mar. 4, 1769, by Rev. Nathaniel Bartlet	43
Mary, d. Aaron & Maria, b. Aug. 15, 1809	105
Morris,* s. [John, Jr. & Zoa], b. Sept. 9, 1788 *(First written "Betsey" and crossed out)	71
Nancy, of Wilton, m. Charles **LEWIS**, of Redding, Mar. 28, [1833], by James A. Batterson	135
Nanny, d. [Daniel & Anne], b. May 5, 1774	41
Rachel, m. Philip **BURRET**, Mar. 1, 1774, by Nathaniel Bartlet	16
Salley, [d. Ele & Mabel], b. Apr. 9, 1786; d. Sept. 20, 1790	17
Sam[ue]l, [s. Zalmon & Huldah], b. June 9, 1797	38
Samuel, m. Laura **JACKSON**, b. of Redding, Nov. 25, 1821, by Rev. Daniel Crocker	111
Samuel Bradley, m. Camilla **LYON**, b. of Redding, Mar. 6, 1825, by Rev. Lemuel B. Hull	120
Sarah, [d. Hezekiah & Anna], b. Sept. 14, 1777	55
Sarah, m. Sturges **SANFORD**, Mar. 10, 1798. Witnesses Lazarus Hull & Wlilly Read	71
Sarah H., m. Charles C. **WINTON**, b. of Redding, May 17, 1848, by Rev. Joseph P. Taylor	161
Thaddeus B., [s. Hezekiah & Abigail], b. Sept. 27, 1792	55
Thaddeus B., m. Eleanor **LYON**, this day [Jan. 1, 1824], by Lemuel B. Hull	117
Ulilla, m. Jedediah **ROGERS**, b. of Redding, Nov. 20, 1805	102
Wilks, s. [John, Jr. & Zoa], b. May 18, 1792	71
William, m. Sarah **HAWLEY**, b. of Redding, Dec. 11, 1753, by Rev. Nathaniel Bartlet	17
William, d. Feb. 11, 1808, ae about 80	101
Wlilly, [s. Hezekiah & Anna], b. Jan. 22, 1780	55
Zalmon, Jr., m. Huldah **GRAY**, Nov. [ ], 1780	38

RICH, Charles B., of Batavia, Genesee Co., N. Y., m. Betsey M. **BARTRAM**, of Redding, Oct. 29, 1833, by Rev. Hawley Sanford   136

RIDER, Harriet E., of Redding, m. David **WOODWARD**, of Watertown, Dec. 21, 1842, by Rev. Daniel Smith   152

Mary C., m. Joseph B. **SHERWOOD**, Sept. [ ], 1850, by Daniel D. Frost, M. G.   166

Stephen R., m. Mary S. **MEEKER**, b. of Redding, Jan. 16, 1849, by Daniel D. Frost   163

	Page
ROBBINS, Ephraim, formerly of Killingley, m. Sarah COUCH, of Redding, June 20, 1769, by Rev. Nathaniel Bartlet	38
ROCKWELL, Alfred, m. Phebe PARSONS, b. of Redding, this day [Nov. 23, 1823], by Jonathan Bartlett, M. G.	117
Charles, m. Mary Ann JONES, Nov. 9, 1842, by David C. Comstock	152
Daniel B., of Ridgebury, m. Sarah CHAPMAN, of Redding, Dec. 12, 1848, by Daniel D. Frost	163
Deborah, of Ridgfield, m. Joel BYINGTON, of Redding, Oct. 1, 1795	102
Reuben, of Southeast, N. Y., m. Annis GRAY, of Redding, Nov. 19, 1839, by Jonathan Bartlett, M. G.	147
ROGERS, Abigail, [d. James], b. Apr. 16, 1776	38
Abigail, m. Daniel BETTS, Nov. 25, 1798. Certified by James Rogers	57
Abigail, m. Daniel BETTS, Nov. 25, 1798	100
Betsey, [d. James], b. Sept. 10, 1778	38
Chloe, m. Joseph HAWLEY, Aug. 3, 1785	63
James, had negro Henry, s. Phillis, b. May 15, 1807	104
Jeddediah, [s. James], b. Dec. 24, 1780	38
Jedediah, m. Ulilla READ, b. of Redding, Nov. 20, 1805	102
Sally, [d. James], b. Nov. 8, 1782	38
Sally, [d. James], d. Mar. 6, 1794	38
Uriah, [s. James], b. Nov. 7, 1773	38
Uriah, [s. James], d. Apr. 13, 1788	38
ROWEL, Harvy, m. Pamelia ANDREWS, Jan. 30, 1839, by Rev. John Crawford	144
ROWLAND, John Stilson, s. Hezekiah & Beulah, b. Mar. 17, 1807	105
Lois, d. Hezekiah & Beulah, b. May 25, 1808	105
Lois, of Redding, m. Hanford HULL, of Newtown, Nov. 24, 1831, by Rev. Lemuel B. Hull	134
Sarah, d. [Hezekiah], b. July 10, 1798	17
Wylys, s. [Hezekiah], b. June 3, 1795	17
ROWLEY, Mercy, m. John PICKIT, Jan. [ ], 1732	14
RUMSEY, Isaac, of Redding, m. Abigail ST. JOHN, of Ridgefield, May 25, 1761, by Rev. Nathaniel Bartlet	17
RUSCO, Elisabeth, m. Philip P. PLATT, Feb. 28, 1788	69
ST. JOHN, Abigail, of Ridgefield, m. Isaac RUMSEY, of Redding, May 25, 1761, by Rev. Nathaniel Bartlet	17
Bela, m. Mary A. HODGES, b. of Redding, Dec. 29, 1850, by James A. Batterson, Dea.	165
SALMON, Anna, d. Asahel & Anna], b. Nov. 21, 1788	51
Asahel, m. Anna WOOD, Sept. 5, 1786, by Rev. Timothy Langdon	51
Asahel Morse, [s. Asahel & Anna], b. May 7, 1795	51
Betsey, [d. Asahel & Anna], b. Feb. 25, 1791; d. Sept. 18, 1794	51
Lyman, [s. Asahel & Anna], b. Aug. 9, 1798	51
Philander, [s. Asahel & Anna], b. July 26, 1805	51
Philander, s. Col. Asahel & Anna, b. July 26, 1805	102
SANFORD, [see also STANFORD], Aaron, m. Lydia HAWLEY, Nov. 2, 1780, by Nathaniel Bartlett	37
Aaron, Jr., [s. Aaron & Lydia], b. July 8, 1786	37

	Page
SANFORD, (cont.)	
Abby, [d. Peter & Abigail], b. Feb. 24, 1797	37
Abiah, [d. Seth & Abiah], b. Dec. 23, 1780	22
Abiah, w. [Seth], d. Feb. 12, 1781	22
Abigail, [d. Oliver & Rachel], b. Dec. 11, 1773	49
Abigail, d. [Lemuel], b. Apr. 30, 1779; d. June 11, 1784	51
Abigail, d. [Ezekiel & Abigail], b. Nov. 10, 1779	70
Abigail, m. Ezra **SANFORD**, Dec. 25, 1781, by Nathaniel Bartlett	53
Abigail, d. [Lemuel], b. Apr. 18, 1784	51
Abigail, 1st w. [Ezra], d. July 25, 1788	53
Abigail, m. Benjamin **GREGORY**, on or about Nov. 14, 1797, by Nathaniel Bartlett	71
Abigail, m. Josiah **CANFIELD**, Oct. 27, 1799, by Rev. Nathaniel Bartlett	99
Abigail, m. Jonathan **BARTLETT**, Apr. 6, 1812	54
Ahaz, [child of Hezekiah & Betsey], b. Jan. 19, 1789	97
Almy, of Redding, m. James **SEELY**, of Weston, this day {May 28, 1824], by Jonathan Bartlett, M. G.	118
Amanda, d. Jonathan R. & Maria, b. Feb. 3, 1810	104
Amelia, [d. Peter & Abigail], b. Jan. 2, 1789	37
Amelia, m. Eben[eze]r Bradley **COLEY**, Oct. 16, 1810, [by] Daniel Crocker	99
Ann, [ ]	39
Ann Augusta, m. Samuel W. **COLEY**, Oct. 18, 1848, by Daniel D. Frost, M. G.	162
Ann Maria, m. Edmund **GODFREY**, Oct. 16, 1848, by Daniel D. Frost, M. G.	162
Anna, d. [Ezra & Abigail], b. Aug. 12, 1782	53
Anna, w. Eli, d. Aug. 27, 1806	101
Annis, m. Israel **CROFUT**, Sept. 19, 1784, certified by Elijah Couch	34
Asahel, [s. Eli & Sarah], b. Apr. 12, 1794	73
Beach, s. [James], b. Oct. 10, 1796	56
Bela, s. Ezra, b. Mar. 4, 1809	105
Benj[ami]n, s. [Ezekiel & Sarah], b. July 17, 1768	18
Betsey, [d. Aaron & Lydia], b. Oct. 5, 1781	37
Betsey, [d. Oliver & Rachel], b. Nov. 25, 1782	49
Betsy, [d. Joel & Huldah], b. Sept. 26, 1795	89
Betsey, 2nd, [d. Hezekiah & Betsey], b. Dec. 3, 1795	97
Betsey, of Redding, m. Nathan **JARVIS**, Jr., of Norwalk, Nov. 16, 1802, by Rev. Jonathan Bartlett, certified by David Sanford	99
Caroline, of Redding, m. Daniel **EDMUNDS**, of Ridgefield, Nov. 28, 1827, by W[illia]m C. Kniffin, M. G.	127
Charles, s. James & Sarah, b. Jan. 7, 1801	102
Charles, of Redding, m. Sarah **SANFORD**, of Weston, Sept. 22, 1844, by Rev. W. F. Collins	154
Clarissa, d. [Ezekiel & Abigail], b. Feb. 23, 1786	70
Clarry, [d. Peter & Abigail], b. Aug. 15, 1792	37
Cyrus, s. Ezra, b. Aug. 25, 1800	105

Page

SANFORD, (cont.)
Cyrus, m. Sarah **HUBBELL**, b. of Redding, Oct. 7, 1826, by W[illia]m C. Kniffin, M. G.	123
Daniel, m. Esther **HULL**, b. of Redding, Apr. 18, 1758, by Rev Nathaniel Bartlet	18
Daniel, [s. David], b. Oct. 3, 1773; d. Feb. 14, 1775	73
Daniel, [s. David], b. Jan. 1, 1776	73
Daniel, d. July 5, 1777	19
Daniel, m. Olive **MOREHOUSE**, Dec. 14, 1799, by Nathaniel Bartlett	77
Daniel, of Redding, m. Anna Maria **AMES**, of Craigvill, N. Y., Apr. 10, 1845, by Morris Hill	157
Daniel S., of Redding, m. Elizabeth **HANFORD**, of Darien, this day [Nov. 17, 1822], by Jonathan Bartlett, M. G.	115
Daniel Stebbens, [s. Eli & Anna], b. Dec. 11, 1795	72
David, [s. Oliver & Rachel], b. July 21, 1769	49
David, d. June 15, 1787	73
David, [s. Ephraim & Molly B.], b. Nov. 15, 1798	77
David, s. Daniel [& Olive], b. Jan. 25, 1799	77
David, m. Lucey **PLATT**, b. of Redding, Sept. 28, 1803	100
David, d. Oct. 4, 1806	101
David, m. Armaziah **BATES**, b. of Redding, Nov 30, 1820, by Rev. Daniel Crocker	109
David Hoyt, s. Jno, 2nd, b. Apr. 10, 1813	107
Deborah, d. Ephraim & Molly B., b. July 28, 1803	102
Deborah, m. Joel **BARLOW**, b. of Redding, Oct. 9, 1821, by Rev. Daniel Crocker	110
Ebenezer, m. Mary **DAUCHY**, Feb. 24, 1787	39
Ebenezer B., m. Sarah **COUCH**, b. of Redding, [Nov.] 25, [1838], by Rev. Jeremiah Miller	144
Eli, m. Anna **STEBBENS**, Nov. 16, 1786, by Rev. Mr. Goodrich. Witnesses Peter Sanford & Hannah Stebbens	72
Eli, m. Sarah **LYON**, Apr. 22, 1792, by Nathaniel Bartlett	73
Elias, m. Hannah **YOUNGS**, Aug. 31, 1786 [witness] Ebenezer Sanford	73
Emily, of Redding, m. Lonson **COLEY**, of Westport, Aug. 30, 1848, by David C. Comstock	162
Enoch, [s. Oliver & Rachel], b. Dec. 18, 1775; d. Feb. 17, 1800	49
Enoch Augustus, m. Eliza Ann **BARLOW**, b. of Redding, Oct. 10, 1821, by Rev. Daniel Crocker	110
Enoe, s. Nathan, b. July 19, 1775	18
Ephraim, [s. Oliver & Rachel], b. Aug. 19, 1771	49
Ephraim, m. Molly B. **BRADLEY**, Dec. 22, 1795, by Rev. James Johnson. Witness Gershom Bradley	77
Esther, d. Stephen, b. Aug. 5, 1775	39
Esther, [d. Eli & Anna], b. Aug. 15, 1787	72
Esther Ann, d. Cyrus & Sarah Ann, b. Oct. 20, 1827	125
Eunice, [d. Aaron & Lydia], b. Aug. 10, 1793	37
Ezekiel, m. Sarah **STURGES**, b.of Redding, Apr. 23, 1767	18
Ezekiel, m. Abigail **STARR**, on or about Nov. [ ], 1773, by	

SANFORD, (cont.)

	Page
Nathaniel Bartlett	70
Ezekiel, s. [Ezekiel & Abigail], b. Sept. 11, 1778; d. Nov. 22, 1778	70
Ezra, m. Abigail **SANFORD**, Dec. 25, 1781, by Nathaniel Bartlett	53
Ezra, [s. Ezra & Abigail], b. July 4, 1788	53
Ezra, s. [Ezra & Abigail], d. Oct. 31, 1794	53
Ezra, m. Charlotte **CRAWFORD**, Sept. 20, 1795, by Nathaniel Bartlett	53
Ezra, d. Dec. 17, 1825	106
Fanny Armeny, d. John, 2nd, b. Nov. 16, 1803	107
Felida, of Redding, m. Norman T. **MIDDLEBROOK**, of Weston, Dec. 15, 1822, by Rev. Ambrose S. Todd	115
Francis A., m. Lucy H. **KNAPP**, b.of Redding, Sept. 16, 1845, by Rev. W. F. Collins	156
George, [s. William & Lydia], b. Sept. 18, 1792	80
George A., m. Susan Caroline **BANKS**, b. of Redding, Mar. 15, 1846, by Morris Hill	158
Giles, [s. William & Lydia], b. June 11, 1798	80
Hannah, m. David **LYON**, b. of Redding, Sept. 19, 1756, by Rev. Nathaniel Bartlet	11
Hannah, m. David **JACKSON**, b. of Redding, Nov. 18, 1762, by Rev. Nathaniel Bartlet	9
Hannah, d. Nathan, b. Feb. 1, 1778	18
Hannah, [d. Aaron & Lydia], b. May 31, 1784	37
Harriet, m. Noah **PARSONS**, b. of Redding, Jan. 27, 1822, by Rev. Daniel Crocker	112
Harry, [s. Peter & Abigail], b. Nov. 14, 1790	37
Harry, s. [Joel & Huldah], b. Nov. 29, 1792	89
Harry, [s. Peter & Abigail], d. May 14, 1794	37
Hawley, [s. Aaron & Lydia], b. July 16, 1789	37
Hawley, m. Sally **KETCHUM**, Nov. 20, 1823, by Rev. Aaron Hunt	117
Hester, m. John L. **HILL**, May 26, 1837, by Rev. Edward J. Darken	141
Hezekiah, b. Jan. 6, 1762; m. Betsey [ ], June 10, 1783	97
Hezekiah, [s. Hezekiah & Betsey], b. Dec. 9, 1785	97
Hezekiah, d. Sept. 16, 1798	37
Hiram, [twin with Polly], [s. Elias & Hannah], b. Apr. 21, 1794	73
Hudson, s. [Joel & Huldah], b. Aug. 18, 1789	89
Huldah, m. Lemuel **LYON**, Oct. 25, 1787, by James Jonson, of Weston. Witnesses James Sanford & Elisabeth Morgain	96
Ira, s. [Ezra & Charlotte], b. Sept. 6, 1796	53
Isaac, s. [James], b. Apr. 23, 1786	56
Isaiah, s. [Joseph & Hepsabeth], b. Apr. 26, 1768	39
James, s. James & Sarah, b. June 10, 1799	102
James & w. Sarah, had s. [ ], b. Oct. 1, 1804	102
James & w. Sarah, had s. [ ], d. Jan. 26, 1805	101
James, Jr., of Redding, m. Eliza **FRENCH**, of Weston, Jan. 27, 1822, by Rev. Ambrose S. Todd	113
Jeremiah, d. June 28, 1777	19
Jeremiah, s. [Elias & Hannah], b. Dec. 15, 1787	73

REDDING VITAL RECORDS

	Page
SANFORD, (cont.)	
Jeremiah, s. Eli & Anna, b. Aug. 21, 1806	103
Jesse Lee, [s. Aaron & Lydia], b. July 27, 1791	37
Joel, m. Huldah **GRIFFIN**, May 1, 1788	89
John, s. Stephen, b. Oct. 4, 1772	39
John, m. Ruth **HOYT**, Dec. 30, 1797, by Nath[anie]l Bartlett	27
John, m. Betty **COUCH**, b. of Redding, Mar. 19, 1822, by Dea. Hawley Sanford	113
John Wheeler, m. Altha **FANTON**, Mar. 5, 1822, by Rev. Laban Clark	113
Jonathan R., m. Maria **DAVIES**, Oct. 17, 1808	104
Jonathan R., Jr., m. Clarissa **READ**, May 16, 1847, by Rev. Daniel D. Frost, at the Cong. Church	159
Jonathan Russel, s. [Lemuel], b. Feb. 11, 1782	51
Jonathan Russel, s. Jonathan R. & Maria, b. Oct. 25, 1819	107
Joseph, m. Hepsabeth **GRIFFIN**, b. of Redding, Nov. 2, 1762, by Rev. Nathaniel Bartlet	39
Joseph, s. Joseph, b. Nov. 15, 1776	39
Joseph, Jr., d. Nov. 25, 1776	39
Julia, d. Lemuel, Jr. & Sarah, b. Sept. 7, 1797	53
Lanson, s. [James], b. Jan. 20, 1789	56
Laura, [d. Eli & Sarah], b. Oct. 10, 1792	73
Lazarus, s. [James], b. Dec. 8, 1791	56
Lemuel, s. [Lemuel], b. July 18, 1769	51
Lemuel, Dea., d. Apr. 25, 1780, in the 81st y. of his age	93
Lemuel, s. [James], b. Nov. 20, 1781	56
Lem[ue]l, Jr., m. Sally **HERON**, b. of Redding, Jan. 1, 1795, by Nathaniel Bartlett	53
Lemuel, d. Mar. 12, 1803	101
Lemuel, s. Jonathan R. & Maria, b. Sept. 18, 1816	107
Lemuel, m. Abby M. **HILL**, b. of Redding, Jan. 13, 1847, by Daniel D. Frost, M. G.	159
Levi, [s. Oliver & Rachel], b. Oct. 6, 1777	49
Levi, m. Abigail A. **FITCH**, Sept. 13, 1801, by Rev. Jonathan Bartlett. Witnesses Oliver Sanford & Rachel Sanford	98
Levi, m. Abigail A. **FITCH**, Sept. 13, 1801, certified by David Sanford	99
Lewis, s. Ezra, b. Nov. 3, 1802	105
Lorrain, [child of Oliver & Rachel], b. Sept. 3, 1787	49
Lorrain, m. Gurdon **BARTRAM**, b. of Redding, Jan. 1, 1804	102
Lucrecia, d. [Lemuel], b. May 4, 1786	51
Lucey, m. David **STARR**, Jr., b. of Redding, Oct. 8, 1778, by Nathaniel Bartlet	50
Lucy, [d. Peter & Abigail], b. Dec. 3, 1794	37
Lucy, of Redding, m. Elnathan W. **SEELEY**, of Philadelphia, Oct. 2, 1825, by W[illia]m C. Kniffin	121
Lydia, [d. Hezekiah & Betsey], b. Mar. 19, 1784	97
Lydia, of Redding, m. Aaron Sanford **HYATT**, of Ridgefield, Apr. 20, 1831, by Rev. E. Washburn	132
Lydia, of Redding, m. Henry B. **MEAD** (Rev.), of West Point, N. Y.,	

SANFORD, (cont.)
June 3, 1852, by Rev. J. L. Gilder	168
Lydia Ann, d. [James], b. Aug. 1, 1783	56
Lydia Ann, m. Edward **JACKSON**, Aug. 14, 1826, by Marvin Richardson	122
Lydia Ann, m. Andrew **MEEKER**, b. of Redding, June 16, 1845, by Rev. W. F. Collins	155
Lyman, s. [Elias & Hannah], b. Apr. 21, 1794; d. same day	73
Maria, d. Eli & Anna, b. Oct. 31, 1800	100
Maria, d. Jonathan R. & Maria, d. Nov. 18, 1815, ae 9 wks.	106
Maria, d. Jonathan R. & Maria, b. Sept. 16, 1815	107
Maria, m. John **COUCH**, b. of Redding, May 19, 1822, by Rev. Daniel Crocker	114
Marietta, [d. Ephraim & Molly B.], b. Dec. 19, 1796	77
Marvin C., m. Eliza Ann **BURR**, b.of Redding, Nov. 3, 1841, by Rev. Warner Hoyt, of Ridgefield	153
Mary, m. Timothy **SANFORD**, b. of Redding, Feb. 14, 1762, by Rev. Nathaniel Bartlet	39
Mary, [d. Oliver & Rachel], b. June 24, 1768; d. Aug. 22, 1768	49
Mary, d. [Lemuel], b. May 18, 1776	51
Mary, [d. Oliver & Rachel], b. Aug. 25, 1780; d. Aug. 9, 1800	49
Mary, m. Thomas **PECK**, Mar. 27, 1796, by Rev. Jonathan Bartlett	54
Mary, m. Tho[ma]s **COUCH**, Jr., Sept. 25, 1797, by Jonathan Bartlett	79
Mary, d. Lemuel & Sarah, b. Apr. 21, 1801	53
Mary, d. Ephraim & Molly b., b. May 27, 1805	102
Mary, of Redding, m. Dr. Nehemiah **PERRY**, of Ridgefield, Oct. 10, 1821, by Rev. Daniel Crocker	111
Mary, m. Samuel J. **COLLINS**, b. of Redding, Oct. 22, 1827, by W[illia]m C. Kniffin, M. G.	126
Mary, wid. Lemuel, d. June 23, 1829, ae 84	106
Molley, [d. Joseph & Hepsabeth], b. Aug. 8, 1770; d. July 12, 1771	39
Molly, [d. David], b. June 19, 1771	73
Molly, d. Joseph, b. Mar. 20, 1774	39
Molly, d. [Ezekiel & Abigail], b. Aug. 16, 1774	70
Molly, of Newtown, m. W[illia]m **BEARDSLEY**, of Redding, July 28, 1798, by [ ]. Witnesses Jesse Beardsley, Jr. & Aaron Beardsley	31
Morris, s. Ezra, b. Mar. 17, 1805	105
Myra, d. Ezra, b. Dec. 9, 1807	105
Nancy, of Redding, m. Aaron **GAUL**, of Danbury (colored), Jan. 1, 1822, by Dea. Hawley Sanford	112
Nancy, of Redding, m. Seth **GILBERT**, of Newtown, this day [Mar. 20, 1825], by Rev. Lemuel B. Hull	120
Nathan, s. Nathan, b. Jan. 30, 1783	18
Oliver, of Redding, m. Rachel **COLEY**, of Northfield, Apr. 9, 1767, by Rev. Samuel Sherwood. Witness David Lyon	49
Oliver, d. Mar. 10, 1814, ae 73	106
Oliver Coley, [s. Oliver & Rachel], b. Apr. 29, 1785	49

	Page
SANFORD, (cont.)	
Patty, [d. Ezra & Charlotte], b. Oct. 5, 1797	53
Patty, d. Ezra, d. Aug. 25, 1825	106
Peter, m. Abigail **KEELER**, Jan. 1, [1786*], by Rev. Mr. Camp. Witnesses Timothy Keeler, Jr. & Esther Keeler *(1786 is handwritten in brackets)	37
Philo, s. [Elias & Hannah], b. June 10, 1797	73
Polly, [twin with Hiram, d. Elias & Hannah], b. Apr. 21, 1794	73
Polly, [d. Eli & Sarah], b. Mar. 8, 1797	73
Rebeckah, m. Aaron **BARLOW**, Dec. 27, 1772, by Nathaniel Bartlet	22
Rebeckah, m. Anson **BARLOW**, b. of Redding, Dec. 17, 1772, by Rev. Nathaniel Bartlet [this entry crossed out]	25
Rebecca, w. [Seth], d. Aug. 23, 1775	22
Rebeckah, d. [Ezekiel & Abigail], b. Nov. 10, 1776	70
Rebeckah, w. Dea. Lemuel, d. Mar. 26, 1779, in the 76th y. of her age	93
Rebecca, d. [Elias & Hannah], b. Aug. 10, 1789	73
Rebeckah, m. Hezekiah **HAWLEY**, Apr. 4, 1796, by Jonathan Bartlett	8
Rodah, m. Elijah **BURR**, b. of Redding, Apr. 2, 1767, by Rev. Nathaniel Bartlet	46
Rhoda, d. [Lemuel], b. Mar. 4, 1773	51
Rhoda, m. Jonathan **BARTLET**, Aug. 16, 1795	54
Ruth, d. Nathan, b. Sept. 1, 1773	18
Sabre, [child of Nathan], b. Nov. 30, 1780	18
Sally, [d. Hezekiah & Betsey], b. Oct. 13, 1792	97
Sally, d. [James], b. Feb. 14, 1794	56
Sally M., of Redding, m. Edwin F. **WHEELER**, of Phelps, N. Y., [June] 24, [1838], by Rev. Jeremiah Miller	144
Sam[ue]l, b. Jan. 27, 1771	22
Sam[ue]ll, [s. Seth & Rebecca], b. Jan. 27, 1771	22
Samuel Ward Benedict, s. [John & Ruth], b. Aug. 22, 1798	27
Sarah, d. [Ezekiel & Sarah], b. Dec. 9, 1769; d. Aug. 1, 1791	18
Sarah, 1st w. [Ezekiel], d. Mar. 31, 1771	18
Sarah, [d. David], b. Feb. 18, 1778	73
Sarah, wid. of Capt. Sam[ue]l, d. Nov. 31, 1803	101
Sarah, of Weston, m. Charles **SANFORD**, of Redding, Sept. 22, 1844, by Rev. W. F. Collins	154
Sarah Maria, m. Benjamin S. **BOUGHTON**, b. of Redding, Jan. 19, 1850, by D. D. Frost, M. G.	164
Sena, d. [Joel & Huldah], b. Mar. 15, 1798	89
Seth, m. Rebekah **BURR**, b. of Redding, Apr. 25, 1759, by Rev. Nathaniel Bartlet	18
Seth, Jr., [s. Seth & Rebecca], b. July 7, 1773	22
[Seth], m. Abiah [ ], Apr. 25, 1778	22
Seth, m. Abigail [ ], Aug. 3, 1781	22
Seth, Jr., m. Sarah **COUCH**, 2nd, b. of Redding, Oct. 8, 1803	100
Seth, Jr., & w. Sarah, 2nd, had child b. July 21, 1804	100
Solomon Noble, s. [Joseph & Hepsabeth], b. Feb. 16, 1764	39
Stephen, m. Abigail **WARD**, b. of Redding, Nov. 19, 1768, by	

	Page
SANFORD, (cont.)	
Rev. Nathaniel Bartlet	39
Stephen, [s. Ezra & Abigail], b. Mar. 30, 1785	53
Sturges, m. Sarah **READ**, Mar. 10, 1798. Witnesses Lazarus Hull & Wlilly Read	71
Tabby, d. [Joseph & Hepsabeth], b. May 1, 1772	39
Thomas, s. Jonathan R. & Maria, b. Sept. 27, 1823	117
Timothy, m. Mary **SANFORD**, b. of Redding, Feb. 14, 1762, by Rev. Nathaniel Bartlet	39
Walter, [s. Aaron & Lydia], b. Feb. 18, 1796	37
Walter, m. Maria H. **BOOTH**, Dec. 6, 1821, by Rev. Laban Clark	111
Warren, [s. Ezra & Charlotte], b. July 6, 1799	53
William, m. Lydia **HULL**, Jan. 8, 1792, by Nathaniel Bartlett	80
William, [s. William & Lydia], b. June 19, 1794	80
Zachariah, s. [Joseph & Hepsabeth], b. Nov. 3, 1765	39
Zalmon, [s. David], b. Dec. 25, 1780	73
Zalmon, m. Caroline **PECK**, b. of Redding, Oct. 1, 1822, by Rev. Ambrose S. Todd	115
Zalmon B., s. Hezekiah, d. Jan. 31, 1803	101
Zalmon Booth, [s. Hezekiah & Betsey], b. Dec. 6, 1798	97
SAUNDERS, Zebulon Jennings, s. Aaron & Polly, b. Aug. 5, 1803	100
SCHOONMAKER, Amos S., of Danbury, m. Sarah Ann **HODGES**, of Redding, Aug. 3, 1845, by James A. Batterson, Dea.	156
SEARS, Aaron, of Monroe, m. Polly **HILL**, of Redding, Mar. 16, 1831, by Rev. Lemuel B. Hull	133
SEELEY, SEELY, Elnathan W., of Philadelphia, m. Lucy **SANFORD**, of Redding, Oct. 2, 1825, by W[illia]m C. Kniffin	121
James, of Weston, m. Almy **SANFORD**, of Redding, this day [May 28, 1824], by Jonathan Bartlett, M. G.	118
Nehemiah, Jr., of Redding, m. Sarah **DIBBLE**, of Ridgfield, Sept. 26, 1769, by Rev. Nath[anie]l Bartlet	38
SELLECK, SILLECK, SILLICK, SELLICK, Ann Eliza, of Redding, m. George **EVERTS**, of New Haven, Sept. 26, 1847, by Rev. J. D. Marshall	160
George, of Norwalk, m. Harriet **BANKS**, of Redding, Nov. 28, 1825, by Marvin Richardson	121
Warren W., of Bridgeport, m. Eliza **FOSTER**, of Redding, this day, [Apr. 22, 1839], by Jonathan Bartlett, M. G.	145
W[illia]m B., of Ridgefield, m. Martha A. **MEEKER**, of Redding, Jan. 17, 1843, by Rev. Daniel Smith	152
SHEPARD, SHEPHERD, Lewis B., of Danbury, m. Sarah Ann **BARLOW**, of Sharon, May 4, 1835, by Jared Olmstead, J. P.	138
Sally, of Redding, m. Henry B. **THORP**, of Edwardsville, Ill., this day [Sept. 12, 1824], by Rev. Lemuel B. Hull	119
SHERMAN, Laura Juliaette, of Redding, m. Jonas **BIGGS**, of Weston, Jan. 27, 1851, by Aaron Sanford, J. P.	166
Nelson, of Trumbull, m. Almira **MOREHOUSE**, of Redding, this day [Nov. 15, 1826], by Rev. Lemuel B. Hull	123

	Page
SHERWOOD, Aaron, m. Manlius, N. Y., m. Jane Ann **COUCH**, of Redding, Feb. 29, 1848, by Rev. J. D. Marshall	160-1
Abigail, m. John **RAYMOND** of Redding, Apr. 6, 1766	17
Abigail, [d. John], b. Mar. 24, 1795	94
Albert, of Ridgefield, m. Eleanor **TURKINGTON**, of Redding, Feb. 22, 1842, by Rev. Daniel Smith	151
Alva,of Fairfield, m. Eliza Ann **MARCHANT**, of Redding, this day [Oct. 23, 1835], by Jonathan Bartlett, M. G.	139
Angenett, m. Sherman **BENNETT**, b. of Redding, Jan. 28, 1837, by James A. Batterson, Dea.	141
Anna, m. Timothy **WAKEMAN**, Mar. 28, 1773	82
Betsey, d. Daniel & Ruth, b. Feb. 11, 1797	104
Betsey, d. Daniel, d. May 31, 1798	101
Betsey, 2nd, d. Daniel & Ruth, b. Nov. 12, 1799	104
Daniel, [s. John], b. July 9, 1771	94
Daniel, of Redding, m. Ruth **CHAMBERS**, of Ridgfield, Aug. 30, 1795	103
Daniel, of Redding, m. Sarah Amanda **WALLACE**, of Newtown, June 21, 1840, by Rev. Charles Jarvis Todd	148
Daniel B., of Weston, m. Electa M. **CHAPMAN**, of Redding, Nov. 27, 1827, by W[illia]m C. Kniffin	126
David, m. Angeline **LOCKWOOD**, b. of Redding, Dec. 2, 1850, by Rev. J. L. Gilder	166
Delia, m. Eli **MALLERY**, b. of Redding, this day [Apr. 20, 1825], by Jonathan Bartlett, M. G.	120
Edwards, [s. John], b. Mar. 2, 1791	94
Electa M., m. Edmund B. **LEE**, b. of Redding, Apr. 11, 1848, by Rev. J. D. Marshall	161
Eli, m. Sarah **HULL**, Oct. 25, 1796, by Jonathan Bartlett	87
Eli, s. Eli & Sarah, b. Nov. 14, 1802	100
Esther, m. Barnabard **KEEKER***, Apr. [ ], 1797, by Nathaniel Bartlet *(**KEELER**?)	19
Eunice, [d. John], b. May 30, 1781	94
Eunice, of Redding, m. Wilkey W. **BATTERSON**, of Wilton, July 10, 1831, by James A. Batterson, Dea.	132
Fanney, [d. Jesse & Sarah], b. Dec. 7, 1798	72
Fanny, m. Aaron **GOULD**, July 7, 1820, by Rev. Laban Clark, Int. Pub.	108
Flora, m. Jeremiah **BEERS**, Dec. 12, 1821, by Rev. Laban Clark	111
Hannah, [d. John], b. Feb. 4, 1789	94
Ira, s. Dan[ie]l & Ruth, b. Nov. 5, 1805	104
James Hervey, s. Daniel & Ruth, b. Dec. 6, 1801	104
Jesse, m. Sarah **BRADLEY**, Sept. 20, 1795. Witnesses Joseph Banks & w. Sarah Banks	72
John, [s. John], b. Apr. 24, 1775	94
John, Jr., b. Apr. 24, [ ]; m. Abigail [ ], Feb. 1, 1795	78
Joseph B., m. Mary C. **RIDER**, Sept. [ ] , 1850, by Daniel D. Frost, M. G.	166
Justis, [s. John], b. Mar. 8, 1787	94
Laura, m. Henry **GLOVER**, b. of Redding, Dec. 26, 1841, by	

124 BARBOUR COLLECTION

	Page
SHERWOOD, (cont.)	
Rev. Daniel Smith	151
Lewis, of Weston, m. Eunice **BENEDICT**, of Redding, Apr. 2, 1834, by Rev. W[illia]m L. Strong	137
Maria, d. John, Jr. & Abigail, b. Jan. 16, 1809	104
Mary J., m. Benjamin **MEEKER**, Jr., July 25, 1852, by Rev. D. D. Frost	168
Merinda, of Redding, m. Nelson **SMITH**, of Norwalk, [Oct.] 12, [1823], by Rev. Daniel Crocker	116
Molly, [d. John], b. Apr. 20, 1773	94
Moses, m. Elizabeth T. **DIBBLE**, b. of Redding, Nov. 7, 1850, by Rev. J. L. Gilder	166
Noah J., m. Sarah **WILSON**, b. of Redding, Mar. 17, 1850, by Rev. Jacob Shaw	165
Orill, [child of Eli & Sarah], b. May 22, 1797	87
Patty, [d. Eli & Sarah], b. Jan. 12, 1799	87
Polly, m. George **BATES**, [18]	125
Polly, d. Daniel & Ruth, b. Oct. 17, 1803	104
Polly Buck, d. John & Abigail, b. Jan. 14, 1798	78
Rebeckah, [d. John], b. Mar. 15, 1783	94
Sally M., of Redding, m. Sherman **ICLLIFF***, of Ridgefield, Jan. 30, 1842, by James A. Batterson, Dea. *(Probably "**JELLEFF**")	150
Samuel, [s. John], b. Mar. 24, 1779	94
Sam[ue]l S., of New York, m. Catharine **MEEKER**, of Redding, Apr. 26, 1828, by W[illia]m C. Kniffin, M. G.	127
Sarah, [d. John], b. Mar. 21, 1777	94
Sarah, eldest d. [Jesse & Sarah], b. Apr. 21, 1796	72
William, [s. John], b. Apr. 10, 1785	94
William, m. Laura **PLATT**, b. of Redding, this day [Jan. 1, 1837], by Jonathan Bartlett, M. G.	140
SHUTE, George, m. Angeline **JENNINGS**, b. of Redding, Sept. 5, 1830, by Rev. Oliver E. Amernon	131
SILLIMAN, Elisabeth, m. Isaac **BEACH**, Dec. 7, 1794, by Rev. Stephen W. Stebbens, of Stratford	79
SKELLY, Martha E., of Redding, m. James M. **TURNEY**, of Weston, Mar. 12, 1845, by D. C. Comstock	155
SKILLENGER, Elizabeth, of Redding, m. Aaron **MALLERY**, of Warren, Feb. 14, 1827, by W[illia]m C. Kniffin, M. G.	124
SLOAN, William, m. Mary **READ**, b. of Redding, Mar. 4, 1769, by Rev. Nathaniel Bartlet	43
SMITH, Abel, s. [Samuel & Esther], b. Nov. 24, 1793	95
Brace, see Orace or Horace **SMITH**	120
Burr, of Norwalk, m. Jane **TILLOW**, of Redding, this day [Dec. 31, 1833], by Jonathan Bartlett, M. G.	136
Cha[rle]s, b. June 25, 1790	41
Charles D., of Manlius, N. Y., m. Sarah **MARVIN**, of Redding, this day [Sept. 19, 1831], by Jonathan Bartlett, M. G.	132
Erastus, [s. Joel], b. Feb. 19, 1781	35

	Page
SMITH, (cont.)	
Horace, see Orace or Brace **SMITH**	120
Jesse, s. [Samuel & Esther], b. Feb. 8, 1785	95
Lydia, w. Sam[ue]l, d. Feb. 8, 1776	41
Lydia, b. July 28, 1792; d. Sept. 20, 1793	41
Mabel, [d. Joel], b. Nov. 13, 1787	35
Mary, wid. S. Sam[ue]l, d. Feb. 1, 1814	101
Nehemiah, [s. Joel], b. Sept. 13, 1786; d. Sept. 20, 1786	35
Nehemiah Collins, [s. Joel], b. Sept. 19, 1779; d. Oct. 17, 1789	35
Nelson, of Norwalk, m. Merinda **SHERWOOD**, of Redding, [Oct.] 12, [1823], by Rev. Daniel Crocker	116
Orace*, m. Ruth **OSBORN**, [Apr.] 27, [1825], by Rev. Aaron Hunt *(Brace? Horace?)	120
Phebe, m. Joel **GRAY**, Mar. 18, 1784, by Nathaniel Bartlett	20
Samuel, had negro Pegg, b. Aug. 6, 1773	41
Samuel, s.[Samuel & Esther], b. Sept. 5, 1781	95
Samuel, d. Feb. 1, 1798	41
Sam[ue]l, m. Esther **PERRY**, Aug. 16, 1799. Witness Hezekiah Ogden	95
S. Sam[ue]l, d. Aug. 7, 1809	101
Seth Samuel, s. Samuel & Lydia, b. Sept. 10, 1760	41
S. S. [Seth Samuel], m. Mary **STURGES**, May 25, 1780	41
Sophia, of Redding, m. Abel **CROFUT**, of Danbury, Sept. 23, 1827, by Henry Stead	126
Tho[ma]s G., b. Jan. 1, 1795	41
Tho[ma]s G., d. Jan. 11, 1812	101
Walter, s. [Samuel & Esther], b. May 25, 1783; d. July 6, 1786	95
Walter, s. [Samuel & Esther], b. Aug. 5, 1788	95
William, s. [Samuel & Esther], b. Feb. 20, 1780	95
SNIFFINS, Amelia Louisa, m. Lorenzo Smith **WEED**, Oct. 17, 1841, by Rev. Charles J. Todd	150
SQUIRES, SQUIRE, Aaron, m. Sally H. **BARTRAM**, b. of Redding, Apr. 14, 1835, by Rev. Hawley Sanford	138
Anna, d. Dan[ie]l & Sarah, b. July 13, 1813	125
Betsey, m. Hezekiah **BEERS**, b. of Weston, Jan. 3, 1841, by Rev. Charles J. Todd	149
Daniel, s. Daniel & Sarah, b. Oct. 13, 1807	125
Dan[ie]l, 2nd, s. Daniel & Sarah, b. Aug. 8, 1811	125
Ebenezer, s. Dan[ie]l & Sarah, b. Oct. 7, 1809	125
Eliza, d. Daniel & Sarah, b. Jan. 29, 1806	125
Harriet, m. John **STARR**, Apr. 21, 1844, by David C. Comstock	153
Sarah, of Newtown, m. Joseph **MANCE**, of Newtown, July 19, 1835, by Rev. H. Humphreys	138
Seth, m. Eliza Ann **JOHNSON**, Sept. 9, 1839, by Rev. P. R. Brown	146
Tama, m. David **COLEY**, Dec. 21, 1788	1
STANFORD, [see also **SANFORD**], Ruth, m. Preserved **TAYLOR**, Sept. 10, 1764, by Moses Dickinson	36
STANLEY, Laurany, of Danbury, m. Comfort **STARR**, of Redding Feb. 25, 1807	103

	Page
STARR, Aaron, s. [David, Jr.], b. Mar. 22, 1788; d. Nov. 10, 1788	50
Aaron, s. [David, Jr.], b. Sept. 23, 1792	50
Abigail, m. Ezekiel **SANFORD**, on or about Nov. [ ], 1773, by Nathaniel Bartlett	70
Abigail, w. David, Sr., d. Feb. 7, 1806	101
Ame, d. [David, Jr.], b. July 2, 1785	50
Annis, [d. Edward], b. Mar. 25, 1785	70
Billy, [s. Thomas & Elisabeth], b. Mar. 22, 1797	93
Billy, s. Thomas & Elizabeth, d. June 1, 1804	101
Charles, s. Eli & Mary B., b. Mar. 31, 1801, at Trumbull	100
Clary, [d. Edward], b. Nov. 7, 1787	70
Comfort, s. [David, Jr.], b. Mar. 27, 1783	50
Comfort, of Redding, m. Laurany **STANLEY**, of Danbury, Feb. 25, 1807	103
D. Alonzo, s. David, 3rd & Eunice, b. Aug. 22, 1804	103
David, Jr., m. Lucey **SANFORD**, b. of Redding, Oct. 8, 1778, by Nathaniel Bartlet	50
David, s. [David, Jr.], b. Mar. 12, 1781	50
David, 3rd, m. Eunice **LEE**, b. of Redding, Nov. 24, 1802	100
David, d. Feb. 11, 1810, ae 85 y.	101
Edward, s. Edward, b. Mar. 25, 1804	70
Edward, s. Edward & Abigail, b. Mar. 25, 1804	100
Edward, m. Abigail **COUCH**, b. of Redding, Dec. 9, 1824, by Rev. Lemuel B. Hull	119
Eli, s. [David, Jr.], b. May 18, 1779	50
Eli, of Redding, m. Mary B. **LEE**, of Ridgefield, Mar. 8, 1800	100
Elnathan Sanford, [s. David, Jr.], b. Apr. 1, 1795	50
Fidelia, d. [Edward], b. Jan. 28, 1800	70
Fidelia, m. Charles **MOREHOUSE**, b. of Redding, Mar. 21, 1824, by Rev. Lemuel B. Hull	118
George, m. Anna **DOWNS**, b. of Redding, June 8, 1822, by Hawley Sanford, Elder	114
George, m. Polly **WILCOX**, b. of Redding, Nov. 28, 1844, by Rev W. F. Collins	154
John, m. Harriet **SQUIRE**, Apr. 21, 1844, by David C. Comstock	153
John Beach, [s. Edward], b Apr. 25, 1795	70
Julius Judson, s. Eli & Mary B., b. May 28, 1803	100
Lucy, d. Eli & Mary, b. Jan. 22, 1806	103
Maria Angeline, d. David, b. July 3, 1808	105
Mary, d. [Thomas & Elisabeth], b. July 30, 1793	93
Nabbe, d. [David, Jr.], b. Apr. 28, 1790	50
Rane, [child of Edward], b. July 16, 1791	70
Rebecca, m. Billy **COMSTOCK**, b. of Danbury, Mar. 26, 1797, by Rev. John Ely	59
Rune, m. Aaron **MOREHOUSE**, Aug. 19, 1787	25
Samuel, s. Edward, b. Aug. 1, 1807	70
Samuel, s. Edward & Abigail, b. Aug. 1, 1807	104
Thomas, m. Elisabeth **HILL**, Dec. 15, 1789, by Rev. Mr. Hull.	

STARR, (cont.)

	Page
Witnesses Ezekiel Hill & Rebekah Guyer	93
W[illia]m Oscar, s. David, 3rd & Eunice, b. Oct. 2, 1805	103

STEBBENS, Abigail, m. Thomas N. **COUCH**, Dec. 13, 1787. Witnesses
  Simon Couch & Anna Couch 58
Anna, m. Eli **SANFORD**, Nov. 16, 1786, by Rev. Mr. Goodrich.
  Witnesses Peter Sanford & Hannah Stebbens 72
STERLING, David L., of Ridgefield, m. Cornelia **TILLOW**, of Redding, this
  day {Aug. 30, 1829], by Jonathan Bartlett, M. G. 129
STEVENS, Frederick, of Danbury, m. Rachel **FAIRCHILD**, of Redding, Mar.
  9, 1829, by Rev. Henry Stead 128
  Lorry, [child of Zachariah & Abigail], b. Mar. 7, 1796 77
  Mariah, [d. Zachariah & Abigail], b. July 29, 1798 77
  Samuel, of Darien, m. Mabel **BENEDICT**, of Redding, [Dec.] 11,
    [1831], by Jonathan Bartlett, M. G. 133
  Zachariah, of Ridgbury, m. Abigail **COLEY**, of Redding, Oct. 22, 1794,
    certified by Nathaniel Bartlett 77
STILSON, Lucy, of Newtown, m. Amos **MUNROW**, June 25, 1795.
  Witnesses Elijah Judd & Benj[ami]n Judd 84
STONE, Achsa, of Redding, m. Henry **BARBER**, of Danbury, Nov. 3, 1844,
  by Norris Hill 155
  Nancy, of Redding, m. Hosea O. **PEARCE**, of Danbury, Nov. 20, 1842,
    by Morris Hill 151
STOW, STOWE, Abigail, d. Robert & Anne, b. Apr. 11, 1776 40
  Abigail, [d. Robert & Anna], b. Apr. 11, 1776 82
  Abigail, m. Israel **ADAMS**, Mar. 28, 1796. Witness Anna Barnum 52
  Abraham, [s. Robert & Anna], b. Mar. 14, 1792 82
  Almira, [d. Daniel & Lucy], b. Jan. 28, 1804 76
  Almira, of Redding, m. Ira **WILLIAMS**, of Danbury, Dec. 19, 1824, at
    the house of Daniel Stow, by John Reynolds, Elder 119
  Daniel, b. July 4, 1779; m. Lucy **HOYT***, [   ]   *(First
    written "**BANKS**" and erased) 76
  Daniel, [s. Robert & Anna], b. July 4, 1779 82
  Daniel, d. Oct. 21, 1844, ae 65 y. 77
  Denny, [s. Robert & Anna], b. Aug. [   ], 1785; d. Nov. 23, 1785 82
  Emeline, m. Elias **GLOVER**, Nov. 12, 1837, by John Crawford 143
  Harriet, [d. Daniel & Lucy], b. Dec. 8, 1806 76
  Harriet, of Redding, m. Ebenezer Silliman **JUDD**, of Danbury, Jan. 3,
    1826, by Marvin Richardson 122
  Huldah, [d. Robert & Anna], b. Feb. 16, 1787 82
  Lucy, [d. Daniel & Lucy], b. Oct. 23, 1810 76
  Lucy, of Redding, m. Horace H. **COUCH**, of Danbury, Feb. 2, 1831, by
    Rev. E. Washburn 132
  Lucy, d. Sept. 25, 1844, ae 34 y. 77
  Lucy, w. Daniel, d. Oct. 10, 1859, ae 79 y. 77
  Mary, [d. Daniel & Lucy], b. Sept. 1, 1817 76
  Mary, m. Agur T. **TURNEY**, b. of Redding, Nov. 25, 1835, by Rev. H.
    Humphreys 140

STOW, STOWE, (cont.)

	Page
Myra, of Redding, m. Oliver **MILLER**, of Pound Ridge, N. Y., Dec. 3, 1845, by Morris Hill	157
Polly, [d. Robert & Anna], b. Sept. 20, 1794	82
Polly, [d. Daniel & Lucy], b. Dec. 6, 1818	76
Polly, d. Daniel & Lucy, d. July 1, 1822, ae 3 y. 8 m.	77
Robert, m. Anna **DARROW**, Jan. 26, 1774, certified by Samuel Gold	82
Robert, m. Anne **DARROW**, b. of Redding, Jan. 26, 1775, by Nathaniel Bartlet	40
Robert d. Nov. 5, 1795	82
Robert Hoyt, [s. Daniel & Lucy], b. Oct. 20, 1802	76
Sally, m. Jesse **BANKS**, 3rd, Jan. 3, 1822, by Rev. Laban Clark	112
Sarah, [d. Robert & Anna], b. Oct. 4, 1777; d. June 8, 1777	82
Sarah, [d. Robert & Anna], b. Aug. 11, 1781	82
Sarah, d. July 13, 1804. Entry from Daniel Stowe's Bible	77
Sarah, [d. Daniel & Lucy], b. Mar. 4, 1805	76
Sumner, [s. Robert & Anna], b. Sept. 17, 1783	82
Sumner, 1st, d. Apr. 3, 1808. Entry from Daniel Stowe's Bible	77
Sumner, [s. Daniel & Lucy], b. Mar. 16, 1812	76
STRATTON, Miles, m. Sally **BARLOW**, of Redding, Jan. 28, 1849, by Daniel D. Frost	163
STREET, Hannah, of Ridgbury, m. Joseph **MEEKER**, of Redding, May 4, 1774, in Ridgfield, by Samuel Camp, V. D. M.	33
STUART, Elizabeth, m. Israel **CROFOOT**, June 9, 1803	100
STURGES, Abigail, d. [Benjamin & Rachel], b. Nov. 6, 1754	59
Benj[ami]n, b. Dec. 10, 1728; m. Rachel [ ], Dec. 26, 1747, by Rev. Beach	59
Ebenezer, of Stamford, m. wid. Eunice **MEEKER**, of Redding, July 31, 1803	100
Ebenezer, d. Feb. 25, 1805	101
Electa, m. Summers **BANKS**, b. of Redding, Oct. 10, 1825, by Rev. H. Humphreys	121
Fanny, of Redding, m. William T. **WELDMAN**, of Danbury, this day, [Sept. 22, 1830], by Rev. Lemuel B. Hull	131
Jeremiah, of Redding, m. Anna **FERRY**, of Danbury, Oct. 3, 1837, by Rev. Hawley Sanford	142
Mary, m. S. S. [Seth Samuel] **SMITH**, May 25, 1780	41
Rachel, of Greensfarms, m. Eben[eze]r **COLEY**, of Redding, Nov. 12, 1771	24
Samuel B., of Westport, m. Fanny E. **BURR**, of Redding, Oct. 15, 1845, by Rev. W[illia]m F. Collins	157
Sarah, d. [Benjamin & Rachel], b. Mar. 20, 1749	59
Sarah, m. Ezekiel **SANFORD**, b. of Redding, Apr. 23, 1767	18
SUMMERS, Any*, m. Daniel **LYON**, Jr., Mar. 26, 1789, certified by Daniel Lyon *(Amy?)	65
Martha, m. Jesse **BANKS**, Jr., Dec. 14, 1787, by Hyatt Banks	4
Sarah, m. Hyatt **BANKS**, Dec. 1, 1785	5
TAYLOR, Abigail, [d. Abraham & Sarah], b. June 15, 1787	85

	Page
TAYLOR, (cont.)	
Abraham, [s. Preserved & Ruth], b. Jan. 2, 1765	36
Abraham, m. Sarah **CABLE**, Dec. 1, 1784, by Jno Benedict. Witnesses Preserved Taylor & Justus Whitlock	85
Adah, [d. Preserved & Ruth], b. May 6, 1781	36
Anne, [d. Abraham & Sarah], b. May 24, 1794	85
Assena, m. James **GRAY**, Jr., b. of Redding, Mar. 27, 1760, by Rev. Nath]anie]l Bartlet* *(Crossed out)	7
Assena, m. James **GRAY**, Jr., b. of Redding, Mar. 27, 1760, by Rev. Nathaniel Bartlet	28
David, [s. Abraham & Sarah], b. Aug. 28, 1785	85
Davis, m. Jane **FRISBY**, Dec. 9, 1824, by Nathan Burton	119
Dorcas, [d. Abraham & Sarah], b. Dec. 9, 1789	85
Eliphalet, m. Urania **DARLING**, Mar. 15, 1826, by M. Richardson	122
Esther, [d. Abraham & Sarah], b. Mar. 10, 1797	85
Eunice, [d. Preserved & Ruth], b. July 22, 1773	36
Hannah, [d. Preserved & Ruth], b. Dec. 21, 1769	36
Hannah, [d. Preserved & Ruth], d. Sept. 30, 1774	36
Hannah, [d. Preserved & Ruth], b. [ ] 28, 1779	36
Hepzibah, [d. Abraham & Sarah], b. Feb. 23, 1792	85
Hezekiah D., of Ridgefield, m. Angeline **FOSTER**, of Redding, Nov. 23, 1846, by Morris Hill	158
Lydia, [d. Preserved & Ruth], b. Dec. 4, 1785	36
Preserved, m. Ruth **SANFORD**, Sept. 10, 1764, by Moses Dickinson	36
Preserved, [s. Preserved & Ruth], b. Mar. 6, 1766	36
Rachel, m. Russel **BARTLET**, Feb. 28, 1776, by Rev. Ebenezer Baldwin, of Danbury. Witnesses Nathaniel Bartlet & Daniel C. Bartlet	47
Rhoda, [d. Preserved & Ruth], b. Feb. 7, 1772	36
Roswell, of Wilton, m. Minerva **HODGES**, of Redding, Aug. 16, [1835], by James A. Batterson	138
Ruth, [d. Preserved & Ruth], b. Feb. 26, 1768	36
Ruth, [d. Preserved & Ruth], d. Sept. 30, 1774	36
Ruth, [d. Preserved & Ruth], b. Jan. 19, 1776	36
Sally Keeler, m. John **BURR**, Feb. 4, 1824, by Nathan Burton	119
Seymour, of Fairfield, m. Deborah **GUYER**, of Redding, Nov. 21, 1820, by Rev. Daniel Crocker	109
W[illia]m, of Ridgefield, m. Rachel **BARNUM**, of Redding, Oct. 29, 1826, by W[illia]m C. Kniffin, M. G.	123
Zillah, [d. Preserved & Ruth], b. July 7, 1783	36
TERRY, Sarah, m. Stephen **GRAY**, b.of Redding, Sept. 3, 1758, by Rev. Nath[anie]ll Bartlet	7
THOMAS, Elisabeth, m. Jonathan **PARSONS**, Aug. 22, 1774, by Nathaniel Bartlett	30
W[illia]m H., of Bethlem, m. Edna **TYRREL**, of Redding, Apr. 12, 1835, by Jared Olmstead, J. P.	137
THORP, Abby, of Redding, m. William **MORGAN**, of New York City, Sept. 6, 1841, by Rev. John Crawford	150

THORP, (cont.)
Eli, of Weston, m. Elizabeth **PLATT**, of Redding, Feb. 16, 1845, by
Rev. W. F. Collins 155
Eunice, wid., of Redding, m. Smith **NORTHROP**, of Newtown, this
day, [Apr. 5, 1821], by Calvin Wheeler, Jr., J. P. 113
Henry B., of Edwardsville, Ill., m. Sally **SHEPHERD**, of Redding, this
day [Sept. 12, 1824], by Rev. Lemuel B. Hull 119
Joanna, m. John **DREW**, June 24, 1760 4
Joel, s. [Lyman & Abigail], b. Dec. 8, 1791 12
Lyman, m. Abigail **FAIRCHILD**, Nov. [ ], 1790, by Justus Hull.
Witnesses Stephen Gray & Samuel Hull 12
Orin W., m. Rebecca W. **DREW**, b. of Redding, Apr. 3, 1842, by
David C. Comstock 151
TILLOW, Cornelia, of Redding, m. David L. **STERLING**, of Ridgefield, this
day {Aug. 30, 1829], by Jonathan Bartlett, M. G. 129
Jane, of Redding, m. Burr **SMITH**, of Norwalk, this day {Dec. 31,
1833], by Jonathan Bartlett, M. G. 136
TODD, Seth, m. Deborah **BURR**, b. of Redding, Oct. 1, 1845, by Rev.
W[illia]m F. Collins 156
TOWN, Robert, of Weston, m. Rachel **BURR**, of Redding, Mar. 3, 1839, by
Aaron Sanford, Jr., J. P. 145
TREADWELL, Bradley, m. Fanny **MEEKER**, b. of Redding, Oct. 14, 1844,
by Rev. W. F. Collins 154
Eliza, d. Stephen & Sally, b. Jan. 20, 1810 104
Stephen Wheeler, s. [Stephen & Sally], b. July 15, 1812 104
TURKINGTON, Ann, of Redding, m. Amos **HOYT**, of Danbury, Apr. 10,
[1833], by Rev. Jesse Hunt 136
Eleanor, of Redding, m. Albert **SHERWOOD**, of Ridgefield, Feb. 22,
1842, by Rev. Daniel Smith 151
Oliver, Sr., m. Rachel **CANFIELD**, b. of Redding, Oct. 22, 1849, by
Rev. Jacob Shaw 164
Sarah, of Redding, m. W[illia]m C. **TURNEY**, of Newtown, Oct. 30,
1848, by Rev. Jacob Shaw 163
TURNEY, Agur T., of Redding, m. Mary **STOW**, of Redding, Nov. 25,
1835, by Rev. H. Humphreys 140
Asa Squier, s. Asa, b. Mar. 20, 1804 103
David, of Fairfield, m. Sarah **GOLD**, of Redding, Nov. 4, 1766, by
Rev. Nath[anie]l Bartlet 19
James M., of Weston, m. Martha E. **SKELLY**, of Redding, Mar. 12,
1845, by D. C. Comstock 155
Mary, d. Jan. 29, 1857, ae 38 y. 3 m. 29 d. 77
Mary Ann, m. William Curtis **HURD**, May 25, 1837, by Rev.
Edward J. Darken 141
Rebecca J., of Redding, m. Roswell W. **HURD**, of Newtown, this day,
[Jan. 24, 1836], by Rev. J. Lyman Clark 164
W[illia]m C., of Newtown, m. Sarah **TURKINGTON**, of Redding, Oct.
30, 1848, by Rev. Jacob Shaw 163
TYRREL, **TURREL**, Charlotte, of Weston, m. Joseph **BEACH**, of Sullivan,

TYRREL, TURREL, (cont.)
    N. Y., Jan. 24, [1827], by John M. Heron, J. P., Int. Pub.   124
    Edna, of Redding, m. W[illia]m H. **THOMAS**, of Bethlem,
        Apr. 12, 1835, by Jared Olmstead, J. P.   137
    Nath[anie]l, of the Jersey, m. Abigail **RAMSEY**, of Redding, Jan. 23,
        1770, by Rev. Nathaniel Bartlet   19
VANTINE, John C., of Redding, m. Catherine E. **WANZER**, of Easton, July
    5, 1846, by Rev. J. D. Marshall   159
WAKEMAN, Abigail, m. John **FAIRCHILD**, Jan. 6, 1792. Witnesses
    Stephen Fairchild & Samuel Fairchild   72
    Abaigil, [d. Jabez], b. May 4, 1795   75
    Anna, [d. Timothy & Anna], b. June 10, 1776   82
    Anna, m. Samuel **HULL**, Jan. 22, 1797, by Nath[anie]l Bartlett   26
    Anson, [s. Jabez], b. June 4, 1793   75
    Banks, [s. Jabez], b. Aug. 2, 1789   75
    Clarrena, [d. Jabez], b. May 17, 1791   75
    Ebenezer, [s. Timothy & Anna], b. Apr. 13, 1793   82
    Esther, [d. Jabez], b. May 30, 1798   75
    Falutt(?), [child Jabez], b. June 5, 1787   75
    Harry, of Redding, m. Phyllis **BRADLEY**, of Weston (colored), Oct. 6,
        1839, by Rev. Hawley Sanford   146
    Jabez, [s. Jabez], b. Jan. 22, 1784   75
    Levi, s. William & Polly, b. Dec. 21, 1816   75
    Mary, [d. Timothy & Anna], b. Sept. 11, 1782   82
    Orrilla, d. William & Polly, b. Feb. 24, 1822   75
    Ruth, [d. Timothy & Anna], b. Aug. 30, 1789   82
    Salmon, [s. Timothy & Anna], b. Oct. 3, 1780   82
    Samuel, [s. Timothy & Anna], b. Apr. 6, 1787   82
    Sarah, [d. Timothy & Anna], b. Dec. 17, 1795   82
    Sarah, d. William & Polly, b. Mar. 23, 1820   75
    Timothy, m. Anna **SHERWOOD**, Mar. 28, 1773   82
    Timothy, [s. Timothy & Anna], b. Mar. 7, 1785   82
    Urana, [child of Timothy & Anna], b. June 24, 1778   82
    Uriah, [s. Jabez], b. Aug. 4, 1782   75
    Walker, [s. Timothy & Anna], b. Feb. 5, 1774   82
WALLACE, Sarah Amanda, of Newtown, m. Daniel **SHERWOOD**, of
    Redding, June 21, 1840, by Rev. Charles Jarvis Todd   148
WANZER, Catherine E., of Easton, m. John C. **VANTINE**, of Redding,
    July 5, 1846, by Rev. J. D. Marshall   159
    John, m. Phebe **BENNETT**, b. of Weston, this day [Sept. 10, 1839], by
        Rev. W[illia]m Denison   147
WARD, Abigail, m. Stephen **SANFORD**, b. of Redding, Nov. 19, 1768, by
    Rev. Nathaniel Bartlet   39
    Esther, m. David **JACKSON**, Jan. 23, 1774, by Nathaniel Bartlett   91
WEED, Lorenzo Smith, m. Amelia Louisa **SNIFFINS**, Oct. 17, 1841, by
    Rev. Charles J. Todd   150
    Rachel, m. Justus **GRAY**, Jan. 10, 1780   91
    Zira, of Danbury, m. Zilpha **NORTHRUP**, of Redding,

WEED, (cont.)
    [Sept.] 24, [1823], by Rev. Daniel Crocker   116
WELDMAN, William T., of Danbury, m Fanny **STURGES**, of Redding, this
    day, [Sept. 22, 1830], by Rev. Lemuel B. Hull   131
WELLS, Nathan, of Easton, m. Eunice **GOODSELL**, of Redding, Sept. 19,
    1847, by Rev. J. D. Marshall   161
WHEELER, Damaris, [d. Enos & Hannah], b. Dec. 28, 1777   74
    Dimon, [s. Enos & Hannah], b. Apr. 20, 1761   74
    Edwin F., of Phelps, N. Y., m. Sally M. **SANFORD**, of Redding, [June]
        24, [1838], by Rev. Jeremiah Miller   144
    Enos, m. Hannah **BRADLEY**, May 15, 1760. Witness Martha Wheeler   74
    Enos, Jr., [s. Enos & Hannah], b. July 26, 1772   74
    Esther, [d. Enos & Hannah], b. Jan. 17, 1765   74
    Esther, of Redding, m. Daniel **LEACH**, of Fishkill, N. Y., Apr. 20,
        1830, by Aaron Sanford, Jr., J. P.   130
    Grace, m. John **MOREHOUSE**, Nov. 4, 1784. Certified by Nathaniel
        Bartlett   45
    Grizzel, [s. Enos & Hannah], b. Oct. 2, 1775   74
    Grissel, m. Asahel **DREW**, Nov. 25, 1795. Witnesses Enos Wheeler &
        Peter Wheeler   59
    Hannah, [d. Enos & Hannah], b. Jan. 20, 1767   74
    Hannah, m. Ebenezer **ANDREWS**, June [ ], 1781, by Rev.
        Nath[anie]ll Bartlett   1
    Hannah, m. Eben[eze]r **MERRIT**, Nov. 10, 1782, by Rev. James
        Johnson. Witnesses Calvin Wheeler & Calvin Wheeler, Jr.   97
    Hannah, of Redding, m. Samuel **BEACHER**, of Cheshire, Aug. 22,
        1830, by Aaron Sanford, Jr., J. P.   130
    Jarvis, s. Peter [& Hannah], b. Oct. 31, 1798   74
    John R., m. Jerusha **BRISTOL**, June 27, 1793. Witness Florilla Crofut   75
    Joseph Bristol, [s. John R. & Jerusha], b. Aug. 28, 1796   75
    Lazarus, m. Hannah **GOREHAM**, b. of Redding, Jan. 24, 1773, by Rev.
        Nathaniel Bartlet   21
    Martha, m. Platt **BENNETT**, July 29, 1792   41
    Mehetabel, m. Jesse **BANKS**, b. of Redding, June 11, 1764, by Rev.
        Nathaniel Bartlet   23
    Peter, [s. Enos & Hannah], b. Apr. 1, 1769   74
    Peter, m. Hannah **LEACH**, Nov. 25, 1796, certified by Ebenezer Crofut   74
    Rosell Beers, [child of John R. & Jerusha], b. Apr. 15, 1794   75
    Ruhamah, [d. Enos & Hannah], b. Feb. 28, 1763   74
    Seth, m. Rebeckah **WILLIAMS**, Dec. 28, 1788. Witnesses Thomas
        Starr & James Sanford   95
WHITE, Harriet Almira, of Redding, m. George **POLLY**, of Danbury, Dec.
    23, 1830, by Rev. Hawley Sanford   131
WHITEHEAD, Angelina S., of Redding, m. Morris **JENNINGS**, of
    Ridgefield, Apr. 9, 1845, by D. C. Comstock   155
    Beach, of Redding, m. Sally **JENNINGS**, of Wilton, May 31, [1824], by
        Rev. Daniel Crocker   118
    Eleanor C., of Redding, m. John **PARTRICK**, of Wilton, July 3, 1843,

	Page
WHITEHEAD, (cont.)	
by James A. Batterson, Dea.	153
WHITING, Sarah Maria, d. Samuel & Sally, b. Oct. 28, 1816	107
Sarah Maria, of Redding, m. Thomas **DUTTON**, of Guilford, Nov. 17, 1840, by Rev. D. C. Comstock	149
Stephen Betts, 2nd, s. Sam[ue]l & Sally, b. May 15, 1806	103
WHITLOCK, Adria, [child of Ephraim & Ruth], b. Dec. 3, 1786	74
Dan[ie]l Couch, [s. Ephraim & Ruth], b. May 28, 1790	74
Elisabeth, m. Elias **OLMSTED**, Jan. 5, 1794, by Rev. Samuel Goodrich. Witness Polle Olmsted	81
Ephraim, m. Ruth **CROFOOT**, June 15, 1786, certifed by Israel Crofut	74
Justus, formerly of Greenfield, m. Abigail **MEEKER**, of Redding, July 19, 1781, by Hezekiah Ripley, V. D. M.	13
Mary Esther, m. Henry **BEERS**, b. of Norwalk, Aug. 4, 1852, by Cortis Merchant, J. P.	168
Nathan, m. Mary **LYON**, Mar. 3, 1793, witnesses Jesse Beardsley & Daniel Beardsley	75
Sam[ue]l, s. [Nathan & Mary], b. Sept. 3, 1794	75
Stephen Crofoot, [s. Ephraim & Ruth], b. May 22, 1788	74
Walter, s. [Justus & Abigail], b. Feb. 22, 1782	13
Zalmon, of Danbury, m. Eunice **GILBERT**, of Redding, Oct. 17, 1839, by Rev. Charles J. Todd	146
WILCOX, Nathan E., m. Hannah W. **BANKS**, Sept. 17, 1837, by John Crawford	142
Nathan E., m. Polly **FAIRCHILD**, Dec. 12, 1841, by Rev. Eli Barnett	150
Polly, m. George **STARR**, b. of Redding, Nov. 28, 1844, by Rev. W. F. Collins	154
WILIMAN, Zeruah Ann, m. Samuel **OLMSTED**, b. of Redding, Sept. 1, 1841, by Rev. Daniel Smith	150
WILLIAMS, Ira, of Danbury, m. Almira **STOW** of Redding, Dec. 19, 1824, at the house of Daniel Stow, by John Reyonlds, Elder	119
Rebeckah, m. Seth **WHEELER**, Dec. 28, 1788. Witnesses Thomas Starr & James Sanford	95
WILSON, Charles, of Ridgefield, m. Sarah Ann **JENKINS**, of Redding, Dec. 26, 1826, by W[illia]m C. Kniffin, M. G.	124
Ebenezer, of Weston, m. Betsey **BARTRAM**, of Redding, Apr. 16, 1835, by Rev. Josiah Bowen	138
Emeline, of Redding, m. James **LORD**, of Monroe, this day [Oct. 4, 1846], by Jonathan Bartlett, M. G.	158
Israel H., of Bethel, m. Sarah **LOCKWOOD**, of Redding, Oct. 16, 1836, by Rev. E. Cole	140
Lydia, of Ridgefield, m. Seymour **GREGORY**, formerly of New Milford, (colored), Mar. 31, 1833, by Rev. Hawley Sanford	135
Sarah, m. Noah J. **SHERWOOD**, b. of Redding, Mar. 17, 1860, by Rev. Jacob Shaw	165
WINTON, Charles C., m. Sarah H. **READ**, b.of Redding, May 17, 1848, by Rev. Joseph P. Taylor	161
Geo[rge] H., of Weston, m. Betsey **READ**, of Redding, Feb. 19, 1845,	

	Page
WINTON, (cont.)	
by D. C. Comstock	155
Laura, m. Noah H. **LINDLEY**, b. of Redding, Nov. 14, 1830, by	
W[illia]m L. Strong	131
Louisa A., m. Eli **LYON**, b. of Redding, Nov. 17, 1839, by Rev.	
Charles J. Todd	147
Mary Rebecca, m. Isaac **BEACH**, b. of Redding, Nov. 1, 1840, by Rev.	
Charles J. Todd	148
WOOD, Anna, m. Ahahel **SALMON**, Sept. 5, 1786, by Rev. Timothy	
Langdon	51
Burr, of Weston, m. Maria **ANDREWS**, of Redding, this day	
[ ], by Jonathan Bartlett, M. G. Recorded Mar. 28, 1827	124
Daniel B., of Danbury, m. Roena **BATES**, of Redding, Mar. 7, 1833, by	
James A. Batterson, Dea.	135
Eunice, m. Jacob C. **BURR**, Feb. [ ], 1787, by Rev. Mr. Goodrich.	
Witness Abel Burr	57
Platt, m. Clarissa **PICKETT**, Mar. 7, 1822, by Levi Brunson	113
Sarah, m. Abel **BURR**, Dec. 20, 1775, by Rev. Mr. Baldwin. Witness	
Anne Salmon	22
Sarah, m. Thomas **BANKS**, Jan. 21, 1792, by Elias Lee. Witnesses	
Sarah Banks & Hannah Banks	83
Thomas, m. Mary Ann **DIKEMAN**, Mar. 10, 1852, by Rev. C. Bartlett	168
WOODROUGH, Warren G., of New Milford, m. Betsey A. **MUNROE**, of	
Redding, Mar. 1, 1843, by Rev. Daniel Smith	152
WOODWARD, David, of Watertown, m. Harriet E. **RIDER**, of Redding,	
Dec. 21, 1842, by Rev. Daniel Smith	152
WORDEN, James, of New York, m. Sarah **KEELER**, of Redding, June 18,	
1837, by Rev. Hawley Sanford	141
WYNKOOP, WINKOOP, Abraham Washborn, s. [John & Esther], b.	
Dec. 4, 1792	43
Betsey, d. [John & Esther], b. Mar. 13, 1800	43
Grozzel, s. [John & Esther], b. Jan. 20, 1791	43
John, m. Esther **GRIFFIN**, eldest d. Joseph, b. of Redding, Mar. 18,	
1790, by Nathaniel Bartlett	43
John, s. [John & Esther], b. Feb. 14, 1795	43
Lelyand, s. John & Esther, b. Sept. 15, 1808	43
YOUNGS, Abraham, s. Richard, b. Dec. 4, 1777	51
Hannah, m. Elias **SANFORD**, Aug. 31, 1786, [witness] Ebenezer	
Sanford	73
NO SURNAME	
Abiah, m. Seth **SANFORD**, Apr. 25, 1778	22
Abigail, b. Sept. 9, 1770; m. John **SHERWOOD**, Jr., Feb. 1, 1795	78
Abigail, m. Seth **SANFORD**, Aug. 3, 1781	22
Betsey, b. Nov. 10, 1763; m. Hezekiah **SANFORD**, June 10, 1783	97
Betsey, b. Oct. 5, 1781; m. John R. **HILL**, Mar. 23, 1799	107
Elisabeth, m. David **CROFOOT**, Nov. 15, 1775, by Rev. [ ]	
Lewis, of Norwalk. Witness Thankful Whitlock	15
Esther, m. Jonathan **MEEKER**, Jr., Jan. 8, 1792, by Rev. Philo Perry.	

	Page
NO SURNAME, (cont.)	
Witnesses Richard Hawley & Richard Hawley, Jr.	21
Rachel, b. Jan. 28, 1729; m. Benj[ami]n **STURGES**, Dec. 26, 1747, by Rev. Beach	59
Rachel, m. Seth **ANDREWS**, May 1, 1782	52

RIDGEFIELD VITAL RECORDS
1709 - 1850

	Vol.	Page
ABANDA, Julia Ann, of Delhi, N. Y., m. Ebenezer **GILBERT**, Jr., of Ridgefield, Jan. 24, 1830, by Samuell M. Phelps	1	172
ABBOT, ABBOTT, Abijah, s. John & Rebecka, b. Oct. 6, 1769	1	22
Abijah, m. Deborah **KNAP[P]**, May 21, 1794	1	97
Alfred, twin with Alvin, s. Caleb & Mary, b. Feb. 23, 1799	1	97
Alvin, twin with Alfred, s. Caleb & Mary, b. Feb. 23, 1799	1	97
Anna, d. Lemuel, Jr. & Rebeckah, b. Aug. 15, 1756	LR1	244
Anne, had s. John, b. Mar. 21, 1762	1	title
Annis, d. Stephen & Elizabeth, b. Aug. 25, 1768	1	21
Arza, s. James & Cate, b. Dec. 17, 1790	1	50
Arza, d. July 17, 1824, ae 33 y. 7 m.	1	224
Aseneth, d. John & Rebecka, b. June 11, 1764	1	22
Benj[ami]n, d. Sept. 22, 1788	1	204
Caleb, s. John & Rebecka, b. Jan. 4, 1773	1	22
Caleb, m. Mary **PORTER**, Dec. 5, 1793	1	97
Cate, d. James & Cate, b. Mar. 8, 1784	1	50
Charity, m. Albert **NASH**, b. of Ridgefield, Mar. 9, 1834, by Rev. Nicholas White	1	179
David, m. Anne **COSIER**, Mar. 19, 1749/50, by Jonathan Ingersoll, V. D. M.	LR1	234
David, s. David & Anne, b. June 25, 1753	LR1	256
David, d. Feb. 12, 1761	1	200
David, Jr., d. May 1, 1764	1	200
Delilah, d. Jonathan & Sarah, b. Dec. 8, [1721]	LR1	203
Eli, s. James & Cate, b. Dec. 25, 1792	1	50
Eliza, of Ridgefield, m. Charles **TAYLOR**, of South Salem, Jan. 20, 1833, by Rev. Charles G. Selleck	1	178
Elizabeth, d. Lemuel & Martha, b. Feb. 27, 1743/4	LR1	237
Elizabeth, d. Stephen & Elizabeth, b. Oct. 27, 1763	1	21
Elizabeth, m. Isaac **NASH**, Mar. 28, 1765	1	150
Elizabeth, m. David Scott **BARLOW**, b. of Ridgefield, Dec. 18, 1831, by Rev. Charles J. Todd	1	175
Eunice, had d. Mary **WHITE**, b. Dec. 2, 1727	LR1	220
Ezra, s. Lemuel & Martha, b. July 21, 1756	LR1	243
Ezra, s. Abijah & Deborah, b. Apr. 2, 1795	1	97
Foster Perry, s. Caleb & Mary, b. May 15, 1815	1	97
Hannah, d. Lemuel & Martha, b. May 3, 1752	LR1	243
Hannah, m. Matthew **NORTHRUP**, Sept. 14, 1769	1	151
Hannah, wid., d. Dec. 4, 1807	1	213
Ira Gregory, s. Caleb & Mary, b. Oct. 23, 1807	1	97
James, s. Lemuel & Martha, b. June 15, 1754	LR1	243

	Vol.	Page
ABBOT, ABBOTT, (cont.)		
James, m. Cate **WOOD**, Mar. 26, 1783	1	153
James, s. James & Cate, b. Feb. 2, 1789	1	50
John, m. Rebeckah **TAYLOR**, Mar. [ ]	LR1	252
John, s. Lemuel & Martha, b. Apr. 1, 1738	LR1	223
John, s. Anne, b. Mar. 21, 1762	1	title
John, s. John & Rebecka, b. Nov. 1, 1767	1	22
John, d. Jan. 1, 1793	1	206
John, s. Caleb & Mary, b. Oct. 14, 1794	1	97
Jno, his wid. [ ], d. Feb. 7, 1796	1	208
John Courtland, s. John & Evelina, b. Sept. 23, 1823	1	106
Jonathan, of Ridgefield, m. Lydia **YOUNG**, of Branford, Apr. 16, [1729], by Samuell Russell	LR1	228
Jonathan, s. Jonathan & Lydia, b. Apr. 29, 1739	LR1	224
Jonathan, Dr., d. Aug. 21, 1751	LR1	217
Jonathan, Dr., d. Aug. 23, 1751	LR1	216
Joshua Porter, s. Caleb & Mary, b. Oct. 11, 1801	1	97
Kate, w. James, d. Aug. 17, 1793	1	206
Lemuel, m. Martha **WOOD**, d. Jonathan & Elizabeth, of Norwalk, Dec. 20, 1732	LR1	229
Lyddia, d. Jonathan & Lyddia, b. Aug. 8, 1736	LR1	220
Lydia, d. Michael & Hannah, b. Apr. 10, 1757	LR1	247
Lydia, d. Jan. 3, 1842, ae 83 y.	1	236
Martha, d. Lemuel & Martha, b. Mar. 16, 1739/40	LR1	224
Martha, d. Lemuel, Jr. & Rebeckah, b. May 3, 176[ ]	1	2
Martha, wid., d. May 17, 1795, ae 80	1	208
Mary, d. Lemuell & Martha, b. Oct. 29, 1747	LR1	240
Mary, d. Lemuel, Jr. & Rebeckah, b. Mar. 10, 176[ ]	1	2
Michael, s. Jonathan & Lidia, b. Apr. 14, 1731	LR1	211
Noah, s. Lemuel, Jr. & Rebeckah, b. Jan. 22, 176[ ]	1	2
Noah, s. Lemuel, Jr. & Rebeckah, b. Jan. 28, 1761	LR1	244
Phebe, d. Samuel & Martha, b. May 24, 1750	LR1	241
Phebe, m. Jeremiah **BURCHARD**, Feb. 5, 1772	1	152
Polly, d. James & Cate, b. Mar. 20, 1787	1	50
Polly, d. James, d. Oct. 27, 1800, ae 13 y. 7 m. 7 d.	1	210
Rebeckah, d. John & Rebeckah, b. Dec. 2, 1765	1	22
Rebeckah, d. Lemuel & Rebeckah, b. Apr. 13, 177[ ]	1	2
Rebeckah, w. Lemuel, 2nd, d. July 3, June 12, 1771 (In the Arnold Copy both dates are written as given here)	1	201
Rebeckah, d. Caleb & Mary, b. Jan. 15, 1796	1	97
Samuel, s. Samuel & Martha, b. June 15, 1734	LR1	218-9
Samuel, Jr., m. Rebeckah **BENEDICT**, Sept. 3, 1755	LR1	252
Samuel, d. July 15, 1791, in the 78th y. of his age	1	205
Sarah, d. Lemuel & Martha, b. Mar. 30, 1742	LR1	236
Sarah, d. Lemuel, Jr. & Rebeckah, b. Oct. 28, 1759	LR1	244
Sarah, d. Sept. 25, 1815, in the state of Georgia	1	220
Silas, s. Lemuel & Rebeckah, b. Sept. 12, 176[ ]	1	2
Stephen, s. Lemuel & Martha, b. Jan. 20. 1735/6	LR1	220

	Vol.	Page
ABBOT, ABBOTT, (cont.)		
Stephen, m. Elizabeth **DAVIS**, Mar. 22, [ ]	LR1	252
William, m. Harriet **SMITH**, Oct. 19, 1842, by Rev. Charles Chettenden	1	193
ALLEN, Barnabus, m. Rachel **STEPHENS**, Feb. 24, 1833, by Nathan Burton	1	176
Burr, m. Katharine **SEYMOUR**, Sept. 18, 1831, by Nathan Burton	1	174
Charles, of Georgetown, m. Harriet **PLATT**, of Ridgefield, May 8, 1848, by Rev. Sylvester S. Strong	1	130
Sarah E., of Ridgefield, m. Hiram **BANKS**, of Danbury, Dec. 24, 1845, by Nathan Burton	1	198
Stephen, Jr., m. Betsey **BENEDICT**, Nov. 26, 1835, by Nathan Burton	1	181
ALVORD, Elisha, Dr., d. Apr. 10, 1812	1	216
AMBLER, Henry F., of Danbury, m. Eliza A. **BATES**, of Ridgefield, Feb. 19, 1843, by Rev. John L. Ambler	1	193
ANDREWS, ANDRUSS, Abigail Blackley, d. John & Dorcas, b. Mar. 1, 1771	1	17
Dorcas, wid., d. Nov. 15, 1804	1	212
James, m. Dorcas **INGERSOLL**, May 5, 1762	1	150
Jeremiah, s. John & Dorcas, b. Feb. 11, 1764	1	17
Jonathan, d. Aug. 14, 1802	1	211
Samuel, s. John & Dorcas, b. Dec. 9, 1767	1	17
ARMSTRONG, Caroline, m. John **SMALLEY**, Apr. 5, 1840, by Nathan Burton, P. T.	1	188
ARNOLD, Abigail, [d. Peleg & Elizabeth], b. Jan. 22, 1789	1	99
Edward N., [s. Peleg & Elizabeth], b. June 19, 1802	1	99
Elizabeth, [d. Peleg & Elizabeth], b. Sept. 11, 1799	1	99
Freelove, [d. Peleg & Elizabeth], b. Dec. 8, 1792	1	99
Freelove, m. Lot **FORESTER**, Nov. 10, 1823, by George Benedict	1	162
John, [s. Peleg & Elizabeth], b. Sept. 10, 1786	1	99
Peleg, [s. Peleg & Elizabeth], b. May 21, 1795	1	99
ATHERTON, Mary, m. David **ROCKWELL**, Jr., Nov. 2, 1760	LR1	234
AUSTEN, Israel W., of Poundridge, N. Y., m. Mary **BANKS**, of Ridgefield, this day [Jan. 19, 1845], by James A. Hawley	1	196
AVERY, William, of Long Island, m. Polly M. **BEERS**, of Ridgefield, May 18, 1841, by Rev. Warner Hoyt	1	190
BAILEY, BALEY, Charles, of Ramulies, Senaca Co., N. Y., m. Julia Ann **MUNROW**, of Ridgefield, Feb. 28, 1840, by Rev. Thomas Sparks	1	188
Charles, d. Apr. 17, 1843, ae about 16 y.	1	237
Frederick, of Danbury, m. Nancy **WHITLOCK**, of Ridgefield, Aug. 3, 1846, by Rev. Henry Olmsted, Jr.	1	127
BAKER, Amos, m. Sarah **STEBBINS**, Nov. 4, 1779	1	155
Amos, s. Amos & Sarah, b. Dec. 6, 1788	1	57
Amos, Dr., d. Mar. 31, 1823	1	223

BAKER, (cont.)

	Vol.	Page
Benjamin, s. Amos & Sarah, b. Nov. 15, 1780	1	57
Benjamin, s. Amos & Sarah, d. Dec. 27, 1780	1	203
Cadalina, m. Samuel **CANFIELD**, b. of Ridgefield, Mar. 9, 1829, by Rev. Henry Stead	1	170
Elizabeth, d. Amos & Sarah, b. Mar. 7, 1785	1	57
Elizabeth, m. Jesse S. **BRADLEY**, Dec. 3, 1805, by Rev. Samuel Goodrich	1	159
Laura, d. Amos & Sarah, b. Jan. 11, 1787	1	57
Sarah, d. Amos & Sarah, b. Jan. 27, 1782	1	57
Sarah, w. Dr. Amos, d. May 14, 1804	1	212
Sarah, d. Feb. 2, 1809, ae 27 y. 6 d.	1	214
BALDWIN, Abigail, d. John & Abigail, b. June 13, 1752	LR1	255
Abigail, w. John, d. [ ], 1808	1	214
Chloe, m. Nathaniel **NORTHRUP**, Nov. 5, 1772	1	151
Esther, d. John & Abigail, b. Oct. 17, 1757	LR1	255
John, m. Abigail **NORTHRUP**, May 7, 17[ ]	1	150
John, d. Nov. 9, 1809	1	215
Lucretia, d. [Samuel S. & Sarah], b. Aug. 30, 1800	1	89
Mary, m. Daries **LOBDELL**, Jan. 16, 1753	LR1	233
Mary, d. Silas & Mary, b. June 10, 1759	LR1	246
Philander, s. [Samuel S. & Sarah], b. Sept. 15, 1798	1	89
Samuel S., m. Sarah **CAMP**, Nov. 10, 1796	1	89
Susannah, had d. Hannah **DIXON**, b. Jan. 9, 1744/5	LR1	255
BANKS, Abigail, [d. Nehemiah & Sarah], b. Dec. 8, 1790	1	85
Adar, m. Thomas **SMITH**, June 11, 1740	LR1	231
Albert, [s. Nehemiah & Sarah], b. Sept. 30, 1797	1	85
Ann, of Ridgefield, m. W[illia]m **BEARDESLEY**, of Wilton, Nov. 28, 1832, by Rev. Charles G. Selleck	1	177
Anna, d. [Nehemiah & Sarah], b. May 11, 1789	1	85
Anna, w. David, d. Mar. 20, 1836	1	232
Bradley, his d. [ ], d. July 18, 1845, ae about 18 y.	1	238
Burr, [s. Nehemiah & Sarah], b. Aug. 17, 1781	1	85
Burr, his infant d. July 21, 1807	1	213
Burr, had infant d. [ ], d. Apr. 22, 1816, ae 2 m.	1	219
Burr, his infant d. Mar. 31 1817	1	220
Daniel, d. Mar. 26, 1842, ae about 52 y.	1	236
David, d. Jan. 15, 1847, ae 82 y.	1	238
Eliphalet, s. [Nehemiah & Sarah], b. Apr. 6, 1795	1	85
Harry, s. Nehemiah, d. May 14, 1801	1	210
Harvey, d. May 10, 1839, ae 41 y.	1	235
Hiram, of Danbury, m. Sarah E. **ALLEN**, of Ridgefield, Dec. 24, 1845, by Nathan Burton	1	198
Jesse, s. Justus, b. Sept. 9, 1830, ae 19 y.	1	228
Justus, d. Aug. 2, 1846, ae about 76	1	238
Lucy, of Ridgefield, m. William **MAYBERRY**, of Norwalk, Aug. 19, 1827, by Samuel M. Phelps	1	168
Mary, [d. Nehemiah & Sarah], b. Feb. 23, 1793	1	85

	Vol.	Page
BANKS, (cont.)		
Mary, of Ridgefield, m. Israel W. **AUSTEN**, of Poundridge, N. Y., this day [Jan. 19, 1845], by James A. Hawley	1	196
Nehemiah, m. Sarah **SHERWOOD**, Jan. 21, 1778	1	85
Nehemiah, twin with Sarah, s. [Nehemiah & Sarah], b. Oct. 10, 1786	1	85
Nehemiah, d. Oct. 5, 1813, in the 27th y. of his age	1	218
Polly, m. Jabez **BEARS**, Jan. [ ], 1790	1	158
Samuel, [s. Nehemiah & Sarah], b. May 2, 1784	1	85
Sarah, twin with Nehemiah, d. [Nehemiah & Sarah], b. Oct. 10, 1786	1	85
Thaddeus, m. Ann **CAIN**, Jan. 11, 1789	1	157
William, s. Burr, d. Sept. 18, 1813	1	218
Zalmon Bradley, s. [Nehemiah & Sarah], b. Nov. 9, 1779	1	85
BARBER, Ira, s. Benjamin & Elizabeth, b. Dec. 9, 1786	1	69
BARBERRY, BARBERY, Benjamin, m. Elizabeth **KEELER**, Sept. 3, 1786	1	156
Elizabeth, w. Benjamin, d. Oct. 28, 1799	1	210
BARKER, Lucretia, Mrs. of Branford, m. Rev. Samuel **CAMP**, of Ridgefield, Oct. 28, 1778, by Rev. Phinehas Robbins, of Branford	1	153
Thomas R., of North Salem, m. Eliza A. **WEBB**, of Ridgefield, Apr. 7, 1847, by Rev. Charles Stearns. Int. Pub.	1	128
BARLOW, Abigail, d. John & Sarah, b. Aug. 13, 1778	1	60
David Scott, m. Elizabeth **ABBOTT**, b. of Ridgefield, Dec. 18, 1831, by Rev. Charles J. Todd	1	175
Elizabeth Sarah, d. John & Sarah, b. Oct. 23, 1783	1	60
Jabez, s. John & Sarah, b. July 16, 1771	1	60
John, s. John & Sarah, b. July 13, 1769	1	60
John, m. Rana **SCOTT**, Nov. 29, 1789	1	158
John, d. Oct. 1, [1848?], ae about 80 y.	1	240
Mansfield, s. John & Sarah, b. Aug. 17, 1773	1	60
Nehemiah, s. John & Sarah, b. Dec. 23, 1781	1	60
Samuel Whitney, s. John & Sarah, b. June 22, 1775	1	60
Sarah Caroline, m. David **PULLING**, 2nd, b. of Ridgefield, Nov. 8, 1829, by Rev. Origen P. Holcomb	1	170
BARNES, BARNS, Ambrose, m. Hannah **BAXTER**, Oct. 12, 1779	1	66
Betsey, [d. Ambrose & Hannah], b. July 10, 1780	1	66
George L., of North Haven, m. Martha R. **BENNET**, of Ridgefield, Mar. 22, 1829, by Samuel M. Phelps	1	169
Orange, [child Ambrose & Hannah], b. Oct. 7, 1786	1	66
Samuel, [s. Ambrose & Hannah], b. May 14, 1784	1	66
BARNUM, Abel, s. Zebulon & Rachel, b. June 27, 1752, at Stratford	1	5 1/2
Abel, m. Hannah **SHERWOOD**, May 31, 1772	1	155
Abel, s. Abel & Hannah, b. Mar. 27, 1779	1	5 1/2
Betsey, d. Abel & Hannah, b. [ ]	1	5 1/2
Charity, d. Abel & Hannah, b. Feb. 29, 1788	1	5 1/2

	Vol.	Page
BARNUM, (cont.)		
Eunice, d. Abel & Hannah, b. May 12, 1782	1	5 1/2
Gerry, of Brookfield, m. Susan **FERGUSON**, of Ridgebury, Mar. 31, 1839, in Ridgebury, by Rev. Lucius Atwater	1	187
Isaac, s. Abel & Hannah, b. Apr. 7, 1775	1	5 1/2
Israel, s. Abel & Hannah, b. May 16, 1776	1	5 1/2
John, s. Abel & Hannah, b. Sept. 13, 1777	1	5 1/2
Mary, d. Abel & Hannah, b. Jan. 4, 1784	1	5 1/2
Rachal, d. Abel & Hannah, b. Oct. 7, 1780	1	5 1/2
Reuben, s. Abel & Hannah, b. Dec. 11, 1772	1	5 1/2
Sally, d. Abel & Hannah, b. [ ]	1	5 1/2
BASSETT, Martin W., m. Elizabeth **FOSTER**, b. of Ridgefield, Apr. 28, 1844, by Rev. Shaller J. Hillyer	1	195
BATES, Elias, [s. Nicholas & Martha], b. Apr. 3, 1722	LR1	210
Eliza A., of Ridgefield, m. Henry F. **AMBLER**, of Danbury, Feb. 19, 1843, by Rev. John L. Ambler	1	193
Ezra, m. Huldah **PLATT**, Mar. 31, 1785	1	156
Hanford, had d. [ ], d. Apr. 1, 1835, ae 5 w.	1	231
Harry, d. [July] 22, [1851], ae 29	1	241
Henry, [s. Nicholas & Martha], b. June 15, 1730	LR1	210
Henry, m. Eunice **WHITLOCK**, b. of Ridgefield, Dec. 17, 1847, by Rev. Henry Olmsted, Jr.	1	129
Henry L., m. Emma **LEE**, b. of Ridgefield, Dec. 18, 1850, by Rev. Nath[anie]l Mead	1	135
Huldah, w. John, d. Oct. 8, 1831, ae 30 y.	1	229
John, [s. Nicholas & Martha], b. May 2, 1724	LR1	210
John, m. Amanda **WHITLOCK**, b. of Ridgefield, Feb. 14, 1832, by Levi Brunson	1	175
John, his w. [ ], d. Aug. 6, 1847, ae 58 y.	1	239
Mary, d. Nicholas & Martha, b. Aug. 31, 1720	LR1	210
Selah, m. Eliza Ann **HUNT**, Dec. 30, 1829, by Nathan Burton	1	170
BATHITE(?), Andrew, of North Salem, m. Jane **BIRDSALL**, of Ridgefield, Dec. 4, 1836, by Rev. Charles G. Selleck	1	183
BATTERSON, Coleman, his child d. Sept. 11, [1843], ae 1 y.	1	237
BAXTER, Hannah, m. Ambrose **BARNS**, Oct. 12, 1779	1	66
Joel, of North Salem, m. Eliza **HOW**, of Ridgefield, Oct. 15, 1826, by Samuel M. Phelps	1	167
John, m. Dorcas **WHITLOCK**, Feb. 4, 1787	1	156
BEARDSLEY, BEARDESLEY, Anne, w. W[illia]m, d. June 21, 1835, ae 42	1	231
Esther, m. Samuel M. **SMITH**, b. of Ridgefield, Oct. 28, 1820, by Rev. Samuell M. Phelps	1	161
W[illia]m, of Wilton, m. Ann **BANKS**, of Ridgefield, Nov. 28, 1832, by Rev. Charles G. Selleck	1	177
BEARS, [see under **BEERS**]		
BEEBE, Isaac, of Lisbon, Ill., m. Mary Ann **THORP**, of Ridgefield, June 16, 1845, by Rev. James A. Hawley	1	197
BEERS, BEARS, Abigail, m. Josiah **SMITH**, 2nd, Nov. 16, 1794	1	82

RIDGEFIELD VITAL RECORDS 143

	Vol.	Page
BEERS, BEARS, (cont.)		
Anthony, his w. [ ], d. July 1, 1810, ae 61	1	215
Anthony, d. Oct. 14, 1820, ae 70 y.	1	222
Bradley, m. Mary E. **SMITH**, b. of Ridgefield, Apr. 24, 1844,		
by James A. Hawley	1	195
Clarry, m. Daniel **SHOLES**, b. of Ridgefield, Sept. 27, 1825,		
by Rev. Origen P. Holcomb	1	164
Cyrus, his w. [ ], d. Sept. 11, 1830	1	228
Daniel, s. Nathan & Martha, b. Feb. 22, 1767	1	50
David, m. Esther **BISHOP**, Feb. 19, 1788	1	156
Delia Ann, of Ridgefield, m. Joseph **GOODSELL**, of Redding,		
Feb. 25, [1838], by Rev. William Bowen, of Redding	1	184
Edmond, his wid., d. Aug. 10, 1848, ae 84 y.	1	240
Eleazer, had d. [ ], d. Jan. 8, 1820, ae 14	1	222
Eleazer, had infant d. Apr. [ ], 1821	1	222
Eleazer, his w. [ ], d. Apr. 4, 1837	1	233
Eleazer, Dea., d. Dec. 24, [1851], ae 71 y.	1	241
Eliza, d. Edmond, d. Apr. 28, [1851], ae [ ]	1	241
Elizabeth, d. Nathan & Martha, b. [ ], 1779	1	50
Elizabeth, d. Apr. 24, 1790	1	205
Elizabeth, m. Seth **BOWTON**, b. of Ridgefield, Aug. 4, 1822,		
by Rev. Samuel M. Phelps	1	161
Hannah, d. Nathan & Martha, b. June 27, 1763	1	50
Hannah, m. Justus **JENNINGS**, Dec. 27, 1781	1	154
Jabez, s. Nathan & Martha, b. Jan. 22, 1765	1	50
Jabez, m. Polly **BANKS**, Jan. [ ], 1790	1	158
Jesse, s. Nathan & Martha, b. [ ], 1781	1	50
Lucy, w. William B., d. Nov. 20, 1832, ae 21 y.	1	229
Lydia Ann, of Ridgefield, m. Peter **CORNEN**, of New York,		
Sept. 5, 1842, by Rev. Warner Hoyt	1	192
Martha, d. Nathan & Martha, b. Mar. 11, 1761	1	50
Mary Delia, of Ridgefield, m. Warren **NICHOLS**, of		
Greenfield, Conn., Apr. 3, 1850, by Rev. Nathaniel Mead	1	133
Nathan, d. July 26, 1793, in the 53rd y. of his age	1	206
Nathan, his child d. May 11, 1840, ae about 3 y.	1	235
Polly, d. Edmond, d. June 11, 1813, ae 22 m.	1	217
Polly M., of Ridgefield, m. William **AVERY**, of Long Island,		
May 18, 1841, by Rev. Warner Hoyt	1	190
Sabra, d. Nathan & Martha, b. Aug. 29, 1773	1	50
Sally Ann, m. Stephen **FRY**, b. of Ridgefield, July 23, 1836, by		
Rev. J. Lyman Clark	1	185
Samuel, s. Nathan & Martha, b. Mar. 3, 1768	1	50
Sarah, m. John **WALKER**, June 3, 1793	1	158
Sarah, wid. Elnathan, d. May [ ], 1810	1	215
Sary, d. Nathan & Martha, b. Sept. 22, 1775	1	50
Sucky, d. Nathan & Martha, b. Aug. 29, 1771	1	50
William, s. Cyrus, d. Feb. 27, 1830, ae 2 y.	1	228
W[illia]m B., m. Lucy **SEAMOUR**, b. of Ridgefield, Jan. 1,		

144   BARBOUR COLLECTION

	Vol.	Page
BEERS, BEARS, (cont.)		
1832, by Rev. Charles G. Selleck	1	176
William W., m. Paulina M. **EDMONDS**, b. of Ridgefield, Sept. 30, 1851, by Rev. Ira Abbott	1	136
BENEDICT, BENEDICK, Aaron, s. Thomas & Jane, b. Apr. 15, 1755	LR1	250
Abiah, d. Timothy & Sarah, b. Dec. 20, 1736	LR1	222
Abiah, m. Samuel **KEELER**, Jr., Mar. 18, 1761	LR1	234
Abigail, d. John, Jr. & Esther, b. Feb. 3, 1780	1	43
Abigail, m. Matthew **SMITH**, 2nd, Feb. 25, 1796	1	82
Abijah, m. Amelia **BULKLEY**, Jan. 17, 1781	1	152
Abijah Bradley, s. Abijah & Amelia, b. Nov. 17, 1784	1	43
Abner, s. Peter & Agniss, b. Nov. 10, 1740	LR1	226
Agness, w. Daniel, d. Jan. 6, 1764	1	200
Agniss, d. Daniel & Mary, b. Aug. 30, 1767	1	19
Alexander, [s. John (s. Benjamin) & Lucy], b. Dec. 22, 1739	LR1	235
Ambrose, his infant d. Apr. 9, 1819	1	221
Ambrose, his w. [ ], d. Sept. 19, 1834, ae 39 y.	1	231
Amelia, d. Abijah & Amelia, b. Apr. 21, 1789	1	43
Amos, s. Benjamin & Mary, b. Sept. 17, [1721/2]	LR1	204
Anna, d. [Matthew & Ruth], b. Feb. 22, 1730	LR1	211
Anne, d. [Joseph & Ann], b. Dec. 17, 1713	LR1	200
Anne, w. Joseph, d. Dec. 9, 1716	LR1	213
Anne, d. James & Joanna, b. July 25, 1757	1	9
Anne, d. Matthew & Elizabeth, b. Feb. 28, 1768	1	15
Anodire, d. [Comfort & Sarah], b. Sept. 5, 1790	1	81
Asahel, 2nd, m. Mariah **BENEDICT**, Nov. 27, 1827, by Nathan Burton	1	167
Benjamin, [s. Benjamin & Mary], b. Oct. 1, 1707	LR1	200
Benjamin, s. [Benjamin] & Hannah, b. Aug. 25, 1737	LR1	221
Benjamin, s. Daniel & Agness, b. Aug. 22, 1754	LR1	245
Benjamin, [twin with Joseph], s. Jesse & Mehetable, b. Jan. 17, 1770	1	1
Benjamin, Dea., d. July 3, 1773	1	201
Benjamin, 2nd, d. Nov. 1, 1819	1	221
Benj[amin], d. July 13, 1847, ae 77 y.	1	239
Betsey, d. [Gamaliel & Hannah], b. Dec. 28, 1789	1	89
Betsey, d. Abijah & Amelia, b. Aug. 19, 1791	1	43
Betsey*, d. [Josiah B. & Esther], b. Apr. 14, 1810 *(Or "Eliza")	1	108
Betsey, m. Stephen **ALLEN**, Jr., Nov. 26, 1835, by Nathan Burton	1	181
Bradley, see Abijah Bradley **BENEDICT**	1	43
Brice, of Danbury, m. Elizabeth Sally **DAN**, of Ridgefield, Mar. 15, 1840, by Rev. T. Sparks	1	188
Catey, d. [Josiah B. & Esther], b. Sept. 14, 1809	1	108
Caty, d. Josiah B., d. Dec. 14, 1835, ae 25	1	232
Charles, s. [Josiah B. & Esther], b. Jan. 27, 1819	1	108

	Vol.	Page
BENEDICT, BENEDICK, (cont.)		
Clark, s. [Gamaliel & Hannah], b. June 8, 1791	1	89
Daniel, m. Agnis [ ], Feb. 13, 1739/40	LR1	231
Daniel, s. Daniel & Agness, b. Apr. 2, 1743	LR1	242
Daniel, s. Ambrose, d. Jan. 8, 1825, ae 20	1	225
Daniel, m. Polly **ROCKWELL**, Feb. 17, 1839, by Nathan Burton, P. T.	1	187
Darius, s. Thomas & Jane, b. Dec. 6, 1758	LR1	250
David, s. Matthew & Elizabeth, b. Feb. 14, 1772	1	15
Delight, d. John & Esther, b. Apr. 25, 1759	LR1	247
Delight, d. June 10, 1812, in her 54th y. School-teacher to Peter Parley	1	217
Dorathy, [d. Benjamin & Mary], b. Nov. 11, 1710	LR1	200
Edward, m. Maria **HOYT**, b. of Ridgefield, Dec. 22, 1830, by Rev. Samuel M. Phelps	1	175
Edwin, m. Katharine **OSBORN**, b. of Ridgefield, Oct. 13, 1833, by Rev. Charles G. Selleck	1	179
Eli, s. Joseph, d. Apr. 11, 1795, ae 1 y.	1	208
Elijah, [s. John (s. Benjamin) & Lucy], b. Oct. 6, 1747	LR1	235
Elijah, s. Matthew & Elizabeth, b. Apr. 17, 1766	1	15
Elijah, s. Matthew & Elizabeth, d. Apr. 18, 1767	1	202
Elijah, 2nd, s. Matthew & Elizabeth, b. Apr. 8, 1770	1	15
Elijah, 2nd, s. Matthew & Elizabeth, d. Mar. 1, 177[ ]	1	202
Eliza, see Betsey **BENEDICT**	1	108
Eliza H., m. Milan H. **MEAD**, b. of Ridgefield, this day [Dec. 10, 1851], by Rev. C. Clark	1	137
Elizabeth, [d. Benjamin & Mary], b. Jan. 17, 1705	LR1	200
Elizabeth, d. Lieut. Benjamin & Mary, m. William **DRINKWATER**, Dec. 18, 1728	LR1	228
Elizabeth, [d. Matthew & Ruth], b. Jan. 2, 1737/8	LR1	211
Elizabeth, d. Jesse & Elizabeth [or Mehitable], b. June 16, 1757	LR1	257
Elizabeth, d. Jesse & Mehitable, b. June 16, 1757	1	1
Elizabeth, d. Matthew & Elizabeth, b. Oct. 31, 1762	1	15
Elizabeth, w. Matthew, d. Nov. 8, 1762	1	200
Elizabeth, d. Daniel & Mary, b. Apr. 14, 1770	1	19
Elizabeth, m. Jasper **MEAD**, Apr. 8, 1779	1	156
Elizabeth, m. Elijah **SMITH**, Oct. [ ]	LR1	252
Emily, of Ridgefield, m. Thomas **NORTHRUP**, of Wilton, Oct. 19, 1824, by Samuel M. Phelps	1	165
Epenetus Platt, s. [Comfort & Sarah], b. Feb. 10, 1796	1	81
Esther, d. John & Esther, b. Jan. 12, 1750/1	LR1	247
Esther, d. John & Esther, b. Feb. 25, 1757	LR1	247
Esther, d. John & Esther, d. Mar. 5, 1757	LR1	217
Esther, m. Job **SMITH**, 2nd, Jan. 12, 1780	1	152
Esther, m. Job **SMITH**, 2nd, Jan. 12, 1780	1	154
Esther, d. John, Jr. & Esther, b. Oct. 2, 1784	1	43
Esther, w. Dea. John, d. Feb. 10, 1814, in the		

146 BARBOUR COLLECTION

	Vol.	Page
BENEDICT, BENEDICK, (cont.)		
90th y. of her age	1	218
Esther, d. John, d. Nov. 13, 1834, ae 78	1	231
Ezra, s. Joseph & Mary, b. Aug. 19, 1730	LR1	211
Ezra, [s. Matthew & Ruth], b. Nov. 5, 1741	LR1	211
Ezra, s. Matthew & Ruth, d. Sept. 15, 1745	LR1	215
Ezra, s. Jesse & Mehitable, b. Apr. 8, 1764	1	1
Ezra, m. Susannah **HINE**, Sept. 28, 1783	1	154
Ezra, d. Dec. 30, 1840, ae 77	1	236
Gamaliel, s. Jesse & Elizabeth [or Mehitable], b. Nov. 9, 176[ ]	LR1	257
Gamaliel, m. Hannah **KEELER**, Apr. 24, 1788	1	89
Gamaliel, d. June 20, 1835, ae 75	1	231
Gamaliel Northrup, s. [Gamaliel & Hannah], b. July 14, 1793	1	89
Gideon, s. [Joseph & Ann], b. Mar. 15, 1710	LR1	200
Gideon, of Ridgefield, m. Dorothy **BOSTFORD**, of New Milford, Apr. 11, 1737, by Roger Brownson, J. P.	LR1	221
Gideon, of Ridgefield, m. Dorothy **BOTSFORD**, of New Milford, Apr. 11, 1737, by Roger Brownson, J. P.	LR1	229
Grindell, m. Hannah **KEELER**, Apr. 24, 1788	1	157
Hannah, d. James & Sarah, b. Jan. 29, 1716	LR1	200
Hannah, m. Ephraim **BENNETT**, May 27, 1730	LR1	229
Hannah, d. Squire James & Sarah, d. Mar. 12, 1737	LR1	215
Hannah, d. John & Esther, b. Feb. 27, 1762	1	8
Hannah, d. Thomas & Jane, b. Jan. 9, 1769	1	3
Hannah, m. Jonah **FOSTER**, Oct. 27, 1778	1	96
Hannah Sally, d. Jesse & Mehitable, b. Jan. 4, 1779	1	1
Harriet, d. Abijah & Amelia, b. July 9, 1801	1	43
Harriet, of Ridgefield, m. Thomas **BUTTLER**, of Brooklyn, N. Y., Apr. 17, 1836, by Rev. Charles G. Selleck	1	182
Hiram, s. [Josiah B. & Esther], b. Sept. 11, 1804	1	108
Ira, s. Jesse & Polly, b. Feb. 14, 1819	1	109
Ira, m. Clara **SANDERS**, b. of Ridgefield, Sept. 18, 1823, by Samuell M. Phelps	1	164
Ira, s. Ezra, d. Sept. 30, 1835, in his 43rd y.	1	232
Isaac Oliver, s. Thomas & Jane, b. Aug. 14, 1764	1	3
James, s. James & Sarah, b. Feb. 19, 1719/20	LR1	203
James, m. Mary [ ], May 8, 1740	LR1	232
James, s. James & Mary, b. May 8, 1745	LR1	239
James, s. Daniel & Agness, b. May 30, 1750	LR1	245
James, s. Thomas & Jane, b. Aug. 12, 1762	1	3
James, d. Nov. 25, 1762	1	200
Jane, m. John A. **BENEDICT**, b. of Ridgefield, Oct. 14, 1832, by Rev. Charles G. Selleck	1	177
Jared, his w. [ ], d. Mar. 13, 1810	1	215
Jemima, d. James & Mary, b. July 25, 1749	LR1	241
Jeremiah, [d. Joseph & Susannah], b. May 14, 1735	LR1	221
Jeremiah, s. Joseph & Susannah, b. May 17, 1735	LR1	215

RIDGEFIELD VITAL RECORDS 147

	Vol.	Page
BENEDICT, BENEDICK, (cont.)		
Jesse, [s. Matthew & Ruth], b. Feb. 2, 1735	LR1	211
Jesse, m. Mehitable **NORTHRUP**, Sept. 16, 1756	LR1	252
Jesse, s. Jesse & Elizabeth [or Mehitable], b. Nov. 9, 1758	LR1	257
Jesse, d. Feb. 2, 1805	1	212
Jesse, d. Jan. 4, 1826, ae 29	1	225
Joanna, d. James & Joanna, b. July 25, 1749	1	9
Joel, s. [Josiah B. & Esther], b. July 28, 1802	1	108
Joel T., m. Phebe M. **JONES**, b. of Ridgefield, Feb. 14, 1827, by Samuel M. Phelps	1	167
John, [s. Benjamin & Mary], b. Oct. 15, 1714	LR1	200
John, [twin with Thomas], s. James & Sarah, b. Oct. 4, 1726	LR1	207
John, [s. Matthew & Ruth], b. Apr. 23, 1732	LR1	211
John, s. Matthew & Ruth, b. Apr. 23, 1732	LR1	212
John, s. Matthew & Ruth, d. Apr. 24, 1732	LR1	214
John, m. Lucy [ ], Nov. 29, 1738	LR1	233
John, [s. Matthew & Ruth], b. Sept. 30, 1743	LR1	211
John, [s. John (s. Benjamin) & Lucy], b. June 16, 1745	LR1	235
John, s. James & Mary, b. Apr. 22, 1747	LR1	240
John, m. Esther **STEBBINS**, Jan. 24, 1749/50	LR1	233
John, [twin with Sarah], s. John & Esther, b. Mar. 7, 1753	LR1	247
John, s. Matthew & Elizabeth, b. May 1, 1764	1	15
John, s. [Josiah B. & Esther], b. Mar. 16, 1807	1	108
John, d. July 9, 1814, in his 88th y.	1	218
John, d. Dec. 13, 1823, in the 71st y. of his age	1	224
John, m. Harriet **OLMSTED**, July 2, 1845, by Rev. James A. Hawley	1	197
John, his w. [ ], d. Mar. 28, 1850, ae 31 y.	1	240
John A., m. Jane **BENEDICT**, b. of Ridgefield, Oct. 14, 1832, by Rev. Charles G. Selleck	1	177
Jonathan, s. Joseph & Mary, b. Feb. 2, [1723]	LR1	204
Joseph, s. Joseph & Ann, b. July 29, 1708	LR1	200
Joseph, m. Mary [ ], Mar. 21, 1720/1	LR1	227
Joseph, m. Susannah [ ], May 18, 1732	LR1	230
Joseph, s. Joseph & Susannah, b. Feb. 17, 1732/3	LR1	221
Joseph, s. James & Joanna, b. May 11, 1760	1	9
Joseph, s. Thomas & Jane, b. Oct. 26, 1760	LR1	250
Joseph, s. Daniel & Mary, b. Aug. 19, 1765	1	19
Joseph, [twin with Benjamin], s. Jesse & Mehetable, b. Jan. 17, 1770	1	1
Joseph, m. Joanna **NORTHRUP**, Dec. 23, 1792	1	158
Joseph, d. Aug. 4, 1838, ae 68 y.	1	234
Joseph Sturgis, s. Joseph & Joanna, b. May 29, 1803	1	99
Josiah, s. Peter & Mary, b. Sept. 24, 1736	LR1	220
Josiah, s. Peter & Mary, d. Dec. 7, 1736	LR1	213
Josiah, his w. [ ], d. Nov. 14, [1851], ae 75	1	241
Josiah B., m. Esther **TERRELL**, Oct. 30, 1799	1	108
Josiah Baldwin, s. John, Jr. & Esther, b. Nov. 6, 1778	1	43

148 BARBOUR COLLECTION

	Vol.	Page
BENEDICT, BENEDICK, (cont.)		
Julia A., m. Almon **HICKOCK**, May 3, 1842, by Nathan Burton, P. T.	1	192
Katey, [d. John, Jr. & Esther], b. Aug. 7, 1795; d. Mar. 20, 1804	1	43
Katy, d. John, Jr., d. Mar. 20, 1804	1	211
Lewis, s. Jesse & Mehetable, b. Dec. 7, 1773	1	1
Lewis, of New York City, m. Harriet **JONES**, of Ridgefield, Sept. 1, 1840, by Rev. Joseph Fuller	1	189
Lucy, [d. John (s. Benjamin) & Lucy], b. June 6, 1741	LR1	235
Lucy, d. [Josiah B. & Esther], b. Oct. 14, 1800	1	108
Lucy, d. Josiah B., d. Oct. 24, 1817	1	220
Lucy, [d. Josiah B. & Esther], d. Oct. 25, 1817, ae 17 y. 11 d.	1	108
Marah, d. Benj[amin] & Hannah, b. Apr. 30, 1735	LR1	221
Mariah, m. Asahel **BENEDICT**, 2nd, Nov. 27, 1827, by Nathan Burton	1	167
Martha, d. James & Sarah, b. Apr. 15, [1723]	LR1	204
Martha, d. James & Joanna, b. June 16, 1751	1	9
Martha, d. Daniel & Agness, b. Jan. 14, 1757	LR1	245
Mary, [d. Benjamin & Mary], b. Mar. 15, 1711	LR1	200
Mary, d. Joseph & Mary, b. July 25, [1726]	LR1	206
Mary, w. Peter, d. Oct. 12, 1736	LR1	213
Mary, d. Peter & Agniss, b. Dec. 24, 1738	LR1	226
Mary, d. Dan[ie]ll & Agnes, b. Nov. 15, 1740	LR1	225
Mary, d. James & Mary, b. Mar. 31, 1741	LR1	239
Mary, w. Capt. Benjamin, d. Nov. 30, 1771	1	201
Mary, d. Benj[ami]n, d. Apr. 15, 1827, ae 14 y.	1	226
Mary, m. Nathan **SMITH**, Dec. [ ]	LR1	252
Matilda, d. Joseph & Joanna, b. Dec. 6, 1798	1	99
Matthew, m. Ruth **KEELER**, d. John, late of Norwalk, Dec. 8, 1727	LR1	228
Matthew, s. Matthew & Ruth, b. Oct. 28, 1728	LR1	211
Matthew, Capt. d. July 7, 1757	LR1	217
Matthew, s. Matthew & Elizabeth, b. Oct. 6, 1759	LR1	257
Matthew, s. Matthew & Elizabeth, d. Oct. 8, 1759	LR1	217
Matthew, s. Matthew & Elizabeth, b. Nov. 23, 1760	LR1	257
Matthew, m. Elizabeth **POMERY**, Nov. [ ]	LR1	252
Mead, had infant s. [ ], d. Oct. 13, 1835, ae 1 y.	1	232
Mead, had d. [ ], d. Oct. 19, 1835, ae 4 y.	1	232
Mead, his w. [ ], d. Aug. 26, [1850], ae about 52 y.	1	240
Mehitable,d. Jesse & Mehitable, b. Oct. 11, 1762	1	1
Mehitable, w. Jesse, d. Dec. 11, 1804, ae 66	1	212
Mehetabel, w. Ezra, d. Dec. 26, 1831, ae 69	1	229
Nancy, m. Daniel **NEWCOMB**, Nov. 20, 1832, by Nathan Burton	1	177
Oscano, s. J. Harvey, d. Apr. 3, 1837, ae 3 y.	1	233
Peter, s. James & Sarah, b. Mar. 20. 1714	LR1	200
Peter, m. Mary **PARISH**, Oct. 29, 1734	LR1	229

BENEDICT, BENEDICK, (cont.)

	Vol.	Page
Peter, s. Peter & Mary, d. Aug. 10, 1735	LR1	215
Peter, s. Peter & Mary, b. Aug. 10, 1735	LR1	218-9
Peter, m. Agniss [ ], June 23, 1737	LR1	231
Phebe, d. James & Sarah, b. Mar. 4, [1718]	LR1	202
Phebe, d. [Matthew & Ruth], b. Aug. 3, 1739	LR1	211
Phebe, d. James & Jemima, b. Aug. 14, 1753	LR1	255
Phebe, d. James & Joanna, b. Aug. 14, 1753	1	9
Philip Lewis, s. Thomas & Jane, b. Sept. 4, 1767	1	3
Philip Lewis, s. Thomas & Jane, d. Oct. 4, 1767	1	200
Polly, [d. John, Jr. & Esther], b. Aug. 16, 1792	1	43
Polly, w. Jesse, d. Feb. 26, 1824, ae 24	1	224
Polly, w. Benjamin, d. Jan. 1, 1839, ae 60 y. 3 m.	1	234
Racheall, d. Benjamin & Mary, b. June 14, [1721]	LR1	203
Rachal, d. Daniel & Agniss, b. Feb. 27, 1745/6	LR1	242
Rebecca, m. Ebenezer **LOBDELL**, Dec. 28, 1732	LR1	229
Rebeckah, m. Samuel **ABBOTT**, Jr., Sept. 3, 1755	LR1	252
Rhoda, d. Benjamin & Hannah, b. Oct. 13, 1732	LR1	221
Ruth, d. James & Sarah, b. Dec. 3, 1711	LR1	200
Ruth, m. Thomas **ROCKWELL**, May 18, 1732	LR1	230
Ruth, [d. Matthew & Ruth], b. Mar. 24, 1733	LR1	211
Ruth, d. Jesse & Mehitable, b. Aug. 6, 1766	1	1
Ruth, m. Matthew **KEELER**, Jr., Jan. 4, 1780	1	156
Sally, m. John J. **ROCKWELL**, b. of Ridgefield, Oct. 28, 1823, by Nathan Burton	1	162
Sally Mary, d. Joseph & Joanna, b. Jan. 23, 1796	1	99
Samuell, [s. Benjamin & Mary], b. Nov. 27, 1716	LR1	200
Sam[ue]ll, s. Benjamin & Mary, b. June 29, [1719]	LR1	203
Samuel, s. Capt. Benjamin, d. Oct. 13, 1740	LR1	215
Samuel, [s. John (s. Benjamin) & Lucy], b Apr. 26, 1743	LR1	235
Sam[ue]ll, d. July 30, [1842], ae 20 y.	1	236
Samuel Andross, s. [Jesse & Polly], b. Aug. 10, 1822	1	109
Sam[ue]l Pitman, s. Joseph & Mary, b. Jan. 31, 1721/2	LR1	204
Sarah, d. James & Sarah, b. May 23, 1709	LR1	200
Sarah, m. Gideon **SMITH**, Dec. 9, 1731	LR1	229
Sarah, d. Timothy & Sarah, b. Apr. 13, 1735	LR1	222
Sarah, d. James & Mary, b. Feb. 6, 1743/4	LR1	239
Sarah, d. Daniel & Agness, b. May 13, 1752	LR1	245
Sarah, [twin with John], d. John & Esther, b. Mar. 7, 1753	LR1	247
Sarah, m. Bartholomew **WEED**, June 12, 1754, by Jonathan Ingersoll, V. D. M.	LR1	252
Sarah, m. James **SMITH**, Mar. 7, 1764	1	150
Sarah, w. Capt. Timothy, d. Jan. 19, 1765	1	200
Sarah, d. Thomas & Jane, b. Mar. 18, 1766	1	3
Sarah, m. Jabez **KEELER**, Apr. 20, 1777	1	66
Sarah, m. Phinehas **DOOLITTLE**, Mar. 7, 1782	1	153
Sarah, d. John, Jr. & Esther, b. Feb. 22, 1787	1	43
Sarah, w. Ambrose, d. Dec. 28, 1831, ae 56	1	229

	Vol.	Page
BENEDICT, BENEDICK, (cont.)		
Sarah, d. Mead, d. Sept. 26, 1835, ae 7	1	232
Susannah, [d. Joseph & Susannah], b. Mar. 25, 1736	LR1	221
Susannah, w. Ezra, d. Sept. 10, 1801	1	210
Thaddeus, s. Jesse & Mehitable, b. Jan. 6, 1772	1	1
Thaddeus, m. Huldah **MARVIN**, Jan. 19, 1794	1	159
Thadis Mead, s. Joseph & Joanna, b. Jan. 3, 1801	1	99
Thankfull, d. Benjamin & Mary, b. June 23, 1727	LR1	208
Thomas, [twin with John], s. James & Sarah], b. Oct. 4, 1726	LR1	207
Thomas, m. Jane **GUN[N]**, May 27, 1752	LR1	234
Thomas, s. Thomas & Jane, b. Feb. 27, 1753	LR1	250
Thomas B., m. Harriet **WOOSTER**, Nov. 14, 1827, by Nathan Burton	1	167
Thomas Platt, s. Comfort & Sarah, b. May 19, 17[ ]	1	81
Timothy, m. Sarah **SMITH**, Jan. 24, 1733/4	LR1	230
Timothy, s. Timothy & Sarah, b. Sept. 27, 1740	LR1	225
Timothy, Jr., d. June 21, 1757	LR1	217
Timothy, had Dorcas (colored), d. Jan. 10, 1760	LR1	217
Timothy, m. Elizabeth **STREET**, Oct. 9, 1765	1	150
Timothy, Capt., d. May 12, 1791, in the 81st y. of his age	1	205
William, s. James & Joanna, b. July 14, 1755	1	9
W[illia]m, his child d. Oct. 6, 1834, ae 2 w.	1	231
W[illia]m N., of New York, m. Elizabeth **KEELER**, of Ridgefiled, Dec. 30, 1832, by Rev. Charles G. Selleck	1	178
BENJAMIN, Joel, his child d. Nov. 27, 1839, ae 2	1	235
Joel S., m. Harriet **MILLS**, b. of Ridgefield, Apr. 13, 1834, by Levi Brunson	1	179
BENNETT, BENNET, BENNIT, BENNITT, Abel, s. Stephen & Mary, b. Apr. 7, 1782	1	52
Abel, M. D., of Leroy, N. Y., m. Mary B. **BUCKLEY**, of Ridgefield, [ ], by Rev. Nathaniel Mead. Recorded May 26, 1851	1	135
Abigail, d. Samuel & Abigail, b. Apr. 2, 1746	1	41
Abigail, d. Samuel & Abigail, d. Jan. 10, 1770	1	202
Antoinette, m. Benjamin A. **DENTON**, b. of Ridgefield, this day, [Oct. 16, 1850], by Rev. C. Clark	1	134
Benj[ami]n, s. [Ezra & Susanna], b. May 28, 1795	1	62
Betty, d. Stephen & Mary, b. Mar. 11, 1777	1	52
Clara, [d. Ezra & Susanna], b. Jan. 29, 1788	1	62
Daniel, s. Trobridge & Sarah, b. Nov. 23, 1771	1	31
Daniel, Jr., d. Aug. 22, 1793	1	206
Deborah, m. Benjamin **WILLSON**, June 2, 1737	LR1	229
Ebenezer O., m. Laura **SCOTT**, Dec. 30, 1830, by Nathan Burton	1	173
Eli Barnet, s. Stephen & Lucy, b. June 16, 1792	1	52
Eliphalet, s. Stephen & Elizabeth, b. Aug. 31, 1772	1	52
Elizabeth, m. Jonah **SMITH**, Dec. 29, 1726	LR1	227
Ellener, d. Samuel & Abigail, b. May 30, 1743	1	41

	Vol.	Page
BENNETT, BENNET, BENNIT, BENNITT, (cont.)		
Ephraim, m. Hannah **BENEDICT**, May 27, 1730	LR1	229
Ezekiel, s. Samuel & Abigail, b. Aug. 23, 1761	1	41
Ezra, s. [Ezra & Susanna], b. Apr. 12, 1790	1	62
Hannah, m. Jonathan **ROCKWELL**, Jr., Jan. 1, 1760	LR1	232
Hannah, w. Eliphalet, d. Mar. 19, 1835	1	231
Ira, s. [Ezra & Susanna], b. July 26, 1793	1	62
James, d. July 27, [1726]	LR1	214
James, s. Ephraim & Hannah, b. Feb. 5, 1731	LR1	212
Jared, s. Ezra & Susanna, b. Jan. 19, 1784	1	62
Jeremiah, s. Josiah & Rachel, b. Aug. 25, 1789	1	70
John, s. Samuel & Abigail, b. May 10, 1759	1	41
John, s. Stephen & Mary, b. July 22, 1780	1	52
John, s. Phalle **NORTHRUP** (single person), b. Dec. 27, 1790	1	69
Joseph, d. May 25, 1790, ae upwards of 80	1	205
Josiah, s. Trobridge & Sarah, b. Sept. 8, 1768	1	31
Josiah, m. Rachel **OSBORN**, Mar. 8, 1789	1	157
Josiah, d. Feb. 20, 1841, ae about 74	1	236
Lois, m. Jacob **DAUCHY**, May 3, 1789	1	69
Martha, m. John **JACKSON**, Nov. 18, 1781	1	154
Martha R., of Ridgefield, m. George L. **BARNES**, of North Haven, Mar. 22, 1829, by Samuel M. Phelps	1	169
Mary, d. Ephraim & Hannah, b. May 5, 1732	LR1	212
Mary, w. Dr. Stephen, d. July 25, 1789	1	205
Mary, w. Samuel, d. Nov. 16, 1789	1	205
Mary Ann, of Ridgefield, m. Charles **DAVIS**, of Wilton, Nov. 7, 1848, by Rev. Sylvester S. Strong	1	131
Nancy, d. Stephen & Mary, b. May 15, 1785	1	52
Olive, m. James **BRADLEY**, Mar. [ ], 1762	1	66
Polly, d. Trobridge & Sarah, b. June 8, 1788	1	31
Sally, m. Lewis **OLMSTED**, Mar. 9, 1795	1	100
Sally, m. David **HANFORD**, Oct. 12, 1837, by Nathan Burton	1	184
Samuel, s. Samuel & Abigail, b. Aug. 23, 1755	1	41
Samuel, s. Samuel & Abigail, d. Dec. 8, 1776	1	202
Sarah, m. Ezekiel **OSBORN**, Nov. 16, 17[ ]	1	150
Sarah, d. Samuel & Abigail, b. Dec. 6, 1751	1	41
Sarah, d. Trobridge & Sarah, b. Mar. 27, 1777	1	31
Sarah, m. Benajah **WORDEN**, Nov. [ ], 1789	1	158
Stephen, Dr., d. Sept. 5, 1802	1	211
Trowbridge, m. Sarah **HINE**, Aug. 20, 1767	1	151
Trowbridge, d. Sept. 4, 1804	1	212
Wakeman, d. June 11, 1840, ae 80 y.	1	235
BERRY, Almyra, [d. George & Lydia], b. Sept. 6, 1802	1	67
Almira, d. George, d. Dec. 17, 1804	1	212
Elizabeth, [d. George & Lydia], b. Oct. 5, 1790	1	67
George, m. Lydia **CRAWFORD**, Oct. 23, 1787	1	156
George, [s. George & Lydia], b. Apr. 29, 1796	1	67
George, d. Mar. 10, 1832, ae 78	1	229

	Vol.	Page
BERRY, (cont.)		
James, [s. George & Lydia], b. Aug. 27, 1800	1	67
John, [s. George & Lydia], b. Sept. 7, 1792	1	67
Lydia, w. George, d. June 5, 1831, ae 69	1	228
Mary, d. George & Lydia, b. May 25, 1786	1	67
Nancy, [s. George & Lydia], b. Feb. 5, 1788	1	67
Sally, [d. George & Lydia], b. Apr. 27, 1798	1	67
William, [s. George & Lydia], b. June 23, 1794	1	67
BETON, Learmore, d. Herman, d. Nov. 13, 1804	1	212
BETTS, Aaron, his child, d. Jan. 2, 1844, ae 1 y.	1	237
Abigail, d. Abraham & Mary, b. July 11, 1762	1	58
Abigail, d. Abraham, d. Dec. 20, 1765	1	203
Abraham, s. Abraham & Mary, b. May 31, 1757	LR1	246
Abraham, s. Abraham & Mary, b. May 31, 1757	1	58
Abraham, s. Abraham, d. Mar. 26, 1780	1	203
Almira, of Wilton, m. Lewis C. **SEYMOUR**, of Ridgefield, Oct. 8, 1823, by Sam[ue]ll M. Phelps	1	164
Anne, d. Gideon & Rachel, b. Mar. 20, 1769	1	26
Anne, m. Gerrel **FOUNTAIN**, May 14, 1787	1	156
Benjamin T., of Wilton, m. Emily **SEYMOUR**, of Ridgefield, May 10, 1826, by Samuel M. Phelps	1	167
Clarry, d. Abraham & Mary, b. Mar. 14, 1768	1	58
Delia, d. Harvey, d. Mar. 11, 1839, ae 16 y.	1	234
Delia Ann, m. John **BORDEN**, b. of Ridgefield, Oct. 26, 1828, by Samuel M. Phelps	1	169
Eunice, d. Abraham & Mary, b. Oct. 13, 1760	LR1	246
Eunice, d. Abraham & Mary, b. Oct. 17, 1760	1	58
Eunice, m. Jared **NORTHRUP**, Apr. 22, 1793	1	158
Fanny A., of Ridgefield, m. Peter **HARKNESS**, of New York City, Apr. 10, 1850, by Rev. Clinton Clark	1	133
Gideon, m. Rachal **SAINT JOHN**, Dec. 20, 1752, by Jonathan Ingersoll, V. D. M.	LR1	234
Gilead, s. Abraham & Mary, b. June 22, 1755	LR1	246
Gilead, s. Abraham & Mary, b. June 22, 175[ ]	1	58
Gilead, s. Abraham, d. Jan. 17, 1778	1	203
Hannah, b. May 10, 1755; m. Jared **OLMSTED**, [ ]	1	38
Hannah, m. Jared **OLMSTED**, Nov. 30, 1773	1	152
Harvey, d. Apr. 27, [1850], ae 54 y.	1	240
John, s. Abraham & Mary, b. Aug. 22, 17[ ]	1	58
Mary, d. Samuell & Judeth, of Norwalk, m. Richard **OLMSTEAD**, Apr. 22, 1714	LR1	227
Mary, d. Abraham & Mary, b. Dec. 12, 1753	LR1	246
Mary, d. Abraham & Mary, b. Dec. 12, 175[ ]	1	58
Mary, m. Benajah **SMITH**, Dec. 13, 1770	1	152
Mary, w. Abraham, d. June 6, 1776	1	203
Matthew, m. Amelia **MUNRO**, Jan. [ ], 1787	1	157
Nathan, s. Gideon & Rachel, b. Aug. 13, 1753	LR1	253
Ruhamah, d. Abraham & Mary, b. July 27, 1765	1	58

	Vol.	Page
BETTS, (cont.)		
Sarah, d. Abraham & Mary, b. Jan. [ ], 1759	1	58
Sarah, d. Abraham & Mary, b. June 7, 1759; d. Oct. 10, 1759	LR1	207
Sarah, d. Gideon & Rachel, b. June 2, 176[ ]	1	26
Sarah, d. Abraham, d. [ ], 1761	1	203
BIRCHARD, BURCHARD, Elias, [s. Uriah], b. Oct. 4, 1795	1	102
Ezra, [s. Uriah], b. Dec. 24, 1799	1	102
Isaiah, d. Feb. [ ], 1794, ae 74	1	207
Jeremiah, m. Phebe **ABBOT**, Feb. 5, 1772	1	152
Jeremiah, s. Jeremiah & Phebe, b. June 11, 1774	1	42
Jeremiah, Jr., d. Aug. [ ], 1777	1	202
Lydia, d. Isaiah & Sarah, b. May 1, 1754	LR1	243
Lydia, m. Abijah **ROCKWELL**, Sept. 30, 1773	1	153
Phebe, m. Matthew **SMITH**, Jan. 10, 1766	1	153
Phebe, d. Jeremiah & Phebe, b. May 17, 1772	1	42
Phebe, w. Jeremiah, d. Sept. 8, 1777	1	202
Phebe, d. Jeremiah, d. Sept. 17, 1777	1	202
Polly, [d. Uriah], b. Apr. 15, 1793	1	102
Sally, [d. Uriah], b. July 6, 1788	1	102
Stephen, s. Jeremiah & Phebe, b. Apr. 9, 1777	1	42
Stephen, d. Sept. 14, 1777	1	202
Uriah, s. Isaiah & Sarah, b. Feb. 23, 1757	LR1	243
Uriah, m. Eunice **TAYLOR**, Oct. 16, 1782	1	152
BIRDSALL, Jane, of Ridgefield, m. Andrew **BATHITE**(?), of North Salem, Dec. 4, 1836, by Rev. Charles G. Selleck	1	183
Jeremiah, d. [, probably 1851], ae 67 y., of Ridgebury	1	241
BISHOP, Ebenezer, of Salem, m. Lucinda **LOBDELL**, June 7, 1790	1	158
Esther, m. David **BEERS**, Feb. 19, 1788	1	156
BLACKMAN, David, his child, d. May 8, 1824, ae 7 y.	1	224
David, d. Oct. 8, 1840, ae about 51 y.	1	235
Eleanor, wid., d. Nov. 20, 1811, ae 56 y.	1	215
John, d. June 6, 1806	1	213
John, d. Jan. 19, 1813, ae 26	1	217
Nehemiah, d. Dec. 2, 1837, ae 40	1	234
Peter, d. Aug. 7, 1805, in the 28th y. or his age	1	212
BODWELL, Levi Munson, [s. Joseph & Sabra], b. Sept. 11, 1803	1	90
William, [s. Joseph & Sabra], b. Feb. 3, 1802	1	90
BOLT, Katy, Mrs., d. Apr. 25, 1790, ae 78	1	205
William, m. Elizabeth **OLMSTED**, Nov. 29, 1781	1	154
BORDEN, John, m. Delia Ann **BETTS**, b. of Ridgefield, Oct. 26, 1828, by Samuel M. Phelps	1	169
BOSTFORD, Dorothy, of New Milford, m. Gideon **BENEDICT**, of Ridgefield, Apr. 11, 1737, by Roger Brownson, J. P.	LR1	221
Dorothy, of New Milford, m. Gideon **BENEDICT**, of Ridgefield, Apr. 11, 1737, by Roger Brownson, J. P.	LR1	229
BOSTWICK, Hannah, m. Samuel **BRADLEY**, Feb. 22, 1786	1	67
BOUTON, BOUGHTON, BOWTON, Anna, m. Timothy **JONES**, Feb. 12, 1806	1	106

154 BARBOUR COLLECTION

	Vol.	Page
BOUTON, BOUGHTON, BOWTON, (cont.)		
Avery, m. Sarah **KEELER**, Apr. 1, 1773	1	155
Avery, d. Apr. 3, 1794, ae 48	1	207
Benjamin, s. Timothy & Martha, b. Mar. 9, 1784	1	47
Currents, d. Timothy, d. July 8, 1815, in the 2nd y. of her age	1	218
Daniel, 2nd, had child d. Sept. 15, 1813, ae 4 y.	1	218
Daniel, his mother d. Nov. 18, 1829, ae 87	1	227
Daniel, had infant s. [ ], d. Jan. 6, 1835	1	231
Delia Ann, of Ridgefield, m. Thomas **SANFORD**, of Danbury, Nov. 19, 1838, by Rev. Thomas Sparks	1	187
Elizabeth, m. Jeremiah **GILBERT**, b. of Ridgefield, Dec. 15, 1844, by Rev. A. S. Francis	1	196
Erastus S., had infant d. Sept. 16, 1828	1	226
Eunice, m. Francis **FAIRCHILD**, June 6, 1830, by Nathan Burton	1	172
Fairchild, d. Jan. 19, 1808	1	213
Hezekiah, d. Jan. 14, 1803, ae 38 y.	1	211
Hiram, had child d. Oct. 1, 1838, ae 4 y.	1	234
Hiram, his child d. Sept. 14, 1839, ae 4 y.	1	235
Hiram, m. Sarah B. **KNAPP**, b. of Ridgefield, Oct. 4, 1846, by Rev. Charles Stearns, Int. Pub.	1	199
Hiram S., m. Rebeckah **SMITH**, b. of Ridgefield, Nov. 10, 1824, by Samuell M. Phelps	1	165
Huldah, d. June 8, 1801	1	210
James, d. June 5, 1833, ae 40	1	230
James Benedict, s. Timothy & Martha, b. Aug. 22, 1779	1	47
Jesse, m. Sally **BOWTON**, [ ], 1795	1	159
Jesse, had infant s. [ ], d. Jan. 25, 1819	1	221
Joel, m. Deborah **ROCKWELL**, [ ], 1795	1	159
John, s. Timothy & Martha, b. May 2, 1770	1	47
Martha, d. Timothy & Martha, b. Dec. 28, 1767	1	47
Mary, m. James **DAUCHY**, Apr. 13, 1786	1	156
Phebe, m. Benjamin **JONES**, Mar. 23, 1790	1	158
Polly, d. Daniel, 2nd, d. Sept. 8, 1813, ae 2 y.	1	218
Rache, m. Edwin **ROCKWELL**, Sept. 14, 1829, by Nathan Burton	1	170
Rufus, d. June 10, 1839, ae 28 y.	1	235
Sally, d. Timothy & Martha, b. May 2, 1773	1	47
Sally, m. James S. **WATEROUS**, [ ], 1795	1	84
Sally, m. James **WAKEMAN**, [ ], 1795	1	159
Sally, m. Jesse **BOWTON**, [ ], 1795	1	159
Sally, d. W[illia]m & Phebe, d. Dec. 3, 1817, ae 9	1	220
Sally, wid., m. Enoch **HOLLY**, b. of Ridgefield, Oct. 19, 1828, by Samuel Stebbins, J. P.	1	168
Sarah Ann, d. Hiram, d. Dec. 4, 1833, ae 3 1/4 y.	1	230
Seth, Jr., d. Aug. 27, 1814, ae 34	1	218
Seth, m. Elizabeth **BEERS**, b. of Ridgefield, Aug. 4, 1822, by Rev. Samuel M. Phelps	1	161

RIDGEFIELD VITAL RECORDS 155

	Vol.	Page
BOUTON, BOUGHTON, BOWTON, (cont.)		
Seth, his w. [ ], d. Jan. 20, 1833, ae 69 y.	1	229
Seth, [of Wilton], d. Dec. 10, 1840, ae 86 y.	1	236
Thaddeus, s. Timothy & Martha, b. May 2, 1777	1	47
Timothy, s. Timothy & Martha, b. Dec. 4, 1786	1	47
Timothy, d. Oct. 27, 1806	1	213
William, m. Polly E. **HOYT**, b. of Ridgefield, Mar. 15, 1829, by Samuel M. Phelps	1	169
Wilson, of Ridgefield, m. Julia Ann **PICK**, of Redding, Sept. 14, 1845, by Rev. James A. Hawley	1	197
-----, wid., & mother of Daniel, d. Nov. 18, 1829, ae 87	1	227
BOWEN, Samuel, s. Rev. [ ], d. Feb. 29, 1832, ae 11 y.	1	229
BOWLER, Elijah, m. Mary **NORTHRUP**, Oct. 27, 1785	1	156
BRADLEY, Abiah, [d. James & Olive], b. May 22, 1775	1	66
Abigail, [d. James & Olive], b. Mar. 28, 1765	1	66
Abigail, m. Benjamin **SELLECK**, Mar. 3, 1783	1	154
Amos B., [s. Isaac S. & Elizabeth], b. Nov. 27, 1818	1	107
Anna, w. Daniel, d. Mar. 2, 1836, ae 70	1	232
Benjamin, s. Benj[amin] & Esther, b. Oct. 19, 1741	LR1	226
Betsey, d. Philip & Molly, b. Feb. 12, 1775	1	21
Billy, s. Daniel, d. Feb. 16, 1793	1	206
Burr, of Onandago, m. Lucy W. **SCOTT**, of Ridgefield, Oct. 24, 1824, by Samuell M. Phelps	1	165
Daniel, m. Ruth **NORTHRUP**, May 10, 1784	1	154
Daniel, his infant s. [ ], d. Sept. 6, 1795, ae 14 d.	1	208
Daniel, had infant d. [ ], d. June 15, 1799	1	209
Eliphalet, s. Benj[amin] & Esther, b. Jan. 25, 1738/9	LR1	226
Elizabeth, w. Jesse S., d. Feb. 19, 1844, ae 59 y.	1	237
Esther, d. Philip & Molly, b. May 7, 1773	1	21
Esther, m. David **KEELER**, Feb. 23, 179[ ]	1	80
Esther, m. David **WHEELER***, Feb. 23, 1794 *(**KEELER**?)	1	158
Esther, see Esther **KEELER**	1	241
Eunice, of Ridgefield, m. George **DICKENS**, of Danbury, Oct. 18, 1848, by Rev. Sylvester S. Strong	1	131
Eunice, of Rigefield, m. George **DICKENS**, of Redding, Oct. 18, 1848, by Rev. Sylvester S. Strong	1	131
Ezekiel, [s. James & Olive], b. Feb. 26, 1770	1	66
Francis, [s. Isaac S. & Elizabeth], b. Nov. 6, 1815	1	107
Harriet Emeline, d. Philip & Polly, b. Apr. 9, 1803	1	99
Howard, [s. James & Olive], b. June 8, 1777	1	66
Jabez Burr, s. Philip & Molly, b. Feb. 18, 1768	1	21
Jabez Burr, d. Dec. 15, 1811, in the 44th y. of his age	1	215
James, m. Olive **BENNET**, Mar. [ ], 1762	1	66
James, [s. James & Olive], b. Apr. 2, 1768	1	66
James, & w. Olive had 2 infants d. Aug. 12, 1781	1	66
James, d. July 4, 1784	1	66
Jesse, s. Philip & Molly, b. Aug. 27, 1782	1	21
Jesse B., [s. Isaac S. & Elizabeth], b. Apr. 4, 1811; d. [ ]	1	107

BRADLEY, (cont.)

	Vol.	Page
Jesse Baker, s. Jesse S., d. June 16, 1812, ae 14 m.	1	217
Jesse S., m. Elizabeth **BAKER**, Dec. 3, 1805, by Rev. Samuel Goodrich	1	159
Jesse S., [s. Isaac S. & Elizabeth], b. May 5, 1813	1	107
Jesse S., d. May 24, 1833, in the 51st y. of his age	1	203
Jesse S., m. Mary E. **SMITH**, July 1, 1838, by Rev. Joseph Fuller	1	186
Lewis, [s. James & Olive], b. Aug. 15, 1782	1	66
Mary, w. Philip, d. Apr. 9, 1812, ae 31 y. 1 m. 20 d.	1	216
Mary Ann, d. Apr. 1, 1836, ae 25 y.	1	232
Mary Anna, [d. Philip & Polly], b. Aug. 11, 1810	1	99
Molly, d. Philip Burr & Molly, b. Sept. 13, 1766	1	21
Molly, m. Samuel **DAUCHY**, Dec. 6, 1789	1	157
Philip, s. Philip & Molly, b. Sept. 17, 1770	1	21
Philip, m. Polly **KEELER**, May 9, 1802	1	159
Philip, had negro girl Emily, d. Nov. 26, 1831, ae 17	1	229
Philip, d. Dec. 27, 1844, ae 74 y.	1	238
Philip B., [s. Isaac S. & Elizabeth], b. Jan. 5, 1809	1	107
Philip Burr, Col. (a revolutionary officer), b. Mar. 26, 1738, d. Jan. 4, 1821, in the 83rd y. of his age	1	222
Philip Edward, s. Philip & Polly, b. July 19, 1809; d. July 29, 1809, ae 10 d.	1	99
Philip Edward, s. Philip, d. July 29, 1809, ae 10 d.	1	214
Polly, m. Alfred **SMITH**, b. of Ridgefield, Jan. 9, 1823, by Rev. Samuel M. Phelps	1	161
Rachel, m. Nathan **DAUCHY**, 2nd, Nov. 13, 1794	1	159
Ruth, d. Philip & Molly, b. Oct. 10, 1771	1	21
Ruth, m. Nathan **DAUCHY**, Jr., Nov. 13, 1794	1	103
Ruth, m. Nathan **DAUCHY**, 2nd, Nov. 13, 1794	1	159
Ruth, wid., d. Jan. 14, 1815	1	218
Ruth, wid. Col. Philip, d. Dec. 9, 1837, in the 93rd y. of her age	1	234
Sally Feret, d. Philip & Molly, b. July 11, 1780	1	21
Samuel, [s. James & Olive], b. Mar. 26, 1763	1	66
Samuel, m. Hannah **BOSTWICK**, Feb. 22, 1786	1	67
Sarah S., d. Isaac S. & Elizabeth, b. Nov. 12, 1806	1	107
Sarah S., m. Nathan **SMITH**, Jr., b. of Ridgefield, Nov. 15, 1825, by Samuell M. Phelps	1	166
Stephen, d. June 25, 1807	1	213
Widing, [s. James & Olive], b. Sept. 16, 1772	1	66
William H., [s. Isaac S. & Elizabeth], b. Nov. 29, 1816	1	107

BRANDAGE, Reuben G., of Greenwich, m. Julia H. **SANDERLAND**, of Ridgefield, Feb. 2, 1851, by Rev. Nathaniel Mead — 1 135

BRIANT, [see under **BRYANT**]

BRINKERHOFF, [see also **BUNKERHOOF**], Betsey, [d. George J. & Susanna], b. Aug. 21, 1790 — 1 77

	Vol.	Page
BRINKERHOFF, (cont.)		
Isaac, d. Jan. 31, 1841, ae 30	1	236
Sally, d. George J. & Susanna, b. Sept. 22, 1788	1	77
Susanna, m. John **TITUS**, Jan. 5, 1794	1	77
BRONSON, BRUNSON, Daniel, of Danbury, m. Clarissa **MILLS**, of Ridgefield, Dec. 31, 1837, by James Coleman, Elder	1	184
-----, d. June 13, 1847, ae 32 y.	1	239
BROOKMAN, William, d. Aug. 29, 1820, in his 64th y.	1	222
BROOKS, Dan[ie]ll, s. Eben[eze]r & Jane, b. Mar. 26, 1741	LR1	223
Ebenezer, m. Jane **SAINT JOHN**, d. Capt. [ ], Aug. 27, 1730	LR1	228
Ebenez[e]r, s. Eben[eze]r & Jane, b. July 6, 1731	LR1	218-9
Elizabeth, m. Thomas **WILLSON**, Jan. 30, 1729	LR1	228
Elizabeth, d. Eben[eze]r & Jane, b. July 18, 1737	LR1	221
Elizabeth, w. Eben[eze]r, d. Nov. 17, 1745	LR1	215
Elizabeth, m. Daniel **JACKSON**, Apr. 5, [ ]	LR1	252
Jane, d. Eben[eze]r & Jane, b. Apr. 8, 1733	LR1	218-9
Jeremiah, s. Jonathan & Sarah, b. Apr. 22, 1750	LR1	249
John, s. Jonathan & Sarah, b. Dec. 4, 1755	LR1	249
Jonathan, m. Sarah [ ], Apr. 9, 1744	LR1	232
Jonathan, s. Jonathan & Sarah, b. Sept. 30, 1745	LR1	239
Joseph, s. Ebenezer & Jane, b. May 21, 1745	LR1	238
Martha, d. Jonathan & Sarah, b. Feb. 20, 1752	LR1	249
Mary, d. Eben[eze]r & Jane, b. Sept. 14, 1735	LR1	218-9
Phebe, d. Jonathan & Sarah, b. Nov. 12, 1746	LR1	239
Rebeckah, d. Ebenezer & Jane, b. Dec. 18, 1742	LR1	237
Ruth, d. Jonathan & Sarah, b. Nov. 9, 1753	LR1	249
Samuel, s. Eben[eze]r & Jane, b. May 10, 1739	LR1	224
Sarah, d. Jonathan & Sarah, b. Feb. 16, 1749	LR1	249
BROWN, Bostwick, s. Daniel & Abigail, b. Oct. 17, 1763	1	27
Daniel, s. Daniel & Abigail, b. Mar. 11, 1770	1	27
David, m. Abigail **NORTHRUP**, Feb. 10, 1763	1	150
David, s. Robert, d. Mar. 23, 1830, ae 5 y.	1	228
Elizabeth, d. Daniel & Abigail, b. Feb. 26, 1769	1	27
Hannah, b. Aug. 22, 1762	1	71
Hannah, m. David **PERRY**, [ ]	1	71
Martha, d. Daniel & Abigail, b. Aug. 24, 1773	1	27
Nabbe, d. Daniel & Abigail, b. Dec. 3, 1766	1	27
Nathan, m. Polly **KEELER**, Mar. 18, 1787	1	156
Parnel, d. Daniel & Abigail, b. July 1, 1765	1	27
Sarah Maria, m. John R. **SMITH**, b. of Ridgefield, Oct. 12, 1842, by Rev. Warner Hoyt	1	192
Silas W., of South Salem, m. Jane E. **MEAD**, of Ridgefield, Oct. 11, 1838, by Rev. Joseph Fuller	1	186
Solomon, of Poundridge, N. Y., m. Sally **WILLIAMS**, of Ridgefield, Nov. 7, 1821, by Rev. Samuel M. Phelps	1	161
BROWNING, Betsey, m. James **SHERWOOD**, b. of Danbury, May 21, 1848, by Rev. James A. Hawley	1	129

BARBOUR COLLECTION

	Vol.	Page
BRUCE, William W., of Tecumsah, Mich., m. Elizabeth B.		
GILBERT, of Ridgefield, June 8, 1841, by A. Sparks	1	190
BRUNDRIDGE, Nathan, m. Hannah **KELLOGG**, Feb. 21, 1788	1	156
BRUSH, Abigail, d. [Eliphalet & Abigail], b. Apr. 17, 1780	1	87
Abigail, 2nd w. Eliphalet, d. May 11, 1791	1	87
Abner, s. [Eliphalet & Eunice], b. Apr. 28, 1801	1	87
Alma, d. [Eliphalet & Abigail], b. June 21, 1783	1	87
Amelia, d. Philip & Ruth, b. Mar. 20, 1799	1	91
Ardel, s. [Eliphalet & Abigail], b. Aug. 20, 1781	1	87
Arza, s. [Eliphalet & Eunice], b. Dec. 5, 1794	1	87
Arza, d. Dec. 20, 1826, ae 32	1	226
Conkling, s. Philip & Ruth, b. Mar. 8, 1794	1	91
Deborah, m. John **MOREHOUSE**, Mar. 14, 17[ ]	LR1	252
Eli, s. {Eliphalet & Abigail], b. July 24, 1785	1	87
Eliphalet, m. Hannah **HAMILTON**, Jan. 13, 1773	1	87
Eliphalet s. Eliphalet & Hannah, b. Mar. 21, 1774	1	87
Eliphalet, m. 2nd w. Abigail **DUNNING**, Nov. 11, 1777	1	87
Eliphalet, Capt. his w. [ ], d. May 10, 1791	1	205
Eliphalet, m. 3rd w. wid. Eunice **LEE**, Jan. 8, 1792	1	87
Eliphalet, m. Eunice **LEE**, Jan. 8, 1792	1	158
Eliphalet, d. June 8, 1846, ae 97 y. 6 m.	1	238
Eunice, d. Eliphalet & Eunice, b. Apr. 5, 1793	1	87
Hannah, w. Eliphalet, d. Apr. 3, 1774	1	87
Hannah, d. Eliphalet & Abigail, b. Mar. 13, 1779	1	87
Henry C., m. Clarissa **ST. JOHN**, b. of Ridgefield, Nov. 4,		
1841, by Rev. Joseph Fuller	1	191
Hull, s. [Eliphalet & Eunice], b. Jan. 30, 1797	1	87
Jarvis, s. Philip & Ruth, b. Jan. 6, 1797	1	91
Jarvis, m. Sarah **KEELER**, Sept. 4, 1827, by Nathan Burton	1	167
Nathaniel, s. Philip & Ruth, b. Mar. 10, 1787	1	91
Oliver B., s. [Eliphalet & Abigail], b. Dec. 9, 1787	1	87
Philetus, s. Philip & Ruth, b. Feb. 7, 1789	1	91
Polly, d. Philip & Ruth, b. May 6, 1791	1	91
Polly, d. [Eliphalet & Eunice], b. Dec. 31, 1798	1	87
Polly, m. James S. **ROCKWELL**, Nov. 2, 1831, by Nathan		
Burton	1	174
BRYANT, BRIANT, Hannah, w. Sam[ue]l, d. June 4, 1789	1	205
Smith, d. Sept. 16, 1816, ae 17 y.	1	219
BUCKLEY, [see also **BULKLEY**], Mary B., of Ridgefield, m. Abel		
BENNETT, M. D., of Leroy, N. Y., [ ], by		
Rev. Nathaniel Mead. Recorded May 26, 1851	1	135
BULKLEY, [see also **BUCKLEY**], Amelia, m. Abijah **BENEDICT**,		
Jan. 17, 1781	1	152
Bradley, d. May 7, 1825, ae 56	1	224
George, of South Port, m. Harriet **KELLOGG**, of Ridgefield,		
Mar. 30, 1851, by Rev. William Staunton	1	136
BUNDY, John, m. Sarah **NICHOLS**, Sept. 26, 1753, by Jonathan		
Ingersoll, V. D. M.	LR1	234

	Vol.	Page
BUNDY, (cont.)		
Sarah, d. John & Sarah, b. Aug. 13, 1754	LR1	257
Sarah, d. John & Sarah, b. Aug. 13, 1754	1	17
Sarah, m. William **WHITNEY**, Aug. 11, 1773	1	152
BUNKERHOOF, [see also **BRINKERHOFF**], Isaac*, m. Mary B. **GILBERT**, b. of Ridgefield, Oct. 24, 1832, by Rev. Nicholas White *(Written "Isaac **BRINKERHOFF**?)	1	177
BURCHARD, [see under **BIRCHARD**]		
BURLING, Lancaster D., of New York, m. Rebecca D. **GILBERT**, of Ridgefield, Mar. 14, 1849, by Rev. Sylvester S. Strong	1	131
BURR, Amelia,of Reading, m. Noah **TAYLOR**, of Ridgefield, Apr. 18, 1821, by Samuel M. Phelps	1	161
Anna, of Reading, m. Nehemiah **MEAD**, of Ridgefield, Mar. 12, 1822, by Rev. Samuel M. Phelps	1	161
Caroline, d. David, d. Jan. 28, 1833	1	229
David, his d. [ ], d. July 2, 1832, ae 14 y.	1	229
David Barlow, m. Abigail **DIBBLE**, b. of Ridgefield, [Apr.] 12, [1825], by Rev. Origen S. Holcomb	1	163
Delia, w. Zalmon S., d. May 9, 1824, ae 27	1	224
Grace, m. Joseph **JACKSON**, Dec. 5, 1750	1	150
Hannah, m. Thomas **HYATT**, [ ]	1	150
Jacob, of Redding, m. Polly **WHITLOCK**, of Ridgefield, this day, [Apr. 7, 1830], by Rev. Origen P. Holcomb	1	171
John, d. Mar. 24, 1825, ae 74 y.	1	224
Mary, m. Josiah **STEBBINS**, Dec. 7, 1771	1	151
Mary P., of Ridgebury, m. Jacob **LOBDELL**, of North Salem, Sept. 22, 1843, by Rev. Z. B. Burr	1	194
Polly, w. Jacob, d. Jan. 23, 1831	1	228
Sam[ue]ll, m. Sarah **LOBDELL**, Mar. [ ], 1793	1	158
Sarah, m. John **JONES**, Oct. 29, 1777	1	155
Seth, of Redding, m. Elizabeth **LOBDELL**, Jan. 26, 1790	1	158
Zalmon, his w. [ ], d. Mar. 11, [1843], ae 42 y.	1	236
Zalmon S., m. Sally **MEAD**, b. of Ridgefield, May 22, 1825, by Samuell M. Phelps	1	166
Zebulon, m. Delia **FOSTER**, b. of Ridgefield, Feb. 11, 1823, by Rev. Oliver Tuttle	1	161
BURRETT, [see also **BURRILL**], Betsey, of Ridgefield, m. Dr. Joel **FOSTER**, of Redding, June 13, 1843, by David C. Comstock	1	194
Wakeman, Jr., had child d. Oct. 20, 1836, ae 3 y.	1	233
BURRILL, [see also **BURRETT**], Amelia, w. Wakeman, d. Dec. 17, 1833, ae 87	1	230
BURT, Abigail, [d. Benjamin & Sarah], b. Nov. 8, 1709	LR1	199
Abigail, twin with Sarah, d. Christopher & Joanna, b. Apr. 14, 1732	LR1	212
Anna, m. Gideon **SCOTT**, Oct. 17, 1779	1	76
Asa, m. Sarah **STEBBINS**, Jan. 3, 1797	1	159
Asa, his infant s. [ ], d. Oct. 16, 1797	1	209

160   BARBOUR COLLECTION

	Vol.	Page
BURT, (cont.)		
Belden, s. Joshua & Lydia, b. May 11, 1775	1	34
Benjamin, [s. Benjamin & Sarah], b. Feb. 5, 1707/8	LR1	199
Benjamin, [s. Seaborn & Susannah], b. Dec. 29, 1741	LR1	247
Charles, d. Jan. 29, 1819, ae 21 y.	1	221
Charlotte, d. [Sept.] 24, [1843], ae about 57 y.	1	237
Christopher, s. Benjamin & Sarah, b. Apr. 14, 1704	LR1	199
Christopher, m. Joanna **SAINT JOHN**, d. Capt. [ ], Dec. 21, 1727	LR1	228
Daniell, s. Benjamin & Sarah, b. July 8, 1716; bp. July 15, [ ]	LR1	199
David, [s. Seaborn & Susannah], b. Feb. 12, 1750	LR1	247
Edwin, m. Rachel **DEAN**, Feb. 2, 1830, by Nathan Burton	1	171
Hachaliah, s. Joshua & Lydia, b. May 3, 1773	1	34
Jeremiah, s. Joshua & Lydia, b. Mar. 6, 1771	1	34
Jeremiah, d. Oct. 15, 1794, ae 23	1	207
John, [s. Benjamin & Sarah], b. Nov. 9, 1711	LR1	199
John, s. Christopher & Joanna, b. Aug. 14, 1729	LR1	211
John, s. Joshua & Lydia, b. May 2, 1781	1	34
Joseph, s. Christopher & Joanna, b. Sept. 8, 1742	LR1	236
Joshua, [s. Seaborn & Susannah], b. Mar. 21, 1743	LR1	247
Joshua, m. Lydia **SMITH**, Sept. 12, 1770	1	151
Joshua, s. Joshua & Lydia, b. Mar. 24, 1777	1	34
Joshua, Jr., his infant, d. Dec. 16, 1809	1	215
Joshua, Jr., had child d. May 23, 1817	1	220
Joshua, d. Nov. 6, 1817, ae 75	1	220
Joshua, d. Apr. 20, 1830, ae 57 y. 27 d.	1	228
Lucy, d. Jeremiah & Urania, b. July 7, 1794	1	76
Lydia, wid. Joshua, d. May 31, 1829, ae 80	1	227
Mary, d. Christopher & Johanna, b. Oct. 28, 1736	LR1	222
Mary, [d. Seaborn & Susannah], b. May 12, 1746	LR1	247
Polly, w. Joshua, 2nd, d. Feb. 22, 1808	1	213
Polly Smith, of Ridgefield, m. Stephen **MARSHALL**, of New Canaan, Mar. 10, 1829, by Samuel M. Phelps	1	169
Sam[ue]ll, s. Christopher & Joanna, b. Jan. 19, 1734	LR1	218-9
Sarah, [d. Benjamin & Sarah], b. June 4, 1714	LR1	199
Sarah, twin with Abigail, d. Christopher & Joanna, b. Apr. 14, 1732	LR1	212
Seaborn, s. Benjamin & Sarah, b. July 4, 1706	LR1	199
Stephen, m. Clarissa **MEAD**, b. of Ridgefield, Jan. 1, 1845, by Rev. A. S. Francis	1	197
Susannah, [d. Seaborn & Susannah], b. Aug. 18, 1748	LR1	247
Susannah, wid., d. Dec. 21, 1803, in the 94th y. of her age	1	211
Thankful, d. Benjamin & Sarah, b. Oct. 9, 1718	LR1	202
Thankfull, d. Benjamin & Sarah, d. Sept. 22, [1719]	LR1	213
Thankfull, d. Benjamin & Sarah, b. Nov. 1, [1721]	LR1	203
Thankfull, [d. Seaborn & Susannah], b. Nov. 3, 1738	LR1	247
Thankfull, m. George **FOLLIETT**, Sept. [ ]	LR1	252

	Vol.	Page
BURT, (cont.)		
Theodorius, d. Mar. 23, 1822	1	223
Theophilus, [s. Seaborn & Susannah], b. May 14, 1752; d. Sept. [ ], 1753	LR1	247
Theophilus, 2nd, [s. Seaborn & Susannah], b. Mar. 31, 1756	LR1	247
-----, wid., d. [May] 1847	1	239
BURTIS, Andrew, of New Canaan, m. Margaret **POWEL**, Mar. 3, [1847], by Rev. Charles Stearnes	1	127
BURTON, Hannah, m. Augustus D. **SLOSSON**, Mar. 15, 1840, by Nathan Burton, P. T.	1	188
BUTTERFIELD, Sarah, m. William **PLATT**, Apr. 16, 1838, by Nathan Burton	1	185
BUTTLER, Thomas, of Brooklyn, N. Y., m. Harriet **BENEDICT**, of Ridgefield, Apr. 17, 1836, by Rev. Charles G. Selleck	1	182
BYINGTON, Nathan, m. Abby **STEBBINS**, b. of Ridgefield, July 7, 1840, by Rev. Joseph Fuller	1	189
Polly, w. Nathan, d. Nov. 17, 1844, ae 34, y.	1	238
CABLE, Sarah, m. Abraham **TAYLOR**, Dec. 1, 1784	1	155
CAIN, Ann, m. Thaddeus **BANKS**, Jan. 11, 1789	1	157
Daniel, s. Hugh & Hannah, d. Apr. 8, 1783	1	203
Hannah, wid., d. Oct. 31, 1828, ae 75 y.	1	227
Hugh, d. Apr. 11, 1808	1	214
CAMP, Anne, d. Rev. Samuel & Mary*, b. Mar. 8, 1775 *(Hannah?)	1	30
Anne, d. Rev. Samuell, d. Oct. 16, 1777	1	203
Hannah, w. Rev. Samuel, d. Sept. 25, 1777	1	203
Lucretia, w. Rev. Samuell, d. Feb. 2, 1782	1	203
Mary, d. Rev. Samuel & Hannah, b. June 10, 1773	1	30
Philander, s. Rev. Samuel & Hannah, b. Sept. 15, 1779	1	30
Samuel, Rev., m. Mrs. Hannah **GARNSEY**, Sept. 21, 1769, by Joseph Bellamy, V. D. M.	1	151
Samuel, Rev. of Ridgefield, m. Mrs. Lucretia **BARKER**, of Branford, Oct. 28, 1778, by Rev. Phinehas Robbins, of Branford	1	153
Samuel, Rev., m. Mrs. Mary **NORTHRUP**, b. of Ridgefield, Oct. 17, 1782, by John Benedict, J. P.	1	153
Samuel, Rev., d. Mar. 10, 1813	1	217
Samuel Abiel, s. Rev. Sam[ue]ll & Hannah, b. Mar. 8, 1771	1	30
Samuel Abiel, d. Nov. 11, 1809	1	215
Sarah, d. Rev. Samuel & Hannah, b. Jan. 15, 1782	1	30
Sarah, m. Samuel S. **BALDWIN**, Nov. 10, 1796	1	89
CAMPBELL, Julia, of Ridgefield, m. Joseph A. **INGERSOLL**, of Westchester Co., N. Y., Apr. 4, 1828, by Samuel M. Phelps	1	169
CANFIELD, Alpheas, d. Nov. 25, 1842, ae 62 y.	1	236
Charles F., of Bedford West Chester Co., N. Y., m. Rachel A. **OLMSTED**, of Ridgefield, Feb. 19, 1849, by Rev. Sylvester S. Strong	1	131

	Vol.	Page
CANFIELD, (cont.)		
Cloe, d. Timothy & Keziah, b. Dec. 20, 1748	LR1	210
Ebenezer, s. Timothy & Keziah, b. Nov. 4, 1733	LR1	218-9
Elijah, s. Timothy & Kezia, b. Apr. 4, 1739	LR1	224
Eliza, of Ridgefield, m. Joseph S. **FERRIS**, of Milford, Oct. 16, 1836, by Rev. J. Lyman Clarke	1	185
Gould, d. Aug. [ ], 1836	1	232
Josephus, d. Mar. 8, 1821, in the 12th y. of his age	1	222
Mary, d. Timothy & Keziah, b. Oct. 25, 1730	LR1	211
Marry E., of Ridgefield, m. Ezra N. **HOYT**, of Lewisboro, Dec. 13, 1843, by Rev. A. S. Francis	1	194
Morris H., m. Margaret **NORTHROP**, of Ridgefield, this day, [June 16, 1852], by Rev. David H. Short	1	138
Patience, d. Ebenezer, of Norwalk, m. Joseph **CRAMPTON**, Dec. 29, 1714	LR1	227
Phebe, d. Timothy & Keziah, b. Dec. 31, 1731	LR1	211
Rachel, w. Charles, d. Dec. 19, [1849]	1	240
Roswell, of Stamford, m. Julia Ann **OLMSTED**, of Ridgefield, Oct. 27, 1827, by Samuel M. Phelps	1	168
Rufus, had infant d. Mar. [ ], 1836, ae 3 m.	1	232
Samuel, m. Cadalina **BAKER**, b. of Ridgefield, Mar. 9, 1829, by Rev. Henry Stead	1	170
Samuel, his w. [ ], d. May 26, 1833, ae 24 y.	1	230
Sarah, m. Jesse **COVERT**, b. of Ridgefield, Sept. 30, 1827, by Samuel M. Phelps	1	168
Silas, s. Timothy & Keziah, b. Apr. 24, 1741	LR1	225
Thaddeus, s. Timothy & Kezia, b. Apr. 22, 1744	LR1	238
Timothy, m. Kezia [ ], Nov. 19, 1729, by Stephen Munson	LR1	228
Timothy, s. Timothy & Keziah, b. Sept. 2, 1736	LR1	221
CASTLE, Aaron, s. William & Catharine, b. Jan. 7, 1764	1	6
Cate, d. William & Catharine, b. Jan. 28, 1769	1	6
Elijah, s. William & Catharine, b. Jan. 22, 1760	1	6
Mary, d. William & Catharine, b. Oct. 30, 1756	1	6
Sarah, d. William & Catharine, b. Mar. 20, 1766	1	6
CASWELL, Charles, of Burlington, Otsego Co., N. Y., m. Mrs. Sally **KEELER**, of Ridgefield, Oct. 16, 1842, by Rev. Warner Hoyt	1	193
CHAMBERS, Anna, [d. Nathan & Ruth], b. Apr. 27, 1779	1	74
Catharine, [d. Nathan & Ruth], b. Jan. 1, 1787; d. May 15, 1787	1	74
Caty, [d. Nathan & Ruth], b. Mar. 18, 1788	1	74
Hannah, [d. Nathan & Ruth], b. Mar. 28, 1790	1	74
Harmon, of Redding, m. Harriet E. **DISBROW**, of Ridgefield, Feb. 5, 1833, by Rev. Charles G. Selleck	1	178
Lucy, [d. Nathan & Ruth], b. Jan. 19, 1792	1	74
Mary, [d. Nathan & Ruth], b. Sept. 3, 1784	1	74
Nathan, [s. Nathan & Ruth], b. Mar. 10, 1794	1	74

	Vol.	Page
CHAMBERS, (cont.)		
Thomas, d. Feb. 2, 1798, ae 78 y.	1	209
-----, wid., d. Mar. 13, 1810, in the 89th y. of her age	1	215
CHAPMAN, Charles, d. [1849], in New York, bd. in Ridgefield	1	240
Elijah, of Tolland, m. Sarah **KEELER**, of Ridgefield, Oct. 20, 1783	1	155
CHASE, Jeremiah, m. Esther **WHITNEY**, Jan. 29, 1771	1	151
CHITESTER, Daniel, his w. [ ], d. Mar. 17, 1807	1	213
Daniel, d. Dec. 5, 1810	1	215
CHURCH, Anson, d. Jan. 27, 1833, ae 25 y.	1	229
Bela St. John, [s. Samuel & Jane], b. Jan. 3, 1817	1	109
Francis, [s. Samuel & Jane], b. Sept. 5, 1821	1	109
Harmon Betts, [s. Samuel & Jane], b. Jan. 8, 1824	1	109
Samuel, b. Aug. 18, 1783; m. Jane **KEELER**, Apr. 27, 1813	1	109
Stephen Keeler, [s. Samuel & Jane], b. Aug. 7, 1814	1	109
CLARK, CLARKE, Augustus, m. Charlotte M. **CROCKER**, b. of Ridgefield, Oct. 16, 1836, by Rev. J. Lyman Clarke	1	185
Ephraim, m. Sarah **SMITH**, Jan. 8, 1784	1	154
Esther, m. Richard **WHITNEE**, Dec. 18, 1745	LR1	233
Fletcher, s. Rev. Theodorius, d. Feb. 11, 1818	1	220
Lois C., of Litchfield, m. Edward O. **TUTTLE**, of Ridgefield, Feb. 19, 1845, by Rev. A. S. Francis	1	196
Martin E., his w. [ ], d. Sept. 20, 1845, ae 24 y.	1	238
Martin E., m. Mary E. **GILBERT**, b. of Ridgefield, Nov. 15, 1846, by Charles Stearnes, Int. Pub. Nov. 15, 1846	1	199
William E., m. Mary **GRUMMAN**, b. of Ridgefield, Oct. 6, 1833, by Rev. Charles J. Todd	1	179
-----, wid. & d. of Dan[ie]ll **SMITH**, d. [Sept.] 22, [1851]	1	241
-----, Capt. had chid d. [ ], in New York, ae 2 y., bd. in Richfield	1	234
CLOSE, Mary, m. Joseph **MEAD**, Apr. 31, 1772	1	151
COHEN, Emily L., m. W[illia]m H. **SEYMOUR**, b. of Norwalk, Jan. 30, 1848, by Rev. L. B. Burr	1	129
COLE, Abigail, d. Ichabod & Ruth, b. July 2, 1748	LR1	242
Almira B., of Wilton, m. William H. **JELLEFF**, of Ridgefield, May 12, 1845, by Rev. A. S. Francis	1	197
Ezra, [s. Timothy & Delilah], b. Apr. 26, 1751	LR1	251
Hannah, d. Ichabod & Ruth, b. Feb. 9, 1740/1	LR1	226
Hezekiah, s. Ichabod & Ruth, b. Apr. 19, 1743	LR1	236
Ichabod, m. Ruth [ ], b. Mar. 14, 1734	LR1	229
Jesse, s. Ichabod & Mindwell, b. Aug. 16, 1752	LR1	244
Jonathan, s. Ichabod & Ruth, b. Oct. 13, 1745	LR1	238
Mary, d. Ichabod & Ruth, b. Jan. 30, 1738/9	LR1	223
Ruth, d. Ichabod & Ruth, b. Dec. 14, 1736	LR1	222
Ruth, w. Ichabod, d. Feb. 5, 1750/1	LR1	216
Samuel, s. Ichabod & Ruth, b. Jan. 9, 1734/5	LR1	222
Samuel, s. Ichabod & Ruth, d. Dec. 1, 1736	LR1	215
Sarah, [d. Timothy & Delilah], b. Apr. 4, 1748	LR1	251

COLE, (cont.)

	Vol.	Page
Sarah, d. Timothy & Delilah, d. Sept. 6, 1751	LR1	216
Timothy, [s. Timothy & Delilah], b. Mar. 28, 1746/7	LR1	251
William, m. Mary A. **FIELD**, Oct. 16, 1840, by Nathan Burton, Pastor	1	189
COLEMAN, James, Rev., d. Feb. 4, 1842, ae 75 y.	1	236
Martha, m. Zalmon S. **MAIN**, b. of Ridgefield, Mar. 22, 1840, by Rev. T. Sparks	1	188
COLEY, Daniel, his w. [ ], d. Oct. 5, 1796	1	208
Eunice, d. Daniel & Sarah, b. Nov. 6, 1772	1	57
Ezra, s. Daniel & Sarah, d. Dec. 30, 1776	1	203
Rebeckah, d. Daniel & Sarah, b. June 17, 1768	1	57
Sarah, d. Daniel & Sarah, b. Apr. 30, 1765	1	57
Sarah, w. Daniel, d. Nov. 16, 1773	1	203
Stephen, s. Daniel & Sarah, d. Aug. 23, 1774	1	203
COLLINS, Samuel B., of Chicago, Ill., m. Sarah **SHERWOOD**, of Ridgefield, Aug. 23, 1841, by Rev. Warner Hoyt	1	190
COMSTOCK, Martha, m.Ambros **OLMSTEAD**, July 1, 1742	LR1	234
Mary, m. Thaddeus **STURGIS**, Nov. 23, 1769	1	151
Matthias, of New Canaan, m. Sarah **SMITH**, of Ridgefield, Feb. 26, 1834, by Rev. Charles G. Selleck	1	179
Stephen, d. Apr. 28, 1825, ae 18 y.	1	224
William, of New Canaan, m. Polly **KEELER**, of Ridgefield, Feb. 8, 1826, by Samuel M. Phelps	1	167
COOK, Samuel, of Huntington, Conn., m. Minerva **GILBERT**, of Ridgefield, May 9, 1836, by Levi Brunson	1	182
COOLEDGE, Henry, of New York, m. Margaret **HAWLY**, of Ridgefield, Nov. 3, 1847, by Rev. James A. Hawley	1	128
CORNEN, Peter, of New York, m. Lydia Ann **BEERS**, of Ridgefield, Sept. 5, 1842, by Rev. Warner Hoyt	1	192
CORNWELL, Sarah, m. Denton **MILLS**, Feb. 29, 1760	1	155
Sarah, m. Denton **MILLS**, Feb. 29, [ ]	LR1	252
Sarah, m. Paul **KEELER**, Feb. 7, 1775	1	152
COSIER, Anne, m. David **ABBOTT**, Mar. 19, 1749/50, by Jonathan Ingersoll, V. D. M.	LR1	234
Anne, had d. Mary, b. [ ]	1	title
Mary, d. Anne, b. [ ]	1	title
COUCH, Abigail, w. Joseph, d. Dec. 23, 1819	1	221
Abigail, 2nd w. Joseph, d. [ ]	1	222
Anne, m. Theophilus **STEBBINS**, July 7, 1750	LR1	234
Sarah, wid. of Thomas, of Fairfield, West Parish, m. Timothy **KEELER**, Nov. 10, 1736	LR1	229
Sarah, m. Stephen **SMITH**, Jan. 2, 1744/5	LR1	231
Stephen, m. Anne **EDMOND**, Jan. 29, 1784	1	154
Thomas N., m. Abigail **STEBBINS**, Dec. 30, 1787	1	157
COVERT, Betsey Ann, d. Nov. [ ], 1842, ae 14 y.	1	236
Jesse, m. Sarah **CANFIELD**, b. of Ridgefield, Sept. 30, 1827, by Samuel M. Phelps	1	168

RIDGEFIELD VITAL RECORDS 165

	Vol.	Page
COVERT, (cont.)		
Jesse, d. June 24, 1836, ae 37	1	232
CRAFT, Heron, of Southeast, m. Mrs. Betty **WEED**, of Ridgefield,		
May 5, 1822, by Oliver Tuttle	1	160
CRAMER, Merian, wid., d. Oct. 16, 1799, ae 97 y.	1	210
CRAMPTON, Abigail, d. Joseph & Patience, b. Aug. 20, [1719]	LR1	203
Joseph, m. Patience **CANFIELD**, d. Ebenezer, of Norwalk,		
Dec. 29, 1714	LR1	227
Joseph & w. Patience, had child b. Aug. 11, [1718]; d. Aug.		
12, [1718]	LR1	202
Joseph & w. Patience, had child d. Aug. 12, [1718], ae 1 d.	LR1	213
Mary, d. Joseph & Patience, b. Nov. 5, 1715	LR1	199
Sarah, d. Joseph & Patience, b. May 5, [1714]	LR1	202
CRANE, Esther, m. Daniel **SMITH**, Jan. 11, 1795	1	95
Esther, m. Daniel **SMITH**, 2nd, Jan. 11, 1795	1	159
CRANK, Hannah, Mrs., m. James **LEASON**, b. of Ridgefield, Mar.		
31, 1846, by Rev. Shaller J. Hillyer	1	198
Timothy, of Fishkill, m. Hannah **DUNNING**, of Ridgefield,		
Mar. 4, 1838, by James Coleman, Elder	1	184
CRAW, Jacob, d. Aug. 24, [1850]	1	240
CRAWFORD, [see also **CROFUT**], Esther A., m. George **KEELER**,		
b. of Ridgefield, Aug. 31, 1829, by Samuell M. Phelps	1	171
Jeremiah, s. Lydia, b. Mar. 6, 1783	1	67
Jeremiah, s. Lydia, b. [ ]	1	title
Lydia, had s. Jeremiah, b. Mar. 6, 1783	1	67
Lydia, m. George **BERRY**, Oct. 23, 1787	1	156
Lydia, had s. Jeremiah, b. [ ]	1	title
CROCKER, Almira, w. W[illia]m, d. Mar. 21, 1824, ae 38	1	224
Ann, Mrs., d. Oct. [ ], 1837, in Upper Alton, Ill.	1	234
Ann A., of Ridgefield, m. Jere A. **SCOTT**, of Moumee City,		
O., Sept. 18, 1837, by Charles G. Selleck	1	183
Charlotte M., m. Augustus **CLARK**, b. of Ridgefield, Oct. 16,		
1836, by Rev. J. Lyman Clarke	1	185
Charlotte Maria, [d. William & Maria], b. July 19, 1819	1	111
George Dauchy, [s. William & Maria], b. Dec. 25, 1822	1	111
Mary Ann, [d. William & Maria], b. Aug. 24, 1816	1	111
William, m. Maria **DAUCHY**, Sept. 22, 1813	1	111
William, m. Mrs. Anna **SMITH**, b. of Ridgefield, Aug. 22,		
[1824], by Rev. Daniel Crocker	1	163
William, d. Feb. 17, 1835, in the 45th y. of his age	1	231
William Austin, [s. William & Maria], b. June 3, 1814	1	111
CROFUT, CRAWFUT, CROFUTT, [see also **CRAWFORD**],		
Ebenezer, [s. Joseph & Lydia], b. Jan. 23, 1727/8	LR1	226
Ebenezer, [s. Joseph & Lydia], b. Apr. 30, 1730	LR1	226
Elizabeth, [d. Joseph & Lydia], b. July 1, 1734	LR1	226
George, of Huntington, m. Charity **HULL**, of Ridgefield, Apr.		
1, 1828, by Samuel M. Phelps	1	168
Harriet E., m. Comfort S. **GRIFFIN**, Aug. 23, 1826, by		

	Vol.	Page
CROFUT, CRAWFUT, CROFUTT, (cont.)		
Nathan Burton	1	166
Lydia, [d. Joseph & Lydia], b. Dec. 13, 1736	LR1	226
Phebe, [d. Joseph & Lydia], b. Feb. 3, 1731/2	LR1	226
Sarah, [d. Joseph & Lydia], b. Mar. 4, 1739/40	LR1	226
Stephen, of Philips, N. Y., m. Betsey **SELLECK**, of Ridgefield, Nov. 2, 1823, by Nathan Burton	1	162
CURTIS, CURTISS, Elizabeth, of Sheffield, m. John Gilbert **MONROW**, of Ridgefield, Oct. 23, 1832, by Rev. Charles G. Selleck	1	176
Hannah, m. William **MUNRO**, Jr., Apr. 3, 1798	1	82
Hiram, had infant d. Dec. 7, 1835, ae 4 m.	1	232
DAGGETT, Horace, of N[ ] Haven, m. Jane **HAWLEY**, of Ridgefield, Oct. 22, 1832, by Rev. C. G. Selleck	1	177
Jane, w. Horace, d. of William **HAWLEY**, d. Sept. 10, 1836, in the 27th y. of her age, at Colton Gosport Miss.	1	232
DANFORD, Moses B., of Redding, m. Mary **HOWLAND**, of Ridgefield, Aug. 24, 1846, by Rev. Henry Olmsted, Jr.	1	127
DANN, DAN, Amos, s. William & Ruth, b. Feb. 24, 1798	1	91
David, m. Lois **DAUCHY**, b. of Ridgefield, Jan. 20, 1850, by Rev. Nathaniel Mead	1	132
Ebenezer W., of West Port, m. Mary E. **STAPLES**, of Ridgefield, Oct. 10, 1843, by Rev A. S. Francis	1	194
Eliza A., m. John S. **STAPLEY**, b. of Ridgefield, May 11, 1847, by Charles Stearns	1	128
Elizabeth Sally, of Ridgefield, m. Brice **BENEDICT**, of Danbury, Mar. 15, 1840, by Rev. T. Sparks	1	188
Ezra, m. Ruth **HYATT**, May 7, 1783	1	154
Ezra, d. May 7, 1795, ae 32 y.	1	208
Hannah, w. Bouton, d. June 24, 1820	1	222
Harriet, of Ridgefield, m. Josiah **WEBB**, of Monroe, Co., of Orange, N. Y., Feb. 16, 1835, by Levi Brunson	1	180
Harry, s. W[illia]m & Ruth, b. May 19, 1799	1	91
John Rockwell, s. W[illia]m & Ruth, b. Nov. 2, 1800	1	91
Mary Augusta, of Ridgefield, m. W[illia]m W. **TOMPKINS**, of New Canaan, [ ], by Rev. T. Sparks. Recorded Jan. 3, 1840	1	187
Phebe, of Ridgefield, m. Granville **WEED**, of Danbury, Nov. 26, 1846, by Rev. Z. B. Burr	1	198
Polly, m. Abel **PULLING**, b. of Ridgefield, Mar. 9, 1845, by Rev. A. S. Francis	1	197
Ruth, wid., d. May 3, 1809, in the 48th y. of her age	1	214
Sarah, m. Abraham G. **KEELER**, Apr. 25, 1801	1	92
William, m. Ruth **KEELER**, May 25, 1797	1	91
-----, wid. her child d. May 17, 1796, ae 2 y.	1	208
-----, Mrs., d. May 10, 1837, ae 76	1	233
DARLING, Abby, of Redding, m. Chauncey **EDMOND**, of Ridgefield, Nov. 5, 1823, by Samuell M. Phelps	1	164

	Vol.	Page
DARLING, (cont.)		
Benjamin, d. Dec. 16, 1787, in the 86th y. of his age	1	204
Henry, m. Elizabeth B. **SCOTT**, b. of Ridgefield, Nov. 3,		
1831, by Rev. C. G. Selleck	1	174
DAUCHY, Abigail, w. Charles, d. May 9, 1814	1	218
Adah, d. John & Anna, b. Mar. 13, 1769	1	17
Almira, [d. Nathan & Mary], b. Feb. 26, 1786	1	79
Amy, d. Dan[ie]ll & Lois, b. Feb. 19, 1798	1	43
Amy, of Ridgefield, m. John **SARLES**, of Poundridge, N. Y.,		
Nov. 22, 1833, by Rev. Charles J. Todd	1	179
Anna, wid. John, d. Mar. 31, 1812, in the 66th y. of her age	1	216
Burr, [s. Samuell & Molly], b. Feb. 7, 1796	1	76
Calvin, s. Daniel & Lois, b. Apr. 10, 1787	1	43
Calvin, had s. [ ], d. Aug. 26, 1819	1	221
Calvin, his w. [ ], d. Apr. 7, 1820, ae 26	1	222
Calvin, d. July 20, 1833, in the 47th y. of his age	1	230
Charles, [s. Jacob & Lois], b. Sept. 27, 1791	1	69
Charles, [s. Nathan, Jr. & Ruth], b. Jan. 21, 1805	1	103
Charles, had infant d. July 24, 1814	1	218
Charles, m. Fanny **SEELEY**, [Sept.] 27, [1820], by Rev.		
Charles Smith	1	160
Charles, had infant d. [ ], d. Aug. 20, 1821, ae 7 d.	1	223
Charles, d. June 24, 1833, in the 42nd y. of his age	1	230
Charles, his w. [ ], d. Dec. [, 1850], ae 32	1	241
Charles, d. Jan. [ ], 1851, ae 34	1	241
Charlotte, [d. Samuell & Molly], b. July 31, 1793	1	76
Clara, d. Dan[ie]ll & Lois, b. Oct. 13, 1795	1	43
Daniel, s. Vivas & Hannah, b. Jan. 23, 1752	LR1	249
Daniel, m. Lois **NORTHRUP**, Dec. 24, 1778	1	152
Daniel, d. July 25, 1807, in the 56th y. of his age	1	213
David, [s. Jacob & Lois], b. July 18, 1790	1	69
David, m. Anna **MEAD**, b. of Ridgefield, Feb. 9, 1825, by		
Samuell M. Phelps	1	165
David, d. Sept. 2, 1827, ae 37 y. 1 m. 15 d.	1	226
David, of Ridgefield, m. Lydia **OAKLEY**, of Danbury, Nov.		
24, 1833, by Rev. Charles J. Todd	1	179
Deborah, d. John & Anna, b. Mar. 13, 1767	1	17
Deborah, m. Enoch **HOLLY**, Feb. 3, 1785	1	155
Delia, [s. Sam[ue]ll & Molly], b. Jan. 26, 1790	1	76
Edward, s. David, d. Sept. 17, 1821, ae 15 m.	1	223
Electa, [d. Nathan & Mary], b. Mar. 4, 1782	1	79
Elizabeth, m. James **JONES**, Mar. 18, 1760	LR1	252
Elizabeth, d. John & Anna, b. Jan. 6, 1776	1	17
Esther, [d. Samuel & Molly], b. Mar. 21, 1799	1	76
Eunice, d. Philip & Mary, b. Nov. 2, 1768	1	22
Eunice, m. Isaac **OLMSTED**, Apr. 21, 1793	1	78
Eunice, m. Isaac **OLMSTED**, Apr. 21, 1793	1	158
Frances, d. Jacob, Jr., d. Aug. 25, 1827	1	226

BARBOUR COLLECTION

DAUCHY, (cont.)

	Vol.	Page
George, [s. Nathan, Jr. & Ruth], b. Apr. 19, 1800	1	103
George, d. Sept. 25, [1850], ae 28 y.	1	240
Grace, d. John & Anna, b. Sept. 8, 1774	1	17
Grace, m. Daniel **KEELER**, 2nd, Jan. 1, 1792	1	157
Hannah, w. Capt. Vivas, d. Sept. 10, 1754	LR1	217
Hannah, d. Philip & Mary, b. Feb. 21, 1772	1	22
Hannah, d. Daniel & Lois, b. July 15, 1781	1	43
Henry B., [s. Nathan, Jr. & Ruth], b. Apr. 24, 1795	1	103
Jacob, s. Vivas & Mary, b. Mar. 8, 1768	1	15
Jacob, m. Lois **BENNETT**, May 3, 1789	1	69
Jacob, [s. Jacob & Lois], b. Mar. 21, 1799	1	69
Jacob, his w. [ ], d. June 27, 1841, ae about 72 y.	1	236
James, s. Vivas & Rachal, b. Nov. 30, 1734	LR1	223
James, s. John & Anna, b. Feb. 12, 1765	1	17
James, m. Mary **BOUTON**, Apr. 13, 1786	1	156
Jeremiah, s. Vivas & Mary, b. Nov. 1, 1755	LR1	249
Jeremiah, [s. Nathan & Mary], b. May 20, 1777; d. Aug. [ ], 1778	1	79
Jeremiah, [twin with Polly], s. [Nathan & Mary], b. July 23, 1779	1	79
Jeremiah, m. Clarissa **OLMSTED**, b. of Ridgefield, Nov. 16, 1826, by Samuel M. Phelps	1	167
Jerusha, w. Calvin, d. Nov. 20, 1809	1	215
Jerusha, d. Calvin, d. Jan. 8, 1810	1	215
Jesse B., [s. Nathan, Jr. & Ruth], b. Oct. 24, 1796	1	103
John, d. May 13, 1809, ae 67 y.	1	214
Josiah, [s. Jacob & Lois], b. Mar. 17, 1794	1	69
Keeler, [s. Jacob & Lois], b. Jan. 8, 1801	1	69
Keeler, m. Mary E. **STEBBINS**, Oct. 16, 1831, by Rev. Charles J. Todd	1	174
Keeler, had infant s. [ ], s. b. Nov. 5, 1833	1	230
Lois, d. Daniel & Lois, b. June 9, 1779	1	43
Lois, wid., d. Aug. 23, 1813	1	217
Lois, m. David **DANN**, b. of Ridgefield, Jan. 20, 1850, by Rev. Nathaniel Mead	1	132
Lucy, d. Jeremiah & Elizabeth, b. Dec. 12, 1782	1	49
Luther, s. Jeremiah & Elizabeth, b. Jan. 11, 1781	1	49
Luther, s. Daniel & Lois, b. Nov. 17, 1790	1	43
Luther, his w. [ ], d. Aug. 11, 1820, ae 45	1	222
Margaret, d. Jacob, Jr., d. Aug. 26, 1827	1	226
Maria, [d. Samuell & Molly], b. Dec. 1, 1797	1	76
Maria, d. Samuell, d. Mar. 24, 1799	1	209
Maria, m. William **CROCKER**, Sept. 22, 1813	1	111
Mary, m. Gamaliel **NORTHRUP**, Jan. 3, 1723/4	LR1	227
Mary, d. Vivus & Rachal, b. Nov. 25, 1736	LR1	223
Mary, d. Vivas & Mary, b. Mar. 18, 1764	1	15
Mary, m. Ebenezer **SANFORD**, Feb. 22, 1787	1	157

	Vol.	Page
DAUCHY, (cont.)		
Mary, wid., d. Nov. 20, 1805, ae 39 y.	1	212
Mary, wid., d. May 22, 1816, ae 91	1	219
Mary, wid. Philip, d. Sept. 7, 1832, ae 90	1	229
Mary, w. Nathan, d. Aug. 7, 1837, in the 88th y. of her age	1	233
Mary, m. Bartlett **FOLLETT**, Aug. [ ]	LR1	252
Nathan, s. Vivas & Rachel, b. Jan. 29, 1746/7	LR1	240
Nathan, m. Mary **SMITH**, Nov. 3, 1768	1	79
Nathan, [s. Nathan & Mary], b. May 16, 1773	1	79
Nathan, Jr., m. Ruth **BRADLEY**, Nov. 13, 1794	1	103
Nathan, 2nd, m. Ruth **BRADLEY**, Nov. 13, 1794	1	159
Nathan, 2nd, m. Rachel **BRADLEY**, Nov. 13, 1794	1	159
Nathan, Jr. & w. Ruth, had s. [ ], b. [ ], 1799; d. Sept. 3, 1801	1	103
Nathan, Jr., had s. [ ], d. Sept. 3, 1801	1	210
Nathan, Capt., d. Apr. 14, 1824, in his 77th y.	1	224
Phebe, [d. Jacob & Lois], b. Feb. 28, 1805	1	69
Phebe, m. Nathaniel D. **HAIGHT**, b. of Ridgefield, July 4, 1825, by Rev. Origen S. Holcomb	1	163
Philip, s. Vivas & Rachel, b. Jan. 12, 1743/4	LR1	237
Philip, m. Mary **JONES**, May 22, 1764	1	150
Philip & w. Mary, d. d. [ ], b. Feb. 26, 1766; d. [ ], ae about 4 d.	1	22
Philip, [s. Jacob & Lois], b. Dec. 20, 1795	1	69
Philip, d. Apr. 30, 1822, ae 79 y.	1	223
Philip, d. Aug. 23, 1839, ae 43	1	235
Philo, [s. Samuell & Molly], b. Sept. 14, 1791	1	76
Polly, [d. Nathan & Mary], b. Mar. 8, 1775; d. Aug. [ ], 1778	1	79
Polly, [twin with Jeremiah], d. [Nathan & Mary], b. July 23, 1779	1	79
Polly, d. Daniel & Lois, b. Oct. 3, 1793	1	43
Polly, m. Gould **ROCKWELL**, Mar. 14, 1807	1	104
Polly, w. David, d. Oct. 3, 1824, ae 31	1	224
Polly Sanford, [d. Jacob & Lois], b. Nov. 20, 1797	1	69
Rachal, w. Vivas, d. Nov. 20, 1748	LR1	216
Rachel, d. Philip & Mary, b. June 9, 1765	1	22
Rachel, m. Aaron **STEWART**, of Norwalk, June [ ], 1787	1	157
Rachel, [d. Jacob & Lois], b. Feb. 26, 1803	1	69
Ruth, d. John & Anna, b. June 6, 1771	1	17
Samuel, [s. Nathan & Mary], b. July 1, 1769	1	79
Samuel, m. Molly **BRADLEY**, Dec. 6, 1789	1	157
Samuel, [s. Samuel & Molly], b. Jan. 11, 1800	1	76
Samuel, d. Aug. 29, 1800, ae 31 y.	1	210
Sarah, [d. Nathan & Mary], b. Apr. 27, 1771; d. June 4, 1773	1	79
Sarah, d. John & Anna, b. Aug. 15, 1780	1	17
Sarah, m. Epenetus **HOW**, Jr., Dec. 24, 1807	1	104
Thomas, s. Vivas & Mary, b. Nov. 5, 1757	LR1	249

170 BARBOUR COLLECTION

	Vol.	Page
DAUCHY, (cont.)		
Thomas, s. Daniel & Lois, b. July 13, 1784	1	43
Vivus, m. Rachel **WALLACE**, Nov. 28, 1732	LR1	230
Vivus, s. Vivus & Rachal, b. Oct. 7, 1738	LR1	223
Vivus, Ens., m. Hannah **SHERWOOD**, Mar. 24, 1750/1, by Jonathan Ingersoll, V. D. M.	LR1	233
Vivus, s. Vivas & Mary, b. Dec. 8, 1759	LR1	249
Vivus, s. John & Anna, b. May 20, 1778	1	17
Vivus, d. Dec. 16, 1795, ae 89; b. [ ],1706	1	208
Wallace, s. John & Anna, b. Oct. 4, 1782	1	17
Watts, [s. Jacob & Lois], b. Dec. 31, 1792	1	69
DAVIS, Charles, of Wilton, m. Mary Ann **BENNETT**, of Ridgefield, Nov. 7, 1848, by Rev. Sylvester S. Strong	1	131
David, his w. [ ], d. Nov. [ ], 1846	1	238
Elizabeth, m. Stephen **ABBOT**, Mar. 22, [ ]	LR1	252
Jabez, s. Daniel & Sarah, b. Mar. 13, 1759	LR1	198
Sarah, d. Daniel & Sarah, b. July 21, 1755	LR1	198
DAWSE, [see also **DOWSON**], Thomas, d. Jan. 3, 1790	1	205
DAYTON, Joseph P., of New Castle, N. Y., m. Samantha **WHEELER**, of Ridgefield, this day [Dec. 24, 1851], by Timothy Jones, J. P.	1	137
DEAN, Benjamin, d. Dec. 11, 1804	1	212
Daniel, d. Sept. 12, 1794, ae 84	1	207
Daniel, d. Mar. 1, 1808	1	213
Daniel, d. Mar. 19, 1818, in the 48th y. of his age	1	221
Esther, d. Dec. 29, 1806, ae 30 y.	1	213
Harry, d. Nov. 7, [1851], ae [ ]	1	241
Mary, w. Daniel, d. Dec. 31, 1793, ae 84	1	207
Mary, wid., d. Nov. 25, 1820, ae 86 y.	1	222
Mary, Mrs., d. Nov. 23, 1844, ae 65	1	237
Polly, d. Feb. 22, 1809, ae 36 y.	1	214
Rachel, m. Edwin **BURT**, Feb. 2, 1830, by Nathan Burton	1	171
Ruhamah, m. Jonah **NORTHRUP**, Jan. 21, 1790	1	158
Sarah, m. Theophilus **RUSCO**, of Poundridge, Jan. 1, 1793	1	158
DeFOREST, DeFORREST, [see also **FORRESTER**], Hezekiah, [s. Hezekiah & Polly], b. Jan. 22, 1770	1	79
Hezekiah, m. Polly **OLMSTED**, Apr. [ ], 1792	1	158
Hiram Olmsted, s. Hezekiah & Polly, b. Mar. 20, 1794	1	79
James Henry, d. Sept. 23, 1846, ae 10 y. 8 m.	1	238
Laurania, m. Timothy **KEELER**, 3rd, Dec. 14, 1788	1	74
LeGrand, s. Hezekiah & Polly, b. Feb. 28, 1792; d. Nov. 23, 1794	1	79
William, m. Esther **DICKINS**, Jan. 2, 1836, by Nathan Burton	1	181
-----, m. [ ] **NORRIS**, [ ], 1795	1	159
DeFREES, Abigail, w. John, d. May 8, 1818	1	221
John, d. Sept. 28, 1828, ae 86 y.	1	226
DeLAVAN, John, m. Martha **KEELER**, Oct. 6, 1785	1	156
DEMON, Thomas, m. Esther **SMITH**, Dec. 11, 1787	1	157

RIDGEFIELD VITAL RECORDS 171

	Vol.	Page
DENTON, Benjamin A., m. Antoinette **BENNETT**, b. of Ridgefield, this day, [Oct. 16, 1850], by Rev. C. Clark	1	134
DIBBLE, Abigail, m. David Barlow **BURR**, b. of Ridgefield, [Apr.] 12, [1825], by Rev Origen S. Holcomb	1	163
Abijah, s. Catharine, b. Sept. 3, 1765	1	1
Catharine, had s. Abijah, b. Sept. 3, 1765	1	1
Mary, d. John & Mary, b. Oct. 5, 1731	LR1	212
DICKENS, DICKINS, Arnold, d. Aug. 26, 1834, ae 78	1	230
David, had child d. [, probably 1851], ae 5 y., & child d. [, probably 1851], ae 7 y.	1	241
Esther, m. William **DeFOREST**, Jan. 2, 1836, by Nathan Burton	1	181
George, d. Aug. 11, 1834, ae 7 y.	1	230
George, of Redding, m. Eunice **BRADLEY**, of Ridgefield, Oct. 18, 1848, by Rev. Sylvester S. Strong	1	131
George, of Danbury, m. Eunice **BRADLEY**, of Ridgefield, Oct. 18, 1848, by Rev. Sylvester S. Strong	1	131
Lewis, his s. [ ], d. June 9, 1832, ae about 4 y.	1	229
Rachel, wid., d. Apr. 15, 1848, ae 83	1	239
-----, s. [ ], d. Jan. 22, 1794	1	207
DICKERSON, [see under **RICKERSON**]		
DIKEMAN, DYKEMAN, DYKERMAN, Aaron B., of Wilton, m. Sarah Ann **MEAD**, of Ridgefield, Jan. 18, 1830, by Samuell M. Phelps	1	171
Cyrus, s. Sam[ue]ll & Sally, b. Feb. 4, 1799	1	90
David, of Danbury, m. Lucretia **PULLING**, of Ridgefield, Feb. 3, 1847, by Rev. Charles Stearnes	1	127
Elizabeth, [d. Jonathan & Hannah], b. Apr. 31, 1786	1	65
Jonathan, m. Hannah **STREET**, May 1, 1785	1	155
Julian, d. Sam[ue]ll & Sally, b. Mar. 15, 1801	1	90
Neran, of Danbury, m. May J. **SMITH**, of Ridgefield, Mar. 26, 1848, by Rev. Sylvester S. Strong	1	130
Samuel, b. Nov. 2, 1774, at Redding; m. Sally **KELLOGG**, d. Epenetus of Norwalk, [ ]	1	90
Samuel, m. Sally **KELLOGG**, Apr. 19, 1798, at Norwalk	1	159
DIMERATT, Elizabeth, d. Michael, b. Feb. 23, 1738/9	LR1	224
John, s. Michael, b. July 13, 1734	LR1	221
Mary, d. Michael, b. Oct. 29, 1736	LR1	221
Ziporah, d. Michael, b. Mar. 23, 1730	LR1	221
DISBROW, Harriet E., of Ridgefield, m. Harmon **CHAMBERS**, of Redding, Feb. 5, 1833, by Rev. Charles G. Selleck	1	178
Henry, of New Canaan, m. Clarissa **NORTHROP**, of Ridgefield, Nov. 26, 1843, by Rev. A. S. Francis	1	194
Levi, d. Mar. 2, 1824, ae 65	1	224
-----, Mr., d. May 14, 1812, ae 94	1	217
DIXON, Hannah, d. Susannah **BALDWIN**, b. Jan. 9, 1744/5	LR1	255
Jane C., m. Lockwood **OLMSTED**, b. of Ridgefield, July 18, 1836, by Rev. Charles G. Selleck	1	182

	Vol.	Page
DODGE, -----, Mrs., d. Feb. [ ], 1850, ae about 84 at Dr. Kendalls	1	240
DOLE, Laura, d. James & Almira, b. Mar. 17, 1785	1	57
DOOLITTLE, Daniel, s. Joseph & Abigail, b. Dec. 12, 1758	1	5
Joseph, m. Abigail **ROCKWELL**, Aug. 10, 1757	1	150
Phebe, d. Joseph & Rachel, b. Feb. 17, 1744/5	LR1	237
Phebe, d. Jan. 24, 1745/6	LR1	215
Phinehas, m. Sarah **BENEDICT**, Mar. 7, 1782	1	153
Polly, d. Phinehas & Sarah, b. Apr. 10, 1783	1	51
Reuben, s. Joseph & Abigail, b. Apr. 19, 1761	1	5
Sarah, d. Joseph & Abigail, b. Jan. 8, 1759	1	5
DOTY, John, d. Mar. 5, 1812	1	216
DOUGLASS, Abigail, d. John & Mary, b. Jan. 10, 1735/6	LR1	226
Anna, d. John & Mary, b. Aug. 18, 1740	LR1	226
Jonathan, s. John & Mary, b. Nov. 8, 1733	LR1	226
Mary, d. John & Mary, b. Feb. last, 1737/8	LR1	226
DOWNS, Anna, b. Sept. 7, 1803; m. William H. **KEELER**, s. Jonah, Aug. 27, 1826	1	110
DOWSON, [see also **DAWSE**], Stephen, [s. Thomas & Mary], b. Dec. 9, 1777	1	65
DREW, John, m. Eliza **ROCKWELL**, Oct. 31, 1837, by Nathan Burton	1	184
DRINKWATER, John, s. William & Elizabeth, b. July 7, 1731	LR1	211
Thomas, s. William & Elizabeth, b. Nov. 3, 1729	LR1	210
William, m. Elizabeth **BENEDICT**, d. Lieut. Benjamin & Mary, Dec. 18, 1728	LR1	228
DUNHAM, Abigail, m. Jonathan **OSBORN**, May 3, 1764	1	150
DUNNING, Abigail, m. Eliphalet **BRUSH**, Nov. 11, 1777	1	87
David, d. June 7, 1833, ae 80	1	230
Hannah, m. Timothy **KEELER**, Dec. 13, 1780	1	156
Hannah, m. John **ST. JOHN**, Jan. 30, 1788	1	157
Hannah, of Ridgefield, m. Timothy **CRANK**, of Fishkill, Mar. 4, 1838, by James Coleman, Elder	1	184
DURANT, Benjamin, of Danbury, m. Sally Maria **ELEIZER**, of Ridgefield, Aug. 29, 1830, by Rev. Oliver E. Ammerman	1	172
DURFEE, -----, wid., d. Oct. 9, 1832, ae 91	1	229
EAMES, Harris, of New Brunswick, N. J., m. Maria **HYATT**, of Ridgefield, Sept. 26, 1830, by Rev. Oliver E. Ammerman	1	172
EDMOND, EDMONDS, EDMUNDS, Aaron, had infant d. Aug. 6, 1819	1	221
Anne, m. Stephen **COUCH**, Jan. 29, 1784	1	154
Chauncey, of Ridgefield, m. Abby **DARLING**, of Redding, Nov. 5, 1823, by Samuell M. Phelps	1	164
Cyrus, d. Oct. 2, 1827	1	226
Daniel L., his grand child d. Sept. 27, 1840	1	235
Daniel Lee, [s. Robert Stiles & Polly], b. Oct. 16, 1792	1	58
David, s. Robert & Rachel, b. May 15, 1778	1	55
David, his child d. Apr. 6, 1838, ae 3 y.	1	234
Eliza Esther, of Ridgefield, m. Legrand **SANFORD**, of		

	Vol.	Page
EDMOND, EDMONDS, EDMUNDS, (cont.)		
Redding, Oct. 14, 1829, by Samuell M. Phelps	1	171
Elizabeth E., of Ridgefield, m. John C. **SMALL**, of New York City, Nov. 29, 1849, by Rev. Nathaniel Mead	1	132
Harriet M., of Ridgefield, m. Ezra B. **KELLOGG**, of Danbury, Sept. 22, 1845, by Charles Stearns, Int. Pub.	1	197
Laura, [d. Robert Stiles & Polly], b. Dec. 30, 1790	1	58
Lee, his d. [ ], d. Sept. [ ], 1837, ae about 18 y.	1	233
Lee, his d. [ ], d. July 9, 1840, ae 23 y.	1	235
Margaret, m. Elias **LEE**, Oct. 24, 1787	1	156
Mary, of Ridgefield, m. Eli **FOOT**, of Weston, Nov. 26, 1823, by Sam[ue]ll M. Phelps	1	164
Mary, m. James **MEAD**, b. of Ridgefield, Dec. 3, 1834, by Rev. Charles G. Selleck	1	180
Paulina M., m. William W. **BEERS**, b. of Ridgefield, Sept. 30, 1851, by Rev. Ira Abbott	1	136
Polly, wid., d. July 27, 1835, ae 66	1	231
Robert, d. May 6, 1819, ae 92	1	221
Robert S., d. Jan. 12, 1813, ae 43	1	217
Robert Stiles, m. Polly **LEE**, Mar. 31, 1790	1	58
Sally, d. Cyrus, d. Mar. 25, 1798	1	209
Sarah, d. Sept. 22, 1830, ae 29 y.	1	228
Stiles, d. Apr. [1849], ae about 40	1	240
W[illia]m, his d. [ ], d. Sept. 2, 1835, ae 8	1	232
William L., m. Betsey **JELLIFF**, Jan. 7, 1829, by Rev. Stephen Saunders, of South Salem, Westchester Co., N. Y.	1	173
William L., d. May 21, 1832	1	229
William Wallace, s. Aaron, d. Dec. 30, 1826	1	226
ELEIZER, Sally Maria, of Ridgefield, m. Benjamin **DURANT**, of Danbury, Aug. 29, 1830, by Rev. Oliver E. Ammerman	1	172
ELIAS, Henry, s. Henry & Abigail, b. May 26, 1753	LR1	243
Jacob, s. Henry & Abigail, b. Apr. 7, 1751	LR1	241
Mary, d. Henry & Abigail, b. Feb. 14, 1747/8	LR1	243
ELIS, Armanus, m. Abigail **SHERWOOD**, Mar. 16, 1745/6, by Joseph Lamson	LR1	232
ELMER, Abigail, m. Silas **KEELER**, Apr. 14, 1746, by Rev. William Gaylord, of Wilton	LR1	234
ESMOND, Esther, d. Aug. 4, 1832, ae 37 y.	1	229
EVERIT, Elizabeth, m. John **NORTHRUP**, Mar. 6, 1776	1	152
FAIRBANKS, Arsena, d. David & Hannah, b. May 28, 179[ ]	1	86
David, s. Samuel & Mehitable, b. Apr. 13, 177[ ]	1	50
David, m. Hannah **ST. JOHN**, Apr. 5, 1795	1	86
Gamaliel, s. Samuel & Mehitable, b. Mar. 30, 1760	1	50
Mehitable, d. Samuel & Mehitable, b. Oct. 14, 176[ ]	1	50
Mehetable, m. Azor **SMITH**, Feb. 28, 1790	1	158
Mercy, d. Samuel & Mehitable, b. Nov. 13, 1776	1	50
Samuel, s. Samuel & Mehitable, b. Nov. 27, 1757	1	50
Samuel, d. May 25, 1794, ae 62	1	207

	Vol.	Page
FAIRBANKS, (cont.)		
Susannah, d. Samuel & Mehitable, b. Dec. 24, 1768	1	50
FAIRCHILD, Andrew, of Redding, m. Betsey **LEE**, of Ridgefield, Feb. [ ], 1821, by Samuel M. Phelps	1	161
Francis, m. Eunice **BOUGHTON**, June 6, 1830, by Nathan Burton	1	172
Gilbert, d. Oct. 31, 1835, ae 76 y.	1	232
Hannah, w. Gilbert, d. Nov. 24, 1816	1	220
Hannah, Mrs., d. June 19, 1839, ae 76 y.	1	235
Hezekiah, twin with Rhoda, s. Hezekiah, d. Aug. 14, 1812, ae 5 d.	1	217
Hezekiah, had d. [ ], d. May 9, 1817, ae 7 y.	1	220
John T., m. Electa **FIELD**, Feb. 3, 1830, by Nathan Burt	1	171
Mary, m. Daniel F. **SEYMOUR**, Feb. 19, 1840, by Nathan Burton, P. T.	1	188
Rhoda, twin with Hezekiah, d. Hezekiah, d. Aug. 14, 1812, ae 5 d.	1	217
Samuell, his w. [ ], d. Mar. 31, 1811	1	215
Samuel, d. Oct. 9, 1820, in the 88th y. of his age	1	222
FARQUHAR, FORQUHAR, Betty, d. Robert & Susannah, b. Jan. 11, 1756	LR1	255
Deborah, [d. Robert & Deborah], b. Oct. 20, 1744	LR1	235
Deborah, w. Robert, d. Mar. 2, 1747	LR1	216
Ebenezer, s. Robert & Susannah, b. Aug. 11, 1753	LR1	235
John, [s. Robert & Deborah], b. Oct. 27, 1742	LR1	235
Mary, [d. Robert & Deborah], b. Nov. 28, 1740	LR1	235
FENN, W[illia]m, Dr. his mother (wid.), d. Aug. 6, [1846], ae about 95	1	238
FERGUSON, Eliza, m. Harvey **GATES**, [Dec.] 23, [1824], by George Benedict	1	163
Susan, of Ridgebury, m. Gerry **BARNUM**, of Brookfield, Mar. 31, 1839, in Ridgebury, by Rev. Lucius Atwater	1	187
FERRIS, Joseph S., of Milford, m. Eliza **CANFIELD**, of Ridgefield, Oct. 16, 1836, by Rev. J. Lyman Clarke	1	185
-----, Mr., d. [, probably 1851], ae about 80 y.	1	241
FIELD, Deborah B., of South East, m. Harry **STONE**, of Danbury, this day [Mar. 27, 1844], at the house of Barnabus Allen, Ridgebury, by Rev. Rollin S. Stone, of Danbury	1	195
Electa, m. John T. **FAIRCHILD**, Feb. 3, 1830, by Nathan Burt	1	171
John, of Amenia, N. Y., m. Mary Jane **SMITH**, of Ridgefield, Dec. 14, 1851, by Rev. Ira Abbott	1	137
Mary A., m. William **COLE**, Oct. 16, 1840, by Nathan Burton, Pastor	1	189
FILLOW, Rufus, of West Port, m. Sally **HOYT**, of Ridgefield, May 17, 1847, by Rev. James A. Hawley	1	128
FINCH, FINTCH, [see also **RITCH**], Augustine N., m. Catharine M. **OLMSTED**, b. of Ridgefield, Aug. 28, 1832, by Rev. Charles G. Selleck	1	176

	Vol.	Page
FINCH, FINTCH, (cont.)		
Nelson S., of Wilton, m. Catharine Ann **LYON**, of Ridgefield, Sept. 21, 1842, by Rev. Warner Hoyt	1	192
Rebeckah, m. John **MILLS**, Dec. 2, 1784	1	153
FITCH, James Platt, of Wilton, m. Cynthia **MEAD**, of Ridgefield, Dec. 25, 1834, by Rev. Charles G. Selleck	1	180
FLETCHER, Challe, d. Thomas & Elizabeth, b. Dec. 27, 1783	1	57
David, s.Thomas & Elizabeth, b. Aug. 12, 1781	1	57
Isaac, s. Thomas & Elizabeth, b. June 5, 1788	1	57
Joseph, s. Thomas & Elizabeth, b. Apr. 19, 1786	1	57
Thomas, m. Elizabeth **NORTHRUP**, Dec. 31, 1778	1	153
Thomas, s.Thomas & Elizabeth, b. Aug. 28, 1779	1	57
FLYNN, James, d. Sept. [ ], 1837	1	234
James, had d. [ ], d. Sept. [ ], 1837, ae about 12 y.	1	234
James, m. Jane **HOWLAND**, b. of Ridgefield, Feb. 24, 1852, by Rev. Ira Abbott	1	137
Jane Ann, of Ridgefield, m. Frederick **OLMSTED**, of Redding, Feb. 5, 1843, by Rev. Warner Hoyt	1	193
FOLLIET, FOLLETT, FOLHOTTS, Anna, d. George & Thankfull, b. Apr. 17, 1767	1	9
Anne, w. Joseph, d. May 8, 1788	1	204
Bartlet, s. Joseph & Annah, b. Jan. 12, 1735/6	1	72
Bartlett, m. Mary **DAUCHY**, Aug. [ ]	LR1	252
Betsey, d. Jeremiah & Mary, b. Apr. 22, 1791	1	78
Betsey, d. Jeremiah & Polly, b. Apr. 22, 1791	1	80
Dorcas, d. George & Thankfull, b. Feb. 18, 1761	1	9
Dorcas, d. George & Thankfull, b. Feb. 28, 1761	LR1	255
George, s. Joseph & Annah, b. Apr. 30, 1732	1	72
George, m. Thankfull **BURT**, Sept. [ ]	LR1	252
George, s. George & Thankfull, b. June 26, 1763	1	9
Hannah, d. Joseph & Anna, b Sept. 13, 1738	LR1	245
Harriet, d. Jeremiah & Polly, b. Mar. 23, 1798	1	80
James, s. Bartlett & Mary, b. Apr. 8, 1761	LR1	256
James Lewis, s. George & Thankfull, b. Jan. 2, 1765	1	9
Jeremiah, s. George & Thankfull, b. July 17, 1766	1	9
Jeremiah, m. Polly **SHERMAN**, Jan. 12, 1790	1	80
Jeremiah, m. Polly **SHERMAN**, Jan. 12, 1790	1	158
John, s. Joseph & Anna, b. Aug. 22, 1754	LR1	245
Joseph, of Marblehead, m. Annah **TENGUE**, of New London, Mar. 6, 1730/1	1	72
Joseph, d. July 30, 1794, ae 86	1	207
Lewis, s. Jeremiah & Polly, b. Sept. 11, 1803	1	80
Pers, s. Jeremiah & Polly, b. Nov. 12, 1804	1	80
Polly, d. Jeremiah & Polly, b. Oct. 29, 1795	1	80
Polly, w. Jeremiah, d. Feb. 18, 1808	1	214
Rebeckah, d. Joseph & Anna, b. Jan. 9, 1740/1	LR1	245
Sally, d. Jeremiah & Polly, b. Dec. 25, 1800	1	80

	Vol.	Page
FOLLIET, FOLLETT, FOLHOTTS, (cont.)		
Sarah, d. Joseph & Anna, b. July 6, 1749	LR1	245
Sarah, m. Jacob **ROSSEGUIE**, 2nd, Apr. 14, 1780	1	154
Sarah, of Ridgefield, m. Zachariah **PORTER**, of Danbury, Feb. 11, 1829, by Samuel M. Phelps	1	169
Seaborn, s. George & Thankfull, b. Dec. 12, 1768	1	9
Sherman, s. Jeremiah & Polly, b. Sept. 8, 1807	1	80
Susannah, d. George & Thankfull, b. Apr. 4, 1762	1	9
Susannah, m. Elijah **SMITH**, Jr., Nov. 14, 1779	1	154
FOOT, Betsey, d. Oct. 19, 1823	1	223
Eli, of Weston, m. Mary **EDMOND**, of Ridgefield, Nov. 26, 1823, by Sam[ue]ll M. Phelps	1	164
Eli, his mother, d. Dec. 17, 1830, at his house	1	228
FORQUHAR, [see under **FARQUHAR**]		
FORRESTER, FORESTER, [see also **DeFOREST**], Ann, d. [William & Sarah], b. Aug. 10, 1780; d. May 9, 1789	1	65
Arthur, b. Apr. 19, 1757; m. Jemima [ ]	1	63
Arthur, [s. Arthur & Jemima], b. Sept. 7, 1784	1	63
Elizabeth, d. [William & Sarah], b. Feb. 15, 1788; d. Feb. 12, 1790	1	65
Frederick, [s. Arthur & Jemima], b. July 10, 1780	1	63
George, s. Lot & Hannah, b. Sept. 7, 1818	1	101
Hiram Mead, s. Lot & Hannah, b. Nov. 21, 1813	1	101
Jane, d. [William & Sarah], b. Nov. 7, 1769	1	65
Jane, [d. Arthur & Jemima], b. May 31, 1778	1	63
Jane, m. Benjamin **FOWLER**, Feb. 10, 1785	1	155
Jane Anne, d. Lot & Hannah, b. Nov. 22, 1815	1	101
Jean, d. William & Sarah, b. Nov. 7, 17[ ]	1	32
Lot, [s. Arthur & Jemima], b. Feb. 12, 1782	1	63
Lot, m. Hannah **MEAD**, Nov. 15, 1803	1	101
Lot, m. Freelove **ARNOLD**, Nov. 10, 1823, by George Benedict	1	162
Maria, d. Lot & Hannah, b. June 19, 1804	1	101
Maria, m. Lyman **KEELER**, Dec. 15, 1824, by George Benedict	1	163
Rufus, s. Lot & Hannah, b. Aug. 21, 1811	1	101
Sally, d. Lot & Hannah, b. Feb. 20, 1808	1	101
Sally, m. George B. **ROCKWELL**, Sept. 30, 1832, by Nathan Burton	1	176
Sarah, d. [William & Sarah], b. June 11, 1775; d. Apr. 4, 1791	1	65
William, m. Sarah [ ], Dec. 8, 1768	1	65
William, s. Lot & Hannah, b. Apr. 18, 1806	1	101
William, d. Jan. 29, 1809	1	214
FOSTER, Abiah, d. Joseph & Zibiah, b. Jan. 30, 1749/50	LR1	253
Abigail, d. Jonah & Abigail, b. Dec. 26, 1750	LR1	198
Abigail, d. Timothy & Desire, b. Mar. 20, 1785	1	43
Abigail, w. Capt. Jonah, d. Oct. 31, 1791	1	206
Albert, s. Joseph & Zibiah, b. Oct. 10, 1751	LR1	253

	Vol.	Page
FOSTER, (cont.)		
Anna, [twin with Isaac], d. Josiah & Anna, b. June 12, 1766	1	24
Anne, d. Josiah & Anne, b. July 19, 1756	LR1	224
Arnold Washington, s. Timothy & Desire, b. Mar. 19, 1776	1	43
Benjamin, of Redding, m. Mary **KEELER**, of Ridgefield, Jan. 11, 1847, by Rev. Henry Olmsted, Jr.	1	127
Chloe, [twin with Mary], d. Josiah & Anna, b. May 30, 1764	1	24
Daniel, s. [Jonah & Hannah], b. Jan. 17, 1779	1	96
Daniel, d. July 28, 1798, ae 20 y.	1	209
Delia, m. Zebulon **BURR**, b. of Ridgefield, Feb. 11, 1823, by Rev. Oliver Tuttle	1	161
Delight, d. [Jonah & Hannah], b. Jan. 29, 1797	1	96
Ebenezer, s. [Jonah & Hannah], b. Oct. 3, 1787	1	96
Elizabeth, d. Joseph & Zibiah, b. Aug. 26, 1753	LR1	253
Elizabeth, m. Martin W. **BASSETT**, b. of Ridgefield, Apr. 28, 1844, by Rev. Shaller J. Hillyer	1	195
Epenetus, s. Jonah & Abigail, b. Dec. 1, 1753	LR1	198
Esther, d. [Jonah & Hannah], b. Feb. 28, 1790	1	96
Esther Ann, of Ridgefield, m. Samuel H. **NORTHRUP**, of Lewisboro, N. Y., Oct. 4, 1852, by Rev. Shaller J. Hillyer	1	138
Hannah, d. Timothy & Sarah, b. Dec. 10, 1749	LR1	245
Hannah, d. Capt. Jonah, d. Aug. 22, 1789	1	205
Hannah, [twin with Jonah], d. [Jonah & Hannah], b. Dec. 8, 1793	1	96
Hannah, wid., d. Dec. 22, 1834, ae 72 y. 9 m. 20 d.	1	231
Isaac, [twin with Anna], s. Josiah & Anna, b. June 12, 1766	1	24
James Sears, s. Timothy & Desire, b. Aug. 11, 1774	1	43
Joel, s. [Jonah & Hannah], b. Nov. 8, 1780	1	96
Joel, Dr., of Redding, m. Betsey **BURRETT**, of Ridgefield, June 13, 1843, by David C. Comstock	1	194
John, s. Josiah & Anna, b. Dec. 15, 1750	LR1	244
John Benedict, s. [Jonah & Hannah], b. Jan. 17, 1785	1	96
Jonah, m. Abigail [ ], Oct. 15, 1745	LR1	233
Jonah, s. Timothy & Sarah, b. Nov. 14, 1751	LR1	245
Jonah, m. Hannah **BENEDICT**, Oct. 27, 1778	1	96
Jonah, [twin with Hannah], s. [Jonah & Hannah], b. Dec. 8, 1793	11	96
Jonah, d. Dec. 17, 1815, ae 69	1	219
Jonah, m. Sally **HUNT**, b. of Ridgefield, [Mar.] 14, [1821], by Oliver Tuttle	1	160
Jonah, d. Aug. 27, 1840, ae 46 y.	1	235
Joseph, m. Zabiah [ ], Feb. 22, 1748/9	LR1	233
Josiah, s. Josiah & Anna, b. Jan. 3, 1746/7	LR1	240
Keziah, d. Josiah & Anna, b. Mar. 15, 1748/9	LR1	244
Libia, d. June 3, 1790, ae 72	1	205
Mary, [twin with Chloe], d. Josiah & Anna, b. May 30, 1764	1	24
Mary Amelia, d. Jonah & Sally, b. Mar. 22, 1822	1	109
Molly, d. Joseph & Zibiah, b. Apr. 18, 1756	LR1	253

	Vol.	Page
FOSTER, (cont.)		
Nathan, s. Jonah & Abigail, b. May 11, 1747	LR1	198
Nathaniel, s. Timothy & Desire, b. Sept. 21, 1778	1	43
Sally, d. Timothy & Desire, b. May 22, 1781	1	43
Sarah, w. Timothy, d. Nov. 24, 1751	LR1	216
Sarah, d. [Jonah & Hannah], b. Jan. 20, 1783	1	96
Susan M., m. John J. **JARVIS**, Oct. 1, 1851, by Rev. Shaller J. Hillyer	1	136
Thomas, s. Josiah & Anne, b. Sept. 25, 1758	LR1	244
Thomas, s. Josiah & Anna, b. Sept. 25, 1758	1	24
Timothy, s. Jonah & Abigail, b. June 8, 1749	LR1	198
Timothy, m. Sarah **SMITH**, Sept. 21, 1749, by Rev. Jonathan Ingersoll	LR1	233
Timothy, m. Desire **SEERS**, Nov. 18, 1772	1	153
Vincent, s. Josiah & Anna, b. Sept. 19, 1754	LR1	244
William, s. Josiah & Anna, b. Apr. 7, 1753	LR1	244
FOUNTAIN, Gerrel, m. Anne **BETTS**, May 14, 1787	1	156
FOWLER, Benjamin, m. Jane **FORRESTER**, Feb. 10, 1785	1	155
Benjamin, s. Benjamin & Jane, b. Oct. 22, 17[ ]	1	65
Rebeckah, Mrs., d. May 2, 1832, ae 76 y.	1	229
William, s. Benjamin & Jane, b. Apr. 1, 1788; d. Feb. 8, 1794	1	65
William, s. Benjamin & Jane, b. Apr. 1, 1788	1	67
FRAZIER, Edmond, of Sully, Ireland, d. Mar. 23, 1788, ae 64 y. at the house of Petter Waddy	1	204
FREEMAN, Jack, m. Elizabeth **JACKLEN**, June 24, 1784	1	154
FRENCH, Reuben, of Hingham, Mass., m. Emeline **HOWE**, of Ridgefield, Feb. 4, 1836, at the house of William Howe, by Rev. Shaller J. Hillyer, of North Salem, N. Y.	1	181
FRY, Stephen, m. Sally Ann **BEERS**, b. of Ridgefield, July 23, 1836, by Rev. J. Lyman Clark	1	185
GARNSEY, Hannah, Mrs., m. Rev. Samuel **CAMP**, Sept. 21, 1769, by Joseph Bellamy, V. D. M.	1	151
-----, Mr. his s. [ ], d. Sept. 2, 1835, ae 1 y.	1	232
GATES, Abigail, d. Samuel & Rachel, b. Sept. 10, 1746	LR1	246
Abigail, d. Jonathan & Sarah, b. Aug. 25, 1772	1	52
Amos, [s. Stephen & Mary], b. Dec. 30, 1797	1	105
Anner, [d. Stephen & Mary], b. May 15, 1804	1	105
Betty, d. Samuel & Rachel, b. Apr. 7, 1748	LR1	246
Daniel, s. [Samuel, Sr. & Sarah], b. Oct. 20, 1741	LR1	236
Eli, [s. Stephen & Mary], b. Aug. 15, 1791	1	105
Eli, m. Mrs. Sally **GRANNIS**, b. of Ridgefield, Mar. 12, 1851, by Hezekiah Scott, J. P.	1	134
Elijah, s. Samuel & Rachel, b. Mar. 16, 1749/50	LR1	246
Hannah, m. Ira **KEELER**, Mar. 14, 1832, by Nathan Burton	1	176
Harvey, [s. Stephen & Mary], b. Sept. 6, 1802	1	105
Harvey, m. Eliza **FERGUSON**, [Dec.] 23, [1824], by George Benedict	1	163
James, s. Samuel & Rachel, b. Aug. 15, 1752	LR1	246

RIDGEFIELD VITAL RECORDS

	Vol.	Page
GATES, (cont.)		
James, s. Jonathan & Sarah, b. June 29, 1774	1	52
Jonathan, s. Sam[ue]ll & Rachall, b. Dec. 5, 1734	LR1	222
Levi, [s. Stephen & Mary], b. Feb. 20, 1794	1	105
Luther, 2nd, d. Feb. 26, 1826	1	225
Lydia, d. Jonathan & Sarah, b. Sept. 1, 1778	1	52
Lydia, [d. Stephen & Mary], b. Aug. 10, 1800	1	105
Lydia, of Ridgefield, m. Solomon **WOOD**, of New York State, Jan. 20, 1823, by Rev. Samuel M. Phelps	1	162
Mariette, m. William A. **JENNINGS**, b. of Ridgefield, Sept. 23, 1850, by Rev. Nathaniel Mead	1	134
Mary, w. Sam[ue]ll, d. Mar. 26, 1732	LR1	214
Mary, d. Sam[ue]ll & Rachall, b. Jan. 27, 1738/9	LR1	222
Mary, d. Jonathan & Sarah, b. Oct. 20, 1781	1	52
Mary, d. Jonathan & Sarah, d. Feb. 12, 1782	1	203
Mary, m. Stephen **GATES**, Nov. 21, 1789	1	105
Mary P., [d. Stephen & Mary], b. Sept. 28, 1796	1	105
Nehemiah, s. Jonathan & Sarah, b. Aug. 25, 1770	1	52
Phebe, d. Samuel, Sr. & Sarah, b. July 20, 1739	LR1	236
Rachal, d. Samuel & Rachel, b. Apr. 16, 1743	LR1	246
Rachel, m. Zachariah **STEVENS**, Dec. 7, 1763; d. Jan. 12, 1768	1	75
Rachel, d. Jonathan & Sarah, b. Aug. 22, 1776	1	52
Sam[ue]ll, m. Rachal [ ], Apr. 1, 1734	LR1	230
Samuel, s. Sam[ue]ll & Rachall, b. Dec. 3, 1736	LR1	222
Samuel, s. Jonathan & Sarah, b. May 2, 1783	1	52
Samuel, d. Sept. 30, 1793, ae 84	1	206
Sarah, d. Sam[ue]ll & Sarah, b. Sept. 10, 1733	LR1	218-9
Sarah, d. Jonathan & Sarah, b. Oct. 23, 1768	1	52
Simeon, [s. Stephen & Mary], b. Apr. 26, 1809	1	105
Stephen, s. Sam[ue]ll & Sarah, b. July 11, 1737	LR1	223
Stephen, s. Jonathan & Sarah, b. Dec. 31, 1767	1	52
Stephen, m. Mary **GATES**, Nov. 21, 1789	1	105
Stephen, [s. Stephen & Mary], b. July 26, 1806	1	105
Stephen, d. Apr. 21, 1812, in the 45th y. of his age	1	217
Thomas, s. Samuel & Rachel, b. Jan. 6, 1740/1	LR1	246
GAYLORD, Ruth, of New Milford, m. Sam[ue]ll **SMITH**, of Ridgefield, Dec. 24, 1740, by Rev. D. Boardman	LR1	231
GEDNEY, GIDNEY, David C., of Westchester Co., N. Y., m. Amelia **OLMSTED**, of Ridgefield, Sept. 7, 1825, by Samuell M. Phelps	1	166
David C., his child, d. Jan. 28, 1831	1	228
Peter J., of New Canaan, m. Abby L. **OLMSTED**, of Ridgefield, Oct. 26, 1834, by Rev. Charles G. Selleck	1	180
W[illia]m Henry, s. David C., d. Jan. 7, 1830, ae 17 m. 3 d.	1	227
GILBERT, Abigail, d. Isaac & Mary, b. July 16, 1775	1	42
Abigail, d. Isaac & Mary, d. Oct. 10, 1777	1	202
Abigail, w. Alba, d. of John **SCOTT**, d. July 25, 1817, ae 23 y.	1	220

	Vol.	Page
GILBERT, (cont.)		
Abijah, s. Josiah & Elizabeth, b. Jan. 20, 1735/6	LR1	220
Abner, [s. Ebenezer & Rebeckah], b. Jan. 10, 1745	LR1	251
Abner, s. Ebenezer & Rebeckah, b. Jan. 10, 1745	1	16
Abner, [s. Abner], b. Apr. 28, 1772; d. Sept. 9, 1778	1	95
Abner, [s. Abner], b. Nov. 15, 1780	1	95
Abner, s. [Abner, Jr. & Laura], b. Feb. 24, 1808	1	107
Abner, d. Mar. 1, 1820, ae 75 y.	1	222
Abner, Jr., of Danbury, m. Frances M. **LEWIS**, of Ridgefield, Sept. 18, 1838, by Rev. Joseph Fuller	1	186
An[n], d. Abner, d. Jan. 10, 1829	1	227
Asher, Dr., d. Sept. 14, 1850, ae about 56 y.	1	241
Baxter, s. Daton & Lydia, b. Jan. 3, 1807	1	102
Benjamin, of Ridgefield, m. Phebe L. **REED**, of West Stockbridge, [Feb. 4, 1852], by Rev. Ira Abbott	1	137
Betsey, d. Isaac & Mary, b. Feb. [ ], 1774	1	42
Betsey, w. Jabes M., d. Mar. 29, 1805	1	212
Betsey, m. Daniel **LOVEJOY**, b. of Ridgefield, Oct. 28, 1828, by Rev. John Lovejoy	1	168
Caroline, d. [Abner, Jr. & Laura], b. May 5, 1806	1	107
Caroline, m. Richard **RANDALL**, b. of Ridgefield, May 5, 1825, by Samuell M. Phelps	1	165
Charles, d. Aug. last, 1835	1	232
Charles, his wid. [ ], d. Dec. 5, 1838, ae about 28 y.	1	234
Daniel B., s. Jabez M., d. Sept. 30, 1817, ae 3	1	220
Daton, [s. Abner], b. Aug. 14, 1774; d. Aug. 31, 1778	1	95
Daton, [s. Abner], b. Sept. 19, 1783	1	95
Daton, s. Daton & Lydia, b. Dec. 1, 1812	1	102
David, s. Eben[eze]r & Rebeckah, b. Apr. 26, 1755	1	16
David, his child, d. Sept. [ ], 1803	1	211
David, d. July 5, 1835	1	231
David, his d. [ ], d. Aug. 24, 1843, ae 5 y.	1	237
David, d. Mar. 15, 1845, ae 47 y.	1	238
David, his wid. [ ], d. Mar. 23, [1852], ae about 89	1	242
David, [s. Ebenezer & Rebeckah], [ ]	LR1	251
Ebenezer, s. Eben[eze]r & Rebeckah, b. Feb. 6, 1749	1	16
Ebenezer, [s. Ebenezer & Rebeckah], b. Feb. 6, 1749/50	LR1	251
Ebenezer, d. Apr. 18, 1798, ae 85 y.	1	209
Ebenezer, Jr., of Ridgefield, m. Julia Ann **ABANDA**, of Delhi, N. Y., Jan. 24, 1830, by Samuell M. Phelps	1	172
Ebenezer, his w. [ ], d. Sept. 19, 1840, ae 66 y.	1	235
Elias, his child d. Dec. 1, 1840, ae 3 y.	1	235
Elias, had s. [ ], d. Oct. [ ], 1851	1	241
Elisha, [s. Ebenezer & Rebeckah], b. May 4, 1738	LR1	251
Elisha, his w. [ ], d. May 24, 1825	1	225
Elizabeth, d. Josiah & Elizabeth, b. Mar. 1, 1731/2	LR1	212
Elizabeth, m. John A. **LEESON**, b. of Ridgefield, Apr. 16, 1840, by Rev. T. Sparks	1	188

GILBERT, (cont.)

	Vol.	Page
Elizabeth B., of Ridgefield, m. William W. **BRUCE**, of Tecumsah, Mich., June 8, 1841, by A. Sparks	1	190
Ephraim, s. Josiah & Elizabeth, b. Apr. 1, 1740	LR1	226
Esther Ann, d. Joel, d. Jan. 17, 1813	1	218
Grace, wid. of Jonathan, d. Mar. 15, 1812, at Redding	1	216
Hannah, m. David **HOYT**, Sept. 29, 1784	1	155
Hannah, m. Samuel **HOYT**, Sept. 21, 1788	1	157
Hannah A., m. Jared **MEAD**, Oct. 28, 1834, by Rev. Josiah Bowen	1	181
Harriet, d. Jabez M., d. Dec. 20, 1830, in the 18th y. of her age	1	228
Harvey, [s. Abner], b. Oct. 5, 1780; d. [ ]	1	95
Harvey, had infant d. [ ], d. Aug. 22, 1824	1	224
Harvey, d. June 14, 1837	1	233
Hester Ann, of Ridgefield, m. Erie **PRUDY**, of North Salem, West Chester Co., N. Y., Feb. 24, 1839, by Rev. Thomas Sparks	1	187
Hezekiah, [s. Ebenezer & Rebeckah], b. Oct. 14, 1735	LR1	251
Hezekiah, s. Hezekiah & Tameson, b. Oct. 10, 176[ ]	1	16
Huldah, [d. Abner], b. Nov. 25, 1781	1	95
Isaac, [s. Ebenezer & Rebeckah], b. Oct. 21, 1742	LR1	251
Ithamar, s. Hezekiah & Tameson, b. Aug. 19, 176[ ]	1	16
Jabez M., his infant, d. May 3, 1808	1	214
Jabez M., his w. [ ], d. Feb. 12, 1839, ae 54 y.	1	234
Jabes Mix, m. Betsey **JONES**, Nov. 23, 1802	1	101
Jacob, s. Daton & Lydia, b. July 9, 1815	1	102
James, s. Jabez M. & Betsey, b. June 6, 1803	1	101
Jeremiah, m. Elizabeth **BOUTON**, b. of Ridgefield, Dec. 15, 1844, by Rev. A. S. Francis	1	196
Job, [s. Ebenezer & Rebeckah], b. Feb. 21, 1747	LR1	251
Joel, s. Ebenezer & Rebeckah, b. Feb. 21, 1747	1	16
Joel, d. Dec. 18, 1834, ae 49	1	231
Joel Abbot, s. [Abner, Jr. & Laura], b. Mar. 22, 1811	1	107
Joel Abbot, s. Abner & Laura, d. Aug. 6, 1825, ae 14 y.	1	225
John, s. Hezekiah & Tameson, b. Sept. 11, 1762	1	16
John, of Wilton, m. Betsey **SCOTT**, of Ridgefield, Mar. 31, 1822, by Rev. Samuel M. Phelps	1	161
Jonathan, d. Jan. 29, 1806, in the 37th y. of his age	1	212
Josiah, m. Elizabeth **SMITH**, June 8, 1726	LR1	227
Josiah, m. Phebe **LOBDELL**, Dec. 12, 1762	1	151
Laura, w. Minor, d. Feb. 3, 1844, ae 57 y.	1	237
Laura B., of Ridgefield, m. William E. **RANDALL**, of New York City, June 22, 1836, by Rev. John B. Beach	1	185
Laura Baker, d. [Abner, Jr. & Laura], b. June 22, 1815	1	107
Lois, [d. Josiah & Elizabeth], b. Aug. 19, 1727	LR1	208
Lucretia, d. Isaac J., d. June 13, 1829, ae 7 m.	1	227
Lydia, wid., d. Apr. 23, 1787, ae 86 y.	1	204

GILBERT, (cont.)

	Vol.	Page
Lydia, w. Daton, d. of Azariah & Elethia Smith, b. Sept. 13, 1788	1	102
Margaret, of Ridgefield, m. Hawley **HULL**, of Lewisboro, N. Y., this eve, [Oct. 13, 1846], by Rev. James A. Hawley	1	198
Martha, [d. Abner], b. Dec. 7, 1776; d. Sept. 19, 1778	1	95
Martha, [d. Abner], b. Apr. 25, 1779; d. Nov. 26, 1801	1	95
Martha, w. Abner, d. Apr. 10, 1808	1	214
Martha, d. Daton & Lydia, b. Nov. 30, 1808	1	102
Martha, d. Abner, d. Nov. 1, 1825, in the 5th y. of her age	1	225
Mary Ann, of Ridgefield, m. David N. **SHERWOOD**, of Darien, Apr. 26, 1840, by Rev. Warner Hoyt	1	189
Mary B., m. Isaac **BUNKERHOOF**, b. of Ridgefield, Oct. 24, 1832, by Rev. Nicholas White	1	177
Mary E., m. Martin E. **CLARK**, b. of Ridgefield, Nov. 15, 1846, by Charles Stearnes. Int. Pub. Nov. 15, 1846	1	199
Miner, his wid., d. Dec. 24, 1841, ae about 86 y.	1	236
Minerva, of Ridgefield, m. Samuel **COOK**, of Huntington, May 9, 1836, by Levi Brunson	1	182
Nathan, [s. Josiah & Elizabeth], b. Apr. 24, 1729	LR1	208
Patty, d. Abner, Jr. & Laura, b. July 4, 1803; d. Apr. 13, 1805	1	107
Phebe, d. Isaac & Mary, b. Dec. 11, 1780	1	42
Phebe, d. May 7, 1812, in the 32nd y. of her age	1	217
Polly, d. Nov. 26, 1801	1	211
Polly*, d. Abner, Jr., d. Apr. 13, 1805 *(Patty written over)	1	212
Prudence, m. David **MORRIS**, Oct. 30, 1786	1	70
Prudence, m. David **MORRIS**, Oct. 30, 1786	1	157
Rebeckah, [d. Ebenezer & Rebeckah], b. Nov. 14, 1740	LR1	251
Rebeckah, d. Hezekiah & Tameson, b. Oct. 22, 176[ ]	1	16
Rebeckah, wid., d. Jan. 10, 1801, ae 88	1	210
Rebecca D., of Ridgefield, m. Lancaster D. **BURLING**, of New York, Mar. 14, 1849, by Rev. Sylvester S. Strong	1	131
Richard Lee, [s. Abner, Jr. & Laura], b. Mar. 4, 1820	1	107
Rowland, s. Isaac & Mary, b. Mar. 20, 1772	1	42
Ruth, d. Nov. 23, 1819, ae 43 y.	1	221
Sally, d. Jan. 4, 1820, in the 29th y. of her age	1	221
Samuel, [s. Ebenezer & Rebeckah], b. Aug. 17, 1752	LR1	251
Samuel, s. Eben[eze]r & Rebeckah, b. Aug. 17, 1752	1	16
Samuel, his child d. Feb. [ ], 1850, ae 3 y.	1	240
Sarah, d. Hezekiah & Tameson, b. Sept. 9, 1758	LR1	207
Sarah, [d. Isaac & Mary], b. Dec. 12, 1782	1	42
Sarah, d. [Abner Jr. & Laura], b. July 11, 1813	1	107
Sarah, d. Jabez M., d. May 28, 1830, ae 5 y.	1	228
Sarah, of Ridgefield, m. Clark P. **SMITH**, of North Salem, Sept. 9, 1834, by Rev. Charles G. Selleck	1	180
Sarah R., m. Samuel C. **HAWLEY**, b. of Ridgefield, Oct. 11, 1846, by Charles Stearnes. Int. Pub.	1	199
Smith, s. Daton & Lydia, b. Oct. 22, 1810	1	102

	Vol.	Page

GILBERT, (cont.)
| Tameson, d. Hezekiah & Tameson, b. Jan. 1, 1759 | LR1 | 207 |
| Ward, s. Josiah & Phebe, b. Feb. 9, 1770 | 1 | 30 |

GODFREY, Julia A., of Ridgefield, m. William E. **PARTRICK**, of
Wilton, Sept. 5, 1852, by Rev. Charles Stearns	1	138
Nathan, d. Jan. 14, 1800	1	210
Polly, wid., d. Jan. [, 1852], ae about 50	1	242
Timothy W., of Wilton, m. Susan **MILLS**, of Ridgefield, Oct. 8, 1834, by Rev. Charles G. Selleck	1	180

GOODRICH, Abigail, [d. Benjamin & Hannah], b. Feb. 26, 1739/40 | LR1 | 235
Abigail, m. Hezekiah **OSBURN**, Apr. 13, 1759	LR1	232
Abigail, [d. Rev. Samuel & Elizabeth], b. Nov. 29, 1788	1	64
Benjamin, m. Hannah **OLMSTEAD**, Mar. 22, 1737/8	LR1	230
Benjamin, [s. Benjamin & Hannah], b. Jan. 17, 1741/2	LR1	235
Betsey, [d. Rev. Samuel & Elizabeth], b. Apr. 26, 1787	1	64
Charles Augustus, [s. Rev. Samuel & Elizabeth], b. Aug. 19, 1790	1	64
Daniel, s. Benj[ami]n & Hannah, b. Dec. 9, 1738	LR1	224
Daniel, [s. Benjamin & Hannah], b. [ ]	LR1	235
David, [s. Benjamin & Hannah], b. July 22, 1747	LR1	235
Eleazur, [s. Benjamin & Hannah], b. Sept. 19, 1751	LR1	235
Elihu Chauncey, [s. Rev. Samuel & Elizabeth], b. Nov. 18, 1795	1	64
Emila Chauncey, d. Rev. Samuell, d. Oct. [ ], 1803	1	211
Ezekiel, s. Benjamin & Hannah, b. Aug. 31, 1749	LR1	241
Hannah, [d. Benjamin & Hannah], b. Oct. 23, 1753	LR1	235
Hezekiah, s. Benjamin & Hannah, b. Dec. 15, 1755	LR1	235
Jeremiah, s. Benjamin & Hannah, b. Nov. 16, 1757	LR1	235
Josiah, s. Benjamin & Hannah, b. Apr. 20, 1760	LR1	235
Katharine, [d. Rev. Samuel & Elizabeth], b. Dec. 2, 1791	1	64
Millecent, m. Nathan **OLMSTEAD**, Dec. 4, 1740, by David Goodrich, J. P.	LR1	231
Nathan, [s. Benjamin & Hannah], b. Sept. 21, 1745	LR1	235
Sally, [d. Rev. Samuel & Elizabeth], b. Aug. 7, 1785, at Saybrook	1	64
Samuel, [s. Benjamin & Hannah], b. Dec. 6, 1743	LR1	235
Samuel, Rev. m. Elizabeth [ ], July 29, 1784	1	64
Samuel G., [s. Rev. Samuel & Elizabeth], b. Aug. 19, 1793	1	64
Silas Chauncey, s. Rev. Samuell, d. June 9, 1797, ae about 20 m.	1	209

GOODSELL, Joseph, of Redding, m. Delia Ann **BEERS**, of
| Ridgefield, Feb. 25, [1838], by Rev. William Bowen, of Redding | 1 | 184 |

GORHAM, William, of New Fairfield, m. Elsey **MUNRO**, of
| Ridgefield, Apr. 8, 1827, by Samuel M. Phelps | 1 | 168 |

GOULD, Jane, of Redding, m. Abraham **PINE**, of Ridgefield, Mar.
| 30, 1831, by Levi Brunson | 1 | 173 |

GRANNIS, Sally, Mrs. m. Eli **GATES**, b. of Ridgefield, Mar. 12,

	Vol.	Page
GRANNIS, (cont.)		
1851, by Hezekiah Scott, J. P.	1	134
GRAVES, Heman, d. May 8, 1808	1	214
GRAY, Charles, s. Lockwood, d. Jan. 16, 1830, in the 8th y. of his age	1	227
Eliza, d. Jan. 18, 1834, ae 16 y. 8 d.	1	230
Euncie, m. Elijah **ROCKWELL**, Nov. 18, 176[ ]	1	150
Laura S., m. Daniel N. **SHERWOOD**, b. of Ridgefield, July 31, 1850, by Rev. W[illia]m Staunton	1	136
Lockwood, m. Sally **SMITH**, b. of Ridgefield, May 3, 1831, by Samuel Stebbins, J. P.	1	173
Lockwood, his s. [ ], d. Dec. 12, 1848	1	240
Lockwood, his w. [ ], d. July 22, [1849], ae 60 y.	1	240
Polly, w. Lockwood, d. Dec. 3, 1828	1	227
Sarah Ann, m. Hiram **ROBERTS**, b. of Ridgefield, Feb. 18, 1830, by Samuell M. Phelps	1	172
GREGORY, Benjamin, [s. Eleazer & Polly], b. June 1, 1796	1	83
Betsey, [d. Eleazer & Polly], b. May 4, 1804	1	83
Betsey, m. John E. **STUDWELL** b. of Ridgefield, June 28, 1828, by Samuel M. Phelps	1	169
Burr, his d. [ ], d. Feb. 28, 1850, ae 1 y.	1	240
Charles, [s. Eleazer & Polly], b. June 3, 1807	1	83
Charles, of Saugatuck, m. Hannah **JENNINGS**, of Ridgefield, Oct. 12, 1828, by Samuel M. Phelps	1	169
Clara, d. Zaccheas & Margaret, b. Jan. 31, 1766	1	19
Clara, [d. Eleazer & Polly], b. Jan. 12, 1801	1	83
Comfort, d. Zaccheas & Margaret, b. Jan. [ ], 1770	1	19
Damares, d. Nov. 20, 1815, ae 68	1	219
Elezeia, s. Zaccheas & Margaret, b. Aug. 20, 1769	1	19
Eleazer, m. Polly **HINE**, Oct. 19, 1793	1	83
Eleazer, m. Polly **HINES**, Oct. 19, 1793	1	158
Eleazer, d. Apr. 21, 1812, in the 43rd y. of his age	1	216
Hannah, m. James **RIDER**, this eve [Jan. 31, 1847], by Rev. James Hawley	1	127
Hiram, d. July 19, 1814, ae 19	1	218
Cumphey*, m. Reuben **ROCKWELL**, Feb. 1, 1795 *(Humphey)	1	88
Lucy, d. Nov. 13, 1826	1	225
Molly, wid., d. June 25, 1851, ae 80 y.	1	241
Polly, [d. Eleazer & Polly], b. Sept. 30, 1794	1	83
Priscilla, wid., d. Nov. 15, 1821, in the 59th y. of her age	1	223
Rebekah, m. Elnathan **STURGIS**, Dec. 21, 1782	1	154
Zaccheus, d. June [ ], 1804	1	212
GRENO, Mary, b. Mar. 16, 1754; m James **LIVESEY**, Sept. 16, 1773	1	68
GRIFFIN, Comfort S., m. Harriet E. **CROFUT**, Aug. 23, 1826, by Nathan Burton	1	166
GRUMMAN, GRUMAN, Augusta, d. Charles, d. [, 1847],		

RIDGEFIELD VITAL RECORDS 185

	Vol.	Page
GRUMMAN, GRUMAN, (cont.)		
ae 1 y.	1	239
Betty, d. Ebenezer & Daborah, b. Mar. 15, 1743/4	LR1	237
Caleb, d. Dec. 7, 1825, in New York City	1	225
Caleb, his wid. d. May [ ], 1848, ae [ ]	1	239
Charles, s. Caleb, d. Nov. 11, 1815	1	219
Charles, m. Elizabeth R. **NASH**, b. of Ridgefield, Nov. 10, 1841, by Rev. Joseph Fuller	1	191
Charles, d. Aug. 6, 1847, ae 28 y.	1	239
Cyrus B., m. Sophia **PERRY**, b. of Ridgefield, Apr. 22, 1838, by Rev. Joseph Fuller	1	186
Ebenezer, m. Deborah [ ], Nov. 12, 1742	LR1	232
Ebenezer, s. Ebenezer & Deborah, b. June 25, 1746	LR1	240
Harriet, m. Sherwood **MEAD**, b. of Ridgefield, Nov. 23, 1825, by Samuel M. Phelps	1	166
Josiah N., of Ridgefield, m. Mary J. **HAYES**, of Lewisboro, N. Y., Nov. 21, 1847, by Rev. Henry Olmsted, Jr.	1	129
Lois, m. Timothy **SHERWOOD**, Oct. 6, 1803	1	159
Mary, m. William E. **CLARK**, b. of Ridgefield, Oct. 6, 1833, by Rev. Charles J. Todd	1	179
Sam[ue]ll B., had two infant children, d. Oct. 14, 1815, ae 10 y., & another infant child, d. Oct. 16, 1815, ae 12 d.	1	219
GUNN, Jane, m. Thomas **BENEDICT**, May 27, 1752	LR1	234
HAIGHT, [see also **HOYT**], Nathaniel D., m. Phebe **DAUCHY**, b. of Ridgefield, July 4, 1825, by Rev. Origen S. Holcomb	1	163
HALL, Abner, s. Josiah & Abigail, b. Aug. 10, 1785	1	44
Bradley, m. Mary **HALL**, Jan. 14, 1794	1	158
Henry, s. Josiah & Abigail, b. Aug. 21, 1774	1	44
Mary, m. Bradley **HALL**, Jan. 14, 1794	1	158
Mary Chapman, d. Bradley, d. Mar. 21, 1812, in the 3rd y. of her age	1	216
Molly, d. Josiah & Abigail, b. Dec. 26, 1777	1	44
Phebe, d. Josiah & Abigail, b. June 11, 1783	1	44
Sally, d. Silas & Elizabeth, b. May 15, 1790	1	75
Sarah, d. Josiah & Abigail, b. Apr. 15, 1775	1	44
Silas, m. Elizabeth **HOYT**, May 4, 1788	1	157
HAMILTON, Hannah, m. Eliphalet **BRUSH**, Jan. 13, 1773	1	87
HAMLIN, Abigail, m. as 2nd w. Zachariah **STEVENS**, May 5, 1768	1	75
HANDLEY, Thomas, s. Thomas, d. Dec. 7, 1823, ae 18 m.	1	224
HANFORD, Charles A., his w. [ ], d. Aug. 21, [1844], ae 41 y.	1	237
David, m. Sally **BENNETT**, Oct. 12, 1837, by Nathan Burton	1	184
HARKNESS, Peter, of New York City, m. Fanny A. **BETTS**, of Ridgefield, Apr. 10, 1850, by Rev. Clinton Clark	1	133
HARRINGTON, Daniel James, s. Asael & Polly, b. Aug. 28, 1808	1	103
Newel, m. Catharine **KEELER**, b. of Ridgefield, Dec. 15, 1833, at Georgetown, by Rev. Nicholas White	1	178
Sally Minerva, d. Asael & Polly, b. Nov. 6, 1806	1	103

186   BARBOUR COLLECTION

	Vol.	Page
HARRISON, George J., Rev. of Franklin, m. Elizabeth **JEWETT**, of Ridgefield, Apr. 26, 1849, by Rev. James A. Hawley	1	132
HATFIELD, John, m. Polly **SELLECK**, Aug. 29, 1825, by by Nathan Burton	1	163
HAVILAND, HAVELAND, Jacob, d. July 12, 1825, ae 68	1	225
Reed, d. Nov. 19, 1835, ae 42 y.	1	232
Reid, had s. [ ], d. Sept. 15, 1834, ae 5 y.	1	231
Sarah, wid., d. Nov. 17, 1829, ae 63	1	227
-----, Mrs., d. Mar. 24, 1804, ae 92	1	212
HAWKINS, John W., his w. [ ], d. Dec. 17, 1837, ae [ ]	1	234
W[illia]m W., m. Amelia A. **SMITH**, b. of Ridgefield, June 26, 1840, by Rev. Joseph Fuller	1	189
-----, Mr. had d. [ ], d. Mar. [ ], 1815	1	218
HAWLEY, HAWLY, Abigail, d. Thomas & Abigail, b. Jan. 1, 1715/6	LR1	199
Abigail, d. Joseph & Abigail, b. Oct. 18, 1745	LR1	238
Abigail, d. Joseph & Abigail, d. Oct. 29, 1745	LR1	215
Abigail, Mrs., d. Apr. 17, 1749	LR1	216
Abigail, d. Thomas & Elizabeth, b. Oct. 24, 1749	LR1	241
Abigai, m. James **ROCKWELL**, Oct. 17, 176[ ]	1	150
Betsey, d. Hezekiah, d. Jan. 1, 1793	1	296
Catharine, of Ridgefield, m. W[illia]m S. **LOCKWOOD**, of N[ ] Haven, Oct. 26, 1831, by Rev. C. G. Selleck	1	174
Daniel, [s. Elisha & Charity], b. Sept. 6, 1795; d. [ ]	1	70
Deborah, w. Dea. Ebenezer, d. Mar. 30, 1812, in the 60th y. of her age	1	216
Dorathy, d. Thomas & Abigail, b. Feb. 27, [1719/20]	LR1	203
Dorothy, d. Joseph & Abigail, b. Nov. 30, 1746	LR1	239
Ebenezer, s. Thomas & Abigail, b. Dec. 10, 1729	LR1	210
Ebenezer, d. Nov. 25, 1749	LR1	216
Ebenezer, s. Thomas & Elizabeth, b. Mar. 31, 1753	LR1	254
Ebenezer, m. Deborah **STEBBINS**, Apr. 10, 1783	1	154
Ebenezer, s. Thomas, d. Aug. 9, 1807, in New York	1	213
Ebenezer, had infant d. [ ], d. Jan. 2, 1815	1	218
Ebenezer, Dea., d. Oct. 12, 1821, ae 68 y.	1	223
Ebenezer, of South Salem, N. Y., m. Harriet **OLMSTED**, of Ridgefield, May 12, 1835, by Rev. Charles G. Selleck	1	182
Ebenezer, 2nd, d. Aug. 4, 1837, ae 23, y.	1	238
Ebenezer G., s. Gould & Betsey, b. Mar. 1, 1810	1	104
Edward, d. Sept. 1, 1837, ae 20 y.	1	233
Elijah, s. Thomas & Abigail, b. May 16, [1718]	LR1	202
Elijah, d. Aug. 17, 1740*, ae 19 y., at New(?) Haven, bd. at Ridgefield *(Probably 1840)	1	235
Elijah, m. Hannah [ ], Oct. 26, 1742	LR1	232
Elijah, s. Elijah & Hannah, b. June 5, 1753	LR1	248
Elisha, s. Thomas & Elizabeth, b. Mar. 9, 1759	LR1	254
Elisha, m. Charity **JUDSON**, Dec. 31, 1786	1	70
Elisha, m. Charity **JUDSON**, Dec. 31, 1786	1	156

RIDGEFIELD VITAL RECORDS 187

	Vol.	Page
HAWLEY, HAWLY, (cont.)		
Elisha, [s. Elisha & Charity], b. Oct. 20, 1788; d. [ ]	1	70
Elisha, d. Apr. 18, 1850, ae 91 y.	1	240
Elizabeth, d. William, d. Aug. 24, 1835, ae 21 y.	1	231
Elizabeth A., m. Thaddeus **HOYT**, b. of Ridgefield, Nov. 2, 1841, by Rev. Joseph Fuller	1	191
Enoch, had child d. July 11, 1837	1	233
Enoch, s. of Walter, d. July 11, 1837	1	233
Ezekiell, s. Thomas, b. Apr. 15, 1713	LR1	199
Ezekiel, s. Elijah & Hannah, b. Mar. 10, 1745/6	LR1	239
Ezekiel, d. Mar. 11, 1745/6	LR1	215
Gould, m. Betsey **STEBBINS**, Jan. 19, 1809	1	104
Hannah, d. Thomas & Abigail, b. Apr. 15, 1728	LR1	209
Hannah, d. Elijah & Hannah, b. Jan. 29, 1743/4	LR1	239
Harriet O., m. Rufus N. **SEYMOUR**, Mar. 17, 1841, by Rev. Joseph Fuller	1	190
Harriet O., Mrs., m. Rufus **SEYMOUR**, b. of Ridgefield, Mar. 17, 1841, by Rev. Joseph Fuller	1	191
Henry, d. Dec. 18, 1846, ae 20 y.	1	238
Hezekiah, m. Ann **JONES**, Oct. 26, 1788	1	157
Hezekiah, d. Oct. 1, 1826, ae 70 y.	1	225
Hezekiah, his wid., d. Oct. 10, 1838, ae 82 y.	1	234
Irad, [s. Elisha & Charity,]	1	70
Jane, of Ridgefield, m. Horace **DAGGETT**, of N[ ] Haven, Oct. 22, 1832, by Rev. C. G. Selleck	1	177
Jane, see Jane **DAGGETT**	1	232
John, s. Nathan & Sarah, b. Feb. 10, 1751	LR1	243
John Gold, s. Thomas & Elizabeth, b. June 5, 1751	LR1	241
Joseph, s. Thomas, b. May 16, 1714	LR1	199
Joseph, m. Abigail [ ], Nov. 8, 1744	LR1	232
Joseph, s. Nathan & Sarah, b. Mar. 8, 1748/9	LR1	243
Joseph, Lieut., d. Apr. 15, 1749	LR1	216
Joseph, s. Thomas & Elizabeth, b. June 15, 1764	1	12
Joseph, m. Phebe **SMITH**, Dec. 5, 1791	1	158
Judson, [s. Elisha & Charity], b. Dec. 19, 1790; d. [ ]	1	70
Lidia, d. Thomas & Abigail, b. July 29, 1725	LR1	205
Margaret, of Ridgefield, m. Henry **COOLEDGE**, of New York, Nov. 3, 1847, by Rev. James A. Hawley	1	128
Molly, d. Elijah & Hannah, b. Nov. 1, 1751	LR1	248
Molly, d. Elijah & Hannah, d. Mar. 16, 1752	LR1	216
Molly, 2nd, d. Elijah & Hannah, b. Apr. 4, 1756	LR1	248
Nathan, s. Thomas & Abigail, b. Nov. 16, [1723]	LR1	204
Nathan, m. Sarah [ ], July 3, 1746	LR1	232
Ruth, d. Joseph & Abigail, b. Dec. 10, 174[ ]	LR1	243
Ruth, m. Caleb **SMTIH**, Oct. 28, 1767	1	150
Samuel C., m. Sarah R. **GILBERT**, b. of Ridgefield, Oct. 11, 1846, by Charles Stearnes. Int. Pub.	1	199
Sarah, w. Nathan, d. Jan. 13, 1754	LR1	216

188 BARBOUR COLLECTION

	Vol.	Page
HAWLEY, HAWLY, (cont.)		
Stiles, [s. Elisha & Charity], b. Apr. 8, 1799, "drowned in Ill."	1	70
Talcott, s. Thomas & Elizabeth, b. Nov. 17, 1762	1	12
Talcott, d. Sept. 11, 1807, in the 44th y. of his age	1	213
Thomas, s. Thomas & Abigaill, b. Feb. 20, [1721/2]	LR1	204
Thomas, Rev., d. Nov. 8, 1738, "ae 49 Sept. 10, preceeding"	LR1	215
Thomas, m. Elizabeth [ ], Jan. 13, 1747/8	LR1	233
Thomas, s. Thomas & Elizabeth, b. Feb. 28, 1755	LR1	254
Thomas, d. Nov. 20, 1840, ae 85 y.; b. [ ] 1755	1	235
Thomas Chauncey, [s. Elisha & Charity], b. Jan. 7, 1802	1	70
Walter, d. July 11, 1837. He, his s. Enoch and a child of Enoch's were all killed by lightning	1	233
William, had infant s. [ ], d. Nov. 14, 1825, ae 2 m. 8 d.	1	225
William, had female d. Sept. 14, 1834, ae 18 y., at his house	1	231
-----, Mr., d. June 2, 1836	1	232
HAYES, Clara, m. Abijah **HYATT**, Apr. 24, 1797	1	88
Mary J., of Lewisboro, N. Y., m. Josiah N. **GRUMMAN**, of Ridgefield, Nov. 21, 1847, by Rev. Henry Olmsted, Jr.	1	129
HIBBERT, Edwin W., of New Haven, m. Catharine A. **KNAPP**, of Ridgefield, Oct. 4, 1846, by Rev. Charles Stearns. Int. Pub.	1	199
HICKOCK, HICKOX, HICKCOCK, Almon, m. Julia A. **BENEDICT**, May 3, 1842, by Nathan Burton, P. T.	1	192
Amy, m. John **WILSON**, Jan. 16, 1783	1	154
Ebenezer, s. Miriam, b. Mar. 11, 1774	1	69
Miriam, had s. Ebenezer, b. Mar. 11, 1774	1	69
Miriam, m. Josiah **LOBDELL**, Oct. 7, 1787	1	69
Miriam, m. Josiah **LOBDELL**, Oct. 7, 1787	1	157
Rhoda, d. Jan. 4, 1832	1	229
HILL, Moses, of Winthrop, Kennebeck Co., Me., m. Phebe Munrow **ROCKWELL**, of Ridgefield, May 25, 1831, by Rev. Hawley Sanford	1	173
HINE, HINES, Abigail, m. Joseph **STEBBINS**, Jr., Apr. 11, 1791	1	157
Abigail, m. Joseph **STEBBINS**, 2nd, Apr. 11, 1792	1	73
Ambros, s. Isaac & Anne, b. June 14, 1775	1	3
Anne, d. Isaac & Anne, b. July 5, 1761	1	3
Benjamin, s. Isaac & Anne, b. Feb. 13, 1764	1	3
Betsey, d. Newton & Mary, b. June 20, 1785	1	46
Charles, s. Newton & Mary, b. Feb. 25, 1789; d. Oct. 16, 1792	1	46
Elijah, s. Isaac & Anne, b. June 28, 1771	1	3
Isaac, s. Isaac & Anne, b. Oct. 4, 1765	1	3
Jane, m. Stephen **REMINGTON**, Oct. 29, 1767	1	71
Jared, s. Newton & Mary, b. Apr. 1, 1787	1	46
Jared, s. Newton, d. May 13, 1799, ae 12 y.	1	209
Josiah, d. June 25, 1790, ae 80	1	205
Lois, d. Isaac & Anne, b. Jan. 14, 1758	1	3
Mehitabel, w. Josiah, d. Apr. 27, 1767	1	201

	Vol.	Page
HINE, HINES, (cont.)		
Newton, m. Mary **WILLIAMS**, Mar. 8, 1781	1	156
Newton, his infant, d. June 21, 1794	1	207
Olive, d. Isaac & Anne, b. Jan. 28, 1769	1	3
Polly, m. Eleazer **GREGORY**, Oct. 19, 1793	1	83
Polly, m. Eleazer **GREGORY**, Oct. 19, 1793	1	158
Sally, d. Newton & Mary, b. Aug. 10, 1782	1	46
Sarah, m. Trowbridge **BENNET**, Aug. 20, 1767	1	151
Susannah, m. Ezra **BENEDICT**, Sept. 28, 1783	1	154
HOBART, Jeremiah, [s. Joseph & Sarah], b. Dec. 29, 1730	LR1	206
Joseph, m. Sarah **ROCKWELL**, May 29, 1723	LR1	227
Joseph, [s. Joseph & Sarah], b. July 7, 1724	LR1	206
Joseph, m. Ruth **PERRY**, Jan. 3, 1748/9, by Jonathan Ingersoll, V. D. M.	LR1	234
Joseph, s. Joseph & Ruth, b. Aug. 15, 1751	LR1	247
Phebe, m. Nathan **WILLSON**, June 5, 1727	LR1	228
Phebe, [d. Joseph & Sarah], b. Feb. 25, 1728	LR1	206
Rebecca, [d. Joseph & Sarah], b. Nov. 13, 1726	LR1	206
Sarah, [d. Joseph & Sarah], b. July 27, 1725	LR1	206
Sarah, d. Joseph & Ruth, b. Oct. 30, 1749	LR1	247
Thomas, [s. Joseph & Sarah], b. Aug. 6, 1729	LR1	206
HOLLAND, Robert, m. Grace **KEELER**, b.of Ridgefield, June 26, 1842, by Rev. Charles Chettenden	1	192
HOLLEBERT, [see also **HURLBURT**], Esther, m. Ens. John **ROCKWELL**, Nov. 22, 1769	1	151
HOLLY, Abby, d. [Walter & Phalle], b. May 13, 1799	1	89
Betsey Ann, d. Walter & Elizabeth, b. Aug. 12, 1816	1	89
Darius, s. [Walter & Phalle], b. Aug. 16, 1797	1	89
Deborah, w. Enoch, d. May 24, 1824, ae 57	1	224
Elnathan, d. Aug. 28, 1814, ae 49	1	218
Enoch, m. Deborah **DAUCHY**, Feb. 3, 1785	1	155
Enoch, s. Walter & Elizabeth, b. July 17, 1814	1	89
Enoch, m. wid. Sally **BOUTON**, b. of Ridgefield, Oct. 19, 1828, by Samuel Stebbins, J. P.	1	168
Katy, d. [Walter & Phalle], b. May 19, 1804	1	89
Mary, d. Daniel & Abigail, of Bedford, m. Joseph **LEES**, Feb. 12, 1735/6	LR1	229
Phalle, w. Walter, d. Dec. 26, 1810, ae 46	1	215
Walter, m. Phalle **NORTHRUP**, Nov. 5, 1795	1	89
Walter, s. [Walter & Phalle], b. July 16, 1801	1	89
HOLMES, Abraham, m. Esther **SMITH**, b. of Ridgefield, Dec. 20, 1825, by Samuel M. Phelps	1	167
Abraham, his child d. Feb. 20, [1847], ae 3 y.	1	239
HOOD, Robert S., of New York, m. Caroline F. **SUNDERLAND**, of Ridgefield, May 17, 1852, by Rev. Shaler J. Hillyer	1	138
HOPKINS, Betsey, see Elizabeth Hopkins	1	200
Elizabeth, or Betsey, d. July 12, 1767	1	200
HORTON, Cornelius, of York Town, m. Orilla **KEELER**, of		

BARBOUR COLLECTION

	Vol.	Page
HORTON, (cont.)		
Ridgefield, Dec. 7, 1823, by Sam[ue]ll M. Phelps	1	164
Samuel, m. Mary **PULLING**, Dec. 4, 1830, by Nathan Burton	1	173
HOW, HOWE, Betsey, d. Epenetus & Elizabeth, b. Dec. 28, 1771	1	18
Charles, s. Epenetus & Sarah, b. Jan. 27, 1810	1	104
Clark, s. Epenetus & Sarah, b. Sept. 20, 1813	1	104
David Ward, his w. [ ], d. Nov. 15, 1836	1	233
Eliza, of Ridgefield, m. Joel **BAXTER**, of North Salem, Oct. 15, 1826, by Samuel M. Phelps	1	167
Elizabeth, d. Epenetus & Elizabeth, b. June 16, 1781	1	18
Elizabeth, d. Epenetus, d. Jan. 12, 1784	1	203
Elizabeth, d. Epenetus, d. Feb. 10, 1784	1	203
Elizabeth, w. Epenetus, d. Sept. 3, 1814, ae 69	1	218
Emeline, of Ridgefield, m. Reuben **FRENCH**, of Hingham, Mass., Feb. 4, 1836, at the house of William Howe, by Rev. Shaller J. Hillyer, of North Salem, N. Y.	1	181
Epenetus, s. Epenetus & Elizabeth, b. July 26, 1773	1	18
Epenetus, Jr., m. Sarah **DAUCHY**, Dec. 24, 1807	1	104
Epenetus, Jr., had infant, d. Feb. 19, 1809	1	214
Epenetus, d. Sept. 9, 1815	1	219
Eunice, d. Epenetus & Elizabeth, b. July 25, 1776	1	18
Harriet, d. Epenetus & Sarah, b. Oct. 19, 1811	1	104
Isaac, s. Epenetus & Elizabeth, b. Jan. 25, 1774	1	18
Isaac, d. June 12, 1774	1	201
John, 2nd, s. Epenetus & Elizabeth, b. Mar. 2, 176[ ]	1	18
John, s. Epenetus & Elizabeth, b. June 12, 1765	1	18
John, s. Epenetus & Elizabeth, d. Dec. 9, 1765	1	200
John, m. Polly **ROCKWELL**, July [ ], 1792	1	158
John, s. William & Polly, b. July 20, 1793	1	77
Miriam, d. Epenetus & Elizabeth, b. Jan. 2, 176[ ]	1	18
Meriam, m. Abijah **OLMSTED**, Apr. 4, 1784	1	155
Nancy, d. Epenetus & Elizabeth, b. July 25, 1776	1	18
Nancy, m. W[illia]m **NAIL**, Jr., Dec. 20, 1829, by Nathan Burton	1	170
Polly, w. John, d. Jan. 11, 1793	1	206
Sally, d. Epenetus & Elizabeth, b. Nov. 25, 1778	1	18
William, s. Epenetus & Elizabeth, b. Dec. 27, 1769	1	18
William Sturgis, s. Epenetus & Sarah, b. Sept. 17, 1815	1	104
HOWARD, Ury, of New Milford, Conn., m. Ruth **MUFFIT**, of Ridgefield, Nov. 24, 1834, by Elias Blanchard, J. P.	1	180
HOWLAND, Ann, of Ridgefield, m. Henry Burr **PLATT**, of Redding, Dec. 18, 1850, by Nathaniel Mead, J. P.	1	135
Jane, m. James **FLYNN**, b. of Ridgefield, Feb. 4, 1852, by Rev. Ira Abbott	1	137
Mary, of Ridgefield, m. Moses B. **DANFORD**, of Redding, Aug. 24, 1846, by Rev. Henry Olmsted, Jr.	1	127
Phebe, m. Philip Burr **KEELER**, b. of Ridgefield, Dec. 18, 1850, by Rev. Nathaniel Mead	1	135

RIDGEFIELD VITAL RECORDS

	Vol.	Page
HOYLE, Abigail, [d. Samuel & Elizabeth], b. May 13, 1793	1	81
Anne, [d. Samuel & Elizabeth], b. May 10, 1784	1	81
Ebenezer, [s. Samuel & Elizabeth], b. Nov. 14, 1779	1	81
Lewis, [s. Samuel & Elizabeth], b. Aug. 24, 1782	1	81
Polly, [d. Samuel & Elizabeth], b. Feb. 6, 1795	1	81
William, [s. Samuel & Elizabeth], b. May 17, 1786	1	81
HOYT, [see also **HAIGHT**], Abigail, d. Benjamin & Sarah, b. Dec. 18, [1719]	LR1	203
Abigail, m. Richard **OLMSTEAD**, Jan. 13, 1740/1	LR1	232
Abigail, m. Nathan **LOBDELL**, Jan. 10, 1793	1	158
Adah, m Nathaniel **SEYMOUR**, Jan. 21, 1790	1	158
Arleban, s. Matthew & Mary, b. Mar. 13, 1784	1	33
Asa, s. Matthew & Mary, b. Dec. 16, 1781	1	33
Benjamin, m. Sarah [ ], Mar. 21, 1716	LR1	227
Benjamin, s. Benjamin & Sarah, b. Dec. 4, [1721/2]	LR1	204
Benjamin, m. Patience [ ], Aug. 28, 1751	LR1	233
Benjamin, d. Feb. 16, 1759	1	201
Benjamin, d. Feb. 11, 1810	1	215
Betsey Ann, m. Charles **JARVIS**, b. of Ridgefield, Jan. 26, 1845, by Rev. A. S. Francis	1	196
David, s. Benjamin & Sarah, b. Dec. 6, 1729	LR1	210
David, m. Hannah **GILBERT**, Sept. 29, 1784	1	155
David, d. Apr. 5, 1798, ae 67 y.	1	209
Dorcas, m. Jonah C. **KEELER**, b. of Ridgefield, Aug. 7, 1832, by Rev. Charles G. Selleck	1	176
Dorcas, see Dorcas **KEELER**	1	229
Eben, m. Polly **STEBBINS**, Nov. 22, 1800	1	159
Edwin S., of Ridgefield, m. Mary G. **KEELER**, of Wilton, this day, [Feb. 19, 1851], by Rev. C. Clark	1	134
Elizabeth, m. Silas **HALL**, May 4, 1788	1	157
Elizabeth, of Ridgefield, m. Daniel **LAMEREAUX**, of Orange Co., N. Y., Mar. 28, 1827, by Samuel M. Phelps	1	168
Elizabeth, wid., d. Jan. 15, 1840, ae 82	1	235
Ezra N., of Lewisboro, m. Marry E. **CANFIELD**, of Ridgefield, Dec. 13, 1843, by Rev. A. S. Francis	1	194
Henry, of South Salem, N. Y., m. Polly **STALL**, of Ridgefield, Nov. 13, 1839, by Rev. T. Sparks	1	187
Hezekiah, of Salem, m. Phebe **HOYT**, of Ridgefield, Dec. 17, 1789	1	158
Jonathan, m. Adah **OLMSTED**, Mar. 6, 1786	1	156
Jonathan, d. Dec. 11, 1786	1	204
Jonathan, d. Oct. 8, 1818, ae 32 y.	1	221
Lucretia Ann, m. Lewis **HUNT**, b. of Ridgefield, Mar. 1, 1846, by Rev. Shaller J. Hillyer	1	198
Lydia, m. Ezekiel **OLMSTEAD**, Mar. 11, 1750/1, by Jonathan Ingersoll, V. D. M.	LR1	233
Maria, d. Ebenezer & Polly, b. Oct. 9, 1801	1	100
Maria, m. Edward **BENEDICT**, b. of Ridgefield, Dec. 22,		

HOYT, (cont.)

	Vol.	Page
1830, by Rev. Samuel M. Phelps	1	175
Mary, d. Benjamin & Sarah, b. Sept. 19, [1724/5]	LR1	205
Mary, m. Timothy **KEELER**, July 19, 1744	LR1	231
Nancy A., m. John W. **MILLER**, b. of Ridgefield, May 31, 1840, by Rev. Thomas Sparks	1	188
Patience, wid., d. Apr. 25, 1812, ae 83	1	216
Phebe, m. John **KEELER**, Sept. 17, 1767	1	68
Phebe, d. Matthew & Mary, b. Sept. 28, 1779	1	33
Phebe, of Ridgefield, m Hezekiah **HOYT**, of Salem, Dec. 17, 1789	1	158
Polly, w. Ebenezer, d. Dec. 14, 1811 ae 33 y.	1	215
Polly, m. Seth **SMITH**, b. of Ridgefield, Feb. 13, 1822, by Samuel M. Phelps	1	161
Polly E., m. William **BOUTON**, b. of Ridgefield, Mar. 15, 1829, by Samuel M. Phelps	1	169
Prudence, d. Benjamin & Prudence, b. Jan. 22, 1767	1	25
Rachel, m. Ward **STURGIS**, Apr. 27, 1788	1	157
Rebeckah, m. Aaron **NORTHRUP**, Jan. 25, 1743/4	LR1	232
Ruhamah, d. Matthew & Mary, b. Mar. 23, 1776	1	33
Sally, of Ridgefield, m. Rufus **FILLOW**, of West Port, May 17, 1847, by Rev. James A. Hawley	1	128
Samuel, m. Hannah **GILBERT**, Sept. 21, 1788	1	157
Samuel, 2nd, his d. [ ], d. June [ ], 1806	1	213
Samuel, d. Sept. 18, 1819, ae 65	1	221
Sarah, d. Benjamin & Sarah, b. Oct. 14, [1714]	LR1	202
Sarah, d. Feb. 9, 1759	1	201
Sarah, d Matthew & Mary, b. Sept. 20, 1777	1	33
Sarah, m. Robert **WILSON**, Apr. 1, 1779	1	154
Stebbins, s. Ebenezer & Polly, b. Nov. 10, 1803	1	100
Thaddeus, m. Elizabeth A. **HAWLEY**, b. of Ridgefield, Nov. 2, 1841, by Rev. Joseph Fuller	1	191
Warner, Rev., d. Oct. 18, 1844, ae 34 y.	1	237
Warren, his d. [Mrs. **MILLER**], d. July 30, 1842, ae 22 y.	1	236
William R., of Lewisboro, N. Y., m. Mary **JEWETT**, of Ridgefield, Sept. 6, 1843, by Rev. James A. Hawley	1	194

HUBBELL, Caroline, d. Polly, d. July 14, 1825, ae 4 y.   1   225
Polly, had d. Caroline, d. July 14, 1825, ae 4 y.   1   225
Polly, m. Keeler **ST. JOHN**, b. of Ridgefield, Dec. 22, 1833, by Rev. Charles G. Selleck   1   179
Polly, m. Sylvester **WILLIAMS**, b. of Ridgefield, Mar. 2, 1851, by Hezekiah Scott, J. P.   1   134
Susan, of Redding, m. Bradley **HULL**, of Ridgefield, Mar. 29, 1824, by Samuell M. Phelps   1   165
Uriah, had child d. Apr. 15, 1840, ae 2 y.   1   235
Wakeman, m. Julia A. **LYNES**, Sept. 2, 1829, by Nathan Burton   1   170

HULL, Bradley, m. Mary **HULL**, Jan. 14, 1794   1   80

	Vol.	Page
HULL, (cont.)		
Bradley, his w. [ ], d. Nov. 1, 1823	1	224
Bradley, of Ridgefield, m. Susan **HUBBELL**, of Redding, Mar. 29, 1824, by Samuell M. Phelps	1	165
Bradley, d. May 26, 1833	1	230
Burr, s. [Bradley & Mary], b. Jan. 10, 1795	1	80
Charity, of Ridgefield, m. George **CROFUT**, of Huntington, Apr. 1, 1828, by Samuel M. Phelps	1	168
Eliza A., m. Nathaniel K. **WOOD**, b. of Ridgefield, Oct. 10, 1847, by Rev. Sylvester Strong	1	130
Elizabeth, w. Silas, d. Oct. 23, 1787	1	204
Hannah, m. Philip **KEELER**, Jan. 8, 1784	1	154
Hawley, of Lewisboro, N. Y., m. Margaret **GILBERT**, of Ridgefield, this eve {Oct. 13, 1846], by Rev. James A. Hawley	1	198
Huldah, m Jeremiah **KEELER**, Apr. 23, 1788	1	157
Mary, m. Bradley **HULL**, Jan. 14, 1794	1	80
Mary Polly, d. Bradley, d. June 17, 1813, ae 1 y. 17 d.	1	217
Sarah, b. Mar. 22, 1749; m. James **SMITH**, s. Gideon, Mar. 18, 1767	1	36
Sarah, m. James **SMITH**, Mar. 18, 1767	1	151
Silas, d. Nov. 14, 1803, ae 65 y.	1	211
HUNT, Clarissa, m. George **MEAD**, Oct. 4, 1827, by Nathan Burton	1	167
Clark, his w. [ ], d. Sept. 21, 1838, ae 26 y.	1	234
Eliza Ann, m. Selah **BATES**, Dec. 30, 1829, by Nathan Burton	1	170
Lewis, m. Lucretia Ann **HOYT**, b. of Ridgefield, Mar. 1, 1845, by Rev. Shaller J. Hillyer	1	198
Sally, m. Jonah **FOSTER**, b. of Ridgefield, [Mar.] 14, [1821], by Oliver Tuttle	1	160
Timothy, d. Jan. 12, 1835, ae 68	1	231
HURLBURT, [see also **HOLLEBERT**], Azor, s. Azor & Mary, b. Aug. 3, 1771	1	39
David, s. Azor & Mary, b. June 28, 1769	1	39
Sarah, d. Azor & Mary, b. Sept. 11, 1766	1	39
Uriah, s. Azor & Mary, b. Aug. 21, 1773	1	39
HUSTED, Alfred W., of New Haven, m. Lucy **NORTHRUP**, of Ridgefield, Sept. 2, 1851, by Rev. Clinton Clark	1	135
HYATT, Abigail, d. Thomas & Experience, b. Dec. 6, [1719/20]	LR1	203
Abigail, d. Thomas & Experience, d. Oct. 6, 1736	LR1	215
Abigail, d. Thomas & Hannah, b. Oct. 29, 1743	LR1	238
Abijah, s. Thomas & Elizabeth, b. May 25, 1777	1	41
Abijah, m. Clara **HAYES**, Apr. 24, 1797	1	88
Caroline, m. Thomas B. **ROCKWELL**, b. of Ridgefield, Dec. 30, 1829, by Rev. E. Washburn	1	170
Charles, s. John B., d. Feb. 18, [1852]. "Killed on New York & Erie R. R., bd. in Ridgefield"	1	242
Charles Smith, s. Abijah & Clara, b. June 9, 1798	1	88
Electa, w. Aaron S., d. Oct. 11, 1830, ae 24 y., at Wilton	1	228

BARBOUR COLLECTION

HYATT, (cont.)

	Vol.	Page
Elizabeth, [d. Thomas & Experience], [b.] Oct. 25, 1711	LR1	201
Elizabeth, d. Thomas, m. David **ROCKWELL**, Aug. 29, 1731	LR1	228
Elizabeth, d. Thomas & Hannah, b. Apr. 20, 1759	LR1	198
Elizabeth, w. Thomas, d. Nov. 11, 1828, ae 70 y.	1	227
Esther, d. Thomas & Hannah, b. Jan. 18, 1755	LR1	198
Esther, d. Uzziel & Rachel, b. Aug. 10, 1777	1	41
Experience, d. Apr. 19, 1773	1	201
George A., of Waterbury, m. Nancy Emily **SMITH**, of Ridgefield, Jan. 14, 1852, by Rev. Ira Abbott	1	137
Hannah, d. Thomas & Experience, b. Aug. 15, 1702	LR1	201
Hannah, m. James **SCOTT**, Apr. 24, 1722	LR1	227
Hannah, d. [Thomas & Hannah], b. Aug. 31, 1745	LR1	238
Hannah, wid., d. Jan. 30, 1789	1	205
John, s. Thomas & Hannah, b. Mar. 16, 1757	LR1	198
John, s. Thomas & Hannah, d. Nov. 8, 1759	LR1	217
Maria, of Ridgefield, m. Harris **EAMES**, of New Brunswick, N. H., Sept. 26, 1830, by Rev. Oliver E. Ammerman	1	172
Mary, [d. Thomas & Experience], b. Sept. 17, 1705	LR1	201
Mary, m. Joseph **OSBURN**, Apr. 18, 1728	LR1	228
Mary, d. Thomas & Hannah, b. July 16, 1763	1	3
Mary, m. Isaiah **SMITH**, Jan. 2, 1796	1	87
Mary, m. Isaiah **SMITH**, Feb. 1, 1796	1	159
Olive, d. Uzziel & Rachel, b. July 14, 1775	1	41
Philip, s. John, d. [July 7, 1851], ae 29	1	241
Rachel, d. Uzziel & Rachel, b. June 19, 1783	1	41
Rachel, w. Uzziel, d. July 4, 1783	1	203
Rebecca, d. Thomas & Experience, b. June 20, [1723]	LR1	204
Ruth, d. Thomas & Hannah, b. July 30, 1761	1	3
Ruth, m. Ezra **DANN**, May 7, 1783	1	154
Sarah, d. Thomas & Hannah, b. Jan. 31, 1750/1	LR1	210
Sarah, d. Uzziel & Rachel, b. Apr. 11, 1773	1	41
Thomas, [s. Thomas & Experience b.] Jan. 10, 1714	LR1	201
Thomas, s. Thomas & Hannah, b. Feb. 9, 1752/3	LR1	210
Thomas, d. Dec. 27, 1759	LR1	217
Thomas, m. Elizabeth **SMITH**, Sept. 11, 1776	1	155
Thomas, d. Dec. 14, 1782	1	203
Thomas, m. Hannah **BURR**, [ ]	1	150
Uzzill, [s. Thomas & Experience], d. Dec. 10, 1708	LR1	201
Uzziel, s. Thomas & Experience, d. Feb. 14, 1712	LR1	213
Uzziel, s. Thomas & Hannah, b. May 16, 1748	LR1	210
Uzziel, m. Rachel **SMITH**, Nov. 28, 1770	1	151
Uzziah, m Hannah **STEVENS**, Nov. 27, 1783	1	155
Uzziel, d. May 8, 1817	1	220
William, s. Uzziel & Rachel, b. May 4, 1780	1	41
William, s. Uzziel, d. Feb. 26, 1782	1	203
Zibiah, d. Tho[ma]s & Experience, b. Mar. 2, [1718]	LR1	202
INGERSOLL, Abigail, d. Rev. Jonathan & Dorcas, b. May 7, 1751	LR1	242

	Vol.	Page
INGERSOLL, (cont.)		
Abigail, m. Daniel **OLMSTED**, Oct. 22, 1769	1	150
Ann, d. Jonathan & Dorcas, b. Apr. 5, 1765	1	17
Anne, Mrs., m. John **KING**, Apr. 22, 1784	1	152
Anne, d. Moses & Ruth, b. Mar. 12, 1791	1	70
Anne, d. Moses, d. Aug. 15, 1793	1	206
David, s. Moses & Ruth, b. Feb. 28, 1793	1	70
David, d. July 29, 1811, in the 19th y. of his age	1	215
Dorcas, d. Rev. Jonathan & Dorcas, b. Oct. 15, 1743	LR1	236
Dorcas, m. James **ANDREWS**, May 5, 1762	1	150
Dorcas, wid. Rev. [ ], d. Sept. 26, 1811, in the 86th y. of her age	1	215
Esther, d. Rev. Jonathan & Dorcas, b. Aug. 10, 1760	LR1	242
Esther, m. Ebenezer **OLMSTED**, Jan. 17, 1779	1	153
Hannah, d. Rev. Jonathan & Dorcas, b. Apr. 9, 1756	LR1	242
Hannah, m. Josiah **RAYMOND**, Mar. 4, 1780	1	154
Harvey, s. Moses & Ruth, b. Dec. 1, 1797	1	70
Jane Ann, d. Moses & Ruth, b. Jan. 22, 1810	1	70
Jonathan, Rev., m. Mrs. Dorcas **MOSS**, Nov. 10, 1740, by Rev. Samuel Cooke, of Stratfield. Int. Pub.	LR1	231
Jonathan, s. Rev. Jonathan & Dorcas, b. Apr. 16, 1747	LR1	240
Joseph, s. Rev. Jonathan & Dorcas, b. Aug. 11, 1753	LR1	242
Joseph, d. July 16, 1819, ae 66 y.	1	221
Joseph A., of Westchester Co., N. Y., m. Julia **CAMPBELL**, of Ridgefield, Apr. 4, 1828, by Samuel M. Phelps	1	169
Mary, d. Rev. Jonathan & Dorcas, b. Dec. 20, 1748	LR1	242
Moses, s. Rev. Jonathan & Dorcas, b. June 9, 1763	LR1	242
Moses, s. Ebenezer & Esther, b. June 3, 1778	1	48
Moses, m. Ruth **SMITH**, Dec. 9, 1787	1	156
Moses, m. Ruth **SMITH**, Dec. 10, 1787	1	157
Nancy, d. Ebenezer & Esther, b. Sept. 30, 178[ ]	1	48
Russell, s. Ebenezer & Esther, b. Dec. 8, 1779	1	48
Ruth, w. Moses, d. Jan. 24, 1817, ae 47 y. 1 m. 20 d.	1	220
Sally, d. Moses & Ruth, b. Mar. 23, 1789	1	70
Samuel, s. Moses & Ruth, b. May 24, 1795	1	70
Samuel, of Bridgeport, m Millesent **SMITH**, of Ridgefield, Feb. 1, 1824, by Samuell M. Phelps	1	165
Sarah, d. Rev. Jonathan & Dorcas, b. Oct. 28, 1741	LR1	236
ISAACS, ISAAC, Abigail, d. Samuell & Mary, b. Oct. 2, 1746	LR1	239
Amanda, of Ridgefield, m. Nathaniel **LAMSON**, of Fishkill, Oct. 28, 1827, by Samuel M. Phelps	1	168
Colman, s. Sam[ue]ll & Mary, b. Sept. 1, 1745	LR1	239
James, s. Sam[ue]ll & Mary, b. Oct. 22, 1747	LR1	198
Sam[ue]ll, m. Mary [ ], Jan. 10, 1744/5	LR1	232
JACKLEN, JACKLIN, Ann, d. Robert & Ann, b. Oct. 7, 1759	1	13
Benjamin, s. Robert & Ann, b. May 6, 1752	1	13
Daniel, s. Robert & Ann, b. Oct. 21, 1749	1	13
Ebenezer, s. Robert & Ann, b. Oct. 22, 1757	1	13

196 BARBOUR COLLECTION

	Vol.	Page
JACKLEN, JACKLIN, (cont.)		
Elizabeth, m. Jack **FREEMAN**, June 24, 1784	1	154
Mary, d. Sam[ue]ll & Sarah, b. Dec. 31, 1742	LR1	251
Thaddeus, s. Robert & Ann, b. June 3, 1761	1	13
JACKSON, Anne, d. John & Martha, b. Dec. 1, 17[ ]	1	32
Betty, d. Daniel & Elizabeth, b. Sept. 22, 1784	1	56
Bille, s. John & Martha, b. Sept. 17, 1782	1	32
Daniel, m. Elizabeth **WHITNEY**, Feb. 20, 1783	1	154
Daniel, m. Elizabeth **BROOKS**, Apr. 5, [ ]	LR1	252
Deborah, d. Daniel & Elizabeth, b. Oct. 16, 1760	LR1	247
Grace, d. Joseph & Grace, b. Jan. 12, 1754	1	5
Jane, m. Thaddeus **OLMSTED**, Dec. 18, 1791	1	158
John, m. Martha **BENNET**, Nov. 18, 1781	1	154
John, d. Dec. 27, 1812	1	217
Joseph, m. Grace **BURR**, Dec. 5, 1750	1	150
Joseph, s. Joseph & Grace, b. Mar. 2, 1756	1	5
Martha, d. Joseph & Grace, b. June 2, 1759	1	5
Martin, d. Oct. 29, 1833	1	230
Mary, d. Daniel & Elizabeth, b. Nov. 24, 1758	LR1	247
Philip Burr, s. Joseph & Grace, b. Sept. 29, 1761	1	5
Sarah, d. Dec. 11, 1843, ae 81 y.	1	237
Stephen, s. Joseph & Grace, b. Oct. 13, 1751	1	5
Tirza, d. Nov. 3, 1800, ae 27 y.	1	210
-----, wid., d. Oct. [ ], 1812	1	217
JAGGER, Joseph, d. Dec. 24, 1802 "supposed to be 100 y. old"	1	211
JARVIS, Charles, m. Betsey Ann **HOYT**, b. of Ridgefield, Jan. 26, 1845, by Rev. A. S. Francis	1	196
Darling, his w. [ ], d. Dec. 2, 1847, ae [ ]	1	239
Darling, m. Fanny **SPELMAN**, b. of Ridgefield, Jan. 7, 1849, by Rev. Sylvester S. Strong	1	131
John J., m. Susan M. **FOSTER**, Oct. 1, 1851, by Rev. Shaller J. Hillyer	1	136
JELLIFF, JELLEFF, JELLOFF, Betsey, m. William L. **EDMONDS**, Jan. 7, 1829, by Rev. Stephen Saunders, of South Salem, Westchester Co., N. Y.	1	173
Dorinda, d. Dec. 13, 1837, ae 26 y.	1	234
Eliza Ann, of Ridgefield, m. Russell **JONES**, of Wilton, June 9, 1824, by Rev. Hawley Sanford	1	162
Juliette, m Nathan C. **MALLORY**, b. of Ridgefield, Jan. 24, 1830, by Rev. Ebenezer Washburn	1	171
Mary, of Ridgefield, m. Roswell **MORGAN**, of Wilton, Jan. 2, 1831, by [Samuel M. Phelps]	1	175
Sturgis, his infant d. Dec. 18, 1803	1	211
Sturgis, his w. [ ], d. [, 1846]	1	238
William H., of Ridgefield, m. Almira B. **COLE**, of Wilton, May 12, 1845, by Rev. A. S. Francis	1	197
-----, Mr., d. Jan. [ ], [1851], ae [ ]	1	241
JENCKS, Hannah, w. Stephen, d. Aug. 11, 1800, ae 28 y. "Teacher		

	Vol.	Page
JENCKS, (cont.)		
of Peter Parley."	1	210
JENNINGS, Abel, m. Phebe Jane **NORTHROP**, b. of Ridgefield,		
May 4, 1842, by Rev. Joseph Fuller	1	192
Albin, had infant s. [ ], d. Mar. 30, 1821	1	222
Fanny, of Ridgefield, m. George **PARTRICK**, of Wilton, Aug.		
20, 1829, by Samuell M. Phelps	1	171
Hannah, of Ridgefield, m. Charles **GREGORY**, of Saugatuck,		
Oct. 12, 1828, by Samuel M. Phelps	1	169
Henry B., of West Port, m. Elizabeth **KEELER**, of Ridgefield,		
Apr. 11, 1850, by Rev. Clinton Clark	1	133
John, of Patterson Putnam Co., N. Y., m. Orra **STURGIS**, of		
Ridgefield, this day [Apr. 14, 1829], by Rev.		
Lemuel B. Hull	1	169
Joseph, s. Joseph & Esther, b. Oct. 18, 1732	LR1	220
Justus, m. Hannah **BEERS**, Dec. 27, 1781	1	154
Moss, his child d. Sept. 27, 1852, ae 2 y.	1	242
William A., m. Mariette **GATES**, b. of Ridgefield, Sept. 23,		
1850, by Rev. Nathaniel Mead	1	134
JEWETT, JEWITT, Elizabeth, [d. Thaddeus & Sarah], b. Nov.		
17, 1824	1	111
Elizabeth, of Ridgefield, m. George J. **HARRISON** (Rev.) of		
Franklin, Apr. 26, 1849, by Rev. James A. Hawley	1	132
Mary, d. Thaddeus & Sarah, b. Sept. 25, 1822	1	111
Mary, of Ridgefield, m. William R. **HOYT**, of Lewisboro,		
N. Y., Sept. 6, 1843, by Rev. James A. Hawley	1	194
Thaddeus, of Galway, N. Y., m. Sally **SMITH**, of Ridgefield,		
Sept. 28, 1821, by Samuel M. Phelps	1	161
JOHNSON, Fanny, d. John & Sarah, b. Dec. 7, 1793	1	62
John, m. Sarah **NORTHRUP**, Mar. 9, 1786	1	156
Judah, d. John & Sarah, b. July 10, 1791	1	62
Squire, s. John & Sarah, b. Apr. 6, 1787	1	62
Ziba, s. John & Sarah, b. Apr. 10, 1789	1	62
Ziba, d. July 18, 1794, ae 5 y.	1	207
JONES, Abigail, d. Jacob & Deborah, b. Mar. 20, 1737	LR1	223
Abigail, m. Joseph **SMITH**, Mar. 16, 1762	1	150
Abigail, d. Jacob, Jr. & Ruth, b. Apr. 7, 1782	1	56
Alvah, d. [Daniel & Elizabeth], b. Oct. 2, 1793	1	106
Ann, m. Hezekiah **HAWLEY**, Oct. 26, 1788	1	157
Ann, w. Capt. Ebenezer, d. Apr. 25, 1819	1	221
Anne, d. Ebenezer & Ann, b. Sept. 23, 1722	1	16
Azor, [s. Ebenezer, Jr. & Hepzibah], b. July 4, 1789	1	98
Benjamin, s. Ebenezer & Ann, b. July 17, 1770	1	16
Benjamin, m. Phebe **BOUTON**, Mar. 23, 1790	1	158
Benjamin, d. Nov. 28, 1843, ae 73	1	237
Betsey, d. John & Rebecka, b. Oct. 19, 1785	1	33
Betsey, m. Jabes Mix **GILBERT**, Nov. 23, 1802	1	101
Clarrissa, of Ridgefield, m. David D. **STURGIS**, of Weston,		

JONES, (cont.)

	Vol.	Page
Nov. 26, 1851, by Rev. Charles Stearnes	1	137
Czar, had negro Elizabeth, d. Aug. 5, 1822, ae 13	1	223
Daniel, s. John & Phebe, b. Feb. 10, 1770	1	33
Daniel, d. Mar. 19, 1835, in the 66th y. of his age	1	231
Daniel, his wid. [ ], d. Aug. 22, 1842, ae [ ]	1	236
Daniel E., s. Philo, d. Dec. 24, 1826, ae 3 y.	1	226
Deborah, d. John & Phebe, b. Mar. 27, 1776	1	33
Deborah, d. John, d. Apr. 19, 1795, ae 19 y.	1	208
Ebenezer, d. June 21, 1821, ae 89 y.	1	222
Ebenezer, s. [Ozar & Sally], b. July 24, 1822	1	110
Ebenezer, s. Jacob & Deborah, b. Aug. 30, 1732	LR1	223
Ebenezer, s. Ebenezer & Ann, b. Nov. 17, 1765	1	16
Ebenezer, m. Hephzibah **OLMSTED**, Feb. 8, 1789	1	157
Ebenezer, his w. [ ], d. Dec. 8, [1851], ae 82 y.	1	241
Ebenezer, d. Dec. 24, [1851], ae 86	1	241
Edward B., s. [Ozar & Sally], b. Dec. 20, 1824	1	110
Edward B., m. Elizabeth **NORTHRUP**, b. of Ridgefield, this day [Sept. 2, 1850], by Rev. C. Clark	1	133
Elizabeth, d. James & Elizabeth, b. Jan. 23, 1762	1	10
Ellin, d. Ebenezer & Ann, b. Oct. 17, 1762	1	16
Hannah, d. James & Elizabeth, b. Dec. 19, 1770	1	24
Harriatt, [d. Ebenezer, Jr. & Hepzibah], b. Feb. 16, 1796	1	98
Harriet, d. [Timothy & Anna], b. Sept. 15, 1810	1	106
Harriet, d. [Ozar & Sally], b. Apr. 13, 1821	1	110
Harriet, of Ridgefield, m. Warren **LOCKWOOD**, of New Canaan, Feb. 13, 1834, by Rev. Charles J. Todd	1	179
Harriet, m. Seth **SMITH**, b. of Ridgefield, Oct. 22, 1834, by Rev. Charles G. Selleck	1	180
Harriet, of Ridgefield, m. Lewis **BENEDICT**, of New York City, Sept. 1, 1840, by Rev. Joseph Fuller	1	189
Isaac, s. Daniel & Elizabeth, b. June 28, 1792	1	106
Isaac, d. Dec. [ ], 1843, in New York; bd. in Ridgefield	1	237
Jacob, Jr., m. Ruth **MORGAN**, Nov. 7, 1781	1	155
Jacob, d. Apr. 11, 1791, in the 85th y. of his age	1	205
Jacob, d. Dec. 29, 1826, in the 78th y. of his age	1	226
James, s. Jacob & Deborah, b. Nov. 16, 1734	LR1	223
James, m. Elizabeth **DAUCHY**, Mar. 18, 1760	LR1	252
James, s. James & Elizabeth, b. Jan. 3, 1773	1	24
James, d. Aug. 17, 1773	1	201
James, d. Aug. 19, 1773	1	201
James, s. James & Elizabeth, d. May 25, 1774	1	201
James, s. Jacob, 2nd & Ruth, b. Jan. 13, 1789	1	56
James J., d. Mar. 30, [1852]	1	242
Job, s. John & Phebe, b. Feb. 17, 1764	1	33
Job, d. June 23, 1828, in the 65th y. of his age	1	226
John, m. Phebe **SMITH**, July 4, 1763	1	151
John, m. Sarah **BURR**, Oct. 29, 1777	1	155

JONES, (cont.)

	Vol.	Page
John, m. Rebeckah **SMITH**, Nov. 7, 1784	1	155
John, s. Jacob & Ruth, b. Sept. 11, 1792	1	56
John, m. Mary **KEELER**, Nov. 14, 1801	1	159
John, d. May 2, 1817, ae 78 y.	1	220
John S., s. [Daniel & Elizabeth], b. Sept. 7, 1797; d. Aug. 28, 1811	1	106
Joseph W., d. [Apr. , 1849], ae 19 y.	1	240
Lewis, s. Jacob, 2nd & Ruth, b. Sept. 30, 1783	1	56
Mary, m. Philip **DAUCHY**, May 22, 1764	1	150
Mary, d. James & Elizabeth, b. Jan. 27, 1769	1	24
Mary, d. James & Elizabeth, d. Nov. 8, 1774	1	201
Mary, d. John & Rebecka, b. Feb. 15, 1790	1	33
Mary, wid., d. Feb. 20, 1819	1	221
Mary, of Ridgefield, m. James A. **WILLIAMS**, of New York, Nov. 16, 1846, by James A. Batterson, Dea.	1	199
Mary Ann, d. [Timothy & Anna], b. Mar. 29, 1815	1	106
Mary S., d. Ozar & Sally, b. Mar. 16, 1820	1	110
Phebe, d. John & Phebe, b. Aug. 13, 1766	1	33
Phebe, d. John & Phebe, d. Oct. 5, 1776	1	202
Phebe, w. John, d. Oct. 24, 1776	1	202
Phebe, d. John & Sarah, b. July 30, 1778	1	33
Phebe, d. John & Phebe, d. Aug. 28, 1784	1	202
Phebe, d. [Daniel & Elizabeth], b. Mar. 18, 1795	1	106
Phebe M., m. Joel T. **BENEDICT**, b. of Ridgefield, Feb. 14, 1827, by Samuel M. Phelps	1	167
Philip, s. James & Elizabeth, b. Dec. 10, 1760	LR1	238
Philo W., s. [Daniel & Elizabeth], b. May 27, 1802	1	106
Philo W., m. Rebeckah **LOBDELL**, b. of Ridgefield, Apr. 28, 1823, by Rev. Samuel M. Phelps	1	162
Polly E., d. [Daniel & Elizabeth], b. Jan. 1, 1804	1	106
Rebeckah, w. Jacob, d. June 25, 1789	1	205
Rebeckah, w. John, d. June 29, 1801, ae 53 y.	1	210
Rhoda, m. John **WHITLOCK**, Nov. 15, 1781	1	154
Russell, of Wilton, m. Eliza Ann **JELLIFF**, of Ridgefield, June 9, 1824, by Rev. Hawley Sanford	1	162
Russell, s. Jacob & Ruth, b. [ ]	1	56
Sally, d. [Daniel & Elizabeth], b. Sept. 25, 1807	1	106
Sally, m. Silas **PERKINS**, b. of Ridgefield, Nov. 29, 1829, by Rev. Oregin P. Holcomb	1	170
Sally Caroline, d. [Timothy & Anna], b. Dec. 3, 1806	1	106
Sarah, d. Ebenezer & Ann, b. May 21, 1758	1	16
Sarah, w. John, d. July 15, 1774	1	203
Sarah, d. John & Phebe, b. Aug. 30, 1774	1	33
Sarah, d. John & Phebe, d. June 22, 1777	1	202
Sarah, w. Czar, d. Feb. 1, [1851], ae 60 y.	1	241
Stephen, s. Jacob & Ruth, b. Feb. 4, 1794	1	56
Stephen, m. Esther **WARREN**, b. of Ridgefield, Dec. 6, 1846,		

	Vol.	Page
JONES, (cont.)		
by D. K. Hawley, V. D. M.	1	127
Timothy, s. John & Phebe, b. Jan. 13, 1773	1	33
Timothy, s. John & Phebe, d. Sept. 27, 1776	1	202
Timothy, s. John & Sarah, b. Dec. 28, 1780	1	33
Timothy, m. Anna **BOUTON**, Feb. 12, 1806	1	106
Timothy, d. Mar. 29, 1824, in her 44th y.	1	224
Timothy, his wid., d. Jan. 22, 1844	1	237
Walter, [s. Ebenezer, Jr. & Hepzibah], b. Mar. 16, 1794	1	98
Walter, s. [Ozar & Sally], b. Oct. 18, 1830	1	110
Walter, d. Dec. 1, 1830, ae 36 y. 8 m. 15 d.	1	228
William, [s. Ebenezer, Jr. & Hepzibah], b. Sept. 10, 1815	1	98
William, of Wilton, m. Julia Ann **MEAD**, of Ridgefield, Dec. 24, 1840, by Rev. Joseph Fuller	1	190
W[illia]m Rufus, [s. Ebenezer, Jr. & Hepzibah], b. Oct. 8, 1799	1	98
William Rufus, d. Aug. 21, 1815, ae 15 y. 10 m. 13 d.	1	219
JUDD, Eli, of Bethel, m. Abbey **STARR**, of Ridgefield, Apr. 10, 1845, by James A. Hawley	1	196
Zilpha, m. Clark **SCOTT**, b. of Ridgefield, this day [ ], by Rev. J. Lyman Clarke. Recorded Dec. 12, 1836	1	185
JUDSON, Charity, m. Elisha **HAWLEY**, Dec. 31, 1786	1	70
Charity, m. Elisha **HAWLEY**, Dec. 31, 1786	1	156
JUNE, Laura Ann, m. Burr **SCOTT**, b. of Ridgefield, July 31, 1848, by Rev. Shaller J. Hillyer	1	129
KEELER, Abba, [d. Paul & Sarah], [ ]	1	41
Abiah, d. Samuel, Jr. & Abiah, b. Dec. 15, 176[ ]	1	12
Abiel, s. Nehemiah & Elenor, b. Mar. 12, 1784	1	38
Abigail, d. Jonah & Ruth, b. Oct. 12, [1721/2]	LR1	204
Abigail, d. Timothy & Abigail, b. Feb. 7, [1724]	LR1	204
Abigail, w. Timothy, d. Nov. 24, 1735	LR1	215
Abigail, [d. Samuell & Mary], b. Apr. 7, 1746	LR1	239
Abigail, d. Silas & Abigail, b. May 30, 1750	LR1	249
Abigail, d. Timothy & Mary, b. June 8, 1756	LR1	249
Abigail, m. Stephen **NORRIS**, Mar. 6, 1765	1	81
Abigail, [d. John & Pat], b. July 5, 1785	1	54
Abijah, [d. Jabez & Sarah], b. Apr. 17, 1787	1	66
Abner, [s. John & Phebe], b. Dec. 30, 1778	1	68
Abraham G., m. Sarah **DAN[N]**, Apr. 25, 1801	1	92
Abraham Gray, s. Nehemiah & Elenor, b. July 20, 1777	1	38
Almira, d. Benjamin, d. Mar. 25, 1829	1	227
Amos, s. Thaddeus & Ruth, b. Jan. 15, 1794	1	60
Anna, [d. John & Pat], b. Feb. 18, 1790	1	54
Anna, w. Josiah, d. Dec. 17, 1795, ae 23	1	208
Anna, m. Abijah **ROSSEGUIE**, b. of Ridgefield, Feb. 1, 1829, by Samuel M. Phelps	1	169
Anna, w. W[illia]m H., d. Sept. 8, 1835	1	110
Anne, d. Isaac & Anne, b. Feb. 27, 1753	LR1	253
Anne, [d. Timothy & Esther], b. Nov. 19, 1787	1	40

	Vol.	Page
KEELER, (cont.)		
Anne, w. W[illia]m K., d. June 26, 1835, ae 32	1	231
Asa, s. Paul & Sarah, b. Oct. 1, 1780	1	41
Asa, [s. John & Pat], b. May 13, 1795	1	54
Benjamin, [s. Timothy & Abigail], b. Nov. 24, 1730	LR1	209
Benjamin, s. Joseph & Jane, b. May 23, 1742	LR1	226
Benjamin, s. Timothy & Mary, b. Nov. 13, 1768	1	1
Benjamin, d. Jan. 17, 1791 "shipwrecked at Eatons Neck"	1	205
Benjamin, m. Eunice **OLMSTED**, Feb. [ ], 1794	1	159
Benjamin, s. Benjamin & Eunice, b. Nov. 2, 1796	1	47
Benjamin, 2nd, m. Elizabeth **KELLOGG**, Dec. 22, 1796	1	159
Benj[ami]n, his infant s. [ ], d. Oct. 17, 1797	1	209
Benjamin, 2nd, his child, d. Apr. 18, 1805	1	212
Benjamin, 2nd, d. Mar. 10, 1812	1	216
Benj[ami]n, 2nd, had infant s. [ ], d. Sept. 1, 1827, ae 6 w.	1	226
Benjamin, m. Martha **SMITH**, Oct. 31, 17[ ]	LR1	252
Betsey, d. Thaddeus & Ruth, b. Mar. 14, 1792	1	60
Betsey, d. June 4, 1812, ae 20 y. 2 m. 22 d.	1	217
Betty, d. Silas & Abigail, b. Jan. 3, 1748	LR1	249
Bettey, w. David, d. of Jeremiah **MEAD**, d. Sept. 9, 1828, in the 32nd y. of her age	1	226
Bradley, d. [ ]	1	234
Burr, [s. Jonah & Rebeckah], b. Jan. 30, 1806	1	83
Burr, had child d. Nov. 20, 1839, ae 1	1	235
Caleb, s. John & Pat, b. Apr. 18, 1783	1	54
Caleb, m. Betsey **YOUNG**, b. of Ridgebury, May 9, 1841, by Nathan Burton	1	191
Catharine, m. Newel **HARRINGTON**, b. of Ridgefield, Dec. 15, 1833, at Georgetown, by Rev. Nicholas White	1	178
Catharine, m. Benjamin K. **NORTHRUP**, b. of Ridgefield, Oct. 26, 1847, by Rev. James A. Hawley	1	128
Chloe, d. Isaac & Hannah, b. Mar. 21, 1761	1	13
Clara, [d. Paul & Sarah], [ ]	1	41
Clark, s. Thaddeus, d. Jan. 2, 1815, ae 7 y.	1	218
Daniel, s. Samuel & Mary, b. July 13, 1750	LR1	248
Daniel, [s. John & Phebe], b. Sept. 19, 1770	1	68
Daniel, 2nd, m. Grace **DAUCHY**, Jan. 1, 1792	1	157
Daniel, d. May 17, 1806	1	213
Daniel, d. Apr. 29, 1832, in the 62nd y. of his age	1	229
Daniel K., m. Hannah **PARTRICK**, b. of Ridgefield, Oct. 29, 1827, by Samuel M. Phelps	1	168
David, s. Timothy & Mary, b. Apr. 16, 1750	LR1	241
David, s. Timothy & Mary, d. June 12, 1771	1	201
David, s. Timothy & Esther, b. Apr. 17, 1772	1	40
David, [s. Jabez & Sarah], b. Oct. 18, 1779	1	66
David, s. Benjamin & Eunice, b. Mar. 5, 1799	1	47
David, m. Esther **BRADLEY**, Feb. 23, 179[ ]	1	80

	Vol.	Page
KEELER, (cont.)		
David, m. Bettey **MEAD**, b. of Ridgefield, May 16, 1821, by Samuel M. Phelps	1	161
Davis C., [s. Jonah & Rebeckah], b. Aug. 11, 1811	1	83
Deborah, d. Matthew & Deborah, b. Nov. 1, 1752 (Date conflicts with birth of Ruth **KEELER**)	LR1	255
Deborah, m. Benjamin **STEBBINS**, 3rd, Dec. 12, 1770	1	151
Deborah, [d. Matthew & Ruth (**BENEDICT**)], b. July 31, 1786; d. Oct. 9, 1788	1	63
Deborah, w. Matthew, d. June 4, 1788, ae 55 y.	1	204
Deborah, d. Matthew, Jr., d. Oct. 9, 1788, ae about 3 y.	1	204
Deborah, 2nd, [d. Matthew & Ruth (**BENEDICT**)], b. Mar. 20, 1789	1	63
Delia, d. Jonathan, d. Mar. 20, 1818, ae 20 y.	1	221
Dorcas, d. Matthew & Deborah, b. July 28, 1768	1	1
Dorcas, m. Joel **SAINT JOHN**, Apr. 1, 1791	1	158
Dorcas, m. Joel **SAINT JOHN**, Apr. 21, 1791	1	77
Dorcas, m. Joel **SAINT JOHN**, Apr. 21, 1791	1	157
Dorcas, w. Jonah C., d. of Ebenezer & Theodoshe **HOYT**, d. Oct. 17, 1832, ae 19	1	229
Doria, d. Levi & Dorcas, b. Feb. 4, 1783	1	53
Dorothy, d. Isaac & Hannah, b. Sept. 15, 1759	1	13
Ebenezer, s. Joseph & Jane, b. May 19, 1746	LR1	239
Ebenezer, s. Josiah & Elizabeth, b. Oct. 11, 1774	1	69
Eleanor, w. Capt. Nehemiah, d. Sept. 22, 1811, in the 60th y. of her age	1	216
Elihu, [s. Timothy, 3rd & Laurania], b. Jan. 22, 1790	1	74
Elijah, s. [Joseph & Elizabeth], b. Mar. 17, 1727	LR1	206
Elijah, [s. Isaac & Mary], b. June 26, 1745	LR1	246
Elijah, s. Isaac & Mary, b. July 10, 1745	1	13
Elijah, s. Elijah & Sarah, b. Jan. 12, 1756	LR1	246
Elijah, s. Levi & Dorcas, b. Aug. 31, 1788	1	53
Elijah, had child, d. Apr. 27, 1817	1	220
Eliza, d. David & Esther, b. Mar. 9, 1796	1	80
Eliza, d. Benj[ami]n, d. Mar. 9, 1824, ae 16	1	224
Elizabeth, d. Joseph & Elizabeth, b. Nov. 18, 1708	LR1	199
Elizabeth, m. John **ROCKWELL**, Sept. 3, 1731	LR1	228
Elizabeth, d. Elijah & Sarah, b. Nov. 14, 1762	1	14
Elizabeth, w. Joseph, d. Mar. 16, 1763	1	200
Elizabeth, d. Josiah & Elizabeth, b. Aug. 3, 1766	1	69
Elizabeth, m. Job **SMITH**, Jan. 9, 1771	1	151
Elizabeth, m. Phinehas **SMTIH**, Nov. 4, 1784	1	155
Elizabeth, m. Benjamin **BARBERRY**, Sept. 3, 1786	1	156
Elizabeth, [d. Matthew & Ruth (**BENEDICT**)], b. Feb. 19, 1797	1	63
Elizabeth, wid., d. May 4, 1816	1	219
Elizabeth, d. Matthew, d. Oct. 18, 1825, in the 29th y. of her age	1	225

	Vol.	Page
KEELER, (cont.)		
Elizabeth, m. Daniel **PARTRICK**, b. of Ridgefield, Nov. 23, 1828, by Samuel M. Phelps	1	169
Elizabeth, of Ridgefield, m. W[illia]m N. **BENEDICT**, of New York, Dec. 30, 1832, by Rev. Charles G. Selleck	1	178
Elizabeth, of Ridgefield, m. Henry B. **JENNINGS**, of West Port, Apr. 11, 1850, by Rev. Clinton Clark	1	133
Elizabeth, of Ridgefield, m. George **TROWBRIDGE**, of Bethel, Nov. 4, 1851, by Rev. Ira Abbott	1	136
Elizabeth, of Ridgefield, m. John D. **WHYMBS**, of Derby, May 16, [1852], by Rev. C. Clark	1	138
Enos, s. Elijah & Sarah, b. Oct. 24, 1760	1	14
Esther, [d. Timothy & Esther], b. Aug. 28, 1775	1	40
Esther, [d. Jabez & Sarah], b. Nov. 16, 1777	1	66
Esther, wid. of Timothy, d. Oct. 4, 1818	1	221
Esther, w. Capt. David, d. of Col. Philip B. **BRADLEY**, d. Aug. 10, 1851, ae 78 y.	1	241
Ezra, s. Joseph & Jane, b. July 16, 1748	LR1	248
Ezra, [s. John & Phebe], b. Nov. 13, 1774	1	68
Freelove, d. Elijah & Sarah, b. Jan. 12, 1754	LR1	246
Gabriel, [s. Isaac & Mary], b. Apr. 23, 1749	LR1	246
Gamaliel, s. John & Pat., b. Dec. 13, 177[ ]	1	54
George, m. Esther A. **CRAWFORD**, b. of Ridgefield, Aug. 31, 1829, by Samuell M. Phelps	1	171
George A., [s. Jonah & Rebeckah], b. Dec. 19, 1797	1	83
George Alton, [s. Jonah & Rebeckah], b. Dec. 19, 1797	1	83
George Henry, s. W[illia]m H. & Anna, b. July 22, 1831; d. Sept. 8, 1833	1	110
George Wyllys, s. Timothy, d. Feb. 28, 1796	1	208
Grace, m. Robert **HOLLAND**, b. of Ridgefield, June 26, 1842, by Rev. Charles Chettenden	1	192
Grace, wid. Daniel, d. Aug. [ ], 1849, ae 74	1	240
Hannah, d. Jonah & Ruth, b. Oct. 14, [1719/20]	LR1	203
Hannah, d. Jonah & Ruth, d. Sept. 7, [1722]	LR1	213
Hannah, d. Jonah & Ruth, b. Dec. 13, 1728	LR1	209
Hannah, d. Sam[ue]ll & Mary, b. Aug. 14, 1739	LR1	224
Hannah, [d. Timothy & Abigail], b. Sept. 1, 1741	LR1	209
Hannah, d. Isaac & Hannah, b. Nov. 1, 1757	1	13
Hannah, d. Matthew & Deborah, b. Aug. 5, 1758	LR1	255
Hannah, d. Timothy & Mary, b. Sept. 30, 1762	1	1
Hannah, d. Jeremiah & Hannah, b. July 6, 1765	1	19
Hannah, d. Jeremiah & Hannah, d. July 30, 1765	1	200
Hannah, d. Matthew & Deborah, d. Jan. 6, 176[ ]	1	200
Hannah, d. Samuel & Abiah, b. Jan. 26, 1773	1	12
Hannah, m. Uriah **MEAD**, Jan. 16, 1780	1	154
Hannah, m. Gamaliel **BENEDICT**, Apr. 24, 1788	1	89
Hannah, m. Grindell **BENEDICT**, Apr. 24, 1788	1	157
Hannah, w. Philip, d. Mar. 9, 1826, ae 64	1	225

204 BARBOUR COLLECTION

	Vol.	Page
KEELER, (cont.)		
Hannah, d. Mar. 8, 1827, in the 65th y. of her age	1	226
Hannah, w. Daniel H., d. Jan. 30, 1834, ae 22	1	230
Harriet, d. David & Esther, b. Dec. 5, 1794	1	80
Harriet, d. David, 2nd, d. June 13, 1801	1	210
Henry H., s. W[illia]m H. & Anna, b. June 3, 1835	1	110
Hervey, s. Thaddeus & Ruth, b. Nov. 28, 1786	1	60
Harvey, had infant d. Dec. 20, 1826	1	226
Harvey, had d. [ ], d. May 21, 1832, ae 20 m.	1	229
Huldah, of Ridgefield, m. Holmes **SANDERS**, of Norwalk, May 13, 1826, by Samuel M. Phelps	1	167
Hull, s. Philip, d. June 20, 1803, ae 8 y.	1	211
Ira, s. Thaddeus & Ruth, b. July 1, 1790	1	60
Ira, d. Dec. 23, 1818, ae 29 y., in his passage from New York to Edenton, N. Carolina	1	221
Ira, m. Hannah **GATES**, Mar. 14, 1832, by Nathan Burton	1	176
Isaac, s. Isaac & Mary, b. Aug. 8, 1739	1	13
Isaac, [s. Isaac & Mary], b. Aug. 8, 1739	LR1	246
Isaac, m. Anne **STEBBINS**, Apr. 29, 1752	LR1	234
Isaac, Jr., m. Rachal **NORTHRUP**, Jan. 16, 1760	LR1	234
Isaiah, m. Mellesent **OLMSTED**, Mar. 6, 1760	1	150
Jabez, m. Sarah **BENEDICT**, Apr. 20, 1777	1	66
Jabez, [s. Jabez & Sarah], b. Mar. 1, 1791	1	66
Jabes, his twin infant, d. June 4, [ ]	1	208
Jacob, [s. Isaac & Mary], b. July 1, 1743	LR1	246
Jacob, s. Isaac & Mary, b. July 10, 1743	1	13
James, s. Samuel & Mary, b. June 13, 1749	LR1	248
Jane, d. Joseph & Jane, b. July 24, 1750	LR1	248
Jane, b. Dec. 9, 1789; m. Samuel **CHURCH**, Apr. 27, 1813	1	109
Jeremiah, [s. Timothy & Abigail], b. Apr. 14, 1733	LR1	209
Jeremiah, s. Timothy & Mary, b. May 6, 1760	LR1	249
Jeremiah, m. Hannah **SEYMOUR**, Jan. 15, 1764	1	150
Jeremiah, s. Jeremiah & Hannah, b. Dec. 6, 1766	1	19
Jeremiah, s. Elijah & Elizabeth, b. Aug. 31, 1783	1	44
Jeremiah, s. Levi & Dorcas, b. Aug. 7, 1786	1	53
Jeremiah, m. Huldah **HULL**, Apr. 23, 1788	1	157
Jeremiah, m. Sarah **ST JOHN**, Mar. 20, 1792	1	158
Jeremiah, m. Polly **SAINT JOHN**, Jan. 26, 1796	1	159
Jeremiah, d. Aug. 12, 1831, ae 65	1	228
Jesse Edward, [s. Matthew & Ruth (**BENEDICT**)], b. Sept. 13, 1798	1	63
Joanna, w. Jonathan, d. July 20, 1825, ae 58	1	225
John, s. Joseph & Elizabeth, b. Jan. 11, [1726]	LR1	206
John, m. Sarah **NORTHRUP**, May 30, 1750	LR1	234
John, s. John & Sarah, b. Jan. 10, 1753	LR1	248
John, m. Phebe **HOYT**, Sept. 17, 1767	1	68
John, Jr., m. Pat **OLMSTED**, Dec. 6, 1775	1	153
John, d. Jan. 2, 1782	1	203

	Vol.	Page
KEELER, (cont.)		
John, [s. Jabez & Sarah], b. Apr. 14, 1783	1	66
John, of Ridgebury, d. Dec. 17, 1798, ae 46 y.	1	209
John, s. Levi, d. July 4, 1811	1	215
John, had child d. Feb. 1, 1833, ae 1 y.	1	229
John, m. Ruth **SHERWOOD**, b. of Ridgefield, Oct. 28, [1834], by Rev. Charles G. Selleck	1	180
John, s. Rufus H., d. Jan. [17], 1852	1	242
John Rice, [s. John & Phebe], b. Feb. 3, 1769; d. Oct. 22, 1775	1	68
John Rice, 2nd, [s. John & Phebe], b. Aug. 5, 1786; d. July 29, 1790	1	68
Jonah, m. Ruth **SMITH**, d. Samuel, of Norwalk, Nov. 5, 1713	LR1	227
Jonah, s. Jonah & Ruth, b. Sept. 17, 1714	LR1	200
Jonah, m. Sarah **KENDRICK**, Nov. 1, 1745	1	150
Jonah, s. Elijah & Sarah, b. Apr. 26, 1768	1	14
Jonah, s. Matthew & Deborah, b. June 5, 1772	1	1
Jonah, m. Rebeckah **RAYMOND**, Dec. 30, 1794	1	83
Jonah, d. Apr. 26, 1837, ae 65 y.	1	233
Jonah C., [s. Jonah & Rebeckah], b. Mar. 29, 1808	1	83
Jonah C., m. Dorcas **HOYT**, b. of Ridgefield, Aug. 7, 1832, by Rev. Charles G. Selleck	1	176
Jonah, s. Matthew & Deborah, b. Aug. 2, 1764	1	1
Jonah, s. Matthew & Deborah, d. July 9, 1767	1	200
Jonathan, s. Timothy & Mary, b. May 14, 1758	LR1	249
Jonathan, s. Timothy & Mary, d. Feb. 26, 1761	LR1	217
Jonathan, s. Timothy & Mary, b. Dec. 27, 1765	1	1
Jonathan, m. Anne **STEBBINS**, Aug. 22, 1790	1	158
Jonathan, his infant s. [ ], d. July 4, 1811, ae 4 d.	1	215
Joseph, s. Joseph & Elizabeth, b. Apr. 8, 1713	LR1	199
Joseph, m. Jane **WILLSON**, d. Benjamin & Jane, Feb. 26, 1735/6	LR1	229
Joseph, s. Joseph & Jane, b. Jan. 31, 1739/40	LR1	226
Joseph, d. Nov. 29, 1757	1	200
Joseph, s. Elijah & Sarah, b. Dec. 27, 1766	1	14
Joseph, [s. Jabez & Sarah], b. Dec. 27, 1788	1	66
Joseph, s. Levi & Dorcas, b. Apr. 18, 1794	1	53
Joseph, d. Apr. 30, 1812, ae 18 y. 12 d.	1	216
Josiah, s. Isaac & Mary, b. June 10, 1741	1	13
Josiah, [s. Isaac & Mary], b. June 22, 1741	LR1	246
Josiah, s. Josiah & Elizabeth, b. Feb. 16, 1768	1	69
Josiah Raymond, [s. Jonah & Rebeckah], b. Aug. 22, 1796	1	83
Kitty, w. Jeremiah, 2nd, d. May 14, 1814	1	218
Laurania, [d. John & Pat], b. Aug. 15, 1787	1	54
Leman, s. [Abraham G. & Sarah], b. Oct. 1, 1801	1	92
Leman, see also Lyman		
Lemuel, [s. Timothy, 3rd & Laurania], b. Jan. 3, 1801	1	74
Levi, s. Elijah & Sarah, b. Apr. 3, 1758	LR1	246

KEELER, (cont.)

	Vol.	Page
Levi, s. Elijah & Sarah, b. Apr. 4, 1758	1	14
Levi, m. Dorcas **SMITH**, Jan. 13, 1782	1	154
Levi, m. Dorcas **SMITH**, Jan. 27, 1782	1	155
Levi, d. May 6, 1812, ae 54 y. 1 m. 2 d.	1	217
Levi, his wid., d. Apr. 5, 1843, ae 83 y.	1	237
Lewis, s. Silas & Abigail, b. Apr. 4, 1760	1	18
Lewis, [s. John & Pat], b. Feb. 18, 1792	1	54
Lott, s. Joseph & Elizabeth, b. Feb. 26, [1719/20]	LR1	203
Lucy, d. Paul & Sarah, b. May 9, 1783	1	41
Lucy, d. Benjamin & Eunice, b. Sept. 20, 1801	1	47
Lucy, m. John **SMITH**, b. of Ridgefield, Jan. 9, 1824, by Samuel M. Phelps	1	164
Lidia, d. Jonah & Ruth, b. Oct. 14, 1731	LR1	211
Lydia, d. Silas & Abigail, b. Nov. 4, 1751	LR1	249
Lydia, d. Samuel & Mary, b. May 26, 1757	LR1	248
Lydia, d. Matthew & Deborah, b. Sept. 7, 1776	1	1
Lydia, d. Matthew, d. Mar. 12, 1777	1	202
Lyman, m. Maria **FORRESTER**, Dec. 15, 1824, by George Benedict	1	163
Lyman, [see also Leman]		
Marah, d. Silas & Abigail, b. May 26, 176[ ]	1	18
Mariah, d. David & Esther, b. Jan. 23, 1798	1	80
Martha, d. Silas & Abigail, b. Nov. 1, 175[ ]	1	18
Martha, d. Benjamin & Martha, b. Aug. 28, 1757	LR1	235
Martha, m. John **DeLAVAN**, Oct. 6, 1785	1	156
Martha, wid., d. Oct. 26, 1804, at Charlton	1	212
Martin, s. Elijah & Sarah, b. Jan. 14, 17[ ]	1	14
Martin, s. Joseph & Elizabeth, b. May 13, [1714]	LR1	202
Martin, [s. Jabez & Sarah], b. July 3, 1781	1	66
Mary, [d. Timothy & Abigail], b. Apr. 30, 1738	LR1	209
Mary, d. Timothy & Sarah, b. Apr. 30, 1738	LR1	223
Mary, [d. Samuell & Mary], b. Feb. 14, 1743/4	LR1	239
Mary, d. Timothy & Sarah, d. Nov. 22, 1745	LR1	215
Mary, d. Timothy & Mary, b. Jan. 28, 1745/6	LR1	240
Mary, [d. Isaac & Mary], b. June 3, 1747	LR1	246
Mary, d. Isaac & Mary, b. June 3, 1747	1	13
Mary, m. John **LEE**, Nov. 7, 1764	1	153
Mary, m. Gamaliel **NORTHRUP**, Jr., May 14, 1766	1	151
Mary, w. Timothy, d. June 30, 1777	1	201
Mary, [d. Timothy & Esther], b. Feb. 19, 1781	1	40
Mary, m. John **JONES**, Nov. 14, 1801	1	159
Mary, of Ridgefield, m. Benjamin **FOSTER**, of Redding, Jan. 11, 1847, by Rev. Henry Olmsted, Jr.	1	127
Mary G., of Wilton, m. Edwin S. **HOYT**, of Ridgefield, this day [Feb. 19, 1851], by Rev. C. Clark	1	134
Matilda, [d. Matthew & Ruth (**BENEDICT**)], b. May 7, 1792	1	63
Matilda, of Ridgefield, m. James **WALLACE**, of Troy, N. Y.,		

	Vol.	Page
KEELER, (cont.)		
May 17, 1825, by Samuell M. Phelps	1	166
Matthew, s. Jonah & Ruth, b. Mar. 13, [1724/5]	LR1	205
Matthew & w. Deborah had d. [ ], b. Oct. 5, 1760	1	1
Matthew, s. Matthew & Deborah, b. Apr. 10, 1762	1	1
Matthew, Jr., m. Ruth **BENEDICT**, Jan. 4, 1780	1	156
Matthew, [d. Matthew & Ruth (**BENEDICT**)], b. Dec. 9, 1787	1	63
Matthew, d. Oct. 29, 1795, ae 71	1	208
Matthew, Jr., m. Sally **SMITH**, b. of Ridgefield, Feb. 5, 1823, by Samuell M. Phelps	1	162
Matthew, Jr., had child d. Sept. 5, 1828, ae 3 y.	1	226
Matthew, d. Jan. 28, 1835, ae 73	1	231
Mehetable, d. Nehemiah & Elenor, b. Oct. 12, 1772	1	38
Millesent, m. Thomas **NORTHRUP**, Jr., Nov. 20, 1770	1	152
Moses, [s. John & Phebe], b. Feb. 27, 1773	1	68
Nancy, d. Paul & Sarah, b. Sept. 10, 1776	1	41
Nanna, d. Elijah & Elizabeth, b. Mar. 13, 17[ ]	1	44
Nathaniel, s. Silas & Abigail, b. Oct. 10, 1757	1	18
Nathaniel, s. Isaac, Jr. & Rachel, b. Nov. 3, 1760	LR1	242
Nehemiah, s. Samuel & Mary, b. July 24, 1753	LR1	248
Nehemiah, m. Elenor **ROCKWELL**, June 15, 1772	1	152
Noah, s. Elijah & Elizabeth, b. July 16, 1770	1	44
Orilla, of Ridgefield, m. Cornelius **HORTON**, of York Town, Dec. 7, 1823, by Sam[ue]ll M. Phelps	1	164
Paul, m. Sarah **CORNWELL**, Feb. 7, 1775	1	152
Phebe, d. Joseph & Jane, b. Dec. 24, 1737	LR1	226
Phebe, d. Samuel, Jr. & Abiah, b. Feb. 25, 1763	1	12
Phebe, d. Elijah & Elizabeth, b. May 11, 1766	1	44
Phebe, [d. John & Phebe], b. May 30, 1781	1	68
Phebe, m. Samuel **WORDEN**, Oct. 13, 1785	1	155
Phelinda, d. Matthew, d. Oct. 14, 1809, ae 5 y.	1	214
Philip, d. [ ]	1	234
Philip, m. Hannah **HULL**, Jan. 8, 1784	1	154
Philip Burr, m. Phebe **HOWLAND**, b. of Ridgefield, Dec. 18, 1850, by Rev. Nathaniel Mead	1	135
Polly, d. Elijah & Elizabeth, b. May 31, 1767	1	44
Polly, [d. John & Phebe], b. Feb. 22, 1784	1	68
Polly, m. Nathan **BROWN**, Mar. 18, 1787	1	156
Polly, m. Philip **BRADLEY**, May 9, 1802	1	159
Polly, of Ridgefield, m. William **COMSTOCK**, of New Canaan, Feb. 8, 1826, by Samuel M. Phelps	1	167
Prua, [child of John & Phebe], b. Oct. 15, 1776	1	68
R. Maria, m. Whitman **PECK**, this day [Nov. 6, 1844], by James A. Hawley	1	195
Rachaell, d. Joseph & Eliza, b. Oct. 4, 1706	LR1	199
Rachel, d. Jonah & Ruth, b. May 5, 1727	LR1	209
Rachel, m. Joseph **NICHOLS**, Jr., Nov. 26, 176[ ]	1	150
Rachel, d. Isaac, Jr. & Rachel, b. Jan. 5, 1763	1	11

KEELER, (cont.)

	Vol.	Page
Rachel, w. Isaac, Jr., d. Jan. 17, 1763	1	200
Rachel, d. Isaac, Jr. & Rachel, d. Feb. 7, 1763	1	200
Rachel, d. Elijah & Sarah, b. Nov. 27, 1764	1	14
Rachel, [d. John & Phebe], b. Sept. 11, 1789	1	68
Rachel, [d. Timothy, 3rd & Laurania], b. Mar. 14, 1793	1	74
Rebeckah, d. Elijah & Sarah, b. Apr. 29, 1751	LR1	246
Rebeckah, d. Elijah & Elizabeth, b. Aug. 17, 1768	1	44
Rebecca, wid. Jonah, d. Feb. 26, [1851], ae 77 y.	1	241
Reuben, s. Elijah & Elizabeth, d. Sept. 15, 1778	1	202
Reuben, s. Elijah & Elizabeth, b. Mar. 2, 178[ ]	1	44
Rhoda, d. Silas & Abigail, b. Dec. 30. 1766	1	18
Rhoda, d. Elijah & Elizabeth, d. Aug. 31, 17[ ]	1	202
Roswell, [s. Timothy, 3rd & Laurania], b. Apr. 2, 1791	1	74
Rufus, [s. Jonah & Rebeckah], b. Jan. 18, 1801	1	83
Ruth, d. Jonah & Ruth, b. Dec. 2, [1714]	LR1	202
Ruth, d. Jonah & Ruth, d. Jan. [ ], 1718	LR1	213
Ruth, d. John, late of Norwalk, m. Matthew **BENEDICT**, Dec. 8, 1727	LR1	228
Ruth, d. Jonah, d. Oct. 25, 1745	LR1	217
Ruth, d. Jonah & Ruth, d. Apr. 1, 1752	1	200
Ruth, d. Matthew & Deborah, b. Dec. 1, 1752 (Conflicts with date of Deborah's birth)	LR1	255
Ruth, w. Jonah, d. Nov. 1, 1754	1	200
Ruthy, d. Nehemiah & Elenor, b. Mar. 7, 1780	1	38
Ruth, m. Thaddeus **KEELER**, May 27, 1784	1	153
Ruth, d. Thaddeus & Ruth, b. Aug. 19, 1788	1	60
Ruth, m. William **DANN**, May 25, 1797	1	91
Ruth, wid., d. June 13, 1814	1	218
Ruth, d. Elisha, d. Sept. 4, 1817, ae 1 y.	1	220
Ruth, w. Matthew, d. Nov. 28, 1836, ae 71 y.	1	233
Sally, d. Levi & Dorcas, b. June 7, 1782	1	53
Sally, [d. Matthew & Ruth (**BENEDICT**)], b. Nov. 22, 1794	1	63
Sally, d. Benjamin & Eunice, b. Nov. 25, 1794	1	47
Sally, [d. Timothy, 3rd & Laurania], b. June 12, 1799	1	74
Sally, Mrs., of Ridgefield, m. Charles **CASWELL**, of Burlington, Otsego Co., N. Y., Oct. 16, 1842, by Rev. Warner Hoyt	1	193
Sally, w. Phillip, d. [Dec.] 27, 1848, ae 61	1	240
Sally, wid., d. Jan. 27, 1852, ae 85 y.	1	242
Sally, [d. Paul & Sarah], [b.]	1	41
Salmon, had child d. Apr. 16, 1836, ae 24(?) y.	1	232
Samuell, d. May 19, 1713, in the 68th y. of his age	LR1	213
Samuell, s. Jonah & Ruth, b. Feb. 9, 1716	LR1	200
Samuel, m. Mary [ ], Jan. 22, 1735/6	LR1	230
Samuel, s. Sam[ue]ll & Mary, b. June 23, 1737	LR1	222
Samuel, Jr., m. Abiah **BENEDICT**, Mar. 18, 1761	LR1	234
Samuel, s. Matthew & Deborah, b. July 27, 1766	1	1

	Vol.	Page
KEELER, (cont.)		
Samuel, d. June 30, 1781	1	202
Sarah, d. Joseph & Elizabeth, b. Sept. 22, 1710	LR1	199
Sarah, wid. Sam[ue]ll, d. Apr. 15, 1714	LR1	213
Sarah, d.Timothy & Abigail, b. July 3, [1726]	LR1	206
Sarah, d. Timothy & Abigail, d. Dec. 2, [1726]	LR1	214
Sarah, 2nd, d. [Timothy & Abigail], b. Sept. 26, 1727	LR1	209
Sarah, d. Samuell & Mary, b. Dec. 3, 1741	LR1	239
Sarah, d. Elijah & Sarah, b. Oct. 16, 1749	LR1	246
Sarah, d. John & Sarah, b. July 12, 1751	LR1	248
Sarah, d. Timothy & Mary, b. Apr. 4, 1754	LR1	249
Sarah, d. Matthew & Deborah, b. Sept. 23, 1756	LR1	255
Sarah, had negroes Jenny, d. Tamor, b. Sept. 10, 1758; d. about 1 y. after & Andrew, s. Tamor, b. July 22, 1761	LR1	257
Sarah, had Jenny d. of Tamar (colored), d. Aug. 26, 1759	LR1	217
Sarah, d. Benjamin & Martha, b. Apr. 26, 1760	LR1	235
Sarah, d. Samuel & Abiah, b. Nov. 1, 177[ ]	1	12
Sarah, m. Benajah **NORTHRUP**, May 15, 1771	1	151
Sarah, m. Avery **BOUTON**, Apr. 1, 1773	1	155
Sarah, m. Noah **STARR**, Aug. 11, 1773	1	153
Sarah, d. Josiah & Elizabeth, b. Oct. 2, 1776; d. Sept. 29, 1785	1	69
Sarah, d. John & Pat, b. Nov. 27, 178[ ]	1	54
Sarah, m. Jacob **SMITH**, Mar. 23, 1780	1	152
Sarah, m. Shubael **RUNDLE**, Jan. 10, 1781	1	154
Sarah, w. John, d. Dec. 11, 1781	1	203
Sarah, [d. Timothy & Esther], b. Apr. 27, 1783	1	40
Sarah, of Ridgefield, m. Elijah **CHAPMAN**, of Tolland, Oct. 20, 1783	1	155
Sarah, [d. Jabez & Sarah], b. Feb. 10, 1785	1	66
Sarah, d. Mar. 10, 1787, in the 90th y. of her age	1	204
Sarah, d. Daniel, d. June 23, 1810, ae 9 y.	1	215
Sarah, d. Dan, d. Dec. 17, 1820, ae 37	1	222
Sarah, m. Jarvis **BRUSH**, Sept. 4, 1827, by Nathan Burton	1	167
Sarah E., m. Joseph **PRINDLE**, Oct. 17, 1838, by Nathan Burton, P. T.	1	186
Seth, s. Joseph & Jane, b. June 30, 1744	LR1	237
Silas, s. Joseph & Elizabeth, b. Dec. 3, 1724	LR1	205
Silas, m. Abigail **ELMER**, Apr. 14, 1746, by Rev. William Gaylord, of Wilton	LR1	234
Silas, s. John & Pat, b. Feb. 26, 177[ ]	1	54
Silas, d. May 2, 1774, "information of Jabez **KEELER**"	1	205
Silas, [s. Jabez & Sarah], b. Apr. 11, 1793	1	66
Smith, [s. Timothy, 3rd & Laurania], b. Sept. 11, 1803	1	74
Smith B., [s. Jonah & Rebeckah], b. July 24, 1799	1	83
Solomon, had child d. [ ]	1	234
Solomon Close, s. Thaddeus & Ruth, b. Oct. 26, 1796	1	60
Susannah, d. Elijah & Elizabeth, b. Feb. 3, 178[ ]	1	44
Thaddeus, s. Timothy & Mary, b. Apr. 2, 1752	LR1	249

210 BARBOUR COLLECTION

	Vol.	Page
KEELER, (cont.)		
Thaddeus, s. Jeremiah & Hannah, b. June 28, 1778	1	42
Thaddeus, m. Ruth **KEELER**, May 27, 1784	1	153
Thaddeus, s. Thaddeus & Ruth, b. July 8, 1785	1	60
Thaddeus, d. Mar. 13, 1803, in the 51st y. of his age	1	211
Thaddeus, his w. [ ], d. Dec. 15, 1836, ae 60 y.	1	233
Thaddeus, d. Oct. 8, [1850], ae 72 y.	1	241
Thomas, s. Silas & Abigail, b. Apr. 8, 1762	1	18
Thomas Smith, [s. Levi & Dorcas,]	1	53
Timothy, m Abigail **OSBURN**, d. Richard & Sarah, May 19, 1720	LR1	227
Timothy, s.Timothy & Abigail, b. Oct. 9, [1721]	LR1	203
Timothy, m. Sarah **COUCH**, wid. of Thomas, of Fairfield, West Parish, Nov. 10, 1736	LR1	229
Timothy, m. Mary **HOYT**, July 19, 1744	LR1	231
Timothy, s. Timothy & Mary, b. May 10, 1748	LR1	241
Timothy, d. Aug. 30, 1748	LR1	213
Timothy, s. Samuel, Jr. & Abiah, b. Mar. 20, 1765	1	12
Timothy, 2nd, m. Esther **KELLOGG**, Dec. 6, 1770	1	152
Timothy, m. Hannah **DUNNING**, Dec. 13, 1780	1	156
Timothy, 3rd, m. Laurania **DeFOREST**, Dec. 14, 1788	1	74
Timothy, d. Apr. 1, 1799, ae 78 y.	1	209
Timothy, d. Feb. 1, 1815, ae 66 y.	1	218
Timothy Benedict, [s. Timothy, 3rd & Laurania], b. Jan. 17, 1796	1	74
Urania, d. Josiah & Elizabeth, b. Apr. 7, 1772	1	69
Urania, [child of Paul & Sarah], [ ]	1	41
Walter, s. Timothy & Esther, b. Mar. 11, 1774; d. Sept. 23, 1776	1	40
Walter, 2nd, [s. Timothy & Esther], b. Dec. 31, 1777	1	40
William, s. Paul & Sarah, b. Sept. 20, 1778	1	41
William, [s. Timothy & Esther], b. June 20, 1785	1	40
William, d. Oct. 20, 1827, ae 42 y. 4 m.	1	226
William, s. Benjamin, d. Sept. 10, 1836	1	232
William H., s. Jonah, b. Feb. 24, 1803; m. Anna **DOWNS**, Aug. 27, 1826	1	110
W[illia]m H., m. 2nd w. Esther **MEAD**, Oct. 25, 1835	1	110
William K., [s. Jonah & Rebeckah], b. Feb. 24, 1803	1	83
William K., had s. [ ], d. Sept. 7, 1833, ae 2 y.	1	230
William S., s. W[illia]m K. & Anna, b. Aug. 18, 1827	1	110
William Seymour, s. Benjamin, 3rd, d. May 23, 1808	1	214
Zalmon G., [s. Jonah & Rebeckah], b. Feb. 27, 1810	1	83
-----, wid., d. Nov. 24, 1797, ae 87	1	209
-----, wid., d. July 25, [1839], ae 71	1	235
KELLNER, Patience, m. John **OSBURN**, Sept. 28, 1726	LR1	227
KELLOGG, Alford, s. Samuel, d. May 12, 1815, ae 5	1	218
Amanda, m. Alfred J. **STEVENS**, b. of Ridgefield, Dec. 14, 1834, by Rev. Charles J. Todd	1	179

RIDGEFIELD VITAL RECORDS 211

	Vol.	Page
KELLOGG, (cont.)		
Daniel, Jr., d. Dec. 7, 1794, ae 21	1	207
Daniel, his w. [ ], d. Feb. 19, 1809, ae 66	1	214
Daniel, d. Feb. 4, 1817, ae 90 y.	1	220
Ebenezer, s. Daniel & Elizabeth, b. Dec. 28, 1772	1	42
Elizabeth, m. Benjamin **KEELER**, 2nd, Dec. 22, 1796	1	159
Esther, m. Timothy **KEELER**, 2nd, Dec. 6, 1770	1	152
Ezra B., of Danbury, m Harriet M. **EDMOND**, of Ridgefield, Sept. 22, 1845, by Charles Stearns. Int. Pub.	1	197
Hannah, d. Nathan F. & Hannah, b. Mar. 3, 1785	1	45
Hannah, m Nathan **BRUNDRIDGE**, Feb. 21, 1788	1	156
Harriet, of Ridgefield, m. George **BULKLEY**, of South Port, Mar. 30, 1851, by Rev. William Staunton	1	136
Hielomith, d. Nathan F. & Hannah, b. Feb. 15, 1782	1	45
Isaac, s. Nathan F. & Hannah, b. Jan. 12, 1780	1	45
Joel, [s. Nathan & Hannah], b. July 2, 1792	1	45
Lewis, s. Nathan F. & Hannah, b. Aug. 21, 1787	1	45
Mary Marinda, d. Norman, d. June 8, 1834, ae 1 y.	1	230
Nathan, s. Nathan F. & Hannah, b. Dec. 10, 1789	1	45
Nathan Fairchild, m. Hannah **MOREHOUSE**, Mar. 30, 1779	1	155
Sally, d. Epenetus, of Norwalk, b. May 30, 1777, in Norwalk; m. Samuel **DIKEMAN**, of Redding, [ ]	1	90
Sally, m. Samuel **DIKEMAN**, Apr. 19, 1798, at Norwalk	1	159
Samuel, his child, d. Mar. 9, 1816	1	219
Samuel, had infant d. [ ], d. July 26, 1821	1	222
KELLY, Catharine, d. Crage & Sibbel, b. Aug. 11, 1782	1	54
Elisha, s. Crage & Sibbel, b. Oct. 9, 1783	1	54
John, s. Crage & Sibbel, b. Jan. 24, 1781	1	54
KENDRICK, Sarah, m. Jonah **KEELER**, Nov. 1, 1745	1	150
KETCHUM, Hannah, m. Daniell **OLMSTEAD**, May 9, 1711	LR1	227
KING, Anne Maria, d. Joshua & Anne, b. Mar. 10, 1797	1	61
Charles, s. Joshua & Anne, b. July 1, 1799	1	61
Fanny, d. Joshua & Anne, b. Nov. 15, 1787	1	61
John, m. Mrs. Anne **INGERSOLL**, Apr. 22, 1784	1	152
John F., d. Nov. 28, 1838, ae 46 y.	1	234
John Frances, s. Joshua & Anne, b. June 30, 1792	1	61
Joshua, his w. [ ], d. Dec. 30, 1838, ae 75 y.	1	234
Joshua, Gen., d. Aug. 13, 1839, ae 82	1	235
Joshua Ingersoll, s. Joshua & Anne, b. Aug. 11, 1801	1	61
Katy, d. Joshua & Anne, b. Sept. 14, 1785	1	61
Mary Ann, d. Joshua & Anna, d. Nov. 20, 1828, ae 25 y.	1	227
Rufus Howard, s. Joshua & Anne, b. Nov. 30, 1795	1	61
Zeviah, d. Joshua & Anne, b. Mar. 11, 1790	1	61
KNAPP, KNAP, Catharine A., of Ridgefield, m. Edwin W. **HIBBERT**, of New Haven, Oct. 4, 1846, by Rev. Charles Stearns. Int. Pub.	1	199
Deborah, m. Abijah **ABBOTT**, May 21, 1794	1	97
Mary J., of Ridgefield, m. Henry B. **MORGAN**, of Wilton,		

	Vol.	Page
KNAPP, KNAP, (cont.)		
Nov. 10, 1844, by Rev. Z. Davenport	1	195
Sarah B., m. Hiram **BOUTON**, b. of Ridgefield, Oct. 4, 1846, by Rev. Charles Stearns. Int. Pub.	1	199
KNOX, Hannah, m. William Malbie **LYNES**, Nov. 27, 1842, by Nathan Burton, P. T.	1	193
LAKEWOOD, Abigail, Mrs., d. June 9, 1749	LR1	216
LAMEREAUX, Daniel, of Orange, Co., N. Y., m. Elizabeth **HOYT**, of Ridgefield, Mar. 28, 1827, by Samuel M. Phelps	1	168
LAMSON, Elizabeth, m. Nehemiah **STURGIS**, Nov. 6, 1775	1	155
Nathaniel, of Fishkill, m. Amanda **ISAACS**, of Ridgefield, Oct. 28, 1827, by Samuel M. Phelps	1	168
LANNAN, Catharine, wid., d. Apr. 28, 1846, ae 44 y.	1	238
LAWRENCE, LARRENCE, Robert, of Munroe, N. Y., m Sally **STREET**, of Ridgefield, [Nov.] 5, [1826], by Levi Bronson	1	166
Sarah, m. Benjamin* **THOMAS**, Jr., Feb. 25, 1757, by Jonathan Ingersoll, V. D. M. (*correction (Benjamin scratched out, "Recompence") handwritten in on original manuscript)	LR1	252
Sarah L., m. W[illia]m W. **MORGAN**, Nov. 16, 1842, by Rev. Charles Chettenden	1	193
LEACH, Abigail, [d. Christopher & Mary], b. Aug. 13, 1788	1	74
Christopher, m Mary [ ], May 8, 1786	1	74
Elizabeth Wood, [d. Christopher & Mary], b. Jan. 28, 1790	1	74
James Lakewood, [s. Christopher & Mary], b. Apr. 5, 1774	1	74
Samuel Tubbs, [s. Christopher & Mary], b. June 15, 1787	1	74
Timothy Street, [s. Christopher & Mary], b. May 8, 1786	1	74
LEASON, LEESON, James, m. Mrs. Hannah **CRANK**, b. of Ridgefield, Mar. 31, 1846, by Rev. Shaller J. Hillyer	1	198
James, m. Mrs. Sarah **PULLING**, b. of Ridgefield, Apr. 27, 1847, by Levi Bronson	1	127
John A., m Elizabeth **GILBERT**, b. of Ridgefield, Apr. 16, 1840, by Rev. T. Sparks	1	188
LEE, LEES, [see also **SEE**], Aaron, Capt., d. Feb. 4, 1847, ae 73 y.	1	239
Abigail, d. Joseph & Mary, b. May 8, 1732	LR1	212
Abigail, d. John & Mary, b. Oct. 27, 1766	1	29
Abigail, m. Timothy **ROSSEGUIE**, June 5, 1785	1	156
Benjamin, had child d. [ ]	1	234
Benjamin, his child d. Nov. [ ], 1846	1	238
Betsey, of Ridgefield, m. Andrew **FAIRCHILD**, of Redding, Feb. [ ], 1821, by Samuel M. Phelps	1	161
Charles, s. Aaron, d. Mar. 29, 1813, ae 4 y. 8 m.	1	217
Chloe, d. John & Mary, b. May 5, 1769	1	29
Chloe, d. Aug. 12, 1774	1	203
Daniel, d. Oct. 14, 1833, ae 89 y.	1	230
Eben, had child d. May [ ], 1803	1	211
Edwin, his child d. [, 1842]	1	236

	Vol.	Page
LEE, LEES, (cont.)		
Elias, s. John & Mary, b. June 18, 1765	1	29
Elias, m. Margaret **EDMONDS**, Oct. 24, 1787	1	156
Elijah, m. Isabella **LEE**, Apr. 15, 1786	1	156
Emma, m. Henry L. **BATES**, b. of Ridgefield, Dec. 18, 1850, by Rev. Nath[anie]l Mead	1	135
Esther, w. Daniel, d. Mar. 3, 1798	1	209
Esther A., m. Amos **SMITH**, Jr., b. of Ridgefield, Nov. 28, 1838, by Rev. Joseph Fuller	1	187
Eunice, wid., m. Eliphalet **BRUSH**, Jan. 8, 1792	1	87
Eunice, m. Eliphalet **BRUSH**, Jan. 8, 1792	1	158
Isabella, m. Elijah **LEE**, Apr. 15, 1786	1	156
Joel, s. John & Mary, b. Apr. 12, 1776	1	29
John, s. Joseph & Mary, b. Apr. 30, [1726]	LR1	206
John, m. Mary **KEELER**, Nov. 7, 1764	1	153
Joseph, [s. Joseph & Mary], b. June 22, 1718	LR1	205
Joseph, m. Mary **HOLLY**, d. Daniel & Abigail, of Bedford, Feb. 12, 1735/6	LR1	229
Lucy, w. Aaron, d. Sept. 4, 1833, ae 57	1	230
Lucy, m. Samuel M. **SMITH**, b. of Ridgefield, June 18, 1848, by Rev. Sylvester S. Strong	1	130
Lidia, d. Joseph & Mary, b. Mar. 9, 1729	LR1	209
Mary, [s. Joseph & Mary], b. Sept. 19, 1720	LR1	205
Noah, s. John & Mary, b. Apr. 13, 1773	1	29
Polly, m. Robert Stiles **EDMONDS**, Mar. 31, 1790	1	58
Rebecca, [d. Joseph & Mary], b. Feb. 21, 1723	LR1	205
Ruth, d. John & Mary, b. Jan. 27, 1771	1	29
Sarah, [d. Joseph & Mary], b. Dec. 24, 1736	LR1	205
Sarah, w. William, d. June 25, 1785	1	203
Seth, d. Oct. 14, 1790	1	205
Susannah, d. William, d. Mar. 1, 1785	1	203
William, s. John & Mary, b. July 14, 1778	1	29
William, s. William, d. Sept. 11, 1778	1	203
William, d. Jan. 7, 1791, in the 82nd y. of his age	1	205
William, his s. [ ], d. Sept. 8, 1836	1	232
LEESON, [see under **LEASON**]		
LEWIS, Frances M., of Ridgefield, m. Abner **GILBERT**, Jr., of Danbury, Sept. 18, 1838, by Rev. Joseph Fuller	1	186
Isaac, his w. [ ], d. Feb. 27, 1811	1	215
Joseph C., of Ridgefield, m. Sarah Marianna **PHELPS**, of Ridgefield, May 30, 1824, by Samuel M. Phelps	1	165
Sarah, m. Josiah **MOREHOUSE**, Dec. 5, 1770	1	151
LIVESEY, Aaron, [s. James & Mary], b. July 9, 1774	1	68
Billy, [d. James & Mary], b. Feb. 4, 1792	1	68
David, [s. James & Mary], b. Dec. 25, 1788	1	68
James, b. Oct. 7, 1750; m. Mary **GRENO**, Sept. 16, 1773	1	68
James, [s. James & Mary], b. Aug. 3, 1784	1	68
John, [s. James & Mary], b. June 25, 1779	1	68

	Vol.	Page
LIVESEY, (cont.)		
Polly, [d. James & Mary], b. May 14, 1794	1	68
Richard, [s. James & Mary], b. Nov. 7, 1776	1	68
Sarah, [d. James & Mary], b. Mar. 16, 1782	1	68
LOBDELL, LOBDEL, Abigail, [d. Sam[ue]ll & Rebecca], b. Oct.		
25, 1726	LR1	208
Abigail, d. John & Ruth, b. May 4, 1753	LR1	243
Abigail, m. Sherwood **WHITNEY,** Mar. 9, 1788	1	157
Amy, [d. Josiah & Miriam], b. Mar. 26, 1798	1	69
Anne, m. William **PATTERSON,** Feb. 15, 1760	1	150
Benjamin, d. Jan. 19, 1813, ae 46	1	217
Burrel, [s. Ebenezer & Rebeckah], b. Feb. 24, 1749	LR1	251
Caleb, m. Bethiah **PADDOCK,** July [ ]	LR1	252
Caleb, [s. Joshua & Eunice], b. Feb. 17, 1715/16	LR1	201
Caleb, m. Elizabeth [ ], June 27, 1739	LR1	232
Caleb, s. John & Ruth, b. Jan. 4, 1748/9	LR1	243
Caleb, s. Caleb & Elizabeth, b. June 2, 1753	LR1	247
Caleb, [s. Caleb, Jr. & Susanna], b. Jan. 11, 1781	1	64
Caleb, 2nd, d. Nov. 27, 1801, in the 21st y. of his age	1	211
Caleb, d. Jan. 17, 1802, in the 86th y. of his age	1	211
Daniel, [s. Ebenezer & Rebeckah], b. Mar. 11, 1740	LR1	251
Daniel, s. John & Ruth, b. Sept. 22, 1757	LR1	243
Darius, s. Joshua & Eunice, b. Oct. 8, 1729	LR1	210
Daries, m. Mary **BALDWIN,** Jan. 16, 1753	LR1	233
Ebenezer, s. Joshua & Mary, b. Dec. 1, 1730	LR1	212
Ebenezer, m. Rebecca **BENEDICT,** Dec. 28, 1732	LR1	229
Ebenezer, [s. Ebenezer & Rebeckah], b. July 13, 1735	LR1	251
Ebenezer, d. Mar. 1, 1801	1	210
Elizabeth, d. Joshua & Eunice, b. Nov. 14, 1732	LR1	212
Elizabeth, d. Eben[eze]r & Rebecca, b. Sept. 21, 1733	LR1	218-9
Elizabeth, m. Isaac **NORTHRUP,** Jan. 16, 1752	LR1	234
Elizabeth, m. Henry **WHITNEY,** Dec. 15, 1755, by Jonathan		
Ingersoll, V. D. M.	LR1	252
Elizabeth, m. Seth **BURR,** of Redding, Jan. 26, 1790	1	158
Eunice, [d. Ebenezer & Rebeckah], b. Sept. 17, 1744	LR1	251
Eunice, [d. Josiah & Miriam], b. July 17, 1800	1	69
Eunice, d. Oct. 29, 1825, ae 82 y.	1	225
Hannah, d. John & Ruth, b. June 4, 1755	LR1	243
Jacob, [s. Josiah & Miriam], b. Mar. 14, 1790	1	69
Jacob, s. Josiah, d. Apr. [ ], 1799, ae 11 y.	1	209
Jacob, of North Salem, m. Mary P. **BURR,** of Ridgebury, Sept.		
22, 1843, by Rev. Z. B. Burr	1	194
Jared, s. Ebenezer & Rebeckah, b. Aug. 8, 1759	1	7
Jared, s. Ebenezer & Elizabeth, d. Oct. 29, 1759	1	200
Jared, [s. Josiah & Miriam], b. May 25, 1788	1	69
John, s. Joshua & Eunice, b. Aug. 21, [1721]	LR1	203
John, m. Ruth [ ], June 25, 1744	LR1	232
John, s. John & Ruth, b. Sept. 21, 1746	LR1	240

RIDGEFIELD VITAL RECORDS

	Vol.	Page
LOBDELL, LOBDEL, (cont.)		
Joseph, Jr., m. Mary **REYNOLDS**, Aug. 9, 1725	LR1	227
Joshua, [s. Joshua & Mary], b. Apr. 23, 1727	LR1	207
Josiah, s. Ebenezer & Rebeckah, b. Aug. 14, 1760	1	7
Josiah, m. Miriam **HICKOCK**, Oct. 7, 1787	1	69
Josiah, m. Miriam **HICKOCK**, Oct. 7, 1787	1	157
Josiah, d. June 4, 1837	1	233
Lewis, s. John & Ruth, b. Mar. 7, 1760	LR1	243
Lucinda, m. Ebenezer **BISHOP**, of Salem, June 7, 1790	1	158
Lydia, Mrs. of Ridgefield, m. Daniel **WOOD**, of Danbury, Aug. 26, 1821, by Rev. Levi Bronson	1	160
Mary, d. Sam[ue]ll & Rebecca, b. Apr. 8, [1724/5]	LR1	205
Mary, d. Joshua & Mary, b. Dec. 6, 1725	LR1	207
Mary, d. Darius & Mary, b. Dec. 17, 1752	LR1	250
Miriam, w. Josiah, d. Oct. 21, 1829, ae 69	1	227
Nathan, m. Abigail **HOYT**, Jan. 10, 1793	1	158
Nathan, s. Ebenezer, Jr. & Eunice, b. May 6, 17[ ]	1	8
Paddock, s. Caleb & Bethiah, b. July 20, 1760	LR1	242
Paddock[*], s. [Philip & Sarah], b. Apr. 6, 1790 *(The right name is "Philip Paddock")	1	68
Phebe, m. Josiah **GILBERT**, Dec. 12, 1762	1	151
Philip, s. Caleb & Bethiah, b. Oct. 7, 1761	1	1
Philip, m. Sarah **SMITH**, Sept. 27, 1788	1	68
Philip, m. Sarah **SMITH**, Sept. 28, 1788	1	157
Philip, d. Dec. 19, 1793, ae 32 y.	1	207
Philip Paddock, see Paddock **LOBDELL**	1	68
Polly, [d. Caleb, Jr. & Susanna], b. Nov. 13, 1782	1	64
Rachel, [d. Ebenezer & Rebeckah], b. May 22, 1742	LR1	251
Rebecca, d. Sam[ue]ll & Rebecca, b. Oct. 1, [1723]	LR1	204
Rebeckah, [d. Ebenezer & Rebeckah], b. Feb. 20, 1751	LR1	251
Rebeckah, [d. Josiah & Miriam], b. Feb. 23, 1796	1	69
Rebeckah, w. Ebenezer, d. Aug. 1, 1798, ae 85 y.	1	209
Rebeckah, m. Philo W. **JONES**, b. of Ridgefield, Apr. 28, 1823, by Rev. Samuel M. Phelps	1	162
Ruth, d. John & Ruth, b. Mar. 26, 1745	LR1	238
Ruth, d. May 4, 1797, ae 60	1	209
Samuel, m. Rebecca **SAINT JOHN**, Dec. 26, 1722	LR1	227
Sam[ue]ll s. Sam[ue]ll & Rebecca], b. Sept. 10, 1728	LR1	208
Samuel, [s. Ebenezer & Rebeckah], b. July 12, 1753	LR1	251
Samuel, s. Ebenezer & Rebeckah, b. July 12, 1753	1	7
Sarah, d. Joshua & Eunice, b. Sept. 27, 1714	LR1	201
Sarah, [d. Ebenezer & Rebeckah], b. Sept. 10, 1746	LR1	251
Sarah, d. Ebenezer & Rebeckah, d. Apr. 27, 1751	LR1	216
Sarah, d. Ebenezer & Rebeckah, b. Aug. 5, 1755	1	7
Sarah, d. Ebenezer & Rebeckah, b. Aug. 5, 1759	LR1	256
Sarah, [d. Josiah & Miriam], b. Jan. 4, 1793	1	69
Sarah, m. Sam[ue]ll **BURR**, Mar. [ ], 1793	1	158
Susan, d. Philip Paddock **LOBDELL**, b. Sept. 19, 1815, in		

216 BARBOUR COLLECTION

	Vol.	Page
LOBDELL, LOBDEL, (cont.)		
North Salem, N. Y.; m. Sylvester **MAIN**, of Wilton, May 27, 1838, by Rev. Nathan Burton	1	113-4
Susannah, d. Ebenezer & Rebeckah, b. July 9, 1758	1	7
Susannah, m. Daniel **RIGGS**, Sept. 9, 1784	1	155
Susannah, m. James **SMITH**, Oct. 23, 1785	1	156
Thomas, [s. Ebenezer & Rebeckah], b. Nov. 2, 1737	LR1	251
LOCKWOOD, Gershom, of South Salem, m. Deborah **STAPLES**, of Ridgefield, Apr. 21, 1828, by Ebenezer S. Raymond	1	168
Susannah, m. Timothy **STREET**, Jan. [ ], 176[ ]	1	150
Susannah, m. Timothy **STREET**, June 21, 176[ ]	1	150
Warren, of New Canaan, m. Harriet **JONES**, of Ridgefield, Feb. 13, 1834, by Rev. Charles J. Todd	1	179
W[illia]m S., of N[ ] Haven, m. Catharine **HAWLEY**, of Ridgefield, Oct. 26, 1831, by Rev. C. G. Selleck	1	174
LODER, Charlotte Amelia, of Ridgefield, m. William D. **STONE**, of Carmel, N. Y., Nov. 2, 1847, by Rev. James A. Hawley	1	128
Noah, d. Sept. 30, 1832, ae 59	1	229
Sabina, m. Samuel **SCOTT**, b. of Ridgefield, Nov. 14, 1850, by Rev. C. Clark	1	134
-----, Mr., d. [, 1846]	1	238
LOUNSBURY, Ann Eliza, m. Joel L. **ROCKWELL**, b. of Ridgefield, May 7, 1850, by Rev. Nathaniel Mead	1	133
Elisha S., m. Betsey **SLAUSON**, b. of Ridgefield, Nov. 29, 1843, by Rev. A. S. Francis	1	194
Epenetus, d. July 5, 1829	1	227
LOVEJOY, Daniel, m. Betsey **GILBERT**, b. of Ridgefield, Oct. 28, 1828, by Rev. John Lovejoy	1	168
LOWDER, Abigail, d. [John & Elizabeth], b. Oct. 25, 1734	LR1	220
Abigail, d. John & Eliz[a]beth, d. Nov. 9, 1734	LR1	215
Elizabeth, d. John & Elizabeth, b. June 29, 1733	LR1	220
John, s. John & Elizabeth, b. Aug. 6, 1739	LR1	237
Jonathan, s. John & Elizabeth, b. May 28, 1741	LR1	237
Mary, d. [John & Elizabeth], b. Feb. 4, 1735/6	LR1	220
Mary, d. [John & Elizabeth], d. Mar. 26, 1736	LR1	215
Mary, d. John & Elizabeth, b. Mar. 15, 1737	LR1	222
LYNDE, Mercy, m. Abraham **NASH**, May 19, 1781	1	154
LYNES, Esther, m. Riah **NASH**, Aug. 15, 1782	1	72
Julia A., m. Wakeman **HUBBELL**, Sept. 2, 1829, by Nathan Burton	1	170
Sarah M., m. George **ROCKWELL**, Oct. 16, 1826, by Nathan Burton	1	166
William Malbie, m. Hannah **KNOX**, Nov. 27, 1842, by Nathan Burton, P. T.	1	193
LYON, Catharine Ann, of Ridgefield, m. Nelson S. **FINCH**, of Wilton, Sept. 21, 1842, by Rev. Warner Hoyt	1	192
Hezekiah, d. Dec. 10, 1807, in the 73rd y. of his age	1	213
Hiram, m. Lydia **SCOTT**, b. of Ridgefield, July 5, 1829, by		

	Vol.	Page
LYON, (cont.)		
Samuell M. Phelps	1	171
Isaac, d. Feb. 17, 1849, ae 58 y.	1	240
Sarah J., of Ridgefield, m. John C. **SMITH**, of Middletown, this day [Sept. 16, 1851], by Rev. Clinton Clark	1	136
McCANSEY, David, s. James & Polly, b. July 15, 1770	1	42
Elizabeth, d. James & Polly, b. Aug. 10, 1779	1	42
Jenny, d. James & Polly, b. May 23, 1777	1	42
Jerusha, d. James & Polly, b. Oct. 18, 1768	1	42
Rachel, d. James & Polly, b. July 8, 1772	1	42
MacDONOLD, -----, Mrs. of New York, d. Oct. 18, 1829, ae 27 y., at Major Dickens	1	227
McFARDEN, McFARTHUNG, Elizabeth, [d. Thomas & Martha], b. Aug. 29, 1786	1	72
Thomas, m. Martha **PARSONS**, Aug. 31, 1785	1	72
Thomas, m. Martha **PARSON**, Aug. 31, 1785	1	155
McNIEL, Sarah Ann, m. Eli **ROCKWELL**, Sept. 13, 1840, by Nathan Burton, P. T.	1	189
MAIN, Cynthia Isabelle, [d. Sylvester & Susan (**LOBDELL**)], b. Aug. 17, 1849	1	113-4
Daniel J., Dr., d. Nov. 7, 1844, ae 23 y.	1	237
Hannah, of Ridgefield, m. Thomas **PARDEE**, of Lewisboro, Jan. 23, 1844, by Rev. A. S. Francis	1	194
Helen Ire, [d. Sylvester & Susan (**LOBDELL**)], b. Oct. 21, 1844	1	113-4
Hubert Platt, [s. Sylvester & Susan (**LOBDELL**)], b. Aug. 17, 1839	1	113-4
Julien Sylvester, [s. Sylvester & Susan (**LOBDELL**)], b. Sept. 28, 1841	1	113-4
Sylvester, b. Apr. 18, 1817, in Wilton, m. Susan **LOBDELL**, d. Philip Paddock **LOBDELL**, of North Salem, N. Y., May 27, 1838, by Rev. Nathen Burton	1	113-4
Zalmon s., his w. [ ], d. Sept. 10, 1839, ae about 26	1	235
Zalmon S., m. Martha **COLEMAN**, b. of Ridgefield, Mar. 22, 1840, by Rev. T. Sparks	1	188
Zalmon S., his child d. May [ ], 1847	1	239
MALLORY, Nathan, his w. [ ], d. June 27, 1838, ae 79	1	234
Nathan C., m. Juliette **JELLOFF**, b. of Ridgefield, Jan. 24, 1830, by Rev. Ebenezer Washburn	1	171
MANSFIELD, Huldah, of Ridgefield, m. David **WARREN**, of Danbury, Sept. 3, 1848, by Rev. James A. Hawley	1	130
Huldah, m. David **WARREN**, b. of Danbury, Sept. 3, 1848, by Rev. James A. Hawley	1	132
MARCHANT, Curtis, m. Rebeckah **ROCKWELL**, Oct. 1, 1828, by Nathan Burton	1	168
MARSHALL, Stephen, of New Canaan, m. Polly Smith **BURT**, of Ridgefield, Mar. 10, 1829, by Samuel M. Phelps	1	169
MARVIN, MARVINE, MARWIN, Betsey, d. Uriah & Sarah, b.		

	Vol.	Page
MARVIN, MARVINE, MARWIN, (cont.)		
Mar. 17, 1785	1	19
Betsey, d. Uriah & Sarah, b. Mar. 17, 1785	1	48
Esther, d. Uriah & Sarah, b. June 4, 1776	1	48
Esther, [d. Uriah & Sarah], b. June [ ], 1776	1	19
Esther, d. Feb. 23, 1792	1	206
Hulda, d. Uriah & Sarah, b. Aug. 12, 1770	1	19
Huldah, d. Uriah & Sarah, b. Aug. 12, 1770	1	48
Huldah, m. Thaddeus **BENEDICT**, Jan. 19, 1794	1	159
James, s. Uriah & Sarah, b. May 28, 1766	1	19
James, s. Uriah & Sarah, b. Mar. 28, 1766	1	48
James, his wid., d. Oct. 1, 1828, ae 67 y.	1	226
John Scott, s. Uriah & Sarah, b. Dec. 26, 1773	1	19
John Scott, s. Uriah & Sarah, b. Dec. 26, 1773	1	48
John Scott, d. June 15, 1788, in the 15th y. of his age	1	204
Martha, w. Uriah, d. Oct. 6, 1807	1	213
Nathaniel, [s. Uriah & Sarah], b. May [ ], 1778	1	19
Nathaniel, s. Uriah & Sarah, b. May 9, 1778	1	48
Nathaniel, d. Feb. 8, 1799, ae 20 y.	1	208
Sarah, w. Uriah, d. Feb. 13, 1788	1	204
Uriah, m. Sarah **SCOTT**, May 15, 1765	1	150
MAYBERRY, William, of Norwalk, m. Lucy **BANKS**, of Ridgefield, Aug. 19, 1827, by Samuel M. Phelps	1	168
MEAD, MEADE, Alanson, of South Salem, m. Mariah **OLMSTED**, of Ridgefield, Mar. 19, 1834, by Rev. Charles G. Selleck	1	179
Anna, m. David **DAUCHY**, b. of Ridgefield, Feb. 9, 1825, by Samuell M. Phelps	1	165
Betsey, d. Ezra & Hannah, b. May 10, 1783	1	56
Betty, d. Jeremiah & Betty, b. Feb. 22, 1791	1	44
Bettey, m. David **KEELER**, b. of Ridgefield, May 16, 1821, by Samuel M. Phelps	1	161
Betty, w. Jeremiah, d. May 11, 1832, in the 77th y. of her age	1	229
Bettey, see Bettey **KEELER**	1	226
Charles, s. Seth, d. June 13, 1835, ae 4 y.	1	231
Clarissa, m Stephen **BURT**, b. of Ridgefield, Jan. 1, 1845, by Rev. A. S. Francis	1	197
Cynthia, of Ridgefield, m. James Platt **FITCH**, of Wilton, Dec. 25, 1834, by Rev. Charles G. Selleck	1	180
Edson, had child d. Apr. [ ], 1838, ae 2 y.	1	234
Edward, s. Lewis, d. Aug. 9, 1831, ae 2 y. 2 m.	1	228
Egbert, m. Emily **NORTHRUP**, b. of Ridgefield, Oct. 5, 1836, by Rev. C. G. Selleck	1	183
Eliphalet, [ ]	1	35
Eliza, m. Stephen **OLMSTED**, Jr., b. of Ridgefield, Sept. 12, 1841, by Rev. Warner Hoyt	1	190
Esther, m W[illia]m H. **KEELER**, Oct. 25, 1835	1	110
Ezra, m. Hannah **WILSON**, Mar. 17, 1777	1	155
Ezra, d. Nov. 8, 1840, ae about 84 y.	1	235

	Vol.	Page
MEAD, MEADE, (cont.)		
Fanny, m. Jesse B. **SLAWSON**, b. of Ridgefield, Oct. 12, 1834, by Rev. Charles G. Selleck	1	180
George, m. Clarissa **HUNT**, Oct. 4, 1827, by Nathan Burton	1	167
Hannah, m. Jabes **SMITH**, Nov. 1, 1780	1	154
Hannah, [d. John & Hannah], b. Mar. 21, 1794	1	84
Hannah, m. Lot **FORRESTER**, Nov. 15, 1803	1	101
Harry, s. Ezra, d. July 21, 1795, ae 6 y.	1	208
Harry, [s. John & Hannah], b. June 4, 1796	1	84
Harry, s. Ezra & Hannah, b. Oct. 17, 1796	1	56
Harry, s. John, d. Feb. 14, 1798	1	209
Harry, s. Ezra, d. Apr. 15, 1816	1	219
Harvey, s. [Jeremiah & Betty], b. Apr. 11, 179[ ]	1	44
Henry, s. Ezra & Hannah, b. June 21, 1789	1	56
Hipsey, d. [Jeremiah & Rachel], b. Jan. 23, 1787	1	44
Hiram, d. June 24, 1836, ae 24	1	232
Hyram J., m. Mary **PICKET**, b. of Ridgefield, May 11, 1836, by Rev. Charles G. Selleck	1	182
Israel, s. Joseph & Mary, b. Mar. 9, 1773	1	45
Israel, d. Apr. 29, 1829, ae 56 y. 1 m. 20 d.	1	227
Jabez, s. Joseph & Mary, b. Mar. 29, 1775	1	45
Jabez, d. Dec. 12, 1814, in the 40th y. of his age	1	218
Jacob, s. Nehemiah, 2nd, d. Jan. 16, 1830, ae 4 y.	1	228
James, m. Mary **EDMONDS**, b. of Ridgefield, Dec. 3, 1834, by Rev. Charles G. Selleck	1	180
James, d. Aug. 11, 1840, ae 28 y.	1	235
James, his w. [ ], d. Mar. 7, 1848, ae 74	1	239
James, his child, d. Feb. 11, [ ], ae 1 y.	1	233
James E., m. Cemantha **NORTHRUP**, b. of Ridgefield, July 14, 1833, by Rev. Charles J. Todd	1	178
Jane E., of Ridgefield, m.Silas W. **BROWN**, of South Salem, Oct. 11, 1838, by Rev. Joseph Fuller	1	186
Jared, m. Hannah A. **GILBERT**, Oct. 28, 1834, by Rev. Josiah Bowen	1	181
Jasper, s. Thaddeus & Rebeckah, of Norwalk, b. Feb. 12, 1755	1	5 1/2
Jasper, m. Elizabeth **BENEDICT**, Apr. 8, 1779	1	156
Jeremiah, m. Rachel **SMITH**, Feb. 17, 1779	1	152
Jeremiah, m. Rachel **SMITH**, Feb. 17, 1779	1	154
Jeremiah, m. Bettey **WHITNEY**, Oct. 6, 1784	1	155
Jeremiah, s. [Jeremiah & Rachel], b. Dec. 19, 1788	1	44
Jeremiah, Jr., d. Sept. 27, 1822, in the 34th y. of his age	1	223
Jerre, s. Ezra & Hannah, b. May 16, 1780	1	56
Jesse, s. Jasper & Elizabeth, b. Mar. 18, 1789	1	5 1/2
Jesse Hyson, [s. Jasper,]	1	5 1/2
John, m. Hannah **SHERWOOD**, [ ]	1	84
Joseph, m. Mary **CLOSE**, Apr. 31*, 1772 *(Probably Apr. 30)	1	151
Joseph, m Mary **ROSE**, Apr. 30, 1772	1	152
Joseph, s. Joseph & Mary, b. Dec. 30, 1776	1	45

MEAD, MEADE, (cont.)

	Vol.	Page
Joseph, his infant, d. Sept. 2, 1794	1	207
Joseph, d. Feb. 4, 1814	1	218
Joseph, his w. [ ], d. Aug. 11, 1823, ae 72 y.	1	223
Joseph, his w. [ ], d. Mar. 24, 1837	1	233
Joseph, his w. [ ], d. June 11, 1840, ae 68 y.	1	235
Joseph C., d. Jan. 4, 1827, in the 22nd y. of his age	1	226
Josiah, s. Joseph & Mary, b. Jan. 5, 1779	1	45
Julia Ann, of Ridgfield, m. William **JONES**, of Wilton, Dec. 24, 1840, by Rev. Joseph Fuller	1	190
Lewis, s. Ezra & Hannah, b. Aug. 2, 1777	1	56
Lewis, s. Jeremiah & Rachel, b. June 9, 1785	1	44
Lewis, d. Dec. 5, 1802, in the 26th y., on the Coast of Malabar in the Chinese Sea	1	211
Lewis, had infant s. [ ], d. Oct. 11, 1828	1	227
Lucretia, m. Rufus **NORTHRUP**, Nov. 6, 1831, by Rev. Charles J. Todd	1	174
Martha, m. Jesse **SMITH**, Apr. 26, 1769	1	150
Martha, d. [Apr. , 1849], ae 13	1	240
Mary, w. Joseph, d. July 26, 1789	1	205
Matthew, s. [Jeremiah & Rachel], b. Mar. 29, 1791	1	44
Matthew, s. Jeremiah, d. Apr. 10, 1791	1	210
Milan H., m. Eliza H. **BENEDICT**, b. of Ridgefield, this day, [Dec. 10, 1851], by Rev. C. Clark	1	137
Nehemiah, s. Joseph & Mary, b. Sept. 30, 1781	1	45
Nehemiah, of Ridgefield, m. Anna **BURR**, of Reading, Mar. 12, 1822, by Rev. Samuel M. Phelps	1	161
Nehemiah, had d. [ ], d. Apr. 11, 1823, ae 9	1	223
Nehemiah, 2nd, d. Dec. 21, 1832, ae 51 y.	1	229
Phebe, m. Jonathan **TRESDELL**, Nov. 27, 1785	1	156
Phebe, m. Thaddeus **WHITLOCK**, June 12, 1788	1	157
Polly, d. Jeremiah & Rachel, b. Aug. 13, 1781	1	44
Polly, d. Ezra & Hannah, b. Oct. 10, 1791	1	56
Polly, [d. John & Hannah], b. Dec. 17, 1791	1	84
Polly, d. Ezra, d. Sept. 16, 1795, ae 4 y.	1	208
Polly, d. Ezra & Hannah, b. Feb. 16, 1800	1	56
Polly, d. Ezra, d. Sept. 17, 1801	1	210
Polly, w. Israel, d. Jan. 14, 1828, ae 40	1	226
Rachel, d. Jeremiah & Rachel, b. Mar. 16, 1780	1	44
Rachel, w. Jeremiah, d. Jan. 21, 1782	1	202
Richard, s. Seth, d. [Jan.] 9, [1852], ae 19 y.	1	242
Ruth, wid., d. July 4, 1829	1	227
Sally, d. Jasper & Elizabeth, b. Oct. 31, 1784	1	5 1/2
Sally, m. Zalmon S. **BURR**, b. of Ridgefield, May 22, 1825, by Samuell M. Phelps	1	166
Sally Gastin, [d. Jasper,]	1	5 1/2
Samuel, s. [Jeremiah & Rachel], b. Apr. 17, 1795	1	44
Sarah, m. Benjamin **STEBBINS**, Aug. 14, 1718	LR1	227

	Vol.	Page
MEAD, MEADE, (cont.)		
Sarah, m. John B. **OLMSTED**, b. of Ridgefield, Nov. 17, 1835, by Rev. J. L. Clark	1	181
Sarah Ann, of Ridgefield, m. Aaron B. **DIKEMAN**, of Wilton, Jan. 18, 1830, by Samuell M. Phelps	1	171
Seth, s. [Jeremiah & Rachel], b. Feb. 1, 1792	1	44
Sherwood, m. Harriet **GRUMMAN**, b. of Ridgefield, Nov. 23, 1825, by Samuel M. Phelps	1	166
Stephen D., d. May 7, 1845	1	238
Susannah, d. Nov. 24, 1840, ae 85 y.	1	235
Thaddeus, s. Jasper & Elizabeth, b. Mar. 16, 1781	1	5 1/2
Thadis Ash, [s. Jasper], [ ]	1	5 1/2
Thomas, his d. [ ], d. May 29, 1798, ae 2 y.	1	209
Thomas, d. May 2, 1844, ae about 76	1	237
Uriah, m. Hannah **KEELER**, Jan. 16, 1780	1	154
Walter, s. Ezra & Hannah, b. May 8, 1786	1	56
Whitney, s. [Jeremiah & Betty], b. July 31, 1801	1	44
Whitney, s. Jeremiah, d. Aug. 13, 1801	1	210
-----, Rev., his mother, d. [Mar.] 3, [1850], ae 68	1	240
MERRICK, Ann, d. Jan. 6, 1790	1	205
MERWIN, [see under **MARVIN**]		
MIDDLEBROOK, Henry, of Wilton, m. Harriet E. **OLMSTED**, of Ridgefield, July 8, 1850, by Rev. C. Clark	1	133
MILLER, Benjamin, d. Nov. 17, 1827	1	226
Betsey D., of Roundridge, N. Y., m. George L. **WOOD**, of Danbury, this eve [Feb. 5, 1845], by James A. Hawley	1	196
Enos C., d. Sept. 21, 1847, ae [ ]	1	239
John W., m. Nancy A. **HOYT**, b. of Ridgefield, May 31, 1840, by Rev. Thomas Sparks	1	188
John W., m. Esther **PALMER**, b. of Ridgefield, Oct. 3, 1849, by Rev. Nathaniel Mead	1	132
Justus, d. Oct. 22, [1849]	1	240
Mercy, d. Oct. 22, 1820, ae 15 y.	1	222
-----, Mrs., d. of Warren **HOYT**, d. July 30, 1842, ae 22 y.	1	236
-----, Mr., d. Dec. [ ], 1850	1	241
MILLS, Abigail, m. John **PALMER**, b. of Ridgefield, Sept. 22, 1839, by Rev. T. Sparks	1	187
Clarissa, of Ridgefield, m. Daniel **BRUNSON**, of Danbury, Dec. 31, 1837, by James Coleman, Elder	1	184
Clemente, m. John **SMITH**, Oct. 29, 1751	LR1	234
Denton, m. Sarah **CORNWELL**, Feb. 29, 1760	1	155
Denton, m. Sarah **CORNWELL**, Feb. 29, [ ]	LR1	252
Denton, d. Nov. 6, 1791	1	206
Harriet, m. Joel S. **BENJAMIN**, b. of Ridgefield, Apr. 13, 1834, by Levi Brunson	1	179
Horartia N., his w. [ ], d. Jan. 31, 1844, ae 35 y.	1	237
Horatio W., d. May 17, 1848, ae 39 y.	1	239
John, m. Rebeckah **FINTCH**, Dec. 2, 1784	1	153

MILLS, (cont.)

	Vol.	Page
John, d. Mar. 24, 1840, ae about 66 y.	1	235
Nancy, of Ridgefield, m. Augustus **PURDY**, of North Salem, Jan. 26, 1830, by Levi Brunson	1	171
Rebecca, d. [Dec.] 26, [1847], ae 47	1	239
Susan, of Ridgefield, m. Timothy W. **GODFREY**, of Wilton, Oct. 8, 1834, by Rev. Charles G. Selleck	1	180

MITCHEL, Edward, Rev., d. Aug. 8, 1834, ae 65 y., at the house of Harry Hunt — 1 — 230

MONROE, MAINROW, MONROW, MUNRO, MUNROW,

Amelia, m. Matthew **BETTS**, Jan. [ ], 1787	1	157
Charles, his infant d. Sept. 23, 1830, ae 3 w.	1	228
David, d. Sept. 11, 1831, ae 50	1	228
Elsey, of Ridgefield, m William **GORHAM**, of New Fairfield, Apr. 8, 1827, by Samuel M. Phelps	1	168
Eunice, wid., d. Apr. 4, 1826	1	225
Harriet, d. W[illia]m & Hannah, b. Jan. 24, 1799	1	82
Henry, d. Oct. 5, 1837, ae 23 y.	1	234
John, had infant d. Mar. [ ], 1836, ae 3 d.	1	232
John Gilbert, of Ridgefield, m. Elizabeth **CURTIS**, of Sheffield, Mass., Oct. 23, 1832, by Rev. Charles G. Selleck	1	176
Joseph, d. Mar. 24, 1824	1	224
Julia Ann, of Ridgefield, m.Charles **BAILEY**, of Ramulies, Senaca Co., N. Y., Feb. 28, 1840, by Rev. Thomas Sparks	1	188
Levina, d. Oct. 23, 1794, ae 63	1	207
Polly, of Ridgefield, m. William **MUNROW**, of Danbury, Apr. 10, 1831, by Nathan Burton	1	173
Rebeckah, wid., d. Jan. 1, 1826, ae 81	1	225
Sarah, m. Thomas **WILSON**, Jan. 31, 1841, by Levi Brunson	1	190
Smith, d. Nov. 18, [1850], ae about 64 y.	1	241
William, Jr., m. Hannah **CURTIS**, Apr. 3, 1798	1	82
William, Jr., his s. [ ], d. Mar. 20, 1805	1	212
William, d. May 4, 1813, ae 77 y.	1	217
William, d. Feb. 2, 1826	1	225
William, of Danbury, m. Polly **MUNROW**, of Ridgefield, Apr. 10, 1831, by Nathan Burton	1	173

MOORE, -----, Mr. [his d.], d. Aug. 22, [1851], ae 5 y. — 1 — 241

MOREHOUSE, Abigail, d. James & Abigail, b. Dec. 22, 1759 — LR1 — 254

Abigail, m. Hezekiah **SMITH**, Sept. 4, 1776	1	155
Adonijah, s. Gabriel & Rebeckah, b. Jan. 29, 1740/1	LR1	237
Betty, d. James & Abigail, b. June 22, 1763	LR1	254
Caleb, s. Lemuel & Sarah, b. Feb. 1, 1767	1	25
Daniel, s. Gabriel & Rebeckah, b. Mar. 29, 1742	LR1	237
Gabriel, [s. Lemuel & Mary], b. Sept. 14, 1718	LR1	225
Hannah, [d. Lemuel & Mary], b. Mar. 20, 1737	LR1	225
Hannah, m. Nathan Fairchild **KELLOGG**, Mar. 30, 1779	1	155
Jabez, m. Mary [ ], Nov. 9, 1738	LR1	230

RIDGEFIELD VITAL RECORDS 223

	Vol.	Page
MOREHOUSE, (cont.)		
James, [s. Lemuel & Mary], b. Sept. 3, 1734	LR1	225
James, s. Lemuel & Sarah, b. May 2, 1755	LR1	235
Joel, s. Lemuel & Sarah, b. Aug 10, 1761	1	25
John, [s. Lemuel & Mary], b. June 10, 1739	LR1	225
John, s. John & Deborah, b. Nov. 9, 1762	1	12
John, m. Deborah **BRUSH**, Mar. 14, 17[ ]	LR1	252
John Lewis, s. Josiah & Sarah, b. Dec. 29, 1771	1	33
Joseph, s. John & Deborah, b. Oct. 17, 1760	LR1	253
Joshua, s. Gabriel & Rebeckah, b. Feb. 22, 1743/4	LR1	240
Josiah, m. Sarah **LEWIS**, Dec. 5, 1770	1	151
Lemuel, [s. Lemuel & Mary], b. Dec. 30, 1728	LR1	225
Lemuel, m. Rachal **OSBORN**, June 16, 1750	LR1	234
Lemuel, s. John & Deborah, b. Nov. 13, 1766	1	12
Lemuel, d. Apr. 20, 1768	1	201
Levi, s. Lemuel & Sarah, b. Sept. 16, 1753	LR1	235
Martha, d. [Gabriel & Rebeckah], b. Aug. 7, 1746	LR1	240
Mary, [d. Lemuel & Mary], b. Sept. 4, 1722	LR1	225
Mary, w. Samuel, d. Nov. 1, 1749	LR1	216
Mary, d. Lemuel & Sarah, b. May 19, 1752	LR1	235
Mary, d. John & Deborah, b. Aug. 5, 1764	1	12
Mary, m. Ezekiel **SMITH**, Nov. 29, 1770	1	151
Mary, m. Ezekiel **SMITH**, Nov. 29, 1770	1	152
Mary Eliot, d. Josiah & Sarah, b. Feb. 21, 1775	1	33
Nathan, [s. Lemuel & Mary], b. Jan. 21, 1720	LR1	225
Noah, s. James & Abigail, b. Nov. 12, 1760	LR1	254
Peter, d. July 30, 1828, ae 47 y.	1	226
Rachel, d. Lemuel & Mary, b. Feb. 11, 1727	LR1	225
Rachel, m. Thomas **NORTHRUP**, Mar. 9, 1747/8	LR1	233
Rachel, d. Lemuel & Sarah, b. Jan. 7, 1757	LR1	235
Rebeckah, [d. Lemuel & Mary], b. July 9, 1732	LR1	225
Ruth Smith, d. Lemuel & Sarah, b. Dec. 5, 1758	LR1	242
Sarah, d. Lemuel & Sarah, b. Aug. 11, 1763	1	25
Sarah, m. James **OLMSTED**, b. of Norwalk, Jan. 14, 1789	1	157
Thomas, [s. Lemuel & Mary], b. Nov. 12, 1730	LR1	225
Thomas, s. Samuel, d. Nov. 20, 1749	LR1	216
Thomas, s. John & Deborah, b. Feb. 21, 1759	LR1	253
MORGAN, Eli, d. Feb. 8, 1834, ae 25 y.	1	230
Henry B., of Wilton, m. Mary J. **KNAPP**, of Ridgefield, Nov. 10, 1844, by Rev. Z. Davenport	1	195
Roswell, of Wilton, m. Mary **JELLIFF**, of Ridgefield, Jan. 2, 1831, by [Samuel M. Phelps]	1	175
Ruth, m. Jacob **JONES**, Jr., Nov. 7, 1781	1	155
W[illia]m W., m. Sarah L. **LAWRENCE**, Nov. 16, 1842, by Rev. Charles Chettenden	1	193
MORRIS, Benjamin, s. John & Sibbel, b. Jan. 16, 1774	1	49
Betsey, [d. David & Prudence], b. Dec. 21, 1788	1	70
David, s. John & Sibbel, b. Sept. 22, 1764	1	49

	Vol.	Page
MORRIS, (cont.)		
David, m. Prudence **GILBERT**, Oct. 30, 1786	1	70
David, m. Prudence **GILBERT**, Oct. 30, 1786	1	157
Elizabeth, d. John & Sibbel, b. Oct. 7, 1754 N.S.	1	49
Eunice, d. John & Sibbel, b. Mar. 18, 1760	1	49
Hannah, d. John & Sibbel, b. Oct. 28, 1766	1	49
Hervey, [s. David & Prudence], b. May 26, 1787	1	70
Hiel, s. John & Sibbel, b. Sept. 30, 1762	1	49
John, m. Sibbell **NEWTON**, Nov. 12, 1750	1	152
Newton John, s. John & Sibbel, b. Jan. 13, 1752, O. S.	1	49
Sarah, d. John & Sibbel, b. Sept. 20, 1758	1	49
Sarah, m. Samuel **OLMSTED**, 3rd, Oct. 23, 1784	1	153
Sibbel, d. John & Sibbel, b. Nov. 13, 1756	1	49
MOSS, Dorcas, Mrs., m. Rev. Jonathan **INGERSOLL**, Nov. 10, 1740, by Rev. Samuel Cooke, of Stratfield, Int. Pub.	LR1	231
MUFFIT, Ruth, of Ridgefield, m. Ury **HOWARD**, of New Milford, Conn., Nov. 24, 1834, by Elias Blanchard, J. P.	1	180
NAIL, W[illia]m, Jr., m. Nancy **HOW**, Dec. 20, 1829, by Nathan Burton	1	170
NASH, Abigail, d. Abraham & Rhoda, b. Jan. 30, 1739	1	22
Abin, his wid., d. Nov. 2, 1815, ae 90	1	219
Abraham, s. Abraham & Rhoda, b. Nov. 7, 1740	1	22
Abraham, Jr., m. Sarah **OLMSTED**, Nov. 17, 1762	1	155
Abraham, s. Abraham, Jr. & Sarah, b. June 10, 1780	1	59
Abraham, s. Abraham, Jr., d. Mar. 21, 1781	1	203
Abraham, m. Mercy **LYNDE**, May 19, 1781	1	154
Abraham, 2nd, s. Abraham, Jr. & Sarah, b. Nov. 13, 1783	1	59
Abraham, 2nd, m. Elizabeth **SMTIH**, [ ], 1795	1	159
Abraham, d. June 24, 1801, ae 83 y.	1	210
Abraham, his w. [ ], d. Mar. 28, 1820	1	222
Abraham, d. Nov. 3, 1821	1	223
Agah, d. Abraham, Jr. & Sarah, b. Apr. 21, 1782	1	59
Albert, [s. Lewis L. & Rachel], b. May 22, 1812	1	112
Albert, m. Charity **ABBOT**, b. of Ridgefield, Mar. 9, 1834, by Rev. Nicholas White	1	179
Arnet Alfred, [s. Jacob & Anna], b. Feb. 11, 1800	1	90
Betsey L., [d. Lewis L. & Rachel], b. Feb. 24, 1819	1	112
Carry N., [d. Lewis L. & Rachel], b. Oct. 3, 1817	1	112
Catharine, of Ridgefield, m. Knapp **OSBORN**, of Wilton, July 1, 1829, by Samuell M. Phelps	1	171
Charles, [s. Jared & Rachel], b. Dec. 17, 1793	1	78
Clara Olmsted, [d. Jared & Rachel], b. Nov. 11, 1800	1	78
Cornelia, [d. Lewis L. & Rachel], b. Mar. 18, 1814	1	112
Daniel, s. Abraham, Jr. & Sarah, b. Nov. 24, 1763	1	59
Daniel, m. Olive **NASH**, Apr. 30, 1783	1	86
Daniel Kellogg, [s. Jacob & Anna], b. Mar. 15, 1795	1	90
David, s. Daniel & Olive, b. Nov. 16, 1783	1	86
David, [s. Riah & Esther], b. Aug. 11, 1790	1	72

	Vol.	Page
NASH, (cont.)		
Dorcas, d. Daniel & Olive, b. Feb. 22, 1787	1	86
Elizabeth R., m. Charles **GRUMMAN**, b. of Ridgefield, Nov. 10, 1841, by Rev. Joseph Fuller	1	191
Ezra, s. Abraham & Rhoda, b. Feb. 25, 1758	1	22
Harry, d. Apr. 18, 1815, ae 19 y. "Was drowned near New York"	1	218
Hawley, [s. Jacob & Anna], b. Aug. 11, 1798	1	90
Hiram O., [s. Lewis L. & Rachel], b. Mar. 22, 1811	1	112
Isaac, s. Abraham & Rhoda, b. Nov. 13, 1744	1	22
Isaac, m. Elizabeth **ABBOT**, Mar. 28, 1765	1	150
Isaac, s. Isaac & Elizabeth, b. July 14, 1766	1	20
Jacob, s. Abraham & Rhoda, b. Aug. 30, 1751	1	22
Jacob, m. Anna **ROCKWELL**, Feb. 7, 1794	1	159
Jacob, had infant, d. Dec. 11, 1804	1	212
Jared, s. Abraham, Jr. & Sarah, b. Aug. 10, 1769	1	59
Jared, m. Rachel **SCRIBNER**, July 7, 1793	1	78
Jared, his w. [ ], d. Mar. 27, 1850, ae 90 y.	1	240
Jey*, d. Feb. 4, [1852], ae 44 y. *(Joy?)	1	242
John, s. Abraham & Rhoda, b. Apr. 13, 1747	1	22
Jonathan, s. Abraham & Rhoda, b. Apr. 14, 1760	1	22
Lavinia, [d. Lewis L. & Rachel], b. June 11, 1827	1	112
Lewis, [s. Riah & Esther], b. Oct. 25, 1784	1	72
Lewis L., b. Oct. 24, 1784; m. Rachel **OLMSTED**, Feb. 18, 1809	1	112
Lewis L., his child d. Dec. 11, 1815, ae 2 y.	1	219
Lewis L., had child d. Oct. 22, 1828, ae 2 y.	1	227
Mary, d. Charles, d. July 19, 1850, ae 21 y. 10 m.	1	240
Olive, m. Daniel **NASH**, Apr. 30, 1783	1	86
Phebe, d. Abraham & Rhoda, b. Nov. 16, 1742	1	22
Phebe, d. Abraham, Jr. & Sarah, b. Feb. 19, 1771	1	59
Rhoda, d. Abraham & Rhoda, b. Oct. 10, 1753	1	22
Riah, s. Abraham & Rhoda, b. Aug. 3, 1763	1	22
Riah, m. Esther **LYNES**, Aug. 15, 1782	1	72
Roxana, w. Charles, d. Feb. 2, 1821	1	222
Sally, [d. Riah & Esther], b. June 1, 1786	1	72
Sally, d. Samuel Olmsted & Sally, b. Nov. 20, 1799	1	67
Sally, d. Biah, d. Mar. 11, 1809, in the 23rd y. of her age	1	214
Sally, d. Lewis L. & Rachel, b. Dec. 21, 1809	1	112
Sally, of Ridgefield, m. Elijah L. **THOMAS**, of Wilton, Jan. 1, 1829, by Rev. Henry Stead	1	168
Samuel, s. Abraham & Rhoda, b. Mar. 13, 1749	1	22
Samuel, s. Abraham, Jr. & Sarah, b. Mar. 12, 1778	1	59
Samuel O., d. Jan. 13, 1831, in the 53rd y. of his age	1	228
Samuel Olmsted, m. Sally **NORTHRUP**, Sept. 13, 1798	1	67
Sarah, d. Abraham, Jr. & Sarah, b. May 5, 1766	1	59
Sarah, w. Abraham, 2nd, d. June 12, 1793	1	206
Sarah, d. Daniel & Olive, b. May 3, 1798	1	86

	Vol.	Page
NASH, (cont.)		
Sarah, w. Samuel, d. Nov. 20, 1799	1	210
NEWCOMB, Daniel, m. Nancy **BENEDICT**, Nov. 20, 1832, by Nathan Burton	1	177
NEWTON, Sibbell, m. John **MORRIS**, Nov. 12, 1750	1	152
NICHOLS, NICHOLLS, Abigail, w. Eliakim, d. May 31, 1763	1	200
Abigail, m. Eliakim **NICHOLS**, Nov. 18, 1764	1	150
Dilly, d. John & Naomi, b. Jan. 11, 1776	1	36
Eliakim, m. Abigail **NICHOLS**, Nov. 18, 1764	1	150
Jared, m. Rachel **SCRIBNER**, [ ], 1794	1	159
John, s. Joseph & Sarah, b. June 22, 1732	LR1	212
John, s. Joseph & Sarah, d. July 6, 1732	LR1	214
John, s. Eliakim & Abigail, b. Nov. 1, 1762	1	13
John, m. Naomi **SHERWOOD**, May 15, 1770	1	151
John, s. John & Naomi, b. Aug. 13, 1770	1	36
Joseph, s. Joseph & Sarah, b. May 27, 1734	LR1	218-9
Joseph, Jr., m. Rachel **KEELER**, Nov. 26, 178[ ]	1	150
Joseph, s. John & Naomi, b. Jan. 15, 1778	1	36
Sarah, d. Joseph & Sarah, b. Feb. 21, 1731	LR1	212
Sarah, m. John **BUNDY**, Sept. 26, 1753, by Jonathan Ingersoll, V. D. M.	LR1	234
Stephen, s. John & Naomi, b. July 9, 1772	1	36
Warren, of Greenfield, Conn., m. Mary Delia **BEERS**, of Ridgefield, Apr. 3, 1850, by Rev. Nathaniel Mead	1	133
William, s. John & Naomi, b. May 17, 1774	1	36
-----, Mrs., her child & grand child of Daniel L. **EDMONDS**, d. Sept. 27, 1840	1	235
NICKERSON, [see also **RICKERSON**], Adah, wid., d. Jan. 16, 1828, ae 59	1	226
Eliphaz, m. Sybel **NORRIS**, Apr. [ ]	LR1	252
Omri, his child, d. Sept. 6, 1810	1	215
NORRIS, Abigail, [d. Stephen & Abigail], b. Sept. 20, 1767; d. Mar. 3, 1768	1	81
Abijah, [s. Stephen & Abigail], b. Apr. 12, 1786	1	81
Betsey, [d. Stephen & Abigail], b. Oct. 10, 1765	1	81
Daniel, [s. Stephen & Abigail], b Feb. 3, 1784	1	81
Erastus D. Lazon, s. [Stephen, Jr. & Elizabeth], b. Sept. 20, 1801	1	92
Frederick A., m. Louis A. **YOUNG**, b. of Ridgefield, Nov. 5, 1844, by Z. B. Burr	1	197
Frederick Augustus, s. Lambert K. & Harriet, b. Aug. 4, 1818	1	98
Hannah, m. Charles **SEYMOUR**, Jan. 29, 1832, by Nathan Burton	1	175
Hannah A., d. [John & Rachel], b. Oct. 21, 1791	1	92
Hiram, s. [John & Rachel], b. Aug. 7, 1801	1	92
James, [s. Stephen & Abigail], b. Oct. 4, 1775	1	81
John, [s. Stephen & Abigail], b. Jan. 20, 1770	1	81
John, m. Rachel **NORTHRUP**, Oct. 20, 1790	1	92

	Vol.	Page
NORRIS, (cont.)		
Keeler, s. [John & Rachel], b. Feb. 21, 1800; d. June 29, 1800	1	92
Lambert Keeler, s. [Stephen, Jr. & Elizabeth], b. Feb. 16, 1797	1	92
Matthew N., s. [John & Rachel], b. Mar. 15, 1798	1	92
Moses, [s. Stephen & Abigail], b. Dec. 17, 1778	1	81
Moses, m. Hepsey [ ], Apr. 26, 1801	1	93
Rachel, d. [John & Rachel], b. Apr. 5, 1796	1	92
Rachel, d. [Stephen, Jr. & Elizabeth], b. Jan. 27, 1800	1	92
Sally, d. [Moses & Hepsey], b. Feb. 7, 1802	1	93
Samuel, [s. Stephen & Abigail], b. Mar. 16, 1789	1	81
Stephen, m. Abigail **KEELER**, Mar. 6, 1765	1	81
Stephen, [s. Stephen & Abigail], b. Mar. 6, 1773	1	81
Stephen, s. [John & Rachel], b. June 20, 1793	1	92
Stephen, Jr., m. Elizabeth [ ], Oct. 1, 1795	1	92
Sybel, m. Eliphaz **NICKERSON**, Apr. [ ]	LR1	252
-----, m. [ ] **DeFOREST**, [ ], 1795	1	159
NORTHRUP, NORTHROP, Aaron, s. Joseph & Susannah, b. Oct. 28, [1719/20]	LR1	203
Aaron, [s. Joseph & Susanna], b. Nov. 30, 1720	LR1	205
Aaron, m. Rebeckah **HOYT**, Jan. 25, 1743/4	LR1	232
Aaron, s. Aaron & Rebeckah, b. June 21, 175[ ]	LR1	248
Aaron, d. May 21, 1768, ae 86	1	204
Aaron, d. Mar. 21, 1802, in the 82nd y. of his age	1	211
Aaron, m. Fanny **OLMSTED**, Apr. 30, 1840, by Rev. Joseph Fuller	1	188
Aaron, 2nd, of Ridgefield, m. Sarah **NORTHROP**, of Lewisboro, N. Y., [Oct.] 22, [1850], by Rev. C. Clark	1	134
Aaron, d. Dec. 10, [1851], ae 68	1	241
Abigail, m. John **BALDWIN**, May 7, 17[ ]	1	150
Abigail, w. Stephen, d. Aug. 22, 1754	LR1	216
Abigail, m. David **BROWN**, Feb. 10, 1763	1	150
Abigail, w. Jared, d. Feb. 14, 1812	1	216
Abraham, [s. Joseph & Susanna], b. Sept. 18, 1722	LR1	205
Allene, d. Joseph & Allene, b. May 13, 1739	LR1	224
Ambrose, s. James & Lydia, b. Apr. 30, 1740	LR1	250
Ambrose, s. James & Lidia, d. Oct. 7, 1745	LR1	217
Amos, twin Eunice, s. James & Abiah, b. Oct. 14, 1784	1	51
Amos, d. Nov. 28, 1801, in the 18th y. of his age	1	211
Anna, d. [Joseph & Allen], b. Sept. 10, 1745	LR1	238
Anne, m. Jonah **SMITH**, Jr., Dec. 24, 1754, by Samuel Smith, J. P.	LR1	234
Anne, d. Eli & Abigail, d. July 18, 1758	1	200
Anne, d. Eli & Abigail, b. May 21, 1760	1	5
Benjah, s. Eli & Abigail, b. Mar. 27, 1752	LR1	243
Benajah, m Sarah **KEELER**, May 15, 1771	1	151
Benjamin, s. James & Lydia, b. Oct. 26, 1747	LR1	250
Benjamin K., m. Catharine **KEELER**, b. of Ridgefield, Oct. 26, 1847, by Rev. James A. Hawley	1	128

NORTHRUP, NORTHROP, (cont.)

	Vol.	Page
Betsey, d. Thomas & Millesent, b. Jan. 8, 1793[sic]	1	39
Bettey, w. John, d. Sept. 8, 1775	1	201
Cemantha, m. James E. **MEAD**, b. of Ridgefield, July 14, 1833, by Rev. Charles J. Todd	1	178
Clara, d. Jonah, d. June 1, 1807	1	213
Clarissa, of Ridgefield, m. Henry **DISBROW**, of New Canaan, Nov. 26, 1843, by Rev. A. S. Francis	1	194
Cyrus, s. Josiah & Rebecka, b. Mar. 17, 1788	1	19
Daniel, [s. Gamaliel], b. July 17, 1733	LR1	207
Daniel, s. Gam[alie]l & Mary, d. Jan. 18, 1738/9	LR1	215
David, s. Isaac & Elizabeth, b. Mar. 20, 1754	LR1	208
Dorcas, d. Eli & Abigail, b. June 22, 1758	1	5
Edward W., m. Sarah E. **SHERWOOD**, b. of Ridgefield, Oct. 16, 1848, by Rev. Sylvester S. Strong	1	130
Edward W., m. Sarah E. **SHERWOOD**, b. of Ridgefield, Oct. 16, 1848, by Rev. Sylvester S. Stong	1	131
Eli, s. Joseph & Susanna, b. Apr. 30, [1718]	LR1	202
Eli, [s. Joseph & Susanna], b. May 1, 1718	LR1	205
Eli, m. Abigail [ ], Jan. 3, 1738/9	LR1	230
Eli, s. Eli & Abigail, b. Feb. 2, 1742/3	LR1	236
Eli, s. Eli & Abigail, d. Nov. 13, 1760	1	200
Elias, s. James & Abiah, b. May 18, 1789	1	51
Elijah, s. Thomas & Mehitable, b. Oct. 8, 1765	1	15
Elizabeth, d. Gamaliel & Mary, b. Oct. [ ], [1724]	LR1	204
Elizabeth, d. Gamaliel & Mary, d. Mar. 14, 1725	LR1	214
Elizabeth, [d. Gamaliel], b. Feb. 29, 1735/6	LR1	207
Elizabeth, d. Isaac & Elizabeth, b. Oct. 28, 1755	LR1	208
Elizabeth, d. Nov. 14, 1776	1	202
Elizabeth, m Thomas **FLETCHER**, Dec. 31, 1778	1	153
Elizabeth, m. Daniel **SMITH**, 2nd, Mar. 1, 1781	1	155
Elizabeth, d. John & Elizabeth, b. May 17, 1783	1	31
Elizabeth, w. Stephen, d. Feb. 20, 1793	1	206
Elizabeth, d. Elizabeth **WILSON**, b. May 16, 1799	1	61
Elizabeth, m. Edward B. **JONES**, b. of Ridgefield, this day, [Sept. 2, 1850], by Rev. C. Clark	1	133
Emila, d. James & Abiah, b. Dec. 3, 1779	1	51
Emily, m. Egbert **MEAD**, b. of Ridgefield, Oct. 5, 1836, by Rev. C. G. Selleck	1	183
Enos, s. John & Rebecca, b. Sept. 14, 1733	LR1	218-9
Esther, d. Eli & Abigail, b. Jan. 18, 1749/50	LR1	243
Eunice, d. Jabez & Sarah, b. Oct. 3, 1735	LR1	223
Eunice, d. Isaac & Elizabeth, b. Feb. 3, 176[ ]	LR1	208
Eunice, m. Thomas **WILSON**, Jan. 27, 1779	1	154
Eunice, m. Thomas **WILSON**, Jan. 27, 1779	1	156
Eunice, twin with Amos, d. James & Abiah, b. Oct. 14, 1784	1	51
Eunice, w. Jared, d. July 10, 1795, ae 35	1	208
Eunice, d. Mar. 3, 1813, in the 18th y. of her age	1	217

NORTHRUP, NORTHROP, (cont.)

	Vol.	Page
Ezra, s. James & Abiah, b. Mar. 10, 1787	1	51
Francis B., of Southeast, N. Y., m. Camilla M. **SEARS**, of Ridgefield, Dec. 25, 1833, by Nathan Burton	1	178
Gamaliel, m. Mary **DAUCHY**, Jan. 3, 1723/4	LR1	227
Gamaliel, [s. Gamaliel], b. May 9, 1730	LR1	207
Gamiel, s. Gamaliel & Mary, d. Sept. 3, 1736	LR1	214
Gamaliel, had negro Ishmael, b. July 21, 1739	LR1	224
Gamaliel, s. Samuell & Mary, b. Dec. 1, 1742	LR1	236
Gamaliel, Jr., m. Mary **KEELER**, May 14, 1766	1	151
Gamaliel, d. Dec. 8, 1784	1	204
Hannah, d. James & Hannah, b. Nov. 16, [1723]	LR1	204
Hannah, d. James & Hannah, b. Aug. 20, 1729	LR1	210
Hannah, d. Aaron & Rebeckah, b. Dec. 5, 1744	LR1	238
Hannah, [d. Gamaliel], b. May 1, 1747	LR1	207
Hannah, m. Stephen **OLMSTEAD**, Aug. 23, 1747	LR1	233
Hannah, d. James & Rachel, b. Feb. 28, 1755	LR1	244
Hannah, d. Sam[ue]ll & Elizabeth, b. Feb. 9, 1771	1	31
Hannah, d. James & Abiah, b. Sept. 8, 1774	1	51
Harriet, m. Jacob B. **SEARS**, b. of Ridgefield, Feb. 4, 1846, by Rev. Z. B. Burr	1	198
Henry, m. Elizabeth **SHERWOOD**, b. of Ridgefield, Oct. 7, 1832, by Rev. Charles J. Todd	1	177
Henry K., his w. [ ], d. Mar. 6, 1837	1	233
Isaac, [s. Joseph & Susanna], b. Nov. 10, 1725	LR1	205
Isaac, m. Elizabeth **LOBDELL**, Jan. 16, 1752	LR1	234
Isaac, s. Isaac & Elizabeth, b. Dec. 24, 1752	LR1	208
Isaac, m. Sarah **SUARD**, Jan. 22, 1772	1	151
Isaac, s. Isaac & Elizabeth, b. Apr. 29, 1777	1	13
Isaac, d. Apr. 27, 1784	1	203
Isaac, d. Mar. 22, 1818, ae 42	1	221
Jabez, m. Sarah [ ], Mar. 6, 1735	LR1	230
Jabez, s. Jabez & Sarah, b. Aug. 14, 1737	LR1	223
James, s. James & Hannah, b. Nov. 9, [1719]	LR1	203
James, Jr., m. Rachal [ ], Jan. 13, 1742/3	LR1	231
James, s. James & Rachal, b. Jan. 22, 1744/5	LR1	238
James, s. James & Rachel, d. Mar. 21, 1749/50	LR1	216
James, s. James & Rachel, b. July 15, 1751	LR1	244
James, Sergt., d. July 11, 1762	LR1	217
James, m. Abiah **ROCKWELL**, Jan. 26, 1774	1	153
James, s. James & Abiah, b. July 14, 1781	1	51
Jane, d. Eli & Abigail, b. Oct. 21, 1747	LR1	240
Jane, m. Zopher **WEEKS**, June 26, 1769	1	151
Jared, s. Aaron & Rebecka, b. Nov. 19, 1761	1	27
Jared, m. Eunice **BETTS**, Apr. 22, 1793	1	158
Jared, d. May 5, 1833, in the 72nd y. of his age	1	230
Joanna, d. Eli & Abigail, b. Aug. 5, 1745	LR1	238
Joanna, d. Eli & Abigail, b. Aug. 6, 1745	LR1	243

NORTHRUP, NORTHROP, (cont.)

	Vol.	Page
Joanna, m. James **STURGIS**, Mar. 18, 1765	1	150
Joanna, m. Joseph **BENEDICT**, Dec. 23, 1792	1	158
John, s. William, of Milford, m. Rebecca **ROBERTS**, Aug. 14, 1728, by Capt. Gunn	LR1	228
John, s. John & Rebecca, b. Jan. 14, 1729	LR1	211
John, s. James & Lydia, b. Nov. 28, 1743	LR1	250
John, s. Jona & Lydia, d. Mar. 20, 1761	LR1	217
John, m. Elizabeth **EVERIT**, Mar. 6, 1776	1	152
John, d. Mar. 2, 1794, in the 91st y. of his age	1	207
John, d. June 8, 1807, ae 80	1	213
John, d. Sept. 3, 1817	1	220
Jonah, d. Mar. 31, 1736	LR1	215
Jonah, s. Isaac & Elizabeth, b. Jan. 30, 1770	1	13
Jonah, m. Ruhamah **DEAN**, Jan. 21, 1790	1	158
Jonah, his w. [ ], d. Jan. 5, 1808	1	213
Jonah, d. Mar. 2, 1812	1	216
Joseph, [s. Joseph & Susanna], b. May 11, 1716	LR1	205
Joseph, s. Joseph & Susannah, b. May [ ], 1716	LR1	201
Joseph, m. Allen [ ], Aug. 9, 1738	LR1	230
Joseph, s. Joseph & Allen, b. Mar. 20, 1742/3	LR1	238
Joseph, s. Aaron & Rebeckah, b. Oct. 16, 1764	1	27
Joseph, had infant, d. Oct. 28, 1799	1	210
Joseph, d. Apr. 14, 1832, in the 68th y. of his age	1	229
Josiah, s. Aaron & Rebeckah, b. May 28, 1759	LR1	248
Josiah, m. Rebeckah **OLMSTED**, Aug. 31, 1779	1	154
Josiah, d. July 17, 1797, ae 38 y.	1	209
Lewis, s. Jabez & Sarah, b. Oct. 14, 1752	LR1	246
Lewis, s. Isaac & Elizabeth, b. Mar. 24, 1773	1	13
Lois, d. Jabez & Sarah, b. Feb. 16, 1743/4	LR1	237
Lois, d. Isaac & Elizabeth, b. July 17, 1757	LR1	208
Lois, m. Daniel **DAUCHY**, Dec. 24, 1778	1	152
Louis, [child of Thomas & Mehitable], b. Jan. 17, 1791	1	15
Lucy, d. Josiah & Rebecka, b. Jan. 11, 1797	1	19
Lucy, of Ridgefield, m. Alfred W. **HUSTED**, of New Haven, Sept. 2, 1851, by Rev. Clinton Clark	1	135
Lydia, d. Thomas & Millesent, b. Apr. 4, 1774	1	39
Margaret, m. Morris H. **CANFIELD**, this day [June 16, 1852], by Rev. David H. Short	1	138
Martha, [d. Gamaliel], b. Dec. 2, 1744	LR1	207
Martha, d. Thomas & Rachel, b. June 8, 1747/8	LR1	244
Martha, w. David, d. May 9, 1830	1	228
Mary, [d. Gamaliel], b. May 26, 1726	LR1	207
Mary, d. John & Rebeckah, b. Sept. 1, 1740	LR1	226
Mary, m. Samuel **SMITH**, Sr., of Norwalk, May 18, 1743	LR1	231
Mary, d. Aaron & Rebeckah, b. Oct. 13, 1746	LR1	248
Mary, d. Samuel & Elizabeth, b. Sept. 15, 1773	1	31
Mary, Mrs., of Ridgefield, m. Rev. Samuel **CAMP**, of		

	Vol.	Page
NORTHRUP, NORTHROP, (cont.)		
Ridgefield, Oct. 17, 1782, by John Benedict, J. P.	1	153
Mary, m. Elijah **BOWLER**, Oct. 27, 1785	1	156
Matthew, s. James & Rachel, b. Apr. 6, 1749	LR1	244
Matthew, m. Hannah **ABBOT**, Sept. 14, 1769	1	151
Matthew, s. Matthew & Hannah, b. Apr. 4, 177[ ]	1	44
Mehetable, d. Gamaliel & Mary, b. May 13, 1738	LR1	224
Mehitable, m. Jesse **BENEDICT**, Sept. 16, 1756	LR1	252
Millicent, d. Aaron & Rebeckah, b. Feb. 25, 1757	LR1	248
Miriam, [d. Joseph & Susanna], b. July 18, 1728	LR1	205
Molle, d. Isaac & Elizabeth, b. Feb. 3, 1768	1	13
Moses, s. Thomas & Mehitable, b. Jan. 17, 1764	1	15
Nancy, d. Josiah & Rebeckah, b. Aug. 29, 1783	1	19
Nathan, s. James & Hannah, b. May 30, [1721]	LR1	203
Nathan, m. Peregrina **SAINT JOHN**, d. Capt. [ ], Aug. 27, 1730	LR1	228
Nathaniel, m. Chloe **BALDWIN**, Nov. 5, 1772	1	151
Pemalla, d. Isaac & Sarah, b. July 1, 1772	1	35
Pholle, d. Isaac & Elizabeth, b. Oct. 26, 1762	1	13
Phalle, single person, had s. David **VERRIAL**, b. Aug. 13, 1787 & John **BENNITT**, b. Dec. 27, 1790	1	69
Phalle, m Walter **HOLLY**, Nov. 5, 1795	1	89
Phebe, d. Matthew & Hannah, b. Mar. 9, 1782	1	44
Phebe Jane, m. Abel **JENNINGS**, b. of Ridgefield, May 4, 1842, by Rev. Joseph Fuller	1	192
Phillip, s. Josiah & Rebecka, b. Oct. 9, 1785	1	19
Philip, had infant d. May [ ], 1823	1	223
Polly, d. Josiah & Rebecka, b. Sept. 12, 1781	1	19
Polly, d. Jared & Eunice, b. Mar. 20, 1794	1	79
Rachal, d. Gamaliell & Mary, b. July 18, 1740	LR1	225
Rachal, d. James & Rachel, b. Jan. 28, 1754	LR1	244
Rachal, w. Thomas, d. Oct. 2, 1759	LR1	217
Rachal, m. Isaac **KEELER**, Jr., Jan. 16, 1760	LR1	234
Rachel, d. Thomas & Millesent, b. Mar. 5, 1772	1	39
Rachel, d. Matthew & Hannah, b. Nov. 29, 1774	1	44
Rachel, m. John **NORRIS**, Oct. 20, 1790	1	92
Rebecca, d. John & Rebecca, b. Sept. 25, 1735	LR1	218-9
Rebeckah, d. Aaron & Rebeckah, b. Mar. 7, 1754	LR1	248
Rebeckah, d. Isaac & Elizabeth, b. July 13, 1759	LR1	208
Rebeckah, w. Aaron, d. Mar. 9, 1800	1	210
Rebecca, wid., d. Mar. 3, 1850, ae 88	1	240
Rufus, m. Lucretia **MEAD**, Nov. 6, 1831, by Rev. Charles J. Todd	1	174
Russell, s. James & Abiah, b. June 15, 1791	1	51
Ruth, d. John & Rebeckah, b. Jan. 11, 1742/3	LR1	237
Ruth, d. Isaac & Elizabeth, b. Sept. 3, 1765	1	13
Ruth, m. Daniel **BRADLEY**, May 10, 1784	1	154
Ruth, d. John & Elizabeth, b. Oct. 6, 1784	1	31

232   BARBOUR COLLECTION

	Vol.	Page
NORTHRUP, NORTHROP, (cont.)		
Sally, m. Samuel Olmsted **NASH**, Sept. 13, 1798	1	67
Samantha, [see under Cemantha]		
Samuel, s. [Joseph & Allen], b. Nov. 26, 1744	LR1	238
Samuel, s. John & Rebeckah, b. Feb. 2, 1746	LR1	246
Samuel, s. James & Rachel, b. Mar. 5, 1746/7	LR1	240
Samuel, m. Prewe **RIGGS**, Nov. 29, 1769	1	151
Samuel, s. Sam[ue]ll & Elizabeth, b. Mar. 16, 1772	1	31
Samuel, s. James & Abiah, b. Aug. 9, 1776	1	51
Samuel, d. Apr. 29, 1802	1	211
Samuel, d. July 26, 1847, ae 33 y.	1	239
Samuel H., of Lewisboro, N. Y., m. Esther Ann **FOSTER**, of Ridgefield, Oct. 4, 1852, by Rev. Shaller J. Hillyer	1	138
Samuel M., m. Sarah **OLMSTED**, b. of Ridgefield, Oct. 3, 1841, by Rev. Warren Hoyt	1	191
Sarah, m. Samuel **SAINT JOHN**, Jr., Mar. 6, 1727/8	LR1	228
Sarah, [d. Gamaliel], b. Apr. 29, 1728	LR1	207
Sarah, d. Jabez & Sarah, b. June 21, 1741	LR1	226
Sarah, d. Aaron & Rebeckah, b. Aug. 22, 1749	LR1	248
Sarah, m. John **KEELER**, May 30, 1750	LR1	234
Sarah, d. Isaac & Elizabeth, b. Mar. 17, 1764	1	13
Sarah, d. Benajah & Sarah, b. Dec. 10, 1771	1	33
Sarah, d. Isaac & Sarah, b. Oct. 3, 1776	1	35
Sarah, d. Josiah & Rebecka, b. Jan. 5, 1780	1	19
Sarah, m. John **JOHNSON**, Mar. 9, 1786	1	156
Sarah, m. Jonathan **SLAWSON**, Feb. 2, 1794	1	83
Sarah, of Lewisboro, N. Y., m. Aaron **NORTHROP**, 2nd, of Ridgefield, [Oct.] 22, [1850], by Rev. C. Clark	1	134
Stephen, s. James & Hannah, b. Dec. 13, 1725	LR1	210
Stephen, d. June 22, 1757	LR1	217
Stephen, s. James & Rachel, b. Jan. 22, 1759	LR1	244
Susannah, m. Thomas **SAINT JOHN**, Mar. [ ]	LR1	252
Susanna, [d. Joseph & Susanna], b. Aug. last, 1714	LR1	205
Susannah, d. Joseph & Eleanor, b. Oct. 20, 1740	LR1	225
Susannah, m Thomas **ST. JOHN**, Mar. 8, 1759	LR1	232
Thaddeus, s. Eli & Abigail, b. Feb. 27, 1763	1	5
Thomas, s. James & Hannah, b. Dec. 5, 1727	LR1	210
Thomas, m. Rachel **MOREHOUSE**, Mar. 9, 1747/8	LR1	233
Thomas, s. Thomas & Rachel, b. Sept. 26, 1751	LR1	244
Thomas, m. Mehetable **ROCKWELL**, Jan. 1, 1760	LR1	232
Thomas, Jr., m. Millesent **KEELER**, Nov. 20, 1770	1	152
Thomas, of Wilton, m. Emily **BENEDICT**, of Ridgefield, Oct. 19, 1824, by Samuell M. Phelps	1	165
William, s. John & Rebecca, b. Oct. 26, 1730	LR1	211
William, s. John & Rebecca, d. Jan. 14, 1734	LR1	215
William, s. John & Rebeckah, b. Feb. 6, 1737/8	LR1	223
William, s. Samuel & Elizabeth, b. Apr. 3, 1769	1	31
William, his child d. [Feb.] 18, [1843], ae 2 y.	1	236

	Vol.	Page
NORTHRUP, NORTHROP, (cont.)		
William H., d. Jan. 24, 1850, ae 17	1	240
W[illia]m N., had child d. [Sept.] 22, [1851], ae 2 y.	1	241
Wilton, s. Eli & Abigail, b. Apr. 7, 1754	LR1	243
NORTON, Henry, m. Roxana **WARREN**, b. of Ridgefield, Oct. 1, 1826, by Samuel M. Phelps	1	167
OAKLEY, Lydia, of Danbury, m. David **DAUCHY**, of Ridgefield, Nov. 24, 1833, by Rev. Charles J. Todd	1	179
OGDEN, Polly, w. Samuel, d. Jan. 14, 1822	1	223
OLMSTED, OLMSTEAD, Aaron, of Wilton, m. Josena **SHERWOOD**, of Ridgefield, Oct. 4, 1846, by Rev. Henry Olmsted, Jr.	1	127
Abby L., of Ridgefield, m. Peter J. **GEDNEY**, of New Canaan, Oct. 26, 1834, by Rev. Charles G. Selleck	1	180
Abby Leonora, d. Nathan & Martha, b. Feb. 20, 1808	1	85
Abiah, d. [Sam[ue]ll & Abiah], b. Jan. 19, 1738/9	LR1	224
Abiah, Mrs., d. Apr. 30, 1796, ae 80 y.	1	208
Abigail, d. Nathan & Sarah, b. Mar. 3, 17[ ]	1	8
Abigail, [d. Ambros & Martha], b. July 5, 1743	LR1	250
Abigail, d. Richard & Abigail, b. Jan. 14, 1743/4	LR1	239
Abigail, w. Richard, d. Apr. 20, 1747	LR1	216
Abigail, m. John **RICHARDS**, Feb. 5, 176[ ]	1	150
Abigail, d. Ezekiel & Lydia, b. Oct. [ ], 176[ ]	1	20
Abigail, d. Justus & Patience, b. July 12, 1760	LR1	198
Abigail, d. Justus & Patience, b. July 12, 1760	1	59
Abigail, m. Zadoc **SHERWOOD**, Nov. 13, 1783	1	153
Abigail, d. David & Abigail, b. Nov. 16, 1792	1	28
Abijah, m. Meriam **HOWE**, Apr. 4, 1784	1	155
Adah, d. David & Elizabeth, b. Nov. 27, 1763	1	40
Adah, m. Jonathan **HOYT**, Mar. 6, 1786	1	156
Alanson, s. Timothy, d. Dec. 5, 1803	1	211
Ambrose, s. Daniell & Hannah, b. May 7, 1719	LR1	203
Ambros, m. Martha **COMSTOCK**, July 1, 1742	LR1	234
Ambros, [s. Ambros & Martha], b. Mar. 10, 1747	LR1	250
Ambrose, d. Apr. 6, 1792	1	206
Amelia, of Ridgefield, m. David C. **GEDNEY**, of Westchester Co., N. Y., Sept. 7, 1825, by Samuell M. Phelps	1	166
Anna, d. Stephen & Hannah, b. Jan. 19, 175[ ]	LR1	249
Anna Lemira, d. [Lewis & Sally], b. Oct. 14, 1804	1	100
Anne, m. Thomas **SEYMOUR**, May 3, 1786	1	156
Anne, d. Samuel & Martha, b. June 29, 1787	1	38
Benjamin, s. Richard & Abigail, b. Dec. 1, 1741	LR1	239
Benjamin, s. Richard & Abigail, d. Oct. 27, 1744	LR1	216
Benjamin, s. Richard & Abigail, b. Nov. 15, 1745	LR1	239
Benjamin Goodrich, s. Hezekiah & Sarah, b. Nov. 30, 1777	1	40
Betsey, d. Justus, Jr. & Betty, b. Oct. 30, 1779	1	40
Betsey, d. Jared & Hannah, b. Mar. 3, 1782	1	38
Betsey Ann, d. Isaac, d. Nov. 25, 1816	1	220

	Vol.	Page
OLMSTED, OLMSTEAD, (cont.)		
Betsey Delia, d. [Lewis & Sally], b. Dec. 7, 1801	1	100
Betty, d. Jonathan & Betty, b. Aug. 22, 1746	LR1	250
Billy, s. David & Abigail, b. June 29, 1778	1	28
Carlisle, s. [Lewis & Sally], b. Sept. 9, 1807	1	100
Caroline, d. Nathan & Martha, b. Apr. 17, 1802	1	85
Caroline, d. Nathan, d. Apr. 10, 1835, ae 34 y.	1	232
Catharine M., m. Augustine N. **FINCH**, b. of Ridgefield, Aug. 28, 1832, by Rev. Charles G. Selleck	1	176
Charles, m. Sarah Esther **SMITH**, b. of Ridgefield, Sept. 26, 1841, by Rev. Warner Hoyt	1	191
Charles Goodrich, s. David & Abigail, b. Aug. 4, 1787	1	28
Chloe, d. Ezekiel & Lydia, b. Mar. 17, 176[ ]	1	20
Clara, d. Nathan & Sarah, b. Oct. 25, 17[ ]	1	8
Clara, had d. Katy, b. Sept. 6, 1784	1	78
Clara, d. Dec. 17, 1794, ae 29	1	207
Clara, twin with Lucretia, [d. Timothy & Huldah], b. Dec. 9, 1795	1	75
Clarissa, m. Jeremiah **DAUCHY**, b. of Ridgefield, Nov. 16, 1826, by Samuel M. Phelps	1	167
Clarissa, d. Mar. 7, [1843], ae 19 y.	1	236
Daniell, m. Hannah **KETCHUM**, May 9, 1711	LR1	227
Daniell, s. Daniell & Hannah, b. Feb. 9, 1712	LR1	199
Daniel, s. Daniel & Hannah, d. Sept. 22, 1730	LR1	213
Daniel, s. Daniel & Hannah, d. Sept. 22, 1730	LR1	214
Daniel, [s. Richard & Mary], b. Sept. 22, 1731	LR1	207
Dan[ie]ll, s. Sam[ue]ll & Abiah, b. June 7, 1737	LR1	224
Daniel, s. Daniel, Jr. & Elizabeth, b. Mar. 22, 1754	LR1	256
Daniel, s. Daniel & Elizabeth, b. Mar. 22, 1754	1	40
Daniel, 2nd, m. Margaret **SMITH**, Jan. 9, 1766	1	151
Daniel, s. Daniel, 2nd & Margaret, b. June 28, 1766	1	34
Daniel, m. Abigail **INGERSOLL**, Oct. 22, 1769	1	150
Daniel, 3rd, m. Joanna **OLMSTED**, Jan. 22, 1772	1	151
Daniel, d. Feb. 7, 1806, in the 75th y. of his age	1	212
Daniel, Jr., of Danbury, m. Army **TAYLOR**, of Ridgefield, Mar. 6, 1822, by S. M. Phelps	1	161
Darius, s. John & Joanna, b. July 7, 1750	LR1	255
David, s. Nathan & Millicent, b. Nov. 20, 1748	LR1	241
David, s. David & Abigail, b. May 21, 1770	1	28
David, 3rd, m. Dorcas **SMITH**, July 6, 1788	1	156
David, m. Dorcas **SMITH**, July 6, 1788	1	157
David, his child d. Dec. 12, 1829, ae 8 m.	1	227
Deborah, d. Daniel & Joanna, b. Aug. 25, 1771	1	35
Delia, d. David, 3rd & Dorcas, b. Jan. 18, 1789	1	62
Dolly, d. Daniel & Joanna, b. Aug. 12, 1778	1	35
Dorcas, d. Samuel & Martha, b. May 26, 1779	1	31
Ebenezer, s. Justus & Patience, b. Oct. 23, 1776	1	59
Ebenezer, m. Esther **INGERSOLL**, Jan. 17, 1779	1	153

OLMSTED, OLMSTEAD, (cont.)

	Vol.	Page
Ebenezer, d. July 19, 1801	1	210
Ebenezer Rockwell, s. Samuel & Martha, b. Oct. 29, 1778	1	31
Edwin B., d. May 12, 1829, ae 23, y.	1	227
Edwin Betts, s. Nathan & Martha, b. May 12, 1806	1	85
Elbert, of Ridgefield, m. Melissa **OLMSTED**, of Wilton, [Oct.] 15, [1845], by Rev. James A. Hawley	1	198
Eliphalet Mead, [s. (?)Daniel & Joanna], [ ]	1	35
Elizabeth, [d. Dan[ie]ll & Hannah], b. Feb. 3, 1727	LR1	208
Elizabeth, m. Benjamin **STEBBINS**, Oct. 8, 1745	LR1	232
Elizabeth, d. Nathan & Millecent, b. July 26, 1746	LR1	240
Elizabeth, d. Daniel & Elizabeth, b. Jan. 30, 1758	LR1	256
Elizabeth, d. Daniel & Elizabeth, b. Jan. 30, 1758	1	40
Elizabeth, m. William **BOLT**, Nov. 29, 1781	1	154
Elizabeth, d. Abijah & Miriam, b. Mar. 29, 1785	1	45
Elizabeth, wid., Daniel, d. Apr. 30, 1822, ae 87 y.	1	223
Emelia, d. Nathan, Jr. & Martha, b. Feb. 15, 1798	1	85
Esther, d. Stephen & Hannah, b. May 3, 1762	1	3
Esther, d. Nathan & Sarah, b. May 3, 1762	1	3
Esther, m. Sands **RAYMOND**, Mar. 8, 1786	1	156
Esther, d. Samuel & Martha, b. June 11, 1787	1	31
Eunice, d. Dan[ie]ll & Elizabeth, b. Dec. 1, 1773	1	40
Eunice, m. Benjamin **KEELER**, Feb. [ ], 1794	1	159
Ezekiel, m. Lydia **HOYT**, Mar. 11, 1750/1, by Jonathan Ingersoll, V. D. M.	LR1	233
Fanny, m. Aaron **NORTHRUP**, Apr. 30, 1840, by Rev. Joseph Fuller	1	188
Frederick, of Redding, m. Jane Ann **FLYNN**, of Ridgefield, Feb. 5, 1843, by Rev. Warner Hoyt	1	193
George Washington, s. David & Abigail, b. Apr. 27, 1776	1	28
Gould, s. Samuel & Martha, b. Feb. 7, 1775	1	38
Gould, his w. [ ], d. Mar. 2, 1824, ae 36	1	224
Hannah, d. Daniell & Hannah, b. July 16, [1721]	LR1	203
Hannah, m. Benjamin **GOODRICH**, Mar. 22, 1737/8	LR1	230
Hannah, d. Jonathan & Betty, b. Jan. 24, 1748	LR1	250
Hannah, d. Ezekiel & Lydia, b. May 6, 175[ ]	1	20
Hannah, d. Stephen & Hannah, b. Aug. 20, 1751	LR1	249
Hannah, d. Justus & Patience, b. Nov. 22, 1772	1	59
Hannah, d. Justus, d. Sept. 3, 1775	1	203
Hannah, w. Stephen, d. Mar. 20, 1779	1	202
Hannah, d. Jared & Hannah, b. Mar. 3, 1780	1	38
Hannah, d. Silas, of Norwalk, m. Silas **ROCKWELL**, Dec. 20, 1781	1	156
Hannah, m. Nathan Gaylord **SMITH**, Apr. 15, 1795	1	79
Hannah, wid. Jered, d. Feb. 18, 1826, ae 71	1	225
Harriet, of Ridgefield, m. William **SMITH**, of North Salem, N. Y., [Nov.] 21, [1830], by Rev. Origin P. Holcomb	1	172
Harriet, of Ridgefield, m. Ebenezer **HAWLEY**, of South Salem, N. Y., May 12, 1835, by Rev. Charles G. Selleck	1	182

236 BARBOUR COLLECTION

	Vol.	Page
OLMSTED, OLMSTEAD, (cont.)		
Harriet, m. John **BENEDICT**, July 2, 1845, by Rev. James A. Hawley	1	197
Harriet E., of Ridgefield, m. Henry **MIDDLEBROOK**, of Wilton, July 8, 1850, by Rev. C. Clark	1	133
Harvey, s. Daniel & Joanna, b. Sept. 1, 1785	1	35
Henry, d. Dec. 22, [1848], ae 61 y.	1	240
Hephzibah, [d. Richard & Mary], b. June 20, 1726	LR1	207
Hephzibah, m John **WHITNEE**, June 15, 1746, by Rev. Jonathan Ingersoll	LR1	233
Hephzibah, m. Ebenezer **JONES**, Feb. 8, 1789	1	157
Hezekiah, s. Nathan & Millicent, b. Dec. 16, 1750	LR1	241
Hezekiah, s. Dan[ie]ll & Elizabeth, b. June 7, 1770	1	40
Hezekiah, d. Aug. 25, [1850], ae [ ]	1	240
Hiram, s. Jared & Hannah, b. May 28, 1795	1	38
Huldah, d. Joseph & Susannah, b. Apr. 21, 1784	1	56
Isaac, s. Samuel & Martha, b. Jan. 17, 1771	1	31
Isaac, m. Eunice **DAUCHY**, Apr. 21, 1793	1	78
Isaac, m. Eunice **DAUCHY**, Apr. 21, 1793	1	158
Isaac, his infant s. [ ], d. Mar. 26, 1798	1	209
Isaac, d. Jan. 10, 1846, ae 75 y.	1	238
J. Burr, his child d. Nov. 22, 1836	1	233
James, s. Stephen & Hannah, b. Sept. 18, 1749	LR1	241
James, s. Stephen & Hannah, b. Sept. 18, 1749	LR1	245
James, s. Nathan & Sarah, b. Dec. 16, 1752	LR1	255
James, s. Nathan & Sarah, d. June 30, 1754	LR1	216
James, s. Stephen & Hannah, d. Feb. 19, 1779	1	202
James, m. Sarah **MOREHOUSE**, b. of Norwalk, Jan. 14, 1789	1	157
Jane, w. James, d. Dec. 4, 1820	1	226
Jared, b. July 1, 1753; m. Hannah **BETTS**, [ ]	1	38
Jared, m. Hannah **BETTS**, Nov. 30, 1773	1	152
Jared, s. Jared & Hannah, b. Feb. 14, 1793	1	38
Jared, s. [Lewis & Sally], b. Aug. 14, 1811	1	100
Jared, d. May 28, 1825, in his 72nd y.	1	225
Jemima, d. Daniel, 2nd & Margaret, b. May 1, 1770	1	34
Jeremiah, s. Matthew & Sarah, b. Sept. 13, 1796	1	108
Jesse, m. Chloe **SMITH**, Mar. 3, 1779	1	154
Jesse Smith, s. David, 3rd & Dorcas, b. Dec. 24, 1792	1	62
Joanna, d. John & Joanna, b. Feb. 7, 1748	LR1	255
Joanna, m. Daniel **OLMSTED**, 3rd, Jan. 22, 1772	1	151
John, s. Richard & Mary, b. Feb. 25, 1714/15	LR1	199
John, s. John & Phebe, b. May 19, 1743	LR1	255
John, s. Daniel & Joanna, b. Sept. 11, 1753	1	35
John, d. Mar. 14, 1800, ae 25 y.	1	210
John B., m. Sarah **MEAD**, b. of Ridgefield, Nov. 17, 1835, by Rev. J. L. Clark	1	181
John Burr, d. Apr. 3, 1838, ae [ ]	1	234
Jonas, s. Jared & Hannah, b. Jan. 31, 1778	1	38

RIDGEFIELD VITAL RECORDS 237

	Vol.	Page
OLMSTED, OLMSTEAD, (cont.)		
Johathan, s. Dan[ie]ll & Hannah, b. Dec. 8, [1723]	LR1	204
Jonathan, s. Ezekiel & Lydia, b. Dec. 23, 1753	LR1	251
Jonathan, s. Ezekiel & Lydia, b. Dec. 23, 175[ ]	1	20
Jonathan, s. Samuel & Martha, b. Dec. 27, 1772	1	31
Jonathan, s. Samuel, 3rd, d. Feb. 27, 1784	1	203
Jonathan, s. Samuel & Martha, b. Dec. 25, 1793	1	31
Jonathan, his infant s. [ ], d. July 12, 1796	1	208
Jonathan, had infant d. July 9, 1820	1	222
Joseph, s. Justus & Patience, b. June 30, 1758	LR1	255
Joseph, s. Justus & Patience, b. June 30, 1758	1	59
Joseph, s. David & Elizabeth, b. Mar. 21, 1768	1	40
Josiah, m. Rebeckah **WHITNEY**, Jan. 18, 1789	1	157
Josiah, his w. [ ], d. Dec. 14, 1843, ae about 83 y.	1	237
Julia Ann, of Ridgefield, m. Roswell **CANFIELD**, of Stamford, Oct. 27, 1827, by Samuel M. Phelps	1	168
Justus, [s. Richard & Mary], b. Jan. 21, 1728/9	LR1	207
Justus, m. Patience [ ], June 10, 1752	LR1	234
Justus, s. Justus & Patience, b. June 20, 1753	1	59
Justus, Jr., m. Betty **WOOD**, Jan. 7, 1777	1	152
Katy, d. Clara, b. Sept. 6, 1784	1	78
Katy, d. Samuel & Martha, b. Mar. 11, 1790	1	31
Ketchum, s. Ezekiel & Lydia, b. May 29, 176[ ]	1	20
Ketchum, s. Ezekiel & Lydia, d. Sept. 22, 1765	1	200
Laura, d. Daniel & Joanna, b. Mar. 18, 1788	1	35
Lavis, s. Daniel & Elizabeth, b. July 27, 1772	1	40
Legrand, [s. Timothy & Huldah], b. Nov. 12, 1797	1	75
Lewis, s. Samuel & Martha, b. Nov. 20, 1771	1	38
Lewis, s. Samuel & Martha, d. Dec. 20, 1771	1	201
Lewis, s. Daniel & Elizabeth, d. Oct. 27, 1772	1	201
Lewis, s. Jared & Hannah, b. Mar. 19, 1774	1	38
Lewis, s. Jeremiah, d. Oct. 5, 1788, ae about 3 y.	1	204
Lewis, m. Sally **BENNETT**, Mar. 9, 1795	1	100
Lewis Benedict, s. Justus, Jr. & Betsey, b. Apr. 11, 178[ ]	1	40
Lockwood, m. Jane C. **DIXON**, b. of Ridgefield, July 18, 1836, by Rev. Charles G. Selleck	1	182
Lucretia, d. Nathan & Sarah, b. Sept. 11, 17[ ]	1	8
Lucretia, m. James **SCOTT**, 2nd, Sept. 6, 1782	1	58
Lucretia, twin with Clara, [d. Timothy & Huldah], b. Dec. 9, 1795	1	75
Lùcretia, w. Roger, d. Mar. 9, 1801, ae 22 y.	1	210
Lucy, d. Jared & Hannah, b. Apr. 24, 1790	1	38
Lucy, d. [Lewis & Sally], b. July 14, 1797	1	100
Lucy, had infant d. [ ], d. Mar. 28, 1812, ae 5 d.	1	216
Lydia, d. Ezekiel & Lydia, b. Oct. 3, 1751	LR1	251
Lydia, d. Ezekiel & Lydia [**HOYT**], b. Oct. 8, 1751	1	20
Marah, d. Richard & Abigail, b. Apr. 20, 1747	LR1	240
Maria, d. David, 3rd & Dorcas, b. Dec. 14, 1791	1	62

BARBOUR COLLECTION

OLMSTED, OLMSTEAD, (cont.)

	Vol.	Page
Mariah, of Ridgefield, m. Alanson **MEAD**, of South Salem, Mar. 19, 1834, by Rev. Charles G. Selleck	1	179
Martha, [d. Ambros & Martha], b. Apr. 14, 1745	LR1	250
Martha, m. Michael **WARREN**, June 23, 1773	1	155
Martha, w. Samuel, d. July 29, 1784	1	203
Martha, w. Samuel, d. May 4, 1794, ae 53	1	207
Martha, wid., d. Aug. 4, 1814, in the 91st y. of her age	1	218
Martha, w. Nathan, d. May 19, 1816, ae 39	1	219
Mary, [d. Richard & Mary], b. Feb. 16, 1737/8	LR1	207
Mary, d. Richard & Mary, d. Aug. 3, 1746	LR1	215
Mary, [d. Ambros & Martha], b. Sept. 3, 1749	LR1	250
Mary, d. Ezekiel & Lydia, b. Sept. 17, 176[ ]	1	20
Mary, d. Justus, Jr. & Betty, b. June 29, 1778	1	40
Mary, d. Jan. 31, 1786, in the 94th y. of her age	1	204
Mary, w. Gould, d. June 17, 1808, ae 24	1	214
Matthew, s. Nathan* & Sarah*, b. Mar. 22, 1750 *(Stephen written) *(Hannah written)	1	3
Matthew, m. Sarah **WHITNEY**, Dec. 21, 1783	1	154
Matthew, his twin s. [ ], d. July 30, 1794	1	207
Matthew, d. Feb. 16, 1847, ae about 86 y.	1	239
Melissa, of Wilton, m. Elbert **OLMSTED**, of Ridgefield, [Oct.] 15, [1845], by Rev. James A. Hawley	1	198
Miles, his child d. Nov. 5, 1842, ae 3 y.	1	236
Millicent, d. Nathan & Millicent, b. Mar. 21, 1741/2	LR1	237
Millicent, w. Nathan, d. Sept. 3, 1751	LR1	216
Mellesent, m. Isaiah **KEELER**, Mar. 6, 1760	1	150
Millicent, d. David & Abigail, b. Aug. 9, 1772	1	28
Molly, d. Justus & Patience, b. Oct. 1, 1763	1	59
Molly, d. Daniel & Elizabeth, b. Dec. 26, 177[ ]	1	40
Molly, d. Justus, d. Sept. 6, 1775	1	203
Moses, d. Apr. [ ], 1798, ae 21 y.	1	209
Nancy, d. Hezekiah & Sarah, b. Mar. 29, 1774	1	40
Nathan, s. Daniel & Hannah, b. Mar. 7, [1714]	LR1	202
Nathan, m. Millecent **GOODRICH**, Dec. 4, 1740, by David Goodrich, J. P.	LR1	231
Nathan, s. Nathan & Millecent, b. May 8, 1744	LR1	237
Nathan, m. Sarah **SMITH**, Feb. 12, 1751/2	LR1	234
Nathan, s. Jared & Hannah, b. Apr. 1, 1776	1	38
Nathan, Jr., m. Martha **WATEROUS**, Apr. 25, 1797	1	159
Nathan, Dea., d. July 30, 1805, in the 89th y. of his age	1	212
Nathan, d. Dec. 6, 1833, ae 56 1/2 y.	1	230
Nathan, d. May 4, [1852], ae 68	1	242
Nathaniel, s. Stephen & Hannah, b. May 27, 1767	1	3
Nehemiah, s. Stephen & Hannah, b. Jan. 7, 1754	LR1	249
Orrin Lewis, s. [Lewis & Sally], b. Nov. 19, 1809	1	100
Pat, m. John **KEELER**, Jr., Dec. 6, 1775	1	153
Peter, s. Hezekiah & Sarah, b. July 27, 1775	1	40

	Vol.	Page
OLMSTED, OLMSTEAD, (cont.)		
Phebe, d. John & Phebe, b. Aug. 20, 1740	LR1	255
Phebe, [d. Ambros & Martha], b. Aug. 7, 1754	LR1	250
Phebe, d. Justus & Patience, b. July 21, 1769	1	59
Phebe, d. Samuel & Martha, b. Oct. 26, 1772	1	38
Phebe, d. Justus, d. Aug. 29, 1775	1	203
Phebe, d. Samuel & Martha, d. Sept. 9, 1796, in the 23rd y. of her age, at Wellstown, N. Y.	1	208
Phebe, d. Jan. 23, 1809, ae 53 y.	1	214
Philip, s. [Lewis & Sally], b. Nov. 11, 1795	1	100
Philip D., d. Dec. 31, 1816, in the 23rd y. of his age	1	220
Philip Dauchy, [s. Isaac & Eunice], b. Jan. 25, 1794	1	78
Philo, d. Jan. 15, 1824	1	224
Polly, d. Nathan & Sarah, b. Jan. 12, 17[ ]	1	8
Polly, d. Samuel & Martha, b. Dec. 7, 1769	1	38
Polly, d. Nathan & Sarah, b. Jan. 12, 1771	1	3
Polly, d. Jared & Hannah, b. May 3, 1786	1	38
Polly, m. Hezekiah **DeFOREST**, Apr. [ ], 1792	1	158
Polly, d. David & Abigail, b. Mar. 14, 1794	1	28
Polly, w. Peter, d. [Jan.] 28, 1847, ae 19	1	238
Priscilla, d. Nathan & Sarah, b. Mar. 1, 1764	1	3
Prudence, d. Nathan & Sarah, b. Nov. 26, 1756	LR1	255
Rachel, d. Nathan & Sarah, b. Oct. 31, 175[ ]	1	8
Rachel, m. Asa **SCRIBNER**, Jan. 10, 1779	1	155
Rachel, d. Jared & Hannah, b. Mar. 18, 1788	1	38
Rachel, b. Mar. 18, 1788; m. Lewis L. **NASH**, Feb. 18, 1809	1	112
Rachel A., of Ridgefield, m. Charles F. **CANFIELD**, of Bedford, West Chester Co., N. Y., Feb. 19, 1849, by Rev. Sylvester S. Strong	1	131
Rebeckah, d. Daniel & Elizabeth, b. Sept. 22, 1761	1	40
Rebeckah, m. Josiah **NORTHRUP**, Aug. 31, 1779	1	154
Richard, m. Mary **BETTS**, d. Samuell & Judeth, of Norwalk, Apr. 22, 1714	LR1	227
Richard, s. Richard & Mary, b. Sept. 15, 1717	LR1	201
Richard, m. Abigail **HOYT**, Jan. 13, 1740/1	LR1	232
Richard, Capt., d. Oct. 16, 1776	1	202
Roger, s. Daniel, Jr. & Elizabeth, b. Mar. 20, 1756	LR1	256
Roger, s. Daniel & Elizabeth, b. Mar. 20, 1756	1	40
Roger, s. Daniel & Joanna, b. May 18, 1776	1	35
Rosanna, d. [Lewis & Sally], b. Feb. 28, 1800	1	100
Ruhamah, d. Justus, Jr. & Bettey, b. Apr. 4, 178[ ]	1	40
Ruhamah, d. Justus, Jr., d. Dec. 4, 1782	1	203
Ruth, [d. Ambros & Martha], b. Aug. 5, 1751	LR1	250
Ruth, d. Mar. 16, 1807	1	213
Sally, d. Hezekiah & Sarah, b. Nov. 26, 1779	1	40
Sally, d. Samuel & Martha, b. July 10, 1781	1	38
Sally, d. Joseph & Susannah, b. Feb. 7, 1783	1	56
Sally, d. Jared & Hannah, b. May 21, 1784	1	38

OLMSTED, OLMSTEAD, (cont.)

	Vol.	Page
Samuel, Jr., m. Martha **WILSON**, Feb. 15, 17[ ]	1	150
Samuell, s. Daniell & Hannah, b. Mar. 27, 1715	LR1	199
Samuel, [s. Richard & Mary], b. June 1, 1734	LR1	207
Sam[ue]ll, m. Abiah **SMITH**, Apr. 15, 1737	LR1	230
Samuel, s. Justus & Patience, b. Feb. 8, 1767	1	59
Samuel, 3rd, m. Martha **ROCKWELL**, Feb. 24, 1767	1	150
Samuel, 3rd, m. Martha **ROCKWELL**, Feb. 24, 1767	1	153
Samuel, s. Samuel & Martha, b. Feb. 7, 1783	1	38
Samuel, 3rd, m. Sarah **MORRIS**, Oct. 23, 1784	1	153
Samuel, d. June 10, 1788, in the 74th y. of his age	1	204
Samuel, 2nd, d. Oct. 14, 1816, ae 70	1	219
Samuel, d. Nov. 23, 1820, ae 86 y.	1	222
Samuel Ketchum, s. Samuel & Martha, b. Feb. 10, 1776	1	31
Samuel S., m. Mary Ann **SMITH**, b. of Ridgefield, Oct. 31, 1832, by Rev. Charles J. Todd	1	177
Sarah, d. John & Joanna, b. June 7, 1744	LR1	255
Sarah, d. Nathan & Sarah, b. Apr. 11, 1754	LR1	255
Sarah, d. Ezekiel & Lydia, b. May 4, 176[ ]	1	20
Sarah, m. Abraham **NASH**, Jr., Nov. 17, 1762	1	155
Sarah, d. David & Elizabeth, b. Mar. 17, 1766	1	40
Sarah, w. Nathan, d. Jan. 10, 1781	1	202
Sarah, d. Samuel & Martha, b. Feb. 10, 1781	1	31
Sarah, d. [Lewis & Sally], b. June 28, 1814	1	100
Sarah, w. Matthew, d. May 22, 1821	1	222
Sarah, wid., d. Nov. 30, 1830, in the 73rd y. of her age, in New York	1	228
Sarah, m. Samuel M. **NORTHROP**, b. of Ridgefield, Oct. 3, 1841, by Rev. Warren Hoyt	1	191
Sarah, wid., d. May 18, 1847, ae 34 y.	1	239
Sarah Ingersoll, d. David & Abigail, b. July 19, 1774	1	28
Sarah J., m. Benj[ami]n **SANFORD**, Dec. 25, 1791	1	158
Seckey, d. Daniel & Joanna, b. Oct. 25, 1780	1	35
Seth, s. Samuel & Martha, b. Apr. 18, 1783	1	31
Smith, [s. Timothy & Huldah], b. Dec. 9, 1793	1	75
Stephen, s. Richard & Mary, b. Mar. 29, 1720	LR1	202
Stephen, s. John & Joanna, b. Oct. 5, 1745	LR1	255
Stephen, m. Hannah **NORTHRUP**, Aug. 23, 1747	LR1	233
Stephen, s. Stephen & Hannah, b. Mar. 8, 1748	LR1	241
Stephen, s. Daniel & Joanna, b. May 13, 1783	1	35
Stephen, his s. [ ], d. Nov. 12, 1820, ae 23 m.	1	222
Stephen, Jr., m. Eliza **MEAD**, b. of Ridgefield, Sept. 12, 1841, by Rev. Warner Hoyt	1	190
Thaddeus, s. Stephen & Hannah, b. Dec. 7, 1764	1	3
Thaddeus, s. Samuel & Martha, b. June 30, 1769	1	31
Thaddeus, m. Jane **JACKSON**, Dec. 18, 1791	1	158
Thaddeus, d. Sept. 30, 1837, ae 23 y.	1	234
Thirza, d. Dan[ie]ll, 2nd & Margaret, b. Apr. 3, 1772	1	34

	Vol.	Page
OLMSTED, OLMSTEAD, (cont.)		
Thomas, s. Richard & Mary, b. Oct. 24, 1722	LR1	205
Thomas, s. Justus & Patience, b. Sept. 20, 1755	1	59
Thomas, s. Justus & Patience, b. Dec. 20, 1755	LR1	198
Thomas, s. Justus & Patience, b. Dec. 20, 1756	LR1	255
Thomas, s. Justus, d. Oct. 16, 1775	1	203
Thomas, s. Samuel & Martha, b. Oct. 7, 1777	1	38
Timothy, s. Nathan & Sarah, b. May 27, 17[ ]	1	8
Timothy, m. Huldah **SANFORD**, Aug. 22, 1791	1	75
Timothy Sanford, [s. Timothy & Huldah], b. June 24, 1792	1	75
Walter, d. Nov. 19, 1834, ae 50	1	231
William, d. July 23, 1836, ae [ ]	1	232
William, see Billy **OLMSTED**	1	28
William Betts, s. [Lewis & Sally], b. Sept. 17, 1816	1	100
William M., m. Mary E. **OSBORN**, b. of Ridgefield, Feb. 18, 1829, by Samuel M. Phelps	1	169
OSBORN, OSBURN, OSBORNE, Aaron, s. David & Rachel, b. Sept. 29, 1735	LR1	221
Aaron, s. Aaron & Hannah, b. Jan. 17, 1776	1	9
Aaron, d. June 13, 1810	1	215
Abigail, [d. Richard & Sarah], b. July [ ], 1702	LR1	199
Abigail, d. Richard & Sarah, m. Timothy **KEELER**, May 19, 1720	LR1	227
Abigail, d. John & Patience, b. July 10, 1740	LR1	225
Abigail, d. Joseph & Mary, b. Mar. 1, 1740/1	LR1	225
Abigail, d. Daniel & Sarah, b. Oct. [ ], 1762	1	4
Abijah, s. Aaron & Hannah, b. Apr. 20, 1760	1	9
Abijah, s. Aaron & Hannah, b. Apr. 20, 1760	LR1	198
Asahel, s. Aaron & Hannah, b. Feb. [ ], 1774	1	9
Daniell, s. Richard & Sarah, b. Oct. 27, [1719]	LR1	203
Daniel, s. John & Patience, b. Dec. 25, 1742	LR1	236
Daniel, s. Daniel & Sarah, b. Nov. 1, 1748	1	4
David, [s. Richard & Sarah], b. Nov. [ ], 1700	LR1	199
David, s. David & Rachel, b. Sept. 25, 1729	LR1	211
David, his wid., d. Feb. 14, 1832, ae 94	1	229
Ebenezer, s. John & Patience, b. May 26, 1738	LR1	223
Elizabeth, d. David & Rachel, b. Sept. 1, 1731	LR1	211
Elizabeth, m. Adams **WHITLOCK**, Feb. 14, 1750	1	150
Ezekiel, m. Sarah **BENNET**, Nov. 16, 17[ ]	1	150
Ezekiel, s. Jonathan & Rebeckah, b. Oct. 16, 1733	LR1	220
Ezekiel, s. Jonathan & Rebeckah, b. July 17, 1748	LR1	198
Ezekiel, s. Ezekiel & Sarah, b. Mar. 9, 1773	1	27
Gamaliel, s. Jonathan & Rebeckah, b. Feb. 11, 1737/8	LR1	223
Gamaliel, s. Jonathan & Rebeckah, b. Aug. 16, 1751	LR1	198
Hannah, wid., d. July 10, 1811, in the 75th y. of her age	1	215
Hezekiah, [s. Richard & Sarah], b. Apr. 30, 1715	LR1	199
Hezekiah, s. Jeremiah & Rebeckah, b. Sept. 5, 1739	LR1	224
Hezekiah, m. Abigail **GOODRICH**, Apr. 13, 1759	LR1	232

242 BARBOUR COLLECTION

	Vol.	Page
OSBORN, OSBURN, OSBORNE, (cont.)		
James, s. David & Rachel, b. Sept. 17, 1733	LR1	221
James, s. John & Patience, b. Jan. 27, 1736/7	LR1	221
James, s. John & Patience, d. Jan. 28, 1736/7	LR1	215
James, s. Hezekiah & Abigail, b. Jan. 23, 1760	LR1	251
Jeremiah, s. Daniel & Sarah, b. Dec. 8, [ ]	1	4
Jeremiah, s. Richard & Sarah, b. Dec. 17, [1714]	LR1	202
Jeremiah, m. Rebeckah [ ], Jan. 11, 1738/9	LR1	230
Jeremiah, s. Jeremiah & Rebeckah, b. Mar. 3, 1740/1	LR1	226
Jeremiah, s. Jeremiah & Rebeckah, d. Mar. 7, 1744/5	LR1	216
Jeremiah, s. Jeremiah & Rebeckah, b. Apr. 30, 1745	LR1	239
Jeremiah, s. Aaron & Hannah, b. Aug. 2, 1757	LR1	198
Jeremiah, s. Aaron & Hannah, b. Aug. 2, 1757	LR1	244
John, [s. Richard & Sarah], b. May [ ], 1704	LR1	199
John, m. Patience **KELLNER**, Sept. 28, 1726	LR1	227
John & w. Patience, had child d. Feb. 14, 1728, before baptism	LR1	214
John, s. John & Patience, b. Nov. 24, 1728	LR1	209
John, s. John & Patience, d. Nov. 25, 1728	LR1	214
John & w. Patience, had child s. b. Oct. 12, 1729	LR1	214
John, s. John & Patience, b. Mar. 2, 1733	LR1	212
Jonah, s. [Jonathan & Rebeckah], b. Oct. 22, 1735	LR1	220
Jonah, m. Dorcas **RICKERSON**, Oct. 1, 1767	1	150
Jonathan, [s. Richard & Sarah], b. Nov. [ ], 1710	LR1	199
Jonathan, m. Rebecca [ ], Jan. 3, 1732/3	LR1	229
Jonathan, m. Abigail **DUNHAM**, May 3, 1764	1	150
Jonathan, s. Ezekiel & Sarah, b. Oct. 10, 1770	1	27
Jonathan, d. Mar. 19, 1790, in the 80th y. of his age	1	205
Joseph, [s. Richard & Sarah], b. Sept. [ ], 1706	LR1	199
Joseph, m. Mary **HYATT**, Apr. 18, 1728	LR1	228
Joseph, s. Joseph & Mary, b. Feb. 11, 1733	LR1	212
Joseph, s. Jonathan & Abigail, b. Feb. 27, 1767	1	20
Joseph, of Danbury, m. Ruamie **WHITLOCK**, May 3, 1789	1	158
Josiah, s. Joseph & Mary, b. Apr. 20, 1738	LR1	223
Josiah, s. Daniel & Sarah, b. Feb. 20, 1746	1	4
Josiah, s. Aaron & Hannah, b. Apr. 23, 1762	1	9
Josiah, m. Hannah **SCOTT**, Aug. 26, 1783	1	154
Katharine, m. Edwin **BENEDICT**, b. of Ridgefield, Oct. 13, 1833, by Rev. Charles G. Selleck	1	179
Knapp, of Wilton, m. Catharine **NASH**, of Ridgefield, July 1, 1829, by Samuell M. Phelps	1	171
Lot, s. David & Rachel, b. Apr. 23, 1744	LR1	241
Mary, d. John & Patience, b. June 5, 1735	LR1	220
Mary, d. Joseph & Mary, b. Feb. 6, 1735/6	LR1	220
Mary, d. Joseph & Mary, d. Mar. 15, 1740/1	LR1	215
Mary, d. Joseph & Mary, b. May 13, 1743	LR1	225
Mary E., m. William M. **OLMSTED**, b. of Ridgefield, Feb. 18, 1829, by Samuel M. Phelps	1	169
Moses, s. David & Rachel, b. Dec. 23, 1737	LR1	241

	Vol.	Page
OSBORN, OSBURN, OSBORNE, (cont.)		
Nancy, w. Azel, d. Jan. 15, 1822, ae 42	1	223
Nathan, s. Joseph & Mary, b. Dec. 3, 1728	LR1	209
Olive, d. Daniel & Sarah, b. June 4, 1759	1	4
Patience, d. John & Patience, b. Feb. 27, 1730/1	LR1	211
Patience, d. John & Patience, d. Apr. 27, 1741	LR1	215
Rachal, m. Lemuel **MOREHOUSE**, June 16, 1750	LR1	234
Rachel, d. Aaron & Hannah, b. July 20, 1771	1	9
Rachel, m. Josiah **BENNETT**, Mar. 8, 1789	1	157
Richard, s. David & Rachel, b. Aug. 4, 1727	LR1	209
Sam[ue]ll, [s. Richard & Sarah], b. Nov. [ ], 1708	LR1	199
Samuell, m. Sarah **SIMKINS**, Jan. 1, 1732/3, by Zachariah Mills, J. P.	LR1	229
Samuel, s. Jonathan & Abigail, b. Jan. 20, 1765	1	20
Sarah, 2nd, d. Daniel & Sarah, b. May [ ]	1	4
Sarah, [d. Richard & Sarah], b. Dec. 12, 1712	LR1	199
Sarah, w. Richard, d. Dec. 6, [1719]	LR1	213
Sarah, d. Joseph & Mary, b. Sept. 27, 1730	LR1	212
Sarah, d. Daniel & Sarah, b. Feb. 6, 175[ ]	1	4
Sarah, d. Daniel & Sarah, d. Oct. [ ], 1752	1	200
Uzziel, s. Joseph & Mary, b. May 29, 1746	LR1	240
William, s. Asel, d. Sept. 23, 1812, in the 3rd y. of his age	1	217
Zadoc, s. Aaron & Hannah, b. May 20, 1765	1	9
PADDOCK, Bethiah, m. Caleb **LOBDELL**, July [ ]	LR1	252
PALMER, Esther, m. John W. **MILLER**, b. of Ridgefield, Oct. 3, 1849, by Rev. Nathaniel Mead	1	132
Henry, m. Ruth **SHERWOOD**, Aug. 26, 1784	1	155
John, m. Abigail **MILLS**, b. of Ridgefield, Sept. 22, 1839, by Rev. T. Sparks	1	187
Mary Elizabeth, d. May 26, [1844], ae 21 y.	1	237
Samuel, had d. [ ], d. May 27, 1835	1	231
PARDEE, Rachel, m. Daniel **SMITH**, Dec. 8, 1774	1	95
Thomas, of Lewisboro, m. Hannah **MAIN**, of Ridgefield, Jan. 23, 1844, by Rev. A. S. Francis	1	194
PARISH, Ann E., of North Salem, N. Y., m. William **SMITH**, 3rd, of Ridgefield, July 9, 1838, by Rev. Thomas Sparks	1	186
Mary, m. Peter **BENEDICT**, Oct. 29, 1734	LR1	229
PARKER, William D., of York Town, N. Y., m. Emily **SHERWOOD**, of Ridgefield, Oct. 23, 1836, by Rev. Charles G. Selleck	1	183
PARKERTON, -----, Mrs., d. [Jan. 28, 1847], ae about 36	1	238
PARMAN, Mary Ann, wid., d. Apr. 5, 1806	1	212
PARMELEE, Noah D., of Somers West Chester Co., N. Y., m. Mary Ann **SMITH**, of Ridgefield, June 1, 1831, by Rev. Charles G. Selleck	1	174
[**PARRISH**], [see under **PARISH**]		
PARSONS, Jonathan, d. May 1, 1801	1	210
Martha, m. Thomas **McFARDEN**, Aug. 31, 1785	1	72

	Vol.	Page
PARSONS (cont.)		
Martha, m. Thomas **McFARTHUNG**, Aug. 31, 1785	1	155
-----, Mr. of Redding, d. Mar. 16, [1852], ae 88 y.	1	242
PARTRICK, Daniel, s. Theophilus & Hannah, b. June 1, 1806	1	101
Daniel, m. Elizabeth **KEELER**, b. of Ridgefield, Nov. 23, 1828, by Samuel M. Phelps	1	169
Edson, d. July [ ], 1848, ae 22	1	239
George, of Wilton, m. Fanny **JENNINGS**, of Ridgefield, Aug. 20, 1829, by Samuell M. Phelps	1	171
Hannah, m. Daniel K. **KEELER**, b. of Ridgefield, Oct. 29, 1827, by Samuel M. Phelps	1	168
Hannah, w. Theophilus, d. Feb. 22, 1829, ae 48	1	227
James, d. Nov. 30, 1822, in the 74th y. of his age	1	223
Stiles, his s. [ ], d. [Apr.] 28, 1842, ae 28 y.	1	236
Theophilus, d. Sept. 15, [1844], ae about 54 y.	1	237
William E., of Wilton, m. Julia A. **GODFREY**, of Ridgefield, Sept. 5, 1852, by Rev. Charles Stearns	1	138
PATTERSON, Betty, d. William & Anne, b. Sept. 26, 1761	1	7
Sarah, d. William & Anne, b. Jan. 5, 1760	1	7
William, m. Anne **LOBDELL**, Feb. 15, 1760	1	150
PAUDEL, Isaac, his child d. Sept. 26, 1846	1	238
PECK, [see also **PICK**], Matthew, his s. [ ], d. Dec. 4, 1793	1	206
Whitman, m. R. Maria **KEELER**, this day [Nov. 6, 1844], by James A. Hawley	1	195
PELHAM, Elisha, d. Apr. 22, 1833, ae 79	1	229
PENOYER, Lewis, of New Canaan, m. Mary **SAUNDERS**, of Ridgefield, Feb. 9, 1835, by Rev. Charles G. Selleck	1	180
PERKINS, Silas, m. Sally **JONES**, b. of Ridgefield, Nov. 29, 1829, by Rev. Oregin P. Holcomb	1	170
PERRY, Anna, d. Solomon & Priscilla, b. Apr. 16, 1758	LR1	247
Betsey, [d. David & Hannah], b. Apr. 16, 1788	1	71
David, m. Hannah **BROWN**, [ ]	1	71
David, s. Solomon & Priscilla, b. May 5, 1768	1	37
David, [s. David & Hannah], b. Oct. 4, 1782	1	71
David, Dr., d. May 21, 1822, ae [ ]	1	223
Esther, m. Augustus **PULLING**, July 17, 1770	1	153
Freeman, s. Solomon & Priscella, b. Oct. 22, 1753	LR1	247
Gilbert, s. Solomon & Priscilla, b. July 9, 1752	LR1	247
Hannah, w. David, b. Aug. 22, 1762	1	71
Hannah, w. Dr. David, d. Nov. 26, 1820, ae 68	1	222
John, [s. David & Hannah], b. May 26, 1786	1	71
John, s. Dr. [ ], d. May 28, 1814, ae 28	1	218
Landas, s. Solomon & Priscilla, b. July 22, 1762	1	37
Lemuel, s. Dr. N[ ], d. May 11, 1832	1	229
Lewis, his child d. June 9, 1841, ae 3 y.	1	236
Lewis C., s. Sturgis L., d. Nov. 17, [1851], ae 21 y.	1	241
Lucy, [d. David & Hannah], b. Dec. 28, 1791	1	71

	Vol.	Page
PERRY, (cont.)		
Lucy, d. Dr. David, d. Feb. 17, 1818, in the 27th y. of her age	1	220
Lucy, d. Feb. 19, 1841, ae 18 y.	1	236
Major Lewis, s. Solomon & Priscilla, b. Apr. 21, 1770	1	37
Mary, w. Dr. N[ ], d. June 4, 1832, ae 31	1	229
Nehemiah, [s. David & Hannah], b. Nov. 5, 1789	1	71
Pennellope, d. Solomon & Priscilla, b. Sept. 10, 1755	LR1	247
Ruth, m. Joseph **HOBART**, Jan. 3, 1748/9, by Jonathan Ingersoll, V. D. M.	LR1	234
Samuel, [s. David & Hannah], b. June 26, 1784	1	71
Samuel, his child d. Nov. 28, [1840], ae about 3 y.	1	235
Sophia, m. Cyrus B. **GRUMAN**, b. of Ridgefield, Apr. 22, 1838, by Rev. Joseph Fuller	1	186
Sturges L., had child d. July 30, 1825, ae 4 y.	1	225
Sturgis L., his d. [ ], d. Aug. 12, 1843, ae 16 y.	1	237
PETERS, Caroline, m. Henry **RILEY**, May 4, 1834, by Levi Brunson	1	179
PHELPS, Samuel Wallace, s. Rev. Samuel M. & Eliza, b. Sept. 10, 1820	1	108
Sarah Marianna, m. Joseph C. **LEWIS**, b. of Ridgefield, May 30, 1824, by Samuel M. Phelps	1	165
PHENIX, John, of New York, m. Catharine **SEYMOUR**, of Ridgefield, Oct. 28, 1829, by Samuell M. Phelps	1	171
PICK*, Julia Ann, of Redding, m. Wilson **BOUTON**, of Ridgefield, Sept. 14, 1845, by Rev. James A. Hawley *(**PECK**?)	1	197
PICKETT, PICKET, Edwin D., d. Apr. 15, 1832, in the 21st y. of his age	1	229
Henry, d. Sept. 22, 1831	1	228
Isabella, of Ridgefield, m. George W. **SLATER**, of Port Chester, N. Y., last eve [May 16, 1848], by Rev. James A. Hawley	1	129
Lewis, d. [, probably 1850], ae [ ]	1	240
Mary, m. Hyram J. **MEAD**, b. of Ridgefield, May 11, 1836, by Rev. Charles G. Selleck	1	182
PIGSLEY, Elenor C., m. Charles **SMITH**, Jr., b. of Ridgefield, Oct. 11, 1846, by Charles Stearns. Int. Pub.	1	199
PIKE, Elizabeth, m. Richard B. **SMITH**, b. of Ridgefield, July 8, 1838, by Rev. Joseph Fuller	1	186
Joel T., d. May 30, 1831, ae 29 y.	1	228
Margaret, m. Hiram L. **SEYMOUR**, b. of Ridgefield, Dec. 26, 1830, by Samuel M. Phelps	1	175
William, his wid. [ ], d. Sept. 15, 1834, ae 72 y.	1	231
PINE, Abraham, of Ridgefield, m. Jane **GOULD**, of Redding, Mar. 30, 1831, by Levi Brunson	1	173
PLATT, Bradley, m. Esther Ann **SELLECK**, Sept. 22, 1833, by Nathan Selleck	1	178
Bradley, his w. [ ], d. May 3, 1840, ae about 24 y.	1	235
David, s. David & Rachel, b. Nov. 5, 1771	1	2

	Vol.	Page
PLATT, (cont.)		
David, d. Sept. 2, 1776	1	202
David, d. Sept. 19, 1776	1	202
Harriet, of Ridgefield, m. Charles **ALLEN**, of Georgetown, May 8, 1848, by Rev. Sylvester S. Strong	1	130
Henry Burr, of Redding, m. Ann **HOWLAND**, of Ridgefield, Dec. 18, 1850, by Nathaniel Mead, J. P.	1	135
Huldah, m. Ezra **BATES**, Mar. 31, 1785	1	156
Isaac, s. Jonas, b. Apr. 13, 1760	1	7
John, d. Sept. 1, 1775	1	202
Mary, w. Obediah, d. Nov. 16, 1771	1	201
Nathan, d. Sept. 23, 1776	1	202
Obadiah, s. Jonas, b. May 17, 1758	1	7
Philip, his wid., d. July 2, 1847, ae over 80 y.	1	239
Sarah, d. David & Rachel, b. Mar. 14, 176[ ]	1	2
Sarah, d. Sept. 15, 1776	1	202
Sarah, m. Joel **STURGIS**, Feb. 20, 1783	1	153
Sarah, m. Noah **RUSCO**, Apr. 27, 1788	1	156
Sarah, wid., d. Aug. 8, [1846], ae 82 y. 10 m. 12 d.	1	238
William, m. Sarah **BUTTERFIELD**, Apr. 16, 1838, by Nathan Burton	1	185
POMERY, Elizabeth, m. Matthew **BENEDICT**, Nov. [ ]	LR1	252
PORTER, Horace, s. wid. Olive, b. Apr. 9, 1791	1	80
Joshua, d. Nov. 8, 1793	1	206
Mary, b. June 14, 1773; m. Caleb **ABBOTT**, Dec. 5, 1793	1	97
Olive, wid. had s. Horace, b. Apr. 9, 1791	1	80
Zachariah, of Danbury, m. Sarah **FOLLIET**, of Ridgefield, Feb. 11, 1829, by Samuel M. Phelps	1	169
POWEL, Margaret, m. Andrew **BURTIS**, of New Canaan, Mar. 3, [1847], by Rev. Charles Stearnes	1	127
PRINDLE, Joseph, m. Sarah E. **KEELER**, Oct. 17, 1838, by Nathan Burton, P. T.	1	186
PRUDY, Erie, of North Salem, West Chester Co., N. Y., m. Hester Ann **GILBERT**, of Ridgefield, Feb. 24, 1839, by Rev. Thomas Sparks	1	187
PUGGSLEY, Joseph F., of Ridgefield, m. Margaret M. **WORDEN**, of Rye, N. Y., Feb. 16, 1845, by Rev. A. S. Francis	1	196
PULLEN, PULLING, Abel, m. Sarah **WHITLOCK**, Dec. 3, 1783	1	153
Abel, s. Abraham & Esther, b. May 13, 1790	1	48
Abel, m. Polly **DAN**, b. of Ridgefield, Mar. 9, 1845, by Rev. A. S. Francis	1	197
Abraham, m. Susanna **WOOD**, Apr. 7, 1779	1	156
Abraham, d. July 4, 1787, ae 84 y.	1	204
Abraham, m. Esther **SEELEY**, Oct. 11, 1787	1	157
Abraham, m. Esther **SILAH**, [**SEELEY**], Oct. 12, 1787	1	156
Abraham, s. Augustus & Esther, b. Dec. 3, 1789	1	55
Abraham, m. Mercy **STEVENS**, Jan. 17, 1793	1	158
Abraham, s. Abraham & Mercy, b. Sept. 24, 1795	1	48

	Vol.	Page
PULLEN, PULLING, (cont.)		
Abraham J., of Danbury, m. Eliza **SMITH**, of Ridgefield, Jan. 1, 1840, by Rev. T. Sparks	1	187
Allethere, d. Augustus & Esther, b. Nov. 7, 1779	1	55
Ammon, s. William & Jane, b. July 11, 1786	1	62
Antoinette, of Ridgefield, m. Benjamin **STEBBINS**, of Brookfield, Dec. 20, 1848, by Rev. Sylvester S. Strong	1	130
Augustus, m. Esther **PERRY**, July 17, 1770	1	153
Beers, s. Abraham & Abigail, b. Nov. 7, 1763	1	55
Beers, his w. [ ], d. June 3, 1818	1	221
Betsey, d. Elias, d. July 1, [probably 1838], ae 27	1	234
Clamenchy, d. Augustus & Esther, b. June 28, 1785	1	55
David, s. Abraham, 2nd & Susannah, b. Aug. 26, 1779	1	48
David, 2nd, m. Sarah Caroline **BARLOW**, of Ridgefield, Nov. 8, 1829, by Rev. Origen P. Holcomb	1	170
Elias, s. Abraaham & Susannah, b. Sept. 2, 1781	1	48
Elias, his w. [ ], d. July 17, 1840, ae about 34 y.	1	235
Elias, d. Nov. 5, 1840, ae about 60 y.	1	235
Ellice Perry, d. Augustus & Esther, b. Feb. 17, 1782	1	55
Esther, d. Augustus & Esther, b. Apr. 23, 1777	1	55
Esther, w. Abraham, d. Nov. 26, 1791	1	206
Josiah, s. Abraham & Esther, b. July 1, 1788	1	48
Josiah, [s. Abraham & Esther (**HYATT** nee **SEELEY**), b. July 1, 1788	1	63
Lois, d. Augustus & Esther, b. Dec. 5, 1770	1	55
Lucretia, of Ridgefield, m. David **DIKEMAN**, of Danbury, Feb. 3, 1847, by Rev. Charles Stearnes	1	127
Maria, d. Beers & Rachel, b. May 24, 1794	1	86
Mary, m. Samuel **HORTON**, Dec. 4, 1830, by Nathan Burton	1	173
Matthew, s. Abraham & Mercy, b. Sept. 7, 1801	1	48
Matthew B., d. Aug. 26, 1822, in the 22nd y. of his age	1	223
Mercy, d. Abraham & Mercy, b. Mar. 27, 179[ ]	1	48
Mercy, w. Abraham, d. Jan. 13, 1805	1	212
Molly, d. Beers & Rachel, b. Sept. 1, 1792	1	86
Polly, d. Augustus & Esther, b. Oct. 3, 1772	1	55
Sam[ue]l, s. Abraham & Mercy, b. May 17, 1794	1	48
Sarah, d. Abraham & Abigail, b. July 7, 1766	1	55
Sarah, Mrs., m. James **LEASON**, b. of Ridgefield, Apr. 27, 1847, by Levi Bronson	1	127
Stephen Bennet, s. Augustus & Esther, b. May 27, 1787	1	55
Susanna, [d. Abraham & Susannah (**SMITH**)], b. Mar. 28, 1786	1	63
Susannah, w. Abraham, d. Aug. 4, 1786	1	204
Susannah, d. Abraham, d. Aug. 29, 1786	1	204
William, s. Abraham & Susannah, b. Nov. 21, 1783	1	48
William, m. Jane **RUSCO**, Nov. 24, 1785	1	156
Zalmond, s. Augustus & Esther, b. Nov. 17, 1774	1	55

PURDY, Augustus, of North Salem, m. Nancy **MILLS**, of

	Vol.	Page
PURDY, (cont.)		
Ridgefield, Jan. 26, 1830, by Levi Brunson	1	171
QUINTARD, Walter C., m. Sarah C. **SMITH**, b. of Ridgefield, Mar. 19, 1837, by Rev. J. Lyman Clark	1	183
RANDALL, Richard, m. Caroline **GILBERT**, b. of Ridgefield, May 5, 1825, by Samuell M. Phelps	1	165
Richard, d. Nov. 16, 1838, ae 48 y.	1	234
William E., of New York City, m. Laura B. **GILBERT**, of Ridgefield, June 22, 1836, by Rev. John B. Beach	1	185
RANSOM, William K., d. Jan. 14, 1830, ae 11 y.	1	227
RAWLEIGH, Philip, of Bridgetown, in Suffolk Co., Great Britain, d. Mar. 26, 1788, ae 38 y., at the house of James Smith (shoemaker)	1	204
RAYGON, Thomas, s. John & Patience, b. Sept. 22, 1756	LR1	255
RAYMOND, Josiah, m. Hannah **INGERSOLL**, Mar. 4, 1780	1	154
Josiah, s. Josiah & Hannah, b. Oct. 23, 1781	1	62
Polly, d. Josiah & Hannah, b. Feb. 7, 1784	1	62
Polly, d. Aug. 14, 1793	1	206
Polly, d. Mar. 22, 1847, ae 49 y.	1	239
Rebeckah, m. Jonah **KEELER**, Dec. 30, 1794	1	83
Sands, m. Esther **OLMSTED**, Mar. 8, 1786	1	156
READ, REED, Aaron, m. Cynthia **SHERWOOD**, June 6, 1841, by Rev. Warner Hoyt	1	190
Elias, d. Oct. 10, 1794, ae 38 y.	1	207
Phebe L., of West Stockbridge, m. Benjamin **GILBERT**, of Ridgefield, [Feb. 4, 1852], by Rev. Ira Abbott	1	137
REMINGTON, Anson, [s. Stephen & Jane], b. May 8, 1786	1	71
Benjamin, [s. Stephen & Jane], b. June 8, 1776	1	71
Benjamin, d. Mar. 10, 1818, in the 42nd y. of his age	1	220
Josiah, [s. Stephen & Jane], b. May 3, 1768	1	71
Stephen, m. Jane **HINE**, Oct. 29, 1767	1	71
Stephen, d. Mar. 1, 1812	1	216
RESSEGUIE, Eunice, wid. James, d. Dec. 13, 1833, ae 83	1	230
REYNOLDS, Lewis, m. Olive **ST. JOHN**, Dec. 10, 1823, by George Benedict	1	162
Mary, m. Joseph **LOBDELL**, Jr., Aug. 9, 1725	LR1	227
RICHARDS, RICHARD, Ambe, s. John & Abigail, b. Sept. 25, 1772	1	26
Isaiah, s. Josiah & Sarah, b. July 22, 1762	1	30
Jara, s. John & Abigail, b. Mar. 12, 1771	1	26
Jeremiah, his infant d. [ ], d. Feb. 14, 1793	1	206
John, s. John & Abigail, b. Jan. 29, 1769	1	26
John, m. Abigail **OLMSTED**, Feb. 5, 176[ ]	1	150
Nathaniel, d. Aug. 27, 1808	1	214
Sam, s. John & Abigail, b. Nov. 18, 1774	1	26
Sarah, d. John & Abigail, b. Apr. 18, 1767	1	26
RICKERSON, [see also **NICKERSON**], Dorcas, m. Jonah **OSBORN**, Oct. 1, 1767	1	150

	Vol.	Page
RIDER, James, his w. [ ], d. [June] 29, [1844], ae about 44 y.	1	237
James, m. Hannah **GREGORY**, this eve [Jan. 31, 1847], by Rev. James Hawley	1	127
Sarah, w. William H., d. Mar. 6, 1829	1	227
RIGGS, Daniel, m. Susannah **LOBDELL**, Sept. 9, 1784	1	155
Daniel, d. June 6, 1793	1	206
Esther, m. Abraham **ROCKWELL**, Nov. 29, 1769	1	151
Esther, d. Joseph & Margaret, b. June 18, 1784	1	57
Isaac, d. Feb. 4, 1837, ae 48	1	233
Jacob, d. Feb. 11, 1847, ae 20 y.	1	239
Prewe, m. Samuel **NORTHRUP**, Nov. 29, 1769	1	151
Susan, d. Aug. 5, 1841, ae 83 y.	1	236
RILEY, Henry, m. Caroline **PETERS**, May 4, 1834, by Levi Brunson	1	179
RITCH*, [see also **FINCH**], Nelson, d. [June] 8, [1847], ae about 17 y. ***(FINCH)**	1	239
ROBERTS, Caleb, d. June 8, 1834, ae 56 y.	1	230
Hiram, m. Sarah Ann **GRAY**, b. of Ridgefield, Feb. 18, 1830, by Samuell M. Phelps	1	172
Hiram, d. June 12, 1831, ae 24 y.	1	228
Levi, d. June [ ], 1841, ae [ ]	1	236
Rebecca, m. John **NORTHRUP**, s. William, of Milford, Aug. 14, 1728, by Capt. Gunn	LR1	228
ROCKWELL, Abel, m. Bettey **ROCKWELL**, Nov. 27, 1799	1	159
Abiah, m. James **NORTHRUP**, Jan. 26, 1774	1	153
Abigail, wid. Jonathan, d. July 8, 1734	LR1	215
Abigail, d. Jonathan & Esther, b. Feb. 3, 1734/5	LR1	223
Abigail, d. David & Elizabeth, b. Jan. 4, 1740/1	LR1	236
Abigail, m. Joseph **DOOLITTLE**, Aug. 10, 1757	1	150
Abigail, d. James & Abigail, b. June 29, 1789	1	46
Abigail, w. Ebenezer, d. Mar. 1, 1813, ae 70	1	217
Abigail, wid., d. Jan. 6, 1821, in the 72nd y. of her age	1	222
Abigail, of Ridgefield, m. Lewis **SMITH**, of Brookfield, Jan. 2, 1842, by Nathan Burton	1	191
Abijah, s. David & Elizabeth, b. July 1, 1751	LR1	246
Abijah, m. Lydia **BURCHARD**, Sept. 30, 1773	1	153
Abner, s. David & Elizabeth, b. Jan. 18, 1746/7	LR1	240
Abraham, s. John & Elizabeth, b. Oct. 5, 1749	LR1	241
Abraham, m. Esther **RIGGS**, Nov. 29, 1769	1	151
Amos, s. [Reuben & Cumphey], b. Dec. 30, 1796	1	88
Anna, d. James & Abigail, b. Mar. 21, 1774	1	46
Anna, m. Jacob **NASH**, Feb. 7, 1794	1	159
Arza, s. [Reuben & Cumphey], b. Mar. 17, 1799	1	88
Benjamin, [s. Jonah & Abigail], b. July 6, 1704	LR1	200
Benjamin, m. Rebecca **WILLSON**, Apr. 15, 1731	LR1	228
Benjamin, s. Benjamin & Rebecca, b. Aug. 13, 1733	LR1	220
Betsey, d. Thaddeus & Mehitable, b. Oct. 15, 1784	1	29

250   BARBOUR COLLECTION

	Vol.	Page
ROCKWELL, (cont.)		
Betsey, d. Thomas & Deborah, b. Sept. 12, 1795	1	98
Betty, d. Daniel & Abigail, b. Nov. 11, 1774	1	15
Bettey, m. Abel **ROCKWELL,** Nov. 27, 1799	1	159
Caleb, s. Daniel & Abigail, b. Oct. 13, 1765	1	15
Charles G., his d. [ ], d. June 5, [1847], ae 11 y.	1	239
Cloe, d. Daniel & Abigail, b. Apr. 13, 1762	LR1	254
Chloe, d. Dan[ie]ll & Abigail, d. May 19, 1775	1	201
Chloe, d. Silas & Hannah, b. Apr. 2, 1784	1	48
Chloe, twin with Coleman, d. Thomas & Deborah, b. Aug. 9, 1799	1	98
Clara, d. [Reuben & Cumphey], b. Oct. 8, 1795	1	88
Clarissa, d. Thaddeus & Mehitable, b. Aug. 16, 1779	1	29
Clarissa, w. Jonathan, d. Apr. 11, 1835, ae 34	1	231
Coleman, twin with Chloe, s. Thomas & Deborah, b. Aug. 9, 1799	1	98
Cynthia, d. Thaddeus & Mehitable, b. Aug. 20, 1776	1	29
Cynthia, d. Thaddeus, d. Mar. 15, 1781	1	202
Cynthia, 2nd, d. Thaddeus & Mehitable, b. July 10, 1781	1	29
Daniel, s. John & Elizabeth, b. Feb. 27, 1735/6	LR1	220
Daniel, m. Abigail **SMITH,** Dec. 18, 1759, by Jonathan Ingersoll, V. D. M.	LR1	252
Daniel & w. Abigail, had s. [ ], b. Aug. 30, 1760	LR1	251
Daniel, s. Daniel & Abigaill, b. Jan. 19, 1764	1	15
Daniel & w. Abigail, had s. [ ], b. Dec. 26, 1769; d. Feb 7, 1770, unbaptized	1	15
Daniel, d. June 13, 1795, in the 60th y. of his age	1	208
David, [s. Jonah & Abigail], b. Oct. 8, 1708	LR1	200
David, m. Elizabeth **HYATT,** d. Thomas, Aug. 29, 1731	LR1	228
David, s. David & Elizabeth, b. Jan. 30, 1734	LR1	218-9
David, Jr., m. Mary **ATHERTON,** Nov. 2, 1760	LR1	234
David, d. May 30, 1788, in the 80th y. of his age	1	204
Deborah, d. Abijah & Lydia, b. [ ] 7, 1775	1	51
Deborah, m. Joel **BOWTON,** [ ], 1795	1	159
Dorcas, d. Thomas & Ruth, b. Feb. 12, 1751/2	LR1	253
Dorcas, d. Thomas & Ruth, d. Mar. 17, 1759	LR1	217
Dorcas, d. James & Abigail, b. Apr. 19, 1770	1	46
Dorcas, m. Nathan **STEBBINS,** May 26, 1791	1	73
Ebenezer, s. Jonathan & Esther, b. Sept. 3, 1742	LR1	237
Ebenezer, m. Abigail **WORDEN,** alias **SMITH,** Nov. 5, 1777	1	152
Ebenezer, d. Dec. 4, 1819	1	221
Ebenezer, d. Dec. 5, 1819	1	222
Edwin, m. Rache[l] **BOUGHTON,** Sept. 14, 1829, by Nathan Burton	1	170
Eleanor, d. John & Elizabeth, b. July 13, 1752	LR1	241
Elenor, m. Nehemiah **KEELER,** June 15, 1772	1	152
Eli, m. Adelia Ann **SMITH,** Dec. 28, 1828, by Nathan Burton	1	169
Eli, m. Sarah Ann **McNIEL,** Sept. 13, 1840, by		

	Vol.	Page
ROCKWELL, (cont.)		
Nathan Burton, P. T.	1	189
Elijah, s. John & Elizabeth, b. Mar. 30, 1745	LR1	240
Elijah, m. Eunice **GRAY**, Nov. 18, 176[ ]	1	150
Eliza, m. John **DREW**, Oct. 31, 1837, by Nathan Burton	1	184
Elizabeth, d. John & Elizabeth, b. July 25, 1732	LR1	212
Elizabeth, d. Jonathan & Esther, b. Oct. 15, 1747	LR1	241
Elizabeth, w. David, d. Feb. 13, 1758	LR1	217
Enos, s. David, Jr. & Mary, b. Oct. 16, 17[ ]	1	4
Esther, d. Jonathan & Esther, b. Dec. 10, 1740	LR1	225
Esther, Mrs., d. May 20, 1796, ae 83	1	208
Eunice, w. Elijah, d. June 2, 1769	1	200
Eunice, d. Silas & Hannah, b. Apr. 7, 1786	1	48
George, m. Sarah M. **LYNES**, Oct. 16, 1826, by Nathan Burton	1	166
George B., m. Sally **FORRESTER**, Sept. 30, 1832, by Nathan Burton	1	176
Gould, s. James & Abigail, b. Dec. 18, 1778	1	46
Gould, m. Polly **DAUCHY**, Mar. 14, 1807	1	104
Gould, [s. Gould & Polly], b. Mar. 6, 1808	1	104
Hannah, m. Ezekiel **WILSON**, Sept. 3, 17[ ], by Jonathan Ingersoll, V. D. M.	LR1	252
Hannah, d. Thomas & Ruth, b. Feb. 24, 1735/6	LR1	223
Hannah, d. David & Elizabeth, b. Aug. 11, 1738	LR1	223
Hannah, d. Jonathan, Jr. & Hannah, b. Oct. 6, 176[ ]	LR1	245
Hannah, m. Isaac **SMITH**, Jr., Dec. 22, 1763	1	150
Hannah, d. Josiah & Mary, b. June 9, 1768	1	23
Harvey Smith, s. Thomas H., d. Feb. 29, 1804	1	211
Henry, d. Mar. 8, 1817	1	220
Isaac, s. David, Jr. & Mary, b. Jan. 6, 17[ ]	1	4
Jabez, d. July 24, 1757	LR1	217
Jabez, s. Josiah & Mary, b. Oct. 8, 1761	1	23
Jabez, s. Josiah & Mary, b. Oct. 8, 1761	LR1	255
James, s. Thomas & Ruth, b. June 9, 1750	LR1	241
James, s. John & Hannah, b. Apr. 12, 1758	LR1	253
James, m. Abigail **HAWLEY**, Oct. 17, 176[ ]	1	150
James, d. Nov. 25, 1808	1	214
James S., m. Polly **BRUSH**, Nov. 2, 1831, by Nathan Burton	1	174
Jane, d. Benjamin & Rebecca, b. Sept. 13, 1735	LR1	220
Jared, s. Josiah & Mary, b. Mar. 7, 1773	1	23
Jeremiah, s. Benjamin & Rebeckah, b. Nov. 12, 1746	LR1	224
Jeremiah, s. John, Jr. & Hannah, b. July 19, 1756	LR1	246
Jeremiah, s. John & Hannah, b. July 19, 1756	LR1	253
Joel L., m. Ann Eliza **LOUNSBURY**, b. of Ridgefield, May 7, 1850, by Rev. Nathaniel Mead	1	133
John, [s. Jonah & Abigail], b. Apr. [ ], 1706	LR1	200
John, m. Elizabeth **KEELER**, Sept. 3, 1731	LR1	228
John, s. John & Elizabeth, b. May 12, 1734	LR1	218-9

ROCKWELL, (cont.)

	Vol.	Page
John, Jr., m. Hannah **SCOTT**, Apr. 16, 1754	LR1	234
John, s. John, Jr. & Hannah, b. Apr. 7, 1755	LR1	246
John, s. John & Hannah, b. Apr. 7, 1755	LR1	253
John, Ens., m. Esther **HOLLEBERT**, Nov. 22, 1769	1	151
John, Ens., d. July 4, 1773	1	201
John J., m. Sally **BENEDICT**, b. of Ridgefield, Oct. 28, 1823, by Nathan Burton	1	162
John Wesley, s. Thomas H., d. Sept. 22, 1824, in the 2nd y. of his age	1	224
Jonathan, [s. Jonah & Abigail], b. Mar. 31, 1711	LR1	200
Jonathan, d. June 19, 1731	LR1	214
Jonathan, m. Esther [ ], Oct. [ ], 1733	LR1	230
Jonathan, s. Jonathan & Esther, b. Jan. 10, 1738/9	LR1	223
Jonathan & w. Esther had s. [ ], b. Dec. 13, 1743	LR1	241
Jonathan, Jr., m. Hannah **BENNETT**, Jan. 1, 1760	LR1	232
Jonathan, d. Sept. 3, 1784	1	203
Joseph, s. David, Jr. & Mary, b. Oct. [ ]	1	4
Josiah, s. Jabez & Keziah, b. July 11, 1737	LR1	222
Josiah, m. Mary **SCOTT**, Sept. 21, 1759	LR1	232
Josiah, s. Josiah & Mary, b. Aug. 28, 1765	1	23
Josiah, m. Mary **SCOTT**, Apr. (?) 21, [ ]	LR1	252
Lewis, s. Silas & Hannah, b. June 17, 1782	1	48
Lucinda, d. James & Abigail, b. Apr. 21, 1785	1	46
Lucy, d. Abraham & Esther, b. May 6, 1783	1	37
Marinda, m. George B. **SEARS**, Sept. 15, 1829, by Nathan Burton	1	170
Martha, d. [Thomas & Ruth], b. Feb. 25, 1742/3	LR1	239
Martha, m. Samuel **OLMSTED**, 3rd, Feb. 24, 1767	1	150
Martha, m. Samuel **OLMSTED**, 3rd, Feb. 24, 1767	1	153
Martin, s. Daniel & Abigail, b. Aug. 27, 1780	1	15
Mary, d. Jabez & Keziah, b. Aug. 23, 1733	LR1	218-9
Mary, d. Jabez & Keziah, d. Aug. 16, 1736	LR1	215
Mary, d. Jonathan & Esther, b. Mar. 9, 1736/7	LR1	223
Mary Jane, of Ridgefield, m. Thomas B. **WARRING**, of North Salem, N. Y., Jan. 28, 1844, by Rev. Shaller J. Hillyer	1	195
Mehetable, d. John & Elizabeth, b. Apr. 11, 1738	LR1	223
Mehetable, m. Thomas **NORTHRUP**, Jan. 1, 1760	LR1	232
Millicent, d. Josiah & Mary, b. Aug. 19, 1763	1	23
Millicent, d. James & Abigail, b. Apr. 25, 1792	1	46
Molly, d. Josiah & Mary, b. July 27, 1759	LR1	255
Nathan, s. Benjamin & Rebeckah, b. Nov. 22, 1737	LR1	223
Obil, s. Abijah & Lydia, b. Dec. 21, 1776; d. [ ], 1871	1	51
Phebe, d. Thomas & Ruth, b. Oct. 14, 1739	LR1	224
Phebe, d. Josiah & Mary, b. Aug. 6, 1770	1	23
Phebe Munrow, of Ridgefield, m. Moses **HILL**, of Winthrop Kennebeck Co., Me., May 25, 1831, by Rev. Hawley Sanford	1	173

	Vol.	Page
ROCKWELL, (cont.)		
Polly, d. James & Abigail, b. Feb. 25, 1772	1	46
Polly, m. John **STOWE**, July [ ], 1792	1	76
Polly, m. John **HOWE***, July [ ], 1792 *(**STOWE**?)	1	158
Polly, d. James & Abigail, b. Dec. 5, 1794	1	46
Polly, d. James, d. Aug. 1, 1798, ae 4 y.	1	209
Polly, m. Daniel **BENEDICT**, Feb. 17, 1839, by Nathan Burton, P. T.	1	187
Rachel, d. John & Hannah, b. [ ], 1762	1	17
Rachel, d. John & Elizabeth, b. Apr. 9, 1840 [probably 1740]	LR1	224
Rebecca, d. Jabez & Keziah, b. Mar. 8, 1735	LR1	218-9
Rebeckah, d. Jabez & Keziah, d. Oct. 8, 1736	LR1	215
Rebeckah, d. David & Elizabeth, b. Mar. 29, 1743	LR1	236
Rebeckah, m. Curtis **MARCHANT**, Oct. 1, 1828, by Nathan Burton	1	168
Reuben, m. Cumphey **GREGORY**, Feb. 1, 1795	1	88
Reuben, s. Ebenezer & Abigail, b. Oct. 11, [ ]	1	34
Reuben, s. David, Jr. & Mary, b. Nov. 6, 17[ ]	1	4
Runa, s. Abraham & Esther, b. Feb. 11, 1773	1	37
Ruth, m. Josiah **STEBBINS**, Feb. [ ]	LR1	252
Ruth, [twin with Sarah], d. Tho[ma]s & Ruth, b. Mar. 1, 1733	LR1	218-9
Ruth, d. Thomas & Ruth, d. Oct. 12, 1736	LR1	215
Ruth, d. Thomas & Ruth, b. Nov. 30, 1737	LR1	223
Ruth, d. Dan[ie]ll & Abigail, b. Apr. 6, 1767	1	15
Ruth, wid., d. June 22, 1807, in the 96th y. of her age, at Salem	1	213
Samuel, s. John & Hannah, b. Oct. 28, 1764	1	17
Samuel D., m. Oville J. **SHERMAN**, Sept. 9, 1832, by Nathan Burton	1	176
Sarah, m. Joseph **HOBART**, May 29, 1723	LR1	227
Sarah, [twin with Ruth], d. Tho[ma]s & Ruth, b. Mar. 1, 1733	LR1	218-9
Sarah, d. John & Elizabeth, b. July 24, 1747	LR1	241
Sarah, m. Thomas **SEAMORE**, Feb. 17, 175[ ]	LR1	234
Sarah, d. Thaddeus & Mehitable, b. Oct. 5, 1772	1	29
Sarah, d. Abijah & Lydia, b. Aug. 1, 1780	1	51
Sarah, d. William & Sarah, b. Dec. 29, 1785	1	60
Sarah, d. Isaac, d. May [ ], 1793	1	206
Seymore, s. Daniel & Abigail, b. Nov. 7, 1777	1	15
Seymour, s. Daniel & Abigail, d. Aug. 25, 1778	1	202
Silas, s. John & Elizabeth, b. Sept. 25, 1742	LR1	237
Silas, s. John & Elizabeth, d. Nov. 20, 1760	LR1	217
Silas, m. Hannah **OLMSTED**, d. Silas, of Norwalk, Dec. 20, 1781	1	156
Stephen, s. Benjamin & Rebeckah, b. Jan. 14, 1739/40	LR1	224
Thaddeus, s. Thomas & Ruth, b. Nov. 23, 1753	LR1	253
Thaddeus, m. Mehetable **SMITH**, Aug. 26, 1770	1	155
Thaddeus, s. Thaddeus & Mehitable, b. Feb. 20, 1771	1	29
Thaddeus, 2nd, d. Oct. 18, 1794, ae 23	1	207

254 BARBOUR COLLECTION

	Vol.	Page
ROCKWELL, (cont.)		
Thankfull, d. Thomas & Ruth, b. May 12, 1744	LR1	239
Thomas, m. Ruth **BENEDICT**, May 18, 1732	LR1	230
Thomas, s. David & Elizabeth, b. May 23, 1745	LR1	239
Thomas, s. [Thomas & Ruth], b. Jan. 16, 1745/6	LR1	239
Thomas, s. Thaddeus & Mehitable, b. Nov. 23, 1774	1	29
Thomas, d. Nov. 4, 1789, in the 87th y. of his age	1	205
Thomas, m. Deborah **TOWNSEND**, July 20, 1795	1	98
Thomas B., m. Caroline **HYATT**, b.of Ridgefield, Dec. 30, 1829, by Rev. E. Washburn	1	170
Thomas H., m. Polly **SMITH**, July 31, 1800	1	159
Thomas Hawley, s. James & Abigail, b. May 21, 1776	1	46
Timothy, s. John & Hannah, b. Dec. 20, 1760	LR1	253
William, s. Ebenezer & Abigail, b. Sept. 20, 1780	1	34
William, s. James & Abigail, b. Feb. 5, 1782	1	46
William, m. Sarah **WORDEN**, June 16, 1785	1	155
William, d. Aug. 21, 1831, ae 75 y. 4 m.	1	228
Zerah, s. Abijah & Lydia, b. Aug. 1, 1786	1	51
-----, Mrs., d. Mar. 9, 1844, ae about 80	1	237
ROCKWOOD, Elizabeth, d. David & Elizabeth, b. Jan. 4, 1731/2	LR1	212
ROSCO, RUSCO, Allen, of South Salem, N. Y., m. Anne **WHITE**, of Ridgefield, Jan. 6, 1836, by Rev. Charles G. Selleck	1	182
Jane, m. William **PULLING**, Nov. 24, 1785	1	156
Jeremiah, s. Jeremiah & Jane, b. May 27, 1775	1	61
Noah, m. Sarah **PLATT**, Apr. 27, 1788	1	156
Theophilus, of Poundridge, m. Sarah **DEAN**, Jan. 1, 1793	1	158
ROSE, Mary, m. Joseph **MEAD**, Apr. 30, 1772	1	152
ROSSEGUIE, Aaron, d. May 20, 1821, ae 27 y.	1	222
Abijah, s. Jacob & Mary, b. Dec. 13, 1754	1	4
Abijah, m. Anna **KEELER**, b. of Ridgefield, Feb. 1, 1829, by Samuel M. Phelps	1	169
Alexander, s. Jacob & Mary, b. May 24, 1759	1	4
Alexander, d. Dec. 28, 1835, ae 76 y.	1	232
Ellen, d. James & Sarah, b. Aug. 5, 1767	1	32
Ellen, d. James & Sarah, b. Aug. 5, 1767	1	35
Ellen, d. James & Sarah, b. Aug. 5, 1767	1	35
Hannah, d. Abraham & Jane, b. May 9, 1756	1	11
Hannah, d. Jan. 24, 1811, at South East	1	215
Isaac, s. James & Sarah, b. Oct. 7, 1772	1	32
Isaac, s. James & Sarah, b. Oct. 7, 1772	1	35
Jacob, s. Jacob & Mary, b. June 1, 1752	1	4
Jacob, 2nd, m. Sarah **FOLLIET**, Apr. 14, 1780	1	154
Jacob, d. Dec. 27, 1801, in the 82nd y. of his age	1	211
Jacob, d. Feb. 21, 1835, in the 83rd y. of his age	1	231
James, m. Sarah **RUMSEY**, Feb. 19, 1766	1	151
James, m. Sarah **RUMSEY**, Feb. 19, 1766	1	152
James, d. Sept. 7, 1830, ae 86 y.	1	228
Jane, m. Nathan **SMITH**, Feb. 18, 1777	1	152

	Vol.	Page
ROSSEGUIE, (cont.)		
Jane, wid., d. July 31, 1797, ae 81	1	209
John, s. Abraham & Jane, b. Apr. 2, 1758	1	11
Lewis, s. Alixander, d. June 26, 1834, ae 27 y.	1	230
Lyman, s. James & Sarah, b. Oct. 29, 1766	1	32
Lyman, s. James & Sarah, b. Oct. 29, 1766	1	35
Lyman, d. Dec. 18, 1791	1	206
Mary, d. Jacob & Mary, b. Apr. 17, 1747	1	4
Mary, d. Mar. 17, 1797, ae 77	1	209
Phebe, d. Abraham & Jane, b. Mar. 8, 1754	1	11
Rachel, d. Abraham & Jane, b. Apr. 11, 1752	1	11
Sarah, w. James, d. Oct. 3, 1791	1	206
Sarah, w. Jacob, d. June 27, 1827	1	226
Seth, s. James & Sarah, b. May 19, 1770	1	32
Seth, s. James & Sarah, b. May 19, 1770	1	35
Timothy, m. Abigail **LEE**, June 5, 1785	1	156
ROWE, David, had infant d. Aug. 9, 1834	1	230
E., had child d. Mar. 15, 1822	1	223
Harriet, m. John **SCOFIELD**, Mar. 1, 1821, by Levi Bronson	1	160
RULY, Edward, m. Lorania **SHAW**, Nov. 4, 1787	1	156
RUMSEY, Sarah, m. James **ROSSEGUIE**, Feb. 19, 1766	1	151
Sarah, m. James **ROSSEGUIE**, Feb. 19, 1766	1	152
RUNDLE, Charles, his infant, d. May 30, 1795	1	208
Samuel, s. Charles, d. Nov. 18, 1794, ae 24 y.	1	207
Shubael, m. Sarah **KEELER**, Jan. 10, 1781	1	154
SAINT JOHN, Abigail, d. Sam[ue]ll & Rebecca, d. Apr. 28, [1720]	LR1	213
Abigail, d. Nathan & Abigail, b. Mar. 27, 1754	LR1	253
Adolphus, [s. Joel & Dorcas], b. Apr. 25, 1792	1	77
Ann, d. David & Mary, b. Feb. 20, 1771	1	39
Anne, d. Matthew & Anne, b. May 1, [1714]	LR1	202
Benjamin, s. Jacob & Phebe, b. July 6, 1768	1	28
Betsey, d. Sam[ue]ll & Chloe, b. Sept. 10, 1795	1	61
Betsey, d. Jacob & Rebeckah, b. June 2, 1798	1	97
Betty, d. Samuel, d. Aug. 27, 1798	1	210
Charles, had child d. Oct. 31, 1815	1	219
Charles, d. Oct. 30, 1823	1	223
Chloe, d. Sam[ue]ll & Chloe, b. Sept. 3, 1807	1	62
Chloe, w. Samuel, d. July 25, 1816, ae 50 y.	1	220
Clarissa, m. Henry C. **BRUSH**, b. of Ridgefield, Nov. 4, 1841, by Rev. Joseph Fuller	1	191
Clark, s. David, d. Aug. 28, 1831, ae 16	1	228
Cynthia, d. Jacob & Rebeckah, b. Sept. 30, 1795	1	97
Daniel, s. Samuel & Sarah, b. July 16, 1748	LR1	241
David, s. Nathan & Hannah, b. May 15, [1726]	LR1	206
David, 2nd, s. Nathan & Hannah, b. Nov. 18, 1738	LR1	240
David, m. Mary **SMITH**, Mar. 13, 1762	1	152
David, s. David & Mary, b. Nov. 7, 1777	1	39
David, d. Mar. 9, 1795, ae 57	1	207

SAINT JOHN, (cont.)

	Vol.	Page
David, his w. [ ], d. Jan. 8, 1823, ae 40	1	223
Dorothy, d. James & Jerusha, b. Aug. 29, 1773	1	2
Edward, s. David, d. Nov. 26, 1834	1	231
Elijah, s. Nathan & Hannah, b. Apr. 20, 1728	LR1	209
Elizabeth, d. James & Jerusha, b. Oct. 13, 176[ ]	1	2
Esther, d. David & Mary, b. Oct. 20, 1773	1	39
Gould L., had child d. Aug. 2, [probably 1833], ae 2 y.	1	230
Gould N., his w. [ ], d. May 10, 1837	1	233
Hannah, d. Nathan & Hannah, b. Apr. 16, [1721/2]	LR1	204
Hannah, d. Nathan & Abigail, b. Feb. 25, 1756	LR1	253
Hannah, w. Samuel, d. Apr. 26, 1765	1	200
Hannah, d. Thomas & Betty, b. Aug. 6, 1769	1	27
Hannah, m. David **FAIRBANKS**, Apr. 5, 1795	1	86
Hannah, d. Jacob & Rebeckah, b. Apr. 4, 1800	1	97
Isaac, his infant d. [ ], d. May 1, 1796	1	208
Isaac, had infant d. [1796]	1	208
Isaac, his infant s. [ ], d. Aug. 11, 1797	1	209
Jacob, s. Samuel & Sarah, b. Aug. 30, 1745	LR1	241
Jacob, s. Thomas & Betty, b. Dec. 3, 1764	1	27
Jacob, m. Ruhama **TAYLOR**, Dec. 23, 1790, by Rev. Joseph Peck. Witnesses Samuel Taylor & Rachel Taylor	1	97
James, s. Samuel & Sarah, b. Oct. 27, 1736	LR1	220
James, s. Thomas & Susannah, b. July 23, 1759	LR1	243
James, s. Thomas & Susanah, d. Dec. 28, 1759	LR1	217
James, s. James & Jerusha, b. Sept. 28, 1760	LR1	243
James, s. Samuel & Chloe, b. Apr. 4, 1800	1	61
James, m. Jerusha **THOMAS**, Apr. 13, [ ]	LR1	252
Jane, d. Capt. [ ], m. Ebenezer **BROOKS**, Aug. 27, 1730	LR1	228
Jared N., had child d. Oct. 21, 1829, ae 3 d.	1	227
Jason, s. Samuel & Chloe, b. Aug. 18, 1804	1	62
Joanna, d. Capt. [ ], m. Christopher **BURT**, Dec. 21, 1727	LR1	228
Joel, m. Dorcas **KEELER**, Apr. 1, 1791	1	158
Joel, m. Dorcas **KEELER**, Apr. 21, 1791	1	77
Joel, m. Dorcas **KEELER**, Apr. 21, 1791	1	157
John, s. Samuel & Sarah, d. Apr. 13, 1746	LR1	216
John, s. Samuel & Sarah, b. Apr. 11, 1753	LR1	241
John, s. Daniel & Abigail, b. Aug. 17, 1777	1	32
John, m. Hannah **DUNNING**, Jan. 30, 1788	1	157
Jonathan, d. July 4, 1826, ae 65	1	225
Keeler, m. Polly **HUBBELL**, b. of Ridgefield, Dec. 22, 1833, by Rev. Charles G. Selleck	1	179
Keeler, his s. [ ], d. Feb. 18, [1847], ae 12 y.	1	239
Keeler, had [d.], d. Sept. 19, [1851], ae 9 y.	1	241
Laura, d. Jacob & Rebeckah, b. Sept. 18, 1791	1	97
Lucinda, d. Samuel & Chloe, b. June 4, 1788	1	61

SAINT JOHN, (cont.)

	Vol.	Page
Mark, s. Matthew & Anne, b. Aug. 15, 1715	LR1	200
Martha, d. Sam[ue]ll & Sarah, b. July 2, 1750	LR1	241
Martha, m. John **THOMAS**, Sept. 19, 1767	1	150
Martha, d. Jacob & Rebeckah, b. Mar. 5, 1794	1	97
Mary, d. Noah & Jane, b. June 4, 1738	LR1	224
Mary, d. James & Jerusha, b. Sept. 4, 1771	1	2
Mary, w. [ ], d. Mar. 5, 1796, ae 59	1	207
Mary Ann, d. David, d. Aug. 19, 1820, ae 13	1	222
Matthew, m. Anne **WHITNE**, d. John, of Norwalk, Oct. 13, 1709	LR1	227
Matthew, s. Matthew & Ann, b. June 23, 1711	LR1	200
Molly, d. Nathan & Abigail, b. Apr. 20, 1759	LR1	253
Molly, d. Nathan & Abigail, d. June 12, 1759	LR1	217
Molly, d. Nathan & Abigail, b. Nov. 17, 1760	LR1	253
Molly, d. David & Mary, b. Feb. 17, 1764	1	39
Molly, d. Apr. 4, 1842, ae 78 y.	1	236
Nathan, m. Hannah [ ], June 7, 1721	LR1	227
Nathan, s. Nathan & Hannah, b. Jan. 26, [1724]	LR1	204
Nathan, s. Noah & Jane, b. Dec. 2, 1739	LR1	224
Nathan, s. Nathan & Abigail, b. Nov. 6, 1765	LR1	253
Noah, s. Daniel & Abigail, b. Apr. 2, 17[ ]	1	32
Noah, m. Jane [ ], Oct. 6, 1737	LR1	230
Olive, d. Thomas & Betty, b. Apr. 7, 1775	1	27
Olive, d. Sam[ue]ll & Chloe, b. Feb. 8, 1798	1	61
Olive, m. Lewis **REYNOLDS**, Dec. 10, 1823, by George Benedict	1	162
Peregrina, d. Capt. [ ], m. Nathan **NORTHRUP**, Aug. 27, 1730	LR1	228
Phebe, d. Jacob & Phebe, b. June 17, 1770	1	28
Phebe, d. Sam[ue]ll & Chloe, b. Aug. 12, 1809	1	62
Polly, m. Jeremiah **KEELER**, Jan. 26, 1796	1	159
Rachel, d. Nathan & Hannah, b. Aug. 14, 1731	LR1	212
Rachal, m. Gideon **BETTS**, Dec. 20, 1752, by Jonathan Ingersoll, V. D. M.	LR1	234
Rachel, d. Thomas & Betty, b. Oct. 27, 1780	1	27
Rebecca, m. Samuel **LOBDELL**, Dec. 26, 1722	LR1	227
Rebeckah, d. Samuell & Sarah, b. June 18, 1743	LR1	237
Rebeckah, d. Samuel & Sarah, b. June 18, 1743	LR1	241
Rebeckah, d. James & Jerusha, b. Aug. 12, 1762	1	2
Ruth, d. David & Mary, b. May 11, 1769	1	39
Ruth, m. Henry **WHITNEY**, [ ], 1794	1	159
Samuel, Jr., m. Sarah **NORTHRUP**, Mar. 6, 1727/8	LR1	228
Sam[ue]ll, s. Sam[ue]ll & Sarah, b. May 4, 1731	LR1	211
Samuell, m. Sarah **WALLIS**, d. James & Mary, Jan. 8, 1735/6	LR1	229
Samuel, s. Thomas & Betty, b. Jan. 3, 1763	1	27
Samuel, d. Nov. 9, 1777	1	202
Samuel, m. Chloe **WEED**, Apr. 6, 1785	1	155

BARBOUR COLLECTION

	Vol.	Page
SAINT JOHN, (cont.)		
Samuel Sidney, s. Thomas, Jr. & Anna, b. Sept. 6, 1806	1	103
Sarah, d. Matthew & Anne, b. Sept. 18, 1713	LR1	200
Sarah, d. Sam[ue]ll & Sarah, b. May 31, 1729	LR1	209
Sarah, w. Sam[ue]ll, d. June 30, 1731	LR1	214
Sarah, d. Nathan & Hannah, b. Oct. 9, 1733	LR1	218-9
Sarah, w. Samuel, d. Jan. 6. 1754	LR1	217
Sarah, d. James & Jerusha, b. Sept. 23, 1758	LR1	243
Sarah, d. David & Mary, b. Jan. 7, 1766	1	39
Sarah, m. Jeremiah **KEELER**, Mar. 20, 1792	1	158
Sarah Benedict, d. Sam[ue]ll & Chloe, b. June 18, 1791	1	61
Stephen, s. Daniel & Abigail, b. Feb. 7, 177[ ]	1	32
Susannah, w. Thomas, d. Aug. 1, 1759	LR1	217
Susanna, d. Thomas & Betty, b. June 25, 1767	1	27
Thomas, s. Sam[ue]ll & Sarah, b. Oct. 12, 1738	LR1	223
Thomas, m. Susannah **NORTHRUP**, Mar. 8, 1759	LR1	232
Thomas, m. Susannah **NORTHRUP**, Mar. [ ]	LR1	252
Thomas, m. Betty **THOMAS**, Apr. 14, 176[ ]	1	150
Thomas, s. Samuel & Chloe, b. Sept. 30, 1785	1	61
Thomas Taylor, s. Jacob & Rebeckah, b. Apr. 12, 1802	1	97
Timothy Weed, s. Sam[ue]l & Chloe, b. Mar. 23, 1802	1	61
Wallace, s. Thomas & Betty, b. Mar. 4, 1772	1	27
William, d. Mar. 14, 1845, ae 27 y.	1	238
Zadock, s. James & Jerusha, b. June 26, 1764	1	2
Zadock, s. Samuel & Chloe, b. June 22, 1793	1	61
Zina, s. Samuel & Chloe, b. Apr. 30, 1789	1	61
SANDERLAND, Julia H., of Ridgefield, m. Reuben G.		
BRANDAGE, of Greenwich, Feb. 2, 1851, by Rev.		
Nathaniel Mead	1	135
Minerva M., m. Henry A. **STUART**, b. of Ridgefield, Mar. 16,		
1851, by Rev. Nathaniel Mead	1	135
SANDERS, [see also **SAUNDERS**], Clara, m. Ira **BENEDICT**, b. of		
Ridgefield, Sept. 18, 1823, by Samuell M. Phelps	1	164
Hannah Jackson, d. Aaron & Polly, b. July 16, 1806	1	103
Holmes, of Norwalk, m. Huldah **KEELER**, of Ridgefield, May		
13, 1826, by Samuel M. Phelps	1	167
Orrin Jackson, s. Aaron & Poly, b. Jan. 6, 1810	1	103
SANFORD, Benj[ami]n, m. Sarah J. **OLMSTED**, Dec. 25, 1791	1	158
Benjamin, [s. Benjamin & Sarah], b. Mar. 15, 1798	1	85
Ebenezer, m. Mary **DAUCHY**, Feb. 22, 1787	1	157
Eli, of Redding, m. Anne **STEBBINS**, Nov. 16, 1786	1	157
Eliza Jane, of Ridgefield, m. Hiram **SMITH**, of North Salem,		
N. Y., May 18, 1846, by Rev. Shaller J. Hillyer	1	198
Ezekiel, s. [Benjamin & Sarah], b. Feb. 12, 1796	1	85
Huldah, m. Timothy **OLMSTED**, Aug. 22, 1791	1	75
Legrand, of Redding, m. Eliza Esther **EDMOND**, of		
Ridgefield, Oct. 14, 1829, by Samuell M. Phelps	1	171
Samuel, d. Dec. 24, 1834	1	231

	Vol.	Page
SANFORD, (cont.)		
Thomas, of Danbury, m. Delia Ann **BOUTON**, of Ridgefield, Nov. 19, 1838, by Rev. Thomas Sparks	1	187
William Henry, s. Benjamin & Sarah, b. May 4, 1794	1	85
SARLES, [see under **SEARLES**]		
SAUNDERS, [see also **SANDERS**], Mary, of Ridgefield, m. Lewis **PENOYER**, of New Canaan, Feb. 9, 1835, by Rev. Charles G. Selleck	1	180
SCOFIELD, John, m. Harriet **ROWE**, Mar. 1, 1821, by Levi Bronson	1	160
SCOTT, Abigail, see Abigail **GILBERT**	1	220
Ame, d. David & Hannah, b. May 10, 1772	1	23
Amelia B., m. Seth **SMITH**, b. of Ridgefield, Mar. 19, 1838, by Rev. Joseph Fuller	1	185
Betsey, of Ridgefield, m. John **GILBERT**, of Wilton, Mar. 31, 1822, by Rev. Samuel M. Phelps	1	161
Bradner, d. Feb. 26, 1834, ae 23 y.	1	230
Burr, m. Laura Ann **JUNE**, b. of Ridgefield, July 31, 1848, by Rev. Shaller J. Hillyer	1	129
Burr, Capt., d. [, 1850], ae 32 y., at Barbadoes	1	240
Caroline, d. Hezekiah, d. Jan. 9, 1850, ae 23 y.	1	240
Charles, s. Hezekiah, d. [Dec.] 29, [1846]	1	238
Clark, m. Zilpha **JUDD**, b. of Ridgefield, this day [ ], by Rev. J. Lyman Clarke. Recorded Dec. 12, 1836	1	185
Daniel Gould, [s. James & Lucretia], b. Apr. 13, 1803	1	58
David, s. [James & Hannah], b. Feb. 25, 1727	LR1	208
David, m. Hannah **SMITH**, Aug. 4, 1751, by Jonathan Ingersoll, V. D. M.	LR1	234
David, s. David & Hannah, b. June 11, 1752	LR1	250
David, d. Feb. 3, 1760	LR1	217
David, s. James & Lucretia, b. Mar. 20, 1785	1	58
David, d. May 21, 1809	1	214
David, had s. [ ], d. Mar. 14, 1813, ae 1 y.	1	217
David, his infant d. May 5, 1825	1	224
Delia, d. James, Jr., d. Aug. 28, 1820	1	222
Eli, s. Gould, d. Sept. 14, 1829, ae 15 y.	1	227
Elizabeth B., m. Henry **DARLING**, b. of Ridgefield, Nov. 3, 1831, by Rev. C. G. Selleck	1	174
Emily, d. David, d. Aug. 10, [1846], ae 13 or 14	1	238
Gideon, s. David & Hannah, b. Dec. 12, 1755	LR1	250
Gideon, m. Anna **BURT**, Oct. 17, 1779	1	76
Gould, s. David & Hannah, b. June 28, 1778	1	23
Goold, of Ridgefield, m. Lucy **WOOD**, of Danbury, Mar. 11, 1802, by Rev. John Ely	1	93
Hannah, [d. James & Hannah], b. Oct. 3, 1731	LR1	208
Hannah, m. John **ROCKWELL**, Jr., Apr. 16, 1754	LR1	234
Hannah, d. David & Hannah, b. Apr. 25, 1765	1	23
Hannah, m. Josiah **OSBORN**, Aug. 26, 1783	1	154

260 BARBOUR COLLECTION

	Vol.	Page
SCOTT, (cont.)		
Hannah, wid., d. Dec. 21, 1829, ae 95	1	227
Hezekiah, [s. James & Lucretia], b. Dec. 25, 1789	1	58
Huldah, d. James & Martha, b. Nov. 26, 1752* *(Perhaps "1751")	LR1	244
Huldah, m. John **WATROUS**, June 12, 1771	1	151
James, s. James & Hannah, b. Feb. 10, [1721/2]	LR1	204
James, m. Hannah **HYATT**, Apr. 24, 1722	LR1	227
James, m. Martha [ ], Mar. 12, 1744/5	LR1	233
James, s. [James & Martha], b. Jan. 14, 1747/8	LR1	244
James, s. James & Martha, d. Oct. 2, 1748	LR1	216
James, s. David & Hannah, b. Jan. 2, 1754	LR1	250
James, 2nd, m. Lucretia **OLMSTED**, Sept. 6, 1782	1	58
James, [s. James & Lucretia], b. Apr. 2, 1792	1	58
James, Capt., d. Mar. 3, 1805	1	212
James, d. Feb. 10, 1826, ae 72	1	225
James, his wid., d. Feb. [ ], 1845, ae about 84 y.	1	238
Jerre, s. David & Hannah, b. Feb. 10, 1770	1	23
Jere, b. [ ], 1770; d. Feb. 18, 1843, ae 73 y.	1	236
Jere, m. Amelia **WAKEMAN**, [ ], 1794	1	159
Jere A., of Moumee City, O., m. Ann A. **CROCKER**, of Ridgefield, Sept. 18, 1837, by Charles G. Selleck	1	183
John, s. James & Martha, b. Apr. 18, 1755	LR1	244
John, d. May 2, 1773	1	201
John, d. June 23, [1852], ae 87	1	242
Laura, m. Ebenezer O. **BENNETT**, Dec. 30, 1830, by Nathan Burton	1	173
Lucretia, [d. James & Lucretia], b. Jan. 15, 1801	1	58
Lucy W., of Ridgefield, m. Burr **BRADLEY**, of Onandago, Oct. 24, 1824, by Samuel M. Phelps	1	165
Lydia, m. Hiram **LYON**, b. of Ridgefield, July 5, 1829, by Samuell M. Phelps	1	171
Martha, d. James & Martha, b. Oct. 6, 1749	LR1	244
Martha, w. James, d. Feb. 5, 1796, ae 72	1	208
Mary, m. Josiah **ROCKWELL**, Apr. (?) 21, [ ]	LR1	252
Mary, m. Josiah **ROCKWELL**, Sept. 21, 1759	LR1	232
Mary Ann, of Ridgefield, m. Lawrence W. **SMITH**, of North Salem, N. Y., Sept. 5, 1847, by Rev. Shaler J. Hillyer	1	128
Nathan, [s. James & Lucretia], b. Dec. 12, 1787	1	58
Nathan, his w.[ ], d. June 9, 1841, ae about 50 y.	1	236
Polly, d. James & Lucretia, b. Mar. 2, 1783	1	58
Polly, d. June 5, 1812, in the 21st y. of her age	1	217
Polly, d. Hezekiah, d. Mar. 17, 1826, ae 13	1	225
Rane, d. David & Hannah, b. Jan. 3, 1768	1	23
Rana, m. John **BARLOW**, Nov. 29, 1789	1	158
Samuel, m. Sabina **LODER**, b. of Ridgefield, Nov. 14, 1850, by Rev. C. Clark	1	134
Sarah, [d. James & Hannah], b. Aug. 12, 1729	LR1	208

	Vol.	Page
SCOTT, (cont.)		
Sarah, d. James & Martha, b. Mar. 14, 1745/6	LR1	244
Sarah, d. David & Hannah, b. Feb. 11, 1758	LR1	250
Sarah, m. Uriah **MARVIN**, May 15, 1765	1	150
Sarah Ann, m. John H. **WOOD**, b. of Ridgefield, Jan. 31, 1836, at the house of Nathan Scott, by Rev. Shaller J. Hillyer	1	181
Smith, [s. James & Lucretia], b. Nov. 1, 1794	1	58
Thadd, s. David & Hannah, b. Sept. 3, 1775	1	23
Thomas, m. Ruth **SEYMOUR**, [ ]	1	76
Thomas, [s. Gideon & Anna], b. [ ]	1	76
Thomas, s. James & Hannah, b. Feb. 3, [1724/5]	LR1	205
Thomas, s. David & Hannah, b. Feb. 14, 1763	1	23
Thomas, m. Ruth **SEYMOUR**, Apr. 21, 1788	1	157
Thomas, d. Sept. 28, 1830, ae 67 y.	1	228
Thomas, his wid., d. Feb. 29, 1848, ae 78 y.	1	239
Timothy Olmsted, [s. James & Lucretia], b. Jan. 12, 1797	1	58
-----, wid., d. Oct. 3, 1843, ae 39 y., at Chauncey Olmsted's	1	237
SCRIBNER, Asa, m. Rachel **OLMSTED**, Jan. 10, 1779	1	155
Elijah P., Capt. of New York, m. Hannah **SMITH**, of Ridgefield, Oct. 29, 1821, by Rev. Samuel M. Phelps	1	161
Julia Ann, d. Roger, d. Sept. 5, 1819	1	221
Lucretia, d. Asa & Rachel, b. June 1, 1779	1	33
Martha, m. Azariah **SMITH**, Nov. 6, 1783	1	154
Mercey, d. Asa & Rachel, b. Dec. 31, 1782	1	33
Rachel, m. Jared **NASH**, July 7, 1793	1	78
Rachel, m. Jared **NICHOLS**, [ ], 1794	1	159
Ruth, m. Henry **WHITNEY**, 2nd, Jan. 17, 1770	1	151
Uriah, m. Elizabeth **WHITLOCK**, Sept. 30, 1783	1	154
Uriah, his w. [ ], d. Aug. 26, 1808	1	214
Uriah, d. June 6, 1810, in the 86th y. of his age	1	215
[SEARLES], SARLES, Ann E., m. Henry A. **STUART**, b. of Ridgefield, Sept. 14, 1846, by Rev. Charles Stearns. Int. Pub. Sept. 11, 1846	1	198
John, of Poundridge, N. Y., m. Amy **DAUCHY**, of Ridgefield, Nov. 22, 1833, by Rev. Charles J. Todd	1	179
SEARS, SEERS, Camilla M., of Ridgefield, m. Francis B. **NORTHRUP**, of Southeast N. Y., Dec. 25, 1833, by Nathan Burton	1	178
Desire, m. Timothy **FOSTER**, Nov. 18, 1772	1	153
George B., m. Marinda **ROCKWELL**, Sept. 15, 1829, by Nathan Burton	1	170
Jacob B., m. Harriet **NORTHROP**, b. of Ridgefield, Feb. 4, 1846, by Rev. Z. B. Burr	1	198
SEE, [see also **LEE**], Betty*, [d. William & Susannah], b. June [ ], 1778 *(Perhaps "Betty **LEE**")	1	65
Ebenezer*, [s. William & Susannah], b. Aug. 31, 1773 *(Ebenezer **LEE**?)	1	65

	Vol.	Page
SEE, (cont.)		
Esther*, [s. William & Susannah], b. Mar. [ ], 1782		
*(Esther **LEE**?)	1	65
Phebe*, [d. William & Susannah], b. July 20, 1776		
*(Phebe **LEE**?)	1	65
Rush*, [s. William & Susannah], b. Sept. 20, 1785		
*(Rush **LEE**?)	1	65
SEELEY, SEALEY, Amos s., of Weston, m. Laura **SHERWOOD**, of Ridgefield, Feb. 19, 1832, by Rev. Charles J. Todd	1	175
Esther, m. Abraham **PULLEN**, Oct. 11, 1787	1	157
Esther*, m. Abraham **PULLEN**, Oct. 12, 1787 *(Written "Esther **SILAH**")	1	156
Fanny, m. Charles **DAUCHY**, [Sept.] 27, [1820], by Rev. Charles Smith	1	160
Jonas, d. Oct. 17, 1813	1	218
SELLECK, Benjamin, m. Abigail **BRADLEY**, Mar. 3, 1783	1	154
Betsey, of Ridgefield, m. Stephen **CRAWFUT**, of Phillips, N. Y., Nov. 2, 1823, by Nathan Burton	1	162
Esther Ann, m. Bradley **PLATT**, Sept. 22, 1833, by Nathan Selleck	1	178
James, m. Phebe **WHEELOCK**, Feb. 26, 1783	1	154
Lewis, had granddaughter d. Sept. [ ], 1826	1	225
Polly, d. Jesse, d. Dec. 11, 1794, ae 2 y.	1	207
Polly, m. John **HATFIELD**, Aug. 29, 1825, by Nathan Burton	1	163
Ruth Smith, w. Lewis, d. Aug. 24, 1826	1	225
[**SEWARD**], [see under **SUARD**]		
SEYMOUR SEAMORE, Abigail, d. Apr. 25, [1848]	1	239
Abijah, s. [Thomas & Sarah], b. July 9, 1762	1	86
Almira, w. Lewis C., d. May 1, 1830, ae 27	1	228
Benjamin, [s. Thomas & Ruth], b. Dec. 16, 1791	1	76
Catharine, of Richfield, m. John **PHENIX**, of New York, Oct. 28, 1829, by Samuell M. Phelps	1	171
Charles, m. Hannah **NORRIS**, Jan. 29, 1832, by Nathan Burton	1	175
Comfort, wid., d. Mar. 4, 1819	1	221
Daniel, s. Matthew & Dinah, b. Apr. 21, 1760	LR1	235
Daniel F., m. Mary **FAIRCHILD**, Feb. 19, 1840, by Nathan Burton, P. T.	1	188
Emily, of Ridgefield, m. Benjamin T. **BETTS**, of Wilton, May 10, 1826, by Samuel M. Phelps	1	167
Hannah, d. Matthew & Hannah, b. Nov. 15, 1737	LR1	221
Hannah, d. Thomas & Sarah, b. Aug. 10, 1758	LR1	208
Hannah, d. Thomas & Sarah, d. Aug. 22, 1758	LR1	217
Hannah, m. Jeremiah **KEELER**, Jan. 15, 1764	1	150
Hannah, d. [Thomas & Sarah], b. Mar. 4, 1775	1	86
Hannah, [d. Thomas & Ruth], b. Aug. 8, 1796	1	76
Henry, s. William H., d. July 21, 1822	1	223
Henry, s. William H., d. Mar. 20, 1826, ae 2 m.	1	225
Hiram L., m. Margaret **PIKE**, b. of Ridgefield, Dec. 26, 1830,		

	Vol.	Page
SEYMOUR, SEAMORE, (cont.)		
by Samuel M. Phelps	1	175
Hiram L., his child d. July [ ], 1846	1	238
Ira, [d. Thomas & Ruth], b. July 14, 1789	1	76
Jared, s. Thomas & Sarah, b. Aug. 3, 1759	LR1	208
Jareed, s. Thomas & Sarah, b. Aug. 13, 1759	1	86
Jared, d. Aug. 6, 1831, ae 72 y. 3 d.	1	228
Jere, wid., d. June 21, [1844], ae about 75 y.	1	237
Katharine, m. Burr **ALLEN**, Sept. 18, 1831, by Nathan Burton	1	174
Lewis C., of Ridgefield, m. Almira **BETTS**, of Wilton, Oct. 8, 1823, by Sam[ue]ll M. Phelps	1	164
Lucy, w. Nathan, Jr., d. July 22, 1816, ae 19	1	219
Lucy, m. W[illia]m B. **BEERS**, b. of Ridgefield, Jan. 1, 1832, by Rev. Charles G. Selleck	1	176
Matthew, m. Hannah **SMITH**, June 14, 1722	LR1	227
Matthew, s. Matthew & Hannah, b. Apr. 7, [1723]	LR1	204
Matt[hew], had negroes Pegg, d. Tamor, b. Dec. 21, 1742, Elizabeth, d. Tamor, b. Oct. 12, 1746, Dover, s. Tamor, b. Aug. 17, 1747, Betty, d. Tamor, b. Sept. 23, 1749, Allen, s. Tamor, b. Nov. 23, 1751 & Naomi, d. Tamor, b. Sept. 10, 1754	LR1	257
Matt[hew], had negro Abigail, d. Tamor, b. Mar. 8, 1761; d. two days after & negro twins of Tamor, b. Jan. 7, 1762; d. three days after	LR1	257
Matthew, s. [Thomas & Sarah], b. Feb. 20, 1765	1	86
Matthew, d. Nov. 24, 1816, ae 94	1	219
Matthew, had negro Nab, d. Sept. 24, 1818, ae 40 y.	1	221
Matthew, d. Feb. 22, 1852, ae 61 y.	1	242
Matthew, d. [ ], ae 77 y.	1	236
Medad, s. Matthew & Dinah, b. Dec. 10, 1761	1	9
Nathan, s. Matthew & Dinah, b. Apr. 15, 1758	LR1	235
Nathan, 2nd, had infant child d. Nov. 25, 1816	1	220
Nathaniel, m. Adah **HOYT**, Jan. 21, 1790	1	158
Nathaniel, his w. [ ], d. Feb. 4, 1843, ae 79	1	236
Nathaniel, d. Jan. 16, 1850, ae 84 y.	1	240
Olive, w. Uriah, d. May 16, 1812	1	217
Rufus, m. Mrs. Harriet O. **HAWLEY**, b. of Ridgefield, Mar. 17, 1841, by Rev. Joseph Fuller	1	191
Rufus N., m. Harriet O. **HAWLEY**, Mar. 17, 1841, by Rev. Joseph Fuller	1	190
Ruth, d. Capt. Matthew, of Norwalk, m. Jabish **SMITH**, June 12, 1729	LR1	229
Ruth, d. [Thomas & Sarah], b. Apr. 8, 1770	1	86
Ruth, m. Thomas **SCOTT**, Apr. 21, 1788	1	157
Ruth, m. Thomas **SCOTT**, [ ]	1	76
Ruth, [d. Thomas & Ruth], b. Dec. 8, 1793	1	76
Sarah, d. Matthew, Jr. & Comfort, b. Aug. 15, 17[ ]	LR1	208
Sarah, d. Matthew & Comfort, b. Sept. 19, 175[ ]	LR1	241

SEYMOUR, SEAMORE, (cont.)

	Vol.	Page
Sarah, d. [Thomas & Sarah], b. Apr. 12, 1773	1	86
Sarah, wid., d. Apr. 27, 1813	1	217
Sarah, d. Feb. 14, 1832, in the 60th y. of her age	1	229
Sarah, d. Mar. 21, [1842], ae 45 y.	1	236
Sherman, his d. [ ], d. Sept. 27, 1846, ae 5 y.	1	238
Thaddeus, s. [Thomas & Sarah], b. Mar. 10, 1782	1	86
Thaddeus, d. May 22, 1834, ae 52 y.	1	230
Thaddeus, Jr., s. Thaddeus, decd., d. Jan. 19, 1837, ae 17 y.	1	233
Thomas, m. Sarah **ROCKWELL**, Feb. 17, 175[ ]	LR1	234
Thomas, s. Thomas & Sarah, b. Dec. 20, 1756	LR1	208
Thomas, s. Thomas & Sarah, b. Dec. 20, 1757	1	86
Thomas, m. Anne **OLMSTED**, May 3, 1786	1	156
Thomas, d. Feb. 15, 1812	1	216
William H., had infant d. Dec. 22, 1826	1	226
W[illia]m H., m. Emily L. **COHEN**, b. of Norwalk, Jan. 30, 1848, by Rev. L. B. Burr	1	129
William W., Dr. his w. [ ], d. Apr. 17, 1839	1	235
SHAW, Lorania, m. Edward **RULY**, Nov. 4, 1787	1	156
SHEETE, Elisha, d. Oct. 6, 1817, ae 29	1	220
SHEPARD, William, his w. [ ], d. Dec. 24, 1816	1	220
SHERMAN, Oville J., m. Samuel D. **ROCKWELL**, Sept. 9, 1832, by Nathan Burton	1	176
Polly, m. Jeremiah **FOLLIET**, Jan. 12, 1790	1	80
Polly, m. Jeremiah **FOLLIET**, Jan. 12, 1790	1	158
Roger M., Hon., d. about Jan. 1, 1845, at Fairfield, in the 72nd y. of his age	1	238
SHERWOOD, Abigail, [d. Daniel & Ruth], b. Apr. 3, 1716	LR1	221
Abigail, m. Armanus **ELIS**, Mar. 16, 1745/6, by Joseph Lamson	LR1	232
Albert, his child, d. Sept. 9, 1843	1	237
Ann, d. Nathan & Lois, b. Mar. 3, 1747/8	LR1	243
Anna, d. Reuben & Rebeckah, b. Feb. 9, 1783	1	54
Anne, m. Abner **WILSON**, June 30, 1768	1	150
Benjamin, s. John & Hannah, b. Apr. 10, 1753	LR1	246
Benjamin, s. Benjamin, d. Apr. 3, 177[ ]	1	202
Benjamin, 2nd, s. Benj[ami]n & Sarah, b. Apr. 20, 177[ ]	1	38
Benjamin, s. Benj[ami]n & Sarah, b. Nov. 6, 177[ ]	1	38
Benjamin, 2nd, s. Benjamin, d. Nov. 17, 177[ ]	1	202
Benjamin, 3rd, s. Benj[ami]n & Sarah, b. July 5, 178[ ]	1	38
Benjamin, d. Apr. 11, 1840, ae about 88 y.	1	235
Benjamin, his wid. [ ], d. Feb. 25, 1848, ae almost 94	1	239
Benj[ami]n, d. June 14, [1851], ae 69 y.	1	241
Betsey, d. [Timothy & Lois], b. July 30, 1807	1	105
Betsey, w. Nehemiah, d. Dec. 26, 1812	1	217
Bettey, m. Nathan **SHERWOOD**, Feb. 10, 1788	1	157
Caroline, d. [Timothy & Lois], b. June 26, 1809	1	105
Christopher, his child d. [probably 1851]	1	241

	Vol.	Page
SHERWOOD, (cont.)		
Clarassee, d. Ben[jamin] & Sarah, b. Apr. 25, 1795	1	38
Cynthia, m. Aaron **READ**, June 6, 1841, by		
Rev. Warner Hoyt	1	190
Daniel, [s. Daniel & Ruth], b. Nov. 21, 1714	LR1	221
Daniel, m. Jerusha [ ], Apr. 29, 1736	LR1	230
Daniel, s. Dan[ie]ll & Jerusha, b. Jan. 21, 1736/7	LR1	224
Daniel, d. May 17, 1766	1	201
Daniel N., m. Laura S. **GRAY**, b. of Ridgefield, July 31, 1850,		
by Rev. W[illia]m Staunton	1	136
David N., of Darien, m. Mary Ann **GILBERT**, of Ridgefield,		
Apr. 26, 1840, by Rev. Warner Hoyt	1	189
Eben, s. Isaac & Naomi, b. Aug. 31, 1771	1	10
Ebenezer, s. Dan[ie]ll & Jerusha, b. Jan. 15, 1738/9	LR1	224
Edward, s. [Timothy & Lois], b. July 3, 1811	1	105
Elizabeth, d. Dan[ie]ll & Jerusha, b. May 5, 1744	LR1	240
Elizabeth, m. Henry **NORTHRUP**, b. of Ridgefield, Oct. 7,		
1832, by Rev. Charles J. Todd	1	177
Emily, of Ridgefield, m. William D. **PARKER**, of York Town,		
N. Y., Oct. 23, 1836, by Rev. Charles G. Selleck	1	183
Esther, d. Isaac & Naomi, b. Nov. 17, 1761	1	10
Esther, m. John **SMITH**, Dec. 10, 1781	1	152
Esther, m. John **SMITH**, Dec. 20, 1781	1	154
Hannah, [d. Daniel & Ruth], b. Mar. 7, 1712	LR1	221
Hannah, d. Nathan & Lois, b. Oct. 2, 1744	LR1	240
Hannah, m. Ens. Vivas **DAUCHY**, Mar. 24, 1750/1, by		
Jonathan Ingersoll, V. D. M.	LR1	233
Hannah, d. Isaac & Naomi, b. July 17, 1754	LR1	248
Hannah, d. Isaac & Naomi, b. July 25, 1754	1	5 1/2
Hannah, d. Benj[ami]n & Sarah, b. Jan. 15, 177[ ]	1	38
Hannah, m. Abel **BARNUM**, May 31, 1772	1	155
Hannah, wid., d. Apr. 15, 1812, in the 85th y. of her age	1	216
Hannah, m. John **MEAD**, [ ]	1	84
Henry, s. Daniel & Jerusha, b. Nov. 18, 1741	LR1	240
Isaac, [s. Daniel & Ruth], b. Feb. 8, 1723/4	LR1	221
Isaac, m. Naomi [ ], Jan. 2, 1746	LR1	233
James, s. Reuben & Rebeckah, b. Feb. 10, 1781	1	54
James, m. Betsey **BROWNING**, b. of Danbury, May 21, 1848,		
by Rev. James A. Hawley	1	129
Joanna, d. Isaac & Naomi, b. Feb. 22, 1752	LR1	248
Joanna, d. Isaac & Naomi, d. Jan. 17, 1754	LR1	217
Joanna, d. Timothy & Lois, b. Jan. 25, 1804	1	105
John, [s. Daniel & Ruth], b. Mar. 15, 1729	LR1	221
John, s. Daniel & Jerusha, b. Dec. 4, 1749	1	8
John, s. Sarah, b. May 4, 1782	1	67
John, s. Benjamin & Sarah, b. Nov. 5, 1784	1	38
John, d. Nov. 2, 1788, in the 90th y. of his age	1	205
John, m. Hannah **STEBBINS**, May [ ]	LR1	252

SHERWOOD, (cont.)

	Vol.	Page
John R., m. Roxana **WARREN**, b. of Ridgefield, Oct. 30, 1842, by Rev. Warner Hoyt	1	193
Josena, of Ridgefield, m. Aaron **OLMSTED**, of Wilton, Oct. 4, 1846, by Rev. Henry Olmsted, Jr.	1	127
Laura, of Ridgefield, m. Amos S. **SEELEY**, of Weston, Feb. 19, 1832, by Rev. Charles J. Todd	1	175
Lemira, d. Zadoc & Abigail, b. May 22, 1784	1	55
Lewis, s. Benj[ami]n & Sarah, b. Oct. 16, 1790	1	38
Lois, d. Nathan & Lois, b. Mar. 5, 1745/6	LR1	240
Lois, w. Timothy, b. Feb. 19, 1785	1	105
Lucy, d. Benj[ami]n & Sarah, b. Feb. 3, 1793	1	38
Mary, d. Daniel & Jerusha, b. Nov. 8, 1747	1	8
Mary, d. Isaac & Naomi, b. May 21, 1759	LR1	248
Naomi, m. John **NICHOLS**, May 15, 1770	1	151
Naomi, d. Jan. 5, 1789	1	205
Nathan, [s. Daniel & Ruth], b. May 16, 1720	LR1	221
Nathan, m. Lois [ ], Jan. 4, 1743/4	LR1	231
Nathan, s. Nathan & Lois, b. Jan. 4, 1751/2	LR1	243
Nathan, s. Isaac & Naomi, b. Feb. 17, 1766	1	10
Nathan, m. Bettey **SHERWOOD**, Feb. 10, 1788	1	157
Nehemiah, d. Dec. 12, 1823, ae 93 y.	1	224
Phebe, d. Benj[ami]n & Sarah, b. Oct. 6, 177[ ]	1	38
Philip, m. Charlotte **WICKSON**, Dec. 27, 1840, by Rev. Warner Hoyt	1	189
Rebeckah, d. Daniell & Ruth, d. Feb. 12, 1719	LR1	213
Rebeckah, w. Lewis, d. May 22, 1838	1	234
Reuben, s. Nathan & Lois, b. Oct. 11, 1754	LR1	243
Reuben, m. Rebeckah **WILSON**, Apr. 8, 1778	1	153
Richard, s. Daniel & Jerusha, b. Mar. 21, 1754	1	8
Ruth, [d. Daniel & Ruth], b. Mar. 29, 1722	LR1	221
Ruth, d. Daniel & Jerusha, b. June 11, 1746	1	8
Ruth, d. Dan[ie]ll & Jerusha, b. June 11, 1746	LR1	240
Ruth, m. Henry **PALMER**, Aug. 26, 1784	1	155
Ruth, d. Aug. 7, 1792	1	206
Ruth, m. John **KEELER**, b. of Ridgefield, Oct. 28, [1834], by Rev. Charles G. Selleck	1	180
Sally Olmsted, d. [Timothy & Lois], b. Oct. 27, 1805	1	105
Samuel, s. Benj[ami]n & Sarah, b. July 25, 1788	1	38
Samuel, of Ballstown, N. Y., m. Mrs. Maria **WHITLOCK**, of New Hartford, Conn., Nov. 15, 1840, by Rev. Warner Hoyt	1	189
Sarah, [d. Daniel & Ruth], b. May 26, 1731	LR1	221
Sarah, d. John & Kezia, b. Apr. 3, 1737	LR1	225
Sarah, d. Daniel & Jerusha, b. Aug. 11, 1751	1	8
Sarah, d. Isaac & Naomi, b. June 12, 1757	LR1	248
Sarah, d. Benj[ami]n & Sarah, b. Feb. 18, 177[ ]	1	38
Sarah, m. Nehemiah **BANKS**, Jan. 21, 1778	1	85

	Vol.	Page
SHERWOOD, (cont.)		
Sarah, had s. John, b. May 4, 1782	1	67
Sarah, wid., d. Jan. 19, 1826	1	225
Sarah, of Ridgefield, m. Samuel B. **COLLINS**, of Chicago, Ill., Aug. 23, 1841, by Rev. Warner Hoyt	1	190
Sarah E., m. Edward W. **NORTHROP**, b. of Ridgefield, Oct. 16, 1848, by Rev. Sylvester S. Strong	1	130
Sarah E., m. Edward W. **NORTHRUP**, b. of Ridgefield, Oct. 16, 1848, by Rev. Sylvester S. Strong	1	131
Sarah Graves, d. Reuben & Rebeckah, b. Nov. 4, 1778	1	54
Seth, s. Benjamin, Jr., d. Aug. 25, 1832, ae 4 y.	1	229
Thomas, d. Nov. 24, 1838, ae 86 y.	1	234
Timothy, s. Benj[ami]n & Sarah, b. Sept. 5, 1780	1	38
Timothy, m. Lois **GRUMMAN**, Oct. 6, 1803	1	159
Timothy, d. May [ ], 1822	1	223
William, .s. Benj[ami]n & Sarah, b. Sept. 23, 1786	1	38
Zadoc, s. Nathan & Lois, b. Apr. 19, 1761	LR1	243
Zadoc, m. Abigail **OLMSTED**, Nov. 13, 1783	1	153
Zalmon, his w. [ ], d. Oct. 6, [1851], ae about 76	1	241
SHINN(?)*, Eliza Ann, d. Sept. 13, 1820, ae 20 y. *(**SKINNER**)	1	222
SHOLES, SHOOLES, SHOLAS, Ann Eliza, of Ridgefield, m. Frederick S. **WEBB**, of Wilton, Apr. 1, [1851], by Rev. William Staunton	1	136
Daniel, m. Clarry **BEERS**, b. of Ridgefield, Sept. 27, 1825, by Rev. Origen P. Holcomb	1	164
-----, Mr. his w. [ ], d. Sept. [ ], 1837, ae [ ]	1	233
SHOVE, Abigail, w. Daniel, d. Nov. 21, 1803, ae 91 y.	1	211
Daniel, d. Feb. 25, 1806, ae 92	1	212
SILAH, Esther, see Esther **SEELEY**	1	156
SILSBEE, Sarah, m. Timothy **WEED**, Dec. 11, 1777	1	63
SIMKINS, Sarah, m. Samuell **OSBURN**, Jan. 1, 1732/3, by Zachariah Mills, J. P.	LR1	229
SKIDMORE, -----, Mr. of New York, his s. [ ], d. July 22, [1852], ae 2 y.	1	242
SKINNER(?)*, Eliza Ann, d. Sept. 13, 1820, ae 20 y. *(**SHINN**?)	1	222
SLATER, George W., of Port Chester, N. Y., m. Isabella **PICKETT**, of Ridgefield, last eve {May 16, 1848}, by Rev. James A. Hawley	1	129
SLAWSON, SLOSSON, SLAUSON, Augustus D., m. Hannah **BURTON**, Mar. 15, 1840, by Nathan Burton, P. T.	1	188
Betsey, m. Elisha S. **LOUNSBURY**, b. of Ridgefield, Nov. 29, 1843, by Rev. A. S. Francis	1	194
Israel, d. Dec. 12, 1835, ae 77	1	232
Jesse B., m. Fanny **MEAD**, b. of Ridgefield, Oct. 12, 1834, by Rev. Charles G. Selleck	1	180
Jonathan, m. Sarah **NORTHRUP**, Feb. 2, 1794	1	83
Lewis, of New Canaan, m. Abbercinda **STUART**, of Ridgefield, Jan. 1, 1822, by Rev. Samuel M. Phelps	1	161

SLAWSON, SLOSSON, SLAUSON, (cont.)

	Vol.	Page
Polly, [d. Jonathan & Sarah], b. Jan. 18, 1795	1	83
-----, Mrs., d. May 2, 1843, ae 79 y.	1	237
SMALL, John C., of New York City, m. Elizabeth E. **EDMONDS,** of Ridgefield, Nov. 29, 1849, by Rev. Nathaniel Mead	1	132
SMALLEY, John, m. Caroline **ARMSTRONG,** Apr. 5, 1840, by Nathan Burton, P. T.	1	188
SMITH, Abby Maria, [d. Josiah, 2nd & Abigail], b. Sept. 11, 1795	1	82
Abel, s. [Stephen & Sarah], b. Dec. 23, 1747	LR1	245
Abel, s. Stephen & Sarah, d. Jan. 14, 1747/8	LR1	216
Abiah, d. [Ebenezer & Sarah], b. Mar. 7, 1716	LR1	201
Abiah, m. Sam[ue]ll **OLMSTEAD,** Apr. 15, 1737	LR1	230
Abiah, d. John & Clement, b. Dec. 12, 1756	LR1	253
Abiah, m. Elijah **SMITH,** of Derby, Oct. 15, 1778	1	153
Abigail, d. Daniel & Betty, b. Feb. 17, 1742/3	LR1	236
Abigail, d. Jacob & Sarah, b. Nov. 17, 1754	LR1	246
Abigail, m. Daniel **ROCKWELL,** Dec. 18, 1759, by Jonathan Ingersoll, V. D. M.	LR1	252
Abigail, d. Joseph & Abigail, b. Aug. 13, 1768	1	11
Abigail, m. Ebenezer **STEBBINS,** June 11, 1776	1	152
Abigail, alias **WORDEN,** m. Ebenezer **ROCKWELL,** Nov. 5, 1777	1	152
Abigail, d. Nathan & Jane, b. May 7, 1781	1	49
Abijah, s. Stephen & Sarah, b. Apr. 18, 1760	LR1	245
Abijah, s. Ezekiel & Mary, b. Oct. 25, 1772	1	37
Abner, s. Nathan & Mary, b. Nov. 9, 1757	LR1	250
Abraham, s. Jabish & Ruth, b. June 6, 1733	LR1	222
Abraham, s. Benajah & Mary, b. Jan. 27, 1774	1	30
Ada, d. Joseph & Abigail, b. Sept. 30, 1773	1	11
Adah, d. Hezekiah & Abigail, b. Mar. 2, 1783	1	52
Adah, wid., d. Feb. 20, 1809, ae 86 y.	1	214
Adelia Ann, m. Eli **ROCKWELL,** Dec. 28, 1828, by Nathan Burton	1	169
Agness, d. Nathan & Mary, b. Oct. 2, 1760	LR1	250
Alford, s. [Isaiah & Mary], b. May 17, 1799	1	87
Alfred, m. Polly **BRADLEY,** b. of Ridgefield, Jan. 9, 1823, by Rev. Samuel M. Phelps	1	161
Amelia A., m. W[illia]m W. **HAWKINS,** b. of Ridgefield, June 26, 1840, by Rev. Joseph Fuller	1	189
Amos, s. John & Clement, b. Nov. 12, 176[ ]	1	24
Amos, Jr., m. Esther A. **LEE,** b. of Ridgefield, Nov. 28, 1838, by Rev. Joseph Fuller	1	187
Andrew, s. Jonah, Jr. & Anne, b. Mar. 8, 1766	1	14
Anna, d. Thomas & Adar, b. Sept. 9, 1746	LR1	239
Anna, [d. Josiah & Joanna], b. Sept. 11, 1788	1	71
Anna, d. Job, 2nd & Esther, b. Dec. 13, 1790	1	47
Anna, Mrs., m. William **CROCKER,** b. of Ridgefield, Aug. 22, [1824], by Rev. Daniel Crocker	1	163

SMITH, (cont.)

	Vol.	Page
Anne, d. Daniel & Betty, b. Mar. 16, 1752	LR1	244
Anne, [d. Stephen & Sarah], b. Oct. 12, 1753	LR1	245
Anne, d. Jonah, Jr. & Anne, b. Dec. 1, 1755	LR1	248
Anne, d. Stephen & Sarah, d. Aug. 1, 1757	LR1	217
Anne, d. Nathan & Jane, b. Aug. 1, 1783	1	49
Anne, wid., d. Oct. 11, 1793	1	206
Azariah, m. Martha **SCRIBNER**, Nov. 6, 1783	1	154
Azariah, d. May 24, 1833, in the 71st y. of his age	1	230
Azariah, his wid., d. Sept. 4, 1841, ae 79 y.	1	236
Azer, s. Daniel, Jr. & Mary, b. Oct. 9, 176[ ]	1	26
Azor, m. Mehetable **FAIRBANKS**, Feb. 28, 1790	1	158
Azor, d. Feb. 20, 1812	1	216
Azor, his wid., d. [Dec.] 20, [1850], ae 84	1	241
Benajah, s. Daniel & Betty, b. Oct. 9, 1749	LR1	244
Benajah, m. Mary **BETTS**, Dec. 13, 1770	1	152
Benedict, [s. Matthew, 2nd & Abigail], b. Jan. 26, 1797	1	82
Benjamin, s. Samuell, 3rd & Ruth, b. Dec. 10, 1741	LR1	236
Benjamin, Lieut., m. Hannah **STEBBINS**, Jan. 11, 1774	1	153
Benj[ami]n, [s. James & Susanna], b. Dec. 20, 1790	1	64
Benjamin, d. Apr. 29, 1823, in the 81st y. of his age	1	223
Benjamin **STEBBINS**, s. Benj[ami]n & Hannah, b. Jan. 5, 1784	1	53
Betsey, [d. James & Sarah], b. Mar. 31, 1779	1	36
Betsey, d. Benjamin & Hannah, b. Apr. 7, 1780	1	41
Betsey, d. Benjamin & Hannah, b. Apr. 7, 1780	1	53
Betsey, d. Job, 2nd & Esther, b. Oct. 27, 1784	1	47
Betsey, d. Hezekiah & Abigail, b. July 29, 1791	1	52
Betsey, [ ]	1	26
Betty, d. Daniel & Betty, b. Aug. 15, 1745	LR1	238
Bettey, w. Daniel, d. Oct. 13, 1798, ae 79 y. 11 m. 6 d.	1	209
Bradley, d. Oct. 9, 1830, ae 30 y.	1	228
Burr, s. [Isaiah & Mary], b. May 9, 1796	1	87
Burr, d. June 2, 1815, ae 19 y.	1	218
Caleb, [s. Jonah & Elizabeth], b. Sept. 11, 1743	LR1	206
Caleb, m. Ruth **HAWLEY**, Oct. 28, 1767	1	150
Caleb, s. Joseph & Abigail, b. Mar. 25, 1771	1	11
Caroline, w. James, d. May 17, 1835, ae 23 y.	1	231
Charles, s. Job & Elizabeth, b. Jan. 17, 1782	1	37
Charles, twin with Chauncey, [s. Phinehas & Elizabeth], b. Aug. 7, 1795	1	35
Charles, Jr., m. Elenor C. **PIGSLEY**, b. of Ridgefield, Oct. 11, 1846, by Charles Stearns. Int. Pub.	1	199
Chauncey, twin with Charles, [s. Phinehas & Elizabeth], b. Aug. 7, 1795	1	35
Chloe, d. Jonah, Jr. & Anne, b. Mar. 5, 1757	LR1	248
Chloe, m. Jesse **OLMSTED**, Mar. 3, 1779	1	154
Clarke, s. Seth, d. Mar. 5, 1834	1	230

SMITH, (cont.)

	Vol.	Page
Clark P., of North Salem, m. Sarah **GILBERT**, of Ridgefield, Sept. 9, 1834, by Rev. Charles G. Selleck	1	180
Clarra, d. Job, 2nd & Esther, b. Sept. 24, 1787	1	47
Clemence, wid., d. Mar. 13, 1828, ae 95	1	226
Cynthia, twin with Sarah, [d. Jeremiah & Lydia], b. May 25, 1789	1	61
Cynthia, d. Jeremiah, d. May 2, 1808, ae 19	1	214
Czar, s. [Daniel & Rachel], b. Jan. 17, 1789	1	95
Czar, d. Mar. 17, 1817, ae 28 y. 2 m.	1	220
Czar, had d. [ ], d. Apr. 1, 1817	1	220
Daniel, s. Daniel, Jr. & Mary, b. Jan. 24, 17[ ]	1	26
Daniell, s. Ebenezer & Sarah, b. Oct. 6, [1719]	LR1	203
Daniel, m. Betty **WHITNEY**, Jan. 25, 1741/2	LR1	231
Daniel, s. Samuell, 4th & Mary, b. June 17, 1745	LR1	238
Daniel, s. Daniel & Betty, b. Sept. 9, 1748	LR1	241
Daniel, Jr., m. Mary **SMITH**, Feb. 25, 176[ ]	1	150
Daniel, m. Rachel **PARDEE**, Dec. 8, 1774	1	95
Daniel, 2nd, m. Elizabeth **NORTHRUP**, Mar. 1, 1781	1	155
Daniel, m. Phebe **WHITNEY**, Jan. 20, 1788	1	157
Daniel, m. Esther **CRANE**, Jan. 11, 1795	1	95
Daniel, 2nd, m. Esther **CRANE**, Jan. 11, 1795	1	159
Daniel, 2nd, d. Mar. 7, 1795, ae 49	1	207
Daniel, d. Aug. 22, 1799, ae 80 y.	1	210
Daniel, 2nd, his infant, d. May 12, 1804	1	212
Daniel, 2nd, his grandchild d. Aug. [ ], 1816	1	219
Daniel, d. Oct. 31, 1823, ae 76 y.	1	224
Daniel, Capt., d. Jan. 19, 1835, ae 67	1	231
Daniel, his wid., d. [Oct.] 12, [1843], ae 77	1	237
Daniel, his child, d. July 10, 1845, ae 2 y.	1	238
Dan[ie]ll, his d. [ ], wid. of [ ] **CLARK**, d. [Sept.] 22, [1851]	1	241
Daniel G., d. Jan. 8, 1825, in the 29th y. of his age	1	224
David, s. Thomas & Hannah, b. June 10, [1718]	LR1	202
David, [s. Josiah & Joanna], b. June 25, 1789	1	71
David, d. Jan. 13, 1793	1	206
Deborah, d. Thomas & Adah, b. Dec. 11, 17[ ]	1	24
Deborah, d. Thomas & Adah, d. Aug. 5, 1766	1	201
Deborah, d. Thomas & Adah, d. Sept. 17, 1766	1	200
Deliverence, w. Levi, d. Apr. 17, 1791	1	205
Dolly, d. Daniel, Jr. & Mary, b. Sept. 17, 17[ ]	1	26
Dorcas, d. Thomas & Adah, b. Aug. 31, 1760	LR1	243
Dorcas, d. Jesse & Martha, b. Oct. 10, 1771	1	28
Dorcas, m. Levi **KEELER**, Jan. 13, 1782	1	154
Dorcas, m. Levi **KEELER**, Jan. 27, 1782	1	155
Dorcas, m. David **OLMSTED**, 3rd, July 6, 1788	1	156
Dorcas, m. David **OLMSTED**, July 6, 1788	1	157
Ebenezer, s. Ebenezer & Hannah, b. Oct. 3, 17[ ]	1	2

SMITH, (cont.)

	Vol.	Page
Ebenezer, s. Ebenezer & Sarah, b. [ ], 15, [1718]	LR1	202
Ebenezer, d. Nov. 4, 1744	LR1	215
Ebenezer, m. Hannah [ ], June 9, 1747	LR1	232
Ebenezer, s. Ebenezer & Hannah, b. Aug. 18, 1752	LR1	242
Ebenezer, s. Ebenezer & Hannah, d. Aug. 9, 1755	LR1	217
Ebenezer, s. Ebenezer & Hannah, d. Aug. 9, 1756	LR1	217
Ebenezer, 2nd. s. Ebenezer & Hannah, b. Oct. 3, 1761	LR1	242
Ebenezer, had child d. June 28, 1808, ae 1 y.	1	214
Ebenezer, d. Oct. 22, 1828, ae 55 y.	1	227
Ebenezer Gould, s. Ebenezer, d. Sept. 6, 1813, in the 3rd y. of his age	1	218
Edmond, s. Daniel, 3rd & Rachel, b. Mar. 22, 1779	1	53
Edmond Pardee, s. [Daniel & Rachel], b. Mar. 22, 1779	1	95
Elijah, s. Gideon & Sarah, b. Dec. 29, 1735	LR1	223
Elijah, of Derby, m. Abiah **SMITH**, Oct. 15, 1778	1	153
Elijah, Jr., m. Susannah **FOLLIET**, Nov. 14, 1779	1	154
Elijah, his negro girl, d. Apr. 2, 1795	1	208
Elijah, d. Apr. 25, 1828, ae 93 y.	1	226
Elijah, m Elizabeth **BENEDICT**, Oct. [ ]	LR1	252
Eliza, [d. Josiah, 2nd & Abigail], b. Oct. 2, 1801	1	82
Eliza, of Ridgefield, m. Abraham J. **PULLEN**, of Danbury, Jan. 1, 1840, by Rev. T. Sparks	1	187
Elizabeth, d. Sam[ue]ll & Elizabeth (of Milford), b. June 30, 1708	LR1	200
Elizabeth, m. Josiah **GILBERT**, June 8, 1726	LR1	227
Elizabeth, [d. Jonah & Elizabeth], b. Nov. 25, 1740	LR1	206
Elizabeth, d. John & Sarah, b. Aug. 31, 1743	LR1	238
Elizabeth, d. Jonah, Jr. & Anne, b. Dec. 14, 1768	1	14
Elizabeth, d. Dec. 16, 1773	1	201
Elizabeth, d. Job & Elizabeth, b. Oct 12, 1775	1	37
Elizabeth, m. Thomas **HYATT**, Sept. 11, 1776	1	155
Elizabeth, d. Jeremiah & Lydia, b. Feb. 28, 1777, d. Sept. 16, 1779	1	61
Elizabeth, 2nd, d. Jeremiah & Lydia, b. Nov. 3, 1780; d. Jan. 7, 1781	1	61
Elizabeth, d. John & Esther, b. June 20, 1785	1	36
Elizabeth, d. Jonah & Anne, d. Apr. 16, 1787	1	204
Elizabeth, [d. Phinehas & Elizabeth], b. Feb. 24, 1791	1	35
Elizabeth, m. Abraham **NASH**, 2nd, [ ], 1795	1	159
Elizabeth, w. Samuel A., d. Sept. 13, 1832, ae 20	1	229
Elizabeth, m. John B. **SMITH**, b. of Ridgefield, Feb. 26, 1843, by Rev. Warner Hoyt	1	194
Elnathan, s. Elijah & Elizabeth, b. Apr. 2, 1766	1	25
Emma, of Ridgefield, m. George **SMITH**, of North Salem, Nov. 11, 1832, by Rev. Charles G. Selleck	1	177
Enos, s. Gideon & Sarah, b. Mar. 6, 1753	LR1	239
Enos, s. Gideon & Sarah, d. Jan. 26, 1772	1	201

SMITH, (cont.)

	Vol.	Page
Ephraim, s. [Gideon & Sarah], b. Apr. 20, 1742	LR1	239
Esther, [d. Jonah & Elizabeth], b. Mar. 4, 1745/6	LR1	206
Esther, m. Thomas **DEMON**, Dec. 11, 1787	1	157
Esther, m. Abraham **HOLMES**, b. of Ridgefield, Dec. 20, 1825, by Samuel M. Phelps	1	167
Esther, w. Walter, d. Aug. 24, 1841, ae 51 y.	1	236
Eunice, d. [Isaiah & Mary], b. Aug. 27, 1797	1	87
Ezekiel, s. Gideon & Sarah, b. June 11, 1749	LR1	239
Ezekiel, m. Mary **MOREHOUSE**, Nov. 29, 1770	1	151
Ezekiel, m. Mary **MOREHOUSE**, Nov. 29, 1770	1	152
Ezra, s. Thomas & Adah, b. Mar. 28, 1758	LR1	243
Ezra, s. Thomas & Adah, d. Aug. 4, 1772	1	201
Ezra, s. John & Rebeckah, b. Dec. 17, 1774	1	36
Ezra, d. Sept. 24, 1833, in the 74th y. of his age	1	230
Fanny, twin with Sally, [d. Thadd & Ruth], b. May 12, 1795	1	88
Gamaliel, s. Samuel, 3rd & Mary, b. Nov. 9, 17[ ]	1	14
Gamaliel, d. Jan. 5, 1782	1	202
George, s. Stephen & Sarah, b. June 12, 1767	LR1	245
George, of North Salem, m. Emma **SMITH**, of Ridgefield, Nov. 11, 1832, by Rev. Charles G. Selleck	1	177
George & w. Emma, had child, d. Mar. [ ], 1837, in New York, bd. in Ridgefield	1	233
George, his child d. Nov. 30, [1840], ae 1 y.	1	235
George, his s. [ ], d. July [ ], [1852], ae about 3 y.	1	242
Gideon, m. Sarah **BENEDICT**, Dec. 9, 1731	LR1	229
Gideon, s. Gideon & Sarah, b. July 27, 1739	LR1	239
Gideon, had negro Ceazer, d. Aug. 2, 1749	LR1	217
Gideon, d. Feb. 7, 1799, ae 91 y.	1	209
Gould, his two infant children, d. Jan. 3, 1795	1	207
Grace, d. Job, 2nd & Esther, b. Feb. 10, 1782	1	47
Grove, s. Daniel & Esther, b. May 30, 1796	1	53
Grove, s. [Daniel & Esther], b. May 30, 1796	1	95
Hannah, m. Matthew **SEAMORE**, June 14, 1722	LR1	227
Hannah, d. Jonah & Elizabeth, b. Nov. 13, 1726	LR1	206
Hannah, d. Gideon & Sarah, b. Sept. 29, 1734	LR1	223
Hannah, d. Ebenezer & Hannah, b. July 13, 1750	LR1	242
Hannah, m. David **SCOTT**, Aug. 4, 1751, by Jonathan Ingersoll, V. D. M.	LR1	234
Hannah, d. Stephen & Sarah, b. Sept. 22, 1755	LR1	245
Hannah, [d. James & Sarah], b. Dec. 17, 1776	1	36
Hannah, d. Benj[ami]n & Hannah, b. Mar. 21, 1788	1	53
Hannah, Mrs., d. Aug. 2, 1793, in the 85th y. of his age	1	206
Hannah, d. Oct. 26, 1809	1	214
Hannah, of Ridgefield, m. Elijah P. **SCRIBNER**, (Capt.), of New York, Oct. 29, 1821, by Rev. Samuel M. Phelps	1	161
Hannah, wid. Benjamin, d. Feb. 12, 1833, ae 82 y. 9 m. at Bedford	1	229

	Vol.	Page
SMITH, (cont.)		
Harriet, w. Seth, d. June 22, 1837, ae [ ]	1	233
Harriet, m. William **ABBOTT**, Oct. 19, 1842, by Rev. Charles Chettenden	1	193
Harry, twin with Stephen, [s. Thadd & Ruth], b. Mar. 16, 1791	1	88
Harvey, s. Job, 2nd & Esther, b. Sept. 29, 1792	1	47
Harvey W., s. [Harvey & Lois], b. Feb. 5, 1821	1	110
Henry, 2nd, d. Sept. 11, 1847, ae 35 y.	1	239
Hezekiah, s. Thomas & Adah, b. Sept. 23, 1755	LR1	243
Hezekiah, m. Abigail **MOREHOUSE**, Sept. 4, 1776	1	155
Hezekiah, d. May 15, 1822, ae 85 y.	1	223
Hiram, of North Salem, N. Y., m. Eliza Jane **SANFORD**, of Ridgefield, May 18, 1846, by Rev. Shaller J. Hillyer	1	198
Huldah, d. Joseph & Abigail, b. July 27, 1766	1	11
Huldah, d. James & Sarah, b. July 8, 1772	1	36
Huldah, d. Ezekiel & Mary, b. Dec. 29, 1782	1	37
Huldah, twin with Major, d. James, decd. & Sarah, b. Feb. 9, 1786	1	36
Huldah, d. Azariah, d. Dec. 23, 1802, ae 17	1	211
Isaac, Jr., m. Hannah **ROCKWELL**, Dec. 22, 1763	1	150
Isaac, d. Apr. 6, 1793, in the 82nd y. of his age	1	206
Isaac, s. Hezekiah & Abigail, b. Dec. 17, 1793	1	52
Isaac, s. [Isaiah & Mary], b. Jan. 24, 1801	1	87
Isaiah, s. Elijah & Elizabeth, d. Apr. 17, 1767	1	201
Isaiah, m. Mary **HYATT**, Jan. 2, 1796	1	87
Isaiah, m. Mary **HYATT**, Feb. 1, 1796	1	159
Isaiah, d. Dec. 25, 1805	1	212
Jabez, s. Jabish & Ruth, b. Dec. 12, 1731	LR1	222
Jabes, m. Hannah **MEAD**, Nov. 1, 1780	1	154
Jabish, m. Ruth **SEAMORE**, d. Capt. Matthew, of Norwalk, June 12, 1729	LR1	229
Jabish, Dea., d. Sept. 22, 1787, in the 82nd y. of his age	1	204
Jacob, s. Samuell & Elizabeth, b. Oct. 6, [1719/20]	LR1	203
Jacob, m. Sarah [ ], Jan. 12, 1748/9	LR1	233
Jacob, s. Jacob & Sarah, b. Oct. 26, 1752	LR1	246
Jacob, m. Sarah **KEELER**, Mar. 23, 1780	1	152
Jacob, d. Apr. 11, 1794, ae 73	1	207
Jacob, [s. Josiah, 2nd & Abigail], b. Feb. 1, 1800	1	82
Jacob, Jr., d. Mar. 11, [ ], in the 38th y. of his age	1	205
James, [s. Jonah & Elizabeth], b. Jan. 7, 1737/8	LR1	206
James, s. [Gideon & Sarah], b. Mar. 6, 1745/6	LR1	239
James, s. Gideon, b. Mar. 6, 1746; m. Sarah **HULL**, Mar. 18, 1767; d. Jan. 27, 1779	1	36
James, m. Sarah **BENEDICT**, Mar. 7, 1764	1	150
James, m. Sarah **HULL**, Mar. 18, 1767	1	151
James, s. Hezekiah, Jr. & Abigail, b. Jan. 14, 1777	1	52
James, m. Susannah **LOBDELL**, Oct. 23, 1785	1	156
James, d. May 12, 1812, ae 74	1	217

SMITH, (cont.)

	Vol.	Page
James B., s. Harvey & Lois, b. Dec. 11, 1816	1	110
Jane, d. Benjamin, d. Sept. 27, 1814, ae 39	1	218
Jane, w. Nathan, d. Feb. 11, 1823, ae 74 y.	1	223
Jemima, d. James & Sarah, b. July 25, 1766	1	18
Jeremiah, s. John & Sarah, b. Oct. 10, 1752	LR1	244
Jeremiah, s. Joseph & Abigail, b. Jan. 13, 1763	1	11
Jeremiah, s. Matthew & Phebe, b. May 15, 1767	1	47
Jeremiah, m. Lydia **SMITH**, Sept. 25, 1776	1	156
Jeremiah, s. John & Esther, b. Aug. 21, 1782	1	46
Jeremiah, s. John & Esther, d. Jan. 28, 1783	1	202
Jeremiah, [s. Jeremiah & Lydia], b. July 4, 1787; d. Aug. 25, 1787	1	61
Jeremiah, s. Hezekiah & Abigail, b. Feb. 6, 1796	1	52
Jeremiah, his wid., d. Nov. 15, 1813, ae 89	1	237
Jeremiah, d. Dec. 22, 1837, in the 85th y. of his age	1	234
Jerusha, d. James & Sarah, b. June 23, 1772	1	18
Jesse, s. Samuel & Ruth, b. Dec. 13, 1748	LR1	242
Jesse, m. Martha **MEAD**, Apr. 26, 1769	1	150
Jesse, s. Benjamin & Hannah, b. Nov. 3, 1789	1	53
Joanna, d. Samuell, 3rd & Ruth, b. Oct. 17, 1743	LR1	236
Joanna, d. Jonah, Jr. & Anne, b. May 21, 1761	LR1	256
Joanna, m. Joseph **STEBBINS**, Feb. 5, 1762	1	150
Joanna, m. Josiah **SMITH**, Apr. 28, 1784	1	154
Joanna, w. Josiah, d. Jan. 2, 1835, ae 73 y.	1	231
Job, m. Sarah **SMITH**, June 25, 1744	LR1	231
Job, s. Job & Sarah, b. Apr. 22, 1747	LR1	198
Job, d. July 5, 1749	LR1	216
Job, s. Daniel & Betty, b. Nov. 3, 1754	LR1	244
Job, m. Elizabeth **KEELER**, Jan. 9, 1771	1	151
Job, 2nd, m. Esther **BENEDICT**, Jan. 12, 1780	1	152
Job, 2nd, m. Esther **BENEDICT**, Jan. 12, 1780	1	154
Job, d. June 6, 1832, ae 78	1	229
Job, his wid., d. [Feb.] 19, [1843], ae 84 y.	1	236
Joel, s. Jabish & Ruth, b. [ ], 9, 1735/6	LR1	222
Joel, s. James & Sarah, b. June 21, 1770	1	36
John, 3rd, m. Rebeckah **SMITH**, July 14, 17[ ]	1	150
John, s. [Samuell & Elizabeth (of Milford)], b. Jan. 12, 1711	LR1	200
John, m. Sarah [ ], Feb. 7, 1739/40	LR1	232
John, s. John & Sarah, b. Oct. 6, 1746	LR1	239
John, m. Clemente **MILLS**, Oct. 29, 1751	LR1	234
John, s. John & Clement, b. Mar. 15, 1759	LR1	253
John, twin with Rebeckah, s. John & Rebeckah, b. Apr. 9, 1773	1	36
John, twin with Rebeckah, s. John & Rebeckah, b. Apr. 9, 1773	1	201
John, d. June 12, 1777	1	202
John, Jr., d. Feb. 28, 1779	1	204

	Vol.	Page
SMITH, (cont.)		
John, s. John, d. Oct. 16, 1781	1	203
John, m. Esther **SHERWOOD**, Dec. 10, 1781	1	152
John, m. Esther **SHERWOOD**, Dec. 20, 1781	1	154
John, s. John & Esther, b. Oct. 11, 1783	1	36
John, s. Jeremiah & Lydia, b. May 16, 1785	1	61
John, [s. James & Susanna], b. Dec. 6, 1787	1	64
John, m. Lucy **KEELER**, b. of Ridgefield, Jan. 9, 1824, by Samuell M. Phelps	1	164
John, d. Aug. 29, 1839, ae 39	1	235
John B., m. Elizabeth **SMITH**, b. of Ridgefield, Feb. 26, 1843, by Rev. Warner Hoyt	1	194
John C., of Middletown, m. Sarah J. **LYON**, of Ridgefield, this day [Sept. 16, 1851], by Rev. Clinton Clark	1	136
John H., of Ridgefield, m. Mary **SMITH**, of West Chester Co., N. Y., Dec. 22, 1830, by Samuel M. Phelps	1	175
John R., m. Sarah Maria **BROWN**, b. of Ridgefield, Oct. 12, 1842, by Rev. Warner Hoyt	1	192
Jonah, m. Elizabeth **BENNETT**, Dec. 29, 1726	LR1	227
Jonah, [s. Jonah & Elizabeth], b. May 7, 1732	LR1	206
Jonah, Jr., m. Anne **NORTHRUP**, Dec. 24, 1754, by Samuel Smith, J. P.	LR1	234
Jonah, Jr. & Ann, had d. [ ], b. Dec. 7, 1759; d. same day, unbaptized	LR1	217
Jonah, s. [Phinehas & Elizabeth], b. Mar. 16, 1789	1	35
Joseph, s. Thomas & Adar, b. May 3, 1742	LR1	236
Joseph, m. Abigail **JONES**, Mar. 16, 1762	1	150
Joseph, of Kartwright, N. Y., d. Oct. 3, 1805, in the 45th y. of his age	1	212
Josiah, m. Joanna **SMITH**, Apr. 28, 1784	1	154
Josiah, twin with July, s. [Thadd & Ruth], b June 3, 1793	1	88
Josiah, 2nd, m. Abigail **BEERS**, Nov. 16, 1794	1	82
Josiah, 2nd, d. Feb. 23, 1808	1	213
Josiah, d. Sept. 7, 1842, ae 82 y.	1	236
Josiah Keeler, s. Phinehas & Elizabeth, b. Mar. 24, 1785	1	35
Julia Elizabeth, d. Nathan, Jr. & Sarah, b. Feb. 27, 1830	1	111
July, twin with Josiah, [child of Thadd & Ruth], b. June 3, 1739	1	88
Kettey, d. [Daniel & Rachel], b. Mar. 24, 1787	1	95
Laune, m. Benjamin L. **STAPLES**, b. of Ridgefield, Sept. 29, 1851, by Rev. Ira Abbott	1	136
Laura, d. Sarah, Jr., d. June [ ], 1789	1	205
Lawrence W., of North Salem, N. Y., m. Mary Ann **SCOTT**, of Ridgefield, Sept. 5, 1847, by Rev. Shaler J. Hillyer	1	128
Levi, s. Jonah, Jr. & Anne, b. July 11, 1764	1	14
Levi, s. Ezekiel & Mary, b. July 26, 1780	1	37
Lewis, s. James & Sarah, b. Oct. 11, 1764	1	18
Lewis, of Brookfield, m. Abigail **ROCKWELL**, of		

SMITH, (cont.)

	Vol.	Page
Ridgefield, Jan. 2, 1842, by Nathan Burton	1	191
Lyoes, d. [May] 19, [1852], ae [ ]	1	242
Lucretia, d. Joseph & Abigail, b. Sept. 13, 1764	1	11
Lucy, d. Benjamin & Hannah, b. Sept. 16, 1776	1	41
Lucy, d. Benjamin & Hannah, b. Sept. 16, 1776	1	53
Lucy, [d. Phinehas & Elizabeth], b. July 7, 1793; d. Apr. 7, 1795	1	35
Lucy, d. Phinehas, d. Apr. 6, 795, ae 2 y.	1	208
Lydia, d. John & Sarah, b. Aug. 6, 1749	LR1	244
Lydia, d. John & Clement, b. Nov. 19, 1752	LR1	253
Lydia, m. Joshua **BURT**, Sept. 12, 1770	1	151
Lydia, m. Jeremiah **SMITH**, Sept. 25, 1776	1	156
Lydia, d. Azariah & Elethia [w. of Daton **GILBERT**], b. Sept. 13, 1788	1	102
Lydia, w. Hezekiah, d. Aug. 7, 1815, ae 78 y.	1	219
Major, s. Daniel, 3rd & Rachel, b. Oct. 4, 1775	1	53
Major, s. [Daniel & Rachel], b. Oct. 14, 1775; d. Aug. 16, 1799	1	95
Major, twin with Huldah, s. James, decd. & Sarah, b. Feb. 9, 1786	1	36
Major, d. Aug. 16, 1799, ae 24 y.	1	210
Major Crane, s. [Daniel & Esther], b. June 11, 1799; d. Oct. 1, 1802	1	95
Major Crane, d. Oct. 1, 1802, in the 4th y. of his age	1	211
Margaret, m. Daniel **OLMSTED**, 2nd, Jan. 9, 1766	1	151
Martha, d. Samuel & Elizabeth (of Milford), b. Feb. 7, [1723]	LR1	204
Martha, d. Samuel & Ruth, b. Aug. 20, 1751	LR1	242
Martha, d. Ebenezer & Hannah, b. Aug. 24, 1756	LR1	242
Martha, m. John **WATEROUS**, May 30, 1782	1	154
Martha, d. May 22, 1796, ae 45	1	208
Martha, m. Benjamin **KEELER**, Oct. 31, 17[ ]	LR1	252
Mary, d. Jonah & Elizabeth, b. Apr. 14, 1730	LR1	206
Mary, d. Jonah & Elizabeth, d. Mar. 25, 1731	LR1	214
Mary, 2nd, d. [Jonah & Elizabeth], b. June 18, 1734	LR1	206
Mary, d. Jonah & Elizabeth, b. June 18, 1734	LR1	218-9
Mary, d. Jacob & Sarah, b. June 10, 1750	LR1	246
Mary, d. Samuel & Mary, b. Aug. 24, 1750	LR1	245
Mary, m. Daniel **SMITH**, Jr., Feb. 25, 176[ ]	1	150
Mary, m. David **SAINT JOHN**, Mar. 13, 1762	1	152
Mary, m. Nathan **DAUCHY**, Nov. 3, 1768	1	79
Mary, w. Daniel, 2nd, d. May 7, 1780	1	202
Mary, w. Samuel, d. Dec. 16, 1781	1	202
Mary, d. Daniel, Jr. & Elizabeth, b. Mar. 17, 1782	1	26
Mary, d. Daniel, 2nd, d. Feb. 25, 1795	1	207
Mary, wid., d. Nov. 25, 1819, ae 94 y.	1	221
Mary, of West Chester Co., N. Y., m. John H. **SMITH**, of Ridgefield, Dec. 22, 1830, by Rev. Samuel M. Phelps	1	175

	Vol.	Page
SMTIH, (cont.)		
Mary Ann, of Ridgefield, m. Noah D. **PARMELEE**, of Somers West Chester Co., N. Y., June 1, 1831, by Rev. Charles G. Selleck	1	174
Mary Ann, m. Samuel S. **OLMSTEAD**, b. of Ridgefield, Oct. 31, 1832, by Rev. Charles J. Todd	1	177
Mary E., m. Jesse S. **BRADLEY**, July 1, 1838, by Rev. Joseph Fuller	1	186
Mary E., m. Bradley **BEERS**, b. of Ridgefield, Apr. 24, 1844, by James A. Hawley	1	195
Mary Jane, of Ridgefield, m. John **FIELD**, of Amenia, N. Y., Dec. 14, 1851, by Rev. Ira Abbott	1	137
Matthew, m. Phebe **BURCHARD**, Jan. 10, 1766	1	153
Matthew, 2nd, m. Abigail **BENEDICT**, Feb. 25, 1796	1	82
Matthew, 2nd, d. July 13, 1813	1	217
May J., of Ridgefield, m. Neran **DIKEMAN**, of Danbury, Mar. 26, 1848, by Rev. Sylvester S. Strong	1	130
Mehetable, d. Ebenezer & Hannah, b. July 3, 1748	LR1	242
Mehitable, d. Thomas & Adah, b. Feb. 14, 175[ ]	LR1	243
Mehetable, m. Thaddeus **ROCKWELL**, Aug. 26, 1770	1	155
Millesent, d. Jesse & Martha, b. Sept. 10, 1776	1	28
Millesent, w. Azariah, Jr., d. May 9, 1812	1	217
Millesent, of Ridgefield, m. Samuel **INGERSOLL**, of Bridgeport, Feb. 1, 1824, by Samuell M. Phelps	1	165
Molly, d. Aug. 4, 1832, ae 83 y.	1	229
Molly, d. Daniel & Betty, b. Oct. 23, [ ]	1	2
Nancy, d. Hezekiah & Abigail, b. Jan. 26, 1781	1	52
Nancy, d. Daniel, 3rd & Rachel, b. Jan. 22, 1783	1	53
Nancy, d. [Daniel & Rachel], b. Jan. 22, 1783	1	95
Nancy Emily, of Ridgefield, m. George A. **HYATT**, of Waterbury, Jan. 14, 1852, by Rev. Ira Abbott	1	137
Nathan, [s. Jonah & Elizabeth], [ ]	LR1	206
Nathan, m. Mary **BENEDICT**, Dec. [ ]	LR1	252
Nathan, [s. Samuell & Elizabeth (of Milford)], b. Sept. 7, 1715	LR1	200
Nathan, s. Sam[ue]ll & Elizabeth [of Milford], d. Jan. 9, [1726] (Entry is followed by date "Feb. 9")	LR1	214
Nathan, s. Jonah & Elizabeth, b. Dec. 11, 1728	LR1	209
Nathan, s. Samuel & Ruth, b. July 17, 1753	LR1	242
Nathan, s. Nathan & Mary, b. June 7, 1759	LR1	250
Nathan, m. Jane **ROSSEGUIE**, Feb. 18, 1777	1	152
Nathan, s. Nathan & Jane, b. Nov. 11, 1788	1	49
Nathan, Jr., m. Sarah S. **BRADLEY**, b. of Ridgefield, Nov. 15, 1825, by Samuell M. Phelps	1	166
Nathan, d. Oct. 1, 1831, ae 78	1	228
Nathan, s. [Nathan, Jr. & Sarah], b. Sept. 3, 1847	1	111
Nathan Gaylord, s. Jesse & Martha, b. June 27, 1773	1	28
Nathan Gaylord, m. Hannah **OLMSTED**, Apr. 15, 1795	1	79
Nehemiah, s. Daniel & Betty, b. Jan. 3, 1757	LR1	244

BARBOUR COLLECTION

	Vol.	Page
SMITH, (cont.)		
Nehemiah, s. Daniel, 3rd & Rachel, b. Feb. 13, 1777	1	53
Nehemiah, s. [Daniel & Rachel], b. Feb. 13, 1777	1	95
Noah, s. Hezekiah & Abigail, b. Feb. 11, 1757* *(1787?)	1	52
Noah, s. Elijah & Elizabeth, b. Mar. 20, 1761	LR1	251
Noah, s. Daniel, Jr. & Mary, b. Mar. 12, 1774	1	26
Noah, s. Ezekiel & Mary, b. Sept. 11, 1775* *(1785?)	1	37
Noah, 2nd, d. Mar. 6, 1829, ae 55	1	227
Noah, his w. [ ], d. Dec. 3, 1842, ae 70 y.	1	236
Northrop, [s. Matthew, 2nd & Abigail], b. Mar. 14, 1807	1	82
Parmenas, s. Hezekiah & Abigail, b. Jan. 21, 1789	1	52
Patience, d. Sam[ue]ll & Elizabeth, of Norwalk, b. Feb. 19, 1727/8	LR1	209
Phebe, d. Job & Sarah, b. Sept. 24, 1745	LR1	238
Phebe, d. John & Clement, b. Nov. 16, 176[ ]	1	24
Phebe, d. Elijah & Elizabeth, b. Feb. 25, 1762	1	25
Phebe, m. John **JONES**, July 4, 1763	1	151
Phebe, d. Jeremiah & Lydia, b. June 21, 1782	1	61
Phebe, m. Joseph **HAWLEY**, Dec. 5, 1791	1	158
Phebe, m. Phenehas **SPELMAN**, Sept. 8, 1798	1	159
Phebe Amanda, [d. Matthew, 2nd & Abigail], b. Jan. 24, 1805	1	82
Phebe Amanda, m. Eli **WHITLOCK**, b. of Ridgefield, Apr. 7, 1827, by Levi Bronson	1	167
Philip, s. Jonah, Jr. & Anne, b. Apr. 24, 1758	LR1	256
Phinehas, s. Jonah, Jr. & Anne, b. May 6, 1763	1	14
Phinehas, m. Elizabeth **KEELER**, Nov. 4, 1784	1	155
Platt, s. [Daniel & Rachel], b. July 24, 1792	1	95
Polly, d. Nathan & Jane, b. Sept. 27, 1778	1	49
Polly, d. Daniel, 3rd & Rachel, b. Feb. 13, 1781	1	53
Polly, d. [Daniel & Rachel], b. Feb. 13, 1781	1	95
Polly, d. Thadd & Ruth, b. Feb. 27, 1786	1	88
Polly, m. Thomas H. **ROCKWELL**, July 31, 1800	1	159
Polly, [d. Matthew, 2nd & Abigail], b. Feb. 5, 1801	1	82
Polly, m. Joseph **WHILLOCK**, b. of Ridgefield, Mar. 24, 1822, by Rev. Samuel M. Phelps	1	161
Polly, w. Seth, d. Oct. 16, 1833, ae 37 y.	1	230
Rachaell, d. Sam[ue]ll & Elizabeth, b. Mar. 27, [1723]	LR1	204
Rachel, d. Samuel & Mary, b. Oct. 23, 1752	LR1	245
Rachel, m. Uzziel **HYATT**, Nov. 28, 1770	1	151
Rachel, d. Jonah, Jr. & Anne, b. Mar. 17, 1771	1	14
Rachel, d. Ezekiel & Mary, b. Jan. 12, 1776	1	37
Rachel, m. Jeremiah **MEAD**, Feb. 17, 1779	1	152
Rachel, m. Jeremiah **MEAD**, Feb. 17, 1779	1	154
Rachel, d. [Daniel & Rachel], b. Apr. 3, 1785	1	95
Rachel, d. Jonah & Anne, d. Apr. 16, 1788	1	204
Rachel, w. Daniel, d. Dec. 20, 1793	1	95
Rachel, w. Daniel, 3rd, d. Dec. 20, 1793, ae 39 y.	1	207
Rebeckah, d. John & Rebeckah, b. Feb. 26, 17[ ]	1	36

	Vol.	Page
SMITH, (cont.)		
Rebeckah, m. John **SMITH**, 3rd, July 14, 17[ ]	1	150
Rebeckah, d. Thomas & Adah, b. Jan. 6, 1748/9	LR1	243
Rebeckah, twin with John, d. John & Rebeckah, b Apr. 9, 1773	1	36
Rebeckah, twin with John, d. John & Rebeckah, d. Apr. 9, 1773	1	201.
Rebeckah, m. John **JONES**, Nov. 7, 1784	1	155
Rebeckah, wid., d. May 27, 1816	1	219
Rebeckah, m. Hiram S. **BOWTON**, b. of Ridgefield, Nov. 10, 1824, by Samuell M. Phelps	1	165
Richard B., m. Elizabeth **PIKE**, b. of Ridgefield, July 8, 1838, by Rev. Joseph Fuller	1	186
Robert, s. Jobe & Rebeckah, d. [ ]	1	201
Rufus, [s. Matthew, 2nd & Abigail], b. May 10, 1799	1	82
Ruhamah, m. Amos **STEARNS**, Sept. 6, 1787	1	156
Ruth, d. Samuel, of Norwalk, m. Jonah **KEELER**, Nov. 5, 1713	LR1	227
Ruth, d. Jabish & Ruth, b. Jan. 16, 1736/7	LR1	222
Ruth, d. Sam[ue]ll, 3rd & Ruth, b. Oct. 13, 1745	LR1	238
Ruth, w. Samuel, d. May 20, 1754	LR1	216
Ruth, d. Caleb & Ruth, b. July 10, 1768	1	25
Ruth, d. Jesse & Martha, b. Dec. 4, 1769	1	28
Ruth, [d. James & Sarah], b. July 5, 1774	1	36
Ruth, w. Josiah, d. Sept. 9, 1776	1	201
Ruth, m. Moses **INGERSOLL**, Dec. 9, 1787	1	156
Ruth, m. Moses **INGERSOLL**, Dec. 10, 1787	1	157
Sally, d. Benjamin & Hannah, b. Oct. 21, 1774	1	41
Sally, d. Benjamin & Hannah, b. Oct. 21, 1774	1	53
Sally, d. Nathan & Jane, b. Apr. 5, 1786	1	49
Sally, d. [Phinehas & Elizabeth], b. Aug. 12, 1787	1	35
Sally, twin with Fanny, [d. Thadd & Ruth], b. May 12, 1795	1	88
Sally, of Ridgefield, m. Thaddeus **JEWITT**, of Galway, N. Y., Sept. 28, 1821, by Samuel M. Phelps	1	161
Sally, m. Matthew **KEELER**, Jr., b. of Ridgefield, Feb. 5, 1823, by Samuell M. Phelps	1	162
Sally, m. Lockwood **GRAY**, b. of Ridgefield, May 3, 1831, by Samuel Stebbins, J. P.	1	173
Samantha, d. [Daniel & Rachel], b. Jan. 10, 1791	1	95
Cemantha, d. Daniel, 4th, d. June 17, 1791	1	206
Sam[ue]ll, [s. Samuell & Elizabeth (of Milford)], b. Jan. 11, 1713	LR1	200
Samuel, m. Sarah [ ], June 13, 1717	LR1	227
Sam[ue]ll & w. Sarah, had child b. dead June 7, [1718]	LR1	213
Samuell, s. Samuell & Sarah, b. July 9, [1719]	LR1	203
Samuell, m. Elizabeth [ ], June 21, 1722 [Norwalk]	LR1	227
Sam[ue]ll, of Ridgefield, m. Ruth **GAYLORD**, of		

SMITH, (cont.)

	Vol.	Page
New Milford, Dec. 24, 1740, by Rev. D. Boardman	LR1	231
Samuel, Sr., of Norwalk, m. Mary **NORTHRUP**, May 18, 1743	LR1	231
Samuel, s. Samuel, 4th & Mary, b. Dec. 21, 1743	LR1	237
Samuel, formerly of Norwalk, d. Jan. 25, 1764	1	200
Samuel, d. May 1, 1778	1	202
Samuel, d. May 1, 1778	1	203
Samuel, s. Benjamin & Hannah, b. Jan. 20, 1782	1	53
Samuel, d. Jan. 20. 1782	1	202
Samuel, 2nd, had d. [ ], d. Mar. 15, 1820	1	222
Samuel, d. Oct. 3, 1823	1	223
Samuel, his wid. [ ], d. Feb. 19, 1833	1	229
Samuel Andrews, s. Dan[ie]ll, Jr. & Elizabeth, b. July 11, 1784	1	26
Samuel M., m. Esther **BEARDSLEY**, b. of Ridgefield, Oct. 28, 1820, by Rev. Samuell M. Phelps	1	161
Samuel M., m. Lucy **LEE**, b. of Ridgefield, June 18, 1848, by Rev. Sylvester S. Strong	1	130
Sarah, d. Ebenezer & Sarah, b. Oct. 13, 1713	LR1	201
Sarah, w. Sam[ue]ll, d. Oct. 22, [1720]	LR1	213
Sarah, d. Sam[ue]ll & Elizabeth, b. Mar. 24, 1724	LR1	204
Sarah, d. Jabish & Ruth, b. Sept. 17, 1730	LR1	222
Sarah, d. Gideon & Sarah, b. Jan. 29, 1732	LR1	218-9
Sarah, m. Timothy **BENEDICT**, Jan. 24, 1733/4	LR1	230
Sarah, d. John & Sarah, b. Dec. 8, 1740	LR1	238
Sarah, m. Job **SMITH**, June 25, 1744	LR1	231
Sarah, d. Stephen & Sarah, b. Oct. 15, 1745	LR1	239
Sarah, d. Stephen & Sarah, b. Oct. 15, 1745	LR1	245
Sarah, d. Samuel, 4th & Mary, b. June 3, 1748	LR1	241
Sarah, m. Timothy **FOSTER**, Sept. 21, 1749, by Rev. Jonathan Ingersoll	LR1	233
Sarah, m. Nathan **OLMSTEAD**, Feb. 12, 1751/2	LR1	234
Sarah, w. Jacob, d. June 6, 1759	LR1	217
Sarah, d. Daniel & Betty, b. Sept. 4, 1759	LR1	244
Sarah, d. John & Clement, b. Sept. 26, 1763	1	24
Sarah, d. Elijah & Elizabeth, b. June 14, 1764	1	25
Sarah, d. James & Sarah, b. July 11, 1768	1	36
Sarah, d. Job & Elizabeth, b. June 20, 1773	1	37
Sarah, d. Dan[ie]ll, Jr. & Mary, b. Apr. 19, 1777	1	26
Sarah, d. John & Rebeckah, b. May 20, 1778	1	36
Sarah, m. Ephraim **CLARK**, Jan. 8, 1784	1	154
Sarah, m. Philip **LOBDELL**, Sept. 27, 1788	1	68
Sarah, m. Philip **LOBDELL**, Sept. 28, 1788	1	157
Sarah, twin with Cynthia, [d. Jeremiah & Lydia], b. May 25, 1789	1	61
Sarah, w. Gideon, d. Oct. 30, 1791	1	206
Sarah, d. May 11, 1797, ae 9 y.	1	209
Sarah, [d. Josiah, 2nd & Abigail], b. June 30, 1797	1	82
Sarah, 3rd, wid., d. Sept. 26, [1801], ae 65	1	210

SMITH, (cont.)

	Vol.	Page
Sarah, w. Stephen, d. Jan. 17, 1802, in the 78th y. of her age	1	211
Sarah, wid. John, d. Apr. 18, 1802, in the 85th y. of her age	1	211
Sarah, wid. of Jacob, d. Mar. 22, 1825, ae 68 1/2	1	224
Sarah, d. Josiah, 2nd, d. Oct. 12, 1829, at Norwalk, in her 33rd y.	1	227
Sarah, of Ridgefield, m. Matthias **COMSTOCK**, of New Canaan, Feb. 26, 1834, by Rev. Charles G. Selleck	1	179
Sarah A., of Ridgefield, m. Edward **TROWBRIDGE**, of New Haven, this day [Aug. 6, 1851], by Rev. C. Clark	1	135
Sarah Ann, d. [Harvey & Lois], b. Sept. 15, 1827	1	110
Sarah C., m. Walter C. **QUINTARD**, b. of Ridgefield, Mar. 19, 1837, by Rev. J. Lyman Clark	1	183
Sarah Esther, m. Charles **OLMSTED**, b. of Ridgefield, Sept. 26, 1841, by Rev. Warner Hoyt	1	191
Seth, m. Polly **HOYT**, b. of Ridgefield, Feb. 13, 1822, by Samuel M. Phelps	1	161
Seth, m. Harriet **JONES**, b. of Ridgefield, Oct. 22, 1834, by Rev. Charles G. Selleck	1	180
Seth, m. Amelia B. **SCOTT**, b.of Ridgefield, Mar. 19, 1838, by Rev. Joseph Fuller	1	185
Seth, had infant d. Mar. 11, 1839	1	234
Stephen, s. Samuel & Elizabeth, b. Sept. 23, [1714]	LR1	202
Stephen, m. Sarah **COUCH**, Jan. 2, 1744/5	LR1	231
Stephen, [s. Stephen & Sarah], b. Apr. 13, 1749	LR1	245
Stephen, d. Apr. 14, 1777	1	201
Stephen, s. Job & Elizabeth, b. Jan. 12, 1780	1	37
Stephen, had negro, d. Feb. 19, 1785	1	203
Stephen, twin with Harry, [s. Thadd & Ruth], b. Mar. 16, 1791; d. Apr. 13, 1791	1	88
Stephen & w. Sarah had negro Nancy, d. Jenny, b. Dec. 14, 1795	1	71
Stephen, testified he had negro Nancy d. Jenny, b. Dec. 14, 1795, to be free at the age of 25 y. Witnesses Philip Bradley & Azor Belden. Sworn to Philip B. Bradley, J. P., May 21, 1798	1	84
Stephen had negro Nancy, d. Jenny, b. Dec.20, 1795	1	71
Stephen, d. Dec. 21, 1798, ae 81 y. 2 m. 27 d.	1	209
Susanna, [d. James & Susanna], b. Feb. 23, 1786	1	64
Susanna, wid., d. Jan. 20, 1810	1	215
Sylvester, d. Dec. 24, 1827, ae 20	1	226
Thaddeus, s. Stephen & Sarah, b. June 12, 1762	LR1	245
Thaddeus, m. Ruth **STEBBINS**, Aug. 4, 1785	1	155
Thomas, s. Thomas & Hannah, b. Oct. 31, 1715	LR1	199
Thomas, m. Adar **BANKS**, June 11, 1740	LR1	231
Thomas, Dea., d. Sept. 15, 1743, ae 67 y.	LR1	215
Thomas, s. Thomas & Adar, b. July 28, 1744	LR1	239
Thomas, s. John & Rebeckah, b. Apr. 20, 177[ ]	1	36

SMTIH, (cont.)

	Vol.	Page
Thomas, s. John & Rebeckah, d. Aug. 14, 1783	1	203
Thomas, 2nd, d. July 22, 1800, ae 56 y.	1	210
Thomas, d. Mar. 21, 1805, in the 94th y. of his age	1	212
Timothy, [s. Matthew, 2nd & Abigail], b. May 5, 1809	1	82
Treat, s. Walter, d. Mar. 18, 1828, ae 17 y.	1	226
Uriah, s. Thomas & Adah, d. Jan. 2, 1782	1	203
Uriah, s. Hezekiah & Abigail, b. Dec. 22, 1784	1	52
William, s. Jacob, Jr. & Sarah, b. Aug. 2, 1752	1	47
William, s. Benajah & Mary, b. Dec. 13, 177[ ]	1	30
William, s. Job & Elizabeth, b. Nov. 20, 1771	1	37
William, s. Nathan G., d. May 7, 1806	1	213
William, of North Salem, N. Y., m. Harriet **OLMSTED**, of Ridgefield, [Nov.] 21, [1830], by Rev. Origin P. Holcomb	1	172
William, 3rd, of Ridgefield, m. Ann E. **PARISH**, of North Salem, N. Y., July 9, 1838, by Rev. Thomas Sparks	1	186
William, d. May 25, 1847, ae 67 y.	1	239
William Gould, [s. Josiah, 2nd & Abigail], b. May 3, 1804	1	82
William H., s. [Harvey & Lois], b. Aug. 13, 1829	1	110
SPELMAN, Fanny, m. Darling **JARVIS**, b. of Ridgefield, Jan. 7, 1849, by Rev. Sylvester S. Strong	1	131
Phenehas, m. Phebe **SMITH**, Sept. 8, 1798	1	159
STALL, Polly, of Ridgefield, m. Henry **HOYT**, of South Salem, N. Y., Nov. 13, 1839, by Rev. T. Sparks	1	187
STAPLES, Benjamin L., m. Laune **SMITH**, b. of Ridgefield, Sept. 29, 1851, by Rev. Ira Abbott	1	136
Betsey, wid., d. Dec. 14, 1828, ae 38 y.	1	227
Deborha, of Ridgefield, m. Gershom **LOCKWOOD**, of South Salem, Apr. 21, 1828, by Ebenezer S. Raymond	1	168
Deborah A., m. John J. **STEVENS**, b. of Ridgefield, Apr. 22, 1846, by Charles Stearnes. Int. Pub.	1	199
Hannah, w. Thomas, d. July 26, 1801	1	210
Jemima, wid., d. Feb. 21, 1835	1	231
Mary E., of Ridgefield, m. Ebenezer W. **DAN**, of West Port, Oct. 10, 1843, by Rev. A. S. Francis	1	194
Molly, wid., d. May 29, 1847, ae 76 y.	1	239
Thomas, d. Dec. 13, 1816, ae 81 y.	1	220
Turney, his s. [ ], d. Dec. 28, 1843, ae 7 y.	1	237
Walter, d. Mar. 10, 1830, ae 60	1	228
William, d. Feb. 7, [1852], ae about 27 y.	1	242
STAPLEY, John S., m. Eliza A. **DANN**, b. of Ridgefield, May 11, 1847, by Charles Stearns	1	128
STARR, Abbey, of Ridgefield, m. Eli **JUDD**, of Bethel, Apr. 10, 1845, by James A. Hawley	1	196
Abigail, d. Samuel & Anne, b. July 22, 1754	LR1	253
Anne, d. Samuel & Anne, b. Nov. 7, 1757	LR1	253
Anne, d. Noah & Sarah, b. Dec. 5, 1778	1	51
Eunice, d. Samuel & Anne, b. Aug. 1, 1765	1	34

	Vol.	Page
STARR, (cont.)		
Hannah, d. Samuel & Anne, b. June 29, 1763	1	34
Keeler, s. Noah & Sarah, b. Nov. 18, 1776	1	51
Mary, d. Sylvanus & Mary, b. Sept. 14, 1760	1	11
Mary, d. Sam[ue]ll & Anne, b. Aug. 1, 1767	1	34
Noah, s. Samuel & Anne, b. Mar. 24, 1753	LR1	253
Noah, m. Sarah **KEELER**, Aug. 11, 1773	1	153
Noah, d. Jan. 6, 1782	1	203
Noah, s. Noah & Sarah, b. June 22, 1782	1	51
Olive, d. Sam[ue]ll & Anne, b. July 11, 1769	1	34
Peter, s. Samuel & Anne, b. Sept. 3, 1757	1	34
Peter, s. Samuel & Anne, b. Sept. 1, 1759	LR1	253
Platt, s. Samuel & Anne, b. July 29, 1761	LR1	253
Platt, s. Samuel & Anne, b. July 29, 1761	1	34
Samuel, s. Sylvanus & Mary, b. Jan. 11, 1758	1	11
Samuel, d. Oct. 17, 1770	1	201
Samuel, s. Samuel & Anne, b. Apr. 1, 1771	1	34
Samuel, s. Noah & Sarah, b. Aug. 24, 1780	1	51
Sarah, d. Samuel & Anne, b. Mar. 27, 1756	LR1	253
Sarah, d. Noah & Sarah, b. Jan. 25, 1774	1	51
Sylvanus, d. June 21, 1762	1	200
Thomas, s. Sylvanus & Mary, b. Dec. 23, 1761	1	11
STEARNS, Amos, m. Ruhamah **SMITH**, Sept. 6, 1787	1	156
STEBBINS, Abby, m. Nathan **BYINGTON**, b. of Ridgefield, July 7,		
1840, by Rev. Joseph Fuller	1	189
Abigail, d. Theophilus & Anne, b. Nov. 17, 1766	1	10
Abigail, d. Ebenezer & Abigail, b. May 21, 177[ ]	1	46
Abigail, m. Thomas N. **COUCH**, Dec. 30, 1787	1	157
Abigail, [d. Nathan & Dorcas], b. June 20, 1813	1	73
Anne, m. Isaac **KEELER**, Apr. 29, 1752	LR1	234
Anne, d. Theophilus & Anne, b. Dec. 12, 1762	1	10
Anne, m. Eli **SANFORD**, of Redding, Nov. 16, 1786	1	157
Anne, m. Jonathan **KEELER**, Aug. 22, 1790	1	158
Benjamin, m. Sarah **MEADE**, Aug. 14, 1718	LR1	227
Benjamin & d. Sarah, had child s. b. Sept. 6, [1719]	LR1	213
Benjamin, had child d. Sept. 3, [1720], unbaptized	LR1	213
Benjamin, s. Benjamin & Sarah, b. Nov. 3, [1721]	LR1	203
Benjamin, s. Benjamin & Elizabeth, b. July 14, 174[ ]	1	56
Benjamin, m. Elizabeth **OLMSTEAD**, Oct. 8, 1745	LR1	232
Benjamin, s. Benjamin & Elizabeth, b. June 13, 1748	LR1	242
Benjamin, s. Ebenezer & Abigail, b. Sept. 26, 177[ ]	1	46
Benjamin, 3rd, m. Deborah **KEELER**, Dec. 12, 1770	1	151
Benjamin, d. Sept. 16, 1780	1	203
Benjamin, s. Benjamin & Ellizabeth, d. Oct. [ ], 1781	1	203
Benjamin, d. Feb. 26, 1803, ae 81 1/2 y.	1	211
Benjamin, of Brookfield, m. Antoinette **PULLING**, of		
Ridgefield, Dec. 20, 1848, by Rev. Sylvester S. Strong	1	130
Betsey, d. Samuel & Ruth, b. Jan. 16, 1785	1	58

STEBBINS, (cont.)

	Vol.	Page
Betsey, m. Gould **HAWLEY**, Jan. 19, 1809	1	104
Cecelia, d. Sam[ue]ll & Ruth, b. July 6, 1802	1	58
Celia, of Ridgefield, m. Amos A. **WATERBURY**, of Stamford, Nov. 26, 1823, by Rev. Oregen S. Holcomb	1	162
Charles, [s. Nathan & Dorcas], b. Apr. 24, 1797	1	73
David, s.Theophilus & Anne, b. Apr. 9, 1759	LR1	256
David, s. Theophilus & Anne, d. Sept. 2, 1761	1	201
David, s. Theophilus & Anne, b. Oct. 7, 1768	1	10
David Mortimor, [s. Nathan & Dorcas], b. May 11, 1810	1	73
Deborah, m. Ebenezer **HAWLEY**, Apr. 10, 1783	1	154
Delia, [d. Nathan & Dorcas], b. Nov. 7, 1804	1	73
Dorcas, d. Josiah & Ruth, b. Dec. 6, 1760	LR1	248
Ebenezer, s. Benjamin & Sarah, b. Jan. 24, 1723	LR1	204
Ebenezer, m. Anne [ ], Jan. 13, 1747/8	LR1	232
Ebenezer, d. Sept. 2, 1749	LR1	216
Ebenezer, s. Benjamin & Elizabeth, b. Nov. 30, 1754	LR1	242
Ebenezer, s. Benjamin & Elizabeth, b. Nov. 30, 1754	1	56
Ebenezer, m. Abigail **SMITH**, June 11, 1776	1	152
Ebenezer, d. Sept. 1, 1808, in the 54th y. of his age	1	214
Elizabeth, d. Benjamin & Elizabeth, b. Aug. 10, 174[ ]	1	56
Elizabeth, d. Benjamin & Elizabeth, b. Aug. 10, 1746	LR1	239
Elizabeth, wid. of Benjamin, d. Mar. 11, 1825, in the 99th y. of her age	1	224
Esther, m. John **BENEDICT**, Jan. 24, 1749/50	LR1	233
Esther, d. Joseph & Joanna, b. Oct. 19, 1781	1	14
Fanny, d. Simon & Eunice, b. May 6, 1793	1	77
Fanny, [d. Nathan & Dorcas], b. Apr. 20, 1800	1	73
Hannah, m. John **SHERWOOD**, May [ ]	LR1	252
Hannah, d. Benjamin & Sarah, b. Mar. 22, 1728	LR1	209
Hannah, d. Benjamin & Elizabeth, b. Apr. 12, 175[ ]	1	56
Hannah, d. Benjamin & Elizabeth, b. Apr. 12, 1750	LR1	242
Hannah, m. Lieut. Benjamin **SMITH**, Jan. 11, 1774	1	153
Hannah, d. Theophilus & Anne, b. May 3, 1777	1	10
Hugh John, [ ], 1807	1	171
Isaac, s. Josiah, d. Oct. 16, 1756	1	201
Isaac, s. Josiah & Ruth, b. Oct. 13, 1766	1	10
Isaac, s. Josiah & Ruth, d. Oct. 16, 1766	1	200
Isaac, s. Joseph & Joanna, b. Feb. 22, 1776	1	14
Isaac, d. Apr. 7, 1825, ae 49 y.	1	224
James, s. Theophilus & Anne, b. Feb. 2, 1761	LR1	256
James, s. Theophilus & Jane, d. Aug. 31, 1777	1	202
James, [s. Nathan & Dorcas], b. Oct. 26, 1794	1	73
James, d. Nov. 10, 1818, in the 25th y. of his age, at Blakeley, in the Alabama Territory	1	221
Jere, [s. Joseph, 2nd & Abigail], b. Sept. 11, 1795	1	73
Jeremiah, s. Ebenezer & Ann, b. Nov. 12, 1748	LR1	241
Jesse, [s. Joseph, 2nd & Abigail], b. Mar. 27, 1794	1	73

STEBBINS, (cont.)

	Vol.	Page
Joanna, d. Joseph & Joanna, b. Apr. 5, 1768	1	14
Joanna, w. Joseph, d. Mar. 7, 1793	1	206
Joanna, d. Sam[ue]ll & Ruth, b. Dec. 24, 1793	1	58
John, s. Theophilus & Anne, b. Feb. 13, 1755	LR1	256
John, s. Simeon & Eunice, b. Feb. 23, 1795	1	77
John, d. Aug. 13, 1797, in New York, ae 24 y.	1	77
John, s. Samuel & Ruth, b. Feb. 1, 1783	1	58
Joseph, s. Benjamin & Sarah, b. July 4, 1735	LR1	220
Joseph, m. Joanna **SMITH**, Feb. 5, 1762	1	150
Joseph, s. Joseph & Joanna, b. Sept. 30, 1766	1	14
Joseph, Jr., m. Abigail **HINE**, Apr. 11, 1791	1	157
Joseph, 2nd, m. Abigail **HINE**, Apr. 11, 1792	1	73
Joseph, Capt., d. Dec. 13, 1794, in the 60th y. of his age	1	207
Joseph, his w. [ ], d. Jan. 14, 1847, ae 72 y.	1	238
Joseph, d. Sept. 26, [1849], ae 83, at Norwalk, bd. Ridgefield	1	240
Josiah, m. Ruth **ROCKWELL**, Feb. [ ]	LR1	252
Josiah, s. Benjamin & Sarah, b. Apr. 21, 1732	LR1	218-9
Josiah, 2nd, s. Josiah & Ruth, b. Feb. 6, 176[ ]	1	10
Josiah, s. Josiah & Ruth (**ROCKWELL**), b. Feb. 8, 1762	1	10
Josiah, s. Josiah & Ruth, d. Sept. 20, 1762	1	200
Josiah, s. Josiah & Ruth, d. Dec. 20, 1767	1	200
Josiah, m. Mary **BURR**, Dec. 7, 1771	1	151
Josiah, s. Ebenezer & Abigail, b. May 16, 1783	1	46
Josiah, Lieut., d. Feb. 12, 1794, in the 61st y. of his age	1	207
Josiah Burr, s. Josiah & Ruth, b. Oct. 17, 1772	1	10
Mary E., m. Keeler **DAUCHY**, Oct. 16, 1831, by Rev. Charles J. Todd	1	174
Mary Emma, d. Sam[ue]ll & Ruth, b. Aug. 21, 1805	1	58
Nathan, s. Joseph & Joanna, b. Oct. 16, 1764	1	14
Nathan, m. Dorcas **ROCKWELL**, May 26, 1791	1	73
Nathan, d. Nov. 27, 1828, ae 64 y. 1 m. 11 d.	1	227
Nathan Gould, [s. Nathan & Dorcas], b. May 28, 1802	1	73
Nehemiah, s. Benjamin & Sarah, b. Nov. 1, 1729	LR1	209
Ormond, s. Ebenezer & Abigail, b. Oct. 23, 1787	1	46
Polly, d. Joseph & Joanna, b. Nov. 26, 1778	1	14
Polly, m. Eben **HOYT**, Nov. 22, 1800	1	159
Ralph, s. Ebenezer & Abigail, b. Oct. 10, 177[ ]	1	46
Russell, [s. Nathan & Dorcas], b. Mar. 1, 1792	1	73
Ruth, w. Josiah, d. Oct. 15, 1756	1	201
Ruth, d. Josiah & Ruth, b. Mar. 15, 1765	1	10
Ruth, w. Lieut. Josiah, d. Oct. 15, 1766	1	200
Ruth, m. Thaddeus **SMITH**, Aug. 4, 1785	1	155
Ruth, d. Samuel & Ruth, b. Sept. 16, 1789	1	58
Sally, d. Joseph & Joanna, b. June 17, 1771	1	14
Sally, d. Sam[ue]ll & Ruth, b. July 26, 1798	1	58
Samuel, s. Joseph & Joanna, b. Feb. 27, 1763	1	14
Samuel, m. Ruth **WILSON**, Jan. 3, 1782	1	155

BARBOUR COLLECTION

	Vol.	Page
STEBBINS, (cont.)		
Samuel, s. Samuel & Ruth, b. July 5, 1796	1	58
Samuel, d. Mar. 27, 1836, ae 73 y. 1 m.	1	232
Samuel, his wid., d. May 8, [1850], ae 89	1	240
Sarah, d. Benj[ami]n & Sarah, b. Apr. 15, 1737	LR1	222
Sarah, d. Benjamin & Elizabeth, b. Dec. 29, 1760	LR1	242
Sarah, d. Benj[ami]n & Elizabeth, b. Dec. 29, 1760	1	56
Sarah, 2nd, d. Theophilus & Sarah*, b. May 28, 177[ ] *(Anne?)	1	10
Sarah, d. Theophilus & Anne, b. Apr. 16, 1771	1	10
Sarah, d. Theophilus & Ann, d. May 31, 1772	1	201
Sarah, d. May 1, 1774, in the 79th y. of her age	1	204
Sarah, m. Amos **BAKER**, Nov. 4, 1779	1	155
Sarah, d. Ebenezer & Abigail, b. June 16, 1785	1	46
Sarah, m. Asa **BURT**, Jan. 3, 1797	1	159
Simeon, m. Eunice **WHITLOCK**, May 15, 1792	1	157
Simon, s. Theophilus & Anne, b. Dec. 5, 1764	1	10
Theophilus, s. Benjamin & Sarah, b. May 16, [1726]	LR1	206
Theophilus, m. Anne **COUCH**, July 7, 1750	LR1	234
Theophilus & Anne, had s. [ ], b. Nov. 4, 1750; d. 18th of the same month, unbaptized	LR1	207
Theophilus, s. Theophilus & Anne, b. Feb. 7, 1752; d. June 14, 1752	LR1	207
Theophilus, had negroes Michael, s. Tamor, b. Sept. 13, 1756 & Tamor & Dinah, d. Dinah, b. June 7, 1759	LR1	257
Theophilus, d. Mar. 24, 1777	1	201
Thomas, s. Theophilus & Anne, b. Apr. 21, 1757	LR1	256
William, s. Samuel & Ruth, b. Oct. 24, 1786	1	58
STEVENS, STEPHENS, Aaron, [s. Zachariah & Abigail], b. Feb. 14, 1769	1	75
Aaron, [s. Zachariah & Abigail], d. Mar. 16, 1769	1	75
Abigail, [d. Zachariah & Abigail], b. Dec. 1, 1781	1	75
Abijah, [s. Zachariah & Abigail], b. Aug. 10, 1779; d. Oct. 8, 1781	1	75
Adah, [d. Zachariah & Abigail], b. June 19, 1777	1	75
Alfred J., m. Amanda **KELLOGG**, b. of Ridgefield, Dec. 14, 1834, by Rev. Charles J. Todd	1	179
Amos, d. Jan. 6, 1806	1	212
Barnabus, [s. Zachariah & Abigail], b. Feb. 8, 1776; d. June 19, 1776	1	75
Elizabeth, [d. Zachariah & Abigail], b. Sept. 16, 1773	1	75
Hannah, m. Uzziah **HYATT**, Nov. 27, 1783	1	155
Jere, d. May 2, 1827	1	226
John J., m. Deborah A. **STAPLES**, b. of Ridgefield, Apr. 22, 1846, by Charles Stearnes. Int. Pub.	1	199
Laura, w. Sylvanus, d. Mar. 16, 1812, ae 23 y. 11 m. 29 d.	1	216
Mercy, m. Abraham **PULLEN**, Jan. 17, 1793	1	158
Oliver, d. Sept. 26, 1824	1	224

	Vol.	Page
STEVENS, STEPHENS, (cont.)		
Rachel, w. Zachariah, d. Jan. 12, 1768	1	75
Rachel, [d. Zachariah & Abigail], b. Jan. 17, 1770	1	75
Rachel, m. Barnabus **ALLEN**, Feb. 24, 1833, by Nathan Burton	1	176
Tryral, [d. Zachariah & Abigail], b. Feb. 4, 1784	1	75
Zachariah, m. Rachel **GATES**, Dec. 7, 1763	1	75
Zachariah, m. 2nd w. Abigail **HAMLIN**, May 5, 1768	1	75
Zachariah, [s. Zachariah & Abigail], b. Jan. 14, 1772	1	75
STEWART, [see under **STUART**]		
STONE, [see also **STOWE**], Harry, of Danbury, m. Deborah B.		
FIELD, of South East, this day [Mar. 27, 1844], at the house of Barnabus Allen, Ridgebury, by Rev. Rollin S. Stone, of Danbury	1	195
William D., of Carmel, N. Y., m. Charlotte Amelia **LODER**, of Ridgefield, Nov. 2, 1847, by Rev. James A. Hawley	1	128
STOWE, [see also **STONE**], John, m. Polly **ROCKWELL**, July [ ], 1792	1	76
Roselle, s. [John & Polly], b. Dec. 13, 1792	1	76
STREET, Betty, d. Timothy & Elizabeth, b. May 1, 1750	LR1	256
Betty, d. Timothy & Susannah, b. Feb. 23, 1770	1	23
Elizabeth, w. Timothy, d. Oct. 19, 1762	1	200
Elizabeth, m. Timothy **BENEDICT**, Oct. 9, 1765	1	150
Hannah, m. Jonathan **DYKEMAN**, May 1, 1785	1	155
John, s. Timothy & Elizabeth, b. Oct. 2, 1756	LR1	246
Lockwood, s. Timothy & Susannah, b. Oct. 17, 1768	1	23
Mary, d. Timothy & Elizabeth, b. June 10, 1752	LR1	256
Mary, w. Timothy & Elizabeth, d. Sept. 2, 1752	LR1	217
Mary, d. Timothy & Elizabeth, b. July 7, 1754	LR1	246
Mary, d. Timothy & Elizabeth, b. July 7, 1754	LR1	256
Sally, of Ridgefield, m. Robert **LAWRENCE**, of Munroe, N. Y., [Nov.] 5, [1826], by Levi Bronson	1	166
Samuel, s. Timothy & Elizabeth, b. Feb. 20, 1760	LR1	246
Sarah, d. Timothy & Elizabeth, b. Dec. 3, 1744	LR1	239
Sarah, d. Timothy & Elizabeth, d. Aug. 2, 1745	LR1	216
Sarah, d. Timothy & Elizabeth, b. Apr. 19, 1748	LR1	256
Timothy, m. Elizabeth [ ], Jan. 31, 1743/4	LR1	232
Timothy, s. [Timothy & Elizabeth], b. May 20, 1746	LR1	239
Timothy, s. Timothy & Elizabeth, b. May 20, 1746	LR1	256
Timothy, m. Susannah **LOCKWOOD**, Jan. [ ], 176[ ]	1	150
Timothy, m. Susannah **LOCKWOOD**, June 21, 176[ ]	1	150
Timothy, d. Sept. 25, 1767	1	200
STUART, STEWART, Aaron, of Norwalk, m. Rachel **DAUCHY**, June [ ], 1787	1	157
Aaron, d. July 10, 1819	1	221
Abbercinda, of Ridgefield, m. Lewis **SLAWSON**, of New Canaan, Jan. 1, 1822, by Rev. Samuel M. Phelps	1	161
Darling, his w. [ ], d. Apr. [ ], 1807	1	213
David, d. Jan. 23, 1837, ae 63 y.	1	233

STUART, STEWART, (cont.)

	Vol.	Page
Deborah, d. June 10, 1795, ae 78	1	208
Henry A., m. Ann E. **SARLES**, b. of Ridgefield, Sept. 14, 1846, by Rev. Charles Stearns. Int. Pub. Sept. 11, 1846	1	198
Henry A., m. Minerva M. **SANDERLAND**, b. of Ridgefield, Mar. 16, 1851, by Rev. Nathaniel Mead	1	135
James, s. Aaron & Rachel, b. May 3, 17[ ]	1	6 1/2
Phebe A., only d. Lewis, d. Mar. 6, 1846, ae 19 y.	1	238
Simeon, d. June 11, 1808, ae 90	1	214
-----, wid. [, probably 1850]	1	240
STUDWELL, Harvey, d. Nov. [ ], 1837	1	234
John E., m. Betsey **GREGORY**, b. of Ridgefield, June 28, 1828, by Samuel M. Phelps	1	169
STURDEVANT, STURTEVANT, Elizabeth, [d. John & 2nd w. [ ], b. Feb. 15, 1713	LR1	201
James, s. John & Kezia, b. Feb. 18, 1735	LR1	218-9
Jane, d. John & Kezia, b. June 6, 1739	LR1	225
John, [s. John & 1st w. [ ], b. Feb. 16, 1710	LR1	201
John, d. July 27, [1717]	LR1	213
John, m. Kezia [ ], Apr. 12, 1732	LR1	229
John, s. John & Kezia, b. Mar. 24, 1733	LR1	218-9
Sam[ue]ll, s. John & 2nd w. [ ], b. Feb. 15, 1715	LR1	201
STURGIS, STURGES, Abigail, d. Joel & Sarah, b. Mar. 21, 1787	1	55
Andia Byvancks(?), d. Thaddeus & Mary, b. June 24, 1783	1	45
Angelina, d. Nehemiah & Elizabeth, b. Apr. 20, 1791	1	64
David D., of Weston, m. Clarrissa **JONES**, of Ridgefield, Nov. 26, 1851, by Rev. Charles Stearnes	1	137
Elizabeth Laura, [d. Nehemiah & Elizabeth], b. Nov. 16, 1786; d. [ ]	1	64
Elizabeth Laura, d. Nehemiah, d. Feb. 25, 1788	1	204
Elnathan, m. Rebeckah **GREGORY**, Dec. 21, 1782	1	154
Elnathan, Jr., d. Apr. 13, 1789	1	205
Elnathan, d. Jan. 2, 1794, ae 84	1	207
Elnathan Joel, s. Joel & Sarah, b. Nov. 28, 1788	1	55
James, m. Joanna **NORTHRUP**, Mar.18, 1765	1	150
James, d. June 12, 1822, ae 85	1	223
Joanna, wid., d. Feb. 5, 1827, ae 81 y.	1	226
Joel, m. Sarah **PLATT**, Feb. 20, 1783	1	153
Joel, d. July 7, 1788	1	204
Judson Turney, s. Nathaniel & Elizabeth, b. Jan. 13, 1781	1	54
Nehemiah, m. Elizabeth **LAMSON**, Nov. 6, 1775	1	155
Nehemiah, his w. [ ], d. Oct. 11, 1822	1	223
Nehemiah, d. Aug. 30, 1827, ae 74 y.	1	226
Orra, d. Nehemiah & Elizabeth, b. June 25, 1789	1	64
Orra, of Ridgefield, m. John **JENNINGS**, of Patterson, Putnam Co., N. Y., this day [Apr. 14, 1829], by Rev. Lemuel B. Hull	1	169
Polly, d. Thaddeus & Mary, b. Mar. 4, 1781	1	45

	Vol.	Page
STURGIS, STURGES, (cont.)		
Sally, d. Thaddeus & Mary, b. July 9, 1785	1	45
Samuel, s. Joel & Sarah, b. May 9, 1784	1	55
Strong, s. Thaddeus & Mary, b. Aug. 6, 1771	1	45
Thaddeus, m. Mary **COMSTOCK**, Nov. 23, 1769	1	151
Thaddeus, d. Sept. 8, 1798, ae 57 y.	1	209
Ward, m. Rachel **HOYT**, Apr. 27, 1788	1	157
William, s. Thaddeus & Mary, b. Apr. 29, 1775	1	45
SUARD, Sarah, m. Isaac **NORTHRUP**, Jan. 22, 1772	1	151
SUNDERLAND, Caroline F., of Ridgefield, m. Robert S. **HOOD**, of New York, May 17, 1852, by Rev. Shaler J. Hillyer	1	138
SYACUS, Ruth, squaw, d. Sept. 7, 1799	1	210
TAYLOR, Abraham, m. Sarah **CABLE**, Dec. 1, 1784	1	155
Abraham, d. Jan. 30, 1813, ae 48	1	217
Abraham, his w. [ ], d. Feb. 24, 1844	1	237
Army*, of Ridgefield, m. Daniel **OLMSTED**, Jr., of Danbury, Mar. 6, 1822, by S. M. Phelps *(Amey?)	1	161
Charles, of South Salem, m. Eliza **ABBOT**, of Ridgefield, Jan. 20, 1833, by Rev. Charles G. Selleck	1	178
Esther, w. Ezra, d. of Joseph & Joanna **STEBBINS**, d. July 12, 1824	1	224
Eunice, m. Uriah **BIRCHARD**, Oct. 16, 1782	1	152
Noah, of Ridgefield, m. Amelia **BURR**, of Reading, Apr. 18, 1821, by Samuel M. Phelps	1	161
Preserved, formerly of Ridgefield, d. May [ ], 1847, in Redding	1	239
Rebeckah, m. John **ABBOT**, Mar. [ ]	LR1	252
Ruhama, m. Jacob **ST. JOHN**, Dec. 23, 1790, by Rev. Joseph Peck. Witnesses Samuel Taylor & Rachel Taylor	1	97
TERRELL, Esther, m. Josiah B. **BENEDICT**, Oct. 30, 1799	1	108
THOMAS, Abraham, s. Recompence & Elizabeth, b. June 30, 1751	LR1	245
Benjamin*, Jr., m. Sarah **LARRANCE**, Feb. 25, 1757, by Jonathan Ingersoll, V. D. M. *(Correction (Benjamin crossed out. "Recompence" handwritten in) in margin of original manuscript)* *(Correction (should be Recompence, Jr.) (Information from Eva A. Thomas, Owego, Tioga Co., N. Y., 10/19/43) (on typed entry inserted in original manuscript)	LR1	252
Benjamin, s. Abraham & Mary, b. June 28, 1772	1	42
Bettey, d. Recompence & Elizabeth, b. Apr. 16, 1742	LR1	240
Betty, m. Thomas **SAINT JOHN**, Apr. 14, 176[ ]	1	150
Daniel, s. Recompence & Elizabeth, b. Nov. 30, 1754	LR1	245
Dinah, d. Recompence, Jr. & Sarah, b. Mar. 12, 1764	1	15
Elijah L., of Wilton, m. Sally **NASH**, of Ridgefield, Jan. 1, 1829, by Rev. Henry Stead	1	168
Elizabeth, d. Recompence & Elizabeth, b. Jan. 18, 1731/2	LR1	222
Elizabeth, d. John & Martha, b. Apr. 9, 1769	1	20
Hannah, d. [Recompence & Elizabeth], b. Apr. 8, 1746	LR1	240

THOMAS, (cont)

	Vol.	Page
James, s. John & Martha, b. Jan. 4, 1768	1	20
James, s. John & Martha, d. Mar. 7, 1768	1	200
Jerusha, d. Recompence & Elizabeth, b. Feb. 17, 1735/6	LR1	222
Jerusha, m. James **SAINT JOHN**, Apr. 13, [ ]	LR1	252
John, s. [Recompence & Elizabeth], b. June 19, 1744	LR1	240
John, m. Martha **ST. JOHN**, Sept. 19, 1767	1	150
John, s. John & Martha, b. May 30, 1777	1	20
Joseph, s. Recompence, Jr. & Sarah, b. May 10, 1754* *(Correction (Original entry gives year as 1751 (six years before mar. of parents); his gravestone at Covert, N. Y., reads: "Joseph **THOMAS** died Oct. 9, 1811, aged 50 years, " which places his birth in 1761) (Information from Eva A. Thomas, Owego, Tioga Co., N. Y., 10/19/43), on typed entry inserted in original manuscript)	1	15
Martha, d. John & Martha, b. July 19, 1779	1	20
Mary, d. Recompence & Elizabeth, b. Mar. 4, 1739/40	LR1	225
Mary, d. Abraham & Mary, b. Mar. 27, 1777	1	42
Phebe, d. Recompence & Elizabeth, b. May 23, 1747	LR1	245
Rebeckah, d. Recompence & Elizabeth, b. Sept. 5, 1756	LR1	245
Recompence, m. Elizabeth [ ], July 26, 1731	LR1	230
Recompence, s. Recompence & Elizabeth, b. Jan. 28, 1733/4	LR1	222
Recompence, d. Apr. 18, 1793, in the 84th y. of his age	1	206
Samuel, s. John & Martha, b. Jan. 18, 1774	1	20
Sarah, d. John & Martha, b. July 18, 1771	1	20
Stephen, s. John & Martha, b. June 3, 1781	1	20
Thomas, s. Recompence & Sarah, b. July 23, 1758	LR1	242
Tushorn(?)*, d. July 10, 1848, ae 71 y. *(Correction (Should be Gershom. (Original record)) (Information from Eva A. Thomas, Owego, Tioga Co., N. Y., 10/19/43), on typed entry inserted in original manuscript)	1	239

THORP, Mary, wid., d. Mar. 23, 1839, ae 61 y.

	1	234
Mary Ann, of Ridgefield, m. Isaac **BEEBE**, of Lisbon, June 16, 1845, by Rev. James A. Hawley	1	197

THRALL, William, his d. [ ], d. Sept. 24, 1831, ae 10 m.

	1	228

TITUS, Charlotte, [d. John & Sarah], b. Feb. 24, 1781

	1	77
John, [s. John & Sarah], b. May 25, 1783	1	77
John, his w. [ ]. d. Oct. [ ], 1792	1	206
John, m. Susanna **BRINKERHOFF**, Jan. 5, 1794	1	77
Polly, d. John & Sarah, b. Dec. 25, 1778	1	77
Sally, [d. John & Sarah], b. Jan. 12, 1791	1	77
Sarah, w. John, d. Oct. 23, 1792	1	77

TOMPKINS, W[illia]m W., of New Canaan, m. Mary Augusta **DAN**, of Ridgefield, [ ], by Rev. T. Sparks. Recorded Jan. 3, 1840

	1	187

TONGUE, Annah, of New London, m. Joseph **FOLLIET**, of Marblehead, Mar. 6, 1730/1

	1	72
Jonathan, s. James & Ruth, b. Feb. 2, 1744/5	LR1	253

	Vol.	Page
TOWNSEND, Deborah, m.Thomas **ROCKWELL**, July 20, 1795	1	98
TROWBRIDGE, Edward, of New Haven, m. Sarah A. **SMITH**, of Ridgefield, this day [Aug. 6, 1851], by Rev. C. Clark	1	135
George, of Bethel, m. Elizabeth **KEELER**, of Ridgefield, Nov. 4, 1851, by Rev. Ira Abbott	1	136
TRUESDALE, TRESDELL, Hannah, w. Jesse, d. Oct. 24, 1806	1	213
Jonathan, m. Phebe **MEAD**, Nov. 27, 1785	1	156
Martha, d. William & Martha, b. Mar. 8, 1729	LR1	210
TRUMBULL, Joseph, s. James, d. Oct. 7, 1800, ae 2 y.	1	210
TRYON, Polly, d. Dec. 22, 1834, ae 49	1	231
TURNBULL, James, s. J[ ], d. Apr. 14, 1798, ae 10 y.	1	209
TUTTLE, Edward O., of Ridgefield, m. Lois C. **CLARK**, of Litchfield, Feb. 19, 1845, by Rev. A. S. Francis	1	196
Susanna, w. Enos, d. Dec. 29, 1801, in the 38th y. of her age	1	211
TYLER, James, s. Edward & Sarah, b. Feb. 16, 1780	1	45
William, s. Edward & Sarah, b. Nov. 21, 1781	1	45
UTTER, Samuel, had s. [ ], d. Nov. 13, 1829	1	227
Samuel, d. Sept. 29, 1842, ae about 63 y.	1	236
VENTRUS, VENTROUS, Benjamin, s. William & Sarah, b. Aug. 12, 1724	LR1	209
William, d. Sept. 9, 1730	LR1	214
VERRIAL, David, s. Phalle **NORTHRUP** (single person), b. Aug. 13, 1787	1	69
WADDY, Alexander, s. Peter & Sarah, b. Dec. 3, 1786	1	35
Ira, s. Peter & Sarah, b. Feb. 8, 1790	1	35
Peter, s. Peter & Sarah, b. Oct. 28, 1782	1	35
Samuel, s. Peter & Sarah, b. Feb. 27, 1781	1	35
William, s. Peter & Sarah, b. Aug. 23, 1784	1	35
William, d. Dec. 7, 1801, in the 17th y. of his age	1	211
WAKEMAN, Amelia, m. Jeremiah **SCOTT**, [ ], 1794	1	159
James, m. Sally **BOUTON**, [ ], 1795	1	159
WALKER, John, m. Sarah **BEERS**, June 3, 1793	1	158
WALLACE, WALLIS, Abigail, d. James & Abigail, b. Dec. 21, 1740	LR1	225
Abijah, s. James & Abigail, b. Aug. 13, 1748	LR1	244
Abraham, s. Rachel, d. of John, b. Feb. 20, 1769	1	21
Agnis, d. James & Mary, b. June 30, 1717	LR1	202
Agness, d. John & Martha, b. Feb. 21, 1765	LR1	256
Epenetus, s. John & Martha, b. Nov. 18, 1766	1	21
Jacob, s. James & Mary, b. Aug. 31, [1721]	LR1	203
Jacob, s. James & Abigail, b. June 17, 1754	LR1	244
Jacob, s. John & Martha, b. June 1, 1759	LR1	256
James, [s. James & Mary], b. Feb. 6, 1713	LR1	201
James, m. Abigail [ ], Feb. 12, 1735/6	LR1	230
James, s. James & Abigail, b. Apr. 30, 1737	LR1	224
James, s. John & Martha, b. July 8, 1762	LR1	256
James, of Troy, N. Y., m. Matilda **KEELER**, of Ridgefield, May 17, 1825, by Samuell M. Phelps	1	166

WALLACE, WALLIS, (cont.)

	Vol.	Page
John, [s. James & Mary], b. Oct. 16, 1709	LR1	201
John, [twin with Martha], s. John & Martha, b. June 2, 1747	LR1	256
Jonathan, s. John & Martha, b. Nov. 18, 1752	LR1	256
Lucy, d. James & Abigail, b. Apr. 10, 1757	LR1	244
Mariah, d. James & Abigail, b. Oct. 22, 1750	LR1	244
Martha, d. James & Mary, b. May 25, [1724/5]	LR1	205
Martha, [twin with John], d. John & Martha, b. June 2, 1747	LR1	256
Mary, d. James & Abigail, b. Aug. 25, 1746	LR1	239
Mary, d. John & Martha, b. Aug. 28, 1769	1	21
Rachell, [d. James & Mary], b. Feb. last, 1711	LR1	201
Rachal, m. Vivus **DAUCHY**, Nov. 28, 1732	LR1	230
Rachel, d. John & Martha, b. Jan. 1, 1749	LR1	256
Rachel, d. John, had s. Abraham, b. Feb. 20, 1769	1	21
Ruth, d. John & Martha, b. Dec. 26, 1756	LR1	256
Samuel, s. John & Martha, b. Nov. 17, 1754	LR1	256
Sarah, [d. James & Mary], b. Dec. 1, 1714	LR1	201
Sarah, d. James & Mary, m. Samuell **SAINT JOHN**, Jan. 8, 1735/6	LR1	229
Sarah, d. James & Abigail, b. July 28, 1752	LR1	244
Thomas, s. James & Mary, b. Apr. 13, 1719	LR1	202
Thomas, s. James & Abigail, b. May 30, 1743	LR1	236
William, s. John & Martha, b. Oct. 16, 1750	LR1	256

WARD, Susannah, m. William SEE*, Mar. 31, 1772   *(Perhaps "LEE"?)

	1	65

WARREN, [see also WARRING], Abigail, d. Michael & Abigail, b. Aug. 7, 1778

	1	49
Antoinette, d. [Daniel & Esther], b. Aug. 25, 1814	1	107
Burr, his w. [ ], d. Jan. 1, 1842	1	236
Catharine, d. [Daniel & Esther], b. Mar. 18, 1812	1	107
Daniel, s. Michael & Abigail, b. Nov. 14, 1774	1	49
Daniel, his w. [ ], d. Feb. 8, [1843], ae [ ]	1	236
David, of Danbury, m. Huldah **MANSFIELD**, of Ridgefield, Sept. 3, 1848, by Rev. James A. Hawley	1	130
David, m. Huldah **MANSFIELD**, of Danbury, Sept. 3, 1848, by Rev. James A. Hawley	1	132
David, of Danbury, m. Huldah **MANSFIELD**, of Danbury, Sept. 3, 1848, by Rev. James A. Hawley	1	132
Esther, m. Stephen **JONES**, b. of Ridgefield, Dec. 6, 1846, by D. K. Hawley, V. D. M.	1	127
Hannah, d. Michael & Abigail, b. Aug. 10, 1776	1	49
Isaac, s. Michael & Abigail, b. Oct. 31, 1780	1	49
Martha, d. Michael & Abigail, b. July 19, 1783	1	49
Martha, w. Michael, d. Apr. 24, 1799, ae 54 y.	1	209
Michael, m. Martha **OLMSTED**, June 23, 1773	1	155
Michael, d. Apr. 8, 1812, ae 69 y.	1	216
Orval, s. Daniel & Esther, b. May 27, 1799; d. Sept. 28, 1815	1	107
Orval, s. Daniel, d. Sept. 28, 1815	1	219

	Vol.	Page
WARREN, (cont.)		
Roxanna, d. [Daniel & Esther], b. Nov. 4, 1804	1	107
Roxana, m. Henry **NORTON**, b. of Ridgefield, Oct. 1, 1826, by Samuel M. Phelps	1	167
Roxana, m. John R. **SHERWOOD**, b. of Ridgefield, Oct. 30, 1842, by Rev. Warner Hoyt	1	193
Rufus, s. [Daniel & Esther], b. Jan. 25, 18[ ]	1	107
Sally, d. [Daniel & Esther], b. Jan. 2, 1801	1	107
Sarah, Mrs., d. Jan. 20, 1838, ae 82 y.	1	234
Shubert, had child d. Dec. 20, 1833, ae 9 y.	1	230
Silas, s. [Daniel & Esther], b. Sept. 20, 1809	1	107
WARRING, WARING, [see also **WARREN**], Jacob, d. Sept. 10, 1833, ae 42	1	230
Thomas B., of North Salem, N. Y., m. Mary Jane **ROCKWELL**, of Ridgefield, Jan. 28, 1844, by Rev. Shaller J. Hillyer	1	195
WATERBURY, Amos A., of Stamford, m. Celia **STEBBINS**, of Ridgefield, Nov. 26, 1823, by Rev. Oregen S. Holcomb	1	162
Charles H., d. Apr. 19, 1832, in the 8th y. of his age	1	229
Elen, wid., d. Apr. 11, 1839, ae 75 y.	1	234
WATROUS, WATEROUS, Eleazer, s. John & Martha, b. Nov. 13, 1786	1	24
Eleazer, d. June 21, 1815, ae 28 y. 7 m. 8 d.	1	218
Huldah, [d. James S. & Sally], b. June 18, 1796	1	84
James Harvey, [s. James S. & Sally], b. Nov. 18, 1812	1	84
James S., m. Sally **BOUTON**, [ ], 1795	1	84
James Scott, s. John & Huldah, b. Feb. 23, 1774	1	24
John, m. Huldah **SCOTT**, June 12, 1771	1	151
John, m. Martha **SMITH**, May 30, 1782	1	154
John, s. John & Martha, b. July 30, 1783	1	24
John, Jr., had infant d. Nov. 29, 1809	1	215
John Bouton, [s. James S. & Sally], b. May 12, 1805	1	84
Lucy, d. John & Huldah, b. Mar. 26, 1776	1	24
Martha, d. John & Huldah, b. Apr. 26, 1778	1	24
Martha, m. Nathan **OLMSTED**, Jr., Apr. 25, 1797	1	159
Martha, w. John, d. Jan. 11, 1804	1	211
Nabbe, d. John & Huldah, b. Apr. 3, 1773	1	24
Ruth, w. Jno, Jr., d. Jan. 14, 1816, ae 27 y. 4 m. 26 d.	1	219
William, [s. James S. & Sally], b. Dec. 29, 1798	1	84
WEBB, Eliza A., of Ridgefield, m. Thomas R. **BARKER**, of North Salem, Apr. 7, 1847, by Rev. Charles Stearns. Int. Pub.	1	128
Epenetus, his w. [ ], d. Oct. 26, 1825	1	225
Epenetus, d. Mar. 22, 1827	1	226
Frederick S., of Wilton, m. Ann Eliza **SHOLAS**, of Ridgefield, Apr. 1, [1851], by Rev. William Staunton	1	136
Josiah, of Monroe, Co. of Orange, N. Y., m. Harriet **DANN**, of Ridgefield, Feb. 16, 1835, by Levi Brunson	1	180
WEED, Abigail, d. Jacob & Abigail, b. May 27, 1763	1	16

	Vol.	Page
WEED, (cont.)		
Anna, d. Jacob & Abigail, d. Aug. 7, 1775	1	202
Anne, d. Jacob & Abigail, b. Nov. 15, 1766	1	16
Anne, d. Jacob & Abigail, b. Feb. 14, 1778	1	16
Azariah, s. Jacob & Abigail, b. July 14, 1771	1	16
Bartholomew, m. Sarah **BENEDICT**, June 12, 1754, by Jonathan Ingersoll, V. D. M.	LR1	252
Bartholomew, [s. Timothy & Sarah], b. Mar. 6, 1793	1	63
Betty, Mrs. of Ridgefield, m. Heron **CRAFT**, of Southeast, May 5, 1822, by Oliver Tuttle	1	160
Burr, d. Feb. [ ], [1851], ae 74	1	241
Cate, d. Jacob & Abigail, b. Mar. 12, 1761	LR1	253
Cate, d. Jacob & Abigail, b. Mar. 12, 1761	1	16
Chloe, d. Bartholomew & Sarah, b. June 27, 1766	1	25
Chloe, m. Samuel **SAINT JOHN**, Apr. 6, 1785	1	155
David, s. Jacob & Abigail, b. Apr. 18, 1765	1	16
David, s. Jabob & Abigail, d. Aug. 7, 1775	1	202
Eli Smith, s. Jacob & Abigail, b. Oct. 27, 1775	1	16
Elijah, s. Bartholomew & Sarah, b. Aug. 30, 1761	LR1	253
Elijah, [s. Timothy & Sarah], b. Aug. 18, 1782	1	63
Granville, of Danbury, m. Phebe **DANN**, of Ridgefield, Nov. 26, 1846, by Rev. Z. B. Burr	1	198
Jacob, s. Jacob & Abigail, b. Aug. 13, 1768	1	16
Joseph Smith, s. Bartholomew & Sarah, b. Sept. 10, 1771	1	25
Joseph Smith, [s. Timothy & Sarah], b. Jan. 2, 1787	1	63
Lydia, [d. Timothy & Sarah], b. Dec. 13, 1788	1	63
Martha, w. Asa, d. Mar. 5, 1817, ae 65 y.	1	220
Polly, [d. Timothy & Sarah], b. July 1, 1784	1	63
Rua, [s. Timothy & Sarah], b. Jan. 28, 1791	1	63
Sarah, d. Bartholomew & Sarah, b. Oct. 6, 1755	LR1	253
Sarah, [d. Timothy & Sarah], b. Oct. 4, 1780	1	63
Silsbee, s. [Timothy & Sarah], b. Mar. 29, 1797	1	63
Thankfull, d. Jacob & Abigail, b. Apr. 4, 1759	LR1	253
Thankfull, d. Jacob & Abigail, b. Apr. 4, 1759	1	16
Timothy, s. Bartholomew & Sarah, b. May 22, 1758	LR1	253
Timothy, m. Sarah **SILSBEE**, Dec. 11, 1777	1	63
Timothy, [s. Timothy & Sarah], b. May 22, 1778	1	63
Timothy, his infant, d. Apr. 8, 1795	1	208
WEEKS, Annis, d. Zophar & Jane, b. Mar. 11, 1777	1	29
David, s. Zophar & Jane, b. Feb. 18, 1773	1	29
Eli, s. Zophar & Jane, b. June 2, 1771	1	29
Jere, s. Zophar & Jane, b. Feb. 6, 1775	1	29
Stephen, s. Zophar & Jane, b. Sept. 8, 1769	1	29
Zopher, m. Jane **NORTHRUP**, June 26, 1769	1	151
WHEELER, Benjamin, had s. [ ], d. Oct. 3, 1820	1	222
Clara, d. Wakeman, d. Dec. 20, 1811, ae 10 m.	1	215
David*, m. Esther **BRADLEY**, Feb. 23, 1794 *(Perhaps "David **KEELER**?")	1	158

	Vol.	Page
WHEELER, (cont.)		
Ichabod, d. Sept. 8, 1829, ae 86 y.	1	227
Ichabod, his wid., d. Feb. 26, 1836, ae 90 y.	1	232
Perry, [d. , probably 1851], ae 42	1	241
Samantha, of Ridgefield, m. Joseph P. **DAYTON**, of New Castle, N. Y., this day [Dec. 24, 1851], by Timothy Jones	1	137
Seth, d. Apr. [ ], 1805	1	212
Simeon, his w. [ ], d. about July 4, 1845	1	238
Simon, d. [Feb.] 18, [1847], ae 72 y. "drowned at Norwalk"	1	239
Wakeman, his child, d. Jan. 3, 1806	1	212
WHEELOCK, Phebe, m. James **SELLECK**, Feb. 26, 1783	1	154
WHITE, Anne, of Ridgefield, m. Allen **ROSCO**, of South Salem, N. Y., Jan. 6, 1836, by Rev. Charles G. Selleck	1	182
Mary, d. Eunice **ABBOTT**, b. Dec. 2, 1727	LR1	220
Sally, d. Uriah & Phebe, b. Oct. 2, 1759	LR1	253
WHITLOCK, Abigail, d. Jonathan & Sarah, b. Oct. 30, 1750	1	6
Abigail, d. Jonathan & Sarah, b. Oct. 30, 1750	1	59
Abigail, d. Thaddeus & Phebe, b. Sept. 27, 1791	1	94
Abraham, s. David & Margarett, b. Feb. 14, 1727	LR1	209
Abraham, s. David & Margarett, d. May 2, [1728]	LR1	214
Abraham, m. Deborah **WOOD**, May 18, 175[ ]	1	150
Abraham, d. Nov. 10, 1843, ae about 67 y.	1	237
Adams, m. Elizabeth **OSBORN**, Feb. 14, 1750	1	150
Almira, w. Abraham, d. Jan. 27, 1828, in the 41st y. of her age	1	226
Amanda, m. John **BATES**, b. of Ridgefield, Feb. 14, 1832, by Levi Brunson	1	175
Arba, had infant s. [ ], d. Mar. 12, 1828, ae 3 m.	1	226
Daniel, s. David & Margaret, b. Sept. 4, 1720	LR1	210
David, s. [David & Margaret], b. Nov. 16, 1723	LR1	210
Dorcas, d. Jonathan & Sarah, b. Nov. 14, 1765	1	59
Dorcas, m. John **BAXTER**, Feb. 4, 1787	1	156
Ellenor, d. Jonathan & Sarah, b. Oct. 16, 1752	1	6
Eli, s. Thaddeus & Phebe, b. Jan. 18, 1807	1	94
Eli, m. Phebe Amanda **SMITH**, b. of Ridgefield, Apr. 7, 1827, by Levi Bronson	1	167
Eli, d. Apr. 1, 1831, in the 25th y. of his age	1	228
Elias P., s. Israel M., d. June 8, 1830, ae 5 y.	1	228
Elias Pulling, s. Israel M., d. Sept. 15, 1823*, ae 3 y. 5 m. *(1833?)	1	230
Ellenor, d. Jonathan & Sarah, b. Sept. 17, 1752	1	59
Eleanor, wid., d. Mar. 27, 1824	1	224
Elizabeth, d. Adams & Elizabeth, b. Jan. 8, 175[ ]	1	6
Elizabeth, m. Uriah **SCRIBNER**, Sept. 30, 1783	1	154
Eunice, m. Simeon **STEBBINS**, May 15, 1792	1	157
Eunice, m. Henry **BATES**, b. of Ridgefield, Dec. 17, 1847, by Rev. Henry Olmsted, Jr.	1	129
Ezra, s. Thaddeus & Phebe, b. Aug. 16, 1798	1	94
H[ ], d. [Sept.] 21, [1847], ae about 20 y.	1	239

WHITLOCK, (cont.)

	Vol.	Page
Hannah, d. Jonathan & Sarah, b. Sept. 15, 1754	1	6
Hannah, d. Jonathan & Sarah, b. Oct. 17, 1754	1	59
Hannah, m. Jonathan **WOOD**, Mar. 7, 1775	1	94
Harry, s. Thaddeus & Phebe, b. Feb. 6, 1805	1	94
Harry, d. Feb. 2, 1827, ae 22 y.	1	226
Henry, s. Jonathan & Sarah, b. Nov. 3, 1761	1	6
Henry, s. Jonathan & Sarah, b. Nov. 3, 1761	1	59
Huldah, d. Jonathan & Sarah, b. Sept. 27, 1767	1	59
Huldah, d. Jonathan, d. Feb. 20, 1772	1	203
Huldah, d. Thaddeus & Phebe, b. June 26, 1790	1	94
Israel M., his child d. Sept. 15, 1823, ae 3 y. 5 m.	1	230
Israel M., his s. [ ], d. Aug. 7, 1850, ae 18 y.	1	240
Israel N., had d. [ ], d. May 7, [1851], ae 15 y.	1	241
Jared Webb, s. Arba, d. Mar. 9, 1825, ae 20 m.	1	224
Jesse, d. Oct. 15, 1835, ae 26 y.	1	232
John, m. Rhoda **JONES**, Nov. 15, 1781	1	154
John, s. Thaddeus & Phebe, b. July 7, 1793	1	94
John, d. May 8, [1845]	1	238
Jonathan, d. July 8, 1788, in the 65th y. of his age	1	204
Joseph, s. Abraham & Deborah, b. Feb. 5, 1760	1	5
Joseph, s. Thaddeus & Phebe, b. July 29, 1801	1	94
Joseph, m. Polly **SMITH**, b. of Ridgefield, Mar. 24, 1822, by Rev. Samuel M. Phelps	1	161
Joseph, 2nd, his child d. Mar. 5, 1831, ae 11 m.	1	228
Joseph, d. Mar. 14, 1844	1	237
Justus, s. Abraham & Deborah, b. Mar. 10, 1753	1	5
Justus, d. Apr. 10, 1803	1	211
Lucy, m. Benjamin **WILSON**, Nov. 26, 1801	1	96
Maria, d. Eli, d. Mar. 1, 1829, in the 2nd y. of her age	1	227
Maria, Mrs. of New Hartford, Conn., m. Samuel **SHERWOOD**, of Ballstown, N. Y., Nov. 15, 1840, by Rev. Warner Hoyt	1	189
Mary, wid., d. Oct. 18, 1801	1	210
Morris K., d. Apr. 17, 1843, ae about 16 y.	1	237
Nancy, of Ridgefield, m. Frederick **BAILEY**, of Danbury, Aug. 3, 1846, by Rev. Henry Olmsted, Jr.	1	127
Naomi, d. Adams & Elizabeth, b. Sept. 15, 1761	1	6
Nathaniel, s. Adams & Elizabeth, b. Mar. 10, 175[ ]	1	6
Oliver, [s. David & Margaret], b. Apr. 28, 1728	LR1	210
Phebe, d. Thaddeus & Phebe, b. Dec. 3, 1808	1	94
Phebe, wid., d. July 27, 1834, ae 73 y.	1	230
Polly, of Ridgefield, m. Jacob **BURR**, of Redding, this day, [Apr. 7, 1830], by Rev. Origen P. Holcomb	1	171
Rachel, d. Adams & Elizabeth, b. Nov. 9, 175[ ]	1	6
Ruamie, m. Joseph **OSBORN**, of Danbury, May 3, 1789	1	158
Rufus, s. Thaddeus & Phebe, b. Aug. 21, 1803	1	94
Ruth, d. Jonathan & Sarah, b. July 4, 1769	1	59

WHITLOCK, (cont.)	Vol.	Page
Ruth, d. Jonathan, d. Jan. 20, 1775	1	203
Ruth, d. Thaddeus & Phebe, b. May 5, 1795	1	94
Ruth, d. Thaddeus, d. Jan. 23, 1816, in the 21st y. of her age	1	219
Samuel, s. Jonathan & Sarah, b. Nov. 5, 1748	1	6
Samuel, s. Jonathan & Sarah, b. Nov. 5, 1748	1	59
Sarah, m. Daniel **WILSON**, Feb. [ ]	LR1	252
Sarah, d. Adams & Elizabeth, b. Sept. 26, 1759	1	6
Sarah, d. Adams & Elizabeth, d. June 7, 1760	1	200
Sarah, d. Jonathan & Sarah, b. Dec. 17, 1763	1	59
Sarah, m. Abel **PULLING**, Dec. 3, 1783	1	153
Seth, s. Jonathan & Sarah, b. Sept. 12, 1757	1	59
Seth, s. Jonathan & Sarah, b. Oct. 27, 1757	1	6
Thaddeus, [s. David & Margaret], b. May 22, 1726	LR1	210
Thaddeus, s. Jonathan & Sarah, b. Dec. 16, 1759	1	6
Thaddeus, s. Jonathan & Sarah, b. Dec. 16, 1759	1	59
Thaddeus, m. Phebe **MEAD**, June 12, 1788	1	157
Thaddeus, s. Thaddeus & Phebe, b. Nov. 4, 1788	1	94
Thaddeus, d. Nov. 30, 1825, in the 66th y. of his age	1	225
Thaddeus, s. Abraham, d. Mar. 15, 1835, ae 22	1	231
Thaddeus, d. June 29, 1841, ae 52 y.	1	236
Thomas, s. Adams & Elizabeth, b. Oct. 23, 1756	1	6
William, s. Thaddeus & Phebe, b. May 6, 1797	1	94
William, d. Feb. 17, 1823, ae 26 y.	1	223
WHITTAMORE, Daniell, s. Amos & Mary, d. Apr. 20, [1721]	LR1	213
WHITNEY, WHITNE, WHITNEE, Abigail, d. Richard & Esther, b. Mar. 28, 1753	LR1	198
Ann, d. Nathan & Sarah, b. Aug. last, 1739	LR1	224
Anne, d. John, of Norwalk, m. Matthew **SAINT JOHN**, Oct. 13, 1709	LR1	227
Anne, d. Daniel & Thankfull, b. May 23, 1748	LR1	241
Benjamin, s. Daniel & Thankfull, b. June 1, 1750	LR1	241
Betsey Clarresee, d. Henry & Ruth, b. May 10, 1789	1	31
Betty, d. Henry & Elizabeth, b. Nov. 7, [1718]	LR1	202
Betty, m. Daniel **SMITH**, Jan. 25, 1741/2	LR1	231
Betty, d. Henry & Elizabeth, b. Apr. 30, 1756	LR1	244
Betty, d. Richard & Esther, b. July 16, 1757	LR1	198
Bettey, m. Jeremiah **MEAD**, Oct. 6, 1784	1	155
Clarrasee, d. Henry & Ruth, b. June 16, 1771; d. July 5, 1785	1	31
Clarissa, d. Henry, Jr. & Ruth, d. July 5, 1785	1	203
Daniel, s. Henry & Elizabeth, b. Apr. 4, [1719]	LR1	203
Daniel, m. Thankfull [ ], Aug. 8, 1741	LR1	231
Daniel, s. Daniell & Thankfull, b. Jan. 12, 1745	LR1	238
Eliakim, s. Nathan & Sarah, b. Nov. 13, [1718]	LR1	202
Eliasaph, s. [Nathan & Sarah], b. Feb. 3, 1716/17	LR1	201
Eliasaph, s. Nathan & Sarah, b. Feb. 3, 1717	LR1	201
Elizabeth, [d. Henry & Elizabeth (**ARMSTEAD**)], b. Aug. 24, 1711	LR1	201
Elizabeth, d. Daniel & Thankfull, b. Nov. 27, 1752	LR1	248

WHITNEY, WHITNE, WHITNEE, (cont.)

	Vol.	Page
Elizabeth, twin with Rebeckah, d. Henry & Elizabeth, b. Feb. 18, 1765	LR1	244
Elizabeth, m. Daniel **JACKSON**, Feb. 20, 1783	1	154
Esther, d. Richard & Esther, b. Oct. 20, 1748	LR1	198
Esther, m. Jeremiah **CHASE**, Jan. 29, 1771	1	151
Henry, [s. Henry & Elizabeth (**ARMSTEAD**)], b. July 29, 1715	LR1	201
Henry, Sr., d. Apr. 26, [1728]	LR1	214
Henry, s. Rich[ar]d & Esther, b. Feb. 28, 1746/7	LR1	198
Henry, m. Elizabeth **LOBDELL**, Dec. 5, 1755, by Jonathan Ingersoll, V. D. M.	LR1	252
Henry, 2nd, m. Ruth **SCRIBNER**, Jan. 17, 1770	1	151
Henry, m. Ruth **ST. JOHN**, [ ], 1794	1	159
Henry, d. July 9, 1794, in the 79th y. of his age	1	207
Henry, Capt., d. Feb. 14, 1813	1	217
Hepzibah, w. John, d. May 20, 1753	LR1	216
Hepzebah, m. Nicholas **WILSON**, Dec. [ ], 1779	1	154
James, s. Henry & Elizabeth, b. Dec. 6, [1724/5]	LR1	205
James, s. James & Lydia, b. May 28, 1751	LR1	249
Jeremiah, s. Nathan & Sarah, b. Sept. 18, 1731	LR1	212
Jerusha, [d. Henry & Elizabeth (**ARMSTEAD**)], b. Dec. 18, 1714	LR1	201
Jerusha, d. Richard & Esther, b. June 28, 1755	LR1	198
John, s. Henry & Elizabeth, b. Jan. 28, 1714	LR1	202
John, m. Hephzibah **OLMSTEAD**, June 15, 1746, by Rev. Jonathan Ingersoll	LR1	233
John, s. John & Hepzibah, b. Apr. 21, 1747	LR1	198
Josiah, s. Nathan & Sarah, b. June 12, 1729	LR1	211
Josiah Anson, s. Richard & Esther, b. Jan. 16, 17[ ]	1	12
Mary, d. Nathan & Sarah, b. Dec. 29, 1715	LR1	201
Mary, d. Daniell & Thankful, b. Sept. 16, 1742	LR1	236
Nabbe, d. William & Sarah, b. Apr. 10, 1774	1	39
Nathan, s. Nathan & Sarah, b. Aug. 13, [1721/2]	LR1	204
Nathan, s. Nathan & Sarah, b. June 11, [1724]	LR1	204
Phebe, m. Daniel **SMITH**, Jan. 20, 1788	1	157
Rebeckah, twin with Elizabeth, d. Henry & Elizabeth, b. Feb. 18, 1765	LR1	244
Rebeckah, m. Josiah **OLMSTED**, Jan. 18, 1789	1	157
Richard, s. Henry & Elizabeth, b. Mar. 29, [1721/2]	LR1	204
Richard, m. Esther **CLARKE**, Dec. 18, 1745	LR1	233
Richard, s. Richard & Esther, b. Dec. 6, 1759	LR1	198
Richard, d. Nov. 18, 1773	1	201
Ruhamah, d. Daniel & Thankful, b. Apr. 10, 1744	LR1	237
Ruth, wid. Henry, d. Aug. 12, 1835, ae 84 y.	1	231
Sally, d. Henry & Ruth, b. Sept. 27, 1786	1	31
Sarah, d. Nathan & Sarah, b. Oct. 25, [1719/20]	LR1	203
Sarah, d. Henry & Elizabeth, b. July 23, 1759	LR1	244
Sarah, d. William & Sarah, b. Apr. 23, 1776	1	39

	Vol.	Page
WHITNEY, WHITNE, WHITNEE, (cont.)		
Sarah, m. Matthew **OLMSTED**, Dec. 21, 1783	1	154
Seth, s. Nathan & Sarah, b. Feb. 8, [1726]	LR1	206
Sherwood, m. Abigail **LOBDELL**, Mar. 9, 1788	1	157
Thomas, s. James & Lydia, b. June 19, 1753	LR1	249
Uriah, s. Nathan & Sarah, b. Nov. 12, 1737	LR1	222
William, s. Richard & Esther, b. Dec. 31, 1750	LR1	198
William, m. Sarah **BUNDY**, Aug. 11, 1773	1	152
-----, wid., d. Aug. 15, 1816, ae 82	1	219
WHYMBS, John D., of Derby, m. Elizabeth **KEELER**, of		
Ridgefield, May 16, [1852], by Rev. C. Clark	1	138
WICKSON, Charlotte, m. Philip **SHERWOOD**, Dec. 27, 1840, by		
Rev. Warner Hoyt	1	189
WILCOX, Chauncey, Rev., d. Jan. 31, 1852, ae 55	1	242
WILLIAMS, Abijah, d. Sept. 20, 1834, ae 55 y.	1	231
Abner Wilson, [s. Samuel & Lemira], b. Jan. 29, 1805	1	73
Anne, [d. Samuel & Lemira], b. May 8, 1794	1	73
Benjamin, [s. Benjamin & Jane], b. June 17, 1709	LR1	201
Bradley, s. Edward, d. July 6, [1851], ae 21	1	241
Hannah, [d. Samuel & Lemira], b. Apr. 9, 1792	1	73
Herman, [s. Samuel & Lemira], b. Mar. 13, 1807	1	73
Huldah, w. Solomon, d. Apr. 14, 1810	1	215
James A., of New York, m. Mary **JONES**, of Ridgefield, Nov.		
16, 1846, by James A. Batterson, Dea.	1	199
Jane, [d. Benjamin & Jane], b. Dec. 28, 1714	LR1	201
John, [s. Samuel & Lemira], b. Nov. 21, 1802	1	73
Mary, [d. Benjamin & Jane], b. July 3, 1712	LR1	201
Mary, m. Newton **HINES**, Mar. 8, 1781	1	156
Merlin, [s. Samuel & Lemira], b. Mar. 22, 1801	1	73
Milo, [s. Samuel & Lemira], b. Sept. 22, 1798	1	73
Sally, of Ridgefield, m. Solomon **BROWN**, of Poundridge,		
N. Y., Nov. 7, 1821, by Rev. Samuel M. Phelps	1	161
Samuel, m. Lemira **WILSON**, b. of Ridgefield, May 26, 1791,		
by Samuel Camp, V. D. M.	1	73
Samuel, [s. Samuel & Lemira], b. Feb. 18, 1796	1	73
Solomon, d. Dec. 4, 1816, ae 57 y.	1	220
Sylvester, m. Polly **HUBBELL**, b. of Ridgefield, Mar. 2, 1851,		
by Hezekiah Scott, J. P.	1	134
Zodack, his child d. Mar. 11, 1845, ae 6 y.	1	238
WILSON, WILLSON, Abiah, d. Benjamin & Deborah, b. Mar.		
4, 1740/1	LR1	226
Abigail, d. Benjamin & Jane, b. Mar. 28, 1721	LR1	203
Abigail, d. Benjamin & Deborah, b. Nov. 10, 1750	LR1	241
Abner, s. [Thomas & Elizabeth], b. June 5, 1744	LR1	240
Abner, m. Anne **SHERWOOD**, June 30, 1768	1	150
Abner Elva, s. Abner & Anne, b. Mar. 11, 1793, at Baulstown	1	26
Alma, d. Thomas & Eunice, b. Nov. 9, 1787	1	61
Ammon, s. Abner & Anne, b. May 27, 1776	1	26

BARBOUR COLLECTION

WILSON, WILLSON, (cont.)

	Vol.	Page
Anne, d. Thomas & Elizabeth, b. Apr. 20, 1734	LR1	218-9
Benjamin, m. Deborah **BENNETT,** June 2, 1737	LR1	229
Benjamin, s. Benjamin & Deborah, b. Nov. 25, 1743	LR1	236
Benjamin, s. Benjamin & Sophira, b. July 7, 1770	1	28
Benjamin, s. Thomas & Eunice, b. Jan. 11, 1782	1	61
Benjamin, m. Lucy **WHITLOCK,** Nov. 26, 1801	1	96
Betsey, d. Nov. 17, 1824, in the 53rd y. of her age	1	224
Bettey, d. Abner & Anne, b. Oct. 3, 1786	1	26
Currents, d. Abner & Ann, d. Oct. 13, 177[ ]	1	202
Currents, d. Abner & Anne, b. Mar. 17, 1774	1	26
Currents Anne, d. Abner & Anne, b. Apr. 17, 1781	1	26
Daniel, s. Thomas & Elizabeth, b. Jan. 21, 1737/8	LR1	223
Daniel, m. Sarah **WHITLOCK,** Feb. [ ]	LR1	252
Deborah, d. Benjamin & Deborah, b. Apr. 4, 1738	LR1	223
Deborah, d. Benjamin & Deborah, b. Apr. 4, 1738	LR1	226
Elizabeth, w. Thomas, d. Dec. 17, 1767	1	200
Elizabeth, d. Sept. 5, 1768	1	200
Elizabeth, d. Tho[ma]s & Elizabeth, b. July 8, 1731	LR1	211
Elizabeth, d. Thomas & Eunice, b. Nov. 8, 1779	1	61
Elizabeth, had d. Elizabeth **NORTHRUP,** b. May 16, 1799	1	61
Elizabeth, m. Seth W. **WOODWARD,** Apr. 12, 1801	1	94
Elizabeth, w. Ezekiel, d. July 22, 1807, in the 82nd y. of her age	1	213
Eunice, w. Thomas, d. Mar. 10, 1812	1	216
Ezekiel, m. Hannah **ROCKWELL,** Sept. 3, 17[ ], by Jonathan Ingersoll, V. D. M.	LR1	252
Ezekiel, s. Nathan & Phebe, b. Nov. 19, 1733	LR1	218-9
Ezekiel, s. Ezekiel & Hannah, b. Sept. 29, 1756	LR1	250
Ezekiel, d. Jan. 17, 1816, in the 83rd y. of his age	1	219
Ezekiel, d. Dec. 24, 1844, ae 89 y.	1	238
Ezra, s. Nathan & Phebe, b. Feb. 14, 1744/5	LR1	237
Ezra, s. Abner & Anne, b. Nov. 29, 1789	1	26
Hannah, d. Ezekiel & Hannah, b. July 18, 175[ ]	1	6
Hannah, d. Daniel & Sarah, b. Mar. 23, 1760	1	7
Hannah, w. Ezekiel, d. Apr. 8, 1765	1	200
Hannah, m. Ezra **MEAD,** Mar. 17, 1777	1	155
Jane, d. Benjamin & Jane, m. Joseph **KEELER,** Feb. 26, 1735/6	LR1	229
Jane, d. [Thomas & Elizabeth], b. Mar. 17, 1746	LR1	240
Jane, d. Benjamin & Deborah, b. Dec. 4, 1748	LR1	241
Jared, s. Nathan & Naomi, b. Dec. 17, 1756	LR1	247
Jeremiah, s. Nathan & Phebe, b. June 2, 1738	LR1	223
Jeremiah, d. Mar. 9, 1816	1	219
John, s. Nathan & Phebe, b. Jan. 27, 1735/6	LR1	220
John, s. John & Mary, b. Oct. 12, 1756	LR1	247
John, m. Amy **HICKOX,** Jan. 16, 1783	1	154
Lemira, d. Abner & Anne, b. Aug. 10, 1769	1	26

	Vol.	Page
WILSON, WILLSON, (cont.)		
Lemira, m. Samuel **WILLIAMS**, b. of Ridgefield, May 26, 1791, by Samuel Camp, V. D. M.	1	73
Lewis, s. Ezekiel & Hannah, b. Jan. 24, 1760	1	6
Lucy, w. Benjamin, d. Sept. 30, 1813	1	218
Lucy, d. May 22, 1827, ae 14 y.	1	226
Lurania, d. Benjamin & Sophria, b. Apr. 3, 1767	1	28
Lydia, d. Benjamin & Deborah, b. Aug. 12, 175[ ]	1	18
Martha, m. Samuel **OLMSTED**, Jr., Feb. 15, 17[ ]	1	150
Mary, d. Thomas & Elizabeth, b. Oct. 6, 1735	LR1	220
Molly, d. John & Mary, b. Jan. 3, 1760	1	21
Nathan, m. Phebe **HOBART**, June 5, 1727	LR1	228
Nathan, s. Nathan & Phebe, b. May 21, 1729	LR1	211
Nathan, d. Mar. 8, 1785, in the 84th y. of his age	1	204
Nicholas, m. Hepzebah **WHITNEY**, Dec. [ ], 1779	1	154
Phebe, d. Nathan & Phebe, b. June 26, 1731	LR1	211
Rebecca, m. Benjamin **ROCKWELL**, Apr. 15, 1731	LR1	228
Rebeckah, d. Benjamin & Deborah, b. Sept. 13, 1755	1	18
Rebeckah, m. Reuben **SHERWOOD**, Apr. 8, 1778	1	153
Robert, m. Sarah **HOYT**, Apr. 1, 1779	1	154
Ruth, d. Ezekiel & Hannah, b. Mar. 2, 1762	1	6
Ruth, m. Samuel **STEBBINS**, Jan. 3, 1782	1	155
Sally, d. Abner & Anne, b. Mar. 4, 1783	1	26
Samuel, s. Benjamin & Deborah, b. July 24, 1739	LR1	226
Samuel, d. Feb. 11, 1822	1	223
Sarah, d. Thomas & Elizabeth, b. Aug. 13, 1742	LR1	240
Sarah, d. Benjamin & Deborah, b. June 14, 1746	LR1	241
Sarah, d. Daniel & Sarah, b. June 19, 1767	1	7
Stephen, s. Nathan & Naomi, b. Feb. 28, 1755	LR1	247
Stephen, s. John & Mary, b. Jan. 27, 1758	LR1	247
Thaddeus, s. Daniel & Sarah, b. Mar. 5, 1763	1	7
Thaddeus, d. Mar. 30, 1798, ae 27	1	209
Thomas, m. Elizabeth **BROOKS**, Jan. 30, 1729	LR1	228
Thomas, s. Thomas & Elizabeth, b. Feb. 2, 1729/30	LR1	210
Thomas, s. Thomas & Elizabeth, d. June 10, 1757	LR1	217
Thomas, s. Benjamin & Deborah, b. Oct. 25, 1757	1	18
Thomas, s. Abner & Anne, b. Feb. 17, 1772	1	26
Thomas, d. Aug. 20, 1775	1	201
Thomas, m. Eunice **NORTHRUP**, Jan. 27, 1779	1	154
Thomas, m. Eunice **NORTHRUP**, Jan. 27, 1779	1	156
Thomas, Dr., his w. [ ], d. Feb. 4, 1840, ae about 80	1	235
Thomas, m. Sarah **MUNROW**, Jan. 31, 1841, by Levi Brunson	1	190
Thomas Rockwell, s. Ezekiel & Hannah, b. Mar. 23, 1763	1	6
WOOD, Abigail, d. Titus & Abigail, b. Oct. 18, [1719/20]	LR1	203
Abigail, d. Titus & Abigail, d. Nov. 2, [1720]	LR1	213
Abigail, d. John & Abigail, b. Dec. 9, 1752	LR1	249
Abigail, w. Jacob, d. Nov. 12, 1788	1	205
Alma, d. Seth W., d. Oct. 10, 1818, ae 13 y.	1	221

WOOD, (cont.)

	Vol.	Page
Anna, d. John & Abigail, b. Feb. 13, 1754	LR1	249
Anne, [d. Daniel & Mary], b. Nov. 24, 1749	LR1	254
Betsey, [d. Jonathan & Hannah], b. Sept. 26, 1784	1	94
Betty, d. Daniel & Mary, b. Sept. 26, 175[ ]	1	4
Betty, m. Justus **OLMSTED**, Jr., Jan. 7, 1777	1	152
Cate, m. James **ABBOT**, Mar. 26, 1783	1	153
Daniel, of Danbury, m. Mrs. Lydia **LOBDELL**, of Ridgefield, Aug. 26, 1821, by Rev. Levi Bronson	1	160
David, s. Jonathan & Elizabeth, b. Jan. 7, [1718]	LR1	202
Deborah, m. Abraham **WHITLOCK**, May 18, 175[ ]	1	150
Eleanor, [d. Jonathan & Hannah], b. Nov. 12, 1786	1	94
George L., of Danbury, m. Betsey D. **MILLER**, of Poundridge, N. Y., this eve [Feb. 5, 1845], by James A. Hawley	1	196
Hannah, w. Jonathan, d. Sept. 16, 1801	1	210
John, s. John & Abigail, b. Apr. 27, 1755	LR1	249
John H., m. Sarah Ann **SCOTT**, b. of Ridgefield, Jan. 31, 1836, at the house of Nathan Scott, by Rev. Shaller J. Hillyer	1	181
Jonathan, m. Elizabeth [ ], May 28, 1715	LR1	227
Jonathan, m. Hannah **WHITLOCK**, Mar. 7, 1775	1	94
Jonathan, his w. [ ], d. Mar. [ ], 1810	1	215
Lucy, of Danbury, m. Goold **SCOTT**, of Ridgefield, Mar. 11, 1802, by Rev. John Ely	1	93
Martha, d. Jonathan & Eliza, b. Feb. 27, 1716	LR1	200
Martha, d. Jonathan & Elizabeth, of Norwalk, m. Lemuel **ABBOTT**, Dec. 20, 1732	LR1	229
Martha, [d. Daniel & Mary], b. Sept. 20, 1752	LR1	254
Mary, wid., d. Nov. 5, 1806, ae 84 y.	1	213
Molly, [d. Jonathan & Hannah], b. Apr. 22, 1789	1	94
Nathan, s. Daniel & Mary, b. Nov. 24, 1754	1	4
Nathaniel K., m. Eliza A. **HULL**, b. of Ridgefield, Oct. 10, 1847, by Rev. Sylvester Strong	1	130
Obadiah, d. Feb. 7, 1791, in Salem, in the 93rd y. of his age	1	205
Rebeckah, d. Timothy & Rebeckah, b. Aug. 15, 1750	LR1	241
Ruth, d. Daniel & Mary, b. Apr. 20, 1757	1	4
Ruth Smith, d. Nathan & Susannah, b. Mar. 4, 1776	1	39
Sarah, [d. Jonathan & Hannah], b. Aug. 2, 1776	1	94
Seth W., [s. Jonathan & Hannah], b. July 19, 1798	1	94
Solomon, of New York State, m. Lydia **GATES**, of Ridgefield, Jan. 20, 1823, by Rev. Samuel M. Phelps	1	162
Susannah, [d. Daniel & Mary], b. Apr. 20, 1748	LR1	254
Susanna, m. Abraham **PULLEN**, Apr. 7, 1779	1	156
Susannah, wid. John, d. Apr. 22, 1802, in the 62nd y. of her age	1	211
Susannah, d. Nov. 10, 1825	1	225
Timothy, m. Rebecca [ ], Nov. 22, 1749	LR1	233
Titus, m. Abigail [ ], Jan. 13, 1720	LR1	227

	Vol.	Page
WOOD, (cont.)		
Titus, s. John & Abigail, b. Nov. 6, 1756	LR1	249
WOODWARD, Seth W., m. Elizabeth **WILSON**, Apr. 12, 1801	1	94
Solomon, [s. Seth W. & Elizabeth], b. Jan. 2, 1802	1	94
WOOSTER, Harriet, m. Thomas B. **BENEDICT**, Nov. 14, 1827, by Rev. Nathan Burton	1	167
WORDEN, Abigail, alias **SMITH**, m. Ebenezer **ROCKWELL**, Nov. 5, 1777	1	152
Benajah, s. Daniel & Abigail, b. Sept. 17, 176[ ]	1	30
Benajah, m. Sarah **BENNETT**, Nov. [ ], 1789	1	158
Harvey, s. Samuel & Phebe, b. Mar. 30, 1786	1	60
Margaret M., of Rye, N. Y., m. Joseph F. **PUGGSLEY**, of Ridgefield, Feb. 16, 1845, by Rev. A. S. Francis	1	196
Samuel, s. Daniel & Abigail, b. Sept. 12, 176[ ]	1	30
Samuel, m. Phebe **KEELER**, Oct. 13, 1785	1	155
Sarah, d. Daniel & Abigail, b. Feb. 16, 17[ ]	1	30
Sarah, m. William **ROCKWELL**, June 16, 1785	1	155
YABBACOM, YABBASON, Elizabeth, wid., d. Dec. 10, 1820, ae 89	1	222
Gilbert, d. Dec. 20, 1807, ae 78	1	213
YOUNG, Betsey, m. Caleb **KEELER**, b. of Ridgebury, May 9, 1841, by Nathan Burton	1	191
Louis A., m. Frederick A. **NORRIS**, b. of Ridgefield, Nov. 5, 1844, by Z. B. Burr	1	197
Lydia, of Branford, m. Jonathan **ABBOTT**, of Ridgefield, Apr. 16, [1729], by Samuell Russell	LR1	228
Sarah, d. John & Lidia, of Branford, b. Mar. 15, 1727	LR1	211
NO SURNAME		
Abigail, m. Titus **WOOD**, Jan. 13, 1720	LR1	227
Abigail, m James **WALLIS**, Feb. 12, 1735/6	LR1	230
Abigail, m. Eli **NORTHRUP**, Jan. 3, 1738/9	LR1	230
Abigail, m. Joseph **HAWLEY**, Nov. 8, 1744	LR1	232
Abigail, m. Jonah **FOSTER**, Oct. 15, 1745	LR1	233
Agniss, m. Peter **BENEDICT**, June 23, 1737	LR1	231
Agnis, m. Daniel **BENEDICT**, Feb. 13, 1739/40	LR1	231
Allen, m. Joseph **NORTHRUP**, Aug. 9, 1738	LR1	230
Anne, m. Ebenezer **STEBBINS**, Jan. 13, 1747/8	LR1	232
Charity, negro, d. Mar. 11, 1812, ae 13	1	216
Deborah, m. Ebenezer **GRUMMAN**, Nov. 12, 1742	LR1	232
Elizabeth, m. Jonathan **WOOD**, May 28, 1715	LR1	227
Elizabeth, m. Samuell **SMITH**, June 21, 1722 [Norwalk]	LR1	227
Elizabeth, m. Recompence **THOMAS**, July 26, 1731	LR1	230
Elizabeth, m. Caleb **LOBDELL**, June 27, 1739	LR1	232
Elizabeth, m. Timothy **STREET**, Jan. 31, 1743/4	LR1	232
Elizabeth, m. Thomas **HAWLEY**, Jan. 13, 1747/8	LR1	233
Elizabeth, m. Rev. Samuel **GOODRICH**, July 29, 1784	1	64
Elizabeth, m. Stephen **NORRIS**, Jr., Oct. 1, 1795	1	92
Esther, m. Jonathan **ROCKWELL**, Oct. [ ], 1733	LR1	230

NO SURNAME, (cont.)

	Vol.	Page
Hannah, m. Nathan **SAINT JOHN**, June 7, 1721	LR1	227
Hannah, m. Elijah **HAWLEY**, Oct. 26, 1742	LR1	232
Hannah, m. Ebenezer **SMITH**, June 9, 1747	LR1	232
Hepsey, m. Moses **NORRIS**, Apr. 26, 1801	1	93
Jane, m. Noah **ST. JOHN**, Oct. 6, 1737	LR1	230
Jemima, b. Sept. 24, 1757; m. Arthur **FORRESTER**, [ ]	1	63
Jerusha, m. Daniel **SHERWOOD**, Apr. 29, 1736	LR1	230
Job, s. Ebenezer & Sarah, b. Feb. 21, [1721/2]	LR1	204
Kezia, m. Timothy **CANFIELD**, Nov. 19, 1729, by Stephen Munson	LR1	228
Kezia, m. John **STURTEVANT**, Apr. 12, 1732	LR1	229
Lois, m. Nathan **SHERWOOD**, Jan. 4, 1743/4	LR1	231
Lucy, m. John **BENEDICT**, Nov. 29, 1738	LR1	233
Martha, m. James **SCOTT**, Mar. 12, 1744/5	LR1	233
Mary, m. Joseph **BENEDICT**, Mar. 21, 1720/1	LR1	227
Mary, m. Samuel **KEELER**, Jan. 22, 1735/6	LR1	230
Mary, m. Jabez **MOREHOUSE**, Nov. 9, 1738	LR1	230
Mary, m. James **BENEDICT**, May 8, 1740	LR1	232
Mary, m. Sam[ue]ll **ISAAC**, Jan. 10, 1744/5	LR1	232
Mary, m. Christopher **LEACH**, May 8, 1786	1	74
Naomi, m. Isaac **SHERWOOD**, Jan. 2, 1746	LR1	233
Patience, m. Benjamin **HOYT**, Aug. 28, 1751	LR1	233
Patience, m. Justus **OLMSTEAD**, June 10, 1752	LR1	234
Rachal, m. Sam[ue]ll **GATES**, Apr. 1, 1734	LR1	230
Rachel, m. James **NORTHRUP**, Jr., Jan. 13, 1742/3	LR1	231
Rebecca, m. Jonathan **OSBURN**, Jan. 3, 1732/3	LR1	229
Rebeckah, m. Jeremiah **OSBURN**, Jan. 11, 1738/9	LR1	230
Rebecca, m. Timothy **WOOD**, Nov. 22, 1749	LR1	233
Ruth, m. Ichabod **COLE**, Mar. 14, 1734	LR1	229
Ruth, m. John **LOBDELL**, June 25, 1744	LR1	232
Sarah, m. Benjamin **HOYT**, Mar. 21, 1716	LR1	227
Sarah, m. Samuel **SMITH**, June 13, 1717	LR1	227
Sarah, m. Jabez **NORTHRUP**, Mar. 6, 1735	LR1	230
Sarah, m. John **SMITH**, Feb. 7, 1739/40	LR1	232
Sarah, m. Jonathan **BROOKS**, Apr. 9, 1744	LR1	232
Sarah, m. Nathan **HAWLEY**, July 3, 1746	LR1	232
Sarah, m. Jacob **SMITH**, Jan. 12, 1748/9	LR1	233
Sarah, m. William **FORRESTER**, Dec. 8, 1768	1	65
Susannah, m. Joseph **BENEDICT**, May 18, 1732	LR1	230
Thankfull, m. Daniel **WHITNE**, Aug. 8, 1741	LR1	231
Zabiah, m. Joseph **FOSTER**, Feb. 22, 1748/9	LR1	233
Zebulon, negro, d. May 4, 1791, in the 80th y. of his age	1	205
-----, strange woman d. Jan. 22, 1848, ae 62	1	239